DATE DUE

DEMCO 38-296

CONTEMPORARY MUSICIANS

Explore your options!

Gale databases are offered in a variety of formats

 The information in this Gale publication is also available in some or all of the formats described here. Your Gale Representative will be happy to fill you in. Call toll-free 1-800-877-GALE.

GaleNet
A number of Gale databases are now available on GaleNet, our new online information resource accessible through the Internet. GaleNet features an easy-to-use end-user interface, the powerful search capabilities of BRS/SEARCH retrieval software and ease of access through the World Wide Web.

Diskette/Magnetic Tape

Many Gale databases are available on diskette or magnetic tape, allowing systemwide access to your most-used information sources through existing computer systems. Data can be delivered on a variety of mediums (DOS-formatted diskettes, 9-track tape, 8mm data tape) and in industry-standard formats (comma-delimited, tagged, fixed-field).

CD-ROM

A variety of Gale titles are available on CD-ROM, offering maximum flexibility and powerful search software.

Online

For your convenience, many Gale databases are available through popular online services, including DIALOG, NEXIS, DataStar, ORBIT, OCLC, Thomson Financial Network's I/Plus Direct, HRIN, Prodigy, Sandpoint's HOOVER, the Library Corporation's NLightN and Telebase Systems.

ISSN 1044-2197

CONTEMPORARY MUSICIANS

PROFILES OF THE PEOPLE IN MUSIC

STACY A. McCONNELL, Editor

VOLUME 21
Includes Cumulative Indexes

GALE

DETROIT · NEW YORK · TORONTO · LONDON

STAFF

Stacy A. McConnell, *Editor*

Maria L. Munoz, *Associate Editor*

Mary Alice Adams, Bill Bennett, Suzanne Bourgoin, Jayne Bowman, Carol Brennan, Gerald Brennan, John Cohassey, Ed Decker, Robert Dupuis, Robert R. Jacobson, Mary Kalfatovic, Judson Knight, K. Michelle Moran, Christine Morrison, John F. Packel, Sean Pollock, Jim Powers, Sonya Shelton, Geri J. Speace, Debra Reilly, Lynn M. Spampinato, B. Kim Taylor, David Wilkins, *Contributing Editors*

Neil E. Walker, *Managing Editor*

Susan M. Trosky, *Permissions Manager*
Maria Franklin, *Permissions Specialist*
Edna Hedblad, *Permissions Assistant*

Mary Beth Trimper, *Production Director*
Deborah Milliken, *Production Assistant*
Cynthia Baldwin, *Product Design Manager*
Barbara J. Yarrow, *Graphic Services Supervisor*
Randy Bassett, *Image Database Supervisor*
Pamela A. Reed, *Photography Coordinator*
Willie Mathis, *Camera Operator*

Cover illustration by John Kleber

This book is printed on acid-free paper that meets the minimum requirements of American National Standard for Information Sciences— Permanence Paper for Printed Library Materials, ANSI Z39.48-1984.

This book is printed on recycled paper that meets Environmental Protection Agency Standards.

ISBN 0-7876-1178-6
ISSN 1044-2197

10 9 8 7 6 5 4 3 2 1

Contents

Introduction

Fills the Information Gap on Today's Musicians

Contemporary Musicians profiles the colorful personalities in the music industry who create or influence the music we hear today. Prior to *Contemporary Musicians,* no quality reference series provided comprehensive information on such a wide range of artists despite keen and ongoing public interest. To find biographical and critical coverage, an information seeker had little choice but to wade through the offerings of the popular press, scan television "infotainment" programs, and search for the occasional published biography or exposé. *Contemporary Musicians* is designed to serve that information seeker, providing in one ongoing source in-depth coverage of the important names on the modern music scene in a format that is both informative and entertaining. Students, researchers, and casual browsers alike can use *Contemporary Musicians* to meet their needs for personal information about music figures; find a selected discography of a musician's recordings; and uncover an insightful essay offering biographical and critical information.

Provides Broad Coverage

Single-volume biographical sources on musicians are limited in scope, often focusing on a handful of performers from a specific musical genre or era. In contrast, *Contemporary Musicians* offers researchers and music devotees a comprehensive, informative, and entertaining alternative. *Contemporary Musicians* is published three times per year, with each volume providing information on more than 80 musical artists and record-industry luminaries from all the genres that form the broad spectrum of contemporary music—pop, rock, jazz, blues, country, New Age, folk, rhythm and blues, gospel, bluegrass, rap, and reggae, to name a few—as well as selected classical artists who have achieved "crossover" success with the general public. *Contemporary Musicians* will also occasionally include profiles of influential nonperforming members of the music community, including producers, promoters, and record company executives. Additionally, beginning with *Contemporary Musicians 11,* each volume features new profiles of a selection of previous *Contemporary Musicians* listees who remain of interest to today's readers and who have been active enough to require completely revised entries.

Includes Popular Features

In *Contemporary Musicians* you'll find popular features that users value:

- **Easy-to-locate data sections:** Vital personal statistics, chronological career summaries, listings of major awards, and mailing addresses, when available, are prominently displayed in a clearly marked box on the second page of each entry.

- **Biographical/critical essays:** Colorful and informative essays trace each subject's personal and professional life, offer representative examples of critical response to the artist's work, and provide entertaining personal sidelights.

- **Selected discographies:** Each entry provides a comprehensive listing of the artist's major recorded works.

- **Photographs:** Most entries include portraits of the subject profiled.

- **Sources for additional information:** This invaluable feature directs the user to selected books, magazines, and newspapers where more information can be obtained.

Helpful Indexes Make It Easy to Find the Information You Need

Each volume of *Contemporary Musicians* features a cumulative Musicians Index, listing names of individual performers and musical groups, and a cumulative Subject Index, which provides the user with a breakdown by primary musical instruments played and by musical genre.

Available in Electronic Formats

Diskette/Magnetic Tape. *Contemporary Musicians* is available for licensing on magnetic tape or diskette in a fielded format. Either the complete database or a custom selection of entries may be ordered. The database is available for internal data processing and nonpublishing purposes only. For more information, call (800) 877-GALE.

Online. *Contemporary Musicians* is available online through Mead Data Central's NEXIS Service in the NEXIS, PEOPLE and SPORTS Libraries in the GALBIO file.

We Welcome Your Suggestions

The editors welcome your comments and suggestions for enhancing and improving *Contemporary Musicians*. If you would like to suggest subjects for inclusion, please submit these names to the editors. Mail comments or suggestions to:

The Editor
Contemporary Musicians
Gale Research
835 Penobscot Bldg.
Detroit, MI 48226-4094
Phone: (800) 347-4253
Fax: (313) 961-6599

Aaliyah

Singer

Photograph by Marc Baptiste. Atlantic Records. Reproduced by permission.

Aaliyah, the sultry hip-hop singer, burst onto the music scene in a flurry of controversy in 1994. She was the latest in a long line of child prodigies to make a mark on the industry, a line that stretches back through Michael Jackson to Little Stevie Wonder and Etta James. The release of Aaliyah's first record was surrounded by an element of soap opera. As it climbed the charts rumors circulated that Aaliyah—who was a mere 14 years old while she was making the record—had eloped with her producer, said to be at least ten years her senior. The publicity could not overshadow Aaliyah's talent, however. Before she graduated from high school in 1997, she had two platinum albums and two number one singles to her credit, and two years of international touring under her belt.

Aaliyah's second album, *One in a Million,* displayed an artistic maturity well beyond her years. The *New York Amsterdam News* wrote: "There is more to the singer than song and dance. Not only has she become 'the highest, most exalted one,' as the true Arabic interpretation of her name suggests, but she has matured into a hip confident performer whose talents and passions range from music and acting, to her commitment to breast cancer research, Alzheimer's disease awareness and her dedication to stay in school until she has completed her education."

Aaliyah Haughton was born in the Bedford-Stuyvesant neighborhood of Brooklyn, New York. When she was five, her parents, Diane and Michael Haughton, moved to Detroit with Aaliyah and her older brother Rashaad. She was surrounded by music from an early age. Her mother's collection of soul, R&B, and popular records was an early and on-going influence. Aaliyah would sing along—with her mother's full encouragement—to the music of Marvin Gaye, the Isley Brothers, Whitney Houston, Johnny Mathis and Barbra Streisand.

At the age of seven Aaliyah started trying out for school plays and singing whenever she could. "I've been singing all my life," she told *Vibe* in 1994. "I sang in my church and school and my parents gave me vocal lessons." She credits her parents for supporting her interest in music and appreciates the fact that they did not shunt her from one audition to another against her will. "I pushed *them,*" she recalled to *Vibe*'s Kris Ex. "I would talk to my mother every day. After school I'd go to her job and be, like, Ma, did anybody call me? Anybody call about signing me? I was into it."

Her uncle, Barry Hankerson, began managing her when she was nine, and Aaliyah's professional career was off and running. She auditioned for TV pilots without success, but continued her voice lessons. A turning point

For the Record . . .

Born Aaliyah Haughton in Brooklyn, NY; daughter of Michael and Diane (nee Hankerson) Haughton.

Released *Age Ain't Nothing but a Number,* 1994; released *One In A Million,* 1996.

Addresses: *Home*—Detroit, MI. *Record Company*—Blackground Enterprises, 15250 Ventura Blvd., Suite 705, Sherman Oaks, CA 91403. *Manager*—Michael and Diane Haughton, Raliah Management, P.O. Box 21847, Detroit, MI 48221.

came when she appeared on the show *Star Search.* "It was really, really cute," she told *Details,* "I sang 'My Funny Valentine,' and I had on a white dress my grandmother made with a little bolero jacket, and special curls in my hair." Although she did not win first place, she soon received the break of a lifetime when she performed for a week in Las Vegas with Gladys Knight, who, incidentally, is Hankerson's ex-wife. Aaliyah got to sing a song half-way through the set, and at the finale she and Knight sang a duet together—"Believe in Yourself."

Protégé or Wife?

When Barry Hankerson founded his own record label, Blackground Enterprises, he signed Aaliyah when she was 14 years old as the label's first act. It was around that time that Hankerson introduced his niece to R. Kelly, a hip-hop musician who was managed by Hankerson's Midwest Entertainment Group. Kelly was to play an important role in Aaliyah's life for the next year or two. "I met Robert before he came out with *Born in the 90s,* Aaliyah told *Vibe.* "He came to my house and I sang for him, and from there we went into the studio." Aaliyah became Kelly's protégé. He took over creative control of what would be her first album, provocatively titled, *Age Ain't Nothing but a Number.*

The title was provocative because of the sensual knowing with which Aaliyah sang. She played down the age issue while promoting the record. "That's not something I really want to discuss," she told *Vibe.* Part of the reason for avoiding the subject were the rumors that were circulating at the time, rumors that Aaliyah and Kelly had eloped. The idea that 24 year old Kelly and Aaliyah—at 14 still very much a minor—were married titillated the

industry for months. *Rolling Stone* even claimed that the Cook County Clerk's Office had a marriage license which proved that Robert Kelly and Aaliyah Haughton, listed on the license to be 18, had been married in Rosemont, Illinois. "I'm not married," she told *Vibe,* "that's all I really want to say about it."

The marriage rumors and the subsequent publicity did not hurt the sales of the album. *Age* went platinum within a year. Its first single, "Back & Forth," spent three weeks at number one in the R&B charts—coincidentally it knocked out R. Kelly's "Your Body's Callin." The record also broke the Top Five on the *Billboard* charts. Aaliyah's second single, "At Your Best (You Are Love)" reached number two on the R&B charts. The singer later recalled being very nervous before the release of "Back and Forth," wondering if people would accept it. Her answer came when the song went gold.

The Girl Can't Sit Still

Aaliyah followed her debut album with nearly a year of touring that took her across the United States and around the world, from Europe to Japan via South Africa. While on the road, Aaliyah maintained a 3.8 grade point average at the Detroit High School for the Performing Arts where she was a dance major. A tutor, under the supervision of Aaliyah's mother who is an educator, traveled with the singer at all times.

After a lengthy tour, Aaliyah was anxious to start work on her next record. It had been such a long time since the release of *Age,* even Aaliyah was wondering if she was only a one-hit wonder. Could the young artist match the success of her first release? "I was a little anxious," she admitted in an Atlantic press release. "You could even say I was a little afraid. I spoke with my family and they helped me realize that it wasn't something I should worry about, that I shouldn't over think the process." Aaliyah's family has been an important factor in her success. She records for a label owned by her uncle and cousin; her father and mother co-manage her; her brother is her creative consultant; and her cousin Jomo was executive producer on her second album.

For her second album, *One in a Million,* the singer chose not to use a single producer, perhaps a way of renouncing R. Kelly who didn't work on the album at all. Eight different producers worked on the album. She also switched distributors, from Jive Records to R&B powerhouse Atlantic. The album was released in fall 1996, and by year's end it was obvious that Aaliyah had scored another big hit. The first single, "If Your Girl Only Knew," zoomed to number one; a year later the record went double platinum and surpassed her first album in sales.

Despite the worldly image created by her records and publicity machine, Aaliyah remains at some level unaffected by her success. Even after *Age* hit the charts she continued to attend high school in Detroit, like any other student—except of course for the world tours and the occasional freshman dogging her for an autograph. The singer, who graduated in June of 1997 and plans to attend college, continues to live at home with her parents. Despite her world tours and the success of *One in a Million,* Aaliyah often wears sunglasses (which have become a kind of trademark) to help overcome her shyness. That carried over to her recording work. "When I'm in the studio, I have to have the lights off— you can't see me 'cause I'm very shy," she told *Vibe.* "I don't mind seeing you in the control room, but you can't see me."

Despite her shyness, Aaliyah remains a very determined artist. When it comes to her music, she knows what she wants and works hard to get it. R&B artist Ginuwine, who appeared in the "One in a Million" video, told *Seventeen* "She's sweet, patient and she'll do a take over and over again until she gets it right." Even at age 14 she had a strong work ethic. "I work every day," she told *Vibe,* "Ev-er-y day." She doesn't want to get caught standing still, or get lumped into one style of music. In late 1997, she recorded "Journey to the Past" for the *Anastasia* soundtrack, a song that is Disney pop rather than R&B. She is interested in getting more involved in acting and dancing, and introduced choreography into her 1997 tour. "These days people are likely to know your music from your videos," she told *Newsday,* so it's nice to be able to include some elements from those in your songs. People really enjoy seeing dance steps or a prop from the video in the stage show."

The future seems limitless for Aaliyah, who has the determination to make any of her dreams come true. She has dreams one wouldn't normally expect from a teenager who is a famous singer. When she was 14 and her records were zooming up the charts, Aaliyah wasn't talking about craving stardom and riches—she wanted to go to college and get a doctorate in music history. Three years later she told *Newsday* she was interested in doing something in indie rock. "I'd love to work with the members from Oasis or Soundgarden. I love their music too." *Vibe* surmised: "Somebody's got to be the one to fulfill our fantasies as we go into the 21st century. Aaliyah may be just the one."

Selected discography

Age Ain't Nothing but a Number, Blackground/Jive, 1994.
One in a Million, Blackground/Atlantic, 1996.
(Contributor) *Anastasia* (soundtrack), 1997.

Sources

Billboard, May 14, 1994.
Essence, January 1997.
Indianapolis Recorder, July 8, 1995.
Newsday, September 12, 1997.
Seventeen, January 1997.
Vibe, September 1994; December 1996, January 1997.

—Gerald E. Brennan

Alabama

Country group

Since it exploded onto the scene in the early 1980s, Alabama has been one of the most popular, best-selling, and most vilified groups in country music—all despite scorn by critics. Michael Bane of the *Encyclopedia of Country Music* wrote, "it was the country music equivalent of fingernails on a chalk board." On the other hand, said Bane, "when the music worked—'Tennessee River' or 'She and I'—it transcended its genre." Part of the negative criticism was probably a normal critic's reaction to a large, loyal and fanatical audience. Between 1980 and 1997 the band has sold more than 57 million records worldwide, including ten platinum, three double platinum, three quadruple platinum albums and one *quintuple* platinum album. They had 41 number one singles, before sales began to slump in the nineties. In other words, instead of multi-platinum sellers they are producing mere million seller albums.

"The first country music supergroup," as Michael Bane called Alabama, got its start when cousins Randy Owen and Teddy Gentry began singing together in the Lookout Mountain Holiness Church up in the hills near the

AP/Wide World Photos, Inc. Reproduced by permission.

won, the three cousins were able to visit the Opry themselves.

While playing music on nights and weekends, the band members held down a variety of day jobs, including hanging dry wall, picking cotton, fixing typewriters, and deejaying. In 1973, despite the skepticism of family and friends they decided to quit their day jobs and devote themselves full-time to music. As if to make the attitude official they renamed themselves Wildcountry and headed off for the wild life in Myrtle Beach, South Carolina.

"When we first got to Myrtle Beach it was an absolute shock," Randy Owen told the *Washington Post*. "People stayed up all night, dancing and playing music, and where we came from nothing like that was going on. People were on vacation and they were acting wild." They played at various clubs before finally settling in at the Bowery, a sweaty joint so small there wasn't even room for dancing. The club was the center of the craziness in Myrtle Beach, and it was where Alabama cut its teeth musically. They did have one advantage, however: they were the only country band in town. But the money they earned came from tips exclusively, so pleasing the crowds was their first priority. The audience could be completely different from one night to the next, demanding anything from rock to R&B to soul music. Wildcountry had to be prepared to play all of it. But, as Owen told the *Post,* they "drew the line at disco."

The Bowery was the band's musical higher education; they learned all the different styles, honing their trademark vocal harmonies to a sharp edge. According to Owen, it taught him that a lead singer couldn't simply stand around and sing, he had to move around on stage. And it helped build their stamina, playing the bar seven years, every night between March and mid-September, five hours at a stretch. "We'd play 'til we got blisters. Then we'd play 'til the blisters popped," recalled Teddy Gentry in the *Comprehensive Country Music Encyclopedia,* "but it sure beat working the swing shift at the sock factory."

By 1977, they were the most popular thing in Myrtle Beach. Fans were traveling to the Bowery from New England and the Midwest in order to hear the band play. That same year they changed their name once and for all to Alabama, and added drummer Mark Herndon two years later. Their first record, which they financed themselves, was released in the late seventies and reached a respectable #77 on the charts. They paid to have some albums pressed as well and would sell them directly to their fans from the stage. Unfortunately, they had been unable to interest any of the larger Nashville

Georgia state line. When they reached their teens they hooked up with another cousin, Jeff Cook, and started playing together around Fort Payne, Alabama. Their band, Young Country, played whatever gigs it could find: local dances, bars, and picnics. Their first *paying* job was at the American Legion hall where they earned the princely sum of $5.37 each. An amusement park in the area hired them not long afterwards and they played there three years running, backing up the various artists passing through town, including some from the Grand Opry. Thanks to a local talent show they record companies in signing them. It wasn't until their third single, "My Home's in Alabama," shot up to the Top 5 and they were asked to perform at the New Faces show at Nashville's annual Country Radio Seminar that their luck changed.

Breaking through Style Barriers

They must have wondered at first if it was *really* changing. "Me and Jeff and Teddy had to stand up on stage without our instruments and sing," Owen told *Billboard*'s Chet Flippo, "and Mark wasn't on stage at all. I wrote the song but I wasn't allowed to play on it." The reason was that the country music establishment at the time still had a heavy prejudice against "bands." Groups that sang, like the Oak Ridge Boys or the Statler Brothers, were perfectly acceptable; but bands that sang *and* played their own instruments were associated with rock 'n' roll, and rock was strictly taboo. Despite the handicap, Alabama electrified the DJs with their renditions of "My Home's in Alabama" and "Tennessee River." RCA responded by singing the band and released the latter tune as their first single. It was an immediate hit and before long it was at the very top of the country charts. RCA's commitment to aggressively promoting Alabama's first album paid off as well. Owen later described RCA's modest expectations to Chet Flippo: "At the beginning, RCA said that if we sold 60,000 albums, they would consider signing us a good deal." The album took off almost immediately and ended up selling over two million copies.

The first Alabama albums, influenced by their work at the Bowery, had a style that Michael Bane, in *The Comprehensive Country Music Encyclopedia* called typical of the pre-Garth Brooks era in country music: "the hardshell Southern bar music filtered through a distinct 1960s pop group sensibility—sort of The Allman Brothers meet The Beatles." By the mid-eighties, with the release of albums like *Roll On* (1984) and *40 Hour Week* (1985), the band had moved toward a more traditional, blue collar country sound. It did not hurt their popularity though—those two albums sold a combined five million plus units and produced eight number one singles.

However one feels about their music, their is no denying that Alabama changed the course of country music. The elements they introduced from other popular music, especially rock, ended the dominance of the traditional Nashville sound. The synthesis they created with rock was a bridge that enabled country to reach a new generation of fans too, new fans country desperately needed at the time. Suddenly country became accept-

able across the nation. And the new fanswere attracted by precisely those qualities that Nashville considered flaws. Naturally, once the millions started rolling in, they weren't flaws any longer. The fact that they were the biggest money machine country music had ever seen was, according to the Country Music Foundation's *Country: The Music and the Musicians,* "Alabama's greatest contribution to country music: Its popularity, especially during the industry's lean years, 1982 to 1986. Alabama's profitability helped RCA take chances on newer performers and to keep deserving but commercially shaky acts, like Gail Davies, on the roster."

Those new fans eventually became more knowledgeable and discriminating about country music, however. As they made a more purist breed of artist popular, typified by Garth Brooks and Dwight Yoakam, in the late eighties, Alabama's fortunes declined, although they did manage to maintain a large and loyal fan base. The band reciprocates that loyalty, taking time after each show to meet fans personally and sign autographs. Their merchandise is very popular, and Alabama was one of the very first country groups to aggressively pursue this avenue of money-making; their well-organized fans are a natural market. The official Alabama fan club has a quarter of a million members, and charges no dues. But members receive, together with regular newsletters, catalogs of Alabama T-shirts, hats, mugs, posters, belts, and more.

Success Follows Alabama into the '90s

By the 1990s the band had become an institution: they had won two Grammys and been voted the "Artist of the Decade" by the Academy of Country Music. Their career began to run on automatic. RCA began feeding them songs, as the band's own songwriting was discouraged. When *In Pictures* was released in 1995 only one cut was an Alabama composition. But around that time they gave up their plane and started touring by bus again, to have time to unwind between shows. The extra off-time on the road gave them more time together and before long the songs were flowing like never before.

When RCA executives visited Fort Payne to talk about a new Alabama album in 1996, they had briefcases full of music like always, but Owen and the band insisted on playing some of their own songs instead. *Dancin' on the Boulevard,* released in 1997, contained seven songs written by Alabama. The album was one of their freshest in years, a mix of styles that looked back to their years playing for tips in Myrtle Beach. With this release, Alabama felt fully in charge of their own career again.

Selected discography

My Heart's in Alabama, RCA, 1980.
Feels So Right, RCA, 1981.
Mountain Music, RCA, 1982.
The Closer You Get, RCA, 1983.
Roll On, RCA, 1984.
40 Hour Week, RCA, 1986.
Alabama Christmas, RCA, 1986.
Alabama's Greatest Hits, RCA, 1986.
Cheap Seats, RCA, 1993.
In Pictures, RCA, 1995.
Dancin' on the Boulevard, RCA, 1997.

Sources

Books

The Comprehensive Country Music Encyclopedia, NY Times
   Books, 1994.

Country: The Music and the Musicians, Abbeville Press,
   1988.

Periodicals

Billboard, September 7, 1985; May 23, 1992; September 2,
   1995; March 1, 1997.
Close-Up, June 1997.
New Country, July 1997.
Washington Post, September 12, 1997.

Online

www.wildcountry.com

Additional information was provided by RCA publicity
materials.

—*Gerald E. Brennan*

Luther Allison

Blues singer, guitarist

At the time of his death in 1997, Luther Allison was at the very top of the blues world. The singer and guitarist had received a total of eight W. C. Handy awards over the prior two years, and was performing to sold-out audiences over the world. He had struggled for 40 years in semi-obscurity—many of those years spent in European self-exile—to reach that peak, only to have his career suddenly ended by terminal cancer.

Allison was born on August 17, 1939, in Mayflower, Arkansas, the fourteenth of 15 children. In 1951, fed up with life in the cotton fields of the South, the family moved to Chicago in search of better opportunities. The family was a musical one. Several of Allison's siblings sang in a gospel group called the Southern Travellers. One of his older brothers, Ollie, soon began working as a guitarist on Chicago's booming South Side blues scene. Seeking to emulate his brother, Luther took up the guitar. By the middle of his teens, Allison was skilled enough to sit in with his brother's band on club dates.

Soon Allison was ready to front his own band, and in 1957 he formed a group called the Rolling Stones, named after a song by blues great Muddy Waters. The band also included another Allison brother, Grant. After changing its name to The Four Jivers, the band quickly became regulars on the Chicago blues club circuit. It was not long before Allison's fiery guitar work caught the attention of Magic Sam, Freddy King, and other fixtures of the competitive West Side blues scene.

For the next decade or so, Allison toiled as a sideman for those and other bandleaders. It was Freddy King who encouraged Allison to start singing. He played supporting roles during this period with such other blues legends as Howlin' Wolf and Muddy Waters. When King started touring nationally, Allison took over his band and his weekly West Side gig. By the end of the 1950s he was one of the bigger acts on the Chicago blues scene.

In 1967 Allison gained national attention when his playing was included on a compilation album released by Delmark Records, called *Sweet Home Chicago*. He followed that up with a Delmark album of his own, *Love Me Mama,* issued in 1969. By this time, Allison had been more or less tabbed as the "next big blues star" out of a generation of hot players coming out of the West Side. This collection of blooming blues stars, which included Otis Rush and Buddy Guy, found ways to incorporate a rock and roll sensibility into their music without sacrificing its blues authenticity.

Meanwhile, Allison had begun taking his band on the road outside of Chicago for the first time, touring with harmonica player Shakey Jake. Allison made huge

Born August 17, 1939, in Mayflower, AR; died August 12, 1997, in Madison, WI; married, wife's name, Fannie Mae (separated); children: Bernard, Luther T.; seven stepchildren.

Formed first band, the Rolling Stones (name subsequently changed to the Four Jivers), 1957; accompanied several blues artists, including Freddy King, Magic Sam, Muddy Waters, and Howlin' Wolf, 1957-59; took over leadership of King's band, c. 1959, and performed in various Chicago venues, 1959-67; appeared on first recording, the compilation *Sweet Home Chicago*, Delmark, 1967; first solo recording, *Love Me Mama*, Delmark, 1969; headlined Ann Arbor Blues Festival, 1969, 70; recorded on Motown Records, 1972-76; moved to Paris in 1979, performed across Europe, 1979-93; returned to U.S. and released *Soul Fixin' Man*, Alligator, 1994; recorded on Alligator label and toured worldwide, 1994-97.

Awards: Blues Foundation, eight W. C. Handy Awards, 1995-97, including Best Blues Entertainer, 1995 and 1996; *Living Blues*, ten Readers' and Critics' Awards.

splashes at the 1969 and 1970 Ann Arbor Blues Festivals in Ann Arbor, Michigan, and it seemed only a matter of time before he would become the biggest blues name in years. He signed a recording contract with Berry Gordy's Motown label. It marked the first time that Motown, a giant in soul music, had signed a blues artist. Allison recorded three albums on Motown: *Bad News is Coming* (1972), *Luther's Blues* (1974), and *Night Life* (1976). Unfortunately, Motown had no idea how to promote blues products, and none of Allison's albums sold very well. In addition, Allison was unhappy with Motown's propensity to "overproduce" his work. He preferred to record in a simpler, more "live" atmosphere.

Gives Paris More Blues

Disillusioned by the failure of his Motown projects, Allison packed up and moved his base of operations to Europe, following in the footsteps of earlier blues expatriates Memphis Slim and Champion Jack Dupree. Settling in Paris in 1979, Allison set out to revitalize his career by concentrating on what he did best—namely

putting on fantastic live shows, in which he exhibited boundless energy, usually exhausting the audience before losing any steam himself. He continued to record as well, turning out albums on European labels such as Melodie and Black & Blue, in addition to the occasional U.S. release on Blind Pig. By the middle of the 1980s, Allison had become arguably the biggest blues star in Europe.

As he gained stature in Europe, Allison continued to court younger listeners by incorporating elements of rock into his music, leading to inevitable comparisons to, among others, Jimi Hendrix. Allison never seemed to mind the association with rock artists, noting the historic connection between the two genres. By the late 1980s, however, Allison was delving back into his hardcore blues roots, combining the hot guitar licks he had honed over the years with a matured vocal style that captured the essence of the wise, world-weary bluesman. His 1984 release *Serious* caught the attention of the people at Chicago-based Alligator Records.

In 1994 Alligator released *Soul Fixin' Man*, Allison's first American album in nearly two decades. The album was a huge hit among blues fans, marking Allison's triumphant return to his native turf. A writer in *Guitar Player* applauded the album's "fever and chills performances," and raved that Allison's "ferocious solos combine the wisdom of a master storyteller with the elegance of B.B. King, the elasticity of Buddy Guy, and the big sting of Albert King."

Back on Top with *Blue Streak*

Allison followed up in 1995 with another Alligator album, *Blue Streak*. Blue Streak not only solidified Allison's comeback, but put him among the elite few at the very top of the blues kingdom and earned him five W. C. Handy awards, the most prestigious in the business for a blues performer. A *Washington Post* writer called it "a sonic roar as soulful as his gospel-shout vocals," and the album remained atop the blues charts for 19 weeks. Allison continued to tour tirelessly all over the world, astonishing fans in North America, Europe, and Japan with the sheer energy of his live shows. Well into his fifties, nearly 30 years after he made his first recordings, Allison summed up his amazing reversal of fortune at the 1995 Chicago Blues Festival: "I'm not only back. I'm unstoppable."

In 1997 Allison released *Reckless*, which would turn out to be his final album. During a July performance, Allison left the stage complaining of dizziness and a loss of coordination. He was taken to the hospital, where he was diagnosed as having inoperable lung cancer and had already spread to other parts of his body. Told that he did not have long to live, the two-time reigning "Blues Entertainer of the Year" canceled the rest of his touring schedule in order to focus on his health. Allison died on August 12, 1997, in Madison, Wisconsin. Although his life ended just as his career was reaching its overdue peak, Allison managed to live just long enough to see his singer/guitarist son Bernard make his debut album, *Born with the Blues*. Allison's career was perhaps best summarized by *Guitar Player*'s Jas Obrecht, who observed that Allison "played the blues as if his life was hanging in the balance."

Selected discography

Albums

Love Me Mama, Delmark, 1969.
Bad News is Coming, Motown, 1972.
Luther's Blues, Motown, 1974.
Night Life, Motown, 1976.
Love Me Papa, Black & Blue, 1977.
Live in Paris, Buda, 1979.
Gonna Be a Live One in Here Tonight, Rumble, 1979.
Life is a Bitch, Melodie, 1984.

Serious, Blind Pig, 1984.
Here I Come, Melodie, 1985.
Hand Me Down My Moonshine, In-Akustik, 1992.
Soul Fixin' Man, Alligator, 1994.
Bad Love, Ruf, 1994.
Blue Streak, Alligator, 1995.
Motown Years, Motown, 1996.
Reckless, Alligator, 1997.

Compilations

Sweet Home Chicago, Delmark, 1967.

Sources

Arizona Republic, August 15, 1997.
Billboard, July 29, 1995; August 23, 1997.
Guardian (London), August 27, 1997.
Guitar Player, February 1995; December 1996.
Independent (London), August 14, 1997.
Living Blues, Autumn 1973.
Melody Maker, September 20, 1980.
Times (London), August 22, 1997.

—Robert R. Jacobson

Anointed

The Christian vocal group Anointed rose from anonymity to their status as one of Christian music's most distinguished vocal groups with the release of their second album, *The Call,* in 1995. Anointed is comprised of Denise "Nee-C" Walls and siblings Steve Crawford and Da'dra Crawford Greathouse. The trio started out as a quartet with Mary Tiller in 1988, in their home town of Columbus, Ohio.

Meeting on Friday nights, the group gathered to practice singing. They'd practice anywhere—in bathrooms or basements ("anywhere the music was good!"), with little thought of recording an album and meeting with success. They were inspired by artists such as the Winans, the Hawkins Family and, Andre Crouch. Crawford told *Release*'s Chris Wells, "It is our desire to create music that supports our vision, which is to bridge the gap across races, across denominations."

Their music incorporates pop, R&B, gospel, uplifting lyrics, and energetic melodies. In addition to being vocalists, they write their own songs. The December

Photograph by Norman Jean Roy. Myrrh Records. Reproduced by permission.

For the Record . . .

Members include **Steve Crawford** (raised in Columbus, OH), vocals; **Da'dra Crawford Greathouse** (raised in Columbus, OH), vocals; **Mary Tiller** (bandmember 1988-96), vocals; **Denise "Nee-C" Walls** (raised in Columbus, OH). Began as quartet in 1988 in their hometown of Columbus, OH, before moving to Nashville in 1995.

Debut album, *Spiritual Love Affair,* released in 1993 on Brainstorm Records and then distributed by Word Records; *The Call* released in 1995 on Myrrh Records, *Under the Influence* released in 1996 on Myrrh Records.

Awards: Three Dove Awards in 1996; Contemporary Gospel Album of the Year, Urban Recorded Song of the Year, and Contemporary Soul Gospel Album all 1996.

Addresses: *Record company*—Myrrh Records, 3319 West End Avenue, Suite 200, Nashville, TN 37203

1996 cover of *Contemporary Christian Music* magazine summed up the band's personal philosophy with a picture of the trio over the caption: "Anointed—Using Their Influence to Promote Unity." According to a Myrrh Records press release: "powerful vocals and smooth, tight harmonies are what separates Anointed from their peers." Andrew Tempest , VP of Marketing at Myrrh notes: "These people could literally sing the phone book and blow people away."

In 1995 they moved to Nashville to broaden their fan base. Greathouse told *Contemporary Christian Music*'s Deara Akins, " When we moved to [Nashville], we really didn't know about how this industry works. We're just beginning to learn about the roles people have at the record label (Myrrh), and we're still trying to understand Christian radio." The group wanted to see more interracial audiences which they succeeded in doing. By 1996, the trio noticed ethnically mixed congregations and black and white promoters, who had never worked together, joining forces on their behalf. Akins noted, "Anointed's recent success set the precedent for R&B artists within Christian music. Unlike general market pop radio, adult contemporary Christian stations have not typically been a big supporter of acts in the R&B or urban genres." Bob Elder, senior buyer for the 185-outlet Family Bookstore chain, told *Billboard*'s Deborah Evans Price, "The exciting thing about a group like Anointed is that you can promote them to your contemporary Christian and gospel customers. Anointed is one of those groups that will bridge the gap."

The members of Anointed were influenced by gospel and R&B music at an early age and were raised in Christian homes, but all three firmly believe that people should be exposed to various types of music. Greathouse explained to Akins, "Take the people who are 'gatekeepers.' If they're familiar with Christian pop, then of course they're only going to gravitate more toward that.... I think more efforts are being made to include both gospel and contemporary Christian music in the same places, but all the changes that need to be made may not happen overnight."

The band's debut album, *Spiritual Love Affair,* was released on Brainstorm Records and then distributed by Word Records in 1993. *Under the Influence,* released in 1996 on Word's Myrrh label, picked up musically where the resoundingly successful *The Call*— also on Myrrh—left off, but offered more of a live performance feel. Band members take turns penning the majority of songs for each release. All three members of the group wrote the songs on *Under the Influence,* but Walls wrote the lion's share for this particular record. Reviewers were positive revealing opinions on *Under the Influence.* Rene Tranthan of *Christian Net* gave the album an A+, calling it "a magnificent showcase of the vocal talents of Anointed.

Along with the accolades and the whirlwind of success came another difficult circumstance: Mary Tiller's exit from the band. She left the group in January of 1996 filing a $2.5 million lawsuit against Anointed and their former manager. The lawsuit claimed sexual harassment by the manager and breach of contract from Anointed. The case created an emotional strain for the members. Greathouse explained to Akin, "There really is no bitterness in our hearts or unforgiveness.... If that were the case, our annointing would be cut off. We wouldn't be effective." Walls added, "(God) is going to allow you to be tried. But you're going to come out pure as gold." Tiller's departure did not affect *Tennessean* writer Tom Roland's review of *Under the Influence.* As Roland stated: "The group may be missing one body, but Anointed remains a complete package."

Epic-Myrrh Union

After the release of *Under the Influence,* Epic Records and the Nashville-based Myrrh Records teamed together to build on the band's broad fan base through a strong push to Christian and mainstream radio and retail. In an interview with *Billboard*'s Price, Myrrh VP/GM Jim Chaffee remarked: "They are very well received in the gospel marketplace ... in the R&B marketplace, and we've had real good success in the contemporary Christian marketplace.... We feel they have the opportunity to reach a world that is way beyond where most contemporary Christian artists are capable of reaching."

The video for the single "In God's Hands Now," from the album *The Call,* was lauded in the mainstream market and received airplay on BET and VH1; the single peaked at No. 40 on *Billboard*'s Hot R&B Singles chart in November of 1995. Epic placed Anointed on a 20-market promotional tour to support the single with the mainstream act at Groove Theory, which gave the group an opportunity for mainstream exposure. As Greathouse told Price: "We never really wanted to be just a gospel ... or contemporary Christian group. And of course, that's one of the most ludicrous things you can ever tell a record company. (They) need to categorize it, and package it. So it has been challenging."

Selected discography

Spiritual Love Affair, Brainstorm Records, 1993.
The Call, Myrrh Records, 1995.
Under the Influence, Myrrh, 1996.

Sources

Billboard, October 19, 1996; November 23, 1996.
Christian Advocate, December 1996.
Christian Net, winter 1996-1997.
Christian Retailing, October 14, 1996.
Contemporary Christian Music, November 1996; December 1996; March 31, 1997.
Release, February/March, 1997.
The Tennessean, November 25, 1996.

—*B. Kimberly Taylor*

Archers of Loaf

Alternative rock band

Chapel Hill, North Carolina's Archers of Loaf have managed to distinguish themselves from other alternative rock bands riding in the wake of Nirvana's epic 1991 crossover to the mainstream. They have done so by maintaining a balance between writing songs for themselves and catering to their fans. Steadfastly avoiding major record label overtures from 1993 to 1997, the band has forsaken the lure of the multi-platinum success of bands like Green Day and Bush. In so doing they have built a mass of critical and listener support and have retained the reigns of creative control.

Yet the Archers have not avoided the limelight just for the sake of doing so, or in opposition to the very idea of a wider audience. As *Village Voice* rock critic and avowed Archers fan Robert Christgau put it in 1995, "unlike many alternabands, right up to the notoriously uneven Pavement, they're not so stricken with incompetence, fear, irony, or disdain that their live efficiency or enthusiasm is ever in question." This is not an unimpressive achievement in an alternative music culture riddled with such self-important negativity.

Photograph by Dennis Kleiman. Alias Records. Reproduced by permission.

The dual Erics, Bachman and Johnson, are the guitar-wielding front men in the Archers of Loaf, and Bachman is the band's singer. The two grew up in Asheville, North Carolina, a small city of 50,000 in the far western part of the state across the Great Smoky Mountains from Knoxville, Tennessee. Both were raised in upper-middle-class homes (Bachman as the son of an insurance salesman), and they met again at the University of North Carolina at Chapel Hill, near the metropolis of Raleigh-Durham. Bachman had studied saxophone for two years at Appalachian State University before transferring to U.N.C. In January of 1992 Bachman and Johnson met bassist Matt Gentling and drummer Mark Price and formed the Archers of Loaf. Usually referred to as simply "the Archers," it isn't clear what the band's name refers to, but its quirkiness is in keeping with song titles like "Hate Paste," "Audiowhore," and "Vocal Shrapnel."

Band Formed at Peak of Chapel Hill Frenzy

The band came together at a time when Chapel Hill's reputation for breeding college music hits had music industry insiders plugging it as the next big scene. Just as in Seattle after Nirvana's mainstream crossover in 1991 and Athens, Georgia (another college town), in the mid-80s following R.E.M.'s meteoric rise, legions of record company talent scouts descended upon Chapel Hill's music scene. Other local bands the Archers shared the spotlight with were Superchunk, Polvo, and Small (also known as Small 23, owing to copyright disputes with other bands apparently using the same self-deprecating moniker). In fact, Bachman was a founding member of Small, as well, contributing to that band's 1993 EP, *Cakes.* But when Small gained record label attention and it came time to choose his allegiance, Bachman stuck with the Archers.

Under a local music fanzine and label called Stay Free, the Archers of Loaf recorded their first single, "Wrong" in late 1992. This release attracted the attention of a number of independent record labels, and the band signed with Burbank, California-based Alias Records. The first album, *Icky Mettle,* was released in 1993 and attracted significant praise in the college/alternative music industry. The first single from the album "Web in Front," gained measurable airplay both on college radio and on MTV. In addition, the album was on the influential *College Music Journal* (*CMJ*) charts for 22 weeks. *Interview* gave *Icky Mettle* the magazine's highest praise, naming the album "Best Indie Rock Album of the Year." The album's varied compositions drew comparisons to a number of sources: the latter-day punk of Washington, D.C.'s Fugazi, the alterna-pop of late-80s indie godfathers the Pixies, and the early 90s low-fidelity, art-school rock of Pavement.

In the fall of 1993, the Archers headlined the Alias Records segment of the *CMJ* music festival in New York, where bands, college music DJs, and label scouts converge annually to observe new talents. Writing in *Rock: the Rough Guide,* critic Jonathan Swift described a live Archers show from the early '90s: "The intensity of Eric Bachman, the dreaminess of Eric Johnson, and the muppet-like qualities of Matt Gentling and Mark Price combine to make one of the most solid live bands touring today."

Spurned Suitors Included Madonna

Continuing their regular recording schedule but offering up a shorter release this time, 1994 saw the band issue *The Archers of Loaf vs. the Greatest of All Time* EP. More punk in style than their previous work, the release again garnered extensive college airplay and also topped *Village Voice* critic Christgau's list of the year's best EPs. This feat prompted many major record labels to call on the band and even prompted singer

Madonna to show up at an Archers performance and try to sign them to her Maverick label. The band spurned all the offers, preferring to stick with the independent Alias. Perhaps this decision was motivated by a desire to avoid the pitfalls of the countless bands who have signed to major labels, only to find themselves dropped after falling short of the required number of album sales. Gentling confessed to the *Village Voice*'s Christgau that the band had a fear of catering to the desires of the marketplace rather than its own original inspiration. "I like the way certain people maintain their privacy," Bachman added. "Like Tom Waits—he's always done what he wants, right?"

Following *The Archers of Loaf vs. the Greatest of All Time*'s release the band embarked on its longest sustained period of touring to date—over 12 months spent traveling across the United States and Europe, including a stop at England's influential Reading Festival. In 1995 the Archers entered the studio with legendary alternative music engineer, Steve Albini, whose long list of credits include *In Utero*, Nirvana's follow up to their multi-platinum *Nevermind*. The result, *Vee Vee*, was another success, spending 14 weeks on the *CMJ*'s Top 50 list and six weeks in the Top 10.

Rolling Stone's review of the album deemed the band "top of the heap" of the Chapel Hill crowd and described the release as follows: "Weirdo song titles ('Underachievers March and Fight Song,' 'Let the Loser Melt') and lyrics stuffed with quips ('the underground is overcrowded') testify to a welcome humor; dissonant guitars lend a wicked edge. And when the Archers settle into full-out rocking—the hammering 'Harnessed in Slums'—they do so with satisfying savagery." That same year Alias also released the first product of Bachman's solo project, Barry Black, a mostly instrumental, experimental amalgam of rock, jazz and folk influences incorporating instruments like the sax, trombone, cello and Brazilian rainstick.

This critical success led the band back to the road, albeit playing in bigger venues and on tour with similarly quirky but slightly better financed bands like the Flaming Lips and Weezer—a group propelled in part by its big-time producer, former Cars front man Ric Ocasek. The Archers also continued their string of annual Alias releases, producing their third album, *The Speed of Cattle,* in early 1996. In contrast to the studio albums, however, this release was an 18-track collection of assorted B-sides, alternate versions of previously released tracks, live recordings, and sessions from the London studios of John Peel. Known as "Peel Sessions," many punk/alternative bands of the last 20 years, from the Buzzcocks to Nirvana, have paid a visit to this studio to record a few songs for limited release.

Even with the lack of new material, *The Speed of Cattle* merited an "A minus" in the *Village Voice*'s "Consumer Guide," and Christgau added, "I say the bits and pieces of the most musical band in Alternia beat the fully realized works of art of mortal road heroes. In fact, I say they are fully realized works of art."

Ever the touring band, the Archers continued to play dates in the United States and Europe up to and following the recording of their next album, *All the Nations Airports,* during March and April of 1996. Released in September of that year, the album was again on the Alias label but this time with the added U.S. distribution muscle of Elektra Records behind it. It was recorded at Ironwood Studios in Seattle and featured slicker production than that on the band's earlier "lo-fi" releases. In contrast to the week spent recording earlier albums, which were essentially taped live, this time the band spent a month just preparing the sound settings. The final product was a similar departure in song writing, including shorter songs, four instrumentals, and a three-song mini-rock opera. "Worst Defense," "Attack of the Killer Bees," and "Rental Sting" were listed as three songs but played as one. The Archers referred to the songs affectionately as "the trilogy."

In January of 1997, the band released another EP on Alias, *Vitus Tinnitus*. Also rereleased that year was the first Archers recording, "Wrong," on an Atlantic Records compilation of songs appearing on the popular but short-lived TV show, *My So-Called Life*. This followed at least five other compilations in the previous two years that featured Archers tracks, including the soundtrack to the movie *Mallrats, Step Right Up: the Songs of Tom Waits,* and a CD to benefit the beloved Chicago indie music venue, Lounge Ax. Furthermore, the single "Harnessed in Slums" from *Vee Vee* was named "one of the best protest songs in indie rock" by *Trouser Press* founder Ira Robbins. This acknowledgment, along with a string of solid indie album releases enabled the Archers to continue following their own inspiration. The band's lasting significance to the music world was deemed by the *Village Voice* to be, "in croaked, wild, intelligent music that's also virtuosic, especially up against the myriad alt bands who fancy themselves players these days."

Selected discography

Icky Mettle (includes "Web in Front"), Alias, 1993.
The Archers of Loaf vs the Greatest of All Time (EP), Alias, 1994.
(Contributor) *Step Right Up: The Songs of Tom Waits,* Manifesto, 1995.

Vee Vee (includes "Underachievers March and Fight Song" and "Let the Loser Melt"), Alias, 1995.

(Contributor) *My So-Called Life,* Atlantic, 1995.

(Contributor) *Mallrats* (soundtrack), MCA, 1995.

The Speed of Cattle (includes "Wrong" and "South Carolina"), Alias, 1996.

All the Nations Airports (includes "Worst Defense," "Attack of the Killer Bees," and "Rental Sting"), Alias, 1996.

(Contributor) *The Lounge Ax Defense and Relocation CD,* Touch & Go, 1996.

Vitus Tinnitus (EP), Alias, 1997.

Sources

Books

Rock: the Rough Guide, Rough Guides Ltd., 1996.
The Trouser Press Guide to '90s Rock, Fireside, 1997.

Periodicals

Guitar Player, November 1996.
Interview, December, 1993.
Melody Maker, October 1, 1994; April 27, 1996, p. 74.
Rolling Stone, March 23, 1995, p. 125.
Village Voice, April 18, 1995, p. 76; October 8, 1996, p. 60.

Online

http://www.iuma.com/Warner
http://wkuweb1.wku.edu/~bob/archers

Additional information was provided by Alias Records publicity materials, 1997.

—*John F. Packel*

Jann Arden

Pop singer, songwriter

Canadian singer/songwriter Jann Arden traveled a circuitous road to success, spending more than a decade singing rock 'n' roll covers and jazz and blues standards in smoky Canadian bars and lounges. She also worked a string of odd jobs to pay the rent, including busking on the street—until she was knocked out and robbed of the four dollars she had earned that day. After a series of failed relationships and a bout with alcoholism, Arden emerged from the fog with a major-label recording contract, a million-selling album, and international fame. Today, she is Alberta's hottest musical export since k.d. lang. Meanwhile, her wicked sense of humor remains intact, sharply contrasting her endearing, melancholy folk/pop songs. "We're going to be doing various songs about despair, heartbreak and loneliness," she once told the crowd at an Edmonton concert, reported Mike Ross in an Arden website article. "We'll be moving on to guilt later, so feel free to slump against the person next to you."

Arden and her two brothers grew up in Springbank, Alberta, a rural town near Calgary in the foothills of the Rocky Mountains. Her father was a construction contractor and her mother was a dental assistant. Friends remember Jann as a happy, rambunctious child who was chronically anxious for approval. "This need was always there, as if she felt it was her responsibility to entertain everyone," a childhood friend told *Chatelaine* magazine. Despite that yearning, however, Arden kept her musical interests quiet. She listened to Karen

Carpenter and ABBA and headed down to the family's basement when she played her hand-me-down guitar and sang her songs. After she was asked to sing one of her compositions at her high school graduation ceremony, her mother said, "We didn't even know you sang."

After high school, Arden moved to Vancouver and began singing with a series of forgettable bar bands. Alcohol was her steadiest companion. "I was making sixty dollars a week, although I usually owed the bar more than I made," she told *Chatelaine.* "I was going home with different people. I thought it was part of the rock 'n' roll life, but it was awful. I didn't like who I was. I can't even think of the specific incidents now, because they're cringes to me. I'm ashamed of that time in my life."

Arden sang covers as varied and Led Zeppelin and Tina Turner to Karen Carpenter and Billie Holiday in bars, lounges, and ski resorts. She worked as a ball washer at a golf course, a singing waitress, and a deckhand on a salmon boat, where she gutted up to 700 fish a day. She tried to launch a solo career, but the booze held her back. "I was 26 and dysfunctional and struggling hard," she said in an interview with *Billboard*'s Timothy White. At about that time Neil MacGonigill, a record promoter who'd grown disillusioned with the music business, took an interest in Arden. He saw enormous potential in her raw talent and offered to manage her career—if she was ready to take her singing seriously. She said she was; they agreed the first step was for Arden to work on her songwriting. Eventually, she quit drinking. "January 20, 1989. You don't forget the date," she told *Chatelaine.*

Success and Yearning

Success, however, remained elusive. Arden and MacGonigill spent nearly three years trying to interest a record company in the young singer. Then, in October 1991, A&M executive Allan Reid heard Arden's demo tape and signed her to a recording contract, giving her the break she needed. Her first album, 1993's *Time for Mercy,* achieved critical and popular success in her homeland. It registered strong sales, went gold in Canada, spawned the hit single "I Would Die for You," and earned two Juno Awards, the Canadian equivalent of the Grammy.

The second album, *Living Under June,* vaulted Arden to international fame. It churned out five singles—"Could I Be Your Girl," "Wonder Drug," "Unloved (a duet with Arden-fan Jackson Browne)," "Good Mother," and "Insensitive." The latter song hit the Top 10 in Canada,

For the Record . . .

Born Jann Arden Richards, March 27, 1962 in Calgary, Alberta; Canada; daughter of Derrell Richards (a construction contractor) and Joan Bentley (a retired dental assistant).

Released three albums on A&M: *Time for Mercy,* 1993; the million-selling *Living Under June,* 1994; and *Happy?,* 1997. Singles include "I Would Die for You," "Could I Be Your Girl," "Good Mother," and "Insensitive." On the strength of *Living Under June,* Arden has appeared on countless TV shows, including *The Late Show with David Letterman, Dick Clark's New Year's Rockin' Eve, Good Morning America,* and *The Rosie O'Donnell Show.* She also hosted the 1997 Juno Awards.

Awards: Junos include Best Solo Performer and Best Video, 1993, and Female Vocalist of the Year, Songwriter of the Year, and Single of the Year, 1995.

Addresses: *Record company*—A&M Records, 595 Madison Ave., New York, NY 10022.

the United States, Italy, and Australia. *Living Under June* sold more than one million copies, earned Arden three more Junos, and kept her touring for more than two years. Meanwhile, the music press raved. *Billboard* editor Timothy White wrote that Arden exhibits a "thrillingly subtle and full-throated vocal vigor that makes *Living Under June* an extraordinary listening adventure." *Elle* magazine stated that the singer "pours out her gorgeous, wise songs with transcendent intensity." *Stereo Review* noted that Arden "crafts smart, provocative songs about complex human relationships and sings them in a wise, knowing soprano.... Arden is usually nothing short of exquisite." *Chatelaine* attributed Arden's wisdom and emotionally revealing songs to her difficult past. "She's still not sure how, early on, her life went from good to bad—the downward spiral that carried her into hard drinking, hard living and scrambling for money before she was 20," the magazine wrote. "The songs on *Living Under June* explore elements of that painful past and reach out with a child's yearning for her parents."

By the time Arden released her third album, 1997's *Happy?,* she was an international recording artist. Yet she remained as down-to-earth as ever. "Album sales change. Jann Arden doesn't," James Muretich wrote in the *Calgary Herald.* "At least not at the core. She is still very much the same Jann she always was, although there've been dramatic changes in her external life, like the way she's gone from hard-drinking to abstaining from liquor, cigarettes and even caffeine." The new album, Muretich noted, "is sparsely arranged but much more richly textured than before.... And her lyrics, buoyed by her powerful vocals—have become more direct, more heart-wrenching, constantly turning melancholy into a thing of beauty, of defiant hope."

Despite the melancholy that invades Arden's songs and the difficult detours she experienced on her way to success, hope permeates her music and her outlook. Although she admits to being used to failure, the artist is proud of her resilience and tenacity. "I used to worry that my songs were too sad or depressing," Arden confessed to Nicholas Jennings of *Maclean's.* "Now, I don't really care because life is about imperfection and making mistakes. It's not a beer commercial. And I feel so much happier that I know that now." Arden's ability to maintain her sense of humor has also been essential to her survival. When asked if her songs are autobiographical, Arden replied to Barbara Wickens of *Maclean's,* "They must be. I couldn't make up that pathetic life."

Selected discography

Time for Mercy, A&M Records, 1993.
Living Under June, A&M Records, 1994.
Happy?, A&M Records, 1997.

Sources

Billboard, April 13, 1994; September 28, 1996.
Calgary Herald, March 5, 1997; February 7, 1997; September 22, 1997.
Chatelaine, October 1995.
Edmonton Journal, March 7, 1997.
Elle, April 1995.
Entertainment Weekly, March 10, 1995.
Hamilton Spectator, September 22, 1997.
Maclean's, April 10, 1995; October 6, 1997; December 23, 1996.
Ottawa Citizen, November 23, 1995.
Southam News, November 23, 1995.
Stereo Review, July 1995.
Variety, June 16, 1995.

Additional information was provided by A&M Records press materials.

—Dave Wilkins

Tina Arena

Pop singer

APWide WOrld Photos, Inc. Reproduced by permission.

At 29 years old, Tina Arena was Australia's most successful female singer. Actually a veteran in the music business, she has been singing professionally for over 20 years. "As an artist, I'm not very one-dimensional," Arena stated in the Auckland *Sunday News.* "I certainly like to diversify. I'm inspired by so many different styles. The listeners would be bored if they kept hearing the same old bloody thing. There's a bit of a rock bitch in me too that likes to come out occasionally."

Her singing style has been characterized as something between rock and R&B. Carole King, Aretha Franklin, and Barbra Streisand were her early music idols. Arena is an international star who writes the lyrics and melodies to most of her songs. "I found strength through writing these songs because I've been able to personally let go and be totally honest," the artist stated in her Epic Center biography. "I'm a believer in honesty and optimism, and I guess that positivity in my character comes through. But all I wanted to do was come up with great songs reflecting my life. I feel most comfortable writing about personal experiences, and that's what I've done."

Arena grew up in suburban Melbourne, the middle of three daughters of Italian immigrants. Born Filippina Arena, her name was abbreviated to Tina in 1975. At age three, she would listen and sing the Spanish, Italian, and French songs that were in the family record collection. The song "You're My World," sung by Daryl Braithwaite, was one she memorized and sang often as a child. Her first performance was at age eight, when she sang "You're My World" in front of 400 guests at a family wedding. The audience loved it so much that they gave her a rallying ovation, which moved the young Arena to tears.

She soon went on to compete in television talent contests, winning three out of the four that she participated in. After one performance, she was asked to be a permanent member of the cast. Almost overnight, she became known as "Tiny Tina" on a show called *Young Talent Time,* a popular Australian TV show. She was a weekly TV star for about seven years, displaying her maturity and confidence in front of the camera. Fortunately, Arena was not overcome by her success. At 16, she went to work as an insurance clerk while also singing live in Melbourne pubs.

Overnight, it seemed Arena went from TV sensation to pop music icon. She grew up performing on-stage, in bars and theatres, on the radio, and on tours. At the age of 21, she started to play in bands, and released her first single, "Turn up the Beat," in 1985. She took a break from singing in 1993 to narrate the nationwide Australian stage production of the *Amazing Technicolour Dreamcoat*. Her 1994 debut album, *Strong As Steel*, was very successful, with the single "I Need Your Body," reaching platinum status.

Soon afterward, she went to Los Angeles in an effort to gain independence, something she didn't have while producing records in Australia. "I've done something that I have wanted to do for many years," Arena proclaimed in her Epic bio. "And going to LA like I did proved that I was very able to do it. It was a fantastic learning experience and I felt a great sense of liberation."

While in the United States, she recorded the album *Don't Ask* in 1996, which marked a milestone for the singer as she felt it was her first independent effort. "I had gotten used to singing other people's songs, but this time they are my songs and my experience so I can sing them like I mean it," Arena stated in her Epic bio. "The record is honest and sincere and simple." *Don't Ask* went platinum ten times in Australia, and was released in the United States in March of 1996, gaining airtime on over 200 radio stations. The single "Chains" focuses on breaking through stereotypes, which was

the way she characterized her own singing career. "I've finally begun believing in my ability," the artist announced in the Sony Music Artist Info website. "I think it's so important to believe in yourself and know that if you work hard, it will pay off." She wrote ten of the 11 songs on the album. "Chains" hit gold after eight weeks, then platinum after 12 weeks. Soon, it reached the Top Ten in Britain and the American Top 40.

Don't Ask went gold in it's first month of release, platinum in six months and over eight times platinum within a year. This made her the highest selling female artist in Australian history. In 1995 Arena toured Europe, appearing on *Top Of The Pops* TV program, which reached an audience of 60 million people. One of the proudest moments of her career was at the Australian Record Industry Awards in October of 1995 when she was awarded the Best Pop Release and Song of the Year for "Chains." She also won the award for the highest selling Australian album and the Best Australian Album Award for *Don't Ask*. In addition, she was awarded Female Artist of the Year. Other accolades she earned were Variety Club Entertainer of the Year, an Advance Australia Foundation award, and a World Music Award.

She returned to Los Angeles in 1996 and 1997 to record her third album, *In Deep*. She wrote four of the songs on the album. Contributions on the other seven songs came from Mick Jones, David Tyson, Christopher Ward, Dean McTaggart, Pam Reswick, and Steve Werfel.

Personal Life Includes Charity

Ralph Carr began to manage Arena's music career and the two were married in December 1995. They live in the inner city of Melbourne. Arena had maintained many of the friendships she formed in high school. According to the Artist Info website, she once told a reporter, "I feel rejuvenated ... I've really taken control of my own destiny. I've made the decisions about where I've wanted to go, what I've wanted to write about, who I've wanted to work with and how I want to be received."

In September of 1997, at the age of 29, Arena announced that she was starting a charitable foundation to help disadvantaged children. "Look, I'm not Mother Teresa," she told Steve McCarty of the *South China Morning Post*. "But I want to give something back to the world; I just like giving so much more than receiving. I've been lucky, I have such a strong support network that I've never had to go jabbing my arm. I didn't fall into any traps like that after the whole child-star business."

She feels her foundation can right some wrongs that she sees in her native country. "The suicide rate among Australian youngsters is climbing," she told McCarty. "Unemployment and dysfunctional families are partly the reason. Some kids just don't have any motivation. I'm hoping to fund youth education pro- grammes by going out and performing at different events, setting up performance camps, giving them a goal."

Selected discography

Strong As Steel, Epic, 1994.
Don't Ask, Epic, 1996.
(Contributor) *One Fine Day* (soundtrack), Epic, 1996.
In Deep, Epic, 1997.

Sources

Periodicals

Billboard, December 14, 1996.
Daily News, April 28, 1996, p. 35.
The Dominion, November 9, 1996, p. 22.
South China Morning Post, September 26, 1997, p. 5.
The Sunday News, August 17, 1997, p. 21.
Time, August 12, 1996; October 14, 1996; September 22, 1997.

Online

www.epiccenter.com/EpicCenter/docs/artistbio.qry?artistid
www.tina-arena.com.au/biog.htm
www.starjump.com/tina/main.htm

—Bill Bennett

Kenny Aronoff

Drummer

Kenny Aronoff never imagined that he would become a rock 'n' roll drummer extraordinaire; trained as a classical percussionist, he reacted with shock when a professor urged him to broaden his instrumental repertoire. "Someday your specialty might be tambourine. Or it might be rock 'n' roll drumset," Aronoff told *Percussive Notes.* "I said, 'Man, I hope not.' [But]I ended up being the drummer I always put down!"

Some 20 years after that exchange, Aronoff is one of the most versatile, sought-after drummers in popular music. *Modern Drummer*'s Rick Mattingly observed that Aronoff's sound is "built on the foundation of traditional American rock music." Writing for *Percussive Notes,* Mattingly called Aronoff "one of the finest rock 'n' roll drummers in the business. His playing is distinguished by a 'less is more' approach in which the beats are fairly simple but always contain that little twist that sets them apart from the norm." That approach is responsible for the remarkable range of music in which Aronoff has made his mark. He has appeared on more than 200 albums since 1980, in styles that range from country

Kenny Aronoff phtograph. Reproduced by permission.

For the Record . . .

Born March 3, 1953, in Albany NY; children: one son, Nik.

Performed with fusion band Stream, winter 1979; recorded and toured with John Mellencamp Band 1980-1996; played as session drummer 1981-1997; toured with various bands 1987-1997; offered drum clinics and private drum lessons, 1970s-1990s.

Awards: Five years #1 Pop/Rock drummer; Honor Roll Pop/Rock Drummer; Three years #1 Studio drummer, all from *Modern Drummer* Readers' Poll.

Addresses: Home—Bloomington, Indiana. E-mail—aronoff1@earthlink.net.

and rock to pop and jazz to the fringes of heavy metal. After getting his start with John Mellencamp, he moved on to artists as diverse as Willie Nelson, Belinda Carlisle, Iggy Pop, and Jon Bon Jovi. Not bad for a guy that never used to care for rock drummers!

Kenny Aronoff was born in Albany, New York, but grew up Stockbridge, Massachusetts. A product of the Sixties, he listened to all the music that was in the air; among his favorites were the Rolling Stones, the Who, the Beatles, Creedence Clearwater Revival, and Jimi Hendrix. Their drummers were to have a decisive influence on his own development. When he was ten he joined his first band—with only a snare drum and cymbal. He learned everything about drumming on his own—he had no formal training on the drum kit until after he graduated from college. He picked up what he could from records, from various method books and from the garage bands he played in throughout junior high and high school. But unlike so many of his peers Aronoff did not dream of being a rock star 'n' roll star; he set sights on playing classical music instead.

Studied Classical Percussion

At the age of 16 he decided to focus on classical music. "My formal training was in classical music," Aronoff told *Musician*, "starting with the summer after my sophomore year in high school when I began studying with Arthur Press of the Boston Symphony Orchestra. That's when I got into the classical stuff, you know, timpani, mallets, snare drums." After high school he attended

the University of Massachusetts School of Music for a year. But after studying with George Gaber at the Aspen Music Festival in the summer of 1972, he transferred to Indiana University where Gaber was teaching. He was concentrating on timpani when Gaber warned him against limiting himself too much: "You have to be a well-rounded percussionist and learn to play all the instruments," Aronoff recalled his teacher telling him in *Percussive Notes*. However, the future drummer did not realize at first how true those words were. "I figured you made a living as an orchestral player," he told *Musician*. But when he graduated from IU in 1976 he faced an unsettling situation: there were no orchestral jobs. Not a single American orchestra was auditioning percussionists. He could have had spots in the Jerusalem Symphony as well as in an orchestra in Quito, Ecuador, but he politely refused both offers.

Without the orchestra job he had been preparing for over the better part of six years, Aronoff changed direction. He moved back East and started studying jazz drumset under Alan Dawson, who had taught at the Berklee School of Music. Drumset was not offered in Indiana's percussion program, a fact Aronoff finds ironic in light of the school's fine jazz program. Jazz drumming was nothing new to Aronoff; he had been interested in jazz since he was a child, when his father had played a John Coltrane album for him.

When Aronoff was getting ready to graduate from Indiana he decided to play a piece for jazz quartet, with himself on drums, as one of his final performance pieces. "It was suggested to me that I shouldn't do that if I wanted to earn a performance certificate. But drumset was as much a part of me as the other instruments," he told *Percussive Notes*, "and my other pieces were very strong." (They were classical pieces by Bartok, Saint-Saëns, and Delecuse.) Aronoff played the jazz "Tribute to Zoltan Kodahly" and was approved for his performance certificate unanimously.

After Dawson and some work under New York studio drummer Gary Chester in the late 1970s, Aronoff moved back to Indiana. Along with David Grissom, he formed a fusion band, called Streamwinner, which played the Midwest and Southern circuits for a while but never managed to make the jump to a nationwide audience.

Percussionist Became Rock Drummer

By the end of the 1970s, Aronoff was playing drumset exclusively. At this time he felt an even stronger contempt for rock drummers than before. "I had no respect whatsoever for simple rock 'n' roll drumming," he confessed to

Percussive Notes. "I only liked heavy fusion and technical drumming like Billy Cobham, Harvey Mason, Alphonse Mougon, Elvin Jones, Joe Morello, Tony Williams, Lenny White and Steve Gadd." So he wasn't entirely prepared for the turn his career was about to take as the 1980s began. He was on his way to Los Angeles for a Lou Rawls audition when he heard that John Mellencamp was looking for a drummer for his band, a rock band. Aronoff dragged his whole kit, 14 drums and 12 cymbals—he had been playing fusion, after all—over to Mellencamp's house and set them up in a small room there. "I remember I tried to play *really loud,*" he told *Musician*'s Alan di Perna. "because I figured it was a rock audition. Ridiculously loud. I think broke three sticks and a cymbal and we only played three songs. John didn't say anything right away, but after he hired me, he said 'Okay, get rid of that drum, that drum, that cymbal, that drum, that cymbal....' I didn't understand it at first, but then I figured it out."

Aronoff spent about two years learning to play rock 'n' roll music with Mellencamp. "I could make the transition because I went back to my roots, back to that Charlie Watts, Keith Moon, Creedence Clearwater approach to rock 'n' roll," he explained to di Perna. "So there's this very schooled part of me, but also this really raw street thing. Sometimes, when I want to get into that really raw state of mind I try to play the drums as if I weren't a drummer."

Session Man and Professor

For 17 years Aronoff was an integral part of Mellencamp's band, and the powerful, innovative sound he developed there did much to define the sound of the band's music. He gives a lot of the credit to Mellencamp, who spurred him on to some of his most inventive ideas. With Mellencamp he felt constantly challenged; Mellencamp's ever-changing approach to recording aided and abetted Aronoff's musical growth. He made the band learn hundreds of songs from the 1960s and 1970s before they even started recording *Scarecrow* in 1985. In contrast, the songs on 1989's *Big Daddy* were recorded in one or two takes, without even the benefit of rehearsals.

In the late 1980s, Mellencamp began taking longer breaks from recording and touring. With time on his hands, Aronoff became a drummer for hire and one of the most in-demand session drummers in popular music. The list of acts with which he has performed includes Bob Dylan, Bob Seger, Marshall Crenshaw, Lyle Lovett, Melissa Etheridge, Bonnie Raitt, and Elton John. Although he is one of the best-paid drummers in music,

he does not maintain his grueling schedule just for the money. "To me it's not about getting quadruple scale," he told *Musician*'s Mattingly. "You have to keep abreast of what's going on. One way for me to keep learning new things is to work constantly."

In the 1990s Aronoff increased his work in drum education. He gave clinics, wrote columns for *Modern Drummer* magazine, and developed instructional videos. In 1993 he became an Associate Professor at his alma mater, Indiana University. There he taught drumset to individual students in the jazz program—the instrument he was unable to study at college. The school gave him a free hand in arranging his courseload around his other professional commitments. He believes he brought a unique perspective to his university teaching. "I know where these students are at," he told *Percussive Notes.* "When I was there I was putting down the kind of drummer I've become, because I didn't understand it." Unfortunately, Aronoff was forced to give up his teaching at IU when his playing schedule became too overwhelming.

While pursuing work outside Mellencamp's band, Aronoff tried extremely hard to coordinate his schedule. He agreed to play a Hong Kong promotional event for executives at Mellencamp's record company, for example, during a short break in his tour with Bob Seger. At the last minute, unexpected problems arose with his flight back to the United States, and he arrived at the arena five minutes before the band began their sound check—but only by hiring a helicopter to fly him in from the airport. Not long afterwards, Aronoff was in the middle of a commitment when Mellencamp called him to play another promotional gig. But there was no way Kenny could get out of the job with such short notice. Because Mellencamp wanted someone who could be available all the time, and Aronoff could not afford to give up his other work, the two parted ways for good.

Played with Boyhood Idol

Aronoff's latest collaboration was with one of his boyhood idols—John Fogerty. Fogerty's album, *Blue Moon Swamp* (1997) took more than four years to make, as he was unable to find a drummer suitable for the project. Aronoff, who said he always believed he would be perfect for Fogerty's music, entered the picture and ended up playing on five of the album's twelve tracks. (Five different drummers worked on the other seven.) For Fogerty, Aronoff's style is his special contribution to the music. "Kenny's time always feels great," Fogerty explained to *Modern Drummer,* "whereas I've had a lot of situations where I'm standing there stomping my left foot trying to keep the thing moving forward. Consider him the best rock 'n' roll drummer in the world."

Aronoff summed up his own role in the music industry in *Percussive Notes:* "I've played rock 'n' roll with Jon Bon Jovi, but I've also played in the orchestra at Tanglewood under Leonard Bernstein. I'm a legitimate guy!"

Selected discography

With John Mellencamp

American Fool, Mercury, 1982.
Uh Huh, Mercury, 1983.
Scarecrow, Mercury, 1985.
The Lonesome Jubilee, Mercury, 1987.
Big Daddy, Mercury, 1989.

With others

Jon Bon Jovi, *Destination Anywhere.*
Bob Dylan, *Under the Red Sky.*
Melissa Etheridge, *Your Little Secret.*
John Fogerty, *Blue Moon Swamp.*
Iggy Pop, *Brick by Brick.*

Buddy Rich Big Band, *Burning for Buddy, Vols. I and II.*
Patty Smyth, *Patty Smyth.*

Videos

Power Workout, Volumes I and II, CPP/Belwin, 1993.

Selected writings

Power Workout, Volumes I and II, CPP/Belwin, 1993
Columnist for *Modern Drummer,* "Rock Perspectives," July 1987 to November 1989.

Sources

Down Beat, June 1993.
Modern Drummer, September 1991; November 1997.
Musician, June 1989; May 1996.
Percussive Notes, April 1993.

Additional information from interview with Kenny Aronoff, December 5, 1997

—*Gerald E. Brennan*

Backstreet Boys

Vocal group

The Backstreet Boys consist of five young men from Orlando, Florida, who took the world by storm in 1995, and two years later became an international phenomenon. They sold over eleven million records worldwide, had four Top Ten singles, and sold out concert venues in Europe, North America, Asia, and Australia. In 1996 they were awarded the MTV Europe Viewers Choice Award, beating out acts like Oasis and Spice Girls as European favorites. Their popularity grew uncontrollably everywhere except in their home country, the United States. It wasn't until 1997 that America heard its first Backstreet Boys album—two years after the rest of the world—and the band launched a tour in an effort to conquer their own country.

The popularity of Backstreet Boys signals a resurgence of the innocent teen music of years past; Backstreet Boys are an old type of act with a new name, "the boy group." Their music appeals mostly to *Tiger Beat* and *Seventeen* crowds, who haven't had a similar fave rave since the New Kids on the Block bowed out in the early 1990s. The rise of the Backstreet Boys coincides with

AP/Wide World Photos, Inc. Reproduced by permission.

the decline of angst-ridden, doom-obsessed indie rock groups like Nirvana. "This music is an aural upper," *Seventeen*'s music editor Susan Kaplow told *USA Today.* "I think consumers and the industry are ready for that." More cynical observers note the similarities in both the group's image—five different male archetypes—and the demographics of their fans—teen and pre-teen girls—to that of heart throb groups of the past, like the New Kids, Menudo, and the Bay City Rollers. All those groups flashed by and disappeared without leaving much of a blip on the radar of public consciousness. But the Backstreet Boys say they are different.

Sunshine and Stardom

The band got their start in Orlando, Florida, in the early 1990s. By that time both Disney and MGM studios had established high profiles and were providing lots of work in movies and commercials. Two high school students, A. J. McLean and Howie Dorough, and junior high schooler Nick Carter started running into each other at auditions. They discovered a common interest in singing and soon they were harmonizing together a cappella whenever they had breaks. After a while they decided to form a group, but felt they needed were two more voices to add range and depth to their sound. Through a friend they discovered Kevin Richardson, who was singing in a show at Disney World. Richardson suggested his cousin, Brian Littrell, who was living in Kentucky at the time. Phone calls were made and Littrell agreed to move down to Florida. With the line-up set they adopted the name Backstreet Boys, after Orlando's Backstreet Market, a popular hangout for the city's teens.

They started singing a cappella covers of their favorite songs by groups like Boyz II Men, Shai, and Color Me Badd. Then, they found managers Johnny and Donna Wright. Johnny had been the Road Manager for the New Kids on the Block. "Before I saw them perform I wasn't sure if I wanted to get involved," Donna told *Billboard.* "The New Kids had just finished up two years prior. But hearing them sing just gave me chills running from the back of my heels to the top of my head. I felt like we really had something here." The Wright's company, Wright Stuff Management, developed a strategy to help the Backstreet Boys perfect their showmanship and musicianship while raising visibility among potential fans. They booked them at junior high and high schools as well as at theme parks. The teenage fans shared the Wrights' initial suspicions about Backstreet Boys. Kevin Richardson told *Billboard* "You could tell they were thinking 'What is this, the second coming of the New Kids on the Block?' But once we started singing a cappella and showing them we could really sing, we won them over every time."

Eventually the Wrights got the group booked as openers for veteran acts with a "family" audience, like REO Speedwagon, Kenny G and the Village People. The turning point came in 1994, when Donna Wright had been begging David McPherson, an executive at Jive Records, to give Backstreet Boys a listen. She called McPherson from a Backstreet Boys' show in Cleveland and simply held the phone up. When McPherson played his messages the next day he could hear the sounds of fanatically screaming kids, and soon afterward, Jive signed Backstreet Boys on.

Their single called "We've Got It Goin' On," first released in 1995, did not live up to expectations in the United States, getting no higher than 65 on *Billboard*'s Top 100. But it exploded onto the charts in Germany, and from there Backstreet Boys mania spread throughout Europe. The "boy group" craze already had a foothold in Europe, providing Backstreet Boys with a ready made audience. They brought a unique something extra—they were American, and thus more novel. "We used the success in Germany as a springboard and brought them over to do shows right off the bat. Once that happened, the whole European market opened up." McPherson told *Billboard.*

From Europe the Backstreet Boys' popularity spread throughout the world—Japan, Australia, Canada, Southeast Asia. Their first album, *Backstreet Boys,* released in April 1996, sold over eleven million copies and was certified platinum in 26 different countries. *Backstreet Boys: The Video* was also a number-one seller in Canada for three months. The group toured overseas for 18 months and their concerts recalled the days of High Beatlemania, complete with crowds of crazed teenage girls, narrow escapes out back windows, and screams so loud the music was barely audible. At home in Florida, foreign fans wait in the parking lots outside the apartment houses where the Backstreet Boys live, hoping for autographs. German fans have torn up their lawns for a blade or two of souvenir grass. Yet back in Orlando, the Backstreet Boys pass everywhere in the city unrecognized.

In 1997 the United States was the final frontier for the Backstreet Boys. As 1998 approached and the band prepared for its second U.S. tour, it was looking forward to seeing whether America had taken to them to the degree everyone else had. "I think the (U.S.) market is more ready for a group like us now," Howie Dorough told *USA Today.* "I think at the time we released our first record, alternative, grunge and urban were hot. Now we feel that pop music is starting to come back a little bit." Their album was finally released in the United States in August 1997, nearly a year and a half after the rest of the world heard it for the first time. They included some of their newer songs on the American version, songs that were used on their second international album, *Backstreet's Back.* Jive promoted the album heavily, concentrating on its key female audience. Free Backstreet Boys cassettes were distributed with J.C. Penney make-up, at cheerleader camps, and with books in the teen romance series, "Love Stories." "The Backstreet Boys have made a great choice in selecting their music. When you listen to it you'll know why they are probably going to be the next new thing," wrote Christina Psoros, a 12-year-old reviewer for *Newsday.*

The Backstreet Boys were also working on broadening their musical foundations. All members of the group took up songwriting—though in December 1997 no Backstreet Boys penned number had made it onto a record—and all were learning how to play instruments. In addition, they have focused more attention on dancing, which has become a major part of their stage show. The group realizes that almost everyone in the world expects them to disappear completely after a year or so. Yet the Backstreet Boys are determined to prevent that from happening.

Selected discography

Albums

Backstreet Boys, (International release), Jive/Zomba, 1995.
Backstreet's Back, (International release), Jive/Zomba, 1997.
Backstreet Boys, (American release, additional cuts), 1997.

Videos

The Backstreet Boys: The Video, Jive, 1996.

Sources

Periodicals

Billboard, July 1997.
Newsday, August 19, 1997.
USA Today, April 1, 1997; September 30, 1997.

Online

http://www.varta.de/bsb/intervie.html

Additional information was provided by Jive Records.

—Gerald E. Brennan

Joshua Bell

Violinist

Photograph by Mark Sink. Shirley Kirshbaum & Associates, Inc. Reproduced by permission.

Typically, child prodigies who debut professionally at the age of 14 either continue to live up to grand expectations and grow into accomplished professionals or fade into obscurity. Joshua Bell is a clear example of the former, having performed with classical music greats like Vladimir Ashkenazy and Yo-Yo Ma, recording 15 acclaimed works, touring the world, and pursuing his own compositions. But perhaps his most impressive trait is his passion for the music he plays. Writing in *Interview* magazine, Stephen Greco asserted, "What Joshua Bell does is play the violin. What Joshua Bell *is* is a poet. Onstage ... Bell conjures from his instrument (a 1726 Stradavarius [known as the "Tom Taylor"]) a sound that does nothing less than tell why human beings bother to live."

Bell received his first violin—or "fiddle" as it's referred to affectionately in the field—at the age of five, a gift from his father. The young boy had already become adept at plunking out tunes like "Mary Had a Little Lamb" on a series of rubber bands stretched to different lengths between his dresser drawers, a system he had devised at the age of three or four. Unlike many overachieving young stars, Bell did not come from a family bent on producing a musical prodigy. Growing up in the lush Midwestern hills of Bloomington, Illinois, his father was a psychologist and professor at the University of Indiana, and his mother was a counselor for gifted children. Bell considered himself a "normal kid," and later told Elizabeth McNeil of *People,* "I went to public schools and played a lot of sports." In fact, he was a state tennis champion at the age of ten and was known locally for his athletic achievements rather than his considerable musical prowess.

Furthermore, Bell did not even consider violin his primary interest until about the age of 12, when he was accepted into the renowned Meadowmount music camp in upstate New York. There he met his future mentor, Josef Gingold, a first-rate violinist born in Belorussia and part of a legendary chain of famous musician/teachers which included his teacher, the Belgian virtuoso Eugene Ysaÿe. The camp also awoke Bell from his musical slumbers: "That was a major turning point, going to the camp and hearing all those great players," Bell told Jessica Duchen of *Strad* in 1996. "It was a revelation to me. I had been living very much in my own world and had never heard of Heifetz before!" (Jascha Heifetz is a Russian-born American violin master).

The four weeks of eight-hour-a-day practice at Meadowmount (compared to the hour a day he had devoted up to then), gave Bell the determination to become a professional musician. After much pleading from Bell's parents, Gingold agreed to make an exception regarding

For the Record . . .

Born December 9, 1967, in Bloomington, IN; son of Alan (a psychology professor) and Shirley (a counselor for gifted children) Bell.

Debuted professionally at age 14 with the Philadelphia Orchestra, 1981; signed to London Records, 1986; toured with major orchestras in America, Europe, Australia, and Asia; performed with classical music legends Vladimir Ashkenazy, Sir Neville Mariner, and Yo-Yo Ma; formed the Orion Quartet, 1994; started an annual chamber music festival in London's Wigmore Hall, 1996.

Awards: First prize, *Seventeen Magazine*/General Motors competition, 1981.

Addresses: *Publicist*—IMG Artists, 22 East 71st St., New York, NY 10021; phone: (212) 772-8900; fax: (212) 772-2617. *Home*—New York, NY.

the boy's age and take him on as a full-time student. But it wasn't without regard to the young musician's considerable prospects. Charles Michener, writing for *New York,* quoted the teacher as saying, "Everything about Joshua is special—his charm, his brains, his naturalness. Certainly he's one of the greatest violin talents I've heard in 70 years—he was born to play the instrument. And he has tremendous powers of concentration: As fast as I could give him the repertoire, he absorbed it."

Gingold instilled in Bell a wide variety of musical skills, ranging from "old fashioned" fingerings the teacher had learned from Ysaÿe to the confidence that comes from being able to test one's own ideas and interpretations. But most important was the idea that an artist's inspiration must come from the heart—from a love for the music and a commitment to it. "He really gave me his love for music and for the violin," Bell told *Strad*. "He had the most beautiful sound of any instrumentalist I've ever heard and just having that beautiful sound in my ear had a big impact on me."

Began Professional Career at Age 14

This experience with the gifted teacher led Bell to win first prize in a 1981 *Seventeen Magazine*/General Motors competition at the age of 14. And that victory landed him an audition with Ricardo Muti, conductor of the

Philadelphia Orchestra. Subsequently, Bell made his professional debut as the youngest soloist ever to play a series of concerts with the Philadelphia Orchestra. The ensuing four years saw Bell continue his studies with Gingold and play professionally, as well as indulge his other interests: tennis, basketball, chess, video games, cards, and computers.

In 1987, before Bell's twentieth birthday, London/Decca Records signed the musician to an exclusive recording contract, the company's first with a classical artist in a decade. The interest was evident in the way the label promoted Bell, with his boyish good looks and affecting charm, as a golden opportunity to make classical music more accessible to a wide audience, including young listeners. *People* referred to this marketing as "peddl[ing] him as an upmarket teen idol through a VH-1 video and some hunkish CD cover photos." Not surprisingly, the video was one of the first ever for a classical performer and was broadcast on the Arts & Entertainment and Bravo networks, as well.

Over the next ten years Bell made 13 records for London, including concertos by Brahms, Schumann and Mozart, two Prokovief sonatas for violin and piano, and selections from the Opus of Fritz Kreisler, the Viennese contemporary of Ysaÿe and idol of Bell's teacher, Gingold. This last recording, as was Bell's first Carnegie Hall recital in March 1997, was dedicated to Gingold, who died in 1995.

Performed with Classical Music's Greats

Luminaries with whom Bell performed and recorded between 1987 and his thirtieth birthday in 1997 included some in the best performers in the classical music world: Vladimir Ashkenazy, Sir Neville Mariner and Esa-Pekka Salonen. His performances with the world's leading symphony orchestras were numerous and included the New York, Los Angeles, and London Philharmonic Orchestras; the Boston, Chicago, and London Symphonies; and many of the major orchestras in Europe, Australia, and Asia.

Music critics regularly regarded Bell's live concerts as special events. In an August 1997 review of his performance of a Saint-Saens Violin Concerto at the famed Tanglewood summer music festival in the Berkshire mountains of Massachusetts, the *Boston Globe* praised "the charismatic young Joshua Bell, who is just plain fun to listen to. Bristling with shameless bravura, opinions, humor, and caprice, Bell soars like a lark in lyric moments and tosses off devilish passage work with airy nonchalance, head thrown back and hair madly tossing."

The fascination with Joshua Bell, the child prodigy turned accomplished professional, continued in the 1990s. He made a series of popular appearances beyond the world of classical music. He was featured in a 1993 *Live from Lincoln Center* PBS broadcast, was the subject of a 1995 BBC documentary *Omnibus*, and was included in Arts & Entertainment's *Biography* of Mozart. Guest spots on the *Tonight Show with Johnny Carson*, CNN, and *CBS This Morning* further exposed Bell to the American public. He even modeled for a June 1994 *Travel & Leisure* fashion page in clothes from Brooks Brothers and Paul Stuart.

By 1996 Bell's career kept him busy, with over 100 concerts a year in recital throughout America and Europe. In that year also he signed an unlimited, exclusive recording contract with Sony Classical. The first release, in the spring of 1998, was renowned composer John Corigliano's "The Red Violin Fantasy," the score for the film *The Red Violin*. Bell was hired as artistic advisor, body double, and performing violinist for the film, which traced the fictional history of a rare violin through three centuries.

Forged His Own Diverse Schedule

Other ongoing projects Bell involved himself with in the late 1990s included the Orion Quartet, which was in residency at New York's Lincoln Center; an annual chamber music festival in London's Wigmore Hall, which he founded in 1997; a Gershwin album with composer John Williams; and a collaboration with the celebrated cellist Yo-Yo Ma. Additionally, Bell embarked on the unusual task of composing his own cadenzas for the major violin concertos. The cadenza is a soloist's elaboration on the themes of the concerto that follows certain progressions but leaves a significant amount to the artist's creativity. Speaking to *Gramophone*'s Nick Kimberley in 1996, Bell described his performance philosophy: "People say music is about communication. I don't see it that way. In a sense, of course, you're communicating, but music is about one's own relationship with a piece.... In the end you're creating something for yourself, which the audience can then peer into."

Selected discography

Albums

Live from the Spoleto Festival USA, 1986: Kodaly: Duo, op. 7; Mozart: Quartet in F major; Vivaldi: Concerto in D major, MusicMasters, 1986.

Live from the Spoleto Festival USA, 1987: Brahms: Piano Quartet No. 3, MusicMasters, 1987.
Presenting Joshua Bell: Works by Wieniawski, Sibelius, Brahms/Joachim, Paganini, Bloch, Novacek, Schumann, Auer, Falla, Kreisler, Grasse, de Sarasate, London, 1988.
Tchaikovsky: Violin Concerto in D major, op 35; Wieniawski: Violin Concerto No. 2 in D minor, op 22 (with The Cleveland Orchestra; Vladimir Ashkenazy, conductor), London, 1988.
Faure: Violin Sonata No. 1; Debussy: Violin Sonata; Franck: Violin Sonata, London, 1988.
Bruch: Violin Concerto No. 1; Mendelssohn: Violin Concerto in E minor, op 64 (with Orchestra of Academy of St. Martin-in-the-Fields; Neville Marriner, conductor), London, 1988.
Saint-Saens: Violin Concerto No. 3; Lalo: Symphonie Espagnole, London, 1989.
Chausson: Concert pour piano, violon et quator a cordes, op. 21; Ravel: Trio pour piano, violon et violoncelle, London, 1990.
Chausson: Poeme, op. 25; Saint-Saens: Introduction et Rondo Capriccioso, op. 28; Massenet: Meditation de Thais; de Sarasate: Zigeunerweisen, op. 20; Ysaÿe: Caprice d'apres l'Etude en forme de valse de Saint-Saens; Ravel: Tzigane (with The Royal Philharmonic Orchestra; Andrew Litton, conductor), London, 1992.
Mozart: Violin Concerti Nos. 3 & 5; Adagio in E major; Rondo in C major, London, 1992.
Prokofiev: Violin Concerti, Nos. 1 & 2, London, 1993.
Prokofiev: Violin Sonata in F minor, op. 80; 5 Melodies, op. 35; Violin Sonata in D major, op. 94, London, 1995.
The Kreisler Album: Joshua Bell Plays Music by Fritz Kreisler, London, 1996.
Brahms: Violin Concerto in D major, op. 77; Schumann: Violin Concerto in D minor, London, 1996.
Barber: Violin Concerto; Bloch: Baal Shem; William Walton: Violin Concerto, London, 1997.

Documentaries/videos

The Gift, San Francisco Public Television.
Joshua Bell, British Broadcasting Corporation's "Panorama," 1994.
Master Teacher Series Lessons with Ivan Galamian, Meadowmount School of Music, 1984.

Sources

BBC Music Magazine, March 1995.
Boston Globe, August 4, 1997.
Classical Pulse, August/September 1996, pp. 8-10.
Esquire, March 1990.
Gramophone, April 1996; February 1997.
Independent (London), January 25, 1997.

Interview Magazine, 1990.

New York, July 16, 1990, pp. 36-39.

New York Times, October 8, 1995, Arts & Leisure section; March 20, 1997.

People, April 28, 1997, pp. 111-112.

Philadelphia Inquirer, September 17, 1992.

Strad, November 1996, pp. 1168-1170.

Strings, May/June 1995, pp. 36-43; July/August 1996, pp. 54-62.

Travel & Leisure, June 94, p. 86.

USA Today, September 27, 1982.

Additional information was provided by IMG Artists publicity materials, 1997.

—John F. Packel

BlackHawk

Country group

The strong vocal harmonies and talented guitar picking of BlackHawk have made it one of country music's most successful contemporary groups in the industry. Their live performances have been characterized as "electrifying." The group is made up of three successful singers and musicians: Henry Paul, Dave Robbins, and Van Stephenson. "One thing our fans respond to is our energy," stated Paul in the band's online biography. "They see our show as a very genuine presentation—not a staged, choreographed walk-through of showmanship. The live show has a great deal to do with our success as record-sellers."

Performing in over 450 concerts since 1994, this self-described working-class band has relied heavily on county fairs and festivals as an important and profitable way for them to succeed. "We think they're terrific for the fair market," stated Phil Potter of the Don Romeo Agency. "From the first crew guy to Henry Paul, they're great to work with. We call them 'fair friendly' acts." However, there is a downside to playing these types of venues. "One of the things we run into occasionally is VIPs right in front of the stage," stated Stephenson in *Amusement Business.* "From a show standpoint, that keeps us separated from the people we really want to get close to. It puts a barrier between us and the people we connect with."

While the band is serious about their music, their enthusiasm and sense of humor shine through in their performances. According to the *Chicago Tribune,* BlackHawk is "Fun with serious attitude." And *The Tennessean* noted, "What Popeye is to cartoons, BlackHawk is to country music." BlackHawk's agent, John Huie opined, "They're a party band ... they are about having fun."

In 1994, the group's debut album, *BlackHawk,* reached double platinum and had the number one hit "Every Once In Awhile." The album also had four Top Ten singles; "Goodbye Says it All," "Sure Can Smell The Rain," "Down In Flames," and "Just About Right." It rode the country hit charts for over a year and a half, averaging over 9,200 sales a week.

Album Success "Is Strong Enough"

Their second album, *Strong Enough,* reached gold status and had a number one hit and three Top Ten singles. Producers Mark Bright and Tim DuBois helped BlackHawk retain the energy of their live performances on the album. "We're happy we can give the fans the same quality of music they hear on our album," stated Stephenson in the BlackHawk bio. The title of the album got its name from the lead single, "I'm Not Strong Enough to Say No." Robbins notes that the song is about the woes of manhood. The album deals with issues from individual spontaneity to complex relationships. It debuted at No. 4 on *Billboard*'s Country Albums Chart, making *Strong Enough* one of the highest debuts of any country group in history. Other top songs included "Like There Ain't No Yesterday," and "Almost a Memory Now."

In 1966 Paul made his debut performance in a coffee house, and had been influenced by country singers such as Johnny Cash, Johnny Horton, and Merle Haggard. Other influences include Bob Dylan, John Lennon, Jerry Lee Lewis, and the Allman Brothers. He was a member of The Outlaws, a southern rock group that was popular in the mid-1970s and had many chart singles, including the Southern rock classic "Green Grass and High Tides."

As Paul stated in *Amusement Business,* "Back then, we just wanted to make a record, get a buzz on and play for the people. Now it's the reverse. I want to make the best music I can make and interact with the audience ... What we do is totally different from what The Outlaws was ... We're not out there to party, we're out to do a job." He left the group in 1977 to start The Henry Paul Band, which went on to record four albums on Atlantic Records. Paul said that he survived the sometimes destructive lifestyle of rock and moved to the more calm and healthy environment of country music. "In country, you don't have all that extreme behavior—it's missing in the audience, it's missing in the music, and the music speaks so much better for it," Paul told Buddy Seigal of the *Los Angeles Times*. Robbins, who first performed publicly at a piano recital at age six, credits Kenny Rogers, Ronnie Milsap, and Steve Walsh as his early influences. "From 1985 through 1987, I toured quite a bit with groups as a keyboard player and vocalist," stated Robbins in *Amusement Business*. "We went all over the world, including into the U.S.S.R. and Sweden." Considered one of the city's premiere songwriters, Robbins has lived in Nashville since 1979. Stephenson, who had a few pop singles in the early 1980's, is also considered one of Nashville's best songwriters. Among his musical influences are Vince Gill and Don Henley.

On the Road Again

At the request of Willie Nelson, the group performed at the Farm Aid '95 concert. They have also performed on the road with Tim McGraw, Dwight Yoakam, Brooks & Dunn, and Wynonna. In addition to performing with these country superstars, BlackHawk has received numerous awards and substantial recognition. The group was named the *TNN/Music City News* Star of Tomorrow, *Performance Magazine*'s Best new Country Act, and *Radio & Records* magazine's Group of the Year. They were nominees for Group of the Year by the Country Music Association and the Academy of Country Music, and received the BMI Award for "Every Once in a While." The video for the song, "That's Just About Right," was nominated for "Best New Artist Clip of the Year," by *Billboard*. The video mimicked American Folk Artist Howard Finster's life, and he appeared in BlackHawk's video. In January of 1996, The Museum of American Folk Art included the video in an exhibit of Finster's work in New York.

Love and Gravity, BlackHawk's third album, was released on July 29, 1997 and debuted at No. 9 on *Billboard*'s country album charts. Singles from the album include "Hole in My Heart" and "Postmarked Birmingham." "We took some real chances on *Love & Gravity* and the result is an incredibly strong album that clearly shows the evolution of our music," Robbins proclaimed on the band's website. The *Billboard* Previews website agreed, commenting that *Love and Gravity* "finds the members of BlackHawk in peak songwriting form."

In addition to making music, the band is involved in a number of charity projects. They were chosen as "spokespeople" for the Second Harvest Foundation, which distributes over 500 million pounds of food to needy people across the United States. BlackHawk also contributed to a Christmas album called *Country Cares for Kids,* proceeds of which will benefit the St. Jude's Children Research Hospital in Memphis, Tennessee.

Selected discography

BlackHawk, BMG/Arista, 1994.
Strong Enough, BMG/Arista, 1995.
Love and Gravity, BMG/Arista, 1997.

Sources

Periodicals

Amusement Business, June 30, 1997, p. 6; December 20, 1993, p. 11.
Chicago Tribune, October 22, 1995, p. 9.
Los Angeles Times, May 9, 1995, p. 2.
Sun-Sentinel, January 26, 1996, p. 18.

Online

http://www.twangthis.com
http://www.geocities.com
http://www.mb1.musicblvd.com

—*Bill Bennett*

Blind Melon

Alternative rock band

Photograph by Ken Settle. © Ken Settle. Reproduced by permission.

Blind Melon rocketed to stardom in the realm of alternative rock with their self-titled debut album in 1992, which sold more than 3 million copies and reached triple platinum status. Before the untimely death of the group's leader and singer/songwriter Shannon Hoon in October of 1995—and the ensuing demise of the band—Blind Melon consisted of Hoon, bassist Brad Smith, guitarist Rogers Stevens, drummer Glen Graham, and guitarist Christopher Thorn. Blind Melon was a promising, talented new band, appearing on the *Late Show with David Letterman, Saturday Night Live, MTV,* Canada's *MuchMusic,* and in Woodstock '94. The band also performed in concert across the globe with megastars such as The Rolling Stones, Soundgarden, Pearl Jam, Lenny Kravitz, and Neil Young. When Hoon died from a tragic drug overdose in 1995, the band was clearly in the midst of perfecting and defining their unique sound, as well as claiming their fame in the realm of alternative rock.

Richard Shannon Hoon was born on September 26, 1967, in Lafayette, Indiana, the son of Richard, a construction worker, and Nel Hoon. Shannon was hyperactive as a child, but his parents did not want to "put him on drugs," so they enrolled him in karate classes at the age of six. By the time he was nine years old, Hoon had earned a black belt. In 1990, at the age of 23, Hoon met Stevens in Los Angeles after taking a bus from Lafayette to California. Stevens and bassist Smith had moved to L.A. in 1989 from West Point, Mississippi, where they worked on the kill floor of a slaughterhouse, beheading, deshouldering, and gutting as many as 6,000 hogs a day. Stevens met Hoon through a mutual friend; Hoon played a couple of tunes for him, and Stevens was impressed with his voice. They decided, on the spot, to form a band together.

The group's debut album was buoyed by the successful single "No Rain" and its accompanying video, which featured a girl in a bee costume and the band members frolicking in a field. The image that the single and video portrayed was that of upbeat, Grateful Dead-inspired alternative rock, yet the lyrics to "No Rain" revealed a deceptive morbidity with lines like "I don't understand why I sleep all day/and I start to complain that there's no rain." It was this sort of ironic twist that underscored the band's music and, in fact, the band's path to acclaim. In sharp reversal to Blind Melon's debut album, the band's second release in 1995, *Soup,* was not hailed as a commercial success at all, and Hoon himself was a classic study in contrasts. Chris Heath wrote in *Details* magazine, "He was crazy and rude, and yet also unbearably sweet ... There was an incredible spirit about him, wanton and careless, but also somehow innocent and invigorating."

For the Record . . .

Members include **Glen Graham** (born December 5, c. 1967), drums; **Shannon Hoon** (born September 26, 1967, in Lafayette, IN, died October 20, 1995; son of Richard [a construction worker] and Nel Hoon; married, wife's name Lisa Crouse; children: Nico Blue [son]), singer, songwriter; **Brad Smith** (born September 29, c. 1967), bass; **Roger Stevens** (born October 31, c. 1967), guitar; **Christopher Thorn** (born December 16, c. 1967), guitar.

Released *Blind Melon*, 1992, which sold more than 3 million copies and reached triple platinum status; released *Soup*, 1995, released *Nico*, 1996; appeared at Woodstock '94, performed with The Rolling Stones, Soundgarden, Pearl Jam, Lenny Kravitz, and Neil Young; lead singer Hoon died from an accidental drug overdose, 1995; remaining band members decided to release *Nico* and a documentary home video entitled *Letters from a Porcupine*.

Addresses: *Record company*—Capitol Records, Inc, 1750 Vine Street, Hollywood, CA 90028 (213) 462-6252. *Band address*—703 Pier Avenue, #B806, Hermosa Beach, CA 90254.

After *Soup* was recorded in New Orleans and released in the summer of 1995, the band began touring to support the album. The night before October 20, Blind Melon played in Houston and according to Heath, they played poorly and Hoon was distraught over the general course of his career. *Soup* was not receiving much airplay, and reviewers were panning their live performance, although the band had been consistently filling stadiums while on tour. *Soup* was meant to be an eclectic mix of varied musical styles. Stevens told the *Indianapolis Star*'s Marc Allan, "I was, frankly, stunned when the reviews came out and said it was the worst record ever. I knew it wasn't that bad."

Over the Edge

Hoon was snorting large amounts of cocaine while on tour in Houston, fell asleep on a bunk in the tour bus, and died of an overdose by the time the band reached New Orleans. Dawn Marecki wrote in the *William Patterson College Beacon*, "Shannon's death placed the band in a difficult position, never fully reaching their potential. It ... leaves band members wondering, despite themselves, 'What if?'"

Band members dealt with Shannon's death by supporting each other, working through their initial anger and grief together, and deciding to release a tribute album in Hoon's memory, an album that would include most of the band's unreleased material, outtakes, rarities, interviews, and previously unreleased photos. Band members decided to call the final album *Nico*, after Hoon and Lisa Crouse's baby daughter, Nico Blue Hoon, who was only 13 weeks old when he died. The enhanced *Nico* CD also featured concert footage and several full-length videos. The band decided to donate a portion of the proceeds of *Nico* to MAP (Musician's Assistance Program), an organization which helps musicians and others in the music industry recover from drug and alcohol addiction. Along with *Nico*, the band released a documentary home video entitled *Letters from a Porcupine*, which offers an overview of the band's personal and musical progression, as well as footage from numerous club performances, recording sessions, and road trips.

Farewell Disc Lauded, Band Forms Anew

Don Aquilante of the *New York Post* wrote, "What makes the last chapter in the songbook of Blind Melon so sad is that today's release, *Nico*, is so good that you want more, but there isn't any more there." *Nico* included the Steppenwolf cover "The Pusher," the ironically titled "Life Ain't So Shitty," and the eerily truncated "Letters from a Porcupine." The latter was a song that Hoon wrote and wanted to share, so he called Chris Thorn and played the song into his answering machine. Paralleling the end of Blind Melon, Hoon was cut off by the machine in mid-song as he sang his heart out; the song from the answering machine tape was included in *Nico*.

After Hoon's death, the band decided they still wanted to play together, as Stevens claimed that a bond had formed among the remaining four members. They intend to reform with a new singer and a new name and have received over 2,000 demo tapes from musicians hoping to fill the tremendous vacuum Hoon left behind.

Selected discography

Blind Melon, Capitol Records, 1992.
Soup, Capitol Records, 1995.
Nico, Capitol Records, 1996.

Sources

Periodicals

Details, July 1996.
E! Online, November 12, 1996.
The Indianapolis Star, November 12, 1996.
MTV Online, November 15, 1996.
New York Post, November 12, 1996.
William Patterson College Beacon, November 18, 1996.

Online

www.blind-melon.com

—B. Kimberly Taylor

James Bonamy

Country singer

Country music singer James Bonamy is at a point in his career that is teetering on the edge of stardom. Although he had a rough start with his first song called, "Dog on a Toolbox," Bonamy has shown the persistence and talent needed to set a foundation of success in the country music industry. "I haven't set a timeline for myself, but of course, I have dreams. No specific goals, really, except I want to do this for 20 or 30 years. The whole hope for me is to be able to support my family, whether as a singer, a musician, a songwriter, or a producer, for many years, because I love music," Bonamy explained in *The Pantagraph*.

Bonamy was born on April 29, 1972 in Winter Park, Florida, but was raised in Daytona Beach, Orlando, and Tuscaloosa, Alabama. His dad was a car dealer and his mom was a housewife. He has an older brother, and the family was a close knit one that laid the foundation for his success in music. Bonamy's parents brought him to the Grand Ole Opry when he was just five years old. As a kid, he was always singing in the house. At age nine, he sang the Charlie Daniel's hit "The Devil Went Down to Georgia," in a school variety show. At age 12, he went to see Kiss, which was the first concert he attended. The Kenny Rogers song "Love Will Turn You Around," was the first single record he ever bought. In addition to his own musical interests, his father would drive him around in his truck while listening to country singers like Johnny Paycheck, Bobby Bare, Moe Bandy, and Joe Stampley.

Bonamy also hung out with his dad's friends while they all listened to the music of Conway Twitty, Charlie Rich, Merle Haggard, George Jones, and George Strait.

Despite his interest in music, Bonamy excelled at and focused his attention more on sports than he did on his guitar while he was in high school. He earned letters in football, soccer, tennis, and track. What did influence him musically were the rock sounds of groups like Bon Jovi and Poison. He learned to play the songs "Wanted Dead or Alive," and "Every Rose Has Its Thorn," although he favored country music. He went on to the University of Alabama, completing his freshman year. He followed his older brother there, where he watched him play football. It was in college that he realized his calling was in music and not in sports.

Bonamy's Big Break

Bonamy's first big break came at age 19 when he had the chance to sing on "The Country Boy Eddie Show" in Birmingham, Alabama. He had heard that Tammy Wynette had gotten her start on the show. His performance was a success, even though his act was on the air while the farm reports were given. Bonamy then quit college to sing and work in Orlando, Florida's Church Street Station Historical District. There he sang for the house band while supporting himself by working at a gift shop.

He spent two years on stage performing on the Country Music USA show at the Opryland USA theme park and earned a quick following. Chely Wright, Ty Herndon, and Ken Mellons were also successful performers at the show. However, he soon realized that working theme parks was very different from the real music business. Before he left, he met his future wife, Amy Jane, who was from East Texas and was also working at Opryland at the time. "I never thought that I'd be married at this age," Bonamy stated on the Country Stars website. "But when you meet 'the one' you know. It's a strange feeling to be so sure about something. But the more I got to know Amy Jane, the more certain I became."

Unfortunately, Bonamy's debut single, "Dog on a Toolbox," received no airplay. It was withdrawn from release because at the time there were too many country songs that were about dogs. "It was just a case of bad timing," Bonamy explained to Chet Flippo in *Billboard*. "There had been a couple of dog songs out, and ... dog songs don't program. So the label felt it best to pull it." Although the song's lukewarm acceptance set back Bonamy's next release by several months, "What I Live to Do" became a hit, along with the video.

Born April 29, 1972, in Winter Park, FL; son of a car dealer and a housewife; married Amy Jane; children: James Daniel. *Education:* Attended the University of Alabama.

Sang in "The Country Boy Eddie Show" in Birmingham, Alabama at age 19; performed at Opryland USA; moved to Nashville; signed recording contract with Epic Records; released *What I Live to Do,* 1995, and *Roots and Wings,* 1997.

Awards: Named Hot New Country Male by *Entertainment Tonight; Country Music Television*'s Video Pick of the Week for "The Swing"; inducted into the Music Valley Wax Museum.

Addresses: *Fan Club*—P.O. Box 587, Smyrna, TN 37167.

The album *What I Live to Do* is about playing, working, loving, and going the extra mile. Songs on the album like "Amy Jane," "All I Do Is Love Her," and "The Couple," are about understanding people's emotions. "Devil Goes Fishing," and "Jimmy and Jesus," reflect the moral values Bonamy says he got from his upbringing at home. "Making music gives me an opportunity to capture all the things I'm about. We picked the album title because it's true. If you listen to this record, all those songs are different parts of me, who I am and what I'm about," claimed Bonamy in the Country Stars website. "It's family, fun, relationships with other people, believing in something." To him, having fun but keeping a strong sense of moral values are essential for a good life.

Bonamy's second album on Epic Records, *Roots and Wings,* showed a more toe-tapping country music side of him. The album was somewhat of a dedication to his new son. "And that whole roots and wings theme 'a part of me stays grounded so the rest of me can fly,'" remarked *The Tennessean*'s Tom Roland, "is a clever dichotomy that Bonamy is able to get across." Mike Kraski of Sony Entertainment stated in *Billboard* that "This is a deep album. It's a maturation process. James has a much clearer sense of who he is musically, and it shows."

Bonamy is more focused on the direction of his career than ever. Debbie Zavitson, Epic A&R Director, works very closely with him to select songs. About every other week they meet and listen to tapes. On "song day" a publisher comes into the office every half hour and plays three new songs. The first question Bonamy asks himself is, "is the song me?" He believes he should be able to relate to the lyrics before actually recording.

Talents Lauded by Critics

Since his debut on the music scene, Bonamy has received a significant amount of recognition for his efforts. *Entertainment Tonight* selected him as the Hot New Country Male, while the Academy of Country Music nominated him for Top New Male Artist. His single release "The Swing," was Country Music Television's Video Pick of the Week and was once ranked at 27 in their Top 100 Countdown. The hit "I Don't Think I Will," reached No. 1 on *Billboard*'s country chart in 1995. He also became immortalized when he was inducted into the Music Valley Wax Museum.

Bonamy is very devoted to his wife, Amy Jane, who sings back-up vocals in his band, and he often dedicates the last song of his shows to her. Their son, James Daniel, who was born in 1997, travels with them on tour. The four-legged members of the family include Holly, who is part Lab and Border Collie, and Mookie, who is a white Chihuahua. At the family's home in Smyrna, Tennessee, Bonamy cuts the grass and washes and irons his own clothes. His mom, Paula, who runs his fan club, sends eight by ten glossy photos to his female fans that show off her son's wedding ring. "I'm glad they think he's handsome," she stated in *People*. "But hopefully it's the music that counts."

Selected discography

What I Live to Do, Epic, 1995.
Roots and Wings, Epic, 1995.

Sources

Periodicals

The Advocate, October 17, 1996, p. 14D.
Billboard, April 19, 1997.
Dallas Morning News, September 6, 1996, p. 33.
Milwaukee Journal Sentinel, September 13, 1996, p. 17.
Palm Beach Post, October 11, 1996, p. 39.
Pantagraph, March 28, 1997, p. D1.
Sarasota Herald-Tribune, January 24, 1997, p. 8.

Tulsa World, October 1, 1997, p. D3.

USA Today, July 28, 1997, p. 4D.

Online

http://www.countrystars.com

http://www.angelfire.com

—Bill Bennett

The Boo Radleys

British pop band

Martin Carr formed the Boo Radleys with his childhood friend Sice in the late 1980s, in their hometown of Wallasey, England. Wallasey is a suburb located across the River Mersey from Liverpool, the town which produced the group most often cited as the Boo Radleys' primary influence—the Beatles. Other artists who had an acknowledged impact on Carr's songwriting and musical sensibilities include guitar heroes Jimi Hendrix, Brian Setzer, and J Mascis of Dinosaur Jr.

To get their band off the ground, Carr and Sice added bass player Tim Brown and drummer Rob Cieka to their lineup and appropriated the name of the recluse in Harper Lee's classic novel *To Kill a Mockingbird*. The Boo Radleys' official bio from Columbia Records portrayed the teen-aged Carr as a slacker and a dreamer trapped in a soulless town that squashed the ambitions and deadened the hearts of its brightest and most talented citizens—he and Sice included. "But way back in the early 1980s, Martin Carr glimpsed an alternative," the biography said. "Devouring books, films and records with ... Sice, the teen-aged Martin occupied a parallel world to that of his contemporaries, one in which he and his friends were pop stars, beautiful people living decadent lives in a dazzling metropolis a long, long way from this place." For years, however, that world existed only in Carr's head—until he overcame his slacker tendencies and made a commitment to pursue his dream. "I'm really proud," Carr stated in the band's bio, "of the way that we've gone from where we were when we started in Wallasey to where we (are) now. And we've done it just by doing it—not by sitting around waiting for other people to do it, which is what we did for seven years before that, wondering why ... we hadn't been on 'Top of the Pops' when we couldn't play a guitar."

In the summer of 1990, the Boo Radleys released their debut album, *Ichabod and I*, on the indie label Preston's Action! Records. One review described the band's sound at that time as "rudimentary sandblasts," and Carr has called the lyrics from his early compositions "meaningless wank." The band followed *Ichabod and I* with an EP series called *Studies in Brutalised Melody* on Rough Trade Records, which included *Kaleidoscope* (1990), *Every Heaven* (1991), and *Boo Up* (1991) before moving to the Creation label. Creation released *Everything's Alright Forever* in 1992. Afterward, the band changed record companies again, this time to Columbia, and released the critically acclaimed *Giant Steps* in 1994, and *Wake Up* the following year. Writing in *Guitar Player,* Mike Metler noted the remarkably eclectic collection of songs displayed on *Giant Steps*. "Carr bounces from texture to texture like a jumping bean on a trampoline," Metler wrote. "For starters, there's the rasta-fied 'Lazarus,' the Beach Boys-esque break in

For the Record . . .

Members include **Tim Brown,** bass and keyboards; **Martin Carr,** guitar and keyboards; **Rob Cieka,** drums and percussion; and **Sice,** vocals and guitar.

Band formed in Wallasey, England, late 1980s; released debut, *Ichabod and I,* 1990; followed up with *Everything's Alright Forever,* on the Creation label, 1992; moved to Columbia Records for *Giant Steps,* 1994, and *Wake Up,* 1995; then signed with Mercury Records and released *C'mon Kids,* 1997.

Awards: *Giant Steps* earned NME Brat Award for Best Album, 1994.

Addresses: *Record company*—Mercury Records, 825 Eighth Avenue, New York, NY 10019.

Columbia bio, he reflected on his maturation as a lyricist: "It's the duality within. That all started with 'Lazarus,' 'cos that was a song about being a cabbage and saying f—ing get off your arse and do something. But the thing is, I can't think of anything to do. I have no other hobbies when we're not working with the band or I've got no songs to write. And it's hard to listen when Sice is singing sometimes, especially when he's referring to somebody else.... But you have to do it. You have to get on with it. It's the only way I can write. And it's weird, 'cos now these lyrics are very introspective, totally the opposite of universal. I think they're really selfish songs. And of course, they're also for everyone."

Perhaps that peek into Carr's thought process explains his band's "jumping bean" eclecticism and penchant for songs which *Entertainment Weekly* reviewer Mike Flaherty described as "melodically fragmented, lyrically obtuse onslaughts." In any event, while the Boo Radleys may not write a new chapter in the history of rock 'n' roll, they certainly will provide an intriguing footnote.

'Barney (and I),' and the relentless right-channel squeal-back throughout 'Run My Way Runway'."

In 1996 the Boo Radleys changed record labels yet again, this time moving to Mercury, which released the disc *C'mon Kids. Guitar Player's* Metler described the disc as "More hyperactive pop from the witty U.K. combo whose tunes veer druggedly from anthemic bubblegrunge to full-blown psychedelia. The best of the overdubbed raveups attain the sort of ecstatic peaks some associate with Ecstasy." *Stereo Review* magazine went on to explain that the Boos' dramatically varied songs are much more a product of the studio than the concert hall: "Unquestionably the Boo Radleys' metier is the studio. They are disciples of that time and place (the late sixties and early seventies) when musicians aspired to create unified albums that couldn't possibly be duplicated on the stage ... *Giant Steps* is a balm for the ears and a trip for the mind."

Say What?

At times, Carr discusses his music in bewildering, fragmented non sequitars that could have been lifted straight from the rock 'n' roll spoof *Spinal Tap.* In the

Selected discography

Ichabod and I, Preston's Action! Records, 1990.
Kaleidoscope (EP), Rough Trade, 1990.
Every Heaven (EP), Rough Trade, 1991.
Boo Up (EP), Rough Trade, 1991.
Everything's Alright Forever, Creation, 1992.
Giant Steps, Creation/Columbia, 1994.
Wake Up, Columbia, 1995.
C'mon Kids, Mercury, 1997.

Sources

Billboard, October 19, 1996, p. 19.
Entertainment Weekly, April 18, 1997, p. 69.
Guitar Player, March 1994, p. 14; February 1997, p. 151.
Rolling Stone, October 1995, p. 33.
Stereo Review, May 1994, p. 86.

Additional material was taken from the Columbia Records web page.

—Dave Wilkins

Boy Howdy

Country band

When you think of country music, you don't often think of California. Nevertheless, this was the home of Boy Howdy. The group was a four-man West Coast country band that found a successful blend of country and rock that quickly pushed them to the top of the country charts in the mid 1990s. However, around the summer of 1995, the group just as quickly disbanded and has not been singing together since. Some of their top singles like "A Cowboy's Born with a Broken Heart," "She'd Give Anything," and "They Don't Make Them Like That Anymore," found the top of the charts in 1994. But soon afterward, the lead singer for the group, Jeffrey Steele, decided to start a solo singing career. In April 1997, Steele released a single called "A Girl Like You" on MCG/Curb Records, although it received little airplay. At the beginning of 1998, Steele turned his attention towards an acting career instead. He worked in Hollywood and appeared on an episode of the TV series *Murder, She Wrote*.

Two of the band members who are brothers, Larry and Cary Park, played lead guitar for the group. They grew up in a country music family, with their father, Ray Park, making records for the Capitol label, and playing the fiddle for Vern & Ray during the late 1950s and early 1960s in California. Larry, who is the older brother, started playing bluegrass, rock 'n' roll, and country at an early age. Cary started playing a little later in the early 1980s for a military band. "Cary plays the rock influenced stuff really nice," Larry told Chris Gill of *Guitar Player*. "I

do more of the bluegrass type stuff. We play the songs and see who comes up with the best part first." Cary plays an early 1980 Charvel (guitar) with two humbuckers, a single-coil, and a Floyd Rose, plugged into a Fender Bassman reissue. Larry, on the other hand, uses either a two-pickup model with a wrist activated B-bender made by Jimmy Bachman or a three-pickup version with a five-position switch.

Larry was the one who actually founded Boy Howdy while brother Cary played in his own band. Drummer Hugh Wright played for the Park brothers' bands, as well as Jeffrey Steele's, who was a talented singer and bassist. Steele was from Burbank, California, and he grew up being influenced by John Lennon, Paul McCartney, Willie Nelson, Hank Williams, and Kris Kristofferson. At the age of 17, Steele began touring the country as a backup musician. Dwight Yoakam's producer, Pete Anderson, heard Steele's work and included him on Yoakam's album *A Town South of Bakersfield, Vol 2*. The country singer Steve Wariner also admired Steele's songwriting, and sang one of his songs "Where Fools Are King," on his *Laredo* album, which was released in 1990.

It was Wright who always told the Park brothers and Steele that they should form a band. One day, Larry needed a substitute for his band and at the insistence of Wright he called Steele to play for him in 1989 at a chili cookoff in Long Beach, California. As Steele recalled to Gene Harbrecht of the *Dallas Morning News,* "We all played together for the first time and just kind of looked at each other and went, Man, this is going to be good." Soon after, brother Cary joined the group. Since the band wanted to create their own sound and play original material rather than covers, they earned a reputation around L.A. as a "bunch of real bad guys." They began going to other clubs that let them feature their own music. At a place where Elvis and Dwight Yoakam once played, Boy Howdy found success. In 1990, the Foothill Club in Signal Hill, California, was the place where Warner Brother executives first heard and liked the Boy Howdy sound. Subsequently, the band headed to Nashville for its first series of studio recordings. "We gave up all our work and went," Steele told Harbrecht. "We didn't have anywhere to play, but we told our families we'd figure out some way to make money."

Where did Boy Howdy come up with it's name, one that many people thought poked fun at country music? "To us the name's like a celebration of country music," Park explained to Bobby L. Weaver, Jr. of the *Arkansas Democrat-Gazette*. In the old Western movies, you'd see somebody riding off on a horse and they'd say 'Boy Howdy, did you see that guy shoot that gun?' That kind of thing. It's a very Western expression."

After being "discovered" in L.A., the band finished filming a video and scene for the film *Pure Country*, which featured George Strait. Boy Howdy hadn't even released its first album yet, but it was riding high on its future prospects for success. Wright was with band manager Alan Hopper returning to their Dallas, Texas, hotel on a Saturday morning in May of 1992. As they were driving back, they came upon a pickup truck that had spun out on the highway. Wright and others went to aid the driver. Suddenly, a car from the highway smashed into the truck and the rescuers aiding its driver. Two people were killed, and Wright was left struggling for his life.

He had two broken legs, was in a coma for five months, and took many more months to fully recover before he could return to the band. The group continued to perform on the road in Wright's absence, and it struggled with the thought of breaking up. "At one point we thought it was over," Park admitted to Mike Boehm of the *Los Angeles Times*. "We considered stopping, but we thought, 'If we quit now, what's Hugh got to look forward to when he comes around?'" Instead of giving up, the band decided to work even harder, continuing to tour with a stand-in drummer. Meanwhile, Wright's condition had improved and he was released from the hospital in November, 1992.

Resilience is the Word

In early 1992, Curb Records released Boy Howdy's single hit "Our Love Was Meant to Be." That summer their first album, *Welcome to Howdywood*, was released. Unfortunately, the album sold poorly. The first real radio hit for the group was in the spring of 1993 with the single "A Cowboy's Born with a Broken Heart," which reached noumber 12 on the Hot Country Singles & Tracks chart. It was a song that described the lonely life of a rodeo cowboy. This hit was soon followed by the successful release of "She'd Give Anything," song expressing the emotions people commonly experience when searching for love. Country Music Television frequently played the video to "She'd Give Anything," and the song reached Number 13 on the Hot Country Singles & Tracks chart.

In an effort to boost sales, Curb Records tried a new marketing strategy with Boy Howdy in releasing the album *She'd Give Anything*, with just six songs on it. It was released on January 11, 1994. "There are certain artists who are absolute album-sellers ... but when it comes to developing artists, I don't know that anybody buys them for the 10 or 11 songs on the album—God bless us, if we're lucky, three—singles on the album," stated Dennis Hannon, Curb's VP of marketing and sales. The album's packaging denoted that there were only six songs, and it was even marked "Specially Priced" in the cover's artwork. The price of the album was also dropped to reflect that it was an abbreviated album.

Boy Howdy's next album, *Born That Way*, was released in 1995. However, difficulties with the record distribution had delayed its release and that of other singles for several months. The album also went through two name changes. First, "Plan B" was going to be the title, then "Bigger Fish to Fry," before they settled on *Born That Way*.

With the difficulties in releasing their third album, it seemed the writing was on the wall for this band. Steele's wife soon moved back to Nashville, which was a precursor to where Steele would soon focus his energy and attention. His business interests were there, along with the premier writers in the industry that he wanted to collaborate with. The group quietly disbanded, with Steele going his own way.

Selected discography

Welcome to Howdywood, Curb Records, 1992.
She'd Give Anything, Curb Records, 1994.
Born That Way, Curb Records, 1995.

Sources

Periodicals

Arkansas Democrat-Gazette, October 14, 1994, p. 5.
Billboard, January 15, 1994, p. 24.

Guitar Player, August 1993, 14.
Los Angeles Times, January 31, 1994,
The Orange County Register, November 21, 1994, p. F02;
    July 4, 1994, p. F02.

Online

http://www.kickincountry.com

—*Bill Bennett*

Brad

Rock band

Although Brad may sound like a one-person project, nobody in the group is named Brad. When they formed, some considered Brad a side project for guitarist Stone Gossard. In 1992 he had garnered the most fame and notoriety with the rock group Pearl Jam. However, every member of Brad had some recognition for working in another project. As Eric Flannigan wrote in *Wall of Sound*, "With so many other commitments, the members of Brad are making music together purely because they want to."

Before Brad began recording together, singer Shawn Smith and drummer Regan Hagar played together in Satchel. At the same time, Smith also sang for the band Pigeonhed. Gossard played guitar for the mega-hit band Pearl Jam, and bass player Jeremy Toback had developed a solo career. Each had his own musical outlet. Yet in the early 1990s, the four members discovered a special dynamic when they played together.

The seeds of the band were planted in the early 1980s in the rich soil of Seattle, Washington. Regan Hagar played in a band called Malfunkshun with a singer named Andrew Wood. They rehearsed in the same space as another band called Green River, which included guitarist Stone Gossard and bassist Jeff Ament. The two bands became acquainted, and eventually, Gossard, Ament, and Wood formed a band called Mother Love Bone.

The musical and personal friendships continued to crossover. While Mother Love Bone started to garner attention, Gossard, Ament, Wood, and Hagar often played cover tunes in the clubs around Seattle using different band names. In 1990 Andrew Wood died of a drug overdose just before the release of Mother Love Bone's debut album. Gossard and Ament formed another band called Pearl Jam, which quickly took off.

Meanwhile, Regan Hagar met a singer named Shawn Smith and they formed their own band called Satchel. When Gossard was on hiatus from touring and recording with Pearl Jam, he would often jam with his longtime friends in Satchel. Gossard also teamed up with Hagar to form a small record label called Loosegroove Records. Since they had played together so much informally, Smith, Hagar, and Gossard decided to start their own project together.

More than a thousand miles south of Seattle, in Los Angeles, California, bassist Jeremy Toback was playing his own music in clubs and coffeehouses around town. He took a trip up to the Northwest's Emerald City to visit his friend Alex Rosenast, who owned the club Rock Candy. Pearl Jam had shot a video for their single

"Alive" in the club, where Gossard later met Toback. As Brad began to form, the band realized they still needed a bass player. So Gossard's roommate suggested he call Toback. "I said, 'Stone, you haven't heard me play,'" Toback recalled to Jeff Gordinier in *Santa Barbara News-Press.* "And he said, 'Aw, don't worry about it.'"

Shades of Seattle Rock

When Toback flew up to Seattle, Brad began recording its first release in October of 1992. Loosegroove Records' bio of the band described them as unique among the rock groups from Seattle: "They have all the propulsive power long associated with Seattle rock, but none of the style's lyrical self-pity or grunge guitar clichés, and sometimes are thrown slightly off-kilter by rhythmic undercurrents, weird synth lines, and unexpected falsetto vocals."

When the four members originally went into the recording studio, they had no idea whether or not the project would work. "There was no guarantee that anything was going to happen," Toback told Gordinier, "and the only way something *would* happen was if everyone could just get along and play music together. If someone had been sitting there kissing Stone's butt, or just being in awe of him, it wouldn't have worked out."

Although the opportunity came out of nowhere for Jeremy Toback, he had no problems treating Gossard like just another member of the band. Before Brad, Toback was primarily interested in jazz, rather than rock n' roll. He graduated from Princeton University in 1988 with a degree in English. Afterward, he moved to Los Angeles to try to break into a musical career and played with several bands before discovering that he would rather be a solo artist. He began writing, rehearsing, and performing around town.

Not long after the recording sessions ended, Brad signed a record contract with Epic records for their debut album. However, the band was yet to change its name. They had called themselves Shame until they discovered a man named Brad already owned the rights to the name. According to some sources, the foursome decided to call the band "Brad" as a tribute to the owner of the name Shame. However, Gossard told Jim Greer in *Spin* that the story is just a rumor. "Brad is a slice of Americana, really," he said. "It's sort of an American name. It's just ... Brad."

Shame, their debut, arrived in stores in 1993. Based on the history of its members, the album received critical attention. Greg Fasolino wrote in a *Creem* review, "*Shame* boasts the sheen of spontaneity—an elusive, one-take resonance that sounds refreshing and natural."

Foundations magazine reported that "Contemplative and moody, this disc is necessary for those quiet evenings when you want to shut out the world and hang with some friends that understand. Brad are those friends, and this piece of art must become part of everyone's collection."

"Most people will view Brad as a Pearl Jam side project from Stone Gossard," a critic wrote in *Intensity.* "But personally, Brad is a million times better than Pearl Jam, and considering how great the music on this LP is, Pearl Jam could very well be a mere side project for Gossard."

One aspect of Brad's sound that many singled was Shawn Smith's vocal style. Deborah Frost of *Entertainment Weekly* described his sound as "closer to Top 40 mavens Daryl Hall and Elton John than to Seattle-sound gods Chris Cornell [of Soundgarden] and Eddie Vedder [of Pearl Jam]."

Returned to Recording After Years

After the release of *Shame,* the members of Brad returned to their main musical paths. They didn't go on tour or even perform live. In 1994 they regrouped to contribute a song to the soundtrack for the movie *Threesome.* Brad didn't reconvene in the studio again until the fall of 1996. They spent three weeks together, with co-producer Nick DiDia at Litho Studios in Seattle to record their next LP, *Interiors.* "We came in and did it with no rehearsal," Hagar said in Brad's record company bio, "whereas the first one was rehearsed for five days."

"The first record was really supposed to be demos," continued Smith. "We didn't know it was gonna be a record until we were a week into it. My writing skills were at a very early stage, too. On this record, I was way more together."

Epic released *Interiors* on June 3, 1997. The record included guest performances by Pearl Jam guitarist Mike McCready and solo percussionist Basheri Johnson. "The Day Brings" became the first single. John Taft, who had directed videos for Pearl Jam, directed the video for "The Day Brings." Then, on July 7, 1997, Brad began its first tour of the United States. However, Jeremy Toback had already booked a promotional tour for his solo album *Perfect Flux Thing,* so Satchel bassist Mike Berg filled in for him on the tour. "Touring is key to getting these songs heard by more people than just ourselves and the people who heard *Shame,*" Gossard said in Brad's bio.

Once the tour was over, the members of Brad returned to their other commitments. Yet they all planned to continue pursuing the rare musical dynamic they had unleashed in Brad. "It's something very family-like, and I think it feels the same way for the other guys," Gossard told Erik Flannigan in *Wall of Sound.* The unconventional process, energy, and sound Brad produces all point back to the idea that they're doing it because they want to.

Selected discography

Shame, Epic Records, 1993.
(Contributor) *Threesome* (soundtrack), Epic Soundtrax, 1994.
Interiors, Epic Records, 1997.

Sources

Creem, March 1993.
Entertainment Weekly, April 30, 1993; April 29, 1994.
Foundations, May 14, 1993.
Intensity, November 1993.
Mail Tribune, July 7, 1993.
Nerve, April/May 1993.
Paperback Jukebox, June 1993.
Santa Barbara News-Press, February 26, 1993.
Spin, May 1993.

Additional information was obtained from the Epic Records artist update website.

—Sonya Shelton

Ray Brown

Jazz bassist

Best known as a contributing member of the bebop jazz movement and a member of the Oscar Peterson Trio, jazz bassist Ray Brown performed with jazz giants from Dizzy Gillespie and Charlie Parker to his wife Ella Fitzgerald. Despite Fitzgerald's short-lived marriage to Brown (1947-1953), she remained a life-long friend and musical associate. A disciple of the 1940s Oscar Pettiford school of jazz bass, Brown developed an individual style renown for its tastefully executed rhythmic lines within the context of ensemble accompaniment. His talent reflects such breadth and diversity that he was the most cited musician in the first edition of the *Penguin Guide to Recorded Jazz* (1992). Unlike many of the founders of bebop bass, Brown still performs and has earned a successful living as a studio musician, record producer, and nightclub owner.

Raymond Matthews Brown was born in Pittsburgh, Pennsylvania, on October 13, 1926. He took piano lessons at age eight and gained knowledge of the keyboard through memorizing the recordings of Fats Waller. A member of the high school orchestra, he soon

Photograph by Jeff Sedlik. Telarc International Corporation. Reproduced by permission.

For the Record . . .

Born Raymond Matthews Brown, October 13, 1926, in Pittsburgh, PA; married Ella Fitzgerald (jazz vocalist), December 10, 1947 (divorced 1953); children: Ray Jr.

Began playing music professionally in high school; performed with Jimmy Hinsley's band and Snookum Russell's territory band, 1944; arrived in New York City and joined Dizzy Gillespie's group, 1945; performed with Gillespie's big band until 1947; backed Ella Fitzgerald and performed with the Milt Jackson Quartet, c. 1948; recorded with Charlie Parker and appeared at the Philharmonic jazz series, early 1950s; became founding member of the Oscar Peterson Trio, 1952; left Peterson's Trio, moved to Hollywood, California, and worked as a freelance performer and studio musician, 1965; became one of the founding members of The L.A. Four, 1974; became a regular solo recording and performing artist, late 1970s.

Addresses: Record company—Telarc Records, 23307 Commerce Park Road, Cleveland, OH 44122.

found himself overwhelmed by the number of pianists among his classmates. "There must have been 14 piano players in it. And 12 of them were chicks who could read anything on sight," explained Brown in *Jazz Masters of the Forties.* In the book *Oscar Peterson: The Will to Swing,* Brown revealed the main reason for ending his study of piano: "I just couldn't find my way on it. It just didn't give me what I wanted." Soon afterward, Brown, unable to afford a trombone, switched to bass, an instrument provided by the school's music department.

Making the Switch

Brown's new musical role model emerged in Duke Ellington's innovative bassist, Jimmy Blanton. As he told Jack Tracey in *Down Beat,* "I just began digging into Blanton because I saw he had it covered—there was nobody else. There he was, right in the middle of all those fabulous records the Ellington band was making at the time, and I didn't see any need to listen to anybody else." As a teenager Brown played local engagements. Despite offers by bandleaders, he followed his mother's advice and finished high school

before performing on the road with regional territory bands. After graduating in 1944, he performed an eight-month stint in Jimmy Hinsley's band. Around this time, Brown fell under the influence of bassists Leroy "Slam" Stewart and Oscar Pettiford, a prime mover of a modern jazz bass approach. He next joined the territory band of Snookum Russell. Eight months later, while on the road with Russell, Brown followed the suggestion of fellow band members and moved to New York City.

New York City and 52nd Street

In 1945 Brown arrived in New York City, and during his first night visited Fifty-Second Street—"Swing Street," a mob-controlled thoroughfare lined with various jazz clubs. That evening he encountered pianist Hank Jones, a musical associate, who introduced him to Dizzy Gillespie. That same evening, Gillespie, prompted by Jones' recommendation, hired Brown without an audition. Attending the band's rehearsal the next day, Brown—a 19-year-old musician still largely unfamiliar with many of bebop's innovators—discovered that his fellow bandmembers were Charlie Parker, Bud Powell, and Max Roach. "If I had known those guys any better I would have probably never gone to the rehearsal," admitted Brown in *Jazz Journal International.* "The only guy I knew something about was Dizzy because some of his records had filtered down through the south where I'd been playing with a territory band." The group's leader, however, immediately recognized the talent of his young bassist. As Gillespie commented, in his memoir *To Be or Not to Bop,* "Ray Brown, on bass, played the strongest, most fluid and imaginative bass lines in modern jazz at the time, with the exception of Oscar Pettiford." Shortly afterward, Gillespie added Detroit-born vibraphonist Milt Jackson. In *Jazz Masters of the Forties,* Brown recounted his early years with Jackson: "We were inseparable. They called us twins."

In 1945 Brown appeared with Gillespie at Billy Berg's night club in Hollywood, California, an engagement which, with the exception of a small coterie of bebop followers, failed to generate a favorable response from west coast listeners. In Gillespie's memoir *To Be or Not to Bop,* Brown summarized the band's Hollywood stint: "The music wasn't received well at all. They didn't know what we were playing; they didn't understand it." During the winter of 1946, Gillespie returned to New York and opened at Clark Monroe's Spotlite on 52nd Street with a band consisting of Brown, Milt Jackson, Stan Levey, Al Haig, and alto saxophonist Sonny Stitt. In *To Be or Not to Bop,* Brown modestly described his role in the sextet, "I was the least competent guy in the group. And they made something out of me." In May of 1946, the sextet recorded for the Musicraft label, cutting the sides such as "One Bass Hit"—featuring Brown's bass talents—and "Oop Bop Sh' Bam,' and "That's Earl Brother." On Feb 5, 1946, Brown took part in one of Charlie Parker's sessions for the Dial label, recording such numbers as "Diggin' Diz."

In 1946 Gillespie formed his second big band, using the same six-member line-up. On February 22, 1946, Brown appeared with Gillespie's big band for a RCA/Victor session organized by pianist and jazz critic Leonard Feather. As Feather wrote in his work *Inside Jazz,* "Victor wanted an all-star group featuring some of the Esquire winners, so we used J.C. Heard on drums and Don Byas on tenor, along with Dizzy's own men—Milt Jackson, Ray Brown, and Al Haig—and the new guitarist from Cleveland, Bill de Arango." The date produced the numbers "52nd Street Theme," "Night in Tunisia," "Ol' Man Rebop," and "Anthropology." Between May and July of 1946, Brown appeared on such Gillespie recordings as "Our Delight," "Things to Come," and "Rays Idea" (co-written with Gil Fuller). In November of the same year, he cut the classic Gillespie side "Emanon."

In 1947 Gillespie assembled a smaller group inside his big band which included Brown, Milt Jackson, pianist John Lewis and drummer Kenny Clarke. As Jackson told Whitney Baillett, in *American Musicians II,* "We'd play and let the band have a rest. I guess it was Dizzy's idea." Attending an August 1947 Gillespie big band session Brown's bass is heard on such numbers as "Ow!," "Oop-Pop-A-Da," and John Lewis' "Two Bass Hit" which Brown's bass is heard driving the band and, at the composition's close, soloing with force and a controlled sense of melody. On December 10, 1947, Brown married vocalist Ella Fitzgerald in Ohio and moved into a residence on Ditmars Boulevard in the East Elmhurst section of Queens, New York. Soon afterward, the couple adopted a son, Ray Jr.

On the Road with Ella Fitzgerald

After leaving Gillespie's band in 1947, Brown and performed with Fitzgerald on Norman Granz's *Jazz at the Philharmonic* tours and various record dates. "When I left Dizzy," commented Brown in *Ella Fitzgerald,* "the band was getting ready to go to Europe, and I couldn't. I'd just gotten married to Ella Fitzgerald. At that time I was in a bit of a curl between her and wanting to be with her as well. She wanted me to travel with her trio; she had Hank Jones playing piano. So I finally decided I was going to stay in New York." During a concert series in

September 1949, Brown performed when Canadian-born pianist Oscar Peterson made his debut with the tour (according to Brown, he had already performed with Peterson at informal Canadian jam sessions). In 1950 Brown and Peterson performed as a duo, and for the next several years, were also billed on various tours.

In 1950 Brown recorded with Charlie Parker and, between 1950 and 1952, appeared with the Milt Jackson Quartet. The quartet's pianist John Lewis recounted in *The Great Jazz Pianists,* "We were all friends and would play together when Dizzy's band wasn't working." At another Parker session in August 1951, Brown found himself in the company of such sidemen as trumpeter Red Rodney, John Lewis, and drummer Kenny Clarke. Together they backed Parker on sides which included "Swedish Schnapps," "Si Si," "Back Home Blues," and "Lover Man." A few months later, Brown appeared with the Milt Jackson Quartet, and on March 25, 1952 Brown attended a Charlie Parker big band recording session in Hollywood, California.

With the Oscar Peterson Trio

In 1952 Brown and guitarist Irving Ashby became the founding members of the Oscar Peterson Trio. Ashby's replacement, Barney Kessel, performed with the trio a year before Peterson recruited guitarist Herb Ellis who, along with Brown on bass, formed one of the most famed jazz trios of the 1950s. "Herb and I rehearsed all the time," stated Brown in *Oscar Peterson: The Will to Swing.* "For a trio that didn't have any drums, we had it all. Herb and I roomed together and we played everyday. Not just the gig. We played golf in the morning and guitar and bass in the afternoon, and then we would shower, take a nap, go to dinner, and go to the gig. We had it all." Under Peterson's leadership, Brown and Ellis underwent a challenging musical regimen. In *Jazz Journal International,* Brown revealed his admiration for Peterson's reputation as a difficult task master: "If you are not intimidated by absolute professionalism, then you have no problem. Sure he'll throw you a curve from time to time by calling unscheduled numbers or unexpectedly doubling the tempos, but if you're not good enough to handle that, you shouldn't be with Oscar anyway."

By 1953 Brown and Fitzgerald ended their marriage. As Stuart Nicholson noted his book *Ella Fitzgerald,* "Ray remained adamant that he would pursue his career with Oscar Peterson, and the couple had begun to see less and less of each other. Finally, they decided to bring their marriage to and end and filed for a 'quickie' divorce." The divorce was finalized on August 28, 1953 in Juarez, Mexico. Fitzgerald maintained custody of Ray Jr., yet she and Brown remained friends. In November 1953 they, along with Oscar Peterson, appeared at a concert in Japan.

In 1958 Peterson replaced Ellis with drummer Gene Gammage, who stayed with the trio a few months until Peterson recruited drummer Edmund Thigpen. Fortunately, Brown was able to stay with the trio and earn a comfortable living. However, by the early 1960s, the group also proved demanding in its performance schedule. As Brown explained in *Jazz Journal International,* "Some of the tours were really punishing—we'd come to Europe and do 62 one-nighters in 65 days." After his 15-year membership in the Oscar Peterson Trio, Brown left the group in 1965, and settled in Hollywood, where he worked in the areas of publishing, management, and record production. In 1974 he co-founded the L.A. Four with saxophonist Bud Shank, Brazilian guitarist Luarindo Almeida, and drummer Shelly Manne (later replaced by Jeff Hamilton). One of Brown's exemplary studio dates emerged in the 1974 album *Dizzy Gillespie Big 4.*

By 1976 Brown appeared four days a week on the *Merv Griffin Show.* A year later, after two decades of appearing as a sideman on the Contemporary label, Brown recorded the solo effort *Something for Lester,* placing him in the company of pianist Cedar Walton and drummer Elvin Jones. In *Down Beat* Zan Stewart gave the album the magazine's highest rating (five stars), and commented, "Walton and Jones are apropos partners-in sound for the superlative bassist ... Ray's imparts the line to 'Georgia'—what glorious tone he possesses! It continually overwhelms the listener, as does his superb intonation, for Brown is always at the center of each note."

World Class Musician

In a 1980 *Jazz Journal International* interview, Brown told Mike Hennessey, "I'm very fortunate. I'm still able to travel and play various countries and still be liked by the public. I'm able to play what I like to play and as long as people want to listen, that's fine with me." During the 1980s, Brown recorded solo albums for the Concord label as well as releases by the L.A. Four, and numerous guest sessions with pianist Gene Harris. Since his first appearance on Telarc Records in 1989, his albums for the company include the 1994 trio LP (with pianist Benny Green and drummer Jeff Hamilton) *Bass Face, Live at Kuumbwa,* the 1995 work *Seven Steps to Heaven* (with Green and drummer Greg Hutchinson), and the 1997 release *Super Bass.* Brown still performs both as

a leader and accompanist at festivals and concert dates. "During the past decades Brown's sound and skill have remained undimmed, "wrote Thomas Owens, in his 1995 book *Bebop: The Music and Its Players.* "He is an agile, inventive, and often humorous soloist. His arco [bow] technique is excellent, though he seldom reveals it. But he shines most brilliantly as an accompanist. Examples of his beautiful lines are legion." Interviewed in *The Guitar Player Book,* Herb Ellis also lauded the talents of his former music partner: "[Ray Brown] is in a class all by himself. There's is no other bassist in the world for me, and a lot of players feel the same way. On most instruments, when you get to the top echelon it breaks down to personal taste, but I tell you, there are a lot of guys on his tail, but Ray has it all locked up."

Selected discography

Albums

Milt Jackson/Ray Brown, Just the Way It Had to Be, Impulse!, 1973 (recorded from a 1969 session).
Something for Lester, Contemporary, 1977.
Ray Brown Trio Live at the Concord Jazz Festival, Concord, 1979.
Tasty!, Concord Jazz, 1980.
Soular Energy, Concord Jazz, 1985.
Red Hot, Ray Brown Trio, Concord, 1987.
Uptown, Telarc, 1990.
Old Friends, Telarc, 1992.
Three Dimensional, Concord Jazz, 1992.
Bass Face, Live at Kuumbwa, 1994.
Ray Brown Trio, Don't Get Sassy, Telarc, 1994.
Seven Steps to Heaven, Telarc, 1995.
Some of My Best Friends Are ... the Piano Players, Telarc, 1995.
Some of My Best Friends Are ... the Sax Players, Telarc, 1996.
Ray Brown/Milt Jackson, Much In Common, Verve, 1996.
Super Bass, Telarc, 1997.

With Dizzy Gillespie

Groovin' High, Savoy, (reissued material from 1946).
Groovin' with Diz & Co., Black Label Music, 1993, (reissued material from 1946).
Dizzy Gillespie: The Complete RCA Victor Recordings, (reissued material from 1946-1947).

With Charlie Parker

The Legendary Dial Masters Vol. I, Stash Records, 1989 (reissued material from 1946-1947).

Charlie Parker 1949 Jazz at the Philharmonic, Verve, 1993, (originally released on Clef Records).

Charlie Parker Plays the Blues, Verve, (reissued material from 1946-1952).

Charlie Parker With Strings, Verve, (reissued material from 1947-1952).

The Verve Years (1952-54), Verve, 1977.

With Bud Powell

Jazz Giant, Verve.

Blues in the Closet, Verve (material from 1956).

With Oscar Peterson

At the Stratford Shakespearean Festival, Verve.

Night Train, Verve.

The Oscar Peterson Trio Live at Newport, Verve.

Oscar Peterson Trio at the Concertgebouw, Verve.

Oscar Peterson Plays the Cole Porter Song Book, Verve.

Eloquence Limelight, Verve.

We Get Requests, Verve.

The Oscar Peterson Trio with Nelson Riddle, Verve.

Oscar Peterson, Jazz Masters 16, Verve/Polygram, 1994.

With The L.A. Four

The L.A. Four, Concerto De Aranjuez, Concord.

With Gene Harris

The Gene Harris Trio Plus One, Concord, 1986.

Tribute to Count Basie, Concord, 1987.

Listen Here!, Concord, 1989.

At Last, Concord, 1990.

Black and Blue, Concord, 1991.

Compilations

Big Band Jazz: From the Beginnings to the Fifties, Smithsonian Collection of Recordings, 1983.

Sources

Books

Balliett, Whitney, *American Musicians II: Seventy-One Portraits in Jazz,* Oxford University Press, 1996.

Feather, Leonard, *Inside Jazz,* (second edition), Da Capo, 1980.

Gillespie, Dizzy with Al Fraser, *To Be or Not to Bop, Memoirs,* Doubleday & Co., 1979.

Gitler, Ira, *Jazz Masters of the Forties,* Collier Books, 1966.

The Guitar Player Book, by the editors of *Guitar Player Magazine,* (revised and updated), GPI Publications, 1979.

Lees, Gene, *Oscar Peterson: The Will to Swing,* Prima Pub. & Co., 1990.

Lyons, Len, *The Great Jazz Pianists Speaking of Their Lives and Music,* Da Capo, 1983.

Nicholson, Stuart, *Ella Fitzgerald: A Biography of the First Lady of Jazz,* Da Capo, 1993.

Owens, Thomas, *Bebop: The Music and Its Players,* Oxford University Press, 1995.

Periodicals

Down Beat, January 29, 1976, pp. 12-13, 33; November, 1979, p. 42.

Jazz Journal International, July 1980, pp. 8-9.

—*John Cohassey*

Brownstone

R&B vocal trio

As legend has it, the three singers who founded the group Brownstone were pounding the pavement in their quest for a record contract when they abruptly found themselves facing a terrifying tryout. At one of their many boardroom auditions in the early 1990s, pop deity and record label exec Michael Jackson casually arrived to hear the session. Although the prospect of performing in front of the "King of Pop" triggered an instant case of the jitters for the members of Brownstone, they persevered. When the trio launched into a stunning a capella number, Jackson declared their heartfelt harmonies extraordinary, and soon they were recording their debut album, *From the Bottom Up,* for his fledgling MJJ Music label. After the record's release, critics were as equally impressed as Jackson. "This set stands on its own," stated a review in *Billboard.* "With the trio ... expressing themselves on such flavorful tracks as the enchantingly serene 'Sometimes Dancin,' the soulful rendition of the Eagles classic 'I Can't Tell You Why,' the inspirational 'Don't Cry for Me,' and the hip-hop/G-funk-influenced 'Pass the Lovin.'"

The record, which included a variety of producers, was released in January 1995. It went gold and spawned the hit single "If You Love Me," which climbed to the pop Top 10 and reached No. 2 on the R&B chart. The follow-up single, "Grapevyne," also cracked the R&B Top 10. Brownstone was suddenly in demand. They joined Boyz II Men on a sold-out U.S. tour, performed with Patti LaBelle, Anita Baker, Maze, and Blackstreet. In addition to performing with these renowned stars, Brownstone appeared on *The Soul Train Music Awards, The Lady of Soul Awards,* and the BET network's *Video Soul.* In January 1996, "If You Love Me" received a Grammy nomination for Best R&B Performance by a Duo or Group.

A Lineup Shift

Brownstone was founded by twenty-something singers Nicole Nicci Gilbert, Charmayne Maxee Maxwell, and Monica Mimi Dolby. They came together in Los Angeles, where each had come in search of a music career: Dolby from New Orleans; Gilbert from Detroit; and Maxwell from Guyana. "The threesome began singing together after seeing each other perform at a seemingly endless series of auditions," *Essence* magazine reported in 1995. "There was instant chemistry. Vocally, we had a really strong blend that sounded good," Dolby told the magazine. "We picked our name because brown is the earth and stone is solid." Gilbert has said that shared sense of strength and stability also inhabited the friendship between these three women. "Together," she told *Essence* reporter D.G. "We have a strong foundation and *act* as a unit."

As it turned out, however, that foundation was not enough to keep the threesome intact. Dolby left the group in 1995, reportedly for health reasons. She was replaced by Detroiter Kina Cosper, a college friend of Gilbert's. Cosper acknowledged the pressure she faced in joining the already successful combo. As a new member, "fitting in with the group was a challenge," she admitted in the band's Epic Records biography. "I was nervous when we first started recording the new album. But I'm very excited about how it turned out." She was not the only one feeling the pressure, however, as the realigned trio began recording their second record in mid-1996. "We had to get over the sophomore jitters," Gilbert explained in the Epic bio. "It was really important for us to realize that our job was not to try and outdo the first record, but to make an album of songs from the heart."

Continued Success

They need not have worried. The album, *Still Climbing,* was released in June 1997 and became another critical and popular success for Brownstone. "In these days of sisters with sound-alike voices, Brownstone is one of the few female R&B groups with a distinct vocal style," Jeremy Helligar wrote in *People.* "Their swaying, three-part harmonies build, build, build, then soar into what could pass for a full choir. Unlike many of their counterparts, who seem too attached to mechanical, mid-tempo beats, Brownstone nails the emotional bull's-eye with their torchy, slow rhythm & blues." Helligar went on to say that *Still Climbing* was reminiscent of the late-70s heyday of singing groups like the Emotions and the Jones Girls, when R&B albums offered groups more than a good excuse to flounce about in fancy videos.

On *Still Climbing,* the group continued to work with a variety of writers and producers and again managed to create an album which was both eclectic and cohesive. The record displayed a seamless consistency derived from the threesome's hands-on approach and special touch. Of the 12 tracks on *Still Climbing,* for example, eight were written or co-written by the three group members. Meanwhile, MJJ Music and its partner, Epic Records did their part by launching a strong promotional campaign that pushed *Still Climbing* to retailers, radio stations, and video networks. Brownstone promoted the record during a European tour, then joined singer Keith Sweat for a series of concerts in the United States.

"We didn't necessarily set out in a different direction (on the second record) but we've grown more," Gilbert told *Billboard's* J.R. Reynolds. "One of the things that we're most recognized for is our singing ability, and with the addition of Kina, there's a new energy with [*Still Climbing*] just like when we were recording the first album." The first single released from *Still Climbing,* an R&B standout called "Five Miles to Empty," received solid airplay and reached the R&B Top 10. The video for the song was aired on VH1, the Box, and BET. Gilbert has suggested that, despite Brownstone's lineup change, the new album picked up where the group left off with *From the Bottom Up.* "It shows our vocal and creative growth," she proclaimed in the Epic bio. "And I think it shows that, if we stay focused, we can take this all the way and be one of the best girl groups around." Many listeners would say they've already reached that plateau.

Selected discography

From the Bottom Up, MJJ Music/Epic, 1995.
Still Climbing, MJJ Music/Epic, 1997.

Sources

Billboard, January 21, 1997; July 12, 1997.
Entertainment Weekly, February 10, 1996.
Essence, June 1995.
People, July 14, 1997.

Additional material was taken from the Epic Records web site.

—Dave Wilkins

Camel

Rock group

Discussing the use of lights and films during his band's performances, Camel guitarist and vocalist Andrew Latimer told *Melody Maker* in 1976, "This is the first time we've used films, and I don't want us to get into it too much.... We're not a very bopping band, so it's nice for the audience to have something to watch."

The British progressive rock group Camel formed in 1972 with the blues-rock trio Brew, consisting of Latimer, bassist Doug Ferguson, and drummer Andy Ward. After backing singer Philip Goodhand-Tait on an album, the trio was joined by organist and vocalist Peter Bardens and began rehearsing original material. Camel's sound featured extensive interplay between Latimer's guitar and Bardens's keyboards, underpinned by Ward's swinging percussion. Vocals were not the band's main focus. During the recording of Camel's debut album, the producer suggested that the group find a better singer. After auditioning 30 unsuitable vocalists, the search was abandoned and the recording sessions continued.

The band became a fixture on the English college circuit. In a 1973 interview with *Melody Maker*, Peter Bardens related the importance of these venues to Camel, "I think the college circuit plays a very important part in any new band's future. They are one of those rare places where small bands get the chance to play, and what's more, they are always good payers." One early concert appearance that provided Camel with under-

ground credibility was on October 8, 1973 at the Greasy Truckers' Party at Dingwall's Dance Hall in London. A live cut from that show, "God of Light Revisited Parts 1, 2, and 3" formed one side of a rare double album commemorating the event, which also featured contributions by progressive contemporaries Gong and Henry Cow.

As a result of constant touring, the band's second album *Mirage* sold much better than its self-titled debut. Bardens told *Melody Maker,* "We started the band from scratch. We had no money and no equipment. In three years we've done four tours of Britain, and we're the sort of band that creeps up on you."

Goose Flies Camel Over the Hump

Camel's first taste of success came with its 1975 album *The Snow Goose,* an all-instrumental work based on Paul Gallico's children's book. The album reached both British and American charts. Latimer commented to *Melody Maker* about the writing of the album: "When we'd written the piece we were really pleased, then again, it wasn't until we'd finished the album that we realized what we'd got." Andy Ward continued, *"Snow Goose* has opened up a reaction in the audience and the press that we'd been waiting for for a long time." The band was voted *Melody Maker*'s Brightest Hope in that magazine's 1975 poll, and performed at The Royal Albert Hall with the London Symphony Orchestra.

Moonmadness, released in 1976, featured several songs inspired by the personalities of the band members, including "Chord Change" for Bardens, "Air Born" for Latimer, "Another Night" for Ferguson, and "Lunar Sea" for Ward. Toward the end of the recording sessions for that album, bassist Doug Ferguson left to form the group Head Waiter. His replacement, Richard Sinclair, was the bassist and vocalist for veteran progressive groups Caravan and Hatfield and the North. On *Rain Dances,* Sinclair became the distinctive vocalist Camel had lacked. A *Melody Maker* contributor wrote, "[Sinclair's] vocals were a rare treat, totally unaffected by the Americanisation most rock singers turned to without question, and delivered with a tone and pitch that would delight a choir master."

In 1978 Peter Bardens left Camel, replaced by two more ex-Caravan members, Richard's cousin David Sinclair and Jan Schelhaas, causing Camel to earn the nickname "Caramel" by the music press. The band also added former King Crimson sax and flute player Mel Collins. Before recording sessions could be held, however, Richard and David Sinclair departed.

Members include **Peter Bardens** (member c. 1971-79), organ, keyboards, vocals; **Colin Bass** (joined c. 1979), bass, vocals; **Paul Burgess** (joined c. 1984), drums; **Mel Collins** (member c. 1978-79), sax, flute; **Doug Ferguson** (member c. 1971-76), bass; **Andrew Latimer,** guitar, vocals; **Jan Schelhaas** (member c. 1978-79), keyboards; **Ton Scherpenzeel** (joined c. 1984), keyboards; **David Sinclair** (member c. 1978-79), organ, piano; **Richard Sinclair** (born June 6, 1948, Canterbury, Kent, England; member c. 1977-79), bass, vocals; **Andy Ward** (born September 28, 1952, London, England; member c. 1971-81), drums, percussion.

Formed c. 1971, in London, England; backed Philip Goodhand-Tait on album and tour, 1971; released debut album *Camel* on MCA, 1973; appeared at Greasy Truckers' Party, 1973; played at Royal Albert Hall with London Symphony Orchestra, 1975; formed Camel Productions, 1991.

Addresses: *Record company*—Camel Productions, P. O. Box 4786, Mountain View, CA 94040.

Camel found itself deserted by the British music press during the early eighties, as press attention shifted to punk rock. Despite sellout tours of Europe, the group's records no longer sold well. Andrew Latimer told *Melody Maker* in 1980, "Sometimes it's frustrating if you do something you think is a work of art and it gets totally ignored." Another major setback occurred when Andy Ward left the band due to the pressures of touring and a distaste for the music industry in general, leaving Latimer as the last original member of Camel.

Latimer was pressured by the record company to record more pop-oriented material on 1982's *The Single Factor* which featured members of The Alan Parsons Project. Peter Bardens makes a guest appearance on the track "Sasquatch" along with founding Genesis guitarist Anthony Philips. Following the release of *Stationary Traveller* in 1984, inspired by the social and physical division of Berlin, Camel took a seven-year hiatus.

Andrew Latimer relocated to California during the early nineties, and formed Camel Productions to release new and archival Camel material. Camel's nineties output includes *Dust and Dreams*, inspired by John Steinbeck's *The Grapes of Wrath*. *Harbour of Tears* was inspired by Latimer's search for his family's roots following his father's death. In 1997 Camel completed a world tour, performing to sell-out crowds in nine countries. Latimer and Camel Productions also produce and distribute an annual newsletter which keeps Camel in the public eye.

In addition to a prolific solo career, Bardens enjoyed a brief stint down memory lane with Ward for a nostalgically titled group Mirage, performing a few select dates in 1994. Since leaving Camel in the early eighties, Ward has been involved with several other projects, including progressive rockers Marillion, Richard Sinclair's Caravan of Dreams, and his current band, English psychedelic rockers, The Bevis Frond.

Throughout its 25-year existence, Camel has scaled the heights of fame as well as the depths of mainstream media derision, acquiring a dedicated following along the way. Through Andrew Latimer's company, Camel Productions, Camel remains alive and well.

Selected discography

Albums

(With Philip Goodhand-Tait), *I Think I'll Write a Song,* Vertigo, 1972.
Camel, MCA, 1973, reissued Camel Productions, 1992.
"God of Light Revisited Parts 1, 2, and 3" from *Greasy Truckers' Party,* Greasy Truckers, 1973.
Mirage, Janus, 1974, reissued Deram, 1994.
The Snow Goose, Janus, 1975, reissued Deram, 1994.
Moonmadness, Janus, 1976, reissued London, 1992.
Rain Dances, Janus, 1977, reissued Deram, 1992.
Breathless, Arista, 1978, reissued One Way, 1994.
A Live Record, London, 1978.
I Can See Your House from Here, Arista, 1979, reissued One Way, 1994.
Nude, Passport, 1981, reissued London, 1995.
The Single Factor, Passport, 1982.
Stationary Traveler, Decca, 1984.
Compact Compilation (rec. 1973-1975), Rhino, 1985.
Pressure Points - Live in Concert, Decca, 1985.
Dust and Dreams, Camel Productions, 1991.
Never Let Go, Camel Productions, 1993.
On the Road 1972, Camel Productions, 1993.
Echoes, The Retrospective (rec. 1973-1991), Polygram, 1993.
On the Road 1982, Camel Productions, 1994.
Harbour of Tears, Camel Productions, 1996.
On the Road 1981, Camel Productions, 1997.

Related projects

(With Richard Sinclair, David Sinclair, Jan Schelhaas), Caravan, *Canterbury Tales: The Best of Caravan 1969-1975*, Polygram, 1994.

David Sinclair, *Moon over Man* (recorded 1978), Voiceprint, 1994.

(With Andy Ward and Richard Sinclair), Todd Dillingham, *The Wilde Canterbury Dream*, Voiceprint, 1994.

(With Andy Ward and Richard Sinclair), *Caravan of Dreams*, HTD, 1994.

(With Andy Ward), Adrian Shaw, *Tea for the Hydra*, Woronzow, 1994.

(With Andy Ward), The Bevis Frond, *Sprawl*, Woronzow, 1994.

(With Andy Ward), The Bevis Frond, *Superseeder*, Woronzow, 1995.

(With Andy Ward), Richard Sinclair, *R.S.V.P.*, Sinclair Songs, 1996.

(With Andy Ward), Mary Lou Lord, *Martian Saints* (EP), Kill Rock Stars, 1997.

(With Andy Ward), The Deviants, "Memphis Psychosis" and The Bevis Frond, "Red Hair" from *Ptolemaic Terrascope Terrastock Special Edition CD*, Flydaddy, 1997.

Peter Bardens solo projects

The Answer, Verve, 1970.
Write My Name in Dust, Verve, 1971.
Heart to Heart, Arista, 1979.
Seen One Earth, Capitol, 1987.
Speed of Light, Capitol, 1988.
Watercolours, Miramar, 1991.
Further Than You Know, Miramar, 1993.
(With Mirage), *Double Live*, Voiceprint, 1994.
Big Sky, HTD, 1995.

Sources

Books

Joynson, Vernon, *Tapestry of Delights: The Comprehensive Guide to British Music of the Beat, R&B, Psychedelic, and Progressive Eras 1963-1976*, Borderline Productions, 1995.

Periodicals

Melody Maker, February 3, 1973; July 6, 1974; November 23, 1974; July 12, 1975; September 13, 1975; October 25, 1975; April 10, 1976; September 24, 1977; November 12, 1977; January 19, 1980.

Online

www.tau.ac.il/~ofirz/camel/welcome.htm
www.alpes-net.fr/~bigbang/calyx.html
www.terrascope.org

—Jim Powers

Eric Champion

Christian singer, songwriter, drummer

The 1996 release, *Transformation,* reflects Eric Champion's new sound on the first album released on a multi-record deal with Essential Records/Brentwood Music. Simultaneously, the change in musical style stems from Champion's own spiritual odyssey as he "comes of age." *Transformation* displays a maturation in sound; Champion leaves behind the computer aided techno-sound used on his previous five albums released under the Myrrh label. More recently, he has combined his pop sound with electric guitars, and adds backup rhythm accompaniment. Not surprising, the promotional campaign used to launch, *Transformation,* was entitled, "What's up with Eric?," designed to call attention to his musical metamorphosis into what he feels is more of a modern rock sound. Champion hopes that his 1996 album appeals more to a younger audience than did previous contemporary/pop albums.

Champion seems to have discovered his place in the music world. Since starting in the business at age 18, *Transformation* is his sixth album released. Perhaps becoming a part of the music industry has been a natural progression for Champion. His mother and father were both professional musicians, and as a child he traveled with his family performing in both club and ministry settings. Champion also appeared in commercials as a youngster. In an interview with Frank Chimento, of *7ball* magazine, he stated "we were like a Christian version of the Partridge family." Since his family had been part of the entertainment business since his childhood,

Champion's next step was to find his own personal niche.

When Champion was about 16 years old he discovered computer-generated music. Using keyboards and computers he began creating techno-sounding music. He was influenced by Howard Jones and Thomas Dolby, and the computer assisted musical sound created in the 1980s. Among his other influences were Led Zeppelin, U2, the Beatles, Radiohead, and REM. In 1990, at age 19, he released a self-titled debut album under the Myrrh Record Label. He would go on to produce four more releases with Myrrh Records.

On the 1994 release, *Vertical Reality,* his last release on the Myrrh label, Champion fuses the techno-rock sound with lyrics clearly influenced by his taste for science fiction literature. The Christian theme also weaves through the tapestry of his lyrics. Incorporating fantasy and sci-fi themes, *Vertical Reality* tells the story about a society so assimilated by computers that individuals no longer have the freedom to think for themselves. Their minds and lives are controlled by a massive mainframe computer called "Govtrol," the institution which controls the world. The theme underlying the sci-fi/fantasy is an old one: humankind's search for God. The members of this imaginary society are being controlled by the computers and whatever information is chosen by "Govtrol," to be included in the massive database.

Champion uses the unreal world of sci-fi/fantasy to ask important questions about the individual's relationship to God. In an online interview on the world wide web, he stated that "the theme [of *Vertical Reality*] was simple: getting to know God in a real and closer way, and applying that to your life." The questions raised in *Vertical Reality* may be set in a fantasy landscape, but they are clearly meant for reflection in our current reality.

Sci-Fi with a Message

The messages in *Vertical Reality* reflect Champion's thoughts and feelings about God, and how his music is an expression of his Christian ministry. He hopes to reach young people with his sci-fi/fantasy themes and to make them aware of messages from the Bible. After touring with the Newsboys, Champion realized that he needed to create a focus for himself and his music, otherwise someone else would create it for him. After creating some demos with another band, it became apparent that Champion was creating music in a new direction. He told Chimento that Myrrh Record's reaction to his new sound was something like, "Whoa, we don't know about this." He soon began working with Charlie

For the Record . . .

Son of Bob and Carol Champion.

Recorded five albums between 1990 and 1994 with Myrrh Records; released *Transformation* on Essential Records, 1996; toured with Newsboys.

Addresses: *Record company*—Essential Records/Brentwood Music, publicist, Nina Williams, One Maryland Farms, Suite 200, Brentwood, TN, 37027. *Fan mail*—P.O. Box 25249, Nashville, TN 37202.

Peacock, who encouraged Champion to follow his vision. He decided to leave Myrrh and sign on with Essential Records, where he was given free range in musical expression and was not required to produce a certain sound.

Metamorphosed

The 1996 release, *Transformation,* is the result of Champion following his creative path musically, personally, and spiritually. It's about making changes, as he encourages others to question themselves and their relationship to God. It is also about challenging oneself to reach self-awareness in spite of life's many obstacles. Leaving the computer generated techno-sound behind, *Transformation* explores the rock-grunge world of music. Champion told Leon van Stensel in an online interview that "*Transformation* talks about a very painful and effectful change that happens when you're trying to change from this old sinful man into this new creature. A lot of questions come into play with that and I'm into it myself."

The initial release of *Transformation* sparked controversy with some Christian retailers. After realizing that the image of himself on the CD cover poised with a toy laser gun could be interpreted by some as promoting violence, Champion agreed to tone down the cover photo. Even the setting for *Transformation* was unusual. Rather than recording in a sound studio, Peacock suggested recording it live. A house that Champion fondly called "a Brady Bunch" style house, based on the television show of the same name was rented for the purpose, and was transformed into a studio.

Transformation's first cut "Dress Me Up," weaves a tale about a man who wants to rid himself of his old nature,

and using clothing as a metaphor for change, he wishes to put on the new clothes only God can give. "Life Form," continues the theme of change in one's life, moving either closer to or further away from God. In "Temptannie," he sings about the power of sexual temptations and his fight to overcome them. Then showing his flexibility and sense of humor, he re-invents a song previously recorded by Amy Grant called "Every Heartbeat."

Although Champion's music clearly has Christian themes, he denies being a preacher. He would like to be known primarily as a communicator and an entertainer and he intends for his music to stimulate people to grow. When asked by Chimento what he envisioned as his next step, Champion replied, "It's kind of cross that bridge when you get to it. My goal right now is to find some great guys and put together a great band and just play and play and play." Besides his song writing, he has ideas for comic books, screenplays, and novels. He also dreams about opening a performing arts school for underprivileged children someday.

Selected discography

Eric Champion, Myrrh Records, 1990.
Revolution, Myrrh Records, 1991.
Hot Christmas, Myrrh Records, 1992.
Save the World, Myrrh Records, 1992.
Vertical Reality, Myrrh Records, 1994.
Transformation, Essential Records/Brentwood Music, 1996.

Sources

Periodicals

Billboard, April 6, 1996, p.22.

Online

http://place2b.org/cmp/davidl/albums/champ_05.htm (Christian Music Review Headquarters)
http://users.aol.com/luxvenit/eric1.htm (7ball interview)
http://www.christianmarketplace.com/cba/ind_news.html#Zomba
http://www.cmo.com/cmo/cmo/data/echampion.htm
http://www.omroep.nl/eo/spoor7/spotlight/archive/spotlight.champion.html
http://www.providentmusic.com/tour/?Eric+Champion
http://www.7ball.com/07/07revs.htm

Additional information was provided by Essential Records, publicity materials.

—Debra Reilly

Chumba-wamba

Alternative rock

When Chumbawamba rose to the top of the alternative charts in late 1997 with their rollicking, anthemic smash single "Tubthumping," many assumed they were just another upstart British band. However, the band had been together a decade and a half, and though new to American audiences, were a well-known anarchist-punk-pop act in Britain—and often a target of derision there for their mouthy, anti-establishment stance. Once termed "cuddly cartoon anarchists," the peroxided, 30-ish members of Chumbawamba now found themselves on MTV's *120 Minutes* explaining what their music was all about.

The line-up of Chumbawamba has proved to be more immutable than the British cabinet ministries it has criticized over the years. Most of the band's founding members, who came together in 1983, were still on board when "Tubthumping" hit the charts 14 years later. Their acquaintance and subsequent formation into a band grew out of a "squat," or illegally-occupied dwelling, in the English industrial city of Leeds, where Lou Watts, Danbert "The Cat" Nobacon, Boff, Paul Greco, Alice Nutter, Dunstan Bruce, and Harry Hamer were living communally. They shared their funds, and for much of the decade earned a living by working in various co-operatives.

Leeds had also given birth to the politically-inspired music of bands like the Mekons and Gang of Four, and a miners' strike in 1984 enervated the squat-dwellers into taking action in support of the strikers. It was Margaret Thatcher's second term as prime minister, and the alternately despised or beloved Conservative Party leader was best remembered for her no-nonsense approach in transforming England from a democratic-socialist enclave to a free-market capitalist economy. Breaking the power of England's powerful trade unions was one facet of her government policy. Members of the Leeds squat that became Chumbawamba began collecting money for a local soup kitchen, and eventually started performing to raise money. "Chumbawamba didn't pick members on whether they could actually play anything," according to the band's self-written history published on their website. "The only entrance specifications were an ability to keep time, a hatred of authority and a good heart."

Anarchist Pranksters

At this point the band's musical style leaned heavily toward punk rock, the sound of the disestablishment in England at the moment. They began playing for other benefits, such as animal-rights fund-raisers, but their against-the-grain mentality earned them enemies even among like-minded peers. Chumbawamba drummer Harry Hamer recalled these shows in an interview with *Melody Maker*'s Ian Watson. Their fellow protesters, Hamer said, "were so narrow minded that even though I agreed with them, I'd find myself wanting to tell them I'd just eaten a bacon buttie!" On another occasion, a defanged Clash arrived in Leeds for a concert, and Chumbawamba singer Danbert Nobacon covered Joe Strummer with red paint. The band also protested at Falklands War victory parades, designed and posted a flyer campaign to shoot down Leed's local police helicopter, and even made fun of themselves: Hamer also told Watson in the *Melody Maker* interview that fans in English clubs never recognized him as the drummer, "so I've often slagged off Chumbawamba in the toilet at our gigs, saying how they're all junkies. That they say all these political things, but really they spend all their money on smack. And people so readily believe it!"

Such attitudes earned Chumbawamba ideological enemies even as word-of-mouth support for the band grew. They once did a single entitled "I'm Thick," in response to the skinhead Oi! punk movement then gaining ground in the early 1980s. To mock them, Chumbawamba took a typical Oi! rhythm track and sang the words "I'm thick" over it 64 times. After releasing these and other anarchist-minded songs on cassette for some time, in 1985 Chumbawamba started up their own label, Agit-Prop. Its first single was

For the Record . . .

Members include **Jude Abbott** (joined band, 1995), trumpet, vocals; **Boff**, guitar, vocals; **Dustan Bruce**, vocals, percussion; **Neil Ferguson**, keyboards, guitars; **Paul Greco**, bass; **Harry Hamer**, drums, programming; **Danbert "The Cat" Nobacon**, vocals; **Alice Nutter**, vocals; and **Lou Watts**, vocals, keyboards.

Most band members worked on co-operative work collectives during the 1980s.

Band formed and recorded and sold own cassettes, early 1980s; formed own label, Agit-Prop, 1985; released several singles and LPs, including *Pictures of Starving Children Sell Records,* 1986; signed to One Little Indian label, c. 1993; released several singles and LPs, including the single "Ugh! Your Ugly Houses!"; signed with EMI Europe, May 1997; released "Tubthumping" single and *Tubthumper* LP, summer 1997.

Addresses: *Record company*—Universal Records, 1755 Broadway, 7th Floor, New York, NY 10019. *Website*—

"Revolution," which famed British DJ John Peel began playing on his show. The song eventually reached the charts, and the band followed it that same year with the LP *Pictures of Starving Children Sell Records.* Its title came in response to the 1985 Live Aid campaign to raise money for victims of famine in Africa; band members were repulsed by the "do-gooder" aspect of the well-publicized, world-televised dual concert project, which failed to address the issue of why governments allowed their citizens to starve. Ten years later, "the media now claims that it had grave misgivings about whether Phil Collins's appearing on two continents in the same day would really be a catalyst for lasting change," the band remarked on their 1997 press release; but at the time, Chumbawamba were the target of much criticism for the title.

Changed Musical Direction

The title of their 1987 release, *Never Mind the Ballots,* was a nod to the title of the first Sex Pistols LP, but actually skewered England's 1987 elections in which Thatcher won a third term. During the campaign Chumbawamba had clandestinely promoted themselves as a band called "The Middle," and even won the endorsement of the Liberal Democrat Party; they almost played live at a political event before the ruse was discovered. Their next project also managed to earn them scorn—in 1988 they released a record of a capella folk music, *English Rebel Songs.* The band's more punk-minded fan base became confused. Two years later, Chumbawamba took a completely different direction with *Slap!,* marking their entry into the burgeoning dance-music scene. "We just reached a point where we realised we weren't enjoying shouting `No, no, no!' and pointing at people," Nutter told *Melody Maker* writer Dave Simpson.

Chumbawamba next attempted a record made up entirely of samples taken from artists such as Kylie Minogue and Abba, mixing the cuts into a record they titled *Jesus H. Christ.* It was never released due to legal problems in obtaining publishing rights for the sampled bits, so in response they wrote songs about censorship issues and released *Shhh.* The 1992 effort, wrote Dave Jennings in *Melody Maker,* "is full of dance rhythms, seductive melodies, harmonies and, above all, a mischievous sense of humour."

The following year Chumbawamba signed to a small, leftist-minded label called One Little Indian, which also has the corporate turf of Bjork and Skunk Anansie. One of their first releases for it was an anti-fascist single, "Enough Is Enough," with black English rap act Credit to the Nation. The single caused a stir, as usual, and a record store in Leeds was vandalized by fascist troublemakers for selling it. More controversy came in 1994 with the LP *Anarchy,* which featured a live birth on its cover. Some outlets objected to the graphic nature of the photograph. The record itself was deemed "a breathtaking mix of infectious disco and anthemic pop with the grand operatic scope of a West End musical" by *Melody Maker's* Watson.

Outspoken About Ecstasy

After the release of the "Homophobia" single in May of 1994—which spoke out against anti-gay violence and attitudes—Chumbawamba's turn toward a more music-hall vibe was evident with the 1995 LP *Swinging with Raymond.* Half its tracks were romantic paeans, the other half about hate and other political issues. Around this time Chumbawamba became embroiled in an anti-anti-drug campaign: the British government had launched campaign to alert young people to the dangers of Ecstasy, and used a photo of an actual 18-year-old woman who had died after taking the drug and drinking too much water, which quickly and fatally affected her metabolism.

Chumbawamba objected to the billboard campaign which they perceived as more of a misinformation service; better to use such a platform to warn teenagers not to take Ecstasy and drink gallons of water at the same time—a common phenomenon in overheated rave clubs—than stressing that the "drug" had "killed" this young woman. They hijacked the billboard image and began mailing out their own literature, an act for which they were vilified in the press. The band explained their stance against the anti-Ecstasy campaign on their website: "The [campaign's] aim was to make ecstasy Public Enemy Number 1; ironic considering how many hundreds and thousands die each year from tobacco-related deaths. Both the government and the advertisers make billions from the tobacco industry; the only posters about tobacco desperately try and coax us into buying it." The Chumbawamba website offers fans and enemies alike much fodder, and is done with the typically smart-mouthed, anti-establishment ethos for which the band has gained renown. One section gathers the most scathing press about Chumbawamba, such as one *Melody Maker* assessment of their 1995 LP *Showbusiness!,* in which Andrew Mueller disparaged the band for what he termed their "sheer woolly-mindedness ... Chumbawamba are a one-legged man at an arse-kicking party."

In the spring of 1997, Chumbawamba came under the aegis of EMI Europe, which released a rousing single called "Tubthumping" that summer. Much of their new sound came as result of their collaboration with producer and friend Neil Ferguson, who also played on the record as well. "Tubthumping" became a huge hit in England, in part for its catchy hook and rap-inspired reworking of an old drinking song once commonly heard in working-class English pubs. The song also featured samples from the 1997 British film *Brassed Off,* the story of permanently unemployed miners in England and their brass band. The very term "tubthumper" is a slang term for an impromptu speechmaker, which is what the band soon had an opportunity to become on a global scale.

Superpopstardom

The LP *Tubthumper* was released in the fall of 1997 in the United States on Republic/Universal. Within a few weeks the "Tubthumping" single was No. 1 on alternative charts and its video appeared frequently on MTV. The album itself featured a typically-Chumbawamba mix of musical genres, from drum-and-bass to straightforward dance songs—but behind it all was their continuing anti-establishment vibe. One track addressed homelessness ("The Big Issue"), another the Liverpool dockworkers' strike ("One by One"). "The revolution will not be televised, but in Britain it sometimes makes the charts," wrote Mark Jenkins in *Time Out-New York,* who called the collection "Woody Guthrie recast by Andrew Lloyd Webber."

Putting their newfound-money where their mouths were, Chumbawamba played a series of concerts to benefit a fund for striking Liverpool dockworkers; they also embarked on a small U.S. club-date tour that fall. Success had failed to dampen their anarchist spirit. In response to a query posted on their website, they suggested that fans shoplift the Chumbawamba LP from the larger retail outlets, and even provide a list of British chain stores from which to steal—which "involves fewer moral dilemmas," they wrote, than pilfering from the small independent record retailer. *Evening Standard* journalist Zoe Williams interviewed the band when "Tubthumping" was No. 5 on the London charts, and noted that despite the recent pop-star fame, Chumbawamba try to remain true to their cause. "Everyone's desperate for them to lose the angry anti-system agenda and settle down to some straightforward self-indulgence," Williams wrote. "But it will take more than some media attention to stop them causing trouble."

Selected discography

On Agit-Prop

Pictures of Starving Children Sell Records, 1986.
Never Mind the Ballots, 1987.
English Rebel Songs (10-inch), 1988.
Slap!, 1990.
First Two, 1992.
Shhh, 1992.

On Little Indian

Anarchy, 1994.
Showbusiness! 1995.
Swinging with Raymond, 1995.
(With Casey Orr) *I - Portraits of Anarchists* (includes book), 1996.

On Republic/Universal

Tubthumper, 1997.

Chumbawamba has also recorded singles under the names Skin Disease and Passion Killers, released a double CD with Noam Chomsky on Allied Records, and recorded several singles for various compilations.

Sources

Evening Standard, September 9, 1997, p. 21.
Melody Maker, May 30, 1992, p. 32; September 11, 1993, p. 35; September 18, 1993, p. 2; April 23, 1994, p. 29; April 30, 1994, p. 28; March 11, 1995, p. 41.
Time Out-New York, October 9, 1997.

—*Carol Brennan*

Natalie Cole

Singer

AP/Wide World Photos, Inc. Reproduced by permission.

When singer Natalie Cole was in college at the University of Massachusetts at Amherst, she performed weekends at nightclubs. Prior to one show, a small club displayed a sign that announced her only as Nat "King" Cole's daughter. She was so angry that she scolded the manager of the club; however, 20 years later, Cole reached the pinnacle of her success by "teaming up" with her late father in an album called *Unforgettable with Love.* The album earned seven Grammy awards and stayed on the pop charts for several weeks. For Natalie, it was a special tribute to her legendary father who died of lung cancer when she was only 15.

Natalie is one of five children born to the famous singer Nat King Cole and his wife Maria. Maria sang with Duke Ellington before marrying Nat. Natalie, their second child, was born on February 6, 1950. Cole told *Working Mother* that her childhood was filled with music that her mom and dad liked to hear as well as the music her dad sung. She said, "He never directed me away from any type of music, but it was the kind of music Dad made that's left a lasting impression on me." It did not take long for her to follow in his footsteps. By age six, she appeared on one of her dad's albums. At eleven, she performed briefly in a nightclub act. However, Cole claims her father died never knowing that she wanted a career in singing because she told him she wanted to be a doctor. He never pushed her into singing, as he wanted her to choose her own career. While earning a degree in child psychology from the University of Massachusetts, she realized that she wanted to sing.

Initially, Cole was filled with insecurity when she performed, not knowing if people liked her just because she was the Nat King Cole's daughter. This insecurity caused her to avoid performing the same type of music as her father, who was a big band, jazzy singer and an accomplished pianist in the fifties. He had several hit albums before rock music was marketed to the public. She told *Ebony,* "I spent the first part of my career rebelling against it [her father's music]. Always in the back of my mind I was trying to stay as far away from that stigma as I possibly could." After earning her degree, Cole toured local clubs with a band called Black Magic.

In 1974 she met two producers in Chicago, Chuck Jackson and Marvin Yancy, who wanted to write and produce an album with her. In 1975 Capitol Records released *Inseparable,* launching Cole's solo career. Lauded by critics, the album contained two singles, "This Will Be" and "Inseparable," which quickly climbed the pop and R&B charts. For her effort, Cole won a Grammy award for Best New Artist. While producing the album, Cole and Yancy formed a relationship that

For the Record . . .

Born Natalie Maria Cole, February 6, 1950; daughter of Nathaniel Adam (singer) and Maria (singer, homemaker; maiden name, Hawkins); married Marvin J. Yancy July 30, 1976 (divorced 1979); married Andre Fischer (a music producer), 1989 (divorced 1996); children: Robert. *Education:* B. A. in Psychology from the University of Massachusetts at Amherst

Started singing with her legendary father Nat "King" Cole at age six; performed with group called Black Magic, early 1970s; discovered by music producers including Marvin Yancy, 1974; producers cut first album with her titled *Inseparable*, 1975; recorded four more successful albums throughout 70s including one with Peabo Bryson; drug problem stalled career, 1980; entered drug rehab at Hazelden for six months, 1983; back on the charts with album *Everlasting,* 1987; released *Good to Be Back,* 1989.

Andre Fischer produced next album called *Unforgettable with Love,* which sold over five million copies, 1991; high-tech wizardry created a "duet" with her late father for the single "Unforgettable"; appeared in television series *I'll Fly Away,* 1993; released album *Take a Look,* 1993; released Christmas album *Holly and Ivy,* 1994; starred in USA Cable movie *Lily in Winter,* 1994; released album *Stardust,* 1997.

Awards: Grammy Award for Best New Artist, 1976; seven Grammy Awards in 1992 for *Unforgettable with Love* including Record of the Year, Song of the Year, and Album of the Year; Grammy Award for Best Jazz Vocal, 1994; one gold single, three gold albums; recipient of two Image Awards from the NAACP, 1976, 1977; American Music Award, 1978; Soul Train Award.

Member: AFTRA; National Association of Recording Arts and Sciences; Delta Sigma Delta.

Addresses: *Office*—c/o William Morris Agency, 151 S., East El Camino Dr., Beverly Hills, CA 90212-2704.

led to marriage in 1976. That same year she released *Natalie*. The single "Sophisticated Lady" reached number one on the R&B charts and number 25 on the pop charts. *Thankful* included the successful singles "I've Got Love on My Mind" and "Our Love" in 1977. In 1979

Cole teamed with Peabo Bryson and released *We're the Best of Friends,* another successful album with two hit singles. Her albums sold very well in the seventies—especially since her career was just beginning. However, her personal problems were escalating out of control and soon stalled her initial stardom.

In 1973 Canadian police arrested Cole for possession of heroin. Her problems with drugs did not end until ten years later, and she claimed that the majority of her drug use was in the five years after her son Robert was born in 1977. She also abused cocaine, prescription drugs, acid, and alcohol, admittedly not employing anyone who would not do drugs with her. When her marriage ended in 1979, she called the relationship "short but devastating." In 1983 she finally entered the Hazelden Foundation in Minnesota after a near-fatal car accident. She walked away from the crash physically unharmed but mentally shaken. She stayed at Hazelden for six months before emerging ready to live life drug-free. Every year on November 28, she celebrates the anniversary of the last day she did drugs.

She released an album every year from 1980 to 1985, but Cole did not reach the pop charts again until 1987, when she released *Everlasting*. This album included three singles that reached the top 20 on the pop charts. She also scored two hit duets with Ray Parker Jr. the same year. In 1989 she released *Good to Be Back,* which included the top ten hit "Miss You Like Crazy." That same year Cole met music producer Andre Fischer, who was a drummer for the band Rufus and for Chaka Khan. He wanted to work with Cole on her next album, but was also secretly in love with her. They married and began work on an album that was unforgettable.

The Spirit of Nat King Cole

Unforgettable with Love was released in 1991 to critical acclaim. Not only did Cole admit to being Nat King Cole's daughter on this album, she pledged her complete devotion to her father and his music. She even "felt" his presence while recording. Produced by her husband, the album included 20 songs from Nat King Cole's collection sung by Natalie. Singles included "The Very Thought of You," "Mona Lisa," and "Route 66." Her uncle, Ike Cole, appeared on "Route 66," but the most fascinating effort was "Unforgettable." With a little help from the masters of technology, Cole performed the song as a duet with her father using her father's original recording. The idea was unprecedented and the result was overwhelming. The album sold over five million copies and earned seven Grammy awards including

Album of the Year. "Unforgettable" won both Record of the Year and Song of the Year. *Billboard* called the album's success "an almost complete anomaly in recent chart history—a massive hit album featuring music in a noncontemporary style." *People* gushed, "Like father, like daughter—when the subject is singing and the father was Nat 'King' Cole, the daughter is in for a big compliment." *Playboy* commented, "Natalie has always been a versatile vocalist, so it's no surprise that she possesses the intelligence and the chops to perform this material convincingly."

Elektra Records released *Unforgettable with Love,* but the album's huge success also benefited Capitol Records, which owns the rights to Nat King Cole's recordings. Nat King Cole's 20-song compilation re-entered the charts when Natalie Cole's album hit the top five. Wayne Watkins, a director of catalog development at Capitol, told *Billboard,* "Next to the Beatles, Nat King Cole is the best-selling artist in our catalog. He's even more popular than Sinatra for us." Capitol has since released a four-CD Nat King Cole box set. Warner Reprise Video released a Nat King Cole video compilation that includes a young Natalie Cole in several clips. A book titled *Unforgettable: The Life and Mystique of Nat King Cole,* issued by St. Martin's Press, was published just as Natalie Cole's "Unforgettable" started making waves.

Since Unforgettable

Cole's success in 1991 allowed her to branch into acting, although she did not find it easy. She told *Jet,* "Acting is a little more difficult than singing. The singing process is something that I've done all my life. When you are singing live, you have the audience there, you have all that inspiration going for you. But when you're on the set, it's just you, your co-stars, and the crew." In 1993 she first acted in the television drama series *I'll Fly Away.* She also starred in a USA Cable production called *Lily in Winter* in 1994. Other guest appearances included the *Touched By an Angel* hit drama series on CBS in 1997. However, the majority of Cole's work since "Unforgettable" was recording albums and touring.

In 1993 Cole released *Take a Look,* an album of her performances of 1930s and 40s popular music. *Entertainment Weekly* commented, "Unforgettable sounds almost tentative next to Natalie Cole's latest, which—thanks to a canny selection of mostly unfamiliar old pop, jazz, and show tunes ... moves her definitively out of her father's shadow." Ron Givens of *People* wrote, "Cole carves her own identity while remaining true to her father." The title song from that album, which was once

sung by Aretha Franklin, earned Cole another Grammy award for Best Jazz Vocal Performance. Cole told *Jet,* "This album actually is the album that I've always wanted to do and that is an album of jazz standards with great stuff that my dad turned me on to when I was about ten or eleven years old."

Holly and Ivy, a Christmas album released in 1994, "is a non-traditional album," she told *Jet.* "My approach was very 40ish, very Andrew Sisters, very fun and up." 1996 saw the release of *Stardust,* which included another "duet" with her late father called "When I Fall in Love." *Stardust* contained 19 Cole performances of songs from the 20s through the 50s. Cole told *Billboard,* "I'm a little nervous with this album, because it's the first time that I was really involved with every aspect of a project from start to finish." *Stereo Review* commented, "Only a versatile singer could handle this rich a mix, and Cole proves she's fully up to the challenge."

Cole's marriage to Andre Fischer ended in 1995 when she not only filed for divorce, but requested a restraining order against him. No comment was made by Cole at the time, but she began work on an autobiography titled *Angel on My Shoulder.* HBO will adapt the book for a television movie, starring Cole as herself. From her earliest days growing up with a legendary father, to losing him at 15, then setting out on a very successful career of her own, Cole has plenty of engaging book material.

Selected discography

Inseparable (includes "This Will Be" and "Inseparable"), Capitol, 1975.
Natalie (includes "Sophisticated Lady"), Capitol, 1976.
Thankful (includes "I've Got Love on My Mind" and "Our Love"), Capitol, 1977.
Natalie...Live!, Capitol, 1978.
We're the Best of Friends (with Peabo Bryson), Capitol, 1979.
Don't Look Back, Capitol, 1980.
Happy Love, Capitol, 1981.
I'm Ready, Epic, 1983.
The Natalie Cole Collection, Capitol, 1984.
Dangerous, Modern, 1985.
Everlasting, Manhattan, 1987.
Good to Be Back (includes "Miss You Like Crazy"), EMI, 1989.
Unforgettable with Love (includes "The Very Thought of You," "Mona Lisa," "Route 66," and "Unforgettable"), Elektra, 1991.
Take a Look, Elektra, 1993.
Holly and Ivy, Elektra, 1994.
Stardust (includes "When I Fall in Love"), Elektra, 1996.

Sources

Books

The New Rolling Stone Encyclopedia of Rock & Roll, edited by Patricia Romanowski, Fireside, 1995.

Periodicals

Billboard, August 3, 1991; March 7, 1992; August 31, 1996.
Ebony, October 1991.
Entertainment Weekly, June 25, 1993.
Jet, July 5, 1993; December 19, 1994.
People, July 22, 1991; June 21, 1993.
Playboy, September 1991.
Stereo Review, March 1997.
Working Mother, September 1996.

—Christine Morrison

Linda Davis

Country singer

AP/Wide World Photos, Inc. Reproduced by permission.

After 15 years of playing backup to famous stars like Reba McEntire, Kenny Rogers, and George Strait, Linda Davis has finally carved out a country music singing career of her own. It wasn't an easy road for her. Before her 1996 hit album, *Some Things Are Meant to Be,* Davis had been on five different record labels and had 10 previous singles that never made it to the top-40. Davis told Mike Redmond of the *Indianapolis Star,* "I think '97 is going to be the year I pretty much stand on my own."

Born Linda Kaye Davis on November 26, 1962 in Carthage, Texas, she grew up in a small rural town of 7,500. Her parents Milford Davis and Oneita Davis raised a family of five. Davis grew up in a musically oriented family. "Music was my pastime, my passion, and my hobby. My sister had a piano. I would pick out songs on the keys—gospel songs like 'Dear Lord' and 'Jesus Loves Me.'"

As a teenager, Davis performed on a weekly radio show called the *Louisiana Hayride.* The show was made famous after stars Elvis Presley, Willie Nelson, and Webb Pierce appeared on the same show early in their youth. Davis said, "It was called the 'cradle of stars' and the next step up was the Grand Ole Opry." At the age of 20, she left her small Texas hometown for Nashville. She thought about moving to Dallas instead, since it was bigger and closer to home. However, country music was being made in Nashville, and a few friends of hers who resided there helped give her the courage and support she needed to move there.

In Nashville, Davis started out singing in nightclubs and hotels, seemingly practicing and rehearsing for the bigger times she knew would someday come her way. She sang demo songs for $45, along with commercial spots for Kentucky Fried Chicken and Dr. Pepper. In 1984, she started a duet called Skip and Linda. Skip was Skip Eaton, and the two of them were brought together by Larry McBride, who founded MDJ Records. McBride needed a new singing success after the country group Alabama left the MDJ label. Davis and Eaton didn't even know each other very well, but it was Davis' first record deal and she jumped at the chance to sign it. Slowly, Davis started to attract the attention of Nashville's record producers and songwriters. Deals with Epic and Capitol Nashville soon followed. She made a few songs, but didn't have a big hit. In 1988, she opened for George Strait. Soon after from 1990-91, she opened for Kenny Rogers. All along, she was a patient touring singer. She said, "It's about an hour and 20 minutes before I come on. I'm sitting backstage waiting. Finally it's time for me to go on stage. I sing my songs and for 15 minutes, I'm in heaven."

For the Record . . .

Born Linda Kaye Davis on November 26, 1962 in Carthage, TX; daughter of Milford and Oneita Davis; married, husband's name Lang Scott; children: Hillary.

Awards: Grammy Award (with Reba McEntire), 1993; Country Music Association Award (with McEntire), 1994.

Addresses: *Fan Club*—Linda Davis Fan Club, P.O. Box 121027, Nashville, TN 37212.

The country music star Reba McEntire heard Davis was a regular singer and pianist at the Sheraton in Nashville, and she was interested in her work. When Davis sang two demo songs, "Falling out of Love," and "Rumor Has It," McEntire liked the songs so much that she also chose to sing them in her live performances. Both songs soon became hits for McEntire. Davis and McEntire quickly formed a professional and personal friendship. Since they both were considered to have similar sounding voices, Davis would often demo new songs that McEntire would later sing and turn into hits. Davis thought this was the start of an invaluable learning experience. In an article for The Advocate, Davis shared her feelings on Reba McEntire with contributor, John Wirt: "To learn from the best, like I think Reba is, is something not everybody gets to do. "I feel so privileged. I tell her thank you all the time."

When Reba Calls...

The big opportunity for Davis came when she joined McEntire's band to tour the U.S. Davis became a back-up singer for about four years with the band. Her big break came when she was asked to sing in a live duet with McEntire called "Does He Love You." The story goes that McEntire was looking for a new song for her second greatest hits album. It was thought that country star Wynonna would sing it with McEntire. Davis told Wirt, "Then when it came time to go in and cut it I got a call from the band leader. He said, 'Reba wants you to come in the studio and sing it with her.'" Davis thought that after the recording they would erase her voice and include some other singer's voice with McEntire's. However, it turned out that McEntire wanted her on the song from the start and she thought that her voice with Davis' would easily prove to the record company executives that the two of them together would make for a great duet. This was the break that Davis needed, for before this time, she wasn't that well known in the country music industry. Almost overnight, the two singers shared a Grammy for the recording of "Does He Love You."

Davis Finds Herself in the Spotlight

Davis quickly capitalized on her new found fame. In 1993 she came out with her first album, called *Shoot the Moon,* yet it did not shoot her to the charts. "That one did not have the radio hits," Davis confessed to Wirt. She later admitted that she and the record producers didn't take the time to find good songs for the album. However, the song "In Pictures" was later made into a hit when Randy Owen of Alabama discovered it and sang it to the top of the charts. In an interview with *Tulsa World* contributor, John Wooley, Davis stated: "From this point on, everything is a gift—because finally I can't say, 'Well, it's not getting out there.' That's all I've ever wanted with my music: to be heard. So for everything from here on, I just say, 'Thank you, Lord.'"

In 1993, Davis signed with Arista Nashville records. It proved to be another smart singing career move. She sang the hit single "Some Things Are Meant to Be," which was also the title track on her second album. She broke the Top 20 on the Radio & Records and Gavin Charts, and the video for "Some Things Are Meant to Be" was in the "Hotshot" rotation on Country Music Television. With this big new success, record promoters didn't stop at just promoting her vocal gifts. Davis also found herself packaged as a monthly calendar pinup that was sent to many country radio stations across the U.S. Album photos of Davis featured her in short shorts and exposed midriffs. When the subject came up in an interview with Robert K. Oermann of *The Tennessean,* Davis dismissed the hoopla, "I know this is part of my business, but I don't take that very seriously at all. I've never seen myself as 'cheesecake.'"

Davis and McEntire later went on to sing other duets together, such as "On My Own," and a song featured on Davis' album, "If I Could Live Your Life." McEntire even gave Davis a song that she was going to sing for one of her albums. With the song "There Isn't One," Davis was given the opportunity to turn it into a hit, which Davis quickly did. This was just one of many examples of Reba McEntire's support for Davis' new solo singing career. The money and fame is not what motivates Davis. She wants her listeners to know her through the songs she sings. As Davis told Wirt, "When you're through listening ... you have an idea of the kind of person I am. Hopefully, you think Linda Davis is a regular, fun-loving ... tender-hearted woman."

Selected discography

In a Different Light, Liberty, 1991.
Linda Davis, Capitol, 1992
Shoot for the Moon, Arista, 1994.
Some Things Are Meant to Be, Arista, 1996.

Sources

Periodicals

Advocate, March 22, 1996, p. 10.
Indianapolis Star, July 21, 1996, p. I9.
Pittsburgh Post-Gazette, August 29, 1995, p. B2.
Tennessean. September 8, 1995, p. 1H; February 10, 1996,
    p.1D; April 30, 1997, p. 2G.
Tulsa World, March 10, 1996, p. H3.
USA Today, October 8, 1993, p. 5D.

Online

www.mb1.musicblvd.com

Del Rubio Triplets

Lounge trio

Three was the magic number for Elena, Eadie, and Milly Boyd. For over 50 years, the identical triplets, dressed many times in matching hot pants and go-go boots, mined the archives of rock and pop history for classic hits and new favorites which were vamped and camped up for their legions of fans across the globe. "It's obvious that we were meant to serve God by being together. It reminds me of the blessed Trinity and the sense that each one is individual, the Father, the Son, and the Holy Ghost. But the three together is God. That's the same thing with us three. Each one is individual, and it's our individuality that makes the act what it is. But it's the three together that make the act. The three make the whole. We've sensed that ever since we were little kids, that the three make the whole", explained Eadie, about their togetherness both as a family unit and as the Del Rubio Triplets singing sensation, to Irene Lacher of the *Los Angeles Times.*

Eadie, Milly, and Elena Boyd were born in the Panama Canal Zone during the 1920s. Although their exact age remains a professional secret, it is known that Milly was born first. Elena followed Milly 15 minutes later, while Eadie was born 15 minutes after Elena. In an interview with Lacher, Eadie related the story behind why she, Elena, and Milly were born as triplets, "Daddy always liked to buy two extra of everything. So when the nurse told Mama she had triplets, she said, 'That figures'."

The Del Rubio Triplets were reared and spent their childhood in both Washington, DC and the Panama Canal Zone. At the age of 14, the Del Rubio Triplets visited Los Angeles for the first time with their parents. The trip was their father's idea. He was tired of hearing them talk incessantly about movie stars and was under the assumption that the "field trip" might, once and for all, put the silly Hollywood fantasy notion out of their heads.

Not only did their father's plan backfire—seeing the stars out and about in Beverly Hills only further stoked the fires of glamour and fame in the Del Rubio Triplets' minds—the trip started the transformation of the triplets from the Boyd sisters to the more upscale and classy Del Rubio Triplets.

Shortly after they left high school, the Del Rubio Triplets started to bleach their hair. They had remembered the "effect" blondes had on their father. Commenting on this to Lacher, Elena said, "Daddy brainwashed us with blond hair. He married a brunette, but I'm telling you he was insane over blond hair. He never told us anything about blondes being so wonderful. It was just us watching him put the brakes on to watch the blonde cross the street." Around this time they started performing as dancers, although as Milly told Steve Daugherty from *People,* "Even though we didn't have any talent, we knew we wanted to be in show business."

When they moved to Hollywood, the Del Rubio Triplets started to teach themselves how to sing in order to work the club circuit. On their semi-official website Milly commented, "We had no coach. We learned by listening to records of our favorite singers." They accompanied themselves on guitar as well—three identical Martin guitars that their father had bought for them when they first started out.

What's with the Name?

The word "rubio"—which means blond in Spanish—gave them the root of their stage name as Elena explained to Lacher, "Almost all the Latin people would meet us backstage and call us the rubias. And it sounded so pretty. So I said that would be a name for us." Eadie picked up the story; "We put the Del in front because Del Rubio is so much prettier than just Rubio. It's more musical."

For the Del Rubio Triplets the late 1950s and early 1960s were spent cruising the local lounge circuit as they honed their craft and as that started to wane they embarked on a self financed three year world tour during which they established themselves as "song stylists." It was their mother's stroke in 1965 that brought the Del Rubio Triplets back to America, or more specifically, the hospital where their mother was recovering. Eadie tol Daugherty, "We sang to her in the hospital.... Mom's dying words were 'Don't let anybody persuade you to get out of this business'."

After their mother died, the Del Rubio Triplets went into seclusion and lived off of a small inheritance for five years before they decided to hit the road. The triplets remembered the power of song when they sang to their mother in the hospital, and they wanted to share a little of this joy with others. So they embarked on a tour of retirement homes and hospitals where they played for and entertained the residents, retirees and the sick.

In 1987, the Del Rubio Triplets finally made it to the big time when they were asked to perform at a party for members of Los Angeles's underground art scene and made appearances on such television programs as *Pee Wee's Playhouse, Night Court, Golden Girls, Ellen, Full House, Married with Children,* and MTV.

The following year the Del Rubio Triplets released their first album, *3 Gals, 3 Guitars,* which featured covers of such classic and contemporary rock hits as the Doors' "Light My Fire," the Pointer Sister's "Neutron Dance," the Beatles' "Hey Jude," and the Bangles' "Walk Like an Egyptian."

Three years later the Del Rubio Triplets released *Whip It.* The 1991 release featured uniquely Del Rubio interpretations of the songs "Whip It" by Devo, the Rolling Stones' "Satisfaction," and "Wake up Little Suzy" by the Everly Brothers. While both of the Del Rubio Triplets' cover albums were released on the label Karma, their holiday songfest retrospective, *Jingle Belles,* was released on their own Del Rubio Records label in 1991.

None of the Del Rubio Triplets ever married because, as Eadie told Lacher, "God comes first.... my sisters come second.... Music comes third" and any potential love interest was a distant "fourth."

Selected discography

3 Gals, 3 Guitars (includes "Neutron Dance," and "Light my Fire"), Karma, 1988.
Whip It (includes "Satisfaction," and "Whip It"), Karma, 1991.
Jingle Belles (Christmas album), Del Rubio Records, 1991.

Sources

Periodicals

Los Angeles Times, January 25, 1991, E1.
People, September 5, 1988.
Washington Post, December 25, 1996.

Online

www.geocities.com/WestHollywood/3331/3GalsDisc.html

—*Mary Alice Adams*

Dog's Eye View

Alternative rock

D og's Eye View leader Peter Stuart's emergence on the national scene came as a result of a song called "Everything Falls Apart," and given his penchant for penning moody songs backed by upbeat pop melodies, this fact is somehow fitting. The first single from his band's debut album became a surprise hit in 1996, earning radio and MTV airplay and establishing Stuart as one of the mid-1990s new rock ironists.

Dog's Eye View—which consists of Stuart on guitar and vocals, Tim Bradshaw on guitars, vocals, and piano, Dermot Lynch on bass, and Alan Bezozi on drums and percussion—was assembled by Stuart around 1995 in New York, after Stuart generated a buzz among record company executives for his solo singer-songwriter act.

Music played an early and important role in Stuart's life. Hard-hit by the unexpected death of his father Fredric when he was a young child, Stuart found himself comforted by Cat Stevens' *Tea for the Tillerman*. As Stuart recalled later in his Columbia Records biography, "I went home and put it on. Here was this song called 'Father and Son'; all of a sudden, there was this songwriter who talked about a relationship between a father and a son and that kind of blew my head apart. I've always felt that every generation needs to hear about the same things in a different way because times change and people change.... I've always sought out those transcendent moments where you listen to something and it affects you very deeply." "Waterline," a song from Stuart's debut album, was reportedly written about his father.

A New York native and the product of an upper-middle-class suburban family, Stuart attended high school on Long Island. Educated at Northwestern University, he began his performing career in Chicago, where the view from his basement apartment inspired his band's name.

Stuart started on the road as an acoustic solo artist, playing guitar and singing on the small club circuit. Building a fan base by establishing a mailing list and keeping in touch with listeners through e-mail, Stuart sold more than 6,000 copies of a three-track home-made demo tape that contained early versions of "Waterline" and "Shine," which both also ended up on his debut album.

From Soloist to Band Leader

After spotting Stuart perform, Counting Crows front-man Adam Duritz invited Stuart to tour with Duritz's group. Serving as both an opening act and a roadie, Stuart spent six months on the road with the Crows in 1994—exposure that attracted the attention of Columbia Records executives, who subsequently signed his band to a record contract.

Along with his bandmates, Stuart recorded Dog's Eye View's first album, *Happy Nowhere,* in Woodstock, New York, in a rented house. After writing all of the songs for the record, Stuart also co-produced his band's debut with James Burton. Although promotion for the album started around the fall of 1995, Columbia officially released *Happy Nowhere* on January 30, 1996. Because Stuart was probably best-known to audiences as a solo artist, Columbia's promotional efforts included emphasizing the fact that Dog's Eye View consisted of not only Stuart, but also Bezozi, Bradshaw, and Lynch. The band achieved national prominence via "Everything Falls Apart," one of the singles from that album. The wry song became a radio staple in the summer of 1996. With the single drawing attention to the band, Dog's Eye View spent more than a year on the road in support of the record.

For the band's follow-up, 1997's *Daisy,* the New York-ers of Dog's Eye View headed west to Bear Creek Studio in Woodinville, Washington. By the time the album hit store shelves, Stuart had relocated to Seattle. Produced by Matt Wallace, the more mature *Daisy* featured Duritz as a guest vocalist. Besides Duritz, contributors to the album included multi-instrumentalist

For the Record . . .

Members include **Alan Bezozi,** drums, percussion; **Tim Bradshaw,** guitars, vocals, piano; **Dermot Lynch,** bass; and **Peter Stuart,** vocals, guitar.

Formed in New York after Stuart opened for Counting Crows as a solo artist, circa 1995; released debut album *Happy Nowhere* on Columbia Records, 1996; released second album, *Daisy,* on Columbia, 1997.

Addresses: *Record company*—Columbia Records, 550 Madison Avenue, New York, NY 10022-3211. *Website*—http://www.dogseyeview.com.

and producer Jon Brion, who also co-wrote songs for and worked on former 'Til Tuesday leader Aimee Mann's first two solo records.

A Little Help From His Friends

That Stuart's list of friends and associates reads like a who's who of modern rock has no doubt enhanced his career success. Stuart's pals included the likes of folk singer Jewel, the acclaimed late singer-songwriter Jeff Buckley, and Duritz. He has also toured with Tori Amos, Belly, Catherine Wheel, Cracker and Matthew Sweet.

Contact with more established artists helped teach Stuart important lessons about the music business. Counting Crows "'told me what deals consist of, and I learned what to stand up for and demand and what wasn't worth fighting for," Stuart is quoted as saying in *Billboard.* In the same article, he stated that Amos advised him "'to make your own record, and live or die by it. If you make it for the record company, they might turn against you if it stiffs, and if it's a hit, you might end up thinking it was all because of them and not you.'"

Maintaining control over his work has apparently paid off. Although not all critics have found favor with his work, Stuart has earned high marks for his songwriting skills. In a 1996 review of *Happy Nowhere, People* writer Craig Tomashoff wrote that the album contained "the perfect balance between folkie-style introspective lyrics ... and intensely energetic pop hooks." Reviewing the band's debut, Mark Jenkins of the *Washington Post* wrote that Dog's Eye View "purveys routinely tasteful adult rock," while in a 1997 review of *Daisy,* Jae-Ha Kim of *Entertainment Weekly* lauded Stuart's "knack for marrying bittersweet words with pop melodies to create evocative vignettes."

Since breaking onto the airwaves in 1996, the music business-savvy Stuart has built a career that balances creativity and common sense. As he told Tracey Pepper in a 1997 interview in *Interview,* "It's not about selling the most records; it's about my experience and progress as a human being. In thirty years I want to have learned more about the world."

Selected discography

Happy Nowhere, Columbia Records, 1996.
Daisy, Columbia Records, 1997.

Sources

Billboard, January 6, 1996.
Entertainment Weekly, March 15, 1996; August 22, 1997.
Interview, September 1997.
People, April 22, 1996.
Washington Post, March 22, 1996; September 26, 1997.

Additional information was provided by Columbia Records publicity materials.

—*K. Michelle Moran*

Bob Dylan

Singer, songwriter

AP/Wide World Photos, Inc. Reproduced by permission.

Singer and songwriter Bob Dylan is recognized worldwide for the impact he has had on rock music since his career began in the early 1960s, and has managed to maintain his popularity among fans and critics alike over the ensuing decades. Although known primarily for his caustic and candid lyrics that reveal the defiant stance on authority, politics, and social norms prevalent among the 60's generation of Americans, Dylan's fans are from a variety of age groups, all of whom identify with the raw human emotion expressed in his lyrics. Dylan's own humanity was brought to the public's attention in May, 1997, when the legendary artist canceled a planned European tour and was hospitalized due to a serious health condition called pericarditis. Yet Dylan returned to the stage in August, and released *Time Out of Mind* to rave reviews in September. As further evidence of Dylan's broad appeal and the magnitude of his contributions to music, he performed in Bologna, Italy, in September, 1997, after receiving a special invitation from Pope John Paul II.

Dylan was born Robert Allen Zimmerman on May 24, 1941, in Duluth, Minnesota, to Abraham Zimmerman, a furniture and appliance salesman, and Beatty Stone Zimmerman. In 1947 the family moved to the small town of Hibbing, Minnesota, where Dylan spent an unremarkable childhood. He began writing poems at the age of ten, and as a teenager taught himself to play the piano, harmonica, and guitar. He appreciated a wide variety of music—from country to rock 'n' roll—and admired the works of Elvis Presley, Hank Williams, Little Richard, and Jerry Lee Lewis. Dylan played in many bands during his high school years, including the Golden Chords and Elston Gunn and His Rock Boppers, before enrolling at the University of Minnesota in 1959.

While he was a student at the University of Minnesota in Minneapolis, the artist began performing as a folk singer and musician under the name Bob Dylan at such popular Minneapolis night clubs as Ten O'Clock Scholar cafe and St. Paul's Purple Onion Pizza Parlor. Dylan soon became more involved with his musical career than with his studies, so he dropped out of school in 1960 and headed straight for New York City. The young performer's interest in New York City was based upon his desire to become involved in the folk music scene that was then emerging in the city's Greenwich Village and upon his wish to meet his idol, folk singer Woody Guthrie. Dylan promptly became a popular performer in Greenwich Village coffee houses and night clubs, and also managed to become a regular performer for Guthrie. The young Dylan quickly gained the respect and admiration of his peers in the folk music scene with his ability to compose his own melodies and lyrics at an astonishing pace. He also became well known outside

Born Robert Allen Zimmerman, May 24, 1941, in Duluth, MN; name legally changed August 9, 1962; son of Abraham (a salesman) and Beatty (Stone) Zimmerman; married Sara Lowndes, November 22, 1965 (divorced, 1977); children: Jesse, Maria, Jakob, Samuel, Anna. *Education:* Attended University of Minnesota, 1959-60.

Composed more than five hundred songs since early 1960s; recorded with rock groups including The Band, The Traveling Wilburys (with Jeff Lynne, Tom Petty, George Harrison, and Roy Orbison), The Grateful Dead, and Tom Petty and the Heartbreakers; solo singer and musician in concerts since early 1960s, including appearances at the Newport Folk Festival in 1962 and 1965, the Woodstock Festivals in 1969 and 1994, and the Live Aid benefit concert in 1985; special performance for Pope John Paul II at a Roman Catholic Youth rally in Bologna, Italy, on September 27, 1997

Awards: Tom Paine Award, Emergency Civil Liberties Committee, 1963; honorary Music Degree, Princeton University, 1970; Grammy Awards, Best Rock Vocal Performance, 1979, for "Gotta Serve Somebody"; *Rolling Stone* Music Award, Artist of the Year (tied with Bruce Springsteen), 1975, and Album of the Year, 1975, for *The Basement Tapes* and *Blood on the Tracks;* inducted into the Rock and Roll Hall of Fame, 1988; Commander Dans L'Ordre des Arts et Lettres from the French Minister of Culture, 1990; Lifetime Achievement Award, National Academy of Recording Arts and Sciences, 1991; Grammy Award, 1993, for *World Gone Wrong;* Arts award, Dorothy and Lillian Gish Prize Trust, 1997; Lifetime Achievement Award, John F. Kennedy Center honors, 1997; Three Grammy Awards, Album of the Year, Best Male Rock Performance, and Best Contemporary Folk Album, 1998, for *Time Out of Mind.*

Addresses: *Office*—c/o 264 Cooper Station, New York, NY 10003.

of the folk music scene in New York City in 1961, when *New York Times* critic Robert Shelton witnessed one of his performances at a club called Gerde's Folk City and declared that Dylan was "bursting at the seams with talent."

Dylan was 20 years old when he released his self-titled debut album in 1962. Although most of the songs were cover tunes, Dylan did include two original compositions—"Song to Woody," which was a tribute to Guthrie, and "Talkin' New York." The album achieved limited success, and Dylan followed it in 1963 with *The Freewheelin' Bob Dylan,* which contained more original songs that shared a common theme of protest. Two of the songs from Dylan's second album, "Blowin' in the Wind" and "A Hard Rain's Gonna Fall," became enduring anthems of the 1960s, largely because they definitively illustrate the thoughts and feelings of the counterculture's young members. As confirmation of Dylan's success, the renowned folk group Peter, Paul, and Mary recorded a cover version of "Blowin' in the Wind" that rose to the number two spot on the pop music charts.

The Tide Changes

By the time Dylan released 1964's *The Times They Are A-Changin',* he had been thrust into the role of media spokesperson for the counterculture protest movement which sought to abolish social and political norms. This third album contained the protest song "The Lonesome Death of Hattie Carroll." But at the same time the album was released, Dylan began to express his growing pessimism about the counterculture's ability to affect change, and declared that he was uncomfortable with his role as the movement's mouthpiece. His next album, *Another Side of Bob Dylan,* further evidenced his disillusionment with the counterculture movement, as it contained extremely personal folk ballads and love songs, rather than his trademark protest songs. In 1965 Dylan enraged his folk music following by performing on an electric guitar at the Newport Folk Festival (fans there booed Dylan and his band off the stage) and by releasing *Bringing It All Back Home,* an album on which Dylan returned to his earlier musical influences of rock 'n' roll and rhythm and blues. While the songs on this album remained critical of society, none contained any of the direct references to racism, war, or political activism that had marked his earlier works. The acoustic song "Mr. Tambourine Man" from *Bringing It All Back Home* was soon recorded in an electrified form by the popular 1960s band the Byrds and reached the top of the pop music charts; by that time a new brand of music known as "folk rock" had become widely favored among young Americans.

Dylan continued to record songs that fused his folk and rock influences, using mystical, ominous lyrics filled with imagery and allusions, and in 1965 he released *Highway 61 Revisited.* This album featured songs with themes of alienation, including the well-known "Like a Rolling Stone," which quickly rose to the number two spot on the *Billboard* singles chart. That same year Dylan married Sara Lowndes, a friend of his manager's wife. In 1966 Dylan released *Blonde on Blonde,* which most critics consider among his best albums because it polished the edgy, harsh rock sounds of *Highway 61 Revisited* and introduced music unlike any of its predecessors. Although he was wildly successful, Dylan was suffering from the strains of fame. In the 1971 biography *Bob Dylan,* the artist commented to Anthony Scaduto about his feelings during that period of his life: "The pressures were unbelievable. They were just something you can't imagine unless you go through them yourself. Man, they hurt so much." Similarly, in a 1997 interview with *Newsweek*'s David Gates, Dylan asserted "I'm not the songs. It's like somebody expecting [William] Shakespeare to be Hamlet, or [Wolfgang von] Goethe to be Faust. If you're not prepared for fame, there's really no way you can imagine what a crippling thing it can be."

Knockin' on Death's Door

On July 29, 1966, at the peak of his popularity, Dylan's neck was broken in a near-fatal motorcycle crash. The accident left Dylan with time to recuperate and rest at his Woodstock, New York, home with Sara and their newborn son Jesse. He began reflecting upon his religious beliefs and personal priorities, and wrote songs that reflected his new-found sense of inner peace. Many of these songs were recorded in 1967 with The Band and later released on the 1975 album *The Basement Tapes,* while others were released on Dylan's first album following the motorcycle accident, 1968's *John Wesley Harding.* A primarily slow-paced, acoustical album, *John Wesley Harding* was followed in 1969 by *Nashville Skyline* and in 1970 by *Self Portrait* and *New Morning.* These three albums were greeted with derision by the public and Dylan was criticized severely by his fans for what they perceived as his failure to comment on the harsh realities of the time, namely the Vietnam War and the struggle for racial equality and civil rights for African Americans.

Dylan's first album to reach the number one spot on music charts was his 1974 effort, *Planet Waves,* which he recorded with The Band. Although it was not a critical success, the album led to a flood of interest in Dylan's 1974 tour of the United States, where audience demand for tickets far exceeded available seating for his concerts. Following his 1994 tour, Dylan released *Before the Flood,* a two-album set of music recorded live during the tour; the album rose to number three on music charts.

While Dylan's musical career was on an upswing, his personal life was in a shambles as he became involved in a bitter separation with Sara that included a fierce custody battle over their children. Dylan's 1975 album *Blood on the Tracks* features songs reflecting the sorrow and passion of his personal life at the time; "If You See Her, Say Hello" directly refers to the breakup of his marriage. Most critics hailed *Blood on the Tracks* as Dylan's best album since the 1960s, praising the artist's use of visual imagery to blur distinctions between reality and illusion to challenge everyday ideas about the world. The album's searing songs about love and loss, including "Tangled up in Blue," "Shelter from the Storm," and "Idiot Wind," were well-received by Dylan's fans and the album soon reached number one on the charts. Dylan's 1976 album, *Desire,* which contained a mournful tune entitled "Sara," also reached number one on the charts, and along with *Blood on the Tracks,* achieved widespread success in both the United States and Europe.

Although Dylan's 1978 album *Street Legal* was unpopular with his fans, who feared that the performer's personal crises had interfered with his musical abilities, it did not prepare the fans for what was soon to follow. In 1978, while touring to support *Street Legal,* Dylan experienced a religious vision that he later asserted made him question his moral values and saved him from self-destructive behavior. Pronouncing his belief in fundamentalist Christianity, Dylan began to communicate in his music a concern with religious salvation and the end of the world; many fans expressed displeasure with Dylan's blatant attempts to persuade his listeners to adopt his religious philosophy, but others viewed the lyrics as similar to Dylan's earlier songs about social change and prophecy. Among Dylan's albums during his Christian period, only the 1979 album *Slow Train Coming* was a commercial success, largely due to the popularity of the Grammy Award-winning single "Gotta Serve Somebody."

Dylan Re-invents Himself

In 1983 Dylan released *Infidels,* an album on which he departed from his overtly religious themes and returned to his more complex, emotionally subtle lyrics in songs such as "Jokerman" and "Don't Fall Apart on Me Tonight." Dylan produced his 1985 album, *Empire Burlesque,* which displayed a wide range of musical sounds, from gospel to acoustic ballad. In the mid-1980s, Dylan remained prominent in the public eye by performing with various other music stars, including superstar Michael Jackson, on the 1985 single "We Are the World" and at the Live Aid benefit concert, both which were designed to raise money for famine relief in Ethiopia. Also in 1985, Dylan released *Biograph,* a five-album set that contained previously released material and "bootleg" (unreleased) recordings and which also included Dylan's brief commentaries; the set was highly popular and proved a top seller.

The year 1988 marked the beginning of Dylan's collaboration with the Traveling Wilburys, which was a group made up of Dylan and veteran music stars George Harrison, Jeff Lynne, Roy Orbison, and Tom Petty. The group produced two albums, 1988's *Traveling Wilburys* and *Traveling Wilburys Volume 3*—no second volume was ever recorded—which was released in 1990. In 1988 Dylan was inducted into the Rock and Roll Hall of Fame, and was honored by noted rock star Bruce Springsteen, who commented during the induction ceremony that "Bob [Dylan] freed the mind the way Elvis [Presley] freed the body. He showed us that just because the music was innately physical did not mean that it was anti-intellectual.... He invented a new way a pop singer could sound, broke through the limitations of what a recording artist could achieve, and changed the face of rock and roll forever."

Another Close Call

In May 1997, Dylan was stricken with a sometimes fatal fungal infection called histoplasmosis, which caused the sac surrounding his heart to swell, resulting in a condition known as pericarditis. The news of his subsequent hospitalization concerned numerous music fans, but Dylan was too ill to reflect on the significance of his own mortality. He told *Newsweek*'s David Gates, "Mostly I was in a lot of pain. Pain that was intolerable. That's the only way I can put it." Nevertheless, Dylan recovered, and although he needed to take a variety of medications, he began performing again in August 1997 of that same year. In September Dylan performed for Pope John Paul II—reportedly at the Pope's request—at a eucharistic conference in Bologna, Italy. And in December, 1997, Dylan became the first rock star ever to receive Kennedy Center honors.

In addition to the struggle with illness and the professional accolades that marked Dylan's experience during 1997, the artist's album *Time Out of Mind* was released in September and was greeted with rave reviews. The album also garnered Dylan three Grammy

Awards—Album of the Year, Male Rock Performance (for "Cold Irons Bound"), and Contemporary Folk Album. Critics declared that Dylan had again managed to reinvent himself and provide his fans with a fresh sound. *Time*'s Christopher John Farley applauded the album, pronouncing: "Dylan has found purpose in his inner battle to reignite his imagination. Turning the quest for inspiration itself into relevant rock—that is alchemic magic." And *Newsweek* contributor Karen Schoemer maintained: "*Time Out of Mind* is rewarding precisely because it's so outside the present. In an era defined by novelty hits and slick video edits, it's a reminder that music can mean something more: it can be personal, uncompromised and deeply felt."

Selected discography

Bob Dylan, Columbia, 1962.
The Freewheelin' Bob Dylan, Columbia, 1963.
The Times They Are A-Changin', Columbia, 1964.
Another Side of Bob Dylan, Columbia, 1964.
Bringing It All Back Home, Columbia, 1965.
Highway 61 Revisited, Columbia, 1965.
Blonde on Blonde, Columbia, 1966.
Bob Dylan's Greatest Hits I, Columbia, 1967.
John Wesley Harding, Columbia, 1968.
Nashville Skyline, Columbia, 1969.
New Morning, Columbia, 1970.
Self Portrait, Columbia, 1970.
Bob Dylan's Greatest Hits, Volume II, Columbia, 1971.
Dylan, Columbia, 1973.
Pat Garrett and Billy the Kid, Columbia, 1973.
(With The Band) *Planet Waves,* Asylum, 1974.
Before the Flood, Asylum, 1974.
(With The Band) *The Basement Tapes,* Columbia, 1975.
Blood on the Tracks, Columbia, 1975.
Desire, Columbia, 1976.
Hard Rain, Columbia, 1976.
Street Legal, Columbia, 1978.
Bob Dylan at Budokan, Columbia, 1978.
Bob Dylan: Masterpieces, Columbia, 1978.
Slow Train Coming, Columbia, 1979.
Saved, Columbia, 1980.
Shot of Love, Columbia, 1981.
Infidels, Columbia, 1983.
Real Live, Columbia, 1984.
Empire Burlesque, Columbia, 1985.
Biograph, 3 vols., Columbia, 1985.
Knocked Out Loaded, Columbia, 1986.
(With the Traveling Wilburys) *Traveling Wilburys,* Warner Bros., 1988.
Down in the Groove, Columbia, 1988.
(With the Grateful Dead) *Dylan and the Dead,* Columbia, 1989.

Oh, Mercy, Columbia, 1989.
(With the Traveling Wilburys) *Traveling Wilburys, Volume 3,*
    Warner Bros., 1990.
Under the Red Sky, Columbia, 1990.
Bootleg Series I-III, Columbia, 1991.
Good As I Been to You, Columbia, 1992.
World Gone Wrong, Columbia, 1993.
Bob Dylan 30th Anniversary Concert, Columbia, 1993.
MTV Unplugged, Columbia, 1995.
Bob Dylan's Greatest Hits, Volume III, Columbia, 1995.
Time Out of Mind, Columbia, 1997.

Selected writings

Tarantula (prose), Macmillan, 1971.
Poem to Joanie, Aloes Press, 1972.
Words (poem), J. Cape, 1973.
Writings and Drawings (songs, poems, drawings, and writ-
    ings), Knopf, 1973; expanded edition published as *Lyr-
    ics: 1962-1985,* 1985.
Renaldo and Clara (screenplay), Circuit Films, 1978.

Sources

Books

Scaduto, Anthony, *Bob Dylan,* Grosset & Dunlap, 1971.
Shelton, Robert, *No Direction Home: The Life and Music of
    Bob Dylan,* Beech Tree Books/William Morrow, 1986.
Spitz, Bob, *Dylan: A Biography,* McGraw-Hill, 1989.

Periodicals

Newsweek, October 6, 1997, pp. 62-71.
New York Times, September 29, 1961.
Time, September 29, 1997, p. 87.

Online

http://www.celebsite.com
http://www.usatoday.com/life/dcovmon.htm
http://www.usatoday.com/life/music/lmds040.htm

—Lynn M. Spampinato

Echobelly

Sonya Aurora Madan of Echobelly. Archive Photos. Reproduced by permission.

Bursting onto the pop scene in 1994 with its acclaimed *Everybody's Got One* album, Echobelly has been a prominent force in the British musical invasion of the 1990s. Although often compared to Blondie and obviously influenced by Morrissey, who himself is a big fan of the group, Echobelly has carved out its own unique place with extremely tuneful melodies that cascade between exuberant optimism and vehement attacks against oppression, bigotry, and alienation in the modern world. As was noted by Jori Wiederhorn in a 1995 issue of *Rolling Stone,* "Echobelly's music is a striking paradox, an unlikely melange of sweet, spiky melodies and bleak, shadowy image." Wiederhorn added that the group members "play with a passion and power well beyond their two years as a band."

One of the hallmarks of Echobelly is their apparent joy in their music, even when dealing with less than joyous subjects. "Ms. Madan's clear, cheerful voice sounds optimistic even when she's telling people to go away," wrote Jon Pareles in the *New York Times* about a 1995 performance at Irving Plaza in New York City. Devon Jackson of *Harper's Bazaar* added that the group is "Powerful and spirited, but not at all strident or preachy when railing against injustice, racism, or oppression." The group also has a distinctive multicultural presence with its mix of personnel that includes an Indian-born vocalist, a Swedish guitarist, and a black guitarist. Despite the melting pot nature of the band, singer Madan downplayed it. "The music we make has very little to do with our backgrounds," she told Jackson. "It has to do with our musical tastes. We merge musically."

The most prominent part of Echobelly's success formula is vocalist Sonya Aurora Madan, who is also the group's primary lyricist. Born in Delhi, India, before moving to England at the age of two, Madan had an unusual background for a pop star. Her rigid upbringing made rock n' roll taboo for her as a youngster, and she didn't attend her first rock concert until she was in college. In 1990 she met Glenn Johansson, a guitarist from Sweden who was pursuing a career in music. Johansson had previously edited a Swedish pornographic magazine called *Eros,* which may contribute to the bands' focus on sexual issues in many of their songs. He and Madan dated for a while, then remained friends after breaking up.

In 1993 Madan and Johansson teamed up with bass guitarist Alex Keyser and drummer Andy Henderson, who had previously played with P.J. Harvey's band. Guitarist Debbie Smith, formerly of Curve, came on board in 1994. According to the Epic Records' website, the group came up with the name Echobelly from the

For the Record . . .

Original members included **Andy Henderson,** drums; **Glenn Johansson,** guitar; **Alex Keyser,** bass guitar; **Sonya Aurora Madan,** vocals; **Debbie Smith,** guitar. Later members included **James Harris,** bass guitar.

Group formed, 1993; released *Bellyache* EP on independent Pandemonium label, 1993; signed with Rhythm King label, 1994; performed in Glastonbury and Reading Festivals, U.K., 1994; released first full-length album, *Everybody's Got One,* 1994; toured U.K., U.S., and Japan, 1994; opened for R.E.M. on tour, 1995; performed at spring fashion show for designer Betsey Johnson, 1995; released *On,* 1995; performed at Brighton Music Festival, U.K., 1996; switched to Epic label, 1996; released *Lustre* on Epic, 1997.

Addresses: *Record company*—Epic, P.O. Box 4450, New York, NY 10101-4450.

notion of "being hungry for something." With Madan and Johansson serving as songwriters, Echobelly recorded their debut EP *Bellyache* on the independent Pandemonium label in late 1993. With songs such as "Give Her a Gun" and "Sleeping Hitler," *Bellyache* demonstrated the group's willingness to boldly face provocative issues, both musically and lyrically. The title track was called "a Johansson masterpiece, all throbbing tremelo guitars and pent-up angst," by the Epic website. Dealing with rejection has been a major theme for Echobelly—on the romantic, sexual, cultural, and political fronts.

Bellyache Hooks Fans

The favorable response to *Bellyache* helped Echobelly secure a contract with Rhythm King, which was then part of Epic. Once on board the label, the group made bigger waves on both sides of the Atlantic with their "I Can't Imagine the World without Me" single. *Rolling Stone* said that the song "was filled with memorably aggressive but somewhat one-dimensional pop hooks," while the label's website called it "a slice of pop heaven and undoubtedly the most confident pop record of the year." Now featuring the services of bass guitarist James Harris (Keyser de-

fected due to personal and artistic differences) the group recorded the memorable *Everybody's Got One* album. This release, which included the single "Insomniac," scored big with English fans and reached number eight on the U.K. pop charts. In his review of the album in the *Village Voice,* Barry Waiters asserted that Echobelly created "a '90s strain of power pop that's got the bounce of Blondie with the crunch and ache of Nirvana." Waiters compared Madan's singing to Morrissey's, remarking, "She's got a similarly dramatic, nearly vaudevillian way of sliding up and down a melody, emphasizing certain key words, twisting heartfelt syllables into rueful ironies."

Second Album Built Reputation

As their music received more airplay, Echobelly won admiration from other artists as well. Madonna expressed interest in putting them on her Maverick label, and R.E.M. requested the group as the opening act for their upcoming tour. The band returned to the studio in 1995 to create their next album, *On,* which proved even more popular than its predecessor. Produced by Shaun Slade and Paul Kolderie, who had also produced Hole and Radiohead, *On* was called "eminently listenable" by Tamara Palmer in *Audio.* "Singer and lyricist Sonya Aurora Madan sounds as if she has become more aware of the beauty and strength in her voice, which emerges with a more poised and practiced edge," continued Palmer.

This album focused on more universal themes, instead of the more politically and ethically charged subjects of *Everyone's Got One.* Madan's lyrics often ventured into the seamy side of life, such as the milieu of prostitution and homelessness addressed in "King of the Kerb." "I wanted to challenge myself as a lyricist on a different level on this album," Madan said in *Rolling Stone.* "I want people to tell me what they thought the lyrics are about. I'm not a politician. I'm not interested in changing everybody around me. I'm interested in myself."

While many of the songs lamented the state of things, others on the *On* album celebrated the endless possibilities of the human spirit. In "Great Things," Madan sang "I want to do great things/I don't want to compromise/Want to know what love is/I want to know everything." The album's mostly optimistic feel provides an intriguing contrast with its serious subject matter. As Pareles wrote, "Both music and lyrics examine the tension between order and liberty." Pop hooks were established early in these songs, many of them displaying a sense of impatience that matched the urgency of the lyrics. Listeners in England responded favorably to the album, driving three singles from the release into the U.K.'s Top 20. Sales of the album rose to over 150,000 in England, nearly double that of *Everyone's Got One.*

Health and legal problems interrupted the success of Echobelly in 1995 and 1996. Madan had a serious thyroid problem during her world tour that was potentially life-threatening, but was later cured. The group also had disagreements with Rhythm King after the label moved to Arista. The band chose to stay with Epic, which is part of Sony Music Entertainment. In 1996 Madan also ventured away from the group when she sang on a recording of the club band Lithium, that later released a single called "Ride a Rocket." Smith left the band before the release of *Lustre,* which was scheduled to appear in record stores in the fall of 1997. A single from the album, "The World Is Flat," was released in July of that year. "On *Lustre,* we've brought out the darker side," noted Madan on the Miller Freeman Entertainment website.

Selected discography

Bellyache (EP) Pandemonium, 1993.
Everybody's Got One, Rhythm King, 1994.
On, Rhythm King, 1996.
Lustre, Epic, 1997.

Sources

Periodicals

Audio, June 1996, p. 80.
Elle, March 1995, p. 104.
Harper's Bazaar, February 1996, p. 186.
New York Times, November 30, 1995, p. C16.
Rolling Stone, November 2, 1995, p. 22.
Village Voice, February 28, 1995, p. 50

Online

http://www.primenet.com/~greggh/disc.html
http://www.charanga.com

—*Ed Decker*

Tommy Emmanuel

Instrumentalist

Tommy Emmanuel, one of Australia's foremost instrumentalists, stated in his Epic Records press release: "To me, music is something that is beautiful and positive. If I can pass that torch on to others, then I'm happy." This extraordinary guitarist has attained world renown status, and at 43 years old, is already considered a legend. "To say I'm blessed would be an understatement," he stated in his biography on the Sony Music Artist Info website. "Half the time I'm waiting for someone to pinch me and wake me up from this dream."

William Thomas Emmanuel was born on May 31, 1955 at Muswellbrook, New South Wales, Australia. Emmanuel first started playing at the age of four. The first guitar tune that he learned was Arthur Smith's "Guitar Boogie." In 1960 he started his first band called The Emmanuel Quartet. It was a family affair, with Tommy on rhythm guitar, Phil on lead guitar, Chris on drums, and Virginia on Hawaiian steel guitar. He and his wife Jane have a daughter named Amanda, and he still performs with his brother Phil.

As a young boy, Tommy practiced an average of 16 hours a day, sometimes in pubs. Early in his career, it was evident that he was very ambitious. He has worked with many renown artists in the music industry and has composed and arranged many successful songs. His musical versatility is evident in the different types of musical styles he's played; jazz, rock and roll, blue-grass, country, and even classical. "I never shy away from a word like 'pop', Frank Sinatra is a pop singer, he sings popular music," stated Emmanuel in his online biography. "Bach was a pop composer, and yes, I'm a pop guitar player. I have roots in all sorts of different styles of music, and I'm able to draw on all of that. At the end of the day, the thing that pulls it all together is my sense of melody."

Emmanuel was inspired by the great American guitarists Chet Atkins and Hank B. Marvin of The Shadows. Emmanuel stated in his biography, "I heard a track of [Atkins'] on the radio and did a total backflip. That lovely fingerpicking led to my picking up the guitar. When I was in my mid-teens, I sent Chet a fan letter and he wrote me back—I've still got his letter. In the early '80s, I went to Nashville for the sole purpose of meeting him." Later on in his career, Emmanuel and Atkins turned out to be a successful pair that often performed together. John Anderson from *Newsday* stated, "Emmanuel professes a lifelong passion for Atkins' playing, and he obviously has studied it, because it's hard to tell where the teacher stops and the student starts. They play seamlessly, with a great deal of humor."

Another strong influence in Emmanuel's successful career has been the Maton Guitar. It is made by Maton, a Melbourne company in Australia. The model MS500 solid body was Emmanuel's first Maton, and he started playing it at the age of six. It is his instrument of choice and he owns about eight of them. In June 1988, he was playing a Takamine guitar. At that time, the owner of the company approached him and asked if they could develop a model that met his high playing standards. Emmanuel agreed and the company soon produced the T/E Artist & Signature guitar. This model features Emmanuel's signature engraved into the fingerboard. It is estimated that over 500 have been made. Today, Emmanuel acts as a consultant to the company to ensure the model guitar maintains its high degree of sound quality and playability.

Top Albums and Awards

In 1995 a dream to play with an orchestra was made possible with the production of the album *Classical Gas,* which received widespread fame and went gold in Australia. "It was something I'd wanted to do for many years," the artist stated on the Sony website. "I wanted to try things I'd never tried before, but at the same time I didn't want to bite off more than I could chew." Some of the album was recorded live outdoors with the Australian Philharmonic Orchestra, and the remaindr was recorded in a Melbourne studio with the same ensemble. Many of his most well-known songs are on the album, including "The Journey," "Run a Good Race," "Who Dates Wins," and "Initiation." New songs included "Padre" and "She Never Knew." The album finishes with a "fiery duet" between Emmanuel and Slava Grigoryan, a fast rising 20-year-old Spanish guitar player from Melbourne. "The great thing about an orchestra is their range," the artist state on the Sony website. "They can play with this incredible subtlety, and it can be so beautiful—but when they really rip into something, the volume is just unbelievable. If you're standing next to them, it nearly blows you away."

Critics Can't Get Enough

Another album, *Can't Get Enough,* really brought out the excellence of his acoustic guitar work. Randy Goodrum, a Nashville keyboard player and songwriter, is also on the album, which was recorded in Melbourne, Nashville, and Los Angeles, and was produced by Goodrum and Emmanuel. Warren Hill was on sax, Tom Brechtlein on drums, and Nathan East on brass. Chet Atkins and guitar players Larry Carlton and Robben Ford are three guests on the album. Richie Yorke in the *Sunday Mail* asserted, "On first hearing of the opening track ... you'd swear you were listening to something new and fresh from Steely Dan ... *Can't Get Enough* has all the earmarks of an international hit at a point in musical history when traditional instrumentalists have been in short supply." Emmanuel stated that the song "Inner Voice" was one of the best on the album. "It's an interesting piece of music and I got the idea from a James Taylor song called 'Baby Boom Baby' from the *Never Die Young* album ... it has a real haunting flavour to it ... the eerie sound comes from a Brazilian instrument called the hose, which you swing above your head. Other songs on the album include "Song for Nature," "Stay Close to Me," "Change for Good," "Reggie's Groove," "Drivetime," "How Many Sleeps?" and "Fields of Gold."

Emmanuel Journeys to America

The 1994 all instrumental collection called *The Journey* was his first U.S. release. Others on the album included Chet Atkins on guitar, Joe Walsh on guitar, Jerry Goodman on violin, and Dave Koz on saxophone. *The Journey* was produced by American guitarist Rick Neigher. Twelve songs made up the album, some of which are "Hellos and Goodbyes," "The Journey," "If Your Heart Tells You To," "Amy," "Tailin' the Invisible Man," and "Villa Anita."

Emmanuel's awards include Australia's Best Guitarist in *Juke Magazine* for 1986, 1987, and 1988. He received the 1988 Studio Musician of the Year award in *Bi-Centennial Music Week.* The recipient of numerous *Rolling Stone* awards such as Most Popular Guitarist in1989 and 1990, and Best Guitarist from 1991 through 1994, he also received Australian Adult Contemporary Record of the Year in 1991 and 1993. He was named Australian Performer of the Year by the MO Awards in 1995 and 1997 and also received a gold record for the sales of *Classical Gas.*

Selected discography

From out of Nowhere, 1979.
Dare to Be Different, Sony.
Initiation, Sony.
Up from Down Under, 1987.
No More Goodbyes, Sony.
Can't Get Enough, Sony.
Determination, Sony, 1991.
The Journey, Columbia, 1993.
The Journey Continues, 1994.
Terra Firma, Columbia, 1995.
Classical Gas, Sony, 1995.
Midnight Drive, Higher Octave, 1997.
(With Chet Atkins) *The Day the Finger Pickers Took over the World,* Sony, 1997.

Sources

Periodicals

Billboard, July 8, 1995.
Newsday, April 13, 1997 p. C23.
Tennessean, February 24, 1997.

Online

http://www.tommyemmanuel.aust.com
http://www.music.sony.com

—Bill Bennett

Foreigner

Rock band

S ince their inception in 1976, the Anglo-American band Foreigner has established itself as one of the premiere rock groups to have emerged from the late 1970s music scene. In the United States alone, the band's sales have exceeded 30 million albums and singles.

During Foreigner's worldwide tour for their highly successful and most popular album *4,* both Robert Plant and Jimmy Page—formerly of Led Zeppelin—joined Foreigner on stage in Germany, while singer Sheryl Crow provided some backup vocals on new songs recorded for Foreigner's *Very Best ... and Beyond* album. Some of the many artists who have opened for Foreigner over the globe throughout the years have included Bryan Adams, the Cars, Cheap Trick, the Ramones, and Billy Squier. All of these accomplishments were achieved despite the fact that many music critics derided Foreigner as "formulaic" in their mass-market appeal.

According to the unofficial Foreigner Inside Information website, the band came into existence in early 1976

AP/Wide World Photos, Inc. Reproduced by permission

Members include **Johnny Edwards** (joined group, 1991, left group, 1992), vocals; **Dennis Elliott** (born August 18, 1950, London England, left group, 1992), drums; **Ed Gagliardi** (born February 13, 1952, left group, 1979), bass; **Lou Gramm** (born May 2, 1950, Rochester, NY, left group 1988, rejoined group, 1992), vocals; **Al Greenwood** (born October 20, 1951, New York, NY, left group, 1980), keyboards; **Jeff Jacobs** (joined group, 1993), bass; **Mick Jones** (born December 27, 1944, London, England), guitar and vocals; **Ian McDonald** (born June 25, 1946, London, England, left group 1980), flute, reeds, keyboards, guitar, and vocals; **Mark Schulman** (joined group, 1993, left group 1995), drums; **Bruce Turgon** (born April 25, 1952, joined group, 1993), bass; **Ron Wikso** (born November 18, 1959, joined group, 1995), drums; **Rick Willis** (joined group, 1979, left group 1992), bass.

Group formed, 1976; released self-titled debut on Atlantic, 1977; *Double Vision*, 1978; *Head Games*, 1979; *4*, 1981; *Records*, 1982; *Agent Provocateur*, 1984; *Inside Information*, 1987; *Unusual Heat*, 1991; *The Very Best ... and Beyond*, 1992; *Classic Hits Live*, 1993; signed with Rhythm Safari and released *Mr. Moonlight*, 1995.

Awards: Juno Award for International Single of the Year for "I Want to Know What Love Is," 1985; Platinum certification for *Foreigner*, *Double Vision*, *4*, *Agent Provocateur*, and *Inside Information*.

Addresses: *Record company*—Atlantic, 75 Rockerfeller Plaza, New York, NY 10019.

when Mick Jones met multi-instrumentalist Ian McDonald at a recording session for Ian Lloyd. A few months later, Jones and McDonald created the band Foreigner when they hooked up with four then unknown musicians including lead vocalist Lou Gramm who was the founder and lead singer with the band Black Sheep. The original lineup came into being with the addition of Dennis Elliott on drums, Al Greenwood on keyboards and synthesizers, and Ed Gagliardi on bass.

Their self-titled debut album was released on Atlantic in 1977. The album sold in excess of four million copies in America alone and remained on the *Billboard* Top Twenty for one year. This rather impressive feat was due, in no small part, to the strength of the two Top Ten singles that were released from the album—"Cold as Ice" and "Feels Like the First Time." The success of the album *Foreigner* earned the band a Grammy nomination for Best New Artist of 1977.

Not content to rest on their laurels, Foreigner released *Double Vision* the following year. It was a Top Five album, which continued to further the chart success of Foreigner; two Top Five singles, "Hot Blooded" and the title track joined the steadily growing list of accomplishments the band was tallying up. Foreigner's increased excursions into the top of the charts enabled them to headline the prestigious English summer music celebration known as the Reading Festival in 1978.

Success Follows Foreigner into the '80s

By the advent of the 1980s, the Foreigner line-up was whittled down to a quartet with the loss of Gagliardi and Greenwood and the addition of Rick Willis on bass. The release of *4* in 1981 ushered in Foreigner's biggest sales—a whopping six million. Two more Top Five singles were added to the ever-growing list of hits, "Waiting for a Girl like You" and "Urgent" which featured Junior Walker on saxophone. Additional accolades racked up by *4* included a Grammy nomination for the Best Rock Performance by a Duo or Group with Vocal in 1981 and a Canadian Juno Award nomination for International Album of the Year in 1983. In 1982 Foreigner released their greatest hits album, *Records*.

Two years later Foreigner released *Agent Provocateur*, which eventually went platinum. Foreigner's first number one single "I Want to Know What Love is" was culled from this album and featured backing vocals from the New Jersey Mass Choir. Also charting from this album was the Top Twenty song "That Was Yesterday." "I Want to Know What Love is" was nominated for a Grammy for the Best Pop Performance by a Duo or Group with Vocal in 1985. In that same year, the song took home the Canadian Juno Award for International Single of the Year.

The Beginning of the End

In 1987 Foreigner released *Inside Information*. This album also went platinum and yielded the Top Ten hit "Say You Will." The following year Gramm left the band to pursue a solo career. He reached the top of the charts twice with a Top Ten hit in 1987 and again two years later. Around this time, Jones released a solo album as well, although it barely managed to crack the Top 200 Album chart.

Vocalist Johnny Edwards was brought on board as a replacement for Gramm in 1991 and the band released *Unusual Heat.* By the following year, Edwards was out and Gramm was back in recording three new tracks for Foreigner's *The Very Best ... and Beyond,* which featured backing vocals provided by singer Sheryl Crow. *Classic Hits Live* (1993) was a collection of live material culled from performances all over the globe spanning Foreigner's career from 1977-1985.

Mr. Moonlight was released on Rhythm Safari in 1995 and marked a turning point for Foreigner. According to the Rock Band Home Page website, not only was Jones "playing acoustic guitar more than he ever has for Foreigner, the two most recent additions to the band line-up—bassist Bruce Turgon and keyboardist Jeff Jacobs have contributed some song writing on the album."

In the Rhythm Safari press release for *Mr. Moonlight,* Gramm was quoted as saying, "I always felt that Foreigner never quite lived up to our own expectations, but I think with this album we're taking a big step to where we want to be. I want this to be what it always should have been ... and better than it ever was." The press release went on to add that Jones felt "that the sound of *Mr. Moonlight* not only takes Foreigner further than it's ever gone before, but again puts the band on the map as a competitive entity.... We've really reformed this band.... Part of it is being driven by the new blood in the band, and I think it's done us both [Jones and Gramm] a lot of good." And *Entertainment Weekly*'s Chuck Eddy lauded the album's skillful production: "Almost every track here is as magnificently produced and hookful as the filler on *Double Vision* or *4.*"

Foreigner has also been credited for its significant contribution to rock music for two decades. By the late 1990s, the band was still adding a great deal of energy and vitality to its live performances, and audiences were still responding enthusiastically.

Selected discography

Foreigner (includes "Feels Like the First Time" and "Cold as Ice"), Atlantic, 1977.
Double Vision (includes "Hot Blooded" and "Double Vision"), Atlantic, 1978.
Head Games (includes "Headgames"), Atlantic, 1979.
4 (includes "Waiting for a Girl like You," "Juke Box Hero," and Urgent"), Atlantic, 1981.
Records (greatest hits), Atlantic, 1982.
Agent Provocateur (includes "I Want to Know What Love Is"), Atlantic, 1984.
Inside Information (includes "I Don't Want to Live Without You" and "Say You Will"), Atlantic, 1987.
Unusual Heat, Atlantic, 1991.
Very Best ... and Beyond, Atlantic, 1992.
Classic Hits Live, Atlantic, 1993.
Mr. Moonlight, Rhythm Safari, 1995.

Sources

Periodicals

Amusement Business, May 13, 1993.
Entertainment Weekly, December 17, 1993; February 24, 1995.
People, December 26, 1983; February 4, 1985; August 26, 1991.

Online

http://members.aol.com/insideinfo/foreigner/home.htm

Additional information was provided by Rhythm Safari publicity materials, 1995.

—Mary Alice Adams

Geraldine Fibbers

Punk band

Geraldine Fibbers emerged in 1994 when Carla Bozulich, frontwoman for a confrontational industrial/punk outfit called Ethyl Meatplow, teamed with members of the punk band Glue to play country music. It was intended to be an entertaining side project, but quickly evolved into something more. The group attracted a local following in and around Silver Lake, California, and its debut recording, an independently released ten-inch EP, captured the attention of major record labels. The record, with its distorted covers of George Jones-Dolly Parton songs, became something of a country-punk cult classic. (The indie-label Sympathy for the Record Industry later augmented it with live tracks and released it on CD under the title *What Part of 'Get Thee Gone' Don't You Understand?*)

Geraldine Fibbers "captures the raw heart and soul of country," *Rolling Stone* reported, describing the band's sound as "simmering with a Velvet Underground-like tension and ferocity." In its brief time together, the five-piece unit continually evolved, and a series of lineup changes contributed new styles to the mix—creating a sound that was virtually impossible to categorize. Critics describe the Fibbers' eclectic, genre-fusing sound as intense, hallucinatory, indefinable, disorienting. "I've become fond of the phrase "sickened traditional," Bozulich told *Rolling Stone*. "It's best if you can come up with your own catch phrase, because that way it's you who is responsible for the fiasco that follows."

That stylistic ambiguity did not, however, prevent a major-label bidding war for the band's services. Geraldine Fibbers ultimately signed with Virgin Records and, in 1995, released *Lost Somewhere between the Earth and My Home.* On that album, they maintained their countrified roots while pushing in a variety of musical directions. *Entertainment Weekly*'s Mike Flaherty concluded that "Bozulich's gnashed-teeth rockers and elegiac dirges suggest a summer camp weekend with Patti Smith." *Tampa Tribune* music critic Curtis Ross said the album's standout track, "Get Thee Gone," was structurally similar to Hank Williams' classic "I'm So Lonesome I Could Cry," but sounded as if it had been run "through a horror show of pummeling guitars and squalling fiddle."

The group's sophomore release on Virgin Records, 1997's *Butch,* took a further step in several directions—while Fibbers followers and the music press scrambled to keep up. *Billboard*'s Chris Morris asserted that the album "cuts a broad swath through a variety of musical styles from Gothic pop on 'California Tuffy' to country-fried rock on 'Folks Like Me,' from squalling punk on 'Toybox' to instrumental atmospherics on 'Heliotrope' and 'Claudine.'" The album also included a striking cover of "Yoo Doo Right," which was originally recorded by German experimental rockers Can. *Los Angeles Times* music critic Richard Cromelin wrote that the songs on *Butch* "convey the power of the sexual and emotional needs that drive people into damaging entanglements. Its rich layers of strings—violin, cello, bowed bass—support the edgy-rock foundation, deepening and rounding the moods." Reviewer Rob Brunner of *Entertainment Weekly* suggested that the Fibbers' fans would be disappointed with the disc, which "largely dispenses with hillbilly posturing for straight forward rock riffs and punk bravado.... The Fibbers still sound like a very good band trying to work up the confidence to be themselves."

"I think people were wondering if maybe on our second album we would kind of figure it out, maybe," Bozulich was quoted in *Billboard*. "But it's definitely gotten more severe—the diversity we're exploring is even more severe now."

Emotional Edge

Geraldine Fibbers' popular and critical success followed a long, difficult road for Bozulich. At age 13, she left her parents' home in San Pedro, California, and began hanging out with the local punk band The Minutemen. She endured drug addiction and life on the streets and, in the mid-1980s, began singing with what

For the Record . . .

Members include **Carla Bozulich**, vocals; **Nels Cline**, guitar; **Kevin Fitzgerald**, drums; **Leyna Papach**, violin (replaced Jessy Greene, who had replaced Julie Fowells); and **Bill Tutton**, bass.

Band formed in Silver Lake, CA, 1994; signed with Virgin Records, 1995; released *Lost Somewhere between Heaven and My Home*, 1995, and *Butch*, 1997.

Addresses: *Record company*–Virgin Records, 9247 Alden Drive, Beverly Hills, CA 90210.

Rolling Stone described as a "succession of arty, punk-based noise bands." The last of those was Ethyl Meatplow, which broke up after releasing a single album because band members could not agree whether to add guitars to their electronic, industrial din. Bozulich is proud of her musical diversity. "I think I'm massively influenced by everybody that I love," she reported to Curtis Ross of *American Business Review*, "the product of a whole lifetime of loving and absorbing, humbly admiring art, music, film and literature."

By the time Ethyl Meatplow split, Bozulich had begun performing in Geraldine Fibbers with guitarist Daniel Keenan, stand-up bass player Bill Tutton, drummer Kevin Fitzgerald and violinist Julie Fowells. The first personnel change occurred during a tour in which the Fibbers opened for former Minuteman Mike Watt. Tendinitis sidelined Keenan and one of Watt's bandmates, a talented guitarist named Nels Cline, filled in. Cline ultimately joined the Fibbers full-time—providing, Cromelin wrote, "Beatlesque folk-rock 12-string, Clapton-like clarity and a dissonance that reflects the disorientation" of the characters in the band's songs.

Fowells, meanwhile, was replaced by violinist Jessy Greene, and Greene abruptly left the band after they recorded *Butch* to join the country-roots outfit The Jayhawks. "I guess her boyfriend's in that band," Bozulich remarked cattily in *Billboard* after Greene's defection. "It could be that, or maybe she just likes their

music better." Greene has since been replaced with the latest Fibbers' fiddler, Leyna Papach.

Through all the twists and turns, Geraldine Fibbers' music—which explores territory such as AIDS, homophobia and violently twisted relationships—has consistently journeyed to the emotional outer limits. *Rolling Stone* critic Dudley Saunders described a Fibbers' performance in Cambridge, Massachusetts, this way: "Through a wall of Gothic-country noise, Bozulich's face, even when twisted in a scream, exuded a creepy serenity—smiling dreamily at nothing, staring unnervingly at people in the crowd—while songs of self-hatred, addiction and death dropped lightly from her mouth.... Bozulich painted these images with the meticulousness of a haunted person, leaving the crowd struck by the power of the Bosch-like world she seemed to see everywhere." In the *Los Angeles Times*, Cromelin asserted that Geraldine Fibbers' music "has an urgency, originality and candor that confirm the band as a legitimate successor to X, Concrete Blonde and Jane's Addiction—Los Angeles' indispensable messengers from the emotional frontier." While the myriad of comparisons and categorizations continue, Bozulich, for one, is satisfied and proud of her band's achievements. "I feel like I could stop now," she said, "and be OK."

Selected discography

Lost Somewhere between the Earth and My Home, Virgin, 1995.
Butch, Virgin, 1997.

Sources

Billboard, May 31, 1997.
Buffalo News, September 11, 1997.
Entertainment Weekly, July 28, 1995; July 11, 1997.
Minneapolis Star Tribune, July 27, 1997; September 14, 1997.
People, September 8, 1997.
Rolling Stone, November 2, 1995; October 16, 1997.

—Dave Wilkins

Benny Golson

Saxophonist, composer

While tenor saxophonist and composer Benny Golson may not be a household name, his compositions are among the most frequently recorded jazz standards. Golson summed up his philosophy of writing music to *Down Beat* in 1958, "I feel that the best contribution any writer can make is to create compositions that are impressive, meaningful, and lasting. I think all serious writers consciously or unconsciously strive for this."

Born in Philadelphia, Golson began playing piano at age nine, tenor saxophone at age 14, and composing at age 17. He studied briefly at Howard University where he wrote his first professional arrangements for the school band. Golson's first job after leaving Howard in 1951 was Bull Moose Jackson's rhythm and blues band. There he met pianist and composer Tadd Dameron, whose work Golson had admired. In a *Down Beat* interview, Golson explained that "Tadd's music really ignited the spark for me. After hearing things like 'Our Delight' and 'Lady Bird' ... I wanted to do more than play tenor sax. I wanted to write."

In the early 50s, Dameron included Golson and a promising young trumpet player named Clifford Brown on a recording session. Benny and Clifford developed a close friendship until Brown's death in a car accident in 1956. Golson composed the standard "I Remember Clifford" as an homage to his friend. "At the time of his death", Golson reminisced in 1961 in *Down Beat,* "Brownie was going in his direction more determinedly than anyone I've ever seen. Really, the last two years of his life, he got a hold of what he wanted to do. His imagination was infinite. He always had a bag of surprises."

In 1956 Benny Golson joined trumpet player Dizzy Gillespie's band, accompanying them on U. S. State Department sponsored tours, until 1958, when he became a member of Art Blakey's Jazz Messengers. During this time, Golson was also a leader on several record dates for the Riverside and Contemporary labels. In 1959 Benny and trumpet player Art Farmer cofounded the Jazztet with trombonist Curtis Fuller and pianist McCoy Tyner. Golson was the main writer for this successful group, which won the New Star Award in *Down Beat's* 1960 International Poll.

Golson explained his compositional goals in *Down Beat* in 1960, "Basically, I'd like to stay simple. I'd like to write melodically, and pretty harmonically.... Although I'm not consciously looking for it, maybe I want something that's easy to remember.... Beauty can be simple, beauty can be simplicity." *Down Beat* critic Ralph J. Gleason confirmed the appeal of Golson's compositions, "What is attractive about Golson's writing, of

Born Benjamin Golson, January 25, 1929, in Philadelphia, PA. *Education:* Attended Howard University, late 1940s.

Arranged for Howard University band, late 1940s, performed in Philadelphia jazz scene, early 1950s; performed with the bands of Bull Moose Jackson, Johnny Hodges, Earl Bostic, Dizzy Gillespie and Art Blakey's Jazz Messengers, 1955; composed, recorded albums, and freelanced, 1950s-90s; co-led the Jazztet with Art Farmer, c. 1959-61; scored films and television c. 1960s-70s; performed solo and with reformed Jazztet, 1981-82; appeared in film *A Great Day in Harlem*, 1995.

Awards: (With Jazztet), *Down Beat* New Star Award, 1960.

Addresses: *Record company*—Evidence Music, 1100 East Hector Street, Suite 392, Conshohocken, PA 19428.

course, is that it is not only original, but it is also lyrical and instantly communicative to both musician and fan. That his tunes are a gas to play is obvious from the number of recordings and the people who play them. That they are a gas to hear is, it seems to me, just as obvious."

Following the breakup of the Jazztet in the early 60s, Golson concentrated on composing, and not just jazz tunes. In 1966, he told *Down Beat* that "I used to compose a lot, but as I look back on it, I was composing indiscriminately.... So then I started working a little bit slower and being a littlemore precise about what I was doing." Golson's biggest hit was "Killer Joe" which was recorded by Quincy Jones on his *Walking in Space* album.

In the late 1960s, Golson furthered his studies in compositional technique. He described what he learned to *Jazz Journal International* in 1983, "[My teacher] really opened up vistas for me that I didn't know existed. I became involved in writing music antiphonally, symmetrical, pandiatonic things. After I'd had three or four one-hour sessions with him I got called to do a film in Germany and I used absolutely everything he taught me."

At the urging of Quincy Jones, Golson moved to Hollywood, where he began writing for films and television. His work included *Ironside, M.A.S.H.,* and *Room 222.* Golson did not play jazz during this period; he didn't even take his saxophone out of its case for a decade. By 1975 he was ready to return to playing the saxophone, however, it wasn't easy. He described the process of relearning to *Crescendo International,* "It was like I'd never played the instrument; it felt like a piece of plumbing from the kitchen in my hand. My mind seemed like it wanted to go ahead—my fingers were those of a dead man; my lips were like ripe tomatoes. It was quite a physical struggle. I had no muscles in my lips or jaws... I sounded so bad, I was even embarrassed for my wife to hear me!"

A Triumphant Return to Jazz

Golson eventually returned to the public eye, where audiences welcomed his comeback. In 1982, after playing at a festival in Japan with Art Farmer, the two of them decided to revive the Jazztet. The new Jazztet broke attendance records around the world and received rave reviews. Golson enthused to *Crescendo International,* "The reception for the revived Jazztet was so warm last year that it was almost like coming back home this second time. The enthusiasm of the audiences has been very encouraging for us—it gives us some incentive to go on in that same direction."

The Jazztet was not revived merely for nostalgia's sake. Golson explained to *Crescendo International,* "In twenty years, as you might expect ... our musical approach is just a little different from the way it was then. Although there's some nostalgic things, like 'Whisper Not' ... I've written a lot of new tunes, and we've moved away somewhat from the hard, straight-up-and-down, strict harmonic kind of approach."

Over the course of his 50-year career, Benny Golson has contributed some of the most memorable standards to the jazz repertoire. In addition, he has expressed himself in a variety of musical settings. From jazz standards to film and television soundtracks, his music has found a warm reception around the world.

Selected discography

(With Clifford Brown), *Clifford Brown Memorial,* Original Jazz Classics, 1953.
Benny Golson's New York Scene, Contemporary, 1957.
The Modern Touch, Riverside, 1957.
(With Dizzy Gillespie), *At Newport,* Verve, 1957.

(With Milt Jackson), *Bags' Opus,* Blue Note, 1958.
(With Art Farmer), *Modern Art,* Blue Note, 1958.
The Other Side of Benny Golson, Riverside, 1958.
(With Art Blakey), *Moanin',* Blue Note, 1959.
(With Blue Mitchell), *Out of the Blue,* Riverside, 1958.
(With Blue Mitchell), *Blues on My Mind,* Riverside, 1959.
(With Wynton Kelly), *Kelly Blue,* Riverside, 1959.
(With Philly Joe Jones), *Drums around the World,* Riverside, 1959.
Groovin' with Golson, Prestige, 1959.
(With the Jazztet), *Meet the Jazztet,* Argo, 1960.
Take a Number from 1 to 10, Argo, 1960.
Turning Point, Mercury, 1962.
Free, Argo, 1962.
California Message, Timeless, 1980.
This Is for You, John, Timeless, 1983.
Moment to Moment, Soul Note, 1983.
Time Speaks, Timeless, 1984.
Stardust, Denon, 1987.
Live, Dreyfus, 1989.
Benny Golson Quartet, LRC, 1990.
Domingo, Dreyfus, 1991.
I Remember Miles, Evidence, 1993.

Sources

Books

Cook, Richard and Brian Morton, *The Penguin Guide to Jazz On CD, LP, & Cassette,* Penguin, 1994.
Rosenthal, David, *Hard Bop,* Oxford University Press, 1992.
Wynn, Ron, ed., *The All Music Guide to Jazz,* Miller Freeman Books, 1994.

Periodicals

Crescendo International, November, 1982; May, 1983; September, 1983.
Down Beat, January 9, 1958; May 15, 1958; June 11, 1959; February 4, 1960; September 1, 1960; June 22, 1961; October 12, 1961; February 24, 1966.
Jazz Journal International, December, 1982; January, 1983.
Kansas City Star, May 14, 1995.

Additional information provided by the video, *A Great Day in Harlem,* 1995.

—*Jim Powers*

Bobby Hackett

Jazz musician

AP/Wide World Photos, Inc. Reproduced by permission.

Bobby Hackett, whose music career was generally influenced by Louis Armstrong and Bix Beiderbecke, had a very mellow tone and style to his playing, which was in stark contrast to the other dixieland players of his time. When he started his musical career, he was given the name, "The New Bix," because he sounded very much like Bix Beiderbecke. It would be difficult to label Hackett's music, because his style was so diverse; he played dixieland, swing, and traditional pop. His own career influenced many artists, including Ruby Braff, Miles Davis, and Wild Bill Davison. Other artists that are comparable to Hackett in his time were Charlie Barnet, Ruby Braff, James Dapogny, Al Hirt, Harry James, Yank Lawson, Joe Newman, Bob Scobey, Warren Vache, Bob Wilber, and Ron Altbach.

Robert Leo "Bobby" Hackett was born on January 31, 1915 and died June 7, 1976, at the age of 61. He was one of nine children, and he grew up in Providence, Rhode Island. When he was a young boy, he learned how to play the ukulele, guitar, violin, and cornet. He never finished high school, for he left after his first year to play in a band that frequented a Chinese restaurant in Port Arthur. His guitar playing was featured often on Providence radio when he performed at the Rhodes and Arcadia ballrooms. Early in his career, he started playing for the Cab Calloway Band when he was asked to fill in for an absent member. He also played with the Herbie March Orchestra in Syracuse, New York. He was generally characterized as being a very easy going and gentle man, and one of the jazz world's most renown artists.

New England was Hackett's home, and he spent most of his career there. While he played with Payson Re's band in 1933, he met Pee Wee Russell on Cape Cod. Russell recruited Hackett to play for Teddy Roy's band at a speakeasy called the Crescent Club in Boston. In 1934 Hackett and Johnny Crandon, who was a Harvard Medical Student and band drummer, formed The Harvard Gold Coast Orchestra to play at colleges in New England on weekends. The band, made up of four professional musicians and four medical students, traveled all over New England. Hackett then went on to receive his union card and lived in the area from 1935 to 1936.

While living in New England, Hackett formed his own band. In 1936 he was primarily playing the cornet. He formed a dixieland band to play in Boston at a well-known night club called The Theatrical Club. He asked Teddy Roy, Roger Malencourt, Russ Isaacs, Pat Barbara, Billy Wiles, and Brad Gowans to join him. The band was extremely successful, and it caught the ear of George Frazier, a very well known music reviewer.

Riches soon fell on the owners of The Theatrical Club, for thousands of people heard Hackett and his band play great jazz and dixie. The club grossed over $1 million in 1937, a rather large sum in its day.

However, the band's success was slow to spread to other regions of the country. When they tried to see what success they would have in New York, they could not find any work. Nevertheless, to make a living again, Hackett decided to join the Condon-Marsala Band at the Hickory House in New York. He was so successful there that he went on to regularly perform in Greenwich Village at a nightclub spot called Nicks.

Yet Nicks was not the end of the road for Hackett; he then became a member of the Carnegie Hall Concert in which Benny Goodman performed the famous "I'm Coming Virginia." At this point, Hackett started to record a number of songs with Eddie Condon and his band The Windy City Seven for the record company Commodore. In addition to being part of The Windy City Seven, he was a member of the Lanin Orchestra. Hackett also continued his professional relationships with Eddie Condon, Jack Teagarden, and Teddy Wilson.

In 1939 it seemed that Hackett's professional musical career would place him into large sums of money. He received strong support from the record company MCA to form his own band under their label. Almost overnight, the promise of big money eluded him, as the honey-moon with MCA was short lived. Despite playing at New York's World Fair, the Ben Franklin Hotel in Philadelphia, and the Famous Door, along with numerous recordings, the band was unprofitable within six months of its inception. Amazingly, Hackett also found himself owing MCA $3,000. At this time, Hackett had sights of marrying his childhood sweetheart, yet his poor financial situation prevented him from doing so. He opted to take a job with the group The Musical Knights, which allowed him to spend a great deal of time on Nantucket Island. A high point in his career came in 1940 when he recorded the soundtrack for the film *Second Chorus,* which starred famous dancer and actor Fred Astaire.

From Glenn Miller to Jackie Gleason

Hackett's fortunes would soon turn for the better in the early 1940s. In 1941, he joined the Glenn Miller band. However, he had a terrible time trying to play the cornet due to the dental problems he was experiencing at the time. To compensate for his inability to play wind instruments, he settled on playing the guitar. At this time, Glenn Miller joined the Air Corps in 1942. Meanwhile, Hackett decided to accept a studio job with NBC. He played with Louis Armstrong and the Condon Gang for about a year, and then performed with the Casa Loma Orchestra until 1946, when he formed a new association with ABC, which would last for 15 years. Hackett also continued to play around New York. One of the most notable times in his career was when he had to help lead Louis Armstrong's band during the May 1947 NYC Town Hall Concert. Armstrong was suffering from an ulcer, and the band prospered under Hackett's leadership.

Between 1949 and 1951, television started to become a heavy influence in America, and it proved to be a great advancement for the music industry. Hackett began recording music for Jackie Gleason's production *Music for Lovers.* He was also on other television shows. His music could be heard in many arenas, some of which were modern for the day, such as supermarkets, department stores, and elevators. The smooth sounds of his cornet playing attracted many followers.

In 1957, Hackett created a sextet that toured the United States and Canada. The band recorded *The Gotham Jazz Scene, Jazz Ultimate,* and *Coast Concert.* They were also recorded live at The Embers in 1957. Into the early 1960s, Hackett bands recorded for Columbia and Epic. While his band continued to play constantly on Cape Cod, he also joined Benny Goodman in 1963. He gained much success from being in constant demand from many well known vocalists such as Billie Holiday,

Louis Armstrong, Frank Sinatra, Maxine Sullivan, and Lee Wiley. Later, he also recorded some records for the Verve label.

Finally in 1971, he made Cape Cod his real home. At this time, he also extensively traveled to Japan and Europe to perform. He also formed his own record company while on Cape Cod called Hyannisport Records. One of his most enjoyable times was in 1975 when he was a regular jazz performer at Disney World.

Hackett died of a heart attack in 1976. A former manager of the Hackett band, Jack Bradley, asked the leader of The Clam Shack Serenaders, Gordon Brooks, to play the song "More Than You Know," at his gravesite. Today, that tradition continues every year on June 7 at the Chatham Cemetery. On June 2, 1996, the Cape Cod Jazz Society presented, "I Remember Bobby," which was a memorable tribute to Hackett's enormous career. His life spanned a time when jazz in America was king, and he was everywhere in the middle of it.

Selected discography

Second Chorus, (soundtrack), 1940.
You Stepped out of a Dream, 1943.
Off Minor (Jack Teagarden), 1943.
String of Pearls, 1943.
Vol. 2 - Live at the Roosevelt, 1943.
Jazz In New York, 1943.
And His Orchestra, 1943.
Vol. 2 - Dr. Jazz Series, 1952.
The Gotham Jazz Scene, Capitol, 1957.
Jazz Ultimate, Dormouse, 1957.
Coast Concert, Dormouse, 1957.
Live at the Roosevelt Grill, 1970.
What a Wonderful World (with Teresa Brewer), 1973.

Sources

Books

Balliett, W., *More Ingredients, American Musicians II: Seventy-One Portraits In Jazz*, (NY: Oxford University Press, 1996) pp. 143-51.
Bradley and G. Brooks, *Bobby Hackett*, Unpublished Manuscript, 1996.
Stokes, W.R., *Swing Era New York: Featuring The Jazz Photography of Charles Peterson*, (Philadelphia: Temple University Press, 1994).

Periodicals

Boston Magazine, April 14, 1986.
Cape Cod Standard Times, June 1, 1996.
Down Beat, July 1936.
The Hartford Courant, March 20, 1997.
National Review, July 6, 1992 .
The Providence Journal Bulletin, August 11, 1997.
Sun-Sentinel, January 27, 1995.

Online

http://www.libertyhall.com
http://www.landing.com
http://www.tunes.com

—Bill Bennett

Sammy Hagar

Singer

Archive Photos, Inc. Reproduced by permission.

Uncompromising and determined, singer Sammy Hagar has followed his own creative impulses throughout his more than 25-year career, in spite of criticism and disrespect. He began as the frontman for a band called Montrose, which gained recognition after its demise. After being fired from the band, Sammy Hagar moved on to a 10-year solo career and became known as the "Red Rocker." In 1985, he joined the already successful rock band Van Halen as the group's controversial new lead singer. Then, in 1996, when he was once again ousted, Sammy Hagar quickly and successfully resurrected his solo career.

Sammy Hagar was born on October 13, 1947, in Monterey, California, the youngest of four children. His father was a bantamweight boxing champ the year he was born. Hagar spent most of his childhood in Fontana, California, just east of Los Angeles. His father inspired him to pursue his own boxing career until he was a teenager, and he continued to maintain much of his physical training for many years afterward. At the age of 18, he learned to play guitar, and began his long career in music.

Hagar performed in nightclubs in San Bernardino, California, before moving to San Francisco in the early 1970s. He discovered that an up-and-coming guitarist named Ronnie Montrose was forming his own band, and Hagar started singing for the band Montrose in the summer of 1973. Before the end of the year, Montrose, Hagar, bassist Bill Church and drummer Denny Carmassi released their self-titled debut on Warner Bros. Records. The LP included long-lasting tracks such as "Rock Candy" and "Bad Motor Scooter," which would occasionally be played on radio stations decades later.

In 1974, the Montrose band released *Paper Money* and the band began to gain momentum. "As a high-energy quartet, Montrose succeeded where others have failed due to the accessibility of their material and their razor-sharp arrangements," wrote Barry Taylor in *Billboard*. Later that year, guitarist and bandleader Montrose fired Hagar as the group's lead singer. Hagar and Montrose had a dispute over the band's musical direction and their egos clashed. Montrose said Hagar was "too limited," while Sammy felt stifled. "I was creatively constipated in that band," Hagar later told Evan Hosie in *Rolling Stone*, "but Montrose influenced me a lot."

Eventually, Church and Carmassi both left Montrose to join Hagar's solo project. In 1976, Hagar released his first solo album called *Nine on a Ten Scale* on Capitol Records, and began a fast-paced career. He released his next effort, *Sammy Hagar* — also known as "The Red Album"—in January of the following year, which included the songs "Red," "Crusin' & Boozin'," and "Rock N' Roll Weekend." Then in October of 1977, his next release, *Musical Chairs*, arrived in stores.

From the beginning of his career, Hagar sparked the interest of a wide variety of audiences. Hereceived some criticism for his accessibility, while others condemned him for being too heavy and loud. Evan Hosie wrote in *Rolling Stone*, "It's hard to reconcile such a charming, articulate fellow, who casually talks about life after death and his love of science fiction, with the guy yelling to a half-crazed crowd." His music often reflected his belief in life on other planets, as well as his interest in other mystical subjects.

Early in his career, Hagar toured with popular rock bands such as Kiss and Boston. In 1978, he won the Bay Area Music Award for "Musician of the Year" in San Francisco, California. With his live performances adding to his popularity, he began headlining his own shows in 1979. At the time, his band included Bill Church, guitarist Gary Pihl, keyboardist Alan Fitzgerald, and drummer Chuck Ruff. "One could actually feel the warmth and rapport he had with the audience, especially when he jumped off the stage into the crowd," John Deegan wrote of Hagar in *Billboard*.

"I'm the kind of performer who happens live," Hagar told Jack McDonough in *Billboard*. "It's more coherent for people. People would hear the records and see me onstage and not put the two together." When he went back into the studio to record *Street Machine*, he decided to produce the album himself. It included the tracks "Trans Am (Highway Wonderland)," "Plain Jane," and "This Planet's on Fire (Burn in Hell)." During the same year, singer Bette Midler performed Hagar's song "Keep On Rockin'" in her movie *The Rose*.

In March of 1980, Sammy Hagar released the live album *Loud and Clear*, with performances of Montrose hits like "Bad Motor Scooter" as well a selection of his solo songs, such as "I've Done Everything for You" (which was later made a huge hit by singer Rick Springfield). In June of the same year, he released his next effort, *Danger Zone*, which included tunes like "Love or Money" and "20th Century Man."

In 1981, drummer David Lauser joined Hagar's band, and the group began recording *Standing Hampton* for Hagar's new record label, Geffen Records. The record escalated Hagar's popularity with "I'll Fall in Love Again," "There's Only One Way to Rock," and "Heavy Metal." The latter track also appeared on the *Heavy Metal* film soundtrack. Later, Hagar also contributed songs to other soundtracks such as *Vision Quest, Footloose*, and *Over the Top*.

Hagar began to climb higher up the *Billboard* charts with his next LP, *Three Lock Box*, which included hits like the title track and "Your Love Is Driving Me Crazy." However, Hagar decided to take a slight departure from his solo career in 1984. He teamed up with Journey guitarist Neal Schon, bassist Kenny Aaronson, and drummer Michael Shrieve to form HSAS (derived from the first letters of the members' last names). The group played a number of West Coast concerts and recorded the album *Through the Fire*.

Hagar returned to his solo project in 1985 with his highly successful record *VOA*. Sparked the by the popularity of the hit single "I Can't Drive 55," *VOA* reached platinum within the year. After more than ten years on his own, Sammy Hagar had begun to truly make his mark in rock n' roll.

Joins Van Halen

Then, one day in 1985, Hagar's auto mechanic, Claudio Zampolli, was doing some work on Van Halen guitarist Eddie Van Halen's Lamborghini. Van Halen was looking for a new lead singer to replace David Lee Roth. Zampolli suggested Eddie Van Halen call Sammy Hagar, which he did, right from the mechanic's shop. "I had a gut feeling that it was going to happen," Hagar recalled to David Fricke in *Rolling Stone*. "I told Betsy, my wife, 'These guys are going to hit on me to join this band.' When Eddie called, I got butterflies in my stomach the second he said, 'hi.'"

Hagar flew down from his home near San Francisco to jam with Van Halen in Los Angeles. By the end of the session, Hagar had decided to give up his solo career and join the band. The decision was met with controversy from critics and fans of Van Halen. He had such a different style and persona from David Lee Roth that few thought he could maintain the group's success. In 1986, Van Halen released *5150* with Hagar center stage. The album became Van Halen's first number one album and the new configuration sold out every concert on the tour.

The camaraderie between Hagar and Van Halen was highly publicized, and the foursome displayed an obvious unity in their concert performances. "We had an instant rapport," Hagar commented in *Guitar Player*. "It's a funny thing. I feel like I've known Edward, Michael, and Alex for a long time."

Hagar's enthusiasm and positive attitude revitalized the members of Van Halen. "Sammy's got a very up attitude about everything," *5150* producer Mick Jones told *Rolling Stone*. "He's extremely positive, and that shook everybody out of the doldrums." Eddie Van Halen later told David Wild in *Rolling Stone*, "From the first second, Sammy could do anything I threw at him. Things I had in me that I wanted to express, I was able to do with Sammy singing them."

After the release of *5150*, Hagar had to release another solo album to fulfill his contractual obligations with Geffen Records. Eddie Van Halen played bass on the album and co-produced it with Hagar. Originally released as *Sammy Hagar*, the name was later changed to *I Never Said Goodbye* as a result of a name contest. Van Halen released their next effort *OU812* in 1988.

Becomes Club Owner

Two years later, Hagar led Van Halen into another international business venture. The band opened their own nightclub in Cabo San Lucas, at the tip of Baja California in Mexico. The called the club Cabo Wabo after the song of the same name on *OU812*. "That place had dirt roads when I started going there," Hagar later told *Contemporary Musicians*. "I thought, 'God, if Van Halen ever played down here....' When we stood on-stage, it was so exciting to me because it was the fulfillment one of my dreams."

Hagar later started the tradition of celebrating his birthday at Cabo Wabo every October. Hagar, Van-Halen bass player Michael Anthony, and Hagar's former drummer David Lauser formed a side project that performed at Cabo Wabo several times each year, called Los Tres Gusanos ("The Three Worms"). Hagar eventually bought out the other members of Van Halen and took over the club. Cabo Wabo later became the originator of its own brand of tequila, which began to surface around the United States in 1997.

Around the same time Cabo Wabo opened, Hagar also ventured into the business of fashion. He started his own line of "Red Rocker" clothing and designed a "Red Rocker" mountain bike after becoming an avid cyclist. Eventually, he limited the clothing to sales in shops around Northern California and later just sold it at Cabo Wabo. "It's just a hobby," Hagar told *Contemporary Musicians*. "It's fun, but it's not the way I make a living."

In 1991, Van Halen returned with their next release *For Unlawful Carnal Knowledge* and the monstrous hit "Right Now." After Van Halen's tour for the album, Hagar and his wife Betsy divorced. During the same year, their son Aaron Hagar joined a band called Bloodline with the offspring of other popular musicians from the Doors, the Allman Brothers, and Miles Davis.

Taking a break from the studio, Van Halen released a live album in 1993, called *Live: Right Here, Right Now*. The following year, Sammy Hagar released a greatest hits collection of his solo work, called *Unboxed*, which also included two new songs, "High Hopes" and "Buying My Way into Heaven." He returned with Van Halen in 1995 for the release of *Balance*, which included the hits "Don't Tell Me (What Love Can Do)" and "Can't Stop Lovin' You."

After the tour for *Balance*, Van Halen began to go through some turmoil. The other members of the group demanded Hagar record the song "Humans Being" for the *Twister* soundtrack, while he was expecting his new wife Kari to give birth. After several more business and personal disputes, Hagar split from Van Halen. According to the band, Hagar wanted to be a solo artist. However, Hagar insisted that he was fired. Van Halen rejoined with original singer David Lee Roth to record a few songs for a greatest hits record. Then, former Extreme singer Gary Cherone took Hagar's post. The break-up became highly publicized with no common ground. Although Hagar was devastated by the betrayal, he quickly picked up the pieces. "I can say it was 10 of the greatest years of my life. One miserable year," Hagar told Peter Tilden in *Live*. "I'm more disappointed in how it ended than anything else."

Not long after the split with Van Halen, Hagar met former Grateful Dead drummer Mickey Hart on a plane to Hawaii. Based on his own experience with the death of Grateful Dead guitarist Jerry Garcia, Hart convinced Hagar of the importance of getting right back into making music. Hagar took his advice, and in May of 1997 released *Marching to Mars* on Track Factory/ MCA Records.

On *Marching to Mars,* Hagar recruited contributions from several of his friends, including Mickey Hart, singer Huey Lewis, Guns N' Roses drummer Matt Sorum, Brother Cane guitarist Damon Johnson, and Bootsy Collins. He also recorded the song "Leaving the Warmth of the Womb" with the original members of the Montrose band—Ronnie Montrose, Bill Church, and Denny Carmassi. The first single "Little White Lie," based on his public squabbles with Van Halen, debuted at Number 18 on the *Billboard* charts. It was followed up with the single "Both Sides Now." "I felt like I had something to prove in 1975, when Montrose broke up," Hagar told Melinda Newman in *Billboard* after the release of *Marching to Mars.* "I felt like I had something to prove when I joined Van Halen in 1986, because of David Lee Roth, and I feel the same way now."

Hagar toured with a newly formed band, which included his former drummer David Lauser and his former keyboardist Jesse Harms, along with guitarist Victor Johnson and bass player Mona. At the age of 50, Sammy Hagar had struck out on a new path in his career, without missing a beat. "I don't feel any different from when I was 12 years old," Hagar told *Contemporary Musicians.* "In some ways, nothing changes. Rock n' roll allows you to feel and act any way you want. If I were a lawyer, I wouldn't be able to be the way I am."

Selected discography

Albums

Nine on a Ten Scale, Capitol, 1976.
Sammy Hagar, Capitol, 1977.
Musical Chairs, Capitol, 1977.
Street Machine, Capitol, 1979.
Loud and Clear, Capitol, 1980.
Danger Zone, Capitol, 1980.
(Contributor) *Heavy Metal* (soundtrack), Asylum, 1981.
Standing Hampton, Geffen, 1982.
Three Lock Box, Geffen, 1983.
(Contributor) *Footloose* (soundtrack), Columbia, 1984.
VOA, Geffen, 1985.

(Contributor) *Vision Quest* (soundtrack), Geffen, 1985.
(Contributor) *Over the Top* (soundtrack), CBS, 1986.
Sammy Hagar (a.k.a. *I Never Said Goodbye*), Geffen, 1987.
Unboxed, Geffen, 1994.
Marching to Mars, Track Factory/MCA, 1997.

With Montrose

Montrose, Warner Bros., 1973.
Paper Money, Warner Bros., 1974.

With HSAS
Through the Fire, Geffen, 1984.

With Van Halen

5150, Warner Bros., 1986.
OU812, Warner Bros., 1988.
For Unlawful Carnal Knowledge, Warner Bros., 1991.
Live: Right Here, Right Now, Warner Bros., 1993.
Balance, Warner Bros., 1995.

Sources

Periodicals

Billboard, March 5, 1977; December 24, 1977; February 11, 1978; February 3, 1979; March 17, 1979; January 19, 1980; June 7, 1980; July 12, 1996; April 26, 1997.
Entertainment Weekly, May 23, 1997; April 22, 1994; May 30, 1997.
Guitar Player, September 1980, October 1987.
Library Journal, February 15, 1982.
Los Angeles, August 1992; November 1993.
People, September 3, 1984; June 23, 1986.
Rolling Stone, March 24, 1977; April 1, 1982; June 5, 1986; July 3, 1986; October 22, 1987; February 18, 1993; June 30, 1994; April 6, 1995.
Playboy, October 1991.
Scene Magazine, July 17, 1997.
Stereo Review, June 1982, May 1983, September 1997.
Variety, July 16, 1980.
Wilson Library Bulletin, January 1985.

Online

http://www.clevescene.com/970717/cs0717.htm
http://www.livemag.com/0897/dialog
http://www.mcarecords.com/amp17/noise/hagar.html

—Sonya Shelton

Jan Hammer

Keyboardist, composer

Country & Eastern Music, Inc. Reproduced by permission.

The name Jan Hammer means different things to members of different generations. To fans of fusion in its early 1970s heyday, he is remembered as an integral part of the groundbreaking Mahavishnu Orchestra. To couch potatoes who lounged through the 1980s in front of the tube, he is the guy behind the infectious, driving soundtrack music to *Miami Vice*. In the late 1990s, Hammer is the mostly anonymous composer of scores for countless commercials, TV movies, and feature films. The one consistent theme that has persisted through composer and keyboardist Hammer's long and varied career has been the drive to be original. Hammer has always managed to be on the scene at the dawn of some musical moment; he was on hand for the instant at which jazz and rock collided, and on the day a decade and a half later when the television industry started to pay closer attention to the "audio" part of "audiovisual."

Hammer was born in Prague, Czechoslovakia, on April 17, 1948. His mother, a jazz singer, and his father, a physician who had worked his way through medical school playing bass and vibes, encouraged their son's musical interest from the start. By age four, he was playing the piano, and he began receiving formal training two years later. Hammer's professional debut, accompanying his mother, came when he was 12 years old. Hammer described the house he grew up in to *Down Beat*'s Herb Nolan as, "the jazz center of Prague; every jazz personality passed through, and for a jazz musician it was an ideal place to grow up."

As a high school student, Hammer formed a jazz trio with brothers Miroslav and Alan Vitous, a bassist and drummer respectively. By the time Hammer and Miroslav Vitous—who later became a founding member of the band Weather Report—were awarded first prize honors at the 1966 International Music Competition in Vienna, Austria, Hammer had ditched his original plan to be a doctor in favor of a career in music. He and Miroslav enrolled at the Academy of Muse Arts in Prague, where Hammer immersed himself in the study of classical composition and piano performance from 1966 to 1968. By night he honed his chops in jazz clubs from Munich to Warsaw, picking up jobs as a studio sideman along the way.

When Russian troops invaded Czechoslovakia in 1968, Hammer decided to move to the United States, where he had been offered a scholarship to attend the prestigious Berklee School of Music in Boston. Hammer never really warmed to class work at Berklee, opting instead to devote his energies to finding jobs playing music. Hammer's first U.S. gig, aboard a Boston Harbor cruise boat in November of 1968, netted him

Born April 17, 1948, in Prague, Czechoslovakia; immigrated to the United States, 1968; father was a physician and jazz musician; mother was a jazz singer; married Ivona; children: one daughter, one son. *Education:* Attended Academy of Muse Arts, Prague, 1966-68; attended Berklee College of Music, Boston, MA, 1968.

Jazz pianist in various clubs throughout Czechoslovakia, Poland, and Germany, 1967-68; performed at various venues in Boston area, 1968-70; arranger and piano accompanist for vocalist Sarah Vaughan, 1970-71; member of Mahavishnu Orchestra, 1971-73; leader of Jan Hammer Group, 1973-76; involved in numerous performing and recording projects as composer and/or keyboardist, 1976-; composer of musical scores for many motion pictures and television shows, 1978—; composed and performed soundtrack for NBC series "Miami Vice," 1984-87; Smythe & Co., composer for film, television, and advertising, 1997— .

Awards: International Music Competition, Vienna, Austria, first prize, 1966; Grammy awards, Best Instrumental Composition and Best Pop Instrumental Performance for "Miami Vice Theme," 1985.

Addresses: Management—Elliott Sears Management, 7 Dunham Drive, New Fairfield, CT 06812.

$15.00. From there, he moved on to the Boston Playboy Club, where he secured steady work in the house band. Although quality work was hard to come by, returning to Europe seemed out of the question. Choosing chose to stay in the United States permanently, Hammer applied for and soon was granted citizenship.

Climbing the Mountain

In 1970 Hammer received his first major break when he was asked to join the band of renowned jazz singer Sarah Vaughan. Hammer jumped at the opportunity, and with virtually no advance rehearsal, he joined the trio for 13 months of extensive touring across North America and Japan. When his stint with Vaughan was over, Hammer resettled in New York, where his keyboard skills were much in demand. He performed with the likes of flautist Jeremy Steig and drum great Elvin Jones. Jones, a hero of Hammer's since childhood, liked Hammer's playing enough invite him to work on two of his albums, *On the Mountain* and *Mr. Jones.*

Hammer's historic role in the development of jazz-rock fusion began to take shape in 1971. That year, he began jamming with guitar whiz John McLaughlin. Within a few months, these meetings led to the creation of the Mahavishnu Orchestra, one of the most important fusion bands ever to play a note. Along with Hammer and McLaughlin, this original version of Mahavishnu featured violinist Jerry Goodman, bassist Rick Laird, and drummer Billy Cobham. That lineup recorded three albums over the next two years: *The Inner Mounting Flame, Birds of Fire,* and *Between Nothingness and Eternity.* These albums, and the band's incendiary live concerts, combined the most appealing elements of rock with those of jazz, winning over fans of both idioms in the process. Between 1971 and 1973, Hammer and Mahavishnu played nearly 500 concerts, setting the standard for an entire generation of fusion artists to come.

Hammer's involvement with Mahavishnu also provided the spark for his interest in the synthesizer as an instrument. The synthesizer allowed him to use his keyboard skills in ways previously impossible. The variety of sounds he was able to create ranged from effects usually associated with electric guitar to walls of noise never before heard out of any instrument. Hammer quickly became one of the most innovative synthesizer practitioners in the world.

Left Mahavishnu for Solo Career

By 1973 Hammer was feeling the strain of Mahavishnu's busy touring schedule, which left him precious little time to compose and to indulge his other musical interests. He left the band after its New Year's Eve, December 31, 1973, concert, and embarked on a solo career. Hammer's first post-Mahavishnu project was the album *Like Children,* a collaboration with violinist Goodman. As a solo artist, Hammer's first recording was *The First Seven Days,* which he recorded and produced at his own Red Gate Studio located in his upstate New York farmhouse. Perhaps as a reaction to his work with McLaughlin, *The First Seven Days* was a guitarless album from start to finish. As Hammer finished work on the album, he began assembling the Jan Hammer Group, which featured Steve Kindler—Goodman's replacement in Mahavishnu—on violin, bassist Fernando Saunders, and drummer Tony Smith. The Group's inaugural nationwide tour was a big success.

Part of that success hinged on Hammer's development, in conjunction with technicians at his favorite synthesizer manufacturer, of a portable keyboard that he could wield freely the way a rock guitarist handles his or her instrument. On the momentum of the tour, the Group headed into the studio to record the album *Oh, Yeah?*, which, unlike *The First Seven Days*, contained eight distinct tunes rather than a single run-on concept piece. *Oh, Yeah?* showed an incredibly broad range of styles and influences, from rock and R&B to progressive disco-jazz and Hammer's own strange vision of "country & eastern."

In 1976 Hammer and his band hooked up with guitar hero Jeff Beck to record Beck's blockbuster LP *Wired*. The Hammer Group toured with Beck for the next year. After over 100 concerts, the album *Jeff Beck with the Jan Hammer Group* was released using material recorded live during the tour. Four of the seven tracks on the live album were Hammer compositions. After the end of the band's association with Beck, it released one more album under the name The Jan Hammer Group, the 1977 LP *Melodies*.

During the next several years, Hammer veered away from his jazz roots, more toward a purer rock and roll sound. He released a solo album, *Black Sheep*, then launched a new rock band, called simply Hammer. In the early 1980s Hammer kept busy working on collaborative projects with several artists on both sides of the rock/jazz border. On the rock side, he recorded with Neal Schon of Journey, James Young of Styx, and the Rolling Stones' Mick Jagger. His jazz dabblings included work with guitarists Al DiMeola and John Abercrombie. He also renewed his connection with Jeff Beck, whose album *Flash* included the Grammy-winning (Best Rock Instrumental Performance) Hammer composition "Escape."

Scored Big with *Miami Vice*

Meanwhile, Hammer began to try his hand at writing and recording scores for film and television. His earliest efforts came in 1978, when he wrote theme music for the British television series *The Tube*. In 1981 Hammer composed the score for "Oceans," a Canadian television documentary. Hammer landed his first movie soundtrack job in 1983, composing the original score for *A Night in Heaven*. By that time, Hammer was being showered with offers to compose scores for feature films, made-for-TV movies, documentaries, and commercials. The offer that took his career in a new direction came in 1984, when he began writing music for the television series *Miami Vice*.

Hammer's "Miami Vice Theme" became a number one single, and the show's soundtrack album recorded quadruple platinum sales. Hammer also received Grammy awards for "Best Instrumental Composition" and "Best Pop Instrumental Performance." Over the next four years, Hammer cranked out weekly soundtracks—a total of more than 70 episodes worth—for the show from his home studio. Hammer's work on "Miami Vice" almost single-handedly created a new, pulsing, driving sound for television music that has since been imitated by countless composers for the small screen.

In 1987 Hammer had two million-selling albums: *Miami Vice II* and *Escape from Television*. The following year, he withdrew from the frenzied pace of his full-time *Miami Vice* gig in order to concentrate on other work. He built a new studio on his upstate New York property. From there, Hammer continued to compose mainly for film and television. Demand for his work remained heavy through the rest of the 1980s and into the 1990s. Hammer's scores for television included music for the British TV series *Chancer*, HBO's *Tales from the Crypt*, and two pilots for NBC's *Knight Rider 2000*. For the big screen, Hammer's work included scores for the films *Sunset Heat* and *The Taking of Beverly Hills*. In 1992 Hammer composed and performed original music for *Beyond the Mind's Eye*, a multimedia extravaganza of computer animation and music that spent 112 weeks on *Billboard*'s music video charts.

Hammer released a new album, *Drive*, in 1994, marking the first original, non-soundtrack recording issued under his name in years. After *Drive*, it was back to scoring for Hammer. In 1995 and 1996, Hammer composed scores for at least two feature films, as well as music for several television projects. In 1997 Hammer signed a deal with the New York commercial music production firm Smythe & Co., where he was expected to create music for film, television, and advertising. Although composing for television commercials seems a long way from Hammer's groundbreaking work with Mahavishnu and others, the artist himself sees it as a perfect forum for his talents. In *Shoot* magazine, Hammer revealed his feelings on the subject: "These days, if you want to create wide-ranging or cutting-edge music, the world of advertising is the only place to be."

Selected discography

Solo albums

The First Seven Days, Nemperor, 1975.
(With Jeff Beck) *Wired*, 1976.

Black Sheep, Elektra/Asylum, 1978.
Hammer, Asylum, 1980.
(Contributor) *A Night in Heaven* (soundtrack), A&M, 1983.
(Contributor) *Secret Admirer* (soundtrack), MCA, 1985.
The Early Years, Nemperor, 1986.
Escape from Television, MCA, 1987.
Beyond the Mind's Eye, Miramar/MCA, 1992.
Drive, 1994.

With Mahavishnu Orchestra

The Inner Mounting Flame, Columbia, 1972.
Birds of Fire, Columbia, 1973.
Between Nothingness and Eternity, Columbia, 1973.

With Jan Hammer Group

Melodies, Nemperor, 1976.
Oh, Yeah? Nemperor, 1976.
Jeff Beck with the Jan Hammer Group, Nemperor, 1976.

With Al DiMeola

Electric Rendezvous, Columbia, 1982.
Tour de Force—Live, Columbia, 1983.

With Neal Schon

Untold Passion, Columbia, 1981.
Here to Stay, Columbia, 1983.

Original Television Soundtracks

Miami Vice, 1985.
Miami Vice II, 1986.
Miami Vice III, 1987.
Miami Vice/Greatest Hits, 1989.
Tales from the Crypt, 1992.

Sources

Down Beat, January 26, 1978; June 1985.
Keyboard, September 1985; January 1995.
Musician, May 1988.
Scholastic Update, March 21, 1986.
Shoot, March 21, 1997.

Additional material for this profile was obtained from the liner notes to the CD *Jan Hammer: The Early Years* (Nemperor, 1986) and material provided by Elliott Sears Management.

—*Robert R. Jacobson*

Sophie B. Hawkins

Singer, songwriter, musician

When Sophie B. Hawkins emerged on the charts with her 1992 hit, "Damn, I Wish I Was Your Lover," critics rushed to categorize her. In spite of the song's soulful hook, Hawkins' background was rock and an eclectic array of influences that ranged from David Bowie to Barbra Streisand to African folk music. Sophie Ballantine Hawkins, it turned out, did not fit the established categories.

As a blond who attracted attention with nude pictures in *Interview* magazine, she might seem like another Madonna. But she eschews comparisons to the pop diva, and again, her songs have a passion lacking in most of Madonna's hits. Nor does she fit anyone's attempts to dismiss her as "just another female singer," since she writes her own songs, plays keyboards and percussion, and is heavily involved in production.

Born in New York City in 1967, Hawkins grew up in Manhattan, the youngest of three children. Her parents, a wealthy lawyer and a writer, raised their children in an unorthodox fashion: Hawkins' mother, British novelist

AP/Wide World Photos, Inc. Reproduced by permission.

For the Record . . .

Born Sophie Ballantine Hawkins, 1967, in New York City; daughter of Joan Winthrop (a writer), and a lawyer father.

Studied and performed with drummer Baba Olatunji, early 1980s; toured as percussionist for Bryan Ferry, 1991; obtained recording contract with Columbia Records, released *Tongues and Tails,* with hit "Damn, I Wish I Was Your Lover," 1992; released follow-up, *Whaler,* 1994; moved from New York to Los Angeles, 1996.

Addresses: *Management*—Stiletto Entertainment, 5443 Beethoven St., Los Angeles, CA 90066.

Joan Winthrop, smoked marijuana and would sometimes pull her daughter out of school to go with her to Coney Island. But even her liberal parents were not amused when at age 14 Sophie fell in love and moved in with an older man. The older man was Gordy Ryan, percussionist for an ensemble led by Nigerian master drummer Baba Olatunji, whose troupe lived at the Ansonia Hotel in New York City. Hawkins gained her introduction to them from her aunt Linda, masseuse for Paul Simon, but it was far from her first exposure to the world of music.

"That's Who I Am"

From an early age, Hawkins saw herself as a drummer, and she and her siblings would pretend that they were a band. "I used to set up the couch and chairs and make them into a drum set," she recalled in a Sony website article. "I'd play the `drums' to all the songs and sing the bass parts while my brother and sister would `play guitar' on tennis rackets."

But only Sophie burned with a dream for stardom even at the age of seven. Hawkins told *Rollling Stone*'s David Wild that she "was going to be a Mick Jagger or a David Bowie or a Bob Dylan, whatever it was they did. I remember sitting there, looking out of a window, listening to a record and saying: `That's it. That's who I am.'"

Bowie's name has often come up as a principal influence in Hawkins' early years, and he was closely tied in her mind to the single greatest influence of all: her mother. "I always thought my mother was [German actress and sex symbol] Marlene Dietrich," she reported to Wild. "And to me he was like the male Marlene Dietrich."

At age nine, Hawkins began taking percussion lessons at a Harlem jazz school. Drums were not exactly the instrument of choice for most musically inclined girls, of course, but then Hawkins was always unusual. One day at age 14, she skipped basketball practice and went with her aunt to meet Olatunji and his troupe at their quarters in the Ansonia. Olatunji showed her a few things on the drums that afternoon, then taught her an African song. "When I left three hours later," she told Wild, "my life made sense. This was the incarnation of everything I wanted." Hawkins never went back to basketball, and she soon left her home and school as well, to move in with Gordy Ryan.

Working Toward the Big Break

During the decade between moving in with Ryan and the recording of her first album, Hawkins bounced around from job to job. She sang with a punk band called the Pink Men, formed a group called Sophie's Private Wave, and of course toured with Olatunji's ensemble. (She lived with Ryan until the age of 20.)

Hawkins even gave up singing for awhile, for a stint in performance art and acting. Other non-musical work included tending bar, waiting tables, and coat-checking. She still knew she wanted to be a star, and when she received an offer from Roxy Music founder Bryan Ferry to tour as a percussionist, it might have seemed like the break she was waiting for. But after three months he called her and, though professing that he and the rest of the band liked her style, told her she just didn't mesh with the rest of the band musically. The next day, she said, she woke up crying. She was 24, young for almost any profession except that of popular musician, a realm in which people who break out in their late twenties are considered late bloomers. Desperate and uncertain about her future, she was inspired to write, and came up with the song "Damn, I Wish I Was Your Lover."

Soon afterward, while she was working in the coat-check booth, a man told her that she had a nice speaking voice, and suddenly her demo tape was circulating to various record company executives. A bidding war followed between Sire, Arista, and Columbia, with the latter winning out over the others and signing Hawkins. In 1992, Columbia released her album *Tongues and Tails,* with "Damn, I Wish I Was Your

Lover." The song reached number five on the charts, and *Billboard* called it "a potential single of the year." Hawkins was on her way. "I feel pretty comfortable with the attention that I'm getting lately," she told *Rolling Stone*. "Things are pretty much happening like I always imagined that they would. I remember when I was eighteen ... I told my guitar player that I'd be making my first album when I was twenty-five. So I guess things are basically on schedule."

Uneven Sophomore Years

Hawkins' optimism would remain somewhat unfulfilled. Her follow-up effort, 1994's *Whaler,* received considerably less attention than its predecessor. *Entertainment Weekly*'s Peter Galvin, who apparently could not resist playing on the aquatic (Moby Dick) theme, observed that the album had "sunk."

Hawkins also endured flak from her record company for her nude pictures in *Interview* magazine. But the complaints revolved not around morality, but appearance: Sophie had allowed herself to be photographed without makeup, the executives complained, and did not look "glamorous enough." In response, she told *Details* magazine, "with most women it's posed and they look beautiful and sexy and glamorous. I look like a cow. It doesn't look like I think I'm pretty or have a good body or like I think I'm going to turn somebody on—but why do women always have to turn someone on? So it was a big statement."

Clearly Hawkins marches to her own drummer—herself, much of the time—and that has not always earned her a great deal of good will. She has said that she has only one celebrity friend, comedian Rosie O'Donnell. Not content to identify herself as heterosexual or homosexual, having had both male and female lovers, she has been described as "omnisexual," and has demonstrated an affinity for the works of the feminist author Camille Paglia.

Audiences have remained loyal to Hawkins, and she has a wide fan base on the Internet. Moreover, after an initial tepid response to *Whaler,* she enjoyed a hit single with "As I Lay Me Down," which in June of 1996 earned the all-time record for longest-running single on the *Billboard* Adult Contemporary charts.

A documentary on Hawkins' work, *The Cream Will Rise,* gained critical attention when it debuted on February 11, 1997. She remained in the limelight throughout the year with appearances on ABC's *Politically Incorrect with Bill Maher* in July and the contribution of an Elton John cover, "Border Song," for the soundtrack of the movie *The Associate.* In August of 1997, several newspapers reported that Hawkins, who had moved to L.A. from New York and set up her own recording studio in her house, was working with famed producer Peter Asher on a CD to be entitled *Angels Get My Mansions Ready.*

In a short career that has defied attempts at categorization, Hawkins has established herself with a style that *Rolling Stone* aptly characterized as "[crossing] rhythmically ambitious, sensual dance pop with the introspection of singer-songwriter rock."

Selected discography

Tongues and Tails, Columbia, 1992.
Whaler, Columbia, 1994.
(Contributor) *The Associate* (soundtrack), 1996.

Sources

Advocate, February 6, 1996.
Chicago Tribune, August 24, 1992.
Details, 1995.
Entertainment Weekly, October 1995.
EQ, March 1996.
Harper's Bazaar, January 1992.
Hollywood Reporter, April 6, 1995.
Interview, September 1991; January 1994; February 1994.
Los Angeles Times, May 28, 1996.
Mademoiselle, September 1992.
Musician, October 1, 1994.
New York, April 13, 1992.
New York Times, May 13, 1996.
Rolling Stone, September 3, 1992.
Us, March 1996.
Washington Post, May 16, 1996.

Additional information was provided by Sophie B. Hawkins sites on the World Wide Web.

—*Judson Knight*

INXS

Rock band

Few rock bands have achieved the success and longevity that INXS has enjoyed. Fewer still can claim this without a single personnel change. All six members recorded and performed together for more over 20 years before the death of singer Michael Hutchence on November 22, 1997.

Beginning in Australia, INXS released several albums before making a splash in the United States in 1983. From then on, they shot up the charts with singles like "The One Thing," "Original Sin" and "What You Need," before launching into astounding worldwide sales and recognition with their 1988 release *Kick*. With this album, they swept the charts, received many awards, and completed a 16-month, worldwide tour. "We seemed to be around the corner every month in America, it was hard to ignore us," singer Michael Hutchence told Glenn A. Baker in *Billboard*. Following *Kick*'s success, rumors of a breakup began to circulate.

Although the band did experience some difficulties as a result of their overwhelming success, they relied on

AP/Wide World Photos, Inc. Reproduced by permission.

For the Record . . .

Members include **Garry Gary Beers**, bass; **Andrew Farris**, keyboards; **Jon Farris**, drums; **Tim Farris**, guitar; **Michael Hutchence** (died November 22, 1997) vocals; and **Kirk Pengilly**, guitar/saxophone.

Band formed in Sydney, Australia, 1977; signed with Australian label Deluxe Records, 1979; released self-titled debut in Australia, 1980; signed with WEA Records in Australia and released *Shabooh Shoobah*, 1982; signed North American recording contract with Atlantic Records, 1983; released multi-platinum album *Kick*, 1988; released four more albums on Atlantic, 1990-93; signed with Mercury/Polygram Records, 1993; released two more albums, 1994-97.

Awards: Best International Band and Best International Male (Hutchence), BPI Awards (Britian), 1991; Best International Band, Australian Music Awards, 1991.

Addresses: *Record company*—Mercury/Polygram Records, 825 8th Ave., New York, NY 10019.

their relationship as friends to keep them together. INXS was one of the few bands to emerge into rock stardom in the 1980s and survive into the late 1990s. They attributed their stability to a competitive air of democracy and the ability to keep each other grounded in reality.

Keyboard player Andrew Farris and singer Michael Hutchence met in high school in Sydney, Australia. Farris broke up a fight between Hutchence and a school bully, and the two budding musicians became fast friends. Hutchence, whose father was an Australian importer, grew up in Sydney, as well as Hong Kong, and Los Angeles, California. His mother had taken him to L.A. when his parents split up. "I spent most of my time in the States by myself, writing prose, poems, and stories," Hutchence told Edwin Morris in *Seventeen*. "I came back home with a large collection of things."

Andrew Farris' two brothers, Tim and Jon, were also aspiring musicians. While the Farris brothers were growing up in Perth, Australia, Tim Farris began taking guitar lessons at the age of eight. When he was 13 years old, the family moved to Sydney. Tim and guitarist/saxophone player Kirk Pengilly met and played in a band together. At the time, they attended Forest High School, where they met bassist Garry Gary Beers. Hutchence, Andrew, and drummer Jon Farris attended Davidson High School.

Started as the Farris Brothers

By 1977 Tim Farris and Kirk Pengilly's band had broken up. They decided to form a band with Andrew and Jon, Beers, and Hutchence called The Farris Brothers. According to INXS legend, the band formed on the night Elvis Presley died. "The day I left school was the day I left home was the day I joined the band," Hutchence recalled to Nina Malkin in *Mademoiselle*.

The following year, The Farris Brothers moved to Perth, where they wrote songs, rehearsed, and performed in local hotels and mining towns. After ten months, they returned to Sydney, where their performances grabbed the attention of Garry Morris, who managed the Australian band Midnight Oil. Morris began working with them and was the first to suggest that they change the name of the band.

Although Morris devoted the majority of his time to Midnight Oil, The Farris Brothers had also met booking agent C.M. Murphy. At the time, Murphy was in the process of starting up an independent record label called Deluxe Records, which had a distribution deal with RCA Records. Murphy agreed that the band's name needed to be changed. "Our record company suggested 'In Excess,'" Tim Farris told Steve Dougherty in *People* magazine. The group liked the idea, but wanted the name to really stand out on their posters. So they shortened it to INXS. Jay Cocks later reinforced the same concept in *Time* magazine, "'In excess' would be phonetically correct, but it lacks the cool mystery of those four uppercase letters, which make the lads loom large, like something mythic: six electrified Druids with some new rhythmic spells to weave."

Sparked Interest in Australia

On September 1, 1979, INXS made its performing debut at the Oceanview Hotel in Toukley, Australia. The following May, the group released its first single, "Simple Simon/We Are the Vegetables" on Deluxe Records. In October of 1980, they released their self-titled debut album in Australia, which included the single "Just Keep Walking." The band embarked on a 300-show tour throughout Australia to promote the album. A year later, they released their second LP, *Underneath the*

Colors, which climbed to the Top 15 on the Australian charts.

In April of 1982, Andrew Farris, Hutchence, and Pengilly went on a "pilgrimage" to England and the United States. Armed with a tape of their music, they set out to spread the word on INXS. They signed a new contract with WEA Records in Australia in July of the same year. Their next release, *Shabooh Shoobah* reached the Top Five on the Australian charts. By the following January, they had signed a North American record contract with Atlantic Records.

Reached Out to Global Audience

They debuted in the United States with the single "The One Thing," which quickly climbed to the Top 30 on the *Billboard* charts. The video went into high rotation on MTV, and INXS had begun to make their mark in America. Atlantic re-released *Shabooh Shoobah* in the United States to wide acclaim. David Fricke wrote in *Rolling Stone,* "Most of *Shabooh Shoobah,* the group's American debut, is both novel in approach and stirring in execution."

After the album's release, INXS began a marathon U.S. tour. They played their first New York City headlining show at The Ritz in May of 1983. From there they went to the Us Festival in California, where they received two encore calls from over 300,000 attendees. Then, Atlantic released a mini-LP in August called *Dekadance,* with remixes of four songs from *Shabooh Shoobah.*

Meanwhile, the band continued to receive attention in their homeland. Their "Original Sin" single reached Number One on the Australian charts in January of 1984. *The Swing* was released in May of that year and included the singles "Burn for You" and "Melting in the Sun." It reached double-platinum sales in Australia and became one of the top five selling albums in Australian music history. INXS also received seven Countdown Awards (Australia's version of the Grammy Awards), more than any other group had ever received.

INXS Goes Global

The band's success also began to spread to the rest of the world. They performed their debut show in London, England at The Astoria. In the meantime, Atlantic re-released their earlier albums, *INXS* and *Underneath the Colors* in the United States. In September of 1984, INXS became the first international rock band to play in Guam. In July of 1985, the band's Sydney performance

for the Live Aid benefit concert was broadcast worldwide.

Despite the group's growing popularity, they continued their intense recording and touring schedules. In October of 1985, they released their next album, *Listen Like Thieves,* and its first single, "This Time." By the end of the year, they had taken off on their first headlining tour in the United States. After the hit single "What You Need" was released the following January, *Listen Like Thieves* reached gold status in the America and eventually went platinum. In May of 1986, INXS performed their "If You Got It, Shake It" world tour.

Kicked into High Gear

They went on to headline the "Australian Made" tour of their home country with eight other Australian bands. Three days before the release of *Kick,* INXS returned to the States for the "Calling All Nations" tour. In January of 1988, *Kick* was certified gold and platinum at the same time. Eventually, it sold ten million copies worldwide.

The single "Need You Tonight" became the band's first Number One song on the U.S. charts. The home video *Kick—The Video Flick* also had platinum sales. All three of the subsequent singles from *Kick*—"Devil Inside," "New Sensation," and "Never Tear Us Apart"—reached *Billboard's* Top 10. INXS swept the MTV Video Music Awards in September of 1988 with five awards for the "Need You Tonight/Mediate" video. In January, the group received its first Grammy nomination for "Best Rock Performance by a Group."

After 16 months of touring and overwhelming success, the members decided to take a break from each other. Hutchence recorded an album with Ollie Olsen called *Max Q* and acted in his second feature film called *Frankenstein Unbound* (he had his film debut in *Dogs in Space* in 1986).

Andrew Farris produced Jenny Morris' album *Shiver.* Tim Farris produced a documentary called *Fish in Space,* about big game fishing, for which Jon Farris and Kirk Pengilly performed the score. Beers co-produced the *Here's Looking up Your Address* album for the Australian band Absent Friends.

With all the side projects going on, rumors began to fly about the band's demise. But in November of 1989, INXS began rehearsals for their next album *X.* Released in 1990, the LP was named for the band's tenth anniversary of recording. The single "Suicide Blonde" hit the Top 10 on charts around the world, and *X* went double-platinum in both the United States and Australia. "We've had this Three Musketeers, or Six Musketeers, attitude for so long, and it's still very strong," Hutchence said in *Billboard*. "There's never any talk or any question of ever replacing anybody or changing anything."

In 1991 INXS received another Grammy nomination for "Best Rock Performance by a Group." *USA Today* reported that the band tied for second place in the list of musical artists with the most videos played on MTV. At the time, they had 37 different clips. On their tour, INXS became the first international rock band to play in Mexico since The Doors had performed there nearly 20 years before.

In March of 1991, INXS won BPI Awards in Britain for "Best International Band" and Hutchence was awarded "Best International Male." They also received the award for "Best International Band" at the first Australian Music Awards. Before the end of the year, INXS released a live album and video titled *Live Baby Live.*

Subjected to Post-Peak Gravity

INXS's following release *Welcome to Wherever You Are* began to mark the group's downward slope from the success of *Kick*. Its sales fell just short of the platinum mark—a huge success for some bands, but nowhere near the popularity previously achieved by the band. Yet the group was not discouraged. They released *Full Moon, Dirty Hearts* in 1993, which included two duets with Hutchence: "Please (You've Got That...)" with veteran singer Ray Charles and "Full Moon, Dirty Hearts" with Chrissy Hynde of the rock band the Pretenders.

INXS also made a video album to accompany *Full Moon, Dirty Hearts* with videos for every song. Nine film directors contributed to the project for the 12 songs on the album. It was showcased on MTV, Australia's Channel Nine, and selected movie theaters. Some of the videos were designed in traditional fashion, while others were produced like mini-movies.

By 1994, INXS had switched record labels from Atlantic to Mercury/Polygram, but not before releasing a greatest hits album simply titled *INXS: The Greatest Hits,* on Atlanta, with the addition of two new songs. The band took another long break before releasing their next effort, *Elegantly Wasted* in 1997. The release received some criticism for continuing in the band's same 1980s style. In the band's record company biography, Andrew Farris admitted that their musical style had not

progressed: "Some of it could be us 12, 13 years ago!" But added that, "To keep changing just because you think you have to is not necessarily a good thing."

Some critics commented that they never fit into the musical fashion of their time. They called them "ahead of their time" and "dated" all in the same few paragraphs. "I don't think we've ever fit in," Hutchence said in the band's bio. "Maybe it's a generational thing. Or maybe it's because there's always been the six of us, pulling in six different directions."

On November 22, 1997, INXS received an unexpected shock. Singer Hutchence committed suicide in a hotel room in Sydney, Australia. The band had gathered in their hometown to begin rehearsals for their twentieth anniversary tour. "Michael was the consummate rock star," Australian rock historian Glenn A. Baker told *Associated Press*. "He took upon the role of a rock star comfortably; he floated above the pressures. Why he would choose this moment to throw in the towel I think will always remain a mystery."

Selected discography

INXS, Deluxe Records, 1980; reissued, Atlantic Records, 1984.
Underneath the Colors, Deluxe Records, 1981; reissued, Atlantic Records, 1984.
Shabooh Shoobah, WEA Records, 1982; reissued, Atlantic Records, 1983.
Dekadance, Atlantic Records, 1983.
The Swing, Atlantic Records, 1984.
Listen Like Thieves, Atlantic Records, 1985.
Kick, Atlantic Records, 1987.
X, Atlantic Records, 1990.
Live Baby Live, Atlantic Records, 1991.
Welcome to Wherever You Are, Atlantic Records, 1992.
Full Moon, Dirty Hearts, Atlantic Records, 1993.
INXS: The Greatest Hits, Atlantic Records, 1994.
Elegantly Wasted, Mercury/Polygram, 1997.

Sources

Periodicals

Billboard, November 26, 1988; October 13, 1990; May 9, 1992; November 13, 1993.
Entertainment Weekly, July 24, 1992; November 5, 1993; April 18, 1997.
Guitar Player, March 1991.
Los Angeles Times, August 11, 1997.
Mademoiselle, April 1990.

People, February 1, 1988; July 11, 1988; October 22, 1990; August 17, 1992; May 12, 1997.

Rolling Stone, April 28, 1983; January 14, 1988; June 16, 1988; April 4, 1991; December 9, 1993; February 24, 1994; May 1, 1997.

Seventeen, August 1986.

Time, December 17, 1990.

Online

http://www.geocities.com/SunsetStrip/9224/inxs-bio
http://www.nytimes.com/aponline/l/AP-Obit-Hutchence.html
http://www.umdnj.edu/~kotharne/inxs/inxsology

—*Sonya Shelton*

Israel Vibration

Reggae trio

When polio struck Jamaica in the late 1950s, many of the island nation's children had not been vaccinated against the crippling disease. Three young victims of the epidemic—Cecil (Skelly) Spence, Albert (Apple) Craig, and Lascelle (Wiss) Bulgin—came together at the Mona Rehabilitation Centre in Kingston, a government institution for young polio patients whose families could not afford medical care. "We grow together like brothers," Craig said. The three boys' paths crossed sporadically as they moved among various institutions, according to Roger Steffens, a reggae historian and founding editor of *The Beat*. Through it all, however, they shared a love of music. Spence, for example, played in a band called the Hot Lickers and performed on Jamaican TV when he was 12. Craig started writing songs at an early age and taught himself to play the piano by watching his teacher's hands as she played.

In that unlikely setting, under those traumatic circumstances, a seed was planted which would grow into one of Jamaica's most noted vocal groups—Israel Vibration.

For the Record . . .

Members include **Lascelle** (Wiss) **Bulgin**, vocals; **Albert** (Apple) **Craig**, vocals (left band, 1997); and **Cecil** (Skelly) **Spence**, vocals.

Israel Vibration began performing and recording in their Jamaican homeland, 1970s; the trio released popular roots-reggae recordings in Jamaica before splitting up in 1983; reunited in the U.S. six years later; signed with RAS Records and recorded a string of albums in the 1990s.

Awards: Tower Records/*Pulse!* magazine selected *On the Rock* the best reggae album of 1995.

Addresses: *Record company*—RAS Records, P.O. Box 42517, Washington, DC 20015.

The trio's concerts, Rob Kenner wrote in *Vibe* magazine, are unforgettable. "It's not just the sight of three polio-stricken Rastafarians skanking on stage in a tangle of crutches, braces and dreadlocks. Rather, it's their voices—the sweet, achy way Skelly, Apple and Wiss blend their wails into one irresistible cry," Kenner commented. "When the three of us come together," Spence told Kenner, "the forces combine in a triangle."

Free and Homeless

As a boy, Craig chafed under the restrictions of institutional life. "I was transferred to the Salvation Army Home, then to the Alpha Boys School, which was run by nuns. It was like a prison," he told Steffens. "They beat me up there, and locked me in a room with three iron bars over a little peephole. I used to climb up in a tree. I sit there for days and plan to run away from that place, and I did it. I break through the fence and until this day, I'm free." At age 14, Craig was living on the street, often dizzy from hunger. He washed car windows and begged for spare change, slept in abandoned houses and cars, and bathed at the wharf. "I was like a lonely sheep in the wilderness," he said. "I was like Job."

The teenager turned to the Rastafari religion and the dreadlocked outcasts who practiced it, even though "society saw them as mad people. They never look presentable with their big 'locks and sandals made of car tires," Craig was quoted in *Vibe*. "Some did smell kinda funny, too, 'cause they live inna [sic] bush."

Spence and Bulgin, meanwhile, left the institutional life—although it is unclear whether they "graduated" or were expelled for embracing the Rastafarian lifestyle. Spence, in any event, was kicked off the Jamaican wheelchair basketball team, with which he had traveled to Germany and New Zealand, when he began growing Rasta dreadlocks.

Three Voices

Around 1969, Craig "was living in the bush near the football field at the University of West Indies," Steffens wrote. "Gradually, he, Wiss and Skelly began to hang out together, smoking herb, reading the Bible, reasoning, and—miraculously—learning that the blend of their three voices was attracting an enthusiastic crowd that would clap and cheer and urge them to record their music." The trio crafted a name which reflected both the children of God and the resonance of music. "We are one of those groups that is born great," Craig has said, "because it was put together by a touch of the Almighty."

In 1976, Israel Vibration started recording their songs—they shared lead vocal duties—with support from the noted Roots Radics rhythm section. The group gained recognition beyond their homeland with the album *Same Song*. Music critic James Lien has called the late 1970s a powerful period for Rastafari and reggae, and he noted that "Israel Vibration provided one of the era's most forceful messages of peace and spirituality." Professionally, however, the trio found serenity elusive. "Their musical careers seemed to be taking off but, like many Jamaican artists, Israel Vibration's recording career was set back," according to the group's official bio, "by a local industry plagued ... by questionable accounting practices, musical piracy, and a lack of tour support."

A New Land

In 1983, Craig, Spence and Bulgin parted company and separately traveled to the United States in search of solo careers and better medical care. Eventually, each approached Washington-based RAS Records with hopes of acquiring a recording contract. The label's president, a man known as Doctor Dread in reggae circles, had other ideas, however. Dread was the catalyst behind Israel Vibration's 1989 reunion, which resulted in a string of inspirational and popular roots-reggae releases, including *Strength of My Life, Praises, and On the Rock*. Once again, the trio was supported on stage and in the studio by the Roots

Radics. In the 1990s, the reunited Israel Vibration cracked the reggae and world music charts and the video for their 1995 single "Rudeboy Shufflin" played on the BET network and other cable channels. The song includes the lyric: "Want peace in society, you better put me on your MTV."

Critics took notice. *Pulse* magazine lauded *On the Rock*'s "haunting melodies, forceful rhythm tracks, and absolutely captivating lyrics." A *Washington Post* critic noted Israel Vibration's ability to shift from songs of social injustice to celebratory tunes on the album *Free to Move*: "Both 'Terrorist' and 'Mud Up' bemoan street violence, and 'Livity in the Hood' insists that education is the way out of the concrete jungle." "But this album isn't entirely grim. The bright, sunny 'Pretty Woman' is propelled by a bouncy ska rhythm, while 'Traveling Man' brings a proselytizer's zeal to a road song."

Due to personal differences, Craig left the group in April 1997. Spence and Bulgin, meanwhile, continued to perform under the name Israel Vibration and launched a tour with the Roots Radics. "The three singers have faced considerable difficulties," Jimmy Cawley wrote in *The Boston Globe*, "but reggae is, after all, the music of sufferers who prevail."

Selective discography

Unconquered People, Greensleeves Records, 1980.
Strength of My Life, RAS Records, 1988.
Praises, RAS Records, 1990.
Dub Vibration, RAS Records, 1990.
Why Are You So Craven, RAS Records, 1991.
Forever, RAS Records, 1991.
Vibes Alive, RAS Records, 1992.
Perfect Love and Understanding, Munich Records, 1993.
IV, RAS Records, 1993.
I.V. D.U.B., RAS Records, 1994.
On the Rock, RAS Records, 1995.
Dub the Rock, RAS Records, 1995.
Rudeboy Shufflin, RAS Records, 1995.
Sugar Me, RAS Records, 1995.
The Same Song, Pressure Sounds, 1995.
Free to Move, RAS Records, 1996.
Feeling Irie, RAS Records, 1996.
Live Again!, RAS Records, 1997.
RAS Portraits, RAS Records, 1997.

Sources

Billboard, September 28, 1996.
Boston Globe, September 7, 1996.
Dub Missive, January 1997.
Echoes, September 2, 1995.
Pulse, June 1995.
URB Magazine, January 1996.
Washington Post, August 25, 1996.

Additional information was provided by RAS Records' press materials and the liner notes from the album *IV*.

—*Dave Wilkins*

Boney James

R&B, jazz artist

Boney James has risen in a few short years from a talented session player adaptable to a wide variety of musical styles, to a prominent "contemporary jazz" artist. According to a Morrice's Jazz Review critic, "Since 1992 Boney James has hit the Jazz music scene with hit after astonishing hit. Boney has definitely made his mark on Contemporary Jazz history." James characterizes himself more as an instrumental R&B player than a contemporary jazz artist, citing among his own musical influences such artists as Sly Stone, Stevie Wonder, and Earth, Wind & Fire. James contends in the Boney James website: "My music is firmly based in the R&B tradition." Despite the genre labels, James objects to the categorization of artists as R&B, funk, rock, etc., many of whom "have tremendous elements of jazz in their music—in their harmonies and in the way their songs are structured. Once that music becomes instrumental, all of a sudden it's 'contemporary jazz.' I think the line between the two is much thinner than a lot of people might think."

James was born in Lowell, Massachusetts and grew up in New Rochelle, New York, where he began playing clarinet at age eight before switching to saxophone at age ten. As a teenager, he began to play keyboards after discovering such R&B/jazz fusion artists as Grover Washington Jr., Ronnie Laws, and the Crusaders. While a college student at Berkeley, he joined a Los Angeles-based fusion band called Line One, which opened for artists such as Airto Moreira and the Yellowjackets. James found his calling in his late teens, he told Lucy Tauss in *e.Bop,* when Line One performed "a real show on a real stage. It was at the Improvisation, where they used to have music—now it's just comedy—and there was a P.A. and lights and an audience, and it was just the most fun I ever had in my life. And I just sort of decided right then and there that, wow, this may be the direction I need to be going in, because I felt passionate about it, which I hadn't felt about anything really up to that point. That's when I really decided to be a musician."

James transferred to UCLA and graduated with a degree in history. He soon developed a reputation as a versatile sessions player in L.A., initially more for his keyboard talents than his saxophone abilities. His first stint as a session player was as a keyboard player in a band formed subsequent to Time by Morris Day, and he soon began landing gigs as a session and tour musician with such acts as The Isley Brothers, Vesta Williams, Teena Marie, Randy Crawford, Bobby Caldwell, and Ray Parker, Jr. During this period James met his future wife, actress Lily Mariye, who appears as a regular on the TV show *E.R.* ("She's the one who goes around sticking tubes into people," Boney commented in the Boney James website).

Born in Lowell, MA; grew up in New Rochelle, NY; married, wife's name Lily Mariye (an actor on the TV show *E.R.*); received degree in History at Berkeley; developed a reputation as a versatile sessions player in L.A. with The Isley Brothers, Vesta Williams, Teena Marie, Randy Crawford, Bobby Caldwell, and Ray Parker, Jr., 1980s; recorded first album, *Trust,* on Spindletop Records, 1992; *Backbone,* on Warner Bros. Jazz, became first to top the charts, in 1994; hit "Seduction" broke all records on R & R NAC music charts by holding #1 slot for seventeen consecutive weeks, 1995; single "Nothin' But Love" also achieved #1 hit status on R & R NAC music charts, 1997.

Awards: Gavin Magazine 1996 Smooth Jazz Artist of the Year.

Addresses: *Record company*—Warner Bros. Jazz, 3300 Warner Blvd., Burbank, CA 91510.

After eight years in the circuits, James uncovered an opportunity to pursue a solo career. While touring with Bobby Caldwell in 1991, he met Paul Brown, an engineer/mixer who wanted to become a producer. Brown helped James land a solo deal with a label called Spindletop Records. James's first album, *Trust,* appeared in 1992 and featured James on saxophones and keyboards, as well as (among others) Jeff Carruthers on keyboards, Paul Jackson Jr. on guitars, Lenny Castro on percussion, and Freddie Washington on bass. Although the album attracted little critical or popular attention, it nonetheless reflected the subtle romantic honesty that many observers have detected in James's later work. James specifically wrote one track, "Lily," for his wife Mariye. "I rememberwhen he wrote it," Mariye commented in the Boney James website. "He really wanted to write a song that was reflective of who I am—not just something that he could later say, 'Oh, I'll call that one Lily.' I watched him work at capturing me. There are playful parts, thoughtful parts, sexy parts. It's a real tribute, and very special to me."

Bonified

By the time James recorded his next album, *Backbone,* in 1994, Spindletop Records had folded. Fortunately,

Warner Bros. acquired his contract and released the album, which became his first to top the charts. With a major label solidly behind him, James gained increased airplay on jazz radio stations and in his 1995 album *Seduction,* began playing with such bonified R&B/funk and jazz fusion legends as bassist Me'Shell NdegeOcello and drummer Peter Erskine of Weather Report fame. James's 1995 hit "Seduction" broke all records on the R & R NAC music charts by holding the #1 slot for 17 consecutive weeks, and a cover of the Bill Withers classic "Ain't No Sunshine" gained him further airplay on urban radio.

James commented on the creation of *Seduction* with his producer Paul Brown to Lucy Tauss in *e.Bop.* "We developed a number of tunes that had that sexy, seductive quality to them, and then we started to think, 'Well, let's have the record continue to communicate that.' So we sort of shaped it that way. We don't set out trying to make a sexy record or a funky record. We just set out trying to make a record. And then, once you see which way it's headed, you can continue refining it." Despite the emphasis on romantic moods, however, *Seduction* showcases a wide variety of influences. Funk and Latin rhythms are evident in "Second Nature" and "Got It Goin' On," featuring Me'Shell NdegeOcello. Tauss characterized the album as "an amalgam of styles and musical references." James commented: "To me, it's got a lot of elements of jazz, in that it's highly improvisational and I'm playing a saxophone. It's instrumental, it's blues-based, it's got a lot of jazz in it. But it's also incorporating all kinds of other things: contemporary R&B music or Motown soul music—whatever. It's just my roots, my various roots."

The Right Mix

James combines jazz and funk with more traditional influences in his 1996 record, *Boney's Funky Christmas.* Reprising such holiday favorites as "Jingle Bells" and "Sleigh Ride" with such special guests as vocalist Bobby Caldwell and Dee Harvey, as well as percussionists Lenny Castro and Paulinho Da Costa, and guitarist Paul Jackson, Jr., James places a unique and eclectic spin on the music. James noted to Lynda Lane in *Music Wire:* "Once I decided to do a Christmas album I sat down with my producer Paul Brown and listened to as many other holiday albums as I could find, everyone from Amy Grant, Ella Fitzgerald to Nat King Cole and the Charlie Brown Christmas album. What struck me was that, even though they were all doing pretty much the same material, each artist really gave the songs their distinctive stamp." James added, "I really tried to make these songs my own, to give them a shape and structure that would bring them alive by coming at them from a different angle."

In his 1997 album *Sweet Thing,* James returned to the romantic, contemporary jazz emphases of *Seduction* while drawing from music of the 1970s. On the Music Previews Network, he commented of the album: "I wanted to explore new directions, while at the same time, touch on some of the music that was important to my own development—everything from jazz fusion to Steely Dan. Theresult is a sort of 'live meets loop' approach; modern and retro at the same time." The album features collaborations between James and several prominent musicians, including vocalist Al Jarreau on "I Still Dream" and former Rufus guitarist Tony Maiden on the title cut, a Chaka Khan original. The single "Nothin' But Love" became a #1 hit on the R & R NAC music charts. The anonymous reviewer of BMG Music Service commented: "With its unbeatable recipe of delicious saxophone solos and delectable grooves, Boney James' *Sweet Thing* will nourish your soul as it satisfies your sweet tooth."

James' quick rise to success has instilled in him an ambition to challenge himself further with each subsequent production. He commented to Tauss in *e.Bop:* "Every now and then I really just stop and smell the roses and say, 'Wow, this is what I've always dreamed of, and it's actually happening.' But then you've gotta get back to work. You can't get too satisfied because you start to think you're happening; then probably you would slide back." To James, composition is "like a sculpture … where you start with a big rock and then you sort of chip at it until it starts to take some sort of shape and then you follow that. [You] start with all sorts of vague ideas for songs or vague ideas of things you want to try and do, experiments you want to make or players you want to use. And then you just keep stuffing the pot until finally you can sit back and say, 'You know, I think it's as good as it's going to get,' or 'It's done. It's great. I love it.'"

Selected discography

Trust, Spindletop Records, 1992.
Backbone, Warner Bros., 1994.
Seduction, Warner Bros., 1995.
Boney's Funky Christmas, Warner Bros., 1996.
Sweet Thing, Warner Bros., 1997.

Sources

Periodicals

Music Wire, November 1996.

Online

http://www.jazzreview.com/pmrev14.html
http://www.mpmusic.com/archive/6745.htm
http://www.bmgmusicservice.com/html/genre/86/jazzpg.html
http://www.wbjazz.com/artistBio.cfm?artNum=33
http://www.musicblvd.com/cgi-bin/tw/1826245878604620_105_810605

—Sean Pollock

Jamiroquai

British acid jazz, funk band

Archive Photos, Inc. Reproduced by permission.

Who is that cat-in-the-hat? That "Rad Hatter" is Jason "Jay" Kay, the lively front man for the band, Jamiroquai. Kay has a fondness for oversized, colorful, and sometimes furry stovepipe hats. JK, for short, is the driving force behind the eleven member British band, Jamiroquai, pronounced Jam-ear-o-kwai. Kay admitted in an online interview with Steve Dougherty and Kimberly Chrisman at http://www.xsite.net/, that his signature Dr. Seuss-like hats sometimes worn on stage "are part of my stage character." Perhaps the unusual hats, which sometimes appear to almost swallow him up, helped create an easily recognizable figure in the group's early days.

Right from the start, British fans loved their eclectic musical style with its strong jazz influences, and soulful rhythm and blues sound. The group was received enthusiastically by fans in the club scene. Performing live gives Kay the greatest opportunity to use his theatrical costumes and high energy dance moves. In 1992, their first hit single, "When You Gonna Learn?," was released on independent record label, Acid Jazz. It was an instant success in the U.K. On the basis of this one hit single, and the opinion held by record companies that this band had what it takes to last, competition broke out to sign the new band with a recording company. Sony Music emerged the victor when Jamiroquai signed an eight record deal with them for $1.9 million dollars. The group skyrocketed to fame and fortune in the early 1990s in Great Britain. Their success in the United States was stimulated at the 1997 MTV Video Music Awards. Nominated in ten categories, Jamiroquai walked away with four awards for "Virtual Insanity."

Kay organized the band in 1992. He created the name, Jamiroquai, to pay homage to the Native American nation of the Iroquois. He added the prefix, "Jam," short for jamming. The Iroquois treated the earth they dwelt upon with spiritual reverence. This ecological motif has inspired many of the socially conscious themes in the band's lyrics. In addition to expressing these themes lyrically, Kay personally sewed jackets for band members fashioned from hand woven Native American blankets. Kay posed with his originally designed jacket for *Seventeen* magazine and, he told the magazine's Carl Fysh why he is drawn to the Native American approach to life. "What attracts me is that these people give back to the Earth what they take out. That's something we've got to learn to do."

Kay's expressed ecological ideology collides directly with his actions that has, at times, gained him criticism, particularly in the U.K. Kay and fellow band member, Toby Graffety-Smith have been able to satisfy their

For the Record . . .

Members include **Sola Akingbola**, percussion; **Wallis Buchanan**, didgeridoo; **Darren Galea** (a.k.a. DJD Zire), turntables; **Toby Graffety-Smith**, keyboards; **Simon Katz**, guitar; **Jason** "Jay" **Kay** (born December 30, 1969, Stretford, England), vocals; **Derrick McKenzie** (Born March 27, 1962, Islington, England), drums; **Adrian Revell**, flute and saxophone; **Winston Rollins**, trombone; **Martin Shaw**, trumpet; **Stuart Zender**, bass guitar. Former members include **Nick Van Gelder**, drummer (1993).

Group formed c. 1992 in the United Kingdom; released single "When You Gonna Learn?" on independent label, Acid Jazz, 1992. Signed eight-record deal with Sony Music Entertainment, Inc., under WORK Group, 1992. Released *Emergency on Planet Earth* (Sony, 1993), *The Return of the Space Cowboy* (Sony, 1994), *Travelling without Moving* (Sony, 1996).

Awards: MTV Video Music Awards: Best Video, Best Special Effects, Best Cinematography, and Breakthrough Video for "Virtual Insanity," Video of the Year 1997 Music Video Production Association Awards for "Virtual Insanity," 1997, Grammy Award, for Best Pop Performance by a Duo or Group with Vocal, 1998.

Addresses: *Record company*—Sony Music Entertainment, Inc., WORK Label, Suite 2788, 550 Madison Avenue, New York, NY 10022-3211.

fetishes for expensive, gas guzzling, luxury cars, due to the band's financial success. Kay owns a Lamborghini, two Mercedes, two BMW's, three Ferraris, an Aston Martin, and a Ducati mini-motorcycle. Kay admits that this can be a conflict for him, at least in his music writing. Kay says, that he agonized about using automobiles as the theme in the 1996 release, *Travelling without Moving.* He spoke about this conflict in an online interview at www.jamiroquai.co.uk/, "I love speed, you see. I was a bit worried about what people would say bearing in mind that the first album was about the environment ... Just because I love to drive a fast car, that doesn't mean I believe in chopping trees down."

Their first album released in 1993, *Emergency on Planet Earth,* clearly reflected their socially conscious themes. The lyrics raise serious questions about the state of the planet, racism, and about the continuing arms race by national governments. *Emergency* hit number one on best-seller charts in Britain in 1993, and Jamiroquai became the best selling British debut band for that year. Kay's soulful tenor voice reminiscent of Stevie Wonder backed up with jazzed up rhythm got the music world's attention.

Emergency received mixed reviews in the United States. Reviews found online at http://www.xsite.net, originating from newspapers all over the United States were a mixed bag. Many critics noted resemblances to other soulful sounding artists including Stevie Wonder and Marvin Gaye. One music critic from the *Daily Telegraph,* called Jamiroquai "the funkiest thing this side of James Brown's underpants." Kay used trite phrases like "you blow my mind," and "no more wars," and turned them into inspired pieces. However some critics panned *Emergency* as just more of the same. *Washington Post* reviewer Mark Jenkins wrote that "Jamiroquai's sound is about as revolutionary as a nonreturnable bottle of Pepsi." A reviewer from the *Sunday Times* seemed relieved that the band finally "gets to the heart of the matter." The same reviewer reminds us to "take the political themes in the lyrics with a grain of salt. It's more fun that way." Although Kay's sound may be reminiscent of Stevie Wonder, one reviewer noted, "Stevie Wonder never used a didgeridoo in his recordings."

Far from Extinction

Return of the Space Cowboy, released in 1995, was further proof that their sound had staying power. In Great Britain, the album went platinum. *Return* is a little lighter on political and environmental themes and the reviews were generally favorable. The instrumental sound of Jamiroquai is highly reminiscent of the 1970s with its strong brass influence. The *Washington Post's* Jenkins notes the strong resemblance of *Return* to Blood, Sweat, and Tears' "Spinning Wheel." Josef Woodard of *Entertainment Weekly* seems to enjoy a remembrance of the 1970s sound and notes the influence of Sly Stone. Other critics also point out resemblances to artists and bands of the 1970s and criticize *Return* for lack of originality. Some of the technology used in producing Jamiroquai's sound has been referred to in reviews as "retro"; this contributes to criticism of the group as sounding like a blast from the past.

Jamiroquai's third album, *Travelling without Moving,* released in 1996 has earned the band world wide popularity, going triple platinum in the U.K. and gold in the U.S. *Travelling* contains serious themes that Kay talked about in an online interview at www.jamiroquai.co.uk. Kay said that the album is about "finding technical ways to balance our technology and nature." And, yes it is about a subject near and dear to Kay's heart, cars. *Travelling* was written by the group and produced by Kay with Al Stone. The album shows the level of maturation the band has developed, and sharpens their musical and lyrical style into clearer focus. "Virtual Insanity," a top three hit in the U.K., starts off the album and showcases what Jamiroquai's all about: wonderful melodies and kinda-makes-me think-lyrics. Some topics in lyrics include drugs in "High Times," and the always popular theme of love in "Everyday" with a R & B twist. Switching gears, "Driftin Along" provides us with a reggae sound and "Cosmic Girl," gives us a taste of disco. Jamiroquai's trademark instrument, the didgeridoo, returns for two of the tracks including "Didjerma."

Although *Travelling without Moving* has, without a doubt gained the group worldwide notice, some critics have criticized it as being too mainstream. However, *People* feels Jamiroquai has remained true to it's vision and has created "some unabashedly Wonder-ful music." Hearing Jamiroquai seems to elicit strong feelings in either direction, people seem to either love them or hate them. They have a great variety of musical styles and sounds, from horn sections with jazz elements to disco rhythms. From their early days on the club scene, their music gained acclaim for its boogie-ability. People enjoyed dancing to the beats, regardless of the style or tempo. Walking away with four awards from the MTV Video Music Awards in New York in September of 1997, for their music video of "Virtual Insanity," seems to have solidified the band's place, musically speaking. Win-

ning the awards resulted in a surge of album sales in the U.S. and added further name recognition to Jamiroquai.

Selected discography

Emergency on Planet Earth, Sony Music, 1993.
Return of the Space Cowboy, Sony Music, 1994.
Travelling without Moving, Sony Music, 1996.

Sources

Books

Larkin, Colin, editor. *The Guinness Encyclopedia of Popular Music,* Guinness Publishing, 1995.

Periodicals

Billboard, May 10, 1997, p.72.
Newsweek, August 4, 1997, p.66.
People, January 20, 1997, p. 25.
Rolling Stone, March 20, 1997, p. 104.
Seventeen, October 1993, p. 101.

Online

http://www.hrc.wmin.ac.uk/J'sJoint/
http://www.jamiroquai.co.uk/
http://www.music.sony.com/
http://www.netlink.co.uk/
www.sony.com/Music/ArtistInfo/Jamiroquai
http://xsite.net/~kara/archive

—*Debra Reilly*

Journey

Rock group

One of the most popular bands of the 1980s, Journey blended power rock rhythms with sentimental balladry. Though often dismissed by critics as purveyors of formulaic and bland "corporate rock," millions of record buyers found Journey's expert musicianship and emotional love songs a refreshing relief from the ultra-hipness that characterized so many rock bands of the time. "The group provided a service—a refuge for those wary of the cool detachment of new wave. Journey's keep-on-believing anthems spoke to more people than any ironic David Byrne lyric did," David Browne wrote in *Entertainment Weekly*.

Selling more than 15 million records in the United States, Journey had 17 top 40 singles between 1978 and 1986, including "Faithfully," and "Don't Stop Believin'." Joel Selvin, pop music critic for the *San Francisco Chronicle,* called Journey's "Open Arms," the "track that probably did more to invent the modern rock power ballad than any other single."

Artistic and personal differences led to Journey's breakup in early 1987, when the band was still enjoying tremendous success. After nearly a decade apart, Journey reunited to write and record an album of new material, *Trial by Fire.* Released in October 1996, the album offered Journey's hallmark "power pop" and quickly moved into the top ten. "One of the things we've always known is that there are certain musical directions that fit what (our) chemistry is about. We're going to sink of swim being what we are and not by trying to reinvent ourselves and not by trying to be the flavor of the month," Journey's lead singer Steve Perry explained to Melinda Newman of *Billboard* magazine.

Journey was founded in San Francisco in 1973 by Walter "Herbie" Herbert, a former road manager for the band Santana. "I wanted to orchestrate another major group in the San Francisco tradition of Jefferson Airplane, Santana or Sly and the Family Stone," Herbert told *People* in 1981. Calling themselves the Golden Gate Rhythm Section, Herbert's band initially consisted of bassist Ross Valory and keyboardist Gregg Rolie, both ex-Santana members, guitarist George Tickner, and drummer Prairie Prince. Their first gigs were anonymous back-up work for other groups passing through the Bay Area. In December 1973, sporting the new name Journey, the band made its debut at San Francisco's Winterland Ballroom.

The first of Journey's many personnel changes came in early 1974 when drummer Prince decided to return to his old band, The Tubes. He was replaced by English-born Aynsley Dunbar who had worked with Frank Zappa, Jeff Beck, and John Mayall. Playing a type of instrumentally oriented jazz-rock fusion, Journey quickly became a favorite in the San Francisco area via club dates and local airplay of their demonstration records. In the autumn of 1974, Journey signed a contract with Columbia Records. Their first album, *Journey,* was released in 1975 and sold about 100,000 copies, largely to Bay Area fans and music industry insiders familiar with the instrumental skills of the individual band members. After completion of the first album, Journey embarked on a lengthy U.S. tour in order to increase its nationwide visibility. After the tour, Tickner left the band to attend medical school. He was not replaced and Journey continued with a single guitarist. Two more albums—*Look into the Future,* 1975, and *Next,* 1977—enjoyed larger but still modest sales.

Herbert, who remained the band's manager and guiding force in the 1970s and 1980s, decided Journey would need an overhauling in order to attract a larger following. "Originally, the band was very self-indulgent. A lot of long solo excursions were created specifically to set up Neal Schon for his guitar statements," Herbert told Ben Fong-Torres of *Rolling Stone* in 1980. Herbert engineered a shift away from instrumental numbers toward vocals. Up to this point, vocalist duties were handled by Gregg Rolie, who, as a member of Santana, had sung such hits as "Black Magic Woman."

In the summer of 1977, Robert Fleischmann, a Denver-based singer recruited by Columbia Records joined the band for its tour as the opening act for Emerson, Lake, and Palmer. Fleischmann proved adequate, but unexciting. He was soon fired and replaced by Steve Perry, who had sung with the defunct California band Alien Project. Perry's soaring tenor voice, solid songwriting talent, and exuberant on-stage personality were just what Journey needed to smooth out its rough edges. The band's first album with Perry, *Infinity,* was released in the spring of 1978 and was notably more melodic than earlier Journey efforts. The album was supported with a grueling 171 city tour of North America and Europe, Journey's first as a headlining act. The work paid off and *Infinity* went to number 23 on the U.S. charts. Three singles from the album—"Wheel in the Sky," "Anytime," and "Lights"—were minor hits.

Travelling Some Rough Roads

During the tour problems developed with drummer Dunbar, who was finding it difficult to adapt his free-wheeling playing style to Journey's tighter new material. "He was bored and frustrated with the music," bassist Valory said of Dunbar to *People* in 1981. Dunbar left the band on bad terms in October 1978 and was replaced by Steve Smith, drummer for Montrose, the opening act of Journey's tour. Dunbar later joined Jefferson Starship. From its beginning, Journey had considered itself a family, with band members, manager, road crew, and other support staff integral parts of a unit. Though Dunbar was considered the more accomplished drummer, Smith fit in better with the band's musical and personal attitude. "The problem with Aynsley was that he was anything but a team player. He was doing anything and everything to look great. And he did," Herbert told *Rolling Stone* in 1980. Team spirit was a Journey fundamental. Early on the band and its staff incorporated themselves as Nightmare, Inc. and plowed their earnings back into lights, sound equipment, and trucks, a strategy which enabled them to operate with debt-free independence. Having signed with Columbia Records as a corporation, Journey enjoyed a great deal of control over its albums, down to the choice of artwork, and was free to make endorsement and publicity deals without the approval of Columbia. Another Journey rule was no hard drugs; band members steered clear of heroin, cocaine, and amphetamines.

Journey continued on an upward spiral with the albums *Evolution* (1979) and *Departure* (1980). Songs from the albums, including "Lovin', Touchin', Squeezin'," and "Any Way You Want It," broke into the top 20. A double live album, *Captured* (1980), gave the band its fourth million selling album. A hectic schedule of touring, writing, and recording was too much for keyboardist Gregg Rolie and he left Journey in the spring of 1981. "I'd been on the road for 15 years and it was time to smell the roses," Rolie told *People*. Rolie was replaced by Jonathan Cain, formerly of The Babys.

Escape to the Top

Journey hit the top of the charts in September 1981 with *Escape*, which remained in the top 20 album count for more than a year and eventually sold over nine million copies. The album featured the popular singles "Who's Crying Now?" "Don't Stop Believin'," and the million-selling "Open Arms." Ticket demand put Journey concerts into stadium venues and in 1982, the band pioneered the use of giant video screens to enable fans to see the action on stage. "Our manager had a company put together with us and we sorta guinea pigged that whole system. That was when video was kinda going crazy and everybody was spending money making videos, we thought that the people who deserved to see us were the people that came to our shows," Jonathan Cain said in a 1996 interview with an Atlanta radio station, Star 94.

Though Journey had always prided itself on an easygoing, cooperative attitude, success began to take its toll and egos expanded. The bickering band was able to put together the 1983 album, *Frontiers,* was only kept out of the number one spot on the U.S. charts by Michael Jackson's phenomenal *Thriller.* Singles were "Separate Ways (Worlds Apart)," "Faithfully," and "Send Her My Love."

After an enormously successful U.S. tour with Bryan Adams as an opening act, Journey members decided to take some time off to work on independent projects. The most notable of these projects was lead singer Steve Perry's *Street Talk,* a top selling album of 1984. Perry's music, including the hit singles "Oh, Sherrie" and "Foolish Heart," were hard to distinguish from Journey songs and indicated that the public wanted more Journey.

Journey regrouped in late 1984 to commence work on another album but personality conflicts made progress slow. After several marginally productive months, Smith and Valory were fired from the band, leaving Perry, Schon, and Cain as a three-man operation working with session musicians. Finally released in May 1986, the *Raised on Radio* album was yet another success. Hit singles were "Be Good to Yourself," "Suzanne," "Girl Can't Help It," and "I'll Be Alright Without You."

Saying Goodbye (For Now)

Despite continuing success, the members of Journey knew the end was near. After completing a *Raised on Radio* promotional tour in February 1987, the band went its separate ways. "The constant touring had made me crazy. The road is an addiction, and the audience is the ultimate narcotic. We had been together 10 years, and it was difficult to leave. But I wanted to jump off the merry-go-round before the band drove itself into the ground," Perry told *USA Today* in 1996. Neal Schon said in the Star 94 interview that "We got burned out, we sorta reached the end of the rope ... when you reach that point and its not fun anymore it's time to give it a rest."

In 1988, Columbia released an extremely popular album of Journey's greatest hits. According to *USA Today,* the greatest hits album still sells 500,000 copies annually. Meanwhile, former Journey members continued to work in the music industry. Cain and Schon formed the band Bad English with John Waite who had been with Cain in The Babys. Bad English recorded two albums and had hit single with "When I See You Smile" in 1989. Schon also recorded a number of instrumental solo albums, including *Beyond the Thunder* in 1995 and *Late Nite* in 1989. Steve Perry released a second solo album, *For the Love of Strange Medicine* in 1994.

Coming Back for More

During a promotional tour for his album, Perry, who had not toured with his earlier solo effort, discovered that he enjoyed being a frontman for a band more than being a solo performer. He also noticed the strong audience reaction to the Journey songs included in his act. A severe respiratory problem caused Perry to cut short his tour. While recuperating at home in the Bay Area, Perry was contacted by Columbia Records executives inquiring about the possibility of a Journey reformation. Columbia's interest prompted Perry to phone Cain and the two met at a local coffee shop. "I hadn't talked to him in years ... I said 'Just listen man, before it's too late. For reasons God only knows, there's a lot of people out there who love us, and I saw some of them not too long ago. Maybe it's time to try again'," Perry told *Billboard*.

Perry and Cain then contacted Schon and the three got together to see if they could still write songs as a team.

They were not interested in reforming only to revive their old hits. "We figured that if the songs came together and were as honest as the early ones, then we'd have a reason to make an album. We didn't want to resurrect a dream just to put it on life support," Perry told *USA Today*.

In mid-1995, after Perry, Cain, and Schon came up with some song ideas, Smith and Valory returned to the Journey fold and work commenced on a new album. Tempers occasionally flared in the Marin County, California, studio where the album was recorded but a mellow attitude generally prevailed. Cain told Star 94 that the band members had learned from their past difficulties not to "take a lot of stuff for granted first of all ... Don't take your friendship for granted. If you got something on your mind, come right out with it. It's better to hit people straight on with it. We used to brood, go away and not really confront each other a lot of times." While putting together the new album, Journey hired a new manger, Irving Azoff, who had engineered the successful reunion of The Eagles. "He's done an incredible job with The Eagles, but that didn't have a lot to do with why we picked him. It was more because we all felt overwhelmingly comfortable about working with him," Perry told *Billboard*.

The reunited Journey released *Trial by Fire* in October 1996. As in the past, most critics sneered at or gave begrudging praise to Journey's work but the public responded enthusiastically. The new album quickly went to the number three spot on the U.S. charts, which is not surprising since Journey had retained many of its old fans. The band's fan club, Journey Force, had remained active until 1993, six years after Journey itself had broken up, and a core of diehard followers still puts out a monthly newsletter called *Faithful Ones News*. Also, frequent airplay of Journey songs on adult oriented or "classic" rock radio stations over the years had provided the band with new fans.

Some commentators have attributed the success of the returned Journey to disenchantment with tougher-edged grunge and "alternative" sounds. "Is it just a coincidence that ten years later Journey is back—and selling millions of records alongside Celine Dion, Toni Braxton, Kenny G and other decidedly non-grunge acts—as alternative music slips off the charts and back into relative obscurity?" wrote Lee-Anne Goodman of the *Calgary Herald*. Journey's Schon agrees, telling

Goodman—"I think people are ready for anything that's going to lighten their lives, take some of the darkness out of it, put a smile on their face and not make them want to run out and shoot up heroin."

Selected discography

Albums; on Columbia label

Journey, 1975.
Look to the Future, 1976.
Next, 1977.
Infinity, 1978.
Evolution, 1979.
In the Beginning, 1980.
Departure, 1980.
Captured, 1981.
Escape, 1981.
Frontiers, 1983.
Raised on Radio, 1986.
Greatest Hits, 1988.
Time 3, 1993.
Trial by Fire, 1996.

Sources

Books

Rees, Dafydd, and Luke Crampton. *The Encyclopedia of Rock Stars*. New York: Dorling Kindersley, 1996.

Periodicals

Billboard, October 5, 1996.
Calgary Herald, February 21, 1997.
Entertainment Weekly, October 25, 1996, p.114.
People, October 12, 1981, p.141-145; November 18, 1996, p.25.
Rolling Stone, June 1, 1978, p.22; June 12, 1980. p.8-10.
San Francisco Chronicle, December 13, 1992, p.53.
St. Louis Post-Dispatch, January 17, 1997.
USA Today, November 12, 1996.

Online

www.journey.simplenet.com/journey

—Mary Kalfatovic

Stan Kenton

Jazz pianist, arranger, composer

In 1996, 17 years after the bandleader's death, Scott Yanow of the *All-Music Guide to Jazz,* stated, "There have been few jazz musicians as consistently controversial as Stan Kenton." Some critics have claimed that Kenton expanded the horizons of jazz music, while others considered him pretentious and more interested in overwhelming listeners with volume and power than with creating works of musical substance. He managed to sustain a number of large-scale bands during his more than 35 years of active performing, despite his willingness to stray from proven formulas. "The economics of maintaining a big band for nearly 40 years without pandering to fashion indicated Stan Kenton's great organizational skills, as well as great artistic conviction," noted the *Harmony Illustrated Encyclopedia of Jazz.*

Kenton continually experimented with the big band format, dissolving his bands and reforming new ones that attempted to set new standards in jazz music. Throughout his career he had a knack for recognizing and nurturing new talent, and his sidemen over the years represented an all-star lineup of jazz greats. In fact, J. Bradford Robinson, in his profile of the bandleader in *The New Grove Dictionary of Jazz,* asserted that Kenton's "own considerable talents as arranger and pianist were soon overshadowed by those of his superior sidemen and staff arrangers." Among those who made their way through the Kenton assembly line included Anita O'Day, June Christy, Lee Konitz, Art Pepper, Stan Getz, Zoot Sims, Maynard Ferguson, Kai Winding, Shelly Manne, and Laurindo Almeida.

Stanley Newcomb Kenton began taking piano lessons from his mother, Stella Kenton, after she bought a used upright piano. He was ten years old at the time and two years started taking lessons with a private teacher. After hearing his musician cousins, Billy and Arthur Kenton, play jazz a few years later, he fell in love with the music and decided to pursue a career in it. "From the time I was fourteen years old, I was all music," he told Carole Easton in *Straight Ahead: The Story of Stan Kenton.* "Nothing else ever entered my head." As a teenager Kenton took lessons in jazz piano form an organist at a local theater, and he also learned to play a number of wind instruments. By then he was immersing himself in the latest releases of artists such as George Gershwin, Earl "Fatha" Hines, Benny Carter, and Louis Armstrong. He formed a musical group called The Beltones and performed at school dances, parties, and local clubs.

After graduating form high school in 1930, the music-crazy Kenton scraped out a living as a musician for five dollars a night playing speakeasies and gambling halls

Born Stanley Newcomb Kenton on December 15, 1911, in Wichita, KS; died August 25, 1979, in Hollywood, CA; married three times; three children.

Began taking piano lessons from mother, 1922; formed group in high school called The Belltones; played in speakeasies and other clubs; performed with Everett Hoagland's band, 1930s; played with dance bands of Vido Musso and Gus Arnheim, 1938–39; studied music theory with Charles Dalmores, late 1930s; landed studio jobs in Hollywood, late 1930s; became pianist and assistant conductor for pit band in Hollywood, CA, 1939; formed Artistry in Rhythm Orchestra, 1940; became well-known as bandleader through radio broadcasts and nationwide touring, 1940s; formed Progressive Jazz Band, 1947; assembled Innovations in Modern Music Orchestra, 1950; went on first European tour with band, 1953; organized "A Festival of Modern American Jazz" program, 1954; hosted television show called *Music '55,* 1955; bought Rendezvous Ballroom as home base for his band, 1957; established his first university jazz clinics at Indiana University and Michigan State University, 1959; set up his own promotional organization called The Creative World of Stan Kenton, 1960; formed New Era in Modern Music Orchestra, 1961; created Neophonic Orchestra, 1965; served as guest conductor of Danish Radio Orchestra, Copenhagen, Denmark, 1966; organized clinic for music students at University of Redlands, CA, 1966; produced *The Crusade for Jazz,* a television special, 1968; produced *The Substance of Jazz,* a film designed for educators, 1969; began marketing his own records on his Creative World label, 1970; toured Europe and Japan with his band, 1972–75.

Awards: Best Big Band, *Down Beat,* 1947, 1948; elected to *Down Beat* Music Hall of Fame, 1954; Grammy Award, *Stan Kenton's West Side Story,* 1961; Grammy Award, *Adventures in Jazz,* 1962; Jazz Band of the Year, Society for the Appreciation of Big Bands, 1974; honorary doctorates: Villanova University, Drury College, and University of Redlands, CA.

in San Diego and Las Vegas. His talent began to develop after he joined Everett Hoagland's band, and in the late 1930s he also tickled the ivories in the dance bands of Vido Musso and Gus Arnheim. By this time he was already developing a reputation as a skilled arranger, not to mention a cheerleader who could motivate other musicians to excel. In 1939 Kenton found himself in Hollywood as pianist and assistant conductor for the pit band at Earl Carroll's Vanities theater. A year later he formed his first band, which in 1941 became known as the Artistry in Rhythm Orchestra.

Developed Reputation for Volume

Manned mostly by young, unknown musicians, the Artistry in Rhythm Orchestra became a hit at the Rendezvous Ballroom in Balboa, California. From there Kenton's band increased its popularity with a five-week stint at the Hollywood Palladium. "The group quickly gained notice for its thick, brassy voicings, staccato articulation and sheer volume," remarked Len Lyons and Don Perlo about this band in *Jazz Portraits.* By this time, Kenton was composing his own songs, but they were the least popular of his band's repertoire. While the public received the Artistry in Rhythm Orchestra favorably, jazz critics for the most part did not care for his music, saying his band was too loud, too structured, and without nuance.

Kenton's band became a mainstay on the music scene during the 1940s through steady touring and radio broadcasts. One of its first big hits was "Eager Beaver," a song composed by Kenton that became his band's theme song. He also scored big with "Tampico," "And Her Tears Flowed Like Wine," which featured a vocal by Anita O'Day, and "Across the Alley from the Alamo," sung by June Christy. During the 1940s Kenton helped launch the career of saxophonist Stan Getz , who signed on with the band in 1943 at the age of 16. Two years later he brought in trombonist Kai Winding, trumpeter Ray Wetzel, and bassist Eddie Safranski.

To pursue new types of music other than the jazz standards of the day, Kenton broke up his band and formed the Progressive Jazz Band in 1947. Featuring arrangements by Pete Rugolo that favored heavy brass, and performers such as drummer Shelly Manne, alto saxophonist Art Pepper, guitarist Laurindo Almeida, tenor saxophonist Bob Cooper, and trombonist Milt Bernhart, his new band provoked strong reactions both pro and con. *Down Beat* magazine named the group Best Big Band in 1947 and 1948, but some critics viewed his music unfavorably. "The sheer volume of the music, the screaming trumpet section, immensely structured works that slam in by section on schedule, intimidated the critics who declared Kenton's music empty and pretentious," claimed *The Harmony Illustrated Encyclopedia of Jazz.*

Despite its popularity, Kenton's Progressive Jazz Band broke up in 1948 because the bandleader was pushed to exhaustion by heavy touring. After emerging from temporary retirement, Kenton struck out in yet another musical direction with his Innovations in Modern Music Orchestra. This 43-piece band featured a 16-piece string section that helped Kenton fulfill his desire to merge jazz and classical styles. He was aided in his quest by a lineup of top musicians that included Bud Shank on flute and sax, Pepper, and trumpeters Shorty Rogers, Chico Alvarez, Buddy Childers, and Maynard Ferguson. Now delving into the avant garde, Kenton began performing works by composer Bob Graetinger, whose music was known for its dissonance. Many critics labeled the band as no more than a big band trying to do modern classical music. They largely panned the band's performance of Graetinger's *City of Glass* in 1948, which in a 1993 review by Yanow was referred to as "avant-garde music that still sounds futuristic 45 years later."

In the early 1950s Kenton made an about face by focusing on swing music. He also put together smaller bands and toured with singers like Nat King Cole and Sarah Vaughn. He was a big hit on his European tour in 1953, and later returned there in 1956. In 1952 he formed the first of his new series of more traditional big-band groups called the New Concepts in Artistry and Rhythm Orchestra. "Performing dance tunes, driving modern jazz, and Afro-Cuban-influenced pieces, these groups represent Kenton's most important style and repertory of big-band music," according to *Jazz Portraits*. Among Kenton's most noteworthy recordings during the 1950s were 1954's *The Kenton Era* and 1956's *Cuban Fire*. Kenton "creates a warm ambiance that contrasts his lush, Ellingtonian orchestral charts with his spare, evocative piano lines," noted *Billboard* in its review of a reissue of the 1958 album *The Ballad Style of Stan Kenton*.

Established First College Jazz Clinics

By 1957 Kenton was fed up with touring, which prompted him to buy the Rendezvous Ballroom as a permanent home base for his band. Then he found himself on the road again within a few months, after discovering he could not attract big enough crowds in the same location to make it pay. The versatile Kenton broadened his career once again in 1959 when he founded the first of his university "jazz clinics," at Indiana University and Michigan State University. These clinics, which he later set up in other schools as well, proved to be highly fertile training grounds, and Kenton proved to have a sharp eye for hot new talent.

As rock 'n' roll eroded the popularity of his band in the early 1960s, Kenton branched out again with his New Era in Modern Music Orchestra. This 23-piece ensemble included a mellophonium, a cross between a trumpet and trombone that produced a sound similar to a French horn. Unlike his bands of the past, this Kenton group relied mostly on young performers rather than highly paid established stars. The band recorded eleven albums during its two-year history and received much acclaim for its recordings of the sound track for *West Side Story* and another album called *Adventures in Jazz*.

Kenton's next band was the highly experimental Neophonic Orchestra, which featured 14 brass instrumentalists among its 28 players. The bandleader's high visibility and popularity at this time attracted some top Hollywood musicians and jazz-oriented composers, as well instrumentalists who played with his previous bands. Many critics considered this band to be Kenton's creative peak. As was pointed out in the *Christian Science Monitor* in 1966, "One gets the feeling that this is what Stan Kenton has been working up to all his musical life ... music that has integrity, individuality, and modernity, without bogging down in atonality, electronic gimmicks, and self-conscious abstractions." In an ironic shift from his past history of popular acceptance and critical derision, the Neophonic Orchestra was championed by the critics but lost money. Financial setbacks forced Kenton to bolster his income by performing with a pickup band, recording albums, and making guest spots on television during the late 1960s.

Active Until Death

In the 1970s Kenton devoted more attention to the educational and business ends of his music. By 1975 he was conducting over 100 music clinics a year, as well as four week-long summer clinics on college campuses. At this time he was also distributing various educational materials and stage-band charts, as well as his own albums, with his Creative World company. Still active on the performance circuit with a new band formed in 1970, Kenton toured Europe and Japan during the early and mid 1970s. Various illnesses and hospitalizations slowed him down somewhat, including an aneurysm in 1972, and a cerebral hemorrhage in 1977, before he passed away in 1979. To his dying day he remained highly critical of country music, as well as rock 'n' roll, and had little respect for the musical tastes of people in general. "Sophistication only exists in one or two percent of the masses," he told Thomas Lyles in an interview for the *Washington Star* in 1975. "And that two percent is the two percent that has to support jazz, classical music and the arts. The masses can't communicate with art."

Selected discography

City of Glass, Capitol, 1947.
Innovations in Modern Music, Capitol, 1950.
New Concepts of Artistry in Rhythm, Capitol, 1952.
The Ballad Style of Stan Kenton, Capitol, 1958.
Mellophonium Moods, Status, 1962.
Kenton '76, Creative World, 1975.

Sources

Books

Case, Brian, and Stann Britt, revised and updated by Chrissie Murray, *The Harmony Illustrated Encyclopedia of Jazz, Third Edition,* Harmony Books, p. 106.
Cook, Richard, and Brian Morton, *The Penguin Guide to Jazz on CD, LP, and Cassette,* Penguin Books, 1992, pp. 610–614.

Easton, Carole, *Straight Ahead: The Story of Stan Kenton,* Morrow, 1973.
Erlewine, Michael, Vladimir Bogdanov, Chris Woodstra, and Scott Yanow, *All Music Guide to Jazz, Second Edition,* Miller Freeman Books, 1996, pp. 424–430.
Feather, Leonard, and Ira Gitler, *The Encyclopedia of Jazz in the Seventies,* Horizon Press, 1976, pp. 211–212.
Kernfeld, Barry, editor, *The New Grove Dictionary of Jazz, Volume One,* Macmillan, 1988, p. 648.
Larkin, Colin, editor, *The Guinness Encyclopedia of Popular Music, Volume 3,* Guinness Publishing, 1995, pp. 2281–2282.
Lyons, Len, and Don Perlo, *Jazz Portraits: The Lives and Music of the Jazz Masters,* William Morrow, 1989, pp. 322–324.

Periodicals

Billboard, August 16, 1997, p. 61.
Christian Science Monitor, April 22, 1966.
Stereo Review, December 1, 1996, p. 104.
Washington Star, July 5, 1975.

—*Ed Decker*

Last Poets

Rap band

The roots of rap music can be traced back to the late 1960s. Militant messages decrying the state and society of African-Americans were first vocalized, commented on, and critiqued by the Last Poets—grandfathers of the genre and purveyors of sharp, insightful street poetry, which, when combined with African percussive rhythms, laid the groundwork for future rap artists.

The creative collective known as the Last Poets was formed in Harlem, New York on May 19, 1968—the day known as Malcolm X Day, so named for the slain founder of the Organization of African-American Unity. According to David Mills of the *Washington Post,* three young African-American poets, David Nelson, Gylan Kain, and Abiodun Oyewole, were, "invited to share some culturally correct poetry at a Malcolm X commemoration in Mount Morris Park (now Marcus Garvey Park)." Despite the fact that the trio had no idea about what to do, they took to the stage as the audience chanted the call to arms used by Howard University student protesters when they overran their campus in March 1968. In recounting the Last Poets first performance, Oyewole commented to Mills, "I thought that [the chant] was so hip. I never heard nothing like that on television. So we sang that as we went on stage. Had the entire park singing that. From that moment on, we got gigs."

Mills stated that the Last Poets remained nameless until Nelson found inspiration in the last verse of a poem by William Kgositsile: "When the moment hatches in time's womb, there will be no more art talk. The only poem you will hear will be the spear point pivoted in the punctured marrow of the villain. Therefore, we are the last poets of the world."

Nelson, who has become a minister in the interim, was the first to leave the Last Poets due to a disagreement over the status of the group. Nelson wanted the group to be a free flowing "collective of writers" while Kain and Oyewole preferred a more fixed line-up. Felipe Luciano, befriended by Kain, joined the group after Nelson quit.

Moved by the Music

A performance at Ohio's Antioch College in early 1969 compelled Umar Bin Hassan to join the Last Poets. Bin Hassan—who was working college security at the time—related to Mills, "[I was] into my black militancy thing.... That was it. It [the performance] just blew my head. I guess I understand what people be getting' from us [because of] what I got from them. It's that feeling, that very spiritual thing that comes out and pulls you in and makes you part of the pain, the diaspora.... That was it. I wanted to become a Last Poet." About six months later, Bin Hassan arrived at East Wind—the headquarters of the Last Poets in Harlem.

Shortly after Bin Hassan joined, a bitter fight broke out between the two remaining original Last Poets, Kain and Oyewole. Kain desired to bring Nelson back into the collective while Oyewole was opposed to the notion. The band split in half and each side performed as the Last Poets. The split foreshadowed the troubles that were to come.

Luciano allied himself with Kain and Nelson while the newest Last Poet, Jalal, joined Bin Hassan and Oyewole. A turf war erupted as the two sides engaged in gang tactics to try to rid themselves of the opposition.

In 1969, Kain, Luciano, and Nelson shot the film *Right On!* The film remained out of the spotlight until the other Last Poets—Bin Hassan, Oyewole and Jalal, released their self-titled debut album on Douglas in early 1970. Although radio stations did not play the album, the underground furor the album caused—especially in the African-American community—was significant enough to allow the Last Poets to be booked into the Apollo Theater for a performance. Not long after the record was recorded, Oyewole left the band.

According to the Official Last Poets' website, Oyewole "traveled to the South where he took Willie Kgositsile's

For the Record . . .

Members include **Don Babatunde** (joined group, 1991), congas; **Umar Bin Hassan** (joined group, Spring 1969, left group, March 1972, rejoined group, May 1973, left group, February 1974), poet; **Sulieman El-Hadi** (joined group, May 1972, died, October 1995), poet; **Jalal** (joined group, June 1969), poet; **Gylan Kain** (left group, Spring 1969), poet; **Felipe Luciano** (joined group, Autumn 1968, left group, Spring 1969), poet; **David Nelson** (left group, Autumn 1968), poet; **Nilija** (died, 1981), congas; **Abiodun Oyewole** (left group, Summer 1969), poet.

Group formed in Harlem, NY, May 19, 1968; released *Last Poets* on Douglas, 1970; *This is Madness*, 1971; *At Last* on Blue Thumb, 1974; signed to Celluloid and released *Delights of the Garden*, 1975; *Jazzoerty*, 1985; *Oh! My People* EP, 1985; *Freedom Express*, 1991; signed to Rykodisc and released *Holy Terror*, 1995; signed to Mouth Almighty and released *Time Has Come*, 1997.

Addresses: *Record company*—Rykodisc, Pickering Wharf Building C, Salem, MA 01970. *Agent*—Peter Schwartz, The Agency Group, 1775 Broadway, Suite 433, New York, NY 10021. *Website*—Official Last Poets website: http:// www.trilliumproductions.com/ tlphp.htm.

message to heart. He put down the pen and picked up a gun, and soon found himself convicted for armed robbery [in 1970]. 'I thought being a Last Poet was being a fake revolutionary,' he said of his motivation at the time, 'I wanted to be a real revolutionary.'" He spent four years in a North Carolina prison for his crime. When Oyewole recounted his experience in jail to Mills he said, "People were coming in the joint talking about the Last Poets and I couldn't even tell them who I was." He had to keep his identity secret for fear of reprisals from the prison guards. Oyewole returned to New York after prison and began work as a creative writing consultant for the New York City School System.

The second Last Poets record, *This is Madness,* was released in 1971. It featured Bin Hassan and Jalal. By the time *At Last* was released on Blue Thumb three years later, Sulieman El- Hadi had joined up with Jalal and Bin Hassan. In the interim, Bin Hassan had quit and

rejoined the band only to quit for good after the release of *At Last.*

Throughout the late 1970s and 1980s, Jalal and El-Hadi recorded as the Last Poets. They signed to Celluloid and released *Delights of the Garden* in 1975 and *Jazzoetry* and the EP *Oh! My People* in 1985. That same year, they wrote the book, *Vibes from the Scribes—* a collection of their writings also released under the name the Last Poets.

Not a Resurrection

In 1990, the founding members of the Last Poets staged a comeback tour that lasted only four dates. El-Hadi dismissed this to Mills when he said, "They put in the papers that the Last Poets are being 'resurrected' when we've been working all this time. My vibe is 'Why didn't you jump on board when it was hard times?'" Jalal and El-Hadi released *Freedom Express* as the Last Poets in 1991. Three years later, the Last Poets played 13 dates on Lollapalooza. They also contributed tracks to the *Panther* film soundtrack and *Stolen Moments: Red, Hot + Cool*—an African American AIDS awareness album.

Holy Terror was released on Rykodisc in 1995 and featured Oyewole and recovered crack cocaine addict Bin Hassan as the Last Poets. Guest artists on *Holy Terror* included former Parliament Funkadelic members Bootsy Collins and George Clinton as well as Grand Master Melle Mel. In October of that year, El-Hadi died.

The next year, Oyewole and Bin Hassan collaborated again, although this time it was on a book titled *On a Mission: Selected Poems and a History of the Last Poets.* The Last Poets, Bin Hassan and Oyewole, signed to Mouth Almighty Records in 1997 and released *Time Has Come.*

Commenting on the place of the Last Poets in the rap pantheon, Oyewole said in the Official Last Poets website, "We're no more 'godfathers of the spoken word' than the man in the moon; it comes in a package from the motherland. But we accept that there is work out there that we can do. People need to see a focal point, a beacon, and we don't have no problem with shining, we don't walk away from the fight."

Selected discography

Last Poets, Douglas, 1970.
This is Madness, Douglas, 1971.

At Last, Blue Thumb, 1974.
Delights of the Garden, Celluloid, 1975.
Jazzoetry, Celluloid, 1985.
Oh! My People (EP), Celluloid, 1985.
Freedom Express, Celluloid, 1991.
(Contributor) *Panther* (soundtrack), Mercury, 1995.
(Contributor) *Stolen Moments: Red, Hot + Cool,* (compilation), GRP, 1995.
Holy Terror, Rykodisc, 1995.
Time Has Come, Mouth Almighty, 1997.

Sources

New York Times, September 18, 1996; February 5, 1997.
New York Times Magazine, April 3, 1994.
USA Today, April 30, 1997.
Washington Post, December 12, 1993; June 18, 1997.

—*Mary Alice Adams*

Lightning Seeds

Pop band

The British band the Lightning Seeds is noted for crafting intelligent, hummable pop tunes in a style reminiscent of—and incorporating elements of—the Smiths, the Bee Gees, the Searchers, the Sweet, the Hermits, XTC, the Pet Shop Boys, and World Party. Immensely popular in Britain, where leader Ian Broudie wrote hit songs for television shows and soccer teams, the band was poised for a niche success in the United States in 1997. Rick Shefchik of the *St. Paul Pioneer Press* noted, "The Lightning Seeds are too musical for alternative rock formats, too soft for heavy metal, too new for AOR, and not dancy enough for Top 40 ... nearly every song [on *Dizzy Heights*] sounds like a single, if only singles sounded like this anymore."

When *Jollification* was released in September of 1994, the band consisted only of Ian Broudie of Liverpool; more than 600,000 copies of the album were sold in the U.K. alone and it earned double-platinum selling status. Broudie decided to form a band three months after *Jollification*'s release in order to perform his songs live. In 1994 he formed a full-time band with bass player Martyn Cambell (ex-Rain member), guitarist Paul Hemmings (ex-The La's member), and drummer Chris Sharrock (formerly with the Icicle Works). The singles "Lucky You," "Change," and "Marvellous," attracted new listeners and avid fans, and being able to tour throughout the U.K. and Europe garnered needed publicity and generated favorable reviews for the band.

In 1995 four singles from *Jollification* reached the Top 30 on the U.K. charts; "Change" was their biggest hit, followed by "Marvellous," "Perfect," and the re-released "Lucky You." The band toured Europe with Dodgy, performed at Glastonbury, and appeared on the television shows *Top of the Pops* and *MTV's Most Wanted* in 1995. Broudie also produced the Sleeper's debut album, *Smart* and Salad's single, "Granite Statue," in addition to appearing on Terry Hall's *Rainbow* album in 1995.

The Lightning Seeds were nominated, along with the (winning) band Oasis, for the 1996 Brit Award for Best British Band. They released *Dizzy Heights* in 1996, which reached #11 on the U.K. charts, and the band the Scanners released a dance cover of the Lightning Seeds single "Pure." Contributing to the band's higher profile in the U.S. was the inclusion of their single "You Showed Me," (a Turtles classic), from their *Dizzy Heights* album in the blockbuster Mike Myers comedy, *Austin Powers: International Man of Mystery*.

Broudie Began with Liverpool Punk

Broudie, born in Liverpool in 1959, became a member of the Liverpool-based punk band Big In Japan in 1977. His band members included Holly Johnson, Bill Drummond, and Budgie, later founders of Frankie Goes to Hollywood, The KLF, and Siouxsie & the Banshees respectively. The band stayed together for only a year, and Broudie then joined the Original Mirrors. In 1980 and 1981 Broudie produced the first two Echo & the Bunnymen albums, *Crocodiles* and *Heaven up Here*. He also produced at least three releases by The Fall: *Wah!, Northside,* and *The Primitives*.

In 1983 Broudie and Paul Simpson, formerly of the Wild Swans, founded the duo Care and were signed to the independent label Ghetto. They released two singles, "Flaming Sword," and "My Boyish Days," but met with no commercial success. In 1984 Care released their final single, "Whatever Possessed You," and parted ways. Three years later Broudie produced The Icicle Works' strongest album, *If You Want to Defeat Your Enemy Sing His Song,* and also produced the first and only album released by The Bodines, *Played*.

Broudie founded the Lightning Seeds in 1989 as the band's sole member, using temporary musical help from time to time. He released the singles "Joy" and "Pure" the same year; "Pure" reached #16 on the U.K. charts and eventually became a hit in the United States as well. A year later Broudie released the album *Cloudcuckooland* on the Ghetto label, with Paul Simpson,

Band members include **Ian Broudie** (born 1959, Liverpool, UK, 1959), producer, singer, songwriter, guitarist; **Martyn Campbell** (formerly with Rain), bassist; **Paul Hemmings** (formerly with The La's), guitarist; **Chris Sharrock** (formerly with Icicle Works), drummer.

Band formed, 1989; released *Cloudcuckooland*, 1990, *Sense*, 1992, *Jollification*, 1994, and *Dizzy Heights*, 1996; *Jollification* was released with Ian Broudie as the sole member of the band; more than 600,000 copies of the album were sold in the UK and it earned double-platinum selling status; four singles from *Jollification* reached the Top 30 on the UK charts, band appeared on the television shows *Top of the Pops* and *MTV's Most Wanted*, 1995; "You Showed Me," (a Turtles classic) from *Dizzy Heights* was included in the film *Austin Powers: International Man of Mystery*, 1997.

Addresses: *Record company*—c/o Epic Records, 550 Madison Avenue, New York, NY 10022-3297 (212) 833-7442, fax: (212) 833-5719.

Chris Sharrock, and Ian McNabb as Lightning Seed members. Broudie also produced and played lead guitar on the final Wild Swans album, *Spaceflower* in 1990.

In 1991 Broudie produced *Ray* for Frazier Chorus and co-produced *Jolie* for Bill Pritchard. The Lightning Seeds released *Sense* on the Ghetto/Virgin label in 1992; two of the albums' singles, "Life of Riley" (inspired by Broudie's son), and "Sense" reached the Top 30 on the U.K. charts. "The Life of Riley" soundtracks the goals on the popular U.K. soccer television show, *Match of the Day*, which further ingratiated the band with their U.K. fans. In 1992 Broudie also produced the Dodgy debut release *The Dodgy Album* and the Poppinjays' *Flying Down to Mono Valey* (sic), as well as tracks for Wedding Present's *Hit Parade*. A year later, he produced the debut album by The Frank and Walters, *Trains, Boats, and Planes*, and co-produced Alison Moyet's *Essex* release.

In 1994 the Lightning seeds were signed by Epic Records and the band released its third album, *Jollification*, preceded by the "Lucky You" single. Their subsequent *Dizzy Heights* release in 1996 was lauded in Britain, but American tastes in pop rock didn't always seem to run as sweet. A review of the album in the Baton Rouge *Advocate* declared, "Superbly crafted though it is, the Lightning Seeds' Brit pop may be a bit fluffy for American listeners accustomed to rougher edges." Mark Jenkins of *Time Out New York* wrote, "the album takes honey-glazed melody as its basic concept; a song like 'Sugar Coated Iceberg' is 'Sugar Sugar' gone to college ... At its most cogent, *Dizzy Heights* is all spun-sugar ornament; substance can only spoil the recipe." However, John Kappes of the *Cleveland Plain Dealer* dubbed the Lightning Seeds "New Order without Angst, with considerable sparkle" and Tony Mastrianni of *The Messenger* wrote of *Dizzy Heights*, "A Smashing U.S. release [that] may out pop Oasis for the current classiest British pop band of late."

With their inclusion on the *Austin Powers* soundtrack, their high profile popularity in the U.K., and Broudie's 20 years musical artistry working on their behalf, the Lightning Seeds are poised to invade the American charts. As the band's past experience indicates, it's only a matter of time before the public catches up to them.

Selected discography

Cloudcuckooland, Ghetto Records, 1990.
Sense, Ghetto/Virgin Records, 1992.
Jollification, Epic records, 1994.
Dizzy Heights, Epic Records, 1996.
(Contributor) *Austin Powers: International Man of Mystery* (soundtrack), Hollywood Records, 1997.

Sources

Periodicals

Baton Rouge Advocate, June 13, 1997.
Break, June 18-24, 1997.
Cleveland Plain Dealer, June 27, 1997.
The Messenger, June 17, 1997.
St. Paul Pioneer Press, June 8, 1997.
Time Out New York, July 3-10, 1997.

Online

http://www.epiccenter.com/EpicCenter/docs/ artistbio.qry?artistid=501

—B. Kimberly Taylor

Patty Loveless

Singer

© Ken Settle. Reproduced by permission.

Dubbed "The Heartbreak Kid" in the headline for an April 1997 article by *TV Guide* contributor Dan DeLuca, country singer Patty Loveless has certainly earned her title. Her ability to belt out the sentimental lyrics of her songs in a way that stirs and inspires her listeners is rooted in the fact that, because of her life experiences, she has become all too familiar with tragedy and misery. Nevertheless, her hard-luck past has served as her key to a spectacular present and a promising future, as Loveless's songs continue to top the charts, her albums continue to win, and her personal life continues to become richer and fuller. Loveless, named the Academy of Country Music's female vocalist of the year for both 1996 and 1997, told DeLuca: "I think torch songs and heartache songs reach out to people and say, `Hey, this is life and we've got to live, learn from our mistakes, and continue.' That's what I try to put into the songs. That's what I make music for."

Loveless was born on January 4, 1957 in the Appalachian mining town of Pikeville, Kentucky. Her father, John Ramey, was a coal miner who ultimately died in 1979 of black lung disease, and her mother, Naomi Ramey, was a homemaker who struggled to care for Loveless and her siblings. Loveless began singing at the age of five, primarily to entertain her parents, but by the age of 12 she was singing in her brother Roger's band. Roger introduced his sister to country music stars Dolly Parton and Porter Wagoner in 1971, and Wagoner agreed to give the 14-year-old Loveless a song publishing contract; shortly thereafter the young singer began working with the Wilburn Brothers road show, replacing famous country singer Loretta Lynn, who is Loveless's distant cousin.

It was while working with the road show that Loveless met Wilburn Brothers drummer Terry Lovelace (pronounced "Love-less"). In 1976, despite the disapproval of her family and friends, she married Lovelace and moved to Kings Mountain, North Carolina. In an article by *People* contributor Steve Dougherty, Loveless said that her marriage at the age of 19 was, in part, a rebellion. "So many people had been making decisions for me for so long," she asserted, "I just wanted to feel a sense of freedom." Unfortunately for the singer, her marriage to Lovelace did not turn out as she had planned. Instead, she began abusing drugs and alcohol and singing cover versions of popular rock songs in Charlotte-area night clubs, in order to support the couple's expensive addictions and to make ends meet. Loveless ultimately overcame her substance abuse, and in 1985, she and Lovelace separated. After changing the spelling of her married name to Loveless, she returned to Nashville to try to rekindle her career as a country singer.

For the Record . . .

Born Patty Ramey, January 4, 1957, in Pikeville, KY; daughter of John (a coal miner) and Naomi Ramey; married Terry Lovelace (a drummer), 1976 (divorced, c. 1987); married Emory Gordy, Jr. (a record producer), February, 1989.

Country singer and songwriter, c. 1970—. Singer with brother Roger Ramey's country music band, c. 1970-72; secured a song-publishing contract, c. 1972; worked as the "girl singer" in the Wilburn Brothers road show, c. 1972-76; worked as a singer in night clubs in and near Charlotte, NC, c. 1976-85; moved to Nashville, TN, recorded demo tape with help of Roger Ramey, c. 1985; began recording artist with MCA, 1985-92; recording artist with Sony Music, 1992—.

Awards: Inducted into the Grand Ole Opry, 1988; American Music Award, favorite new country artist, 1989; TNN Music City News Country Award, female artist, 1990; Country Music Association Award, album of the year, 1995, for *When Fallen Angels Fly,* and female vocalist of the year, 1996; Academy of Country Music Awards, both female vocalist of the year, 1996, 1997.

Addresses: *Record company*—Epic, P.O. Box 4450, New York, NY 10101-4450.

With the help of her brother, Roger, Loveless recorded a demo tape and worked to sell it to record labels. While in the elevator on her way to audition for executives at MCA Records, she met Emory Gordy, Jr.—at the time an MCA producer—who would later become her husband. In 1985 Loveless signed with MCA and soon began to receive positive reviews from music critics and industry insiders who predicted that she would one day be a country music superstar. She and Terry Lovelace were divorced in 1987, and in 1988 Loveless was honored as an inductee of the Grand Ole Opry. Loveless's first number one single came in 1989, with "Timber I'm Falling in Love"; that same year she and Gordy were married and she took home an American Music Award for favorite new country artist. Loveless continued to gain notoriety and became increasingly popular among country music fans; in 1990 she was awarded the Tennessee News Network (TNN) Music City News Country Award. The singer's career was most definitely moving her toward stardom.

Between 1990 and 1993 Loveless's luck changed, and she suffered a series of professional and private setbacks. In 1992, in an attempt to revitalize her career, which was in a slump following the sluggish sales of two of her records, Loveless left MCA Records and fired her brother, Roger Ramey, as her manager, a move which caused a rift in their previously close relationship. Before she was able to begin the work of recording fresh material—with her new label, Epic, and her new producer, Emory Gordy—and getting her career back on track, Loveless encountered another personal obstacle; in the fall of 1992 she began experiencing hoarseness, and soon learned that she had developed an aneurysm on her vocal cords. The situation was grave; in order to repair the aneurysm, which left untreated could have destroyed her voice, Loveless had to undergo risky laser surgery, which also had the potential to damage her voice permanently. The surgery was performed on October 21, 1992. After remaining completely silent during November 1992 and recuperating throughout December 1992, Loveless decided to try out her newly-repaired vocal cords and began recording her sixth album in January 1993. The album was an immediate success when it was released in the spring of 1993, and as *People*'s Steve Dougherty termed it, "it was clear that Loveless' luck had turned."

Hidden Past Haunts Luckless Loveless

Unfortunately, despite the promise with which 1993 had begun, Loveless was to suffer yet another personal challenge. In June 1993 a tabloid article with the headline "Patty Loveless Killed Our Baby!" was published. The story, which quoted as its source Loveless's ex-husband Terry Lovelace, revealed that the singer had had an abortion in 1980. Previously no one had known about the terminated pregnancy, and the singer was devastated to have her private misery made public in such a merciless and tasteless manner. In the *People* article by Dougherty Loveless discusses the reasons behind her decision to end her pregnancy, indicating that she was frightened that her excessive drug and alcohol consumption during the pregnancy would have produced birth defects or other health traumas for the fetus, and declaring that "[t]he abortion was a decision Terry and I both made. We swore we would never tell because of the pain it would cause our families." Asserting her belief that her ex-husband was attempting to jeopardize her career out of bitterness, Loveless told Dougherty, "I wish [Lovelace] could just get on. I hope that people will understand and that I'll be forgiven." Lovelace has maintained that he was duped into revealing the secret to the press and never intended to subject Loveless to such public embarrassment.

Loveless managed to overcome her personal crises—even reconciling with her brother Roger—and used her familiarity with tragedy to her advantage, producing emotionally powerful songs that touched the hearts of fans and music experts alike. Matraca Berg, a songwriter who penned Loveless's 1990 hit single "That Kind of Girl" and 1996's "You Can Feel Bad," maintained in an article by *TV Guide*'s Dan DeLuca that Loveless has "a lot of class and she's no puppy. She's lived, and she sings like she believes every word of it. And that's a rare gift." The music industry continued to bestow upon Loveless some of its highest honors. In 1996 Loveless was named female vocalist of the year by both the CMA and the Academy of Country Music (ACM), and in 1997, she repeated as the ACM's female vocalist and was nominated for the CMA's award as well.

Loveless's vocal ability, which DeLuca called "a gut-bucket emotionalism that places her squarely in the sisterhood of soul," has been applauded by critics since the release of her debut album, *Patty Loveless,* in 1985. The praise continued for her 1988 effort, *If My Heart Had Windows* and for *Honky Tonk Angel,* released that same year and containing the number-one single "Timber I'm Falling in Love." Although critics lauded her 1990 album *On down the Line—People*'s Ralph Novak declared that it represented "just plain quality country singing"—as well as 1991's *Up Against My Heart,* neither of the albums managed to reach the level of commercial success Loveless had attained with her previous albums.

Second Chance with Luck and Fame

However, with the 1993 release of *Only What I Feel,* Loveless again joined the ranks of the critically acclaimed and popularly successful country music stars. Recorded after her encounter with laser surgery, the album was hailed by critics as irrefutable evidence that Loveless's voice had come through her ordeal intact. *Billboard*'s Peter Cronin declared that on the album Loveless was "singing with more range, more control, more conviction than ever before, effectively combining powerful delivery with fragile emotion." *Entertainment Weekly* contributor Alanna Nash noted the "restored power and character shadings of Loveless' authentically rural voice," and *People*'s Hal Espen characterized Loveless's vocals as "equal parts Linda Ronstadt and Pasty Cline," referring to her ability to combine elements of traditional country and rock music. The album quickly produced a number-one hit with "Blame It on Your Heart," an up-tempo tune in which Loveless tells her philandering lover that he is respon-

sible for the breakup of their relationship, urging him to "blame it on your lyin', cheatin', cold-dead beatin', two-timin', double-dealin', mean-mistreatin', lovin' heart." *Only What I Feel* also contained the single "How Do I Help You Say Goodbye," a poignant, moving ballad in which Loveless portrays a mother who is attempting to help her child cope first with the loss of a childhood friend, then with the ordeal of a divorce, and finally with the death of the mother herself. That single helped bring *Only What I Feel* out of the sales slump it had entered following the early success of "Blame It on Your Heart," and quickly became a favorite of fans, who expressed how to Loveless the many ways in which the song had touched their hearts. Loveless told *Entertainment Weekly*'s Alanna Nash: "I hope it makes people think.... And to look at death as a long goodbye, and not necessarily something final." The song, backed by the strength of the album on which it appeared,° earned Loveless three 1994 CMA Award nominations for song of the year, album of the year, and female vocalist of the year.

Loveless followed up the success of *Only What I Feel* with her 1994 album, *When Fallen Angels Fly,* which, she told Morris, she wanted "to be one of those that when people listen to it, it gives them some release and hope and encourages them not to give up." The album garnered both critical and popular success, and the single "You Don't Even Know Who I Am" earned Loveless 1996 Grammy Award nominations for best female country vocal performance and best country song. In his review of the album, *Entertainment Weekly*'s Bob Cannon called Loveless's performance "emotionally gripping," and *People*'s Craig Tomashoff offered praise for Loveless's "conversational" tone, contending that "listening to [*When Fallen Angels Fly*] is like chatting with a close friend." Loveless's efforts on *When Fallen Angels Fly* were rewarded in 1995 when she became the first woman artist to win the CMA's Award for album of the year.

Loveless Speaks the Truth

The Trouble with the Truth, Loveless's 1996 album that *People* contributor Craig Tomashoff asserted "builds a bridge" between country, rock, and pop music, was also a critical and popular success, earning Loveless a 1997 Grammy Award nomination for best country album. The album contains the singles "You Can Feel Bad," in which a woman tells her ex-lover that she has successfully gone on with her life after their breakup, and "A Thousand Times a Day," which critics praised for its powerful vocals; *People*'s Tomashoff called Loveless's singing "warm and inviting" and *Entertainment*

Weekly's Nash asserted that Loveless "uses her backwoods soprano—as rural and unassuming as a mountain brook—to best effect" on this song. The album's title song proclaims that the truth has "ruined the taste of the sweetest lies, / Burned through my best alibis," and as *Time* critic Richard Corliss contended: "The way Loveless sings it, the truth ain't pretty, but it sounds as golden as the Gospel."

According to critics, Loveless's 1997 effort, *Long Stretch of Lonesome,* lived up to the high expectations that followed the singer's 1996 CMA and ACM Awards for best female vocalist as well as her 1997 ACM Award for best female vocalist and her 1997 nomination for the CMA's best female vocalist honors. Jeremy Helligar, writing in *Entertainment Weekly,* observed that "Loveless' Appalachian blues sound torchy with hardly a hint of twang," and *People*'s Tomashoff lauded the singer's "silky voice," concluding that "Loveless' words may tell you how tough life can be, but her voice lets you know that things will work out anyway." Interviewed by *TV Guide*'s DeLuca while working on her ninth album, Loveless maintained that she was determined not to let her fame weaken her commitment her singing. Loveless told DeLuca: "I like to keep focused on the work. I'm just looking for songs that stir emotions in me. Because if it moves me, then somebody else is going to be stirred in the same way."

Selected discography

Patty Loveless (includes "After All," "Slow Healing Heart," and "You Are Everything"), MCA,1985, reissued, 1989.
If My Heart Had Windows (includes "A Little Bit on the Lonely Side," "You Saved Me," and "I Can't Get You off My Mind"), MCA, 1988.
Honky Tonk Angel (includes "Timber I'm Falling in Love" and "The Lonely Side of Love"), MCA, 1988.
On down the Line (includes "You Can't Run Away from Your Heart" and "Looking in the Eyes of Love"), MCA, 1990.
Up Against My Heart (includes "I Already Miss You (Like You're Already Gone)" and "If It's the Last Thing I Do"), MCA, 1991.
Greatest Hits, MCA, 1993.
Only What I Feel (includes "Blame It on Your Heart" and "How Can I Help You Say Goodbye"), Epic, 1993.
When Fallen Angels Fly (includes "You Don't Even Know Who I Am" and "I Try to Think about Elvis"), Epic, 1994.
The Trouble with the Truth (includes "You Can Feel Bad" and "A Thousand Times a Day"), Epic, 1996.
Patty Loveless Sings Songs of Love, MCA, 1996.
(With others) *Tin Cup* (soundtrack), Epic, 1996.
Long Stretch of Lonesome (includes "You Don't Seem to Miss Me," a duet with George Jones, and "I Don't Want to Feel Like That"), Epic, 1997.

Sources

Billboard, April 17, 1993, p. 7; April 16, 1994, p. 38; August 13, 1994, p. 1.
Entertainment Weekly, April 23, 1993, p. 56; August 26, 1994, p. 113; September 22, 1995, p. 77; February 2, 1996, p. 56; October 3, 1997, p. 85.
People, June 25, 1990, p. 23; May 3, 1993, p. 25; August 9, 1993, p. 85; September 5, 1994, p. 28; February 12, 1996, p. 27; November 3, 1997, p. 25.
Time, March 11, 1996, p. 71.
TV Guide, April 19, 1997, p. 42.

—Lynn M. Spampinato

Love Spit Love

Alternative rock band

The raspy, darkly unique voice of Richard Butler, former frontman for the Psychedelic Furs, reemerged in the 1990s with Love Spit Love, a band he named after a piece of art he once saw at someone's home. Ironically, both sales and serious appraisal for each of Love Spit Love's releases—their self-titled 1994 debut and 1997's *Trysome Eatone*—have never been able to match the retro appeal that the Furs' music still incites.

Throughout the 1980s, the English-born Butler's scraping voice, combined with the arch, quasi-literary lyrics he penned, gave the Furs its distinctive sound and made them one of the most successful of British post-punk acts in the United States. *Billboard* editor Craig Rosen summed up the Furs' seminal 1980 self-titled debut as a blend of "the rage and raw power of the Sex Pistols with the sophisticated cool of David Bowie and Roxy Music." Butler's talents shone through on a string of alternative gems such as "India" and "Alice's House," but it was for the Furs' more pop-anchored songs like "Love My Way" and "Pretty in Pink" that the band gained mass fandom. They continued to record until the early 1990s; as publicity materials on Love Spit Love reported, eventually Butler "admitted that it had just gotten to the point where he knew what the albums would sound like before they even recorded them."

During the Furs' final tour, Butler struck up a friendship with Richard Fortus, the guitarist for their opening act, Pale Divine. "I got to know Richard over the course of the tour and I had this feeling that a combination of my voice and sense of melody and his versatility and musical strength would be really interesting," Butler recalled in a press release. "When I made the decision to start a new band, he was the first person I called." That moment came shortly after the 1991 tour, and the pair began writing songs together, recruiting New York City musician Frank Ferrer as drummer. Ferrer had played with a band called The Beautiful; when some labels expressed interest in the project, Butler and his new cohorts scrambled to find a compatible bass player to round out what would become Love Spit Love. Butler dragooned his brother Tim into the band, and they departed for Los Angeles to record their debut in early 1994.

Love Spit Love was released in 1994 on the Imago label. It was produced by Dave Jerden, whose resume included projects with Jane's Addiction and the Talking Heads. Comparisons with Butler's former band were inevitable. "Whereas the Psychedelic Furs were the epitome of textured post-punk British pop," wrote Brian Q. Newcomb in *Billboard,* "with Love Spit Love, Butler's voice and Fortus' potent acoustic and electric guitar work have produced a more direct rock sensibility, without sacrificing any of Butler's sense of challenging melody." A cello and mandolin surfaced on some tracks, evidence of Fortus's range of musical abilities. The album's single "Am I Wrong?" did relatively well, reaching No. 3 on *Billboard*'s modern-rock charts, but reviewers were less than effusive in their judgment. *Melody Maker* writer Cathi Unsworth called Love Spit Love's debut "glamour on ice," saddled with a "production as thick as varnish." She gave it a mixed assessment, but did find a gem in the song "Codeine"—"only this once does Butler manage to crawl under your skin," her review noted.

On another of *Love Spit Love*'s tracks, "Seventeen," Butler relinquished his trademark raspy voice and sang in falsetto. The switch was blasted by *Rolling Stone* reviewer Geoffrey Welchman, who likened it "a bad Monty Python impression." However, Welchman also lavished praise upon "Codeine," deeming it a song that "demonstrates the best this band is capable of." Unfortunately, Love Spit Love's debut release would suffer further indignities: the band's Imago label found itself in corporate distress and at one point lost their distribution deal with media conglomerate BMG.

Meanwhile, other labels were finding sales healthy for a series of Psychedelic Furs re-issues, capitalizing on the mid-Nineties nostalgia for the music of the previous decade. Even the music press poked fun at the cottage Furs industry with headlines such as, "Oh Look! It's Another Psychedelic Furs Compilation!" Younger fans

Original members include **Richard Butler**, vocals; **Tim Butler** (left band, c. 1996), bass; **Chris Wilson** (joined band 1996), bass; **Frank Ferrer**, drums; ' **Richard Fortus**, guitar, cello, mandolin.

Butler was a founding member and lead singer of the British new-wave band the Psychedelic Furs; Fortus formerly played guitar in Pale Divine; Ferrer had once been the drummer for The Beautiful.

Band formed, 1991, after a joint Psychedelic Furs/Pale Divine tour; signed to Imago Records, c. 1993; released *Love Spit Love*, 1994; signed to Maverick Records, c. 1996; released second album, *Trysome Eatone*, 1997.

Addresses: *Record company*—Maverick Records, 8000 Beverly Blvd., Los Angeles, CA 90048.

who were introduced to Butler's unique style with the Love Spit Love singles—or on his appearance singing "I Am Anastasia" on Sponge's *Wax Ecstatic* LP—could revisit the Furs experience with such packages as *In the Pink* or *Radio One Sessions*.

After the problems with Imago, Butler and Love Spit Love found a new corporate home with Maverick Records, usually referred to as "Madonna's label." Still, it was nice, cozy quarters for any band, especially given Maverick's success with Alanis Morissette and Prodigy. When it came time to record a follow-up, the band recruited famed producer Ben Grosse, who had worked with both Republica and the Rollins Band. They ensconced themselves in a Massachusetts studio for several weeks to complete *Trysome Eatone*, released the late summer of 1997.

Again, Butler abandoned his usual abrasive growl for a falsetto on the tracks "Believe" and "Little Fist." He told *Billboard*'s Rosen that "it was just something that happened on this record.... Most of these songs were written around my apartment with Richard Fortus, and a lot on acoustic guitar," Butler said. "When he played ['Little Fist'] it just seemed natural to go into that voice." Home for Butler is New York's East Village, and the roughness of the neighborhood—not as tidy and cool as the streets of next-door Greenwich Village—inspired some lyrical visions. "St. Marks [Place] is almost like a Third World street in some ways," Butler told Rosen. "There's this hotel, the St. Marks Hotel, where there's a death every four or five days. `Little Fist' is about some of the people you see walking in and out of there."

Perhaps uncoincidentally, *Trysome Eatone* coincided with fall 1997 release of the penultimate Psychedelic Furs greatest-hits package, the double CD *Should God Forget: A Retrospective*. Meanwhile, Love Spit Love were ready to embark on a U.S. tour before an early 1998 overseas release for *Trysome Eatone*. They planned to cover some old Furs tunes live. "We didn't on the first tour, because we didn't want people to think they were going to get their favorite hits from the Psychedelic Furs," Butler told *Billboard*. "But having established this as a band, I think it's safe to try a couple of Psychedelic Furs songs if I feel like it."

Selected discography

Love Spit Love, Imago, 1994.
Trysome Eatone, Maverick Records, 1997.

Sources

Billboard, June 25, 1994, p. 13; August 9, 1997, p. 9.
Melody Maker, December 10, 1994, p. 30.
Rolling Stone, December 15, 1994, pp. 95-96.

Additional information for this profile was provided by Maverick Records publicity materials, 1997.

—*Carol Brennan*

Ashley MacIsaac

Rock fiddler

Cape Breton, Nova Scotia, is one of the last Celtic communities left in the world. It is here that the two hundred year old tradition of fiddle playing has been cradled. The music retained its traditional sounding style up until Ashley MacIsaac, a fiddle playing rocker, literally collided smack into the music scene. He has turned the world of traditional Celtic music upside down, while also displaying to much of the world through television, an unorthodox variation of the traditional dress look of the Celtic culture.

In an A&M Records press release, MacIsaac made a statement about his fashion choices: "The reason I don't mind wearing platforms and bell bottoms and basically being a fiddle slut is because I still do play in a structured way and it's totally fusion because of that. So I'm not a grunge fiddler, and I'm not a rock fiddler and I'm not a slow Celtic fiddler ... I'm just a Cape Breton fiddler who's learned to put things other ways. It's multi-media to music." Many who listen to him say he perfectly blends the traditional sound of Celtic fiddle with the hard rhythmic beat of rock and roll. He can turn from static beats to smooth ones on a dime.

MacIsaac could easily pass for an extra in the Mel Gibson movie hit, *Braveheart*. He has a threatening look to him, somewhat barbaric and devilish, and his music reflects the same. He stomps in his army boots, has scruffy facial hair, all this while wearing the most traditional looking kilt. He tops off his dress with a feather boa, which was a gift from the American drag queen RuPaul. He is the epitome of in-your-face music rebellion, a Celtic with the cause of turning upside down any notion of a traditional fiddler from some far away land. MacIsaac's father's passion for fiddling rubbed off on his son. MacIsaac once said his father told him, "If you want to play the fiddle get mad at it or don't play it at all. When I go out and do my live show I present the image of angry young man when on stage. It's angst or punk and that's what the Celts were, punks. But it's also about romancing because the Celts were also about that."

MacIsaac got his first musical break when Philip Glass asked him to perform for the 1992 off-Broadway production of *Woyzeck*. The charged-up fiddler hung out in Manhattan clubs, soaking up its rough and caustic atmosphere. This is when he, "started doing more freaky things," he stated in *People*. After his introduction to the world of acting, MacIsaac began to see himself as more than a fiddle player. He parlayed his drama experience into his concert performances, and success followed.

Early Rebellion Tendencies

MacIsaac learned how to step-dance at the age of five and fiddle at the age of eight. In an A&M press release, MacIsaac is accredited with "flagrantly challenging of tradition to re-create, messing it up until it's unclear then forging ahead with his version—a new age fusion of Celtic soundscapes interwoven on a symbiotic tapestry with contemporary forms." In 1984, there was a softer side to the young musician. He performed in front of the pope during his visit to Nova Scotia, and didn't display the stomping antics of his future performances.

MacIsaac's musical roots run deep. His father, Angus, and Stan Chapman, a man from Nova Scotia who trained about 70% of the fiddlers on Cape Breton, taught him and about 600 other fiddlers. In an interview with *Cleveland Plain Dealer* reporter Michael Norman, MacIsaac reflected on Cape Breton and its cultural core. "It was a very traditional family and community. People kept the Scottish customs alive—everything from the fiddling and the square dancing to the food and the language." His music reflects his heritage yet, in his debut release *Hi How Are You Today?*, MacIsaac makes the traditional Celtic fiddle interact with the music from the grunge world in the song "Rusty D-con-STRUCT-tion." "Beaton's Delight," on the other hand, pounds out a more industrial sound, while "Sleep Maggie," has been simply called new age Celtic.

Born February 24, 1975, in Creignish, Cape Breton, Nova Scotia; son of Angus MacIsaac (an electrician and musician).

Learned how to step-dance at the age of 5 and fiddle at the age of eight; performed for the pope, 1984. Major label debut, *Hi How Are You Today?*, was released in 1995 and has sold over 500,000 copies worldwide. Guest featured on albums by Paul Simon, Edie Brickell, David Byrne, The Chieftans, and Philip Glass.

Awards: East Coast Music Award, Best Live Act, 1995; Canadian Music Association Award, 1995; Juno Award, Best New Solo Artist, 1996; Juno Award, Best Roots and Traditional Album-Solo, 1996.

Addresses: *Management*—Jones & Company, 1819 Granville Street, 4th floor, Halifax, Nova Scotia, Canada, B3J 3R1. *Fan club*—Cape Breton Diddleing Association, P.O. Box 25025 Clayton Park RPO, Halifax, NS, Canada, B3M 4H4.

Ashley MacIsaac's audiences span several generations. MacIsaac's hometown audience is no exception. "In Cape Breton, I get grandmothers and 15-year-old moshers at my shows," MacIsaac told Andrew Essex in *Replay* magazine. "The old-timers sit through the punk stuff just to hear one somber Celtic number. If the young ones don't settle down for the slow number, I tell 'em to shut up and listen." While touring Ireland and Scotland in 1996, MacIsaac noticed a slight difference between his Canadian audiences and the ones abroad. As he related to Tiffany Danitz in *Insight,* these audiences had "more of a sense of intrigue, because they had a connection with my music."

A Worldwide Success

This bad-boy rock fiddler has sold over 500,000 copies of the album *Hi How Are You Today?* worldwide. It went platinum in Canada. In the U.S., he gained enough attention from Paul Simon, Edie Brickell, David Byrne, The Chieftans, and Philip Glass to be guest-featured on their albums. He won two 1996 Juno Awards, a 1995 East Coast Music Award, and a Canadian Music Association Award for his own work.

Critics received MacIsaac's 1995 release *Hi How Are You Today?* warmly. Terri Horak of *Billboard* praised MacIsaac for his "pop-fiddle tunes" and noticed that "he took care to keep the traditional tunes pure." Dan Aquilante of the *New York Post* hailed the album as "a Celtic fusion that is a 50/50 mix of raw energy and instrumental dynamics." Many reviewers took notice of MacIsaac's unusual fiddle play. *Saturday Night* contributor Bruce Headlam commented on MacIsaac's technique, calling him "a rhythmic player who makes the impurities of his full stroke—the `dig' at the start of the note, the bounce across the length of the bow—work to the tune's advantage."

When he's not playing the fiddle, MacIsaac indulges in his second passion: American television. He likes to say that he brings the culture of his favorite shows like *Seinfeld, Columbo,* and even *The Andy Griffith Show,* into his Celtic music. While getting his chance to actually step inside his tubular TV world as a guest on *Late Night with Conan O'Brien,* he stunned the late night audience. MacIsaac is a true Scotsman, and as such he does not wear anything under his plaid. The in-studio audience saw more than they expected, and the television viewers saw less since producers censored him from the waist down. MacIsaac was not fazed by the incident, and according to him, "They blurred it so you can't see anything."

Selected discography

Close to the Floor, independently released, 1992.
A Cape Breton Christmas, 1993.
(With others) *Strictly Bass Three,* 1994.
Kumbaya Album, 1995.
Hi How Are You Today?, A&M, 1996
Fine Thank You Very Much!, A&M, 1996.

Sources

Alternative Press, August 23, 1996.
Billboard, April 27, 1996.
Cleveland Plain Dealer, November 22, 1996.
Hits, September 9, 1996.
Insight, August 12, 1996.
Musician, September 1996.
New York Post, June 11, 1996.
People, May 5, 1997.
Replay, August 1996.
San Francisco Examiner-Chronicle, June 2, 1996.
Star-Ledger, July 19, 1996.
Time, December 11, 1995.
Washington Post, November 15, 1996.

Mamas and the Papas

Folk-rock group

Achieving major success with their laid-back folk-rock songs that epitomized the love generation of the late 1960s, the Mamas and the Papas filled the airwaves with their music. Their first hit, "California Dreamin'," was released in 1966, and within two years, the band produced a dozen chart-toppers. Their unique sound was one of the most successful mergers of folk and rock music to date, and resulted in a series of million-selling singles and gold albums. As was stated in *The Harmony Illustrated Encyclopedia of Rock,* the group "combined strong, memorable melodies with soaring vocal harmonies and distinctive folk-rock sound."

The recordings of the Mamas and the Papas were especially lush, featuring elaborate string arrangements and extensive orchestration. "The elaborate productions (by Lou Adler) on their albums prepared the way for the opulent recording style of such groups as Fleetwood Mac in the 1970s," noted *The New Grove Dictionary of American Music. The Harmony Illustrated Encyclopedia of Rock* added that the group "had

AP/Wide World Photos

Original members included **Denny Doherty** (born November 29, 1941, in Halifax, Nova Scotia, Canada), vocals; **Cass Elliot** (born Ellen Cohen, on September 19, 1943, in Alexandria, VA; died July 29, 1974, in London, England), vocals; **John Phillips** (born August 30, 1935, in Parris Island, SC), vocals, guitar; **Michelle Phillips** (born Holly Michelle Gilliam, April 6, 1944, in Long Beach, CA), vocals. Later members included **Elaine "Spanky" McFarlane** (born June 19, 1942, in Peoria, IL), vocals; **Scott McKenzie,** vocals. **Mackenzie Phillips,** vocals.

Group known as the New Journeymen was formed by John Phillips, Michelle Phillips, and Denny Doherty, 1964; moved to Virgin Islands and was joined by Elliot briefly, 1965; relocated to California and was rejoined by Elliot, 1965; contributed backing vocals to Barry McGuire's second album, *This Precious Time,* 1965; signed recording contract with Dunhill label of RCA, 1965; released first single, "California Dreamin'," 1966; had number-one hit with "Monday Monday," 1966; fired Michelle Phillips from group and hired Jill Gibson to replace her, 1966; rehired Michelle Phillips in place of Gibson, 1966; performed at Carnegie Hall, 1966; released "Creeque Alley," an autobiographical song about group's history, 1967; canceled series of appearances in England after Elliot was arrested in London for petty theft, 1967; helped organize and performed at Monterey Pop Festival, 1967; fired Michelle Phillips from group again, 1968; disbanded, 1968; reunited to release *People Like Us* album, 1971; broke up again, 1971; was reformed with John Phillips, Doherty, Mackenzie Phillips (John's daughter), and Elaine McFarlane (formerly of Spanky and Our Gang); added Scott McKenzie to group when Doherty quit; toured as part of "Happy Together Tour" with Turtles, Grass Roots, Gary Lewis, the Buckinghams, and other groups, 1985; participated in "An Evening of California Dreamin'— The Tour" with Brewer & Shipley, Maria Muldaur, Canned Heat, and the New Riders of the Purple Sage, 1988.

Awards: Grammy Award, Best Contemporary (Rock 'n' Roll) Group Performance ("Monday Monday"), 1966; inducted into Rock and Roll Hall of Fame, 1998.

considerable influence on '60s music scene, paving way for more heavyweight protagonists of Aquarian Age."

Critical to the success of the Mamas and the Papas was the significant songwriting talent of John Phillips, who was the chief creative force behind most of the group's big hits. The appeal of the group was also enhanced by the diversity of its four members. John Phillips was rebellious and somewhat philosophical; Denny Doherty was wholesome yet wisecracking; Michelle Philips was quiet; and Cass Elliot was outspoken. Musically, the addition of Elliot to the group was very significant. "With John and Michelle, we had a nice, sweet folk sound," Doherty told *Macleans.* "But with Cass, we suddenly had power."

Developed Talent on Folk Circuit

Despite their association with the California music scene, the Mamas and the Papas nurtured their musical talents in the folk scene of New York City's Greenwich Village. After attending George Washington University and spending a few months at the United States Naval Academy, John Phillips gravitated to New York City in 1957 and started up a folk-singing group called the Journeymen. This band proved popular in folk circles, releasing three albums on Capitol Records. Holly Michelle Gilliam, who had met Phillips at the Hungry I club in San Francisco, joined the group as a singer after coming to New York in hopes of landing modeling jobs. The relationship between Phillips and Gilliam advanced, and the couple were married in 1962, with Gilliam changing her name to Michelle Phillips.

Canadian Doherty cut his musical teeth in the Halifax Three in Nova Scotia, which made two albums for the Epic label. One of the group members was Zal Yanovsky, who later became part of the Lovin' Spoonful. Doherty and Yanovsky later teamed up with Elliot and her first husband, Jim Hendricks, to form Cass Elliot and the Big Three, which later became known as the Mugwumps and included Art Stokes on drums and future Lovin' Spoonful star John Sebastian on harmonica. After the Mugwumps broke up, Doherty joined John and Michelle Phillips to form the New Journeymen. When they traveled to the Virgin Islands in 1965 to rehearse, Elliot quit her job as a waitress and came on board to perform with them.

Phillips soon decided that the group should base themselves in California as well, and after they moved to Los Angeles Elliot rejoined the group. While there, they were introduced to record producer Lou Adler by their friend Barry McGuire, who previously had sung with the New Christy Minstrels. The New Journeymen got their first break by singing backing vocals on McGuire's second solo album, *This Precious Time.* Adler saw their potential and signed a record deal with them for his new Dunhill label in 1965. At this time, the group decided to change its name. After rejecting names like the Magic Circle, the group settled on the Mamas and the Papas.

First Single a Major Hit

Although the Mamas and the Papas recorded "Go Where You Wanna Go" as their debut single, Adler decided that "California Dreamin'" should be their first exposure to the public. Written by John and Michelle Phillips, "California Dreamin'" was originally recorded by McGuire, but it was turned into a Mamas and the Papas song by erasing McGuire's voice and inserting Doherty's. The song made the group an instant sensation in pop music, becoming somewhat of an anthem for California hippies, and topped out at number four on the U.S. hit parade in 1966. *The Guinness Encyclopedia of Popular Music* stated that the song "effectively established the group as arguably the finest vocal ensemble from their era working in the pop field."

Subsequently, the Mamas and the Papas turned out some dozen hit songs in a two-year period. They made the top of the charts with their second single, "Monday Monday," which was also released in 1966. Ironically, everyone in the group except John Phillips disliked the song, according to *Rock Movers & Shakers.* The popularity of this tune and "California Dreamin'" helped propel the group's first album, *If You Can Believe Your Eyes and Ears,* to the top of the U.S. charts in 1966. This album featured many cover songs, and the Mamas and the Papas had success with remakes of "Dancing in the Street" and "Dedicated to the One I Love," the latter of which made it to number two on the U.S. charts.

By the second album, *The Mamas and the Papas,* John Phillips' songs began to dominate the group's recordings. But by this time the group's exceptional musical harmony contrasted sharply with John and Michelle's strained marriage, which by 1966 was starting to fall apart. In July of 1966, Michelle Phillips was fired from the group and replaced for a short time by Jill Gibson, the girlfriend of Jan Berry from the singing duo Jan and Dean, who incidentally resembled Michelle. When John and Michelle reconciled in August of 1966, Michelle rejoined the group, replacing Gibson.

Generating four Top Ten hits in 1996 alone, the Mamas and the Papas became a major concert draw. Their appearances that year included a gig at New York City's prestigious Carnegie Hall. Cass Elliot demonstrated her potential as a solo act in "Words of Love," a number five hit that was largely a showcase for her voice. "Monday Monday" was a big hit in England, and the group traveled there in the winter of 1967 for a series of concerts and television appearances. But after arriving for a concert at Royal Albert Hall in London, Elliot was arrested for allegedly having stolen blankets and keys from the Royal Garden Hotel. Although the charges were dropped after Elliot spent the night in jail, the incident resulted in cancellation of all of the group's appearances as rumors of an impending break-up began spreading.

Beginnings and Endings

In the summer of 1967, Phillips helped organize the Monterey Pop Festival. His composition "San Francisco (Wear Some Flowers in Your Hair)" was sung by Scott McKenzie at the Festival and became a major hit. The Mamas and the Papas' own appearance at the Festival turned out to be the last time all four original members sang live together. In 1968 the other group members fired Michelle Phillips, who then began pursuing acting opportunities. Later that year, the rest of the group broke up to pursue solo careers. "It was a mess," noted Doherty of the group's demise in *Macleans,* admitting that his own affair with Michelle Phillips may have contributed to the marital breakup. "Nobody could have what they wanted."

John Phillips released a solo album called *The Wolf King of L.A.,* and also co-produced Robert Altman's 1970 film *Brewster McCloud* with Lou Adler. Legal problems ensued as Dunhill and the group members sued each other for fraudulent withholding of royalties and breach of contract, with the exception of Elliot, who was continuing to record for the label as a solo performer. The band attempted to reunite in 1971 to create the *People Like Us* album, but the release received negative reviews and perhaps suffered because the individual contributions to the album were taped separately. This failure led the group to break up again.

After this final breakup, members of the Mamas and the Papas went on to pursue other interests. Doherty recorded two solo albums that had little impact, while the creative powers of John Phillips were dissipated by his increasingly severe drug addiction that came close to killing him. Michelle Phillips finally got regular acting work as a cast member of the popular evening soap opera *Knots Landing.* Elliot had the most success as a solo performer, although it was erratic. While she was in England for a series of concerts in 1974, her solo career was cut short when she died of an apparent heart attack.

While living off his royalties in the 1970s for hit songs released in the 1960s, John Phillips claimed in his autobiography, *Papa John,* that his drug use escalated to a $1,000-a-day heroin addiction. He was arrested in 1980 by federal narcotics agents, then sentenced to eight years in prison and a $15,000 fine before the sentence was reduced to 30 days and 250 hours of community service. The arrest turned out to be a wake-up call for Phillips, and he finally stopped using hard drugs. As part of his sentence, Phillips began appearing around the country with his actress daughter Mackenzie to speak out against drug abuse.

Became Active on Nostalgia Circuit

In 1982 Doherty reunited with Phillips in a new version of the group that also included Mackenzie Phillips, and Elaine "Spanky" McFarlane, who was formerly with Spanky and Our Gang. When Doherty defected after the band started touring full-time, he was replaced by Scott McKenzie. The group continued to perform in its new line up on a fairly steady basis, mostly on the nostalgia circuit. In 1985 they were part of the "Happy Together Tour" across the United States that included the Turtles, Grass Roots, Gary Lewis, the Buckinghams, and others. Three years later they were a featured attraction of "An Evening of California Dreamin'— The Tour," along with Brewer & Shipley, Maria Muldaur, Canned Heat, and the New Riders of the Purple Sage. That year John Phillips also scored on the charts as co-writer of the Beach Boys' hit song "Kokomo." *Rolling Stone* honored the Mamas and the Papas that year by naming "California Dreamin'" one of the "100 Best Songs" of the last 25 years.

Both John and Michelle Phillips wrote autobiographies published in 1986 that offered their perspectives on the group's rise and fall. In recent years John Phillips has had a number of health problems and received a liver transplant in 1992. In the 1990s, Doherty found his niche with young audiences as the harbormaster on the hit PBS children's show *Theodore the Tugboat.*

Selected discography

Singles

"California Dreamin'," 1966.
"Monday Monday," 1966.
"I Saw Her Again," 1966.
"Dedicated to the One I Love," 1967.
"Creeque Alley," 1967.

Albums

If You Can Believe Your Eyes and Ears, Dunhill/RCA, 1966
Farewell to the First Golden Era, Dunhill, 1968.
The Mamas and The Papas, Dunhill/RCA, 1968.
A Gathering of Flowers, Dunhill/Probe, 1970.
Sixteen of Their Greatest Hits, Dunhill/Probe, 1970.

Sources

Books

Clifford, Mike, consultant, *The Harmony Illustrated Encyclopedia of Rock, Sixth Edition,* Harmony Books, 1988, p. 107.

Hitchcock, H. Wiley, and Stanley Sadie, editors, *The New Grove Dictionary of American Music,* Volume 3, Macmillan, 1986, p. 166.

Larkin, Colin, editor, *The Guinness Encyclopedia of Popular Music, Volume 4,* Guinness Publishing, 1995, pp. 2680–2681.

Phillips, John, *Papa John: An Autobiography,* Dolphin/Doubleday, 1986.

Phillips, Michelle, *California Dreamin': The True Story of the Mamas and the Papas,* Warner Books, 1986.

Rees, Dafydd, and Luke Crampton, editors, *Rock Movers & Shakers,* ABC-CLIO, 1991, pp. 542–543.

Romanowski, Patricia, and Holly George-Warren, editors, *The New Rolling Stone Encyclopedia of Rock & Roll,* Rolling Stone Press, 1995, pp. 618–619.

Periodicals

Atlanta Constitution, May 3, 1996, section P, p. 9.
Macleans, March 11, 1996, p. 54.
New York Times, October 12, 1997, section 9, p. 3.
Rolling Stone, September 8, 1988, p. 129.

—Ed Decker

Man or Astroman?

Futuristic rock band

Man or Astroman? claim to be not the space-music surf-rockers they appear, but instead, unlikely emissaries from another galaxy who accidentally crashed their spaceship near Auburn, Alabama. Since that day in 1992, Man or Astroman? have released over two dozen seven-inch singles and several full-length albums of dizzying, instrumental guitar virtuosity wedded to sounds derived from the quasi-modern technology of a Hammond organ or Theremin. The band's outrageous live shows have attracted a cult following throughout the United States and across the Atlantic.

Man or Astroman? "sounds a lot like Dick Dale and Link Wray gone amok with a sampler and several bowls of Count Chocula," declared *Guitar Player*. Band members Starcrunch (guitar), Birdstuff (drums), Coco the Electronic Monkey Wizard (bass and a battery of electronic gear), and Dexter X (bass and rhythm guitars for live shows), joined forces in Auburn, Alabama, in 1992 at a time when half of the band was underage and couldn't get into their own shows except through the stage door. "It was pretty much the lack of a scene that spawned Man or Astroman?," Dexter X told *Addicted to Noise*'s Kembrew McLeod. "I think we were more influenced by what didn't exist than what existed. There were no real clubs to play in ... it was like a house party situation or you had to play some stupid fraternity bar. We sort of had to put on our own all-ages punk rock show."

Not surprisingly, members of Man or Astroman? cite the famed television series *Lost in Space* as a big influence, and they liken their own career as musicians to a modern-day version of *Gilligan's Island:* perpetually stranded and stymied by their own incompetence from returning to Grid Sector 24, otherwise known as home. The years spent driving around the country in a van and playing small venues is just a ruse: "We're touring in order to find parts for our ship," Coco told *Pitchfork* interviewer Jason Josephes. They also cite stellar musical influences that range from the early vinyl of surf music pioneer Dick Dale, avant-garde extremists The Residents, the pop singles of Jan and Dean, and a host of other bands ranging from the Ventures to Devo to forgotten new-wave act the Rezillos.

The output from Man or Astroman? include several singles—which they term "scout vessels"—EPs, and full-length releases such as the Estrus label's issuance of *Destroy All Astro-Men!,* in 1994. The 1994 EP *Your Weight on the Moon,* issued by the band's overseas home, One Louder, was described by Cathi Unsworth in *Melody Maker* as "a blast of visceral, ridiculous fun, with impeccably cool credentials." The Washington state-based Estrus would issue numerous other singles

For the Record . . .

Members include **Birdstuff,** drums; **Coco the Electronic Monkey Wizard,** bass, samplers, Theremin, Tesla Coil; **Dexter X,** bass and rhythm guitarist for live shows; **Starcrunch,** guitar.

Band formed in Auburn, Alabama, in 1992.

Addresses: *Record company*—Touch & Go Records, P.O. Box 25520, Chicago, IL 60625. *Website*—http://www.astroman.com.

and LPs such as *Project Infinity.* The 1995 release *Intravenous Television Continuum* covered more theme songs from television shows—in this case, *The Jetsons* and *The Munsters*—but featured authentic Man or Astroman? compositions such as "Out of Limits" and "Tomorrow Plus X" as well. Most of the original songs are instrumentals, but like their other efforts, employ wacky musical appliances such as the Hammond organ or Theremin, an early electronic musical instrument dating back to the 1920s.

Swithching Vessels

Man or Astroman? later switched "anti-gravity vessels," as they refer to their label, to Chicago-based Touch and Go Records. They ran into some potential legal trouble when they borrowed the Sixties-era National Aeronautics and Space Administration (NASA) logo and were instructed, in legal terms, to cease and desist. The band had adapted the now-defunct lettering once seen on astronaut gear, replacing "NASA" with the word "Astro" on their stickers and t-shirts.

Another humorless encounter with earthlaw occurred when they shot their first video for the song "The Miracle of Genuine Pyrex," which first appeared on the EP *1000X.* Music video behemoth MTV requested that the band edit out a few frames where Coco was running about with a flaming television box on his head. As he wrote in his essay entitled "MTV Just Loves Fire!," published on the band's official web site, Coco and other Man or Astroman? members agreed to edit the bit out, but only after a major moral struggle. "I suppose I wouldn't want every kid running around the house with a flaming TV on their head," Coco reflected. "I would much rather them aspire to drug dealing and all the other wonderful things that are also glamorized on MTV."

Live Man or Astroman? shows are a treat. In addition to the occasional flaming television set, other stage props includes a battery of projection screens, vintage Radio Shack computers, slide show, inflatable rockets, and disco lights; television sets replay sci-fi classics or bizarre imagery. One of their first releases for Touch and Go was *Live Transmission from Uranus,* which packaged the aural part of the Man or Astroman? live experience for fans. Recorded at a show in Gainesville, Florida, *Live Transmission* includes a cover of the Pixies' "Manta Ray" as well as the theme song from the sixties television show *The Man from U.N.C.L.E.* Included in the usual Man or Astroman? stage line-up is Stuart the Lounge Lizard, who programs the television sets that show old Godzilla movies from the Sixties or other cheesy sci-fi entertainment. (Not surprisingly, Man or Astroman? are huge fans of the cult cable program *Mystery Science Theater 3000*). Sometimes the sets catch fire, and sometimes the band tosses retro snacks like Twinkies or Moon Pies to the audience.

"You claim to appear onstage in binary form," queried *Guitar Player.* "How does the audience see you?" "Well, there's a protective shield in front of us which is also a holographic viewing device," Man or Astroman? asserted. "If that wasn't there, the audience would just see instruments floating." Often wearing the ubiquitous empty television set as space helmets, band members choreograph their stage movements. "Jerking around in unison, the band suggested what Gene Simmons and Ace Frehley [of KISS] might have looked like if they grew up in Akron, Ohio [the hometown of Devo], went to art school and developed a theory of de-evolution," wrote *Addicted to Noise*'s McLeod. In another *Addicted to Noise* article, Birdstuff explained the band's attitude about live performances that hearken back to the spectacles of GWAR: "It's like if you're just going to go on stage dressed like and act like the people who paid to see you, I mean, what's the point? If you want to do that you might as well work at Pizza Hut or something."

The Future's So Bright...

Man or Astroman? released *Made from Technetium* on Touch and Go in mid-1997. The record, wrote *Rolling Stone*'s Rob O'Connor, "continues the Man or Astroman? tradition of making dexterous instrumental music for the Space Age." There was even a track with vocals—a homage to the call that all cellular device users receive at some point, from the mysterious "Lo Batt." Despite its retro appeal, the music of Man or Astroman? fits in to futuristic recreational pursuits well. When not recording new "scout vessels," members write music for computer games and are planning a

Man or Astroman? CD-ROM—they have already contributed to several such projects—and also hope to begin bit-streaming live broadcasts via the Internet. As Birdstuff conceded in the *Addicted to Noise* interview, "We'd really want to transmit direct to people's neural synapses but the technology isn't there yet."

Selected discography

Destroy All Astro-Men!, Estrus, 1994.
Your Weight on the Moon (EP), One Louder, 1994.
Live Transmission from Uranus, Touch and Go, 1995.
Intravenous Television Continuum, One Louder, 1995.
Experiment Zero, Touch and Go, 1996.
1000X (EP; includes the song "The Miracle of Genuine Pyrex"), Touch and Go, 1997.
Made from Technetium, Touch and Go, 1997.

Released several singles and EPs on both the Estrus and Touch and Go labels since 1993; also released the LP *Project Infinity* on Estrus.

Sources

Addicted to Noise, September 11, 1996; November 1, 1996.
Alternative Press, January 1995, p. 29.
Guitar Player, July 1996, p. 20.
Melody Maker, September 17, 1994, p. 41; April 1, 1995, p. 38; July 29, 1995, p. 32.
Pitchfork, July 5, 1996.
Rolling Stone, September 18, 1997.

—*Carol Brennan*

Richard Marx

Singer, songwriter

Known for his good looks as well as his vocal abilities, Richard Marx was perhaps the prototypical flashy 1980s pop star, making a name for himself as a mainstay of top-40 radio stations and MTV. With the 1997 release of *Flesh and Bone,* his first album since 1994's *Paid Vacation,* Marx joined other stars of the 1980s whose popularity underwent a resurgence as the members of the MTV generation became nostalgic for the sounds of their youth. With the release of his fifth album, Marx, serving as the 1997 Grammy in the Schools spokesperson, aided the fundraising efforts of the National Academy of Recording Arts and Sciences (NARAS) Foundation's campaign to encourage the creative efforts of American students. Although critics have not assessed Marx as a serious artist in terms of his songs, which *Billboard*'s Larry Flick characterized as "radio-friendly nuggets" and "engaging, rock-etched love poems," they have praised his ability to belt out powerful lyrics. Despite any reservations expressed in reviews of his works, Marx attained enormous popular success: his first four albums went multi-platinum, selling more than 20 million copies worldwide.

The son of a commercial jingle-writing father and a jingle-singing mother, Richard Noel Marx—born September 16, 1963 in Chicago, Illinois—spent the better part of his childhood inside recording studios. He began recording jingles himself at the age of five, and as a teenager Marx wrote his own songs. When he was 18, Marx managed, through a series of acquaintances in the music industry, to get a demo he had recorded to singer Lionel Richie, who was at the time still a member of the Commodores. At Richie's urging, Marx moved to Los Angeles, and beginning in 1980, he worked as a background vocalist for a variety of recording artists, including George Benson, Whitney Houston, Dolly Parton, Madonna, Barbra Streisand, Billy Joel, and Julio Iglesias. In addition, Marx provided background vocals for songs on Lionel Richie's solo albums, including the hits "All Night Long (All Night)" and "Running with the Night."

Marx supplemented his work as a background vocalist by writing songs, which were recorded by such artists as Kenny Rogers and the band Chicago. The songwriter also contributed to movie soundtracks, including those for the 1985 films *St. Elmo's Fire* and *The Goonies.* While working as a contributing songwriter for the 1983 John Travolta film *Staying Alive,* the sequel to the wildly popular *Saturday Night Fever,* Marx met Cynthia Rhodes, the movie's female lead. He and Rhodes dated for several years and eventually married in 1989. Despite his success as a songwriter and his frequent contributions as a background vocalist, success as a solo recording artist eluded Marx, until 1987, the year his first album, *Richard Marx,* was released by EMI.

Four singles from the *Richard Marx* album, which ended up at number eight on the album charts, made it to the top of the popular music charts in 1987; one of these singles, the ballad "Hold On to the Nights," was particularly well-liked among pop music fans, and spent several weeks at number one. Other chart-topping songs from Marx's debut album included "Don't Mean Nothing" and "Should Have Known Better," both of which reached the number three spot, and "Endless Summer Nights," which reached number two. The songs, all of which were composed by Marx, displayed his signature romantically raspy, forceful vocal style, and his trademark theme of love, unrequited and otherwise. The corresponding music videos for the songs depicted Marx as a soulful and often lovesick romantic figure, and with his youthful good looks—he was widely popular among MTV viewers, especially female viewers.

Repeated His Offenses

Marx's second album, *Repeat Offender,* was released in 1989 and quickly reached triple-platinum status, producing the two number one singles "Satisfied" and "Right Here Waiting." "Satisfied" was not only popular with fans, it was favored by music critics as well, which

was an unusual achievement for a Marx song; the critics noted that the song departed from Marx's usual romantic-ballad formula and lauded the singer for his powerful, heartfelt vocal performance on the song. "Angelia," another song from *Repeat Offender,* reached number four on the charts in 1989, while "Too Late to Say Goodbye" topped out at number 12 in 1990. "Children of the Night" reached number 13 in 1990; the song commended the efforts of—and raised money for—the Los Angeles-based group called Children of the Night, which provides services for runaway children and teenage prostitutes. With the songs and videos from this second album, Marx established himself as a formidable player in the 1980s music scene.

Rushing Around

In 1991 Marx released *Rush Street,* which, while not as popularly successful as its predecessors, produced three top-twenty singles, including "Take This Heart," which reached number 20, "Keep Coming Back," which reached number 12, and "Hazard," a song that *Entertainment Weekly's* Chuck Eddy dubbed "an oddly spooky flamenco-rock ballad about a riverside murder," which went to number nine. In order to boost the sales of his third album, Marx took part in a publicity stunt that had him play five concerts in a twenty-four hour period, going from one coast of the United States to the other. The mini-tour began at an airport in Baltimore and ended at a Los Angeles airport, with performances at New York, Cleveland, and Chicago airports sandwiched between.

Marx's 1994 effort, *Paid Vacation,* like his earlier albums, was not well-received by critics who deemed the collection simply more of the same rock ballads and top-40s sounds previously released by the singer. Again, however, critics acknowledged Marx's vocal talent, such as *People's* Peter Castro, who conceded that the album was "packed with well-sung songs" and *Entertainment Weekly* contributor Chuck Eddy, who offered a backhanded compliment to Marx with the assertion that *Paid Vacation* contained "some of the most skilled hackwork in the business." Nevertheless, the critics still maintained their dislike for Marx's lyrics and melodies; Castro remarked that the songs on the album were "painfully short on substance." Among the songs on *Paid Vacation,* "One More Try" and "Nothing Left Behind Us" could be heard most often on the radio, and the album was a moderate success.

After three years without releasing a single album, Marx released *Flesh and Bone* in 1997. With superstar guest vocalists such as Luther Vandross and Randy Jackson lending their talents to the mix of songs that were, as always, entirely written by Marx, the album was designed to appeal to the fans who had embraced Marx in the late 1980s and early 1990s. Although critical reception of the album was as always lukewarm, Marx's vocals were deemed somewhat more mature—and at the age of 34 his voice was most definitely more seasoned than it had been on his debut album ten years earlier—and richer than they had been previously. *Entertainment Weekly*'s Jeremy Helligar, although faulting the album for containing what he referred to as "cheesy hallmarks" of the 1980s—cliche-laden lyrics, overdone vocals, and hackneyed arrangements—conceded that on songs such as "Touch of Heaven" Marx is "an occasionally convincing soul man."

A noteworthy fact concerning Marx's fifth solo album was its association with the NARAS Foundation; Marx requested photos, paintings, drawings, short stories, and poems from high school students around the United States, and the winning entries were featured in *Flesh and Bone*'s CD booklet. In addition, Marx donated proceeds from the sales of the first single released from *Flesh and Bone,* "Until I Find You Again," to the NARAS Foundation, and produced five songs submitted by students on an album released with the support of the same organization. The singer was enthusiastic about the project, according to the Richard Marx website, which quoted him as saying: "The idea that I can expose a young short story writer, photographer, poet, painter or songwriter to a mass audience is really exciting. It'd be pretty cool if someone in a position to help even more then sees or hears their work and says, `This is great. Let's open the door for him or her.'" The successful singer and songwriter was also eager for the concept to become more widespread among celebrities, remarking: "I hope other artists will pick up the ball and do similar things. In fact, I hope everybody steals the idea. For once, I want to be plagiarized."

Selected discography

(Contributor) *Staying Alive* (soundtrack), 1983.
(Contributor) *The Goonies* (soundtrack), 1985.
(Contributor) *St. Elmo's Fire* (soundtrack), 1987.
Richard Marx, EMI, 1987, reissued, Capitol, 1991.
Repeat Offender, EMI, 1989, reissued, 1991.
Rush Street, Capitol, 1991.
(Contributor) *A League of Their Own* (soundtrack), 1992.
Paid Vacation, Capitol, 1994.
(Contributor) *Mirror Has Two Faces* (soundtrack), 1996.
Flesh and Bone, Capitol, 1997.
Greatest Hits, Capitol, 1997.

Sources

Periodicals

Billboard, April 27, 1991, p. 1; January 28, 1995, p. 69.
Entertainment Weekly, February 11, 1994, p. 54; April 18, 1997, p. 68.
People, August 1, 1988, p. 106; June 26, 1989, p. 102; February 28, 1994, p. 23.
Variety, April 22, 1991, p. 63.

Online

www.richardmarx.com.

—*Lynn M. Spampinato*

Grant McLennan

Singer, songwriter

Highly regarded as a creator of understated, beautifully melodic music that transcends standard pop formulas, Grant McLennan has managed to elude mainstream stardom despite receiving a bounty of critical acclaim during his career. After more than a decade as part of The Go-Betweens, a group that never broke through to fame, he has continued to earn kudos as a solo act. As Paul Evans in *Rolling Stone* wrote in his review of the singer's *Horsebreaker Star* CD released in 1995, "Grant McLennan is one of today's best songwriters."

McLennan was far removed from the music scene as a child, growing up on a cattle ranch in the Australian outback some 250 miles away from the nearest town. "I wanted to get out of there," McLennan told *Option* about his boyhood in the boondocks. "I knew I wanted something different." One of his favorite groups when he was young was the Monkees, whose pop hooks he found irresistible.

After attending boarding school in Brisbane, McLennan enrolled in the University of Queensland. At college he found a musical soulmate in fellow student Robert Forster, who shared his interest in the new punk music making waves from England. Both of them were also interested in movies and started writing a screenplay together, according to an interview with McLennan in the *New Review of Records*. Initially, McLennan wasn't nearly as interested as Foster in performing music. McLennan had no musical experience and was focusing most of his attention on writing film reviews for the university newspaper, as well as short stories. "We started talking about music, but it took him about a year to persuade me to play with him," McLennan told *Option*.

Eventually, Forster taught McLennan how to play bass guitar so that the two of them could perform together. When the duo was later joined by bassist Robert Vickers, drummer Lindy Morrison, and violinist Amanda Brown, the new group became the Go-Betweens. McLennan then switched from bass to guitar, which he taught himself to play, and also began composing songs. At this time he still had no intention of making music his career.

Initially, McLennan wrote songs that were sung by Forster. He made his singing debut on the Go-Betweens' first album, *Send Me a Lullaby,* which was released in 1982 on the Rough Trade label. During the 1980s the group created a series of highly acclaimed albums that brilliantly merged a folk-style 1960s sound with a harder-edged punk sound, with the different pop strengths of McLennan and Forster merging beautifully.

Born on February 12, 1958, in Rockhampton, Australia. Education: Attended University of Queensland, Australia.

Joined the Go-Betweens, 1977; singing debut with Go-Betweens, 1981; wrote script for film short, *Heather's Glove*, 1981; moved to London, U.K., 1982; switched from bass guitar to guitar, 1983; became solo performer after Go-Betweens disbanded, 1988; recorded an album with Steven Kilbey of Church as Jack Frost; released first solo album, *Watershed*, on Beggars Banquet, 1991; went to U.S. to record *Horsebreaker Star*, 1995; performed in reunion shows with the Go-Betweens, 1997.

Addresses: *Home*—Brisbane, Australia; *Record company*—Beggars Banquet, 580 Broadway, Suite 1004, New York, NY 10012.

As Holly George-Warren wrote in *Option*, "McLennan's buoyant melodies and tuneful tenor vocals perfectly complemented Forster's darker, edgier compositions." Jamie T. Conway in *Melody Maker* also noted, "The greatness of the Go-Betweens lay not in the (peerless) songwriting abilities of Forster and McLennan, but in the fact that the contrasting moods they depicted offset each other beautifully."

McLennan also developed a reputation for being able to churn out new songs at a rapid rate. "Grant was quite prolific," said bassist Vickers in *Option*. "He really had a lot of songs, so many that we'd have to throw out dozens to keep the albums balanced."

Romantic involvements ensued between McLennan and Brown, and also Forster and Morrison, but were follwed by breakups. This created a lot of stress in the Go-Betweens by the late 1980s, hastening the group's demise. McLennan and Forster also wanted to go their separate ways in order to explore new creative directions. "It's not as if I was happy about it, but both Robert and myself had other songs we wanted to do," McLennan told the *New Review of Records*.

McLennan then joined up with Steven Kilbey of Church to record an album under the name Jack Frost, which was recorded in just two weeks. This release was followed by McLennan's first solo album, *Watershed*, which came out on the Beggars Banquet label in 1991.

Watershed offered a more polished pop sound than that offered by the Go-Betweens, proving that McLennan could survive musically without collaborating with Forster.

Released Acclaimed Double Album

Two years after releasing his mostly acoustic *Fireboy* in 1993, McLennan reached his solo peak with the double album *Horsebreaker Star*, which Mark J. Petracca in the *New Review of Records* called "his most arresting and intense work to date." Produced in Athens, Georgia, by John Keane, who also produced R.E.M. and the Indigo Girls, the songs for *Horsebreaker Star* were recorded in just nine days with musicians McLennan had never met before.

The songs on *Horsebreaker Star* covered the pop spectrum, from the countryish "Don't You Cry for Me No More" and "Hot Water," to the haunting strains of "Open Invitation," to the rocking "Dropping You." McLennan's ability to pin down feelings of disillusionment with a catchy lyric was plainly evident in *Horsebreaker Star*. A perfect example is "I'll Call You Wild," where he sings, "People are talking about living in a new Renaissance / Only thing they care about are their tickets to the seance."

Despite being received well by record reviewers, *Horsebreaker Star* did not receive much airplay on radio stations and failed to win McLennan a large following. "It is a challenge that a lot of labels have to deal with when they have a really quality musician, a singer/songwriter who doesn't obviously fit into one format or another," explained Michael Krumper, Altantic's director of product development, in his discussion of McLennan's plight in *Billboard*. McLennan, however, took his relegation to "cult status" in stride. "You can't really think about that, because the average Joe is interested in what Lisa Marie and Michael are eating for breakfast," he commented in *Billboard*. "I'm interested in different things. There's enough people discovering what I do to make me stay optimistic and happy."

Continuing his pace of an album every two years, McLennan came out with *In Your Bright Ray* in 1997. This release confirmed the songwriter's ability to capture many pop moods, ranging from the psychedelic flavor of "Malibu '60" and country feel of "Sea Breeze" to the rocking rush of "Do You See the Lights." A reviewier in *Space* remarked, "From the title track to the final shimmering, beautiful 'The Parade of Shadow,' [McLennan] carves out a niche for himself as a producer of truly sublime adult pop music."

In the summer of 1997, McLennan joined up with the former members of the Go-Betweens for a reunion tour in Europe. He continued to divide his time between performing and writing songs, stories, and film scripts from his base of operation in Brisbane, Australia.

Selected discography

Watershed, Beggars Banquet, 1991.
Fireboy, Beggars Banquet, 1993.
Horsebreaker Star, Beggars Banquet/Atlantic, 1995.
In Your Bright Ray, Beggars Banquet, 1997.

Sources

Periodicals

Billboard, January 21, 1995, p. 16.

Melody Maker, October 27, 1990, p. 29; August 23, 1997.
New Review of Records, 1996.
New York Times, January 12, 1995, p. C16; January 13, 1997, p. C16.
New York Times Magazine, October 29, 1995, p. 34.
Option, September/October 1995, pp. 59–65.
Rolling Stone, February 23, 1995, p. 76.
Space, Autumn 1997.
Village Voice, July 25, 1995, 76.
Vox, September 1997, p. 8

Online

http://www.beggars.com

Additional information for this profile was obtained from publicity materials supplied by Beggars Banquet Records.

—*Ed Decker*

Melvins

In more than a decade testing the limits of hardcore rock, the Melvins have been more successful swaying the course of modern music than finding a commercial niche of their own. *Rolling Stone* magazine, for one, credits the three-man band with being the first to fuse punk and heavy metal—creating the hybrid which fueled the groundbreaking, earth-shaking Seattle grunge sound. In fact, grunge innovators such as Nirvana's Kurt Cobain and Soundgarden guitarist Kim Thayil have cited the Melvins as a major influence—acknowledgment that earned the band the dubious title "Godfathers of Grunge." It is double-edged recognition that the Melvin's frontman, guitarist/vocalist Buzz Osborne, can live with. "People say, 'How do you feel about Nirvana, Soundgarden and Pearl Jam selling all these records?'" Osborne was quoted in *Guitar Player*. "I can understand it; they're a lot more commercial-sounding than we are. I wasn't trying to write 'Black Hole Sun' or 'Smells Like Teen Spirit.' Those songs are fine, and those bands have done well. I'm really happy for them, but none of that stuff concerns me in the least. If it did, we wouldn't be making the kind of records we make. It's our duty to push the limits."

In the process, the Melvins have bounced between a half-dozen or so record labels and created a catalog of nearly a dozen albums and assorted EPs, singles, and live recordings—music variously described as a ponderously slow and heavy, uncompromising, sludgy, scuzzy, inscrutable, slob rock, and ugly noise. The essence of the band's attitude about music is epitomized in Osborne's comments about the song "Goggles" from the 1996 album *Stag*: "I managed to record absolutely the most hideous vocals I've ever done," he told *Guitar Player*'s Mike Rowell. "It doesn't even sound human. It's the most distorted lo-fi vocal you could ever imagine," he said with obvious pride. "Now I've got to do something worse."

Osborne formed the Melvins with a high school buddy, drummer Dale Crover, in the mid-1980s in Aberdeen, Washington—the blue-collar town from which Nirvana would later emerge. Matt Lukin was the first in a series of Melvins' bass players; he went on to play for the Seattle band Mudhoney. Mark Deutrom, the Melvins' one-time producer, has been the band's bassist since the tour supporting the 1993 album *Houdini*—which *Rolling Stone* called "the best heavy metal release of the decade." The album was co-produced by Kurt Cobain, who also played guitar on one track.

As a guitar player, Osborne is primitive, but his taste in instruments is exquisite. "I have a totally ham-fisted guitar technique," he told *Guitar Player*. "I can't read music at all. In fact, I can barely remember the names of the strings. People get hung up on that kind of stuff." Osborne doesn't even bother with the all six strings. "I never use the high string," he said, "so I never have to worry about breaking it.... I just realized I didn't need it." Despite his casual approach to his instrument of choice, Osborne appreciates a fine guitar. He owns four late-model black Les Paul Customs as well as a classic Fender, a Silvertone, and a Rickenbacker.

In the late 1980s, the Melvins released *Gluey Porch Treatments* on Alchemy Records, and *Ozma* on Boner Records. "The sludgy riffing that oozed from early releases," *Billboard* wrote in June 1996, "cemented the band's reputation for off-the-periodical-scale heaviness—a characteristic still present in the Melvins' physically punishing live shows." A few years later, the Melvins reached the big leagues when a major label, Atlantic Records, released the band's headbanging classic *Houdini* and the follow-up *Stoner Witch*. On *Stoner Witch*, which sold 50,000 copies, with especially strong sales in New York and Seattle, the Melvins continued "a journey without maps, destination unknown," Grant Alden wrote in *Rolling Stone*. "The band has become far more adroit than the monochromatic slow, grinding force its own legend would suggest."

Guitar Player's Rowell also recognized the band's evolution: "The Melvins revel in testing boundaries: scuzzy guitar-noise sprees, Melvinized covers of anything from Kiss to the Cars, marathon drum solos and

For the Record . . .

Members include **Dale Crover**, drums; **Mark Deutrom**, bass; **Buzz Osborne**, guitar and vocals.

Formed in Aberdeen, Washington, mid-1980s; released debut album, *Gluey Porch Treatments,* on Alchemy Records, 1987; followed with a series of albums for Boner Records, Your Choice Records, Atlantic, Amphetamine Reptile, and Mammoth; toured over the years with Primus, White Zombie, Rage Against the Machine, and Nine Inch Nails; headlined the second stage on the 1996 Lollapalooza tour.

Addresses: *Record company*—Atlantic/Mammoth Records, 75 Rockefeller Plaza, New York, NY 10019.

the occasional set consisting entirely of one note," Rowell wrote. "Early Melvin's releases ... contained some of the most ponderous sloth-rock ever committed to tape, prompting pigeon-holers to classify them as 'the slowest band on Earth.' While once deserving such a crown, the Melvins have diversified their sound over the years, with more recent releases ... equally likely to contain accessible mid-tempo anthems and bizarre experimental forays."

More label-changing

For the 1996 release, *Stag,* Atlantic relegated the Melvins to a subsidiary label, Mammoth Records—a move which could be construed as comparable to sending a major-league ballplayer to the minors. Osborne, however, didn't see it that way. "At first it looked like we were getting pawned off on a side label, but it didn't take long for me to see that we were going to be in a better situation," he told *Billboard.* "Atlantic puts out about 3,000 records a week, and there were people who dug us there, but to Mammoth we're genuinely a big deal." Mammoth President Jay Faires said the smaller label could provide customized marketing which would double the band's fan base. But radio play was the missing piece in the Melvins' puzzle. "There are 40 or 50 important outlets playing

aggressive bands like Filter, and I certainly think (the Melvins' music) fits in with that mix," Faires said. "They've toured with bands like White Zombie, Rage Against the Machine, and Nine Inch Nails and always gotten a response from that audience."

Musically, *Stag* was a departure for the Melvins. "While chock-full of the band's trademark blunderbuss riffage and inscrutable experimentation," *Guitar Player* wrote, "the album tosses out a few left-field surprises, from trombone and keyboards to chiming pop songs with chipmunk vocals." That album was followed by 1997's *Honky,* which was released by yet another record company, the indie noise label Amphetamine Reptile. Jim Meyer of the *Minneapolis Star Tribune* called *Honky* "an uncompromising noise journey." For his part, Osborne demonstrates no desire to become predictable. "I just do what I enjoy," he told *Billboard*'s David Sprague, "and a certain number of people seem to enjoy it, too. If people want easy entertainment, there's always going to be a Green Day or an Offspring to give it to them; that's not my job."

Selective discography

10 Songs , C/Z Records, 1986.
Gluey Porch Treatments, Alchemy Records, 1987.
Ozma, Boner Records, 1989.
Your Choice Live Series: The Melvins, self-bootlegged live album released on Your Choice Records, 1991.
Bullhead, Boner Records, 1991.
Houdini, Atlantic Records, 1993.
Prick (EP), Amphetamine Reptile, 1994.
Stoner Witch, Atlantic Records, 1994.
Stag, Mammoth Records/Atlantic, 1996.
Honky, Amphetamine Reptile, 1997.

Sources

Billboard, June 8, 1996.
Guitar Player, September 1996.
Minneapolis Star-Tribune, July 4, 1997.
Rolling Stone, January 26, 1995.

Additional information was provided by the Geocities web page and Melvins' press material.

—*Dave Wilkins*

Stephanie Mills

R&B singer

AP/Wide World Photos, Inc. Reproduced by permission.

Stephanie Mills' future on stage was perhaps foretold when, at age nine, she won the highly charged Amateur Hour competition at Harlem's legendary Apollo Theater for six consecutive weeks. Soon afterward, her career quickly progressed, assisted by her talent, hard work, and tenaciousness. She auditioned three times to win the small part of Pansie in the Broadway musical *Maggie Flynn,* in which she performed alongside Shirley Jones and Jack Cassidy. When *Maggie Flynn* closed after three months, Mills moved on to the off-Broadway Negro Ensemble Company Workshop. She also performed with the Isley Brothers and the Spinners and recorded her debut album, *Movin' in the Right Direction,* while still a teenager.

Mills' breakthrough came in 1974, however, when her stunning, gospel-tinged mezzo-soprano landed her the lead role of Dorothy in *The Wiz,* the all-black stage version of L. Frank Baum's classic tale, *The Wonderful Wizard of Oz.* The show was a blockbuster, running from 1974 to 1979, and showcasing Mills in such venues as Carnegie Hall, the Metropolitan Opera House, and Madison Square Garden. As a result, the tiny four-foot, nine-inch singer with the remarkably powerful voice was catapulted to fame. Mills appeared regularly on TV talk and variety shows, released a series of popular R&B albums, won gold records, and was awarded a Tony and a Grammy. Despite all her success at such an early age, Mills would face many professional and personal disappointments.

As the youngest girl in the Mills' household, Stephanie was pampered and doted on by her older siblings. She was drawn to music from a very early age and often entertained her family by singing along with tunes on the radio and performing in school functions. But it was perhaps her membership in the choir at Cornerstone Baptist Church in Brooklyn that allowed her to hone her skills as a gospel singer. The tiny child's big voice was so impressive, in fact, that her brothers and sisters regularly escorted her to talent shows around Brooklyn. Mills' early influences included Diana Ross, Barbra Streisand, Carly Simon and Dolly Parton.

In 1974 Mills captured the attention of Ken Harper, who asked her to audition for *The Wiz,* a black musical he was preparing for Broadway. Mills won the lead role, and spent the next five years as Dorothy. The show's infectious anthem, "Ease on Down the Road," became Mills' trademark. "I had seen the *Wizard of Oz* movie, starring Judy Garland, on television when I was a kid and I had always enjoyed the fantasy," Mills told the *Chicago Tribune* in 1983. "What I had to do was to make Dorothy my role by bringing all of my emotions to the part and thinking about how a little black girl would

For the Record . . .

Born March 22, 1957 (some sources say 1959), in Brooklyn, NY; daughter of Joseph (New York city employee) and Christine (a hairdresser) Mills; married Jeffery Daniels (a musician), 1980 (marriage ended); married Michael Saunders (a radio programmer), 1992. *Education:* Studied at the Juilliard School of Music; gained fame starring in *The Wiz* on Broadway, beginning 1975.

Awards: Tony Award, circa 1976; Grammy Award for Best Female R&B Vocal, 1980; American Music Award for Best Female R&B Vocal, 1981.

Addresses: *Record company*—Casablanca Records, 810 7th Avenue, New York, NY 10019.

react to finding herself in Kansas and meeting a scarecrow and a witch and all those other weird people."

Riding the success of *The Wiz,* Mills became a household name—but it was not enough to land the role of Dorothy in the film version of the musical. That went to her childhood inspiration, Diana Ross. Another professional disappointment involved Mills' short tenure as a recording artist for Motown Records. While she was still touring in *The Wiz,* Jermaine Jackson of the Jackson Five urged Motown executive Berry Gordy to offer her a record contract. Mills recorded a single album for Motown, 1976's *For the First Time,* which was written and produced by the renowned team of Burt Bacharach and Hal David. The album, however, had poor sales, and Motown dropped Mills.

Goodbye Yellow Brick Road

After leaving *The Wiz,* Mills became an opening act for artists such as Teddy Pendergrass, the Commodores and the O'Jays. Before long, she was headlining—and wowing the crowds and critics alike. After her release from Motown, Mills signed with 20th Century Records, which released her next three albums and spawned a series of radio-ready R&B hits. The album *What Cha Gonna Do with My Lovin'* reached No. 8 on the R&B charts in 1979. Mills' follow-up album, *Sweet Sensation,* featured the million-selling, Top 10 pop hit "Never Knew Love Like This Before" and reached No. 3 on the R&B chart. In 1981 Mills released the last of her albums for 20th Century Records, the self-titled

Stephanie, and hit the charts again with "Two Hearts," a duet with Teddy Pendergrass. Her mainstream popularity resulted in the 1980 Grammy Award for Best Female R&B Vocal and the 1981 American Music Award for Best Female R&B Vocal.

Growing up off stage

While the young show biz veteran was enjoying fame on stage and on the radio, however, the first of her three marriages, to Jeffrey Daniels of Shalamar, was crumbling. The pair married in 1980 and divorced after a short, unhappy union. Following the three successful albums on the 20th Century label, Mills signed with Casablanca Records—and her popularity waned. Her four subsequent albums, released between 1982 and 1985, generated only one Top 10 R&B single, "The Medicine Song." The songstress landed a daytime television show on NBC in 1983, although it was short-lived. Mills then returned to her original success, the role of Dorothy, in a revival of *The Wiz* in 1984.

In 1986 and 1987, Mills returned to the top of the R&B charts three times with the singles "I Have Learned to Respect the Power Of Love," "I Feel Good All Over," and "(You're Puttin') A Rush on Me." Despite this comeback, Mills was experiencing personal hardship. A second marriage ended in divorce and unscrupulous handlers had stolen millions from her, according to *Ebony* magazine. "My life has gone through a lot of changes, some good, some bad," the singer told *Ebony* in 1992. "I learned something from all the experiences that has made me the person I am today. I've undergone a spiritual renewal from 1990 to 1992. It has been very educational to me in learning myself, through my music and therapy. I'm really getting to know what Stephanie wants to do. Before, I was just a puppet entertainer. There were things done for me and around me. Now I control everything, and that's a good feeling."

In 1992 Mills' album *Something Real* generated the Top 20 R&B single "All Day, All Night," and she married Michael Saunders, a radio programmer from Charlotte, North Carolina. "She has grown and matured," Sandra Davis wrote in *Notable Black American Women,* "into a graceful, humble, and tenacious African American role model."

Selected discography

Movin' in the Right Direction, Paramount, 1973.
For the First Time, Motown, 1976.

What Cha Gonna Do with My Lovin', 20th Century, 1979.
Sweet Sensation, 20th Century, 1980.
Stephanie, 20th Century, 1981
Tantalizingly Hot, Casablanca, 1982.
Merciless, Casablanca, 1983.
I've Got the Cure, Casablanca, 1984.
Stephanie Mills, MCA, 1985.
If I Were Your Woman, MCA, 1987.
Something Real, 1992.

Sources

Books

Mapp, Edward, *Dictionary of Blacks in the Performing Arts,* Scarecrow Press, Inc., 1990.

Periodicals

Ebony, December 1992.
People, February 10, 1986; August 17, 1987.

—*Dave Wilkins*

Keb' Mo'

Blues artist

Photograph by Jack Vartoogian. © Jack Vartoogian. Reproduced by permission.

Kevin Moore was born in Los Angeles in the early 1950s, but is actually a product of the deep South—possessing the values, music, and religion that black southerners carried with them on their migratory path to California in the first half of the 20th Century. Moore's family and neighbors in their Compton community had roots in the hard soil of Texas, Louisiana, Alabama, and Mississippi. Growing up in that setting, Moore found music all around him—blues on the record player, soul and R&B on the radio, gospel from the choir at his family's Baptist church. "The whole Southern culture kind of blended into one big black community," he told the *Advocate.* "Everybody had church socials, fried chicken on Sunday, staying in church all day. The women wore the hats and gloves to church—and they got happy."

By age ten, Moore played percussion and rhythm instruments in a steel band that regularly landed gigs performing calypso music. He later tackled the trumpet, French horn, and guitar. After high school, Moore performed Top 40 songs and oldies in various cover bands. During that period, one of Moore's bandleaders took him aside, told him his playing "didn't swing," then taught him about the music of New Orleans and its relation to the sounds of the Caribbean and Africa. "He gave me a big lesson. He sat down and listened to record after record with me," Moore was quoted in *Offbeat* magazine. "He turned me on to the Wild Tchoupitoulas and all these other things he had, like the Neville Brothers. And I took it to heart and listened to them, and began to incorporate that kind of swing into my own kind of music, more feel."

In 1973 former Jefferson Starship/Hot Tuna vocalist and violinist Papa John Creach hired Moore to play with his blues/rock outfit. Three years and three albums with Creach's band provided Moore with a steady touring job, songwriting experience, and connections in the Southern California blues scene. From the mid-1970s through the early 1980s, Moore worked in Los Angeles as a session musician and studio arranger. In 1980 he released his debut album *Rainmaker,* on the Chocolate City label, a subsidiary of Casablanca Records. Unfortunately, it attracted little attention.

In 1983 Moore joined the house band at an L.A. club called Marla's Memory Lane, where he learned from bandleader and veteran blues saxophonist, Monk Higgins, and jammed with legends such as Big Joe Turner, Albert Collins, Jimmy Witherspoon and Pee Wee Crayton. "My exposure to Monk Higgins was probably the most important element in developing my understanding of the blues," Moore told the *Detroit News.* He reconnected with the blues in 1990, when the Los

Born Kevin Moore in 1952 in Compton, CA. Moore's stage name, Keb' Mo', is a Black English version of his given name.

Signed with the Epic Records blues label, OKeh, and released self-titled debut, 1994; released *Just Like You,* 1996; performed on *The Late Show with David Letterman, Late Night with Conan O'Brien,* and *The Rosie O'Donnell Show,* 1996; appeared on the series *Touched by an Angel, ABC In Concert,* and *Sessions at West 54th,* 1997.

Performed at the Chicago Blues Festival, Montreaux Jazz Festival, and North Sea Jazz Festival, and his song "Crapped Out Again" was used in the Kevin Costner film *Tin Cup.*

Awards: Named Blues Artist of the Year, 1996, by the Blues Foundation; *Just Like You* earned Grammy Award for Best Contemporary Blues Album, 1996.

Addresses: *Record company*—Epic Records, P.O. Box 4450, New York, NY 10101-4450.

Angeles Theater Center asked him to portray a Delta bluesman in a play called *Rabbit Foot.* "By that time, I had already started listening to Robert Johnson and Big Bill Broonzy," Moore said. "Broonzy really blew my mind. His stuff was so basic, so powerful—that Southern-man, gospelly blues sound. To me, his music was the sound of a man moanin' out in the cotton field, trying to get free."

Keb' Mo' is Born

Moore went on to a role in a Mark Taper Theater production of *Spunk* and portrayed blues master Robert Johnson in a docudrama called *Can't You Hear the Wind Howl?* Meanwhile, he continued playing in L.A. clubs. The name "Keb' Mo'" came about around this time. A drummer friend, Quentin Dennard, gave him his street-slang stage name, Keb' Mo'. "I'd go see Quentin's jazz band on Monday nights, bring my guitar and sit in, start playing the blues," Moore explained in his Epic Records biography. "He'd look over the drums and holler, 'KEB' MO'!' Like, if I was playing jazz I could be Kevin Moore—but if I was gonna play the blues I had to be 'Keb' Mo'!' "

Big changes were in store for Kevin Moore in June of 1994. That's when Epic Records released his album *Keb' Mo'* on its newly revived blues label, OKeh. Moore's musical style demonstrated a timeless quality and his effortless ability to cross cultures and merge genres. The record won praise from the *New York Times, People,* and *Request* magazine, among others. One review compared his vocals to Otis Redding and David Ruffin and lauded his ability to move easily between 12-bar blues to melodic folk-pop ballads. Amid growing notoriety, Moore played music festivals, headlined at clubs and coffeehouses, and charmed large audiences while opening for artists as varied as Jeff Beck, Carlos Santana, Buddy Guy, George Clinton, Joe Cocker, and the Subdudes.

Moore's second record for Epic, *Just Like You,* took him to new heights, winning a Grammy Award for Best Contemporary Blues Album of 1996. "Like Taj Mahal, his closest spiritual precursor, singer-guitarist Keb' Mo' breathes new life into archetypal African-American musical forms," Tom Sinclair wrote in a review of *Just Like You* for *Entertainment Weekly.* "This freewheeling traditionalist works his alchemy on sweet country blues, gritty juke-joint jive, up-tempo R&B, and even breezy, George Benson-style jazz-pop." The *Washington Post* suggested that Moore had created a marketing dilemma for himself with all his genre-hopping. "By shifting his focus back and forth between these styles," the newspaper concluded, "Mo' runs the risk of alienating both blues purists and pop radio programmers. Yet anyone with open ears will recognize him for what he is: gifted and versatile."

Meanwhile, Moore returned to his familial and musical roots—by moving into a house on the edge of the French Quarter in New Orleans. He also shows no sign of reigning in his wandering spirit. "I want to stretch out more, on both ends," he told the *Detroit News.* "I want to go back even further, and dig deeper into the traditional-blues well, but I also want to bring something new to the table creatively, maybe by adding more electric guitar or putting 'today'-type sounds on top of a traditional rhythm section. I'm definitely looking to expand the realm of possibilities with the blues."

Selected discography

Rainmaker, Chocolate City, 1980.
Keb' Mo', OKeh/Epic Records, 1994.
Just Like You, OKeh/ Epic Records, 1996.
(Contributor) *Tin Cup* (soundtrack), Epic, 1996.

Sources

Advocate, April 25, 1997.
Detroit News, October 12, 1995.
Entertainment Weekly, June 12, 1996.
Offbeat, July 1996.
People, July 25, 1994.
Washington Post, August 30, 1996

Additional information provided by Epic Records web page.

—Dave Wilkins

Chante Moore

Pop artist

Pop balladeer Chante Moore enjoyed a resoundingly positive response to her 1991 debut album, *Precious,* and she continued to explore romantic musical terrain with equal success in her second release, *A Love Supreme.* While *Precious* presented her mellow pop style with jazz underpinnings, 1995's *A Love Supreme* instead highlighted her earnestness and playful personality and allowed Moore to grow comfortably into her early success. She cowrote 14 of the songs on her second album and branched out as coproducer as well. Moore fuses soulful ballads with rhythm and blues, pop, and jazz. *YSB* magazine's Sharon Dukes wrote, "Only in her twenties, Moore is a talent whose blend of jazz and R&B continues to surprise and capture listeners from all generations. Listen to the music.... smooth lyrics that swirl and soothe, over sensual notes, but with a strong message."

Moore's first album was so successful that she was featured in a one-hour BET special, *Candlelight and You: Chante Moore Live.* She has been compared to Roberta Flack, Sade, and Diana Ross and has seemingly incorporated elements of all three legendary singers: the dulcet tones of Ross, the thoughtful songwriting ability of Flack, and the smooth elegance of Sade. Moore told Dukes, "You can't grow up in America and not have influences from all the greats. I don't pattern myself after anyone in particular ... I really sound like my mom!"

The youngest of three children, Moore was born to a Church of God in Christ minister and his wife in San Francisco, California. The family moved to San Diego when Moore was twelve. She was raised in a musical atmosphere: her father played the piano and her brother played the drums, and she sang in a church choir throughout her childhood. Although she never performed a public solo because she was too shy, she used to sing at home all the time. She told *Ebony* magazine's Aldore Collier, "My family used to make me be quiet. They would say, 'Shut Up, Chante. Don't sing all the time.'... I sang with all the gospel albums, primarily Andrae Crouch and Edwin Hawkins." Moore's other early influences were Tremaine Hawkins and The Imperials. Her father loved jazz music and played it often at home.

At the age of 16, Moore was asked to play Dorothy in a musical production of *The Whiz.* She told Collier, "That was the first time I ever sang anywhere publicly. This lady from the church asked me to be Dorothy because I was so young ... she wanted me to sing and that didn't make sense. But I learned ... I didn't know I could touch people vocally. A little bug was put in my head." After her experience in *The Whiz,* Moore decided to pursue

For the Record . . .

Born Chante Moore c. 1970 in San Francisco, CA; the youngest of three children; father was a Church of God in Christ minister; moved to San Diego at the age of 12; children: one daughter.

Played Dorothy in a musical production of *The Whiz* at the age of 16; released debut album *Precious* for Silas/MCA Records, 1991; released *A Love Supreme*, 1995.

Awards: Voted "Best Female Vocalist" and "Most Promising Newcomer," *Precious* named the year's best album by Britain's *Blues & Soul* magazine, 1993.

Addresses: Silas/MCA Records, 70 Universal City Plaza, 3rd floor, Universal City, CA 91608 (818) 777-4000.

music professionally. She participated in local musicals in San Diego, and occasionally had the opportunity to meet people in the music industry.

Singer El DeBarge Provided Her Break

In 1989 Moore met singer El DeBarge while performing in the Motown musical *Heat Wave* in Los Angeles. DeBarge went to see the play one evening and met Moore backstage; the two struck up an enduring friendship. She eventually met his manager, Fred Moultrie, who offered to represent Moore as well. At the time, she didn't have a demo tape—so she landed a manager before she had a record deal. A month after retaining Moultrie, he convinced her to sign a contract with MCA Records.

People familiar with Moore's background and musical ability expected her to record gospel music on her debut album, but she explained to Collier, "First I wanted to establish myself ... to do everything else I wanted to do.... The Lord brought me to this. When people tell me, 'There's something special about you.' I tell them it's the Lord because I couldn't do this without him. He's the one who has blessed me."

Moore's debut album for MCA, *Precious,* quickly went gold, as did her second album, *A Love Supreme*, which details the experience of finding the right person, discovering the joys of love, and moving toward a commitment. The album includes Lionel Ritchie's "Sail On,"

Deniece Williams' "Free," and Alicia Myers' "I Want To Thank You." Moore's inspiration for the romantic release was real life: she met and fell in love with actor Kadeem Hardison at a 1995 *NAACP* event, and by 1997 the two had decided to marry.

Groomed for High Profile Career

Louil Silas Jr. launched a joint venture with MCA Records in September of 1992 to create Silas Records, and Moore was the label's first artist. Silas told *Billboard's* David Nathan, "Chante had everything: the musical talent, the personality, charisma, and beauty. I knew right away that she was a long-term career artist. I studied what (Berry Gordy, Jr.) did with Motown, the whole grooming process that helped create real entertainers." When MCA chairman Al Teller told Silas that he could oversee his own label, Silas told Nathan he knew he wanted Moore to be his first artist.

Moore was placed with three different veteran producers, and Bassel Benford and BeBe Winans were each called in to collaborate on one song. Visibility was created for Moore by placing her on the soundtrack for the movie *House Party 2*: she and Keith Washington recorded the duet "Candlelight and You" for the album. A special wardrobe clause was created in Moore's contract for her public appearances, key professional photographers and stylists were utilized, and her video for "Love's Taken Over" was shot in Paris.

BET also played a significant role in Moore's development and visibility. The station covered her video shoots, appearances at parties and record launchings for other artists. In addition, she appeared on *Video Soul, Video LP, Screen Scene,* and *Teen Summit.* Her concert special was aired twice on the station, and her visibility overseas in Canada, France, and England was heightened through concert appearances and tours.

Moore's *Precious* debut held its ground after nine months on the Top R&B Albums chart and close to six months on the *Billboard* 200. Readers of Britain's *Blues & Soul* magazine voted Moore "Best Female Vocalist" and "Most Promising Newcomer" in 1993. The readers also named *Precious* the year's best album. *Precious* delivered two Top 5 R&B hits: "Love's Taken Over," and "It's Alright." Moore also toured with legendary soul artist Barry White on his summer Icon World Tour in 1995. She was asked to contribute to the song "Freedom" for the *Panther* film soundtrack, but she felt the lyrics were too harsh for her to make a genuine contribution. Moore told Jeff Hall of the *Camden Courier-Post,* "I make sure I can send (the album) home to church and not be embarrassed."

Selected discography

(Contributor) *House Party 2: The Pajama Jam* (soundtrack), 1994.
Precious, Silas/MCA Records, 1991.
(Contributor) *Beverly Hills Cop III* (soundtrack), 1994.
A Love Supreme, Silas/MCA Records, 1995.
(Contributor) *New York Undercover* (soundtrack), UNI/MCA, 1995.
(Contributor) *Waiting to Exhale* (soundtrack), BMG/Arista, 1995.

Sources

Akron Beacon Journal, June 1, 1995.
Billboard, July 10, 1993.
BRE, May 2, 1997; July 9, 1993.
Camden Courier-Post, June 16, 1995.
Cleveland Plain Dealer, June 10, 1995.
Durham Herald-Sun, June 16, 1995.
Ebony, May 1995.
Jet, July 22, 1996.
Music Connection, March 15-March 28, 1993.
New Orleans Data News Weekly, December 23, 1995.
Now Magazine, August 1995.
Times-Picayune, December 22, 1995.
Tri-Valley Herald, November 21, 1995.
West County Times, November 24, 1995.
YSB, April 1995.

—*B. Kimberly Taylor*

Najee

Saxophonist, flutist

AP/Wide World Photos, Inc. Reproduced by permission.

ajee has been called one of the finest instrumentalists on the contemporary jazz scene. His smooth pop-jazz style, heavy on rhythm and blues, has gained him a tremendous audience of fans and a series of gold albums. Najee gives the people what they want to hear, and this has been his road to success. Although his aim-to-please attitude has brought criticism from some circles, he told Deni Kasrel of *Jazz Times* online that "when critics come to my concerts, they see the other side. I mix it up...." Najee tours extensively, playing at clubs and music festivals worldwide. After five successful albums, he decided to accept the challenge of something different. In 1995, he released *Najee Plays Songs from the Key of Life: A Tribute to Stevie Wonder,* an all-instrumental interpretation of a Stevie Wonder 1976 classic album.

Born in New York City, Najee grew up in the Jamaica section of Queens. He learned to play the clarinet in elementary school, and by the end of junior high, Najee got his chance to play sax with neighborhood groups. During high school, several instructors introduced him to the big band sound. Frank Foster, Frank Wess, and Jimmy Heath encouraged Najee to listen to the classics and to study jazz. Najee said that prior to participating in the city's Jazzmobile program, "I was mainly into Kool and the Gang, and James Brown." His early mentors from high school also inspired him to learn the flute.

Following high school graduation, Najee performed with Ben E. King and The Main Ingredient. He also supported the Miss Black America world tour in 1976. Subsequently, Najee attended the New England Conservatory of Music in Boston, Massachusetts. At the Conservatory he studied jazz with George Russell and Jaki Byard, as well as playing in the big bands they led.

After finishing at the New England Conservatory of Music, Najee returned to the New York jazz scene in 1982, and his rhythm and blue roots. He performed with The Fatback Band and Chaka Khan. It was during a performance in a New York club with one of Khan's backup singers that Najee's talent attracted Charles Huggins of Hush Productions. An impressed Huggins introduced Najee to executives at EMI Records, who promptly signed him to the EMI label.

His debut album, entitled *Najee's Theme,* was released in 1987. Following this, he set out on a nationwide tour with singer Freddie Jackson. On the road, playing clubs and concerts, he began to develop what would become a very loyal following to his smooth pop-jazz heavily laced with rhythm and blues. The following year, *Day by Day* was released, and in 1990, *Tokyo Blue.* Both albums went gold.

Remaining loyal to producing the contemporary jazz-pop that earned him his early popularity, Najee's fourth album, *Just an Illusion,* was released in 1992. On the track "Deep Inside Your Love," he illustrates his talent for fitting flowing spurts from his saxophone around the vocalists. Patrick Cole of *DownBeat* magazine remarked that he he adds to the vocals "without stealing the show."

Following the release of *Just an Illusion,* Najee toured extensively during 1993 and 1994 with various artists, including superstar Quincy Jones and jazz greats Stanley Clarke, Larry Carlton, and Billy Cobham. Many, including Clarke, were surprised by Najee's ability to hold his own against these musicians because the majority of his work previously had been considered smooth jazz. Najee told Kasrel, "It was a different setting than I'm used to and it allowed me to open up."

Two years later, in 1994, Najee released *Share My World.* He continued to remain true to the familiar, comfortable grooves of smooth pop-jazz, with rhythm and blues undertones. Some of the cuts are fanciful and delicately move along the romantic landscape. He has plenty of opportunity to showcase his soprano saxophone throughout the album, and stays within the safety of previous margins. Only at the very end of the album does he allow a peek at his "jazz chops." This ending is the most noticeable departure from his usual style.

Despite his lack of improvisation, Najee has considerable range and flexibility. Besides playing soprano and tenor sax, he also plays the flute and occasionally keyboards. His background in rhythm and blues remains a strong influence in his work. He has remarked that his influences include Grover Washington, Jr., and Ronnie and Hubert Laws.

Took a New Road

After *Share My World,* Najee was prepared for a challenge. Working with EMI Records president Davitt Sigerson, the two decided upon a change in direction for Najee's next release. They decided to produce an all-instrumental version of Stevie Wonder's 1976 classic, *Songs in the Key of Life.* George Duke was chosen to produce it.

In addition to being a vehicle showcasing Najee's talents as an instrumentalist, a long list of other distinguished musicians were brought together. Some of these included Stanley Clark and Freddy Washington on bass; Ray Fuller, Phil Upchurch, and Paul Jackson, Jr. on guitar; Herbie Hancock and Ronnie Foster on keyboard; Paulino DaCosta and Sheila E. on percussion; and arrangements by Jorge del Barrio, and others. Producer George Duke felt that the musicians should use the same instruments that were used to produce the original recording in 1976. Najee told Kasrel in an interview, "He [Duke] would suggest something and I would say 'I trust you, period.'" Duke had established his reputation during the 1970s, so he had a good grasp and understanding of the period instruments and equipment being used.

Because the original release of *Songs* was a double album set, some of the songs were combined and shortened. Najee wanted to be sure that all of the songs from the original version of Stevie Wonder's album were included in his tribute, and that they were in the same order as the original album.

Developed Voice on Flute

Songs from the Key of Life also provided Najee with an opportunity to break from the standard soprano saxophone. Out of the 18 cuts on the album, Najee plays flute on half of them. Grateful to add a new instrument to his repertoire, he said he was glad to have the chance to emphasize his flute chops for a change. The technical challenge came for Najee in learning how to play the flute as if he were Stevie Wonder's voice. Najee felt that it was a worthwhile effort, and the project also gave him an opportunity to work with some of the legends in the jazz world.

Another treat for Najee was including his young son, Jamal, in on the recording; Jamal's voice can be heard on the special medley combining "Isn't She Lovely" and "Joy Inside My Tears." Creating the tribute to Stevie Wonder also returned Najee to his youth. Najee recalled back in his teens playing in a band called Area Code; the group had played some of the same cuts, including "Knocks Me Off My Feet."

From the first cut, "Love's In Need of Love Today," to the grand finale — the combination of "All Day Sucker" and "Easy Goin' Evening," Najee showcases his talents on the flute, and soprano and alto sax. His nimble fingerings and the talented accompaniment by many of the masters of jazz playing mostly period pieces captures the feel of 1976. From the reggae sound of "Pastime Paradise," to the heart wrenching "If It's Magic," *Najee Plays Songs from the Key of Life* is not only a tribute to Stevie Wonder, but also to Najee's talent as well as all of the skillful musicians featured. Najee told an interviewer from *VIBE* magazine, "...it was an incredible learning experience and I'm happy with how it turned out ... [it was] my opportunity to take us back to this beautiful era."

Selected discography

Najee's Theme, EMI, 1987.
Day by Day, EMI, 1988.
Tokyo Blue, EMI, 1990.
Just an Illusion, EMI, 1992.
Share My World, EMI, 1994.
Najee Plays Songs from the Key of Life: A Tribute to Stevie Wonder, EMI, 1995.

With others

(With Pete Escovedo), *Flying South,* Concord Picante, 1996.
(With Doc Powell), *Laid Back,* Discover, 1996.

Sources

Books

Erlewine, Michael; Bogdanov, Vladmir; Woodstra, Chris; Yanow, Scott, editors, *All Music Guide to Jazz,* Miller Freeman, 1996.

Periodicals

DownBeat, October 1992, p. 41; January 1995, p. 51.
Vibe, October, 1995.

Online

http://cdnow.com
http://www.freeyellow.com/members/earthlydiscoveries/page3.html
http://www.jazzcentralstation.com/
http://www.montego-bay-jamaica.com/jamjazz/target.htm
http://www7.cddb.com/xm/cd/jazz/1410db12.html
http://www.vibe.com/vibe/vibevideo/artists/najee/docs/f-ab1.html
http://www.cduniverse.com/programs/cdubin.exe/frm=ad_mc12
http://206.98.164.240/jcs/station/jazzdest/festivals/essence/index.html

—Debra Reilly

Anita O'Day

Jazz vocalist

AP/Wide World Photos, Inc. Reproduced by permission.

Called "one of the finest singers to emerge from the swing era" by Scott Yanow in the *All Music Guide to Jazz,* Anita O'Day has been hailed as one of the most distinctive voices in the history of jazz. She advanced from a Billie Holiday-type style to her own inventive technique that made her equally adept at interpreting songs as written and improvising with a flair matched by few. O'Day was also the chief inspiration of many famed singers who came to prominence in the 1940s, including June Christy, Chris Connor, and Helen Merrill. She has had one of the longest active careers among jazz singers, now spanning over 60 years. Her tenure in front of the microphone is all the more incredible considering that she was addicted to heroin during many of her peak years.

New York Times writer Stephen Holden reported that during a 1995 performance at Rainbow and Stars in New York City, O'Day remarked: "I'm not a singer; I'm a song stylist." Although her singing approach was inspired by Mildred Bailey, Billie Holiday, Ella Fitzgerald, and Martha Raye, O'Day eventually developed her own style that others found difficult to imitate. Some of her most inventive traits as a singer were "a manner of skipping in front of and behind the beat, and the extensive use of melisma [a group of notes or tones sung on one syllable]," according to Leonard Feather and Ira Gitler in *The Encyclopedia of Jazz in the Seventies.* O'Day also cut a distinctive profile on stage in her early career by appearing in a band jacket and short skirt rather than the more formal dress that was virtually demanded of female singers of her time, causing her to be regarded as an early feminist.

Anita Belle Colton came upon her career as a singer somewhat accidentally. She joined a burlesque show as a teenager, and then was asked to replace a singer who had laryngitis. During the Depression she endured an exhausting tenure as a contestant in dance marathons, at which time she assumed the stage name of O'Day. When she was 19 she scratched out a living by becoming a singing waitress and dice-girl, finally landing some jobs as a singer with local Chicago groups. One of her key venues as a performer was the Off-Beat, a night spot frequented by musicians such as the drummer and band leader Gene Krupa.

A singing job with the Max Miller combo at the Three Deuces club in Chicago gave O'Day the exposure she needed, and two years later she replaced Irene Daye as a singer for Krupa's band. Critical to her success at this time was the addition to the band of trumpeter and vocalist Roy Eldridge, who shared a strong chemistry with O'Day on stage. The two were featured as singers on the recording of "Let Me Off Uptown," which was one

For the Record . . .

Born Anita Belle Colton December 18, 1919, in Chicago, IL.

Began singing as a teenager as a replacement for ill singer in burlesque show, 1930s; worked as a dance-a-thon contestant, 1930s; changed name to O'Day while working as a singing waitress and dice-girl, 1938; sang in Off-Beat club, Chicago, IL, late 1930s; began singing with Max Miller combo at Chicago's Three Deuces, 1939; joined Gene Krupa's band, 1941; had first hit, "Let Me Off Uptown," with Krupa band, 1941; left Krupa band to get married, 1943; sang briefly with Woody Herman's band, 1943; joined Stan Kenton's band, 1944; rejoined Krupa band, 1945; began recording as soloist with Signature label, 1947; sang with various small bands and studio orchestras, 1950s; began long association with Verve label, 1952; started working regularly with drummer John Poole, 1954; received rave reviews for performance in Newport Jazz Festival, 1958; appeared in *The Gene Krupa Story*, 1959; made first tour of Japan, early 1960s; almost died from heroin overdose, 1967; made comeback at Berlin Jazz Festival, 1971; toured England and Europe, 1970–71; formed own record company, Anita O'Day Records (later renamed Emily Records), 1972; performed at Monterey Jazz Festival, 1974; sang at Carnegie Hall and various super clubs in New York, NY, 1974; had special performance at Carnegie Hall to commemorate her 50 years as a singer, 1985; continued to perform and record, 1990s. Film appearances include *The Glenn Miller Story*, 1959; *Zig-Zag*, 1971; *The Outfit*, 1974.

Addresses: *Record company*—Verve Records, 825 8th Ave., 26th fl., New York, NY 10019.

of the first interracial vocal duets on record. This single, which was a major hit, and O'Day's rendition of "That's What You Think" helped make the young singer a hot new star in the early 1940s. In 1941 her new fame was confirmed by *Down Beat* magazine naming her "New Star of the Year," and the following year the magazine cited her as one of the top five big band singers.

After getting married in 1943, O'Day left the Krupa band and moved to California to explore other options as a performer. She joined up with Woody Herman's band for a short period, then quit because she was unable to cope with the band's exhausting schedule of consecutive one-night stands. At that point her manager advised her to sing with Stan Kenton's band, which she did in 1944. More accolades came her way in the mid 1940s, among them designations of best big-band singer by *Down Beat* and "outstanding new star" by *Esquire*. Although her fame grew with Kenton thanks to her renditions of songs such as "And Her Tears Flowed Like Wine," O'Day was not pleased with Kenton's highly controlled approach. As Len Lyons and Don Perlo noted in *Jazz Portraits: The Lives and Music of the Jazz Masters,* "O'Day was uncomfortable with the rigid structure of the music and highbrow attitude of the group."

Her eagerness for a more freewheeling atmosphere brought O'Day back to Krupa's band in 1945, which by then had the services of the bebop-style pianist Dodo Marmaros and clarinetist Buddy DeFranco. After leaving Krupa in 1946, O'Day explored her potential as a solo artist. Her first solo work was recorded on the Signature label in 1947, and on her own she began to demonstrate her exceptional versatility. In his review of *Anita O'Day 1949–1950* on Tono, Yanow wrote that the singer "handles the wide variety of songs (ranging from bop and dated novelties to calypso and 'Tennessee Waltz') with humor and swing, mostly uplifting the occasionally indifferent material."

Blossomed with Verve Label

Starting in 1950, O'Day sang with a number of small bands, and worked as a session singer in the studio. Her career received a major boost after she signed on with the new Verve jazz label produced by Norman Granz. She hit her peak in 1955 with *Anita,* about which Yanow stated: "O'Day is heard near the peak of her powers on such songs as 'You're the Top,' 'Honeysuckle Rose,' an emotional rendition of 'A Nightingale Sang in Berkeley Square,' and 'As Long as I Live.'" Many of her Verve recordings in the mid 1950s featured Monty Budwig on bass, Tal Farlow or Barney Kessel on guitar, and Jimmy Rowles on piano. Since O'Day's rhythmic style was so responsive to percussion, it was no surprise when she hooked up with drummer John Poole as her regular accompanist in 1954 for a professional relationship that lasted 32 years.

As her fame spread during the 1950s, O'Day was in demand for festivals and concerts that featured the greatest jazz stars of her day—including Louis Armstrong, Dinah Washington, George Shearing, and Thelonious Monk. Many fans and critics have attested that the high point of her career was her performance at the Newport Jazz Festival in 1958, which was called "sensational" by Barry Kernfeld in *The New Grove Dictionary of Jazz.* Her versions of "Sweet Georgia Brown" and "Tea for Two" at the Festival brought down the house, and were also preserved in a filmed account of the event.

Strong Soul, Weak Heart

Although still active on the jazz circuit in the 1960s, O'Day began to suffer heart problems as a result of her long-term heroin addiction. She finally stopped using the drug in 1967 after a near fatal overdose. Her career got back on track with a strong performance at the Berlin Jazz Festival in 1970, and she ventured into the business end of her music in 1972 when she formed her own record company, Anita O'Day Records (later known as Emily Records). Many O'Day albums were turned out on her label in the 1970s, and she continued to perform in major festivals and jazz clubs as she approached 60. In 1974 she began appearing frequently at Ye Little Club in Beverly Hills, California, as well as clubs such as Reno Sweeney's in New York City. Meanwhile, her new releases were often received favorably. In his review of *Anita O'Day Live,* a recording of a 1975 performance released for the first time in 1993, Scott Yanow said that "the singer is heard in excellent form."

In 1985 O'Day celebrated her half-century as a singer with a performance in Carnegie Hall. "She still excels at up-tempo rhythms," remarked Len Lyons and Don Perlo in *The Jazz Masters* in 1987, confirming that O'Day had aged well. But by the 1990s, her public appearances had become somewhat erratic. Discussing an O'Day performance at Rainbow and Stars in New York City when she was 75 years old, John Holdung wrote in *Back Stage,* "The voice, while still pure jazz, is now a dim memory possibly best left for recording rather than for public performances in a pricey room." In his review of 1994's *Rules of the Road,* Chris Albertson wrote that the singer "would have been better served leaving us to wonder how she might have sounded today."

It is likely that Anita O'Day's extensive lineup of highly regarded albums and performances will always stand tall among the pantheon of great jazz performers. Brian Priestly concluded in *Jazz: The Rough Guide* that "the many singers who emulated her work, ballads especially, such as June Christy, Chris Connor, and Helen Merrill, came nowhere near to swinging as delightfully as O'Day."

Selected discography

Anita O'Day 1949-1950, Tono.
Anita, Verve, 1955.
Anita O'Day Sings the Winners, Verve, 1958.
All the Sad Young Men, Verve, 1961.
Anita O'Day Live, Star Line, 1976.
Live at the City, Emily, 1979.
A Song for You, Emily, 1984.
Rules of the Road, Pablo, 1994.

Selected writings

High Times, Hard Times (with George Eells), Corgi, 1983.

Sources

Books

Carr, Ian, Digby Fairweather, and Brian Priestley, *Jazz: The Rough Guide,* The Rough Guides, 1995, pp. 479–480.
Case, Brian, and Stann Britt, revised and updated by Chrissie Murray, *The Harmony Illustrated Encyclopedia of Jazz, Third Edition,* Harmony Books, pp. 140–141.
Cook, Richard, and Brian Morton, *The Penguin Guide to Jazz on CD, LP, and Cassette,* Penguin Books, 1992, pp. 819–820.
Erlewine, Michael, Vladimir Bogdanov, Chris Woodsta, and Scott Yanow, *All Music Guide to Jazz, Second Edition,* Miller Freeman Books, 1996, pp. 559–561.
Feather, Leonard, and Ira Gitler, *The Encyclopedia of Jazz in the Seventies,* Horizon Press, 1976, p. 258.
Kernfeld, Barry, editor, *The New Grove Dictionary of Jazz, Volume Two,* Macmillan, 1988, pp. 264–265.
Lyons, Len, and Don Perlo, *Jazz Portraits: The Lives and Music of the Jazz Masters,* William Morrow, 1989, pp. 399–400.
O'Day, Anita and George Eells, *High Times, Hard Times,* Corgi, 1983.

Periodicals

Back Stage, July 14, 1995, p. 11.
New York Times, June 30, 1995, p. C20.
Stereo Review, May 1994, p. 90.

Additional information for this profile was obtained from the Jazz Profiles website of the National Public Radio on the Internet.

—*Ed Decker*

Orchestral Manoeuvres in the Dark

British pop band

The most famous band ever to come out of Liverpool, England may have been the Beatles. In the 1980s, however, the Liverpudlian group cranking out the most catchy pop hits was the synthesizer band Orchestral Manoeuvres in the Dark (OMD). For most of its history, OMD was essentially a two-man operation consisting of Andy McCluskey and Paul Humphreys. During its mid-1980s heyday, the duo recorded a string of commercial hits that put it among the elite of that period's synthesizer-based, dance-friendly pop bands.

Friends since grade school, McCluskey and Humphreys began playing music together during the mid-1970s. Their earliest inspiration was the German electronic band Kraftwerk, which pioneered the use of synthesizers in popular music. McCluskey and Humphreys began noodling around with a collection of primitive electronic gear, and soon began creating original experimental music under the name VCL XI. Over the next few years, one or the other or both of them performed in a series of bands with such names as Hitlerz Underpantz, Dalek I Love You, and Equinox.

In 1977 McCluskey and Humphreys became part of an eight-piece band called The Id. The Id was heavily influenced by the emerging electronic music scene populated by such bands as Cabaret Voltaire and Human League. When The Id began to fizzle, McCluskey and Humphreys reformed as a duo under the most self-indulgent name they could thing of—Orchestral Manoeuvres in the Dark. Playing mostly material salvaged from The Id, OMD made its live debut in October of 1978 at a Liverpool club called Eric's. In addition to its two human members, OMD's third performer was a tape deck named Winston.

The novelty of OMD's sound quickly caught the attention of Factory Records honcho Tony Wilson, who signed the band to its first record contract. OMD's first recording was the single "Electricity," released in May of 1979. The record sold out its first pressing in a couple of weeks, and received heavy radio play in Britain. It led to gigs with other emerging bands of post-punk England, including Joy Division and Echo and the Bunnymen, another band that awarded its drum machine full membership status. While touring in support of new waver Gary Numan, OMD was approached by Din-Disc, a new subsidiary of Virgin Records. They quickly signed with DinDisc, and used their advance money to build their own recording studio.

After a couple more fairly successful singles, OMD struck gold in 1980 with the single "Enola Gay," which sold 2.5 million copies worldwide and reached the top of the charts all over Europe. The group's debut album,

Members include **Martin Cooper** (left band in 1989), keyboards, saxophone; **Malcolm Holmes** (left band in 1989), drums; **Paul Humphreys** (born February 27, 1960, in Liverpool, England; left band in 1989), synthesizers, vocals; and **Andy McCluskey** (born June 24, 1959, in Liverpool, England), bass, synthesizers, vocals.

First live performance as Orchestral Manoeuvres in the Dark in Liverpool, October 1978; signed with Factory Records and released first single, "Electricity," 1979; signed with Virgin Records, 1980; scored first major hit single, "Enola Gay," 1980; broke up, 1989; resurrected by McCluskey with release of album *Sugar Tax,* 1991.

Addresses: *Record company*—Virgin, 30 West 21st St., New York, NY 10010. *Management*—Direct Management Group, Inc., 947 North La Cienega Blvd., Suite G, Los Angeles, CA 90069.

the self-titled *Orchestral Manoeuvres in the Dark,* and their follow up, *Organisation,* both released in 1980, were also big commercial successes. For the next two years, OMD was a fixture at the top of the singles charts, with a string of hits that included "Souvenir," "Joan of Arc," and "Maid of Orleans." Meanwhile, the band replaced Winston with two human musicians, drummer Malcolm Holmes and keyboard/saxophonist Martin Cooper.

An 80s Masterpiece: *Architecture & Morality*

OMD's 1981 album, *Architecture & Morality,* reflected a further refining of the band's trademark sound, which combined a haunting electronically-generated atmosphere with the catchiest brand of pop melodies. *Melody Maker* magazine described the album as "the first true masterpiece of the Eighties." OMD continued to be a prolific hit machine, scoring several hit singles and another four Top Twenty albums. The band's 1983 LP *Dazzle Ships,* was a bit more experimental than its predecessor's, to the dismay of some OMD fans. Almost unified enough to call a concept album, it contained such anti-pop elements as a spoken-word tape collage ("Time Zones") and a piece that featured sounds of ship noises (the title track).

By the mid-1980s, many synth-based bands that had been clearly influenced by OMD, including Soft Cell, Depeche Mode, and Pet Shop Boys, had emerged. OMD scored its first American hits in 1985, with the singles "So in Love" and "Secret" from the album *Crush.* In 1986 the band was heard on the soundtrack for the popular film *Pretty in Pink.* By the time OMD's 1986 album *The Pacific Age* came out, it was becoming clear that the band's popularity had already peaked. Although the LP included a hit single in "Forever (Live and Die)," its critical reception was mixed at best. Writer Dave Castle called it "a weak epilogue" to the staling partnership between McCluskey and Humphreys.

Resurrected by McCluskey

In 1988 the band released *The Best of OMD,* and the following year, with internal tensions mounting, Humphreys left OMD to pursue other musical interests. Humphreys joined forces with old OMD associates Malcolm Holmes and Martin Cooper to form another band, called The Listening Pool, with Humphreys assuming the role frontman and chief songwriter. Meanwhile, McCluskey spent two years writing songs and assembling a new stable of young musicians, and in 1991 he dusted of the OMD name and emerged from the shadows with a new album, *Sugar Tax,* which featured the hit singles "Pandora's Box" and "Sailing on Seven Seas." *Sugar Tax* eventually sold more than two million copies worldwide, and it thrust OMD back into the spotlight after several years of stagnation.

Riding the momentum of *Sugar Tax,* and the hugely successful world tour that accompanied it, McCluskey returned in 1993 with *Liberator,* which, although touted as OMD's most blatantly commercial offering, did not perform as well as its predecessor. "*Liberator* picks up the musical thread of OMD's mid-'80s synth-pop hits," wrote Larry Flick of *Billboard.*

McCluskey and OMD came through with another album, *Universal,* in 1996. This recording included the single "Walking on the Milky Way," which received fairly heavy radio play and fared respectably on the pop charts. Since OMD in its current form is essentially McCluskey's solo operation, its life expectancy is exactly as long as his attention span—at least if loyal fans continue to buy OMD recordings at the levels they have in the past.

McCluskey's fountain of pop hits certainly shows no sign of drying up. "My best songs come from me leaping off into the wild blue yonder," he was quoted as saying in *Billboard.* "It's like therapy. In my day-to-day life, I often steer clear from emotional confrontation. A lot of those tightly tucked feelings wind up in my songs. The challenge is to effectively place them into a three-minute pop tune." For OMD, meeting that challenge has been a formula for lasting pop stardom and acclaim.

Selected discography

Orchestral Manoeuvres in the Dark, Virgin, 1980.
Organisation, Virgin, 1980.
Architecture & Morality, Virgin, 1981.
Dazzle Ships, Virgin, 1983.
Junk Culture, Virgin, 1984.
Crush, Virgin, 1985.
The Pacific Age, Virgin, 1986.
The Best of OMD, Virgin, 1988.
Sugar Tax, Virgin, 1991.
Liberator, Virgin, 1993.
Universal, Virgin, 1996.

Sources

Periodicals

Billboard, July 17, 1993
Creem, June 1982; July 1985.
Melody Maker, April 28, 1984.
Musician, October 1985.
Rolling Stone, August 29, 1985.

Online

www.accessone.com/~fester/omdframe.htm
www.csu.edu.au/faculty/commerce/account/omd/omd.htm

—*Robert R. Jacobson*

Carl Orff

Classical composer, music educator

Archive Photos, Inc. Reproduced by permission.

The work of German composer Carl Orff predates the late twentieth-century renewal of interest in the haunting, unusual melodies of medieval-era religious music by several decades. In the 1930s, Orff was composing works for the stage based on medieval Latin chants, and later revived the classic tales of love, lust, and blood from ancient Greek drama for modern audiences. Yet Orff's most famous work remains *Carmina Burana,* a 1937 homage to life's more earthy pleasures based on a long-lost collection of medieval songs. The melodies he adapted into the stirring *Carmina Burana* have entered popular culture in the form of background music for television commercials and entrance pomp at sporting events. "Orff's chorus seems to transcend period, place, authorship, even meaning," wrote Matthew Gurewitsch of *Carmina Burana*'s lasting legacy in the *Atlantic Monthly.* "Part paean, part lament, it purrs and roars like some titanic flywheel. This is chant the cosmos might sing to itself, as impersonal as a landslide or a tidal wave. The din it makes has all but obliterated its maker."

Orff was born in the Bavarian capital of Munich on July 10, 1895, into a long line of military officers in service to the local princes or the German kaiser. Orff, however, strayed down a far different path from an early age, perhaps inspired by the rich and varied offerings Munich offered to music-lovers. He began piano lessons at age of five, and also took up the organ and cello. As a child he began writing his own musical compositions, and loved to stage puppet shows for his household. As a teenager he set verse by German Romantic poets Friedrich Hoelderlin and Heinrich Heine to music, and had his first compositions published in 1911. He graduated from Munich's music academy, the Akademie der Tonkunst in 1914, and at the age of 20 took a job as the assistant Kapellmeister, or orchestra conductor, at the famed Muenchener Kammerspiele.

Orff stayed at the Kammerspiele from 1915 to 1917, but was drafted into the German Army during the last year of World War I. The long military traditions of the Orff family seemed to have genetically bypassed him, and the demands of war tested him greatly. The following year, upon his return to civilian life and the end of the war, Orff became assistant Kapellmeister at the Nationaltheater in Mannheim, as well as holding the same position at the Landestheater (State Theater) in nearby Darmstadt. In 1919, he returned to Munich and began teaching music; he also studied under Heinrich Kaminski, and it was through this avenue that Orff became interested in Renaissance-era music.

In 1924 Orff and gymnast Dorothea Guenther founded a Munich school for children whose legacy would continue long after their deaths. The Guenther Schule's aim

For the Record . . .

Born, July 10, 1895, in Munich, Germany; died of cancer, March 29, 1982, in Munich, Germany; son of Heinrich and Paula (Koestler) Orff; married to Lise Lotte; children: Godela (daughter). *Education:* Received degree from the Akademie der Tonkunst (Academy of Music), Munich, 1915; studied with Heinrich Kaminski, early 1920s.

Composer and music teacher; assistant Kapellmeister, or orchestra conductor, at the Muenchener Kammerspiele, 1915-17; also served in the same position at the Nationaltheater, Mannheim, and at the Landestheater, Darmstadt, both from 1918-19; co-founded Guenther Schule, Munich, with Dorothea Guenther, 1924; first work for the stage was *Klage der Ariadne,* which premiered in Karlsruhe, Germany, 1925; was active in Munich's Bach Society in the early 1930s and served as its director until 1934; taught a master class at Munich's Hochschule fuer Musik, 1950-60; was an instructor at the Orff School for Music at the Mozarteum Academy for Music and Dramatic Art in Salzburg, Austria, instructor, for over a decade, beginning in 1949; later served as its director until his death in 1982; received honorary doctorates from the Universities of Tuebingen (1955) and Munich (1972).

Awards: Munich Music Prize, 1947; New York Music Critics' Prize, 1954, for *Carmina Burana;* Bremen Music Prize, 1956; Order pour le Merite for Science and Art, West Germany, 1956; Cross of Merit, 1959; Mozart Prize, Basel Goethe foundation, 1969.

was to teach music to children by a set of aesthetic-awareness principles Orff and Guenther had formulated, based on the idea that nearly all human beings are "musical" by nature. Orff wrote the treatise *Schulwerk,* which explained these theories and gave teachers a curriculum of songs and activities employing German folk songs and poetry. Even in the late twentieth century, thousands of teachers around the world are certified in the program, and translated versions of *Schulwerk* incorporate the folklore and literature of each culture. Orff also developed easy-to-learn percussion instruments to use in the program.

Orff penned a number of works for the stage during the 1920s. His adaptation of one of opera's first great works, *Orpheus,* was performed in Mannheim in 1925 with some of the original instruments used in Claudio Monteverdi's 1607 production. The city of Karlsruhe hosted the debuts for Orff's *Klage der Ariadne* ("Ariadne's Lament") and *Tanz der Sproeden* ("Dance of the Merciless Beauties"), also adaptations of Monteverdi operas, in 1925 as well. In the late 1920s, Orff was preoccupied in writing *Schulwerk;* in 1930, the same year its first part was published, Orff was named conductor of Munich's Bach Society. In 1931 he adapted a Bach passion play into a controversial stage version set in rural Bavaria, the maligned *St. Luke Passion,* which set the story of Christ among southern German peasantry.

Fame came to Orff, however, with the 1937 debut of *Carmina Burana,* and the stage work marked a radical new direction in his career as well: he even wrote his publisher instructing him to destroy all his previous works, since the composer felt that his career rightly began here. *Carmina Burana,* or the "Songs of Beuren," was Orff's adaptation of a codex discovered in the archives of a Bavarian monastery in 1803. The manuscript was a collection of songs written down in the thirteenth century, and reflects the popular tastes of that age in its lyrics from wandering minstrels and spoofs written by the Benedictine monks. In the original Vulgar Latin, Old French, and Middle High German, its 200 songs poke fun at organized religion or celebrate carnal pursuits. Others reflect a love of nature or life's gustatory pleasures—a goose on a spit, for instance, sings a comic lament over the fire. The plotless stage work Orff created from this used only about ten percent of the original manuscript—much of it the risqué text—and its performance, though dance and pantomime, won him great praise upon its debut in 1937.

Orff and Hitler's Germany

Carmina Burana, it should be noted, was first staged in Frankfurt am Main's opera house during the height of Nazi power in Germany. Most of the country's artists of this era—the composers, painters, or writers who were not Jewish and had not emigrated—found themselves bound to a strict ideology to celebrate "German" traits in their work. Artists who kept out of trouble during this period have sometimes been looked upon as quasi-collaborators with the fascist regime, and Orff's name has often been mentioned in the same sentence as the phrase "Nazi composer."

Orff, however, was certainly aware of the necessity to keep out of trouble during this time, and it seems unlikely that he was a "favorite" of anyone in power, with the Nazi leadership better remembered for its fondness toward the operas of Richard Wagner. In 1934, when the Munich Bach Society came increasingly under the control of a Nazi group, the Kampfbund, Orff resigned his director's post. The Kampfbund was a government agency set up to weed out modernist or "Jewish" tendencies in all aspects of the arts in Germany.

Furthermore, around the time of *Carmina Burana*'s premier, Orff came to the attention of Heinz Drewes, the newly appointed head of the music section of the ministry of propaganda for the German government. The functionary, according to Michael H. Kater in *The Twisted Muse: Musicians and Their Music in the Third Reich,* "took an immediate dislike to Orff and, while never censuring outright any of the composer's current or future works, successfully intimidated him, keeping him in abeyance until well into the war." Later, Orff would write *Astutuli,* completed in 1945. This allegorical tale slyly criticizing Hitler and the Third Reich was not staged, however, until 1953.

Though he is best remembered for *Carmina Burana,* Orff wrote several other works for the stage. Reflecting his interest in medieval music—the chants of the Gregorian monks, for example—Orff's compositions were repetitious in tone, and often described as "primitive" or "skeletal." The same note might be played continuously, taking minimalist music to new extremes; a performer might be required to sing a "C" 200 times straight in other instances. Orchestras for Orff's compositions usually consisted of a heavy percussion section and banks of pianos, with their pianists instructed in the notation to smash the keys with vigor.

Wrote Work for Actress Daughter

As with *Carmina Burana,* Orff enjoyed the challenge of adapting works from unusual sources. In 1939's *Der Mond* ("The Moon"), which he based on a Brothers Grimm fairy tale, four men steal the moon, with predictably disastrous consequences. *Die Kluge: The Story of the King and the Wise Woman,* which had its first performance in 1943, told the story of a farmer's daughter who gains the love of a despot by solving his riddles. Orff penned *Die Bernauerin* ("The Tragedy of Agnes Bernauer") for his daughter Godela, an actress. It premiered in Stuttgart in 1947 and is still performed annually in the Bavarian city of Augsburg, where some of it is set. In this harsh tale, recounted by a chorus of male witches, the title character is an impoverished young woman from the lower classes who wins the heart of a duke and marries him. For this she is despised as a villain and then lynched.

Orff also adapted the works of others besides Monteverdi and Grimm. His version of Shakespeare's *A Midsummer Night's Dream, Ein Sommernachtstraum,* debuted in 1939 but was revised by Orff a total of six times over the next four decades. Later in his career Orff took the works of the ancient Greek playwrights—upon which the very principles of opera were based—and adapted them for the modern German stage. To do so he used translations from the Greek undertaken in the late eighteenth century by the poet Hoelderlin, whom modern scholars have theorized probably suffered from schizophrenia. Hoelderlin, according to Gurewitsch in the 1995 *Atlantic Monthly* essay, "mimicked the original Greek with breathtaking disdain for accepted German usage, creating in effect a language within a language." Orff's Greek adaptations include *Antigonae* (1949) *Oedipus der Tyrann* (1959), both by Sophocles.

Carmina Burana premiered to American audiences in the late 1950s, and won Orff great acclaim. He continued to adapt the work of the Greek dramatists during the latter years of his career; *Prometheus* (after Aeschylus), debuted in Stuttgart in 1966. One of his last works was written for the 1972 Summer Olympic Games held in Munich. Orff was married more than once and enjoyed his last years on his home on the Lake Ammersee outside Munich. He died of cancer in 1982. A concert hall in Munich, part of a contemporary arts center and home of the Munich Philharmonic, is named in his honor.

Selected writings

Klage der Ariadne (after Monteverdi; title means "Ariadne's Lament"), Karlsruhe, 1925; rev., Gera, 1940.
Orpheus (after Monteverdi), Mannheim, 1925; rev., Munich, 1931; rev., Dresden, 1940.
Tanz der Sproeden (after Monteverdi; title means "Dance of the Merciless Beauties"), Karlsruhe, 1925; rev., Gera, 1940.
St. Luke Passion (after Bach), Munich, 1931.
Carmina Burana (cantiones profanae, medieval Lain lyrics), Frankfurt, 1937.
Der Mond (kleines Welttheater, after Brothers Grimm), Munich, 1939.
Catulli Carmina (luda scaenici; title means "Songs of Catullus"), Leipzig, 1943.
Die Kluge (title means "The Clever Woman"), Frankfurt, 1943.
Die Bernauerin: Bairische Stueck (title means "The Tragedy of Agnes Bernauer"), Stuttgart, 1947.
Antigonae (Sophocles, trans. Hoelderlin), Salzburg, 1949.
Astutuli: Bairsiche Komoedie, Munich, 1953.

Trionfo di Afrodite (concerto scenario; title means "The Triumph of Aphrodite"), Milan, 1953.

Trionfi (includes *Carmina Burana, Catulli carmina, Trionfo di Afrodite;* title means "Triumphs"), Salzburg, 1953.

Comoedia de Christi resurrectione (Osterspiel), Stuttgart, 1957.

Lamenti (includes *Klage der Ariadne, Orpheus, Tanz der Sproeden*), Schwetzingen, 1958.

Oedipus der Tyrann (Sophocles, transl. Hoelderlin), Stuttgart, 1959.

Ludus de nat infante mirificus (Weihnachtsspiel), Stuttgart, 1960.

Ein Sommernachtstraum (after Shakespeare), 1939-62; final version, Stuttgart, 1964.

Prometheus (after Aeschylus), Stuttgart, 1966.

De temporum fine comoedia (Buehnenspiel; title means "Play of the End of Time"), Salzburg, 1973.

Selected discography

Monteverdi Realisation: Lamento d'Arianna, Deutsche Grammophon.

Carmina Burana: Scenic Cantata (with the Bavarian Radio Chorus and Orchestra; title means "Songs of Beuren"), Deutsche Grammophon.

Entrata (with the Viennese State Opera Orchestra), Westminster.

Der Mond: A Narration with Four Episodes (title means "The Moon"), Columbia.

Die Kluge: The Story of the King and the Wise Woman, Angel.

Catulli Carmina: Ludi Scaenici, Deutsche Grammophon.

Die Bernauerin: Ein Bairisches Stueck, Deutsche Grammophon.

Antigonae: Setting of Hoelderlin's Vision of Sophocles' Tragedy, Deutsche Grammophon.

Trionfo di Afrodite: Concerto Scenico, Deutsche Grammophon.

Music for Children, Volumes 1 & 2, Columbia, Volumes 5 & 6, Mundi 2-Harmo.

Sources

Books

Kater, Michael H., *The Twisted Muse: Musicians and Their Music in the Third Reich,* Oxford University Press, 1997.

Liess, Andreas, *Carl Orff,* translated by Adelheid and Herbert Parkin, Calder and Boyars, 1966.

The New Grove Dictionary of Music and Musicians, edited by Stanley Sadie (Volume 13: Muwashsha-Ory), Macmillan, 1980.

Periodicals

Atlantic Monthly, August 1995, pp. 90-93.

New York Times, March 31, 1982, p. B5.

—*Carol Brennan*

Greg Osby

Saxophonist, composer, producer

Photograph by Philip Wong Blue Note Records. Reproduced by permission.

Greg Osby's 1997 album release, *Further Ado,* maintains and deepens the acoustic groove he struck with his previous album. With the release of 1996's *Art Forum,* it seems Osby has come full circle and returned to his stylistic roots. Before these two albums, 1987 was the last time he favored the jazz world with anything faintly resembling an acoustic sound. That was on his first album, *Sound Theater.* Sandwiched between *Further Ado* and *Art Forum,* Osby explored new musical combinations including much that was experimental, improvisational, or radical. He combined the rap/hip-hop sound with jazz. Working to fuse jazz with an African-American street-wise sound has added to Osby's reputation for seeking provocative styles of expression. However, Osby is quick to point out that his two latest albums remain connected to his vision of improvisational jazz, and are not a sell-out to improve album sales. Osby told *Boston Globe* correspondent Bob Blumenthal in a 1997 interview, "I'm an experimentalist and the things I do are based upon contemporary aspects of sound."

Greg Osby was born August 3, 1960 in St. Louis, Missouri. His first instrument was the clarinet. He quickly graduated to the alto saxophone and also learned how to play the flute. At age 15, he began playing professionally. In 1978 he was granted a scholarship to attend Howard University in Washington, D.C. It was at Howard that his radical nature began to show through. He found himself questioning teachers about why they were studying Bach and Mozart. His path to the world of jazz beckoned even in his early years of musical study. In 1980 he enrolled in the Berklee College of Music in Boston—finally, he was home! At Berklee he met many like minded musicians including saxophonists Donald Harrison and Branford Marsalis, bassist Victor Bailey, drummer Marvin "Smitty" Smith, Jeff "Tain" Watts, and guitarist Kevin Eubanks, among others. During his tenure at Berklee, he traveled regularly to New York City on the weekends and sat in on jam sessions. Word of his talent quickly spend through the New York jazz scene; when trumpeter, Jon Faddis, began asking around for a saxophonist who could read and write music, Greg Osby was the name who came to minds and lips.

Osby auditioned for Faddis in April 1983, and in spite of graduation being just a couple of months away, Osby left Berklee and hit the road with Faddis. In an interview with Willard Jenkins from *JazzTimes* online, Osby recalled his tour with Faddis and jazz great, Dizzy Gillespie, who was their guest. "I was really into Cannonball [Adderly], but I was trying to embark on a personalized method of playing and composition, improvisation, and delivery." Gillespie encouraged the young musician to persevere in seeking his own voice on the alto saxo-

Born August 3, 1960, in St. Louis, MO; son of Georgina Osby. *Education:* Attended Howard University in Washington, DC, 1978-80; studied at Berklee College of Music in Boston, MA, 1980-83.

Joined the New York City jazz scene performing with Jon Faddis, 1983; toured with Faddis and Dizzie Gillespie; formed M-Base with Steve Coleman; collaborated with Cassandra Wilson, Andrew Hill, and many other great improvisational jazz artists; on JMT released *Mind Games,* 1989, and *Season of Renewal,* 1990; signed with Blue Note Records and released five albums: *Man-Talk for the Moderns V.X.,* 1991; *3-D Lifestyles,* 1993; *Black Book,* 1995; *Art Forum,* 1996; and *Further Ado,* 1997.

Addresses: *Record company*—Blue Note Records, 304 Park Avenue South, Third Floor, New York, NY 10010. *Website*—Official Greg Osby World Wide Website: www.bluenote.com.

phone. He advised Osby that in spite of negative responses, he should not give up. Other early influences included Herbie Hancock's piece, "Speak Like a Child," Charles Minug's "Ah Um," Duke Ellington's "Indigo," and the collaborative effort of Miles Davis-Gil Evans.

Seeking challenge has been a theme in Osby's career. Upon diving into the New York jazz scene,he often found himself frustrated by his less adventuresome peers. He sought out other musicians who shared his love of exploring musical styles beyond the standard Tin Pan Alley fare. One of these fellow adventurers into the experimental and improvisational jazz world was fellow alto saxophonist, Steve Coleman.

During the 1980's along with Coleman, Osby formed the group known as M-Base. M-base was an acronym standing for Macro Basic Array of Structured Extemporizations. "The original idea," Coleman told Nicky Baxter in *JAZZIZ,* "was to make music that keeps evolving." The group's membership changed over the years. The core members included Jean-Paul Bourelly, guitar; Cassandra Wilson, vocals; Graham Haynes, trumpet and cornet, Osby and Coleman, alto saxophones; Kim Clarke, bass, and Mark Johnson on drums. A literal who's-who of the improvisational scene of the time.

His 1993 album *3-D Lifestyles* may have shocked some. At least one critic noted that the language used in this hip-hop meets jazz album by Osby perhaps should have carried a warning label because of potentially offensive language.

Two years later in 1995, the release of *Black Book* continued his exploration of this radical new form of jazz. Perhaps Osby's early life in the city inspired his use of the harsh, descriptive beat poetry to explore the tenuousness of life in the city where drugs were readily available, and death was merely a heart beat away. In "Pillars of the Community," the lyrics described the affect the environment had on him. "Skeletons stared at me with bulging eyes. I was always close to my piece, but sometimes closer to their cries." His improvisational style continued to thread its way through this work as well. *Black Book* also came forth from his continued need to always enlarge his vistas and seek new directions.

Whether Osby was playing in a recording studio or jamming live, composing pieces or producing them, his unceasing quest seems to focus on increasing his range and versatility as a performer and composer. Never one to be self-satisfied or to remain long in one place musically, he continued seeking various venues which allowed his full expression of himself musically and personally. Osby realizes that many people fail to appreciate his level of comfort in the acoustic environment, since much of what he played previous to *Art Forum* and *Further Ado* were recorded under other artists names, including Andrew Hill, Cassandra Wilson, and Geri Allen.

"Unplugged"

The 1996 release of *Art Forum,* returned Osby to his musical roots and allowed him to express himself in his familiar acoustic environment. However, this album also continued his traditionally radical approach to jazz. Osby told Europe Jazz Network online that, "I've always been one to speak my mind, and I've always been one to play my mind." We see no less than classic Osby on *Art Forum.* Leaving the work of fusing hip-hop and jazz behind, at leastmomentarily, *Art Forum* is more about group cohesiveness than showcasing one artist. From the peaceful rendering of "Mood of Thought," to the fanciful and lovely rendition of "Don't Explain," Osby's accompanied by the thoughtful and artful pianist, James Williams, drummer Jeff "Tain" Watts, vibist Bryan Carrott and bassist, Lonnie Plaxico. Then in an abrupt change of pace and mood, he goes for his "signature slash and burn" in "Miss D'Meena." Although variety among the pieces is apparent, and each piece distinctly stands alone, they appear to be joined together effortlessly into one.

Further Ado, released in 1997, is more completely set in an acoustic environment. Osby knows that many of his fans prefer this style of his work as opposed to the more experimental tangents he explored in earlier releases. His further development in the acoustic arena remains connected to his vision of jazz as improvisation. *Further Ado* has been well received by jazz lovers and provided Osby with an opportunity to showcase his playing. Osby hand picked the musicians accompanying him. They include Jason Moran, piano; Eric Harland, drums; and Lonnie Plaxico and Calvin Jones sharing responsibilities on bass. *Further Ado* also features Tim Hagans, trumpet; Mark Shim, tenor sax; Gleave Guyton, flute, alto flute, and clarinet; and Jeff Haynes on percussion.

Osby composed two cuts to honor various mentors. "Heard," and "Mentor's Prose," are two of his favorites, and are in honor of the late tenor saxophonist, Eddie Harris. "Mentor's Prose" at the same time is in recognition of Andrew Hill, Muhal Richard Abrams, and Von Freeman. In an online interview with Blue Note Records, Osby stated that the result of *Further Ado's* combination of artists working together is something of a "metamorphic small band configuration that changes on a per tune basis. I was going for a more captivating project using instrumental colors and timbres." It sounds like he's accomplished his goal. Although each piece stands independently they all meld together into a dramatic expression that surprises Osby by leaving him feeling somewhat exposed and vulnerable. The sensitive composition of nine original pieces, plus the popular "Tenderly," in the hands of these talented musicians and guided by Osby's muse leave one believing that Osby has realized his goal of cohesiveness and original expression on *Further Ado.*

The sound of jazz is alive and well; jamming live or recording, composing or producing, it seems Osby's restless muse will continue to push him forward into uncharted waters—musically, personally, and philosophically. As he told an interviewer on Blue Note Records online, "It's a personal challenge for me to always be open to change, to be ever evolving. Because comfort has a complacent sound that goes with it, and I don't want to play that."

Selected discography

Greg Osby and Sound Theater, Watt, 1987.
Mind Games, JMT, 1989.
Season of Renewal, JMT, 1990.
Man-Talk for the Moderns V.X., Blue Note Records, 1991.
3-D Lifestyles, Blue Note Records, 1993.
Black Book, Blue Note Records, 1995.
Art Forum, Blue Note Records, 1996.
Further Ado, Blue Note Records, 1997.

With others

(With Steve Coleman) *Strata Institute Cipher Syntax,* JMT.
(With Andrew Hill) *Eternal Spirit,* Blue Note.

Sources

Books

Carr, Ian; Fairweather, Digby; Priestley, Brian, editors, *Jazz: the Rough Guide,* The Rough Guides, 1995.

Periodicals

Audio, March 1997.
Boston Globe, September 28, 1997.
Downbeat, October 1989, p. 26-28.
JAZZIZ, December 1996.
People, August 9, 1993, p. 27.

Online

http://jp.jazzcentralstation.com
http://musiccentral.msn.com
http://www.allmusic.com
http://www.bluenote.com
http://www.ejn.it
http://www.jazzonln.com

—Debra Reilly

The
Pixies

Alternative rock band

Photograph by Ken Settle. © Ken Settle. Reproduced by permission.

Considered one of the most vital American alternative rock bands of the late 1980s, the Pixies attracted a huge European audience, as well as a moderate underground American following, between 1987 and 1993 with their combination of brash, intentionally tasteless punk and post-punk indie guitar rock, classic pop, and surf rock. Although the band never established strong commercial success in the United States, the Pixies' hard rock melodies and subversion of conventional song structures influenced many bands of the 1990s. The band disbanded in 1993, yet its raw, unstudied approach to music, combined with singer/songwriter/guitarist Black Francis' bizarre rants on religion, UFOs, mutilation, and pop culture, spawned a host of imitators that have summarily failed to match the Pixies' in either popularity or reputation. David Fricke of *Rolling Stone* called the Pixies "Boston's best gift to trash pop since the great Mission of Burma, and a roaring foursome who mix and mash abrasive guitar propulsion with [Francis's] quixotic melodicism and brutal, beguiling lyric surrealism."

The Pixies was founded in 1986 in Boston, Massachusetts, by roommates Charles Michael Thomson Kitteridge IV and Joey Santiago. The pair, who had traveled to Boston to attend the University of Massachusetts, decided to publish an ad calling for musicians to form a "Hüsker Dü/ Peter, Paul & Mary band" after checking out the local club scene. Bassist Kim Deal (then Mrs. John Murphy, who reclaimed her maiden name following a divorce in 1986) joined the band shortly after, also introducing drummer David Lovering to Thomson and Santiago. According to Michael Azerrad in *Rolling Stone,* "One day Thompson's father joked about naming his next child Black Francis, and Thompson claimed the name as his own. Santiago chose the band's name by riffling through a dictionary."

Born in Long Beach, California, Francis grew up in Southern California listening to such classic-rock legends as the Rolling Stones and Iggy Pop and attending a Pentecostalist church that instilled in him a congruent sense of religious fundamentalism. An anthropology major at the University of Massachussetts, in Amherst, he dropped out to found the Pixies (originally known as Pixies in Panoply) and quickly became its mouthpiece. Although most press has tended to focus on Francis, Azerrad declared guitarist Santiago "the lifeblood of the Pixies' sound, as well as their unhinged spirit. As someone close to the band only half-joking puts it: 'Joey is completely psycho. He's a dangerous character.'" Ian Gittins in *Melody Maker* characterized Kim Deal as "a regular sunbeam. She's fun to be with and whatever she thinks, she says. She's the drinkin', smokin', rockin' Pixie, the one who keeps the spirits

For the Record . . .

Members include **Black Francis** (born Charles Michael Thomson Kitteridge IV in Long Beach, CA) guitar, vocals; **Joey Santiago**, guitar. Former members include **Kim Deal**, bass; **David Lovering**, drums.

Band founded as Pixies in Panoply by Black Francis; secured a recording deal on UK independent label, 4AD Records, based on demo tapes, 1986; attracted a wide underground popularity for blend of hard-driving, guitar-heavy rock sublime melody and bizarre, surreal lyrics, 1986-1989; burst into the British Top 10 with *Doolittle*, 1989; *Bossanova* widely acknowledged as one of the top albums of the year, 1990; disbanded, 1993.

Addresses: *Record company*—Elektra Entertainment, 75 Rockefeller Plaza, New York, NY 10019.

up." Lovering, perhaps the most reticent member of the band, was often praised by reviewers as well as the purportedly egotistical Francis as perhaps the most gifted and exacting musician in a band of self-taught players.

In 1986, the Pixies played in Boston clubs and recorded a demo tape that eventually found its way into the office of a British independent label, 4AD Records. on the strength of a series of superior demo tapes. Although according to Deal the label found the Pixies' sound "too American, "i.e. loud and obnoxious," the company was quick to sign the quartet and released the demo intact as a mini-LP titled *Come on Pilgrim* in 1987. The album prompted an ecstatic press response in the United Kingdom, with its abrasive, powerful sound and Francis' surreal lyrics. Blotcher noted that "the album offered twisted rockers and ballads, guitar-scarred and coodled, celebrating incest and animals and sex so fine (with an elevator operator). They're charged with a sound as rewarding as scabpicking was when you were a kid. Gleefully reckless. Good nasty fun. The Pixies have the eerie depth of old souls, yet their average of 22, explains their eagerness to offend, to aurally jar and generally rock people off their mental axis."

The Pixies' next album, *Surfer Rosa,* produced in 1988 by Big Blacks' Steve Albini, was more raw and voluminous in sound than its predecessor. The band gener-

ally attributed the change to Albini's dislike for "anything human sounding," which led him to elevate fractured, Jurassic guitar riffs over vocal melody in such hits as "Bone Machine" and "Gigantic." Francis commented to Marlene Goldman in *Alternative Press:* "Albini turned the guitars up real loud. That's not any criticism to him. That's a very basic thing. We' ve worked with a lot of other people and a lot of other people wouldn't dare do that."

Despite *Surfer Rosa*'s instrumental emphasis, Francis's lyrics managed to attract some critical attention for their bizarre juxtaposition of religious and grotesque images. Francis mentioned in OPTION #21 of the repeated incest motif: "'I dunno, Jim Morrison sang about it a lot, didn't he?' He looks around for backup. 'I don't have any sisters or anything! I just had a lot of Bible upbringing. Real hardcore Pentacostal ... you can't get rid of a lot of stuff. You have all the letters of the alphabet to choose from and all the words in the dictionnary, and you start putting things together and it begins to look like something—sort of—but there are lots of missing parts because you're starting off with arbitrary syllables."

With 1989's *Doolittle,* the Pixies burst into the British Top 10. This album retained the rough sound of *Surfer Rosa,* yet reveals a softer touch in Francis's smoother melodies."You just get tired of listening to yourself scream. You just want to sing. So we sang a lot more," Francis told Marlene Goldman in *Alternative Press.* In 1989, the Pixies played over 150 dates on their world tour and became a highly fashionable attraction as much for their emerging grasp of melody as for their hard-driving sound. Their live performances evoked a strongly enthusiastic response in the press and enhanced their growing reputation with such standards as "Debaser,""Wave of Mutilation," and "Bone Machine." Fricke contended that "the way Thompson shoehorns sexual obsession, graphic violence, goofy humor, and religious iconography into musical telegrams—bursts of rage and revelation in 'Wave of Mutilation,' 'I Bleed,' and 'Monkey Gone to Heaven,' a corrosive, compelling meditation on God and garbage—transcends mere naivete."

The latter song, perhaps the band's most endearing single, became the title cut of the Pixies' next album, *Monkey Gone to Heaven* (1989). The song plays on the designation of Man, the Devil, and God into numerological values in Hebrew scriptures (5, 6, and 7, respectively). Speaking to Goldman, Black characteristically disclaimed the significance of his lyrics while hinting at a deeper meaning: "It's a reference from what I understand to be Hebrew numerology, and I don't know a lot about it or any of it really. I just remember someone telling me of the supposed fact that in the Hebrew language, especially in the Bible, you can find lots of references to man in the 5th and Satan in the 6th and God in the 7th. I don't know if there is a spiritual hierarchy or not. But it's a neat little fact, if it is a fact. I didn't go to the library and figure it out."

Change

The Pixies' 1989 album, *Here Comes Your Man,* attracted less attention than its predecessor. The same year, the Pixies contributed to Neil Young's 1989 tribute album, *The Bridge* (covering "Winterlong"), and Deal formed her own all-female band, the Breeders. Over the next two years, Deal found an outlet for her singing and songwriting that she later implied had been stifled in the Pixies, which came to be increasingly dominated by Francis.

The Pixies' 1990 album *Bossanova* which put the Pixies back in the public eye as one of the most widely acknowledged top albums of the year. Deal described the *Bossanova* album as "more Steven Spielberg than David Lynch," with several songs in *Bossanova* reflecting Francis' life-long interest in extraterrestrials. Francis told Roy Wilkinson in *Sounds:* "We've tried to elevate the sci-fi thing, make it more opera-ish, more of a serious rock thing.... We want UFOs to be an acceptable topic. They're romantic." "The Happening" is about aliens in Las Vegas, for example, and "Ana" describes an otherworldly surfer girl. Bossanova also reflects another of Francis' obsessions, surf music. Michael Azerrad commented in *Rolling Stone:* "Bossanova opens with a cover of 'Cecilia Ann,' an early-Sixties obscurity by the Surftones, and the twangy sounds of the genre snake throughout the record."

A League of Their Own

Despite its generally positive critical response and emphasis on patently popular themes, *Bossanova* failed to make an impact on the mainstream charts. Wilkinson commented: "For although a brilliant performance at Reading proved that large-scale shows were no problem to them, Pixies' music remains too quirky, too abrasive for the perceived dictates of daytime radio." Long-time fans of the band's harder-edged early albums complained in some quarters that the Pixies had sold out to commercialism. Francis retorted: "So many people comment on the drastic changes between this record and the last one. And they really aren't listening, because to me it's the same 'old sh**,'

sort of. There are certain things that have changed, but those are obvious—like having more money to spend on your record, so your 'production values' get a little more sophisticated. But it's the same TYPE of material."

The Pixies' next major release, *Trompe le Monde,* returned to the *Sturm und Drang* of their earlier works, prompting some critics to describe it as "the Pixies Heavy Metal album." The rage apparent to many in the 1991 work was perhaps due in part to increasing tensions within the band. Deal barely sang on the record and was reportedly angry that she wasn't allowed any space for her songs on either *Trompe* or *Bossanova.* Following a tense final tour opening for U2, Black Francis disbanded the group in early 1993. Azerrad had reported earlier in *Rolling Stone:* "Frictions reportedly developed within the band toward the end of *Doolittle* tour and the beginning of *Bossanova* sessions," and general rumors in the press were finally confirmed. Speaking on Mark Radcliffe's Radio 5 show *Hit the North,* Black admitted: "Nothing really happened. I decided to disband the group because I didn't want to be in the group any more. I just think that some groups are maybe cut out for the long haul and being together for ten or twenty years, but no way am I going to do that. I don't even know whether I'm going to be in the music business for that long."

Admitting that he failed to inform the group of his decision before announcing its demise to the press, Francis said that he had simply become "bored" with the Pixies. Black Francis inverted his stage name to Frank Black and released his first solo album three months later. Lead guitarist Joey Santiago played with Black; drummer David Lovering also played intermittently with Black before joining Cracker. Deal returned to working with the Breeders, which soon became a much bigger commercial success than any Pixies record in history.

Selected discography

Come on Pilgrim, 4AD/Rough Trade, 1987.
Gigantic, 4AD/Rough Trade, 1988.
Surfer Rosa, 4AD/Rough Trade, 1988.
Surfer Rosa & Come on Pilgrim, 4AD/Rough Trade, 1988.
Doolittle, 4AD/Elektra, 1989.
Here Comes Your Man, 4AD/Elektra, 1989.
Monkey Gone to Heaven, 4AD/Elektra, 1989.
Bossanova, WEA/Elektra Entertainment, 1990.
Dig for Fire, 4AD/Elektra, 1990.
Velouria, 4AD/Elektra, 1990.
Planet of Sound, 4AD/Elektra, 1991.
Trompe le Monde, 4AD/Elektra, 1991.

Death to the Pixies (2 CD set), WEA/Elektra, 1997.
Debaser Part 1 (import, England), 4AD, 1997.
Debaser Part 2 (import, England), 4AD, 1997.

Sources

Periodicals

Alternative Press, September 1989.
Guitar Player, April 1991.
Melody Maker, December 1989; November 3 , 1990; December 14 1991.
Music Express, October 1990.
Musician, February 1992.
New Musical Express, January 23 1993.

OPTION #21, July/August 1988.
Reflex Magazine, May 1988.
Rolling Stone, June 15, 1989; November 1, 1990; February 4, 1993.
Sounds, December 1990.
Spin, November 1996.

Online

http://www.ozemail.com.au/~thrashin/bands.htm#pixies
http://www.pixies.com/uk/
http://www.iol.ie/~bfogarty/pixiepage.htm
http://www.mis.enac.fr/~biel/pixies/

—Sean Pollock

Point of Grace

Christian vocal group

Point of Grace, Christian rock's glamorous and wholesome female quartet, followed their dreams into pop-gospel singing and attained an astounding level of success in a remarkably short period of time. The group, which consists of Denise Jones, Heather Floyd, Shelley Phillips-Breen, and Terry Jones, released their debut album, *Point of Grace,* in 1994. Six songs from the album reached the No. 1 spot on *Billboard*'s Contemporary Christian chart. Point of Grace was hailed by the *New York Times* as a harbinger of the future and an indication that the public wants to listen to messages of hope, redemption, faith, and inspiration. Lynn Keesecker, vice president of the group's label, Word Records, told Bruce Sims of *Gulf Coast Newspapers,* "We are overwhelmed by the success that Point of Grace has accomplished in such a short time ... and foresee the group as attaining a position of major influence in contemporary Christian music."

Nicholas Davidoff of the *New York Times* described Point of Grace as, "a cleverly derivative confection adapted for Christian teen-age consumption from a

Photograph by Michael Haber. Word Records. Reproduced by permission of Michael Haber.

For the Record . . .

Members include vocalists **Heather Floyd** (born 1970 in Abilene, TX); **Denise Jones** (born 1969 in Norman, OK, married to Stuart Jones); **Terry Jones** (born 1970 in Marion County, CA; married to Chris Jones); and **Shelley Phillips** (born c. 1969 in Belleville, IL; married to David Breen).

Jones, Jones, and Floyd formed a teen trio in their Norman, OK, church in high school. The three women attended Ouachita Baptist University in Arkadelphia, AR, as education and music majors; sang as a trio within The Oklahoma Girls; toured local churches as the Ouachitones, 1991; Shelley Phillips joined the band, 1991; switched band name to Say So; traveled to Estes Park, CO, to compete in the Christian Artists Seminar, 1992; signed to Word Records, changed name to Point of Grace, and released self-titled debut album, 1993; released *The Whole Truth*, 1995; released *My Utmost for His Highest*, 1995; released *Life, Love & Other Mysteries* in conjunction with a book also entitled *Life, Love, & Other Mysteries,* published by Simon & Schuster's Pocket Books, 1996.

Awards: Special Event Album of the Year for *My Utmost for His Highest;* America's Christian Music Award for Favorite New Artist, 1994; Dove Awards: New Artist of the Year, 1994; Group of the Year, Pop/Contemporary Album of the Year for *The Whole Truth,* Pop/Contemporary Recorded Song of the Year for "The Great Divide," 1996.

Addresses: *Record company*—Word Records, 3319 West End Avenue, Suite 200, Nashville, TN 37203; (615) 385-9673, ext. 3210.

series of mainstream pop girl-group templates: the Andrews Sisters, the Supremes and En Vogue."

Terry Jones and Denise Jones are not related, they merely happened to marry men with the same last name. While in high school, Jones, Jones, and Floyd formed a teen trio in their Norman, OK, church. The three women then attended Ouachita Baptist University in Arkadelphia, AR, together as education and music majors, and sang as a trio within a larger group called The Oklahoma Girls. Heather Floyd and Denise Jones had been friends since fifth grade, and they met Terry

Jones in eighth grade. Their musical trio was so popular that the women decided to tour local churches on their own in 1991 as the Ouachitones. Shelley Phillips was Denise Jones's roommate at OBU at the time, and she asked if she could join the band as they toured, so the trio became a quartet. They switched to the name Say So, which stemmed from the biblical line "If you are redeemed of the Lord say so," and began singing simply for the fun of it. Denise Jones told the *Springfield News-Sun*'s Lawrence Calder Trump, "We thought it would be fun to spend the summer singing at youth camps and festivals ... at the end of the summer people kept calling us to sing at this banquet and that, and we just kept doing it."

During the summer of 1992, the Say So quartet traveled to Estes Park, CO, to compete in the Christian Artists Seminar, where they met an executive from Word Records. The band was invited to visit Nashville for a demo tape. Word Records then signed the band, at which point they changed their name to Point of Grace. The band's name was inspired by a line that C.S. Lewis wrote: "Christians live each day on the point of God's grace." Word Records is currently the largest company dealing in Christian music in the world.

Floyd told Natalie Nichols of the *Tulsa World,* "We only planned to do it for fun for those couple of months....We went out and were so well-received it just snowballed. Radio just embraced us. We weren't doing it to have Number 1 records, but rather to get the message out, and we're doing just that."

Busting *Billboard* Charts

The 1993 debut Point of Grace album became the strongest-selling debut album in Christian music; the six No. 1 singles from the album rendered Point of Grace ahead of Mariah Carey and Paula Abdul in the record books—each of whom had four No. 1 hits from their debut releases. According to *Billboard* magazine, *Point of Grace* was the first debut album of any genre to have six No. 1 hit singles. The singles on the band's debut release that reached No. 1 on *Billboard*'s Contemporary Christian chart were "I'll Be Believing," "One More Broken Heart," "Jesus Will Still Be There," "Faith, Hope, and Love," "I Have No Doubt," and "No More Pain". The band received a Dove Award for New Artist of the Year in 1994 and a Favorite New Artist Award from the America's Christian Music Award judges.

Point of Grace's second album, *The Whole Truth,* released in 1995 within 20 months of their debut album, had three No. 1 hits on the Contemporary Christian chart: "The Great Divide," "Dying to Reach You," and "Gather at the River." A review of the album in *USA Weekend* concluded, "...Vocal-driven girl pop a la Wilson Phillips.... Incites fits of humming." Following the release of *The Whole Truth*, Point of Grace sold a total of 500,000 units overall by July of 1995, and the band's second album held the No. 1 position on the Sound-Scan Christian retail chart in *CCM Update* for 13 weeks. When the group tours, they generally play to between 1,500 and 3,000 people each performance. The group released an album featuring original recordings by some of gospel music's top artist, titled *My Utmost for His Highest*, and received a Dove Award for Special Event Album of the Year in 1996.

Deep Roots, Broad Appeal

In 1996 the group released *Life, Love & Other Mysteries* in conjunction with a book of the same title, published by Simon & Schuster's Pocket Books. The book details the life story of each group member, and offers inspirational advice to their fans. The release of the book signaled a marketing position for Point of Grace beyond their music; the band was popular enough to offer collective advice and wholesome enough to serve as a Christian example. "It was so obvious ... that they are clearly the future of contemporary Christian music," Sue Carswell, a senior editor at Pocket Books said, "Christian pop is the next sensation and is coming into its own much like the country music industry has done." In 1996 Point of Grace garnered four additional Dove Awards, including Group of the Year.

When Christian artists such as Amy Grant and Michael W. Smith have crossed over into the mainstream market, they have been perceived as having moved afield of their Christian roots. Point of Grace, however, has the potential and resolve to appeal to a mainstream market while retaining their initial vision and purpose. Terry Jones told *Release* magazine's Douglas McKelvey, "What we know about is growing up in the church and being raised in Christian homes. That's us. That's our story." Word/Epic Records distributed Point of Grace's product into the mainstream market after the success of their first album. Denise Jones told Calder Trump, "We never planned to cross over (to pop music). We're not out to judge anybody. We just want to say hey, this worked for us, maybe it could work for you."

Marketable Future

Point of Grace's ideas are worked into rhymes and melodies by more than 35 songwriters. The band also serves as the spokespeople for Mercy Ministries of America, a shelter for unwed mothers and troubled girls. Paul Moore, co-head of the William Morris Agency's Nashville office and the agent responsible for Point of Grace, told *CCM Update*, "Every department at William Morris—film, television, commercials, soundtrack, literary and even theatrical—is exploring ideas for Point of Grace. They are so incredibly marketable."

Point of Grace's Shelley Phillips told *Time* magazine's Patrick E. Cole, "I read John Grisham books. I watch *Friends*. We're not so separated from regular girls. We tell people to give the music a listen and give it a chance."

Heather Floyd summed up the group's philosophy when she told Camerin Courtney of *Today's Christian Woman*, "Our ministry and success are way beyond us. We're just four girls who like to sing and got together, and God has somehow blessed us. *He's* the one—not us—making the impact on others."

Selected discography

Point of Grace, Epic/Word Records, 1993.
The Whole Truth, Epic/Word Records, 1995.
My Utmost for His Highness, Epic/Word Records, 1995.
Life, Love & Other Mysteries, Epic/Word Records, 1996.

Sources

Periodicals

Billboard, August 3, 1996; December 16, 1995; December 9, 1995.
Brio, September 1996.
Contemporary Christian Music Magazine (CCM), September 1996.
Contemporary Christian Music Magazine (CCM) Update, August 19, 1996; July 17, 1995.
Gavin, November 24, 1995.
Gulf Coast Newspapers, September 16, 1995.
The Janesville Gazette, July 28, 1996.
Ladies Home Journal, November 1995.
London Sunday Times, April 2, 1995.
New Music, Summer 1996.
New York Times, February 5, 1995.
Release, November/December 1996.
Saturday Evening Post, March/April 1996.
Seattle Post-Intelligencer, February 11, 1995.
Springfield News-Sun, July 22, 1996; July 18, 1996..
Time, January 22, 1996.

Today's Christian Woman, November/December 1996.
USA Weekend, April 2, 1995.

Online

http://www.epiccenter.com/EpicCenter/docs/
artistbio.qry?artistid=234

—*B. Kimberly Taylor*

Mike Post

Composer, producer, musician

Like Elton John or Mick Jagger, Mike Post's music is a part of everyday culture, extremely well-known to most people in the United States and Europe. Few could fail to recognize the themes to *The Rockford Files, Hill Street Blues,* or the 1981 number-one hit "Believe It or Not" by Joey Scarbury, from *Greatest American Hero.* These are all Post compositions, as are the themes for television shows such as *NYPD Blue, Silk Stalkings, Law and Order, L.A. Law, Magnum P.I., The A-Team, Hunter,* and many more. In addition, Post as producer and musician has left his imprint on well-known hits such as Mason Williams's "Classical Gas," Sonny and Cher's "I Got You Babe," and the 1967 hit "I Just Dropped In (To See What Condition My Condition Was In)" by the First Edition.

Yet Post, unlike highly visible artists such as Mick Jagger or Elton John, can go almost anywhere without being recognized. Many people recognize the music he composes but not the man behind the notes. This lack of visibility fuels many misconceptions about Post. Chief among these misconceptions is the idea that Mike Post is a jazz artist. Certainly his music does have an airy, jazz-like flavor, Post has admitted, but in fact he was never much influenced by jazz. On the contrary, he has confessed to having "a rock 'n' roll heart. I'd quit the business if I could be [Rolling Stones guitarist] Keith Richards."

Keith Richards he may not be, but Post has had a varied career, and in the process established himself as the most successful composer in television history. As evidence of his talent and his massive impact on popular culture, Post has received five Grammy awards, one Emmy, and a BMI Film & Television Richard Kirk Award for Lifetime Achievement.

Born in 1945, Mike Post grew up in the San Fernando Valley outside of Los Angeles. His father, architect Sam Postil, encouraged in him an appreciation for discipline, a key to Post's early and continued success. Yet Post was far from a dedicated student, and he spent his days at Grant High School "playing" on a homemade paper keyboard, which he hid behind an open book while sitting at his desk. For good measure, he wore a pair of dark glasses.

Thus Post survived high school only by keeping close to his first and true love, which was music. From the beginning, he had varied tastes and influences, ranging from the composer Antonin Dvorak to American folk songwriter Stephen Foster to the blues and—of course— rock 'n' roll. Like his idol Ray Charles, Post's instrument was the piano, and by the age of fifteen, he was already playing at clubs. He only graduated from Grant High,

Born 1945, in San Fernando, CA; son of Sam Postil, an architect; married Patty McGettigan; children: Aaron and Jennifer.

Performed session work with a number of bands, formed Wellingbrook Singers and First Edition, played backup guitar for Dean Martin, Sammy Davis Jr., Sonny and Cher mid-1960s; producer on First Edition and Mason Williams hits late 1960s; became musical director of *The Andy Williams Show* 1969; partnership with Pete Carpenter as composer of TV and film theme music 1968-87; continued as composer on shows such as *NYPD Blue.*

Awards: Grammy, 1968, Best Instrumental Arrangement: *Classical Gas*—Mason Williams; Grammy, 1975, Best Instrumental Arrangement: *Rockford Files;* Grammy, 1981, Best Instrumental Composition: *Hill Street Blues;* Grammy, 1981, Best Instrumental Performance: *Hill Street Blues;;* Grammy, 1988, Best Instrumental Composition: *L.A. Law;* BMI Film & Television Richard Kirk Award for Lifetime Achievement, 1994; Emmy, 1996, Main Title Theme Music, *Murder One.*

Addresses: *Management*—Gorfaine-Schwartz Agency, 13245 Riverside Dr., Ste. 450, Sherman Oaks, CA 91423. *Office*—Mike Post Productions, 1007 West Olive Ave., Burbank, CA 91506.

his 1962 graduating class were the Monkees' Mickey Dolenz and actor Tom Selleck, whose *Magnum, P.I.* theme Post would later compose. But that lay far in the future, as did Post's induction to his high school's Hall of Fame, which would occur in 1987—quite an achievement for a bad student.

Post hit the club circuit in L.A., playing with bands who had famous names without the original members who had gained them that fame: Paul and Paula—Post became the new "Paul"—and the Markettes. He played in the house band for a topless club in San Francisco, and then, in an irony that would surely have pleased his teachers back at Grant High, Post realized he wouldn't get anywhere without an education.

So he spent a year studying music, learning how to sight-read and write notation. He formed a folk group called the Wellingbrook Singers, and they toured the U.S. before disbanding. At that point, Post began working as a session musician for artists such as Sammy Davis Jr., Dean Martin, and Dick and Dee Dee. He also spent a year playing backup for Sonny and Cher as a guitarist on songs that included their hit "I Got You Babe."

Pivotal Partnerships

Post soon began to see a place for himself in the production booth. While working as a studio arranger for producer Jimmy Bowen, he helped form the group the First Edition. Later the group's bassist and vocalist, Kenny Rogers, would gain enormous fame, but Post assisted them in their start by producing their first hit in 1967, "I Just Dropped In (To See What Condition My Condition Was In.)"

After his work with First Edition, Post entered into another significant partnership, this time with the multi-talented musician Mason Williams. Post acted as producer/arranger on *The Mason Williams Phonograph Album* (1968), which spawned the hugely successful hit, "Classical Gas." For his work with Williams, Post earned his first Grammy Award—at the age of 23. At 24, he became the youngest person in television history to become musical director for a major talk/variety program when he signed on with *The Andy Williams Show* in 1969.

Welcome to Television

The Andy Williams Show was Post's introduction to the world of television, where he would have his greatest successes in the next three decades. But before this could happen, the self-effacing Post, who had already proven his ability to work well in partnership with others, had to form yet another partnership. This one would become the most significant pairing of his life—other than his marriage to music editor Patty McGettigan, of course—and it would last for the next 19 years.

While playing in a golf tournament in 1968, Post met trombonist and arranger Pete Carpenter. The latter was much older than Post, and it was a time when the "generation gap" made the idea of a collaboration between the two seem like an oddity to everyone but Post and Carpenter. Post recalled in the BMI Music World website: "All of Pete's friends—older jazz guys—thought, oh well, Pete's kind of carrying this kid. Mike's just a rocker. And all of my friends thought, `poor

Mike, he's just carrying this old guy, who really isn't too hip.' All that was baloney."

The two men collaborated on the music for TV producer Stephen J. Cannell's first series, *Toma*. It was a police drama program, and it established a pattern for Post, who would become identified with numerous cop shows in the years to come. Much greater success followed with *Rockford Files*, for which Post composed the distinctive music that earned him a top ten radio hit and another Grammy in 1975.

Over the course of the 1970s and early 1980s, Post composed the music for some feature films, ranging from 1972's *Gidget* to the 1984 Sylvester Stallone-Dolly Parton pairing, *Rhinestone*. He would also produce Parton's smash 1981 album *9 to 5 and Other Jobs*, as well as the debut for singer Joey Scarbury. But it was as a composer of television themes that Post made his name. These included the music for *Greatest American Hero*, which in Scarbury's 1981 rendition became the only TV theme to ever reach number one on the charts. Further top ten exposure followed with the music from *Hill Street Blues*, which featured Larry Carlton on guitar.

Up until 1987, Post worked with Carpenter. Discussing this partnership with Julius Robinson of BMI Music-world, Post recalled: "We never worried about who wrote what ... We did our job. After 18 years, we never even had a handshake agreement or a contract; we just split it all 50/50. We never had an unkind word. Not one argument." When Carpenter was on his deathbed in 1987, he and Post calculated that they had together scored 1,800 hours of television "all done in the back of his house, eating tuna fish sandwiches." Along the way, "we made a big dent in the tradition of ghosting—we always gave contributing writers credit—so we were able to help a lot of other guys start as composers." In 1989, Post and the BMI Foundation established a Pete Carpenter Memorial Fund to benefit young composers.

"I've had at least one show on the air every year since 1970," Post recalled in a 1994 interview on the occasion of receiving the BMI Film & Television Richard Kirk Award for Lifetime Achievement. But rather than sit back and merely rest on what he had established, though, he was already looking toward new challenges in an area that had so far eluded him: songs with lyrics. Referring to himself as "the worst lyricist," Post didn't plan to write the words himself, but to collaborate with someone such as his friend James Nederlander on compositions for Broadway.

It would be fitting if the future found Mike Post, the relatively anonymous composer of many enormously

popular themes, in another collaboration. He continues to draw input from his wife Patty, who refers to him as "hobby-man" because of his many projects, and from children Aaron and Jennifer, who he credits for "keeping me on the cutting edge of new music." Post is as active physically as he is musically, having competed in over 20 marathons from Honolulu to New York City. He was once the third-ranking arm wrestler for his class in the United States, and he enjoys golfing with son Aaron, who is also embarking on a career in the music industry. Not surprisingly, the man whose name is virtually synonymous with TV cop shows regularly donates money to charities that benefit police officers and their families. Part of the profits from his album *Inventions from the Blue Line* go to the Law Enforcement Officers Educational Foundation, which provides college scholarships to children of police officers who perished while in the line of duty.

Selected scores

Film

Rabbit Test, 1978.
Deep in the Heart, 1981.
Running Brave, 1983.
Hadley's Rebellion, 1984.
Rhinestone, 1984.
The River Rat, 1984.

Television pilots/series

The Andy Williams Show, 1969.
Griff, 1973.
Needles and Pins, 1973.
Toma, 1973.
The Rockford Files, 1974.
The Texas Wheelers, 1974.
The Mac Davis Show, 1974.
The Bob Crane Show, 1975.
Charlie Cobb: Nice Night for a Hanging, 1977.
Off the Wall, 1977.
The Black Sheep Squadron, 1977.
ChiPs, 1977.
Richie Brockelman, Private Eye, 1978.
The White Shadow, 1978.
The 416th, 1979.
Operating Room, 1979.
Captain America, 1979.
Captain America II, 1979.
240-Robert, 1979.
Big Shamus, Little Shamus, 1979.
The Duke, 1979.
The Night Rider, 1979.

Stone, 1980.
Tenspeed and Brown Shoe, 1980.
Magnum P.I., 1980.
(With Stephen Geyer) The Greatest American Hero, 1981.
Hill Street Blues, 1981.
Palms Precinct, 1982.
The Powers of Matthew Star, 1982.
The Quest, 1982.
Tales of the Gold Monkey, 1982.
The A-Team, 1983.
Bay City Blues, 1983.
Big John, 1983.
Hardcastle and McCormick, 1983.
Riptide, 1984.
The Rousters, 1983.
Brothers-in-Law, 1985.
L.A. Law, 1986.
The Last Precinct, 1986.
Hooperman, 1987.
J.J. Starbuck, 1987.
Wiseguy, 1987.
Sirens, 1987.
Quantum Leap, 1989.
The Hat Squad, 1992.
Silk Stalkings: Natural Selection, 1994.
NYPD Blue, 1993.
Murder One, 1996.
Brooklyn South, 1997.
Players, 1997.

Television movies

(With Pete Carpenter) Two on a Bench, 1971.
(With Carpenter) Gidget Gets Married, 1972.
Locusts, 1974.
(With Carpenter) The Morning After, 1974.
The Invasion of Johnson County, 1976.
Scott Free, 1976.
Richie Brockelman: Missing 24 Hours, 1976.
Dr. Scorpion, 1978.
Coach of the Year, 1980.
Scout's Honor, 1980.
Will: G. Gordon Liddy, 1982.
Adam, 1983.
Sunset Limousine, 1983.
Hard Knox, 1984.
Heart of a Champion: The Ray Mancini Story, 1985.
Adam: His Song Continues, 1986.
Stingray, 1986.
Destination: America, 1987.
The Ryan White Story, 1989.
B.L. Stryker: The Dancer's Touch, 1989.

B.L. Stryker: Blind Chess, 1989.
Unspeakable Acts, 1990.
Without Her Consent, 1990.
The 100 Lives of Black Jack Savage, 1991.
The Great Pretender, 1991.
(With Velton Ray Bunch) Palace Guard, 1991.
The Rockford Files: I Still Love L.A., 1994.
Jake Lassiter: Justice on the Bayou, 1995.

Television specials

Mac Davis Special, 1975.
Mac Davis Christmas Special, 1975.
Mac Davis Christmas Special ... When I Grow Up, 1976.
Mac Davis Christmas Odyssey, Two Thousand and Ten, 1978.

Selected discography

Albums

(As the Mike Post Coalition) Fused, 1975.
Television Theme Songs, 1982.
Mike Post, 1984.
Music from L.A. Law & Otherwise:
Inventions from the Blue Line (includes the theme from NYPD Blue), American Gramophone, 1994.

Sources

Books

Hubbard, Linda S. and Owen O'Donnell, eds., Contemporary Theatre, Film, and Television, Vol. 6, Gale, 1989.

Periodicals

Billboard, May 7, 1994.
Billboard, May 28, 1994.

Online

http://www.bmi.com/MusicWorld/summer94/MIKEPOST.html

Additional information was provided by Mike Post Productions.

—Judson Knight

Scud Mountain Boys

Country rock band

Northampton, Massachusetts-based Scud Mountain Boys are at heart a rock band, but one might not know it after only a quick listen to the quartet's three albums. In fact, many reviewers have reported almost passing the band up before listening more closely. Writing in *Option,* Brad Lips reported a typical introduction to Scud Mountain Boys: "On a first listen, mood seemed so much the point that I missed their oddly poignant lyrics ('Down by the water, as the waves beat back the sand/I can count the love you gave me on one hand'). I had to challenge my assumptions about innocuous-sounding, hooky ballads, but Scud Mountain Boys are well worth the effort." After a self-released cassette tape, a CD on a tiny record label, and then finally signing with a larger independent label and releasing two recordings, the Scuds broke up in the Fall of 1997. However, the primary songwriter, Joe Pernice, continues to record on Sub Pop Records and is poised for his music to induce the same kind of double take from a much wider audience.

The Scud Mountain Boys began simply as the Scuds in western Massachusetts' Pioneer Valley in 1991. With

Photograph by Chris Toliver. Sub Pop Records. Reproduced by permission.

For the Record . . .

Members include **Stephen Desaulniers** (born June 27, 1965; left group, 1997), vocals, acoustic guitar, piano, and bass; **Joe Pernice** (born July 17, 1967), vocals, acoustic and electric guitars; **Tom Shea** (born February 1, 1968; joined group officially, 1996), drums, mandolin; and **Bruce Tull** (born June 9, 1955), electric guitar, lap steel, pedal steel.

Group formed in Northampton, MA, 1991; changed from hard rock to country rock sound, 1993; contributed to *Hit the Hay* (Swedish compilation) on Sound Asleep Records, 1994; released self-recorded cassette *Pine Box* and *Dance the Night Away* CD on Chunk Records, 1995; signed with Sub Pop Records and released *Massachusetts*, 1996; re-issued *Pine Box* and *Dance the Night Away* as *The Early Year*, 1997; group disbanded, fall 1997; Pernice continued to record with Sub Pop Records, 1997-.

Addresses: *Band*—Scud Mountain Boys, c/o Sub Pop East, 10A Burt St., Dorchester, MA 02124. *Record company*—Sub Pop, 1932 First Avenue, Ste. 1103, Seattle, WA 98101. *Website*—Official Scud Mountain Boys site: www.subpop.com/bands/scud.

the Gulf War going on and all the news about Saddam Hussein's feared Scud missiles, the band latched on to the name. Back then the group played loud rock 'n' roll in local clubs and had an appreciable number of fans who would frequent their live shows. But after those shows ended, the three main members—Joe Pernice (vocals, acoustic and electric guitars), Stephen Desaulniers (vocals, acoustic guitar, piano, and bass), and Bruce Tull (electric guitar, lap steel, pedal steel)—would retreat to Bruce's kitchen to unwind. There, late at night, the trio would break out their old country favorites, playing the songs they thought too quiet and too slow for live performances.

Slowing the Pace

The band found that these were the songs they really lived to play, and that lugging heavy equipment to clubs and stomping their feet on the floor to loud music wasn't their calling. So after the last in a string of flighty drummers had left the group, they decided to make a change—to go "slowcore," as a number of alternative country bands were labeled (in contrast to the "hard-core" punk sound of groups like Dead Kennedys). Adding the country-sounding "mountain" to their name, the re-christened Scud Mountain Boys played their first show around 1993. They described the stripped-down approach to Northampton's *Union-News* music critic Joyce Marcel: "We took simple gear like acoustic guitars. We borrowed the kitchen table from the club. We sat down in chairs around the table, put a lamp on it, and had a convenient place to put our beers and ashtrays.... Then we played our set. We have yet to play a gig standing up." Scud Mountain drummer Tom Shea, then a local musician in a band called Hoola Popper (named after a fishing lure), would occasionally accompany the trio on mandolin for Glen Campbell cover songs.

Made First Recordings in Kitchen

In keeping with their simplified approach, the Scud Mountain Boys preferred to record in the same kitchen that spawned their new direction. They had tried recording in a small studio but found it alienating. Tull later told the fanzine *White Bread* about the experience: "We were very rushed. I was playing in this cold and drafty hallway with my guitar and amp where I couldn't see the rest of the band. I was trying to look through this crack in the doorway to see them." So a four-track recorder captured the sounds for 12 original songs and three covers of songs originally performed by such diverse sources as Jimmy Webb ("Wichita Lineman"), Olivia Newton-John ("Please, Mister Please"), and Cher ("Gypsies, Tramps and Thieves"). Originally sold as the *Pine Box* cassette, the tracks were later released on vinyl by the indie-rock label Chunk Records in 1995.

As an album, *Pine Box* carries the mordant tone set by its title's reference to a plain coffin, and features songs like "There Is No Hell (Like the Hell on This Earth)" and "Freight of Fire." The lyrics tend to the subjects of loss and longing, with a tone of resignation that suggests some inner ability to deal with the pain. Pernice told James Keast of the website *shmooze.net* that he was interviewed by the *New Music Express* and the interviewer's first question was, "Do you have a terrible life?" He replied that he probably would if he didn't have music as an outlet to express himself. Examples of this seem to abound on *Pine Box*. In a line from "Peter Graves' Anatomy" Pernice croons softly, "Old age for a body, decay for a crown/Don't ask for nothin', you'll never be let down." And yet the voice is not one of self-pity. Writing for *Addicted to Noise*, Chris Nelson described Pernice's vocal quality as one that "can convey the deepest of emotions without sounding contrived or melodramatic, a gift that is intensified by the fact that he happens to be an excellent writer whose poetic imagery brings to life his painful, tragic stories."

Later in 1995 the Scud Mountain Boys recorded another set of tracks which became *Dance the Night Away* on Chunk. Including more four-track kitchen recordings, as well as others made a 24-track studio, the CD-only release featured drums on a few songs, another Jimmy Webb cover ("Where's the Playground Susie") and similar lyrical themes. As with the first record, soft sounds mask dark thoughts, and simple words are deceptively suggestive. Ira Robbins, of the *Trouser Press Guide to '90s Rock*, claimed that with *Dance the Night Away* "the Scuds barely disturb the silence as they whisper such slightly bent inventions as 'Letter to Bread' and 'Television' ('send me a show/you're the only world I know'). Although able to rouse themselves to a mild roots-rock roar...[they] make understatement far more engrossing."

Signed to Sub Pop Records

As word of these two powerful records spread beyond Massachusetts, a number of record labels became interested in the band. "There's a million bands out there. It's unexpected," Tull told *Union-News* critic Marcel after the group signed with Seattle-based Warner Brothers affiliate Sub Pop Records. "We were a dinky band from Northampton, kind of unorthodox, and we probably didn't play more than ten gigs out of Northampton." Opting for a drummer to fill out the sound, the band brought accompanist Shea on board as a full-time member and set about recording *Massachusetts*, a 14-song album with a number of more upbeat songs with drums and electric guitar. Released in April of 1996, *Massachusetts* unleashed the floodgates of critical acclaim that had eluded its less-known predecessors. The *New Musical Express* rated the record a nine (out of ten) and opined, "Joe Pernice has the golden voice of the damaged, regret oozing from every word like wounded honey ... render[ing] glorious the utter inevitability of failure....The best broken love and bad drug cocktail songs written in many a year." Acknowledging the vast difference between Scud Mountain Boys and their country music forbears on the one hand, and new crossover stars like Garth Brooks on the other, *Rolling Stone* called the album, "country in that the songs are the honest, homespun sort that characterized country before it picked up a blow-dryer."

Although the band's sound has often been labeled as country music, the Scud Mountain Boys clearly see themselves as casting a wider net than that. As music writer James Keast put it on the *shmooze.net* website,

"While the Scuds may be lumped in with Son Volt, Wilco and any number of other bands who are moving back to the traditional sounds of Hank Williams, they take their inspiration as much from hooky '70s AM pop as from the dirty country road of Johnny Cash." This assessment is borne out by the band's covers of artists like Cher and Olivia Newton-John. Scud guitarist Tull defined the band's style this way for the *Union-News*: "We're roots rock, but steeped in a real punk tradition and with a decided country flavor."

So Much To Do, So Little Time

With the success of *Massachusetts* bringing increased demand for the first two albums, Sub Pop re-issued them as a double CD in 1997. That year also found the band adjusting to a full-time musical career. Pernice, for one, had to reconcile the new career path with the master's degree in creative writing he had completed in 1996. Finding himself with a lot more time to write songs, he stacked up a few albums' worth in a short period of time. He also devoted some creative energy to the Pernice Brothers—a side project with his brother, Bob, and recently departed Scud bass player, Desaulniers—and recorded a single, "Jimmy Coma/Monkey Suit."

Perhaps this outside effort was a sign of discord among the band's members, as the Scud Mountain Boys disbanded abruptly in the fall of 1997. Pernice remained on Sub Pop Records, however, and continued to explore what he found lurking in the cracks between rock, pop, country, and other musical influences. He told Keast that the world could expect more 'round-the-kitchen-table musical stories from future releases: "I think the arrangements might get a little more complex, but none of us like particularly polished recordings. We like the little mistakes and stuff."

Selected discography

(Contributor) *Hit the Hay* (compilation), Sound Asleep [Sweden], 1994.
(Contributor) *Homegrown Harvest* (compilation), 1994.
"Television" (7" single split with Steve Westfield & the Slow Band), Chunk, 1994.
Pine Box (originally cassette, then vinyl only), Chunk, 1995.
Dance the Night Away (CD only), Chunk, 1995.
"Knievel ½ Way" (7" single), Sub Pop, 1995.
Massachusetts, Sub Pop, 1996.
The Early Year (double CD *Pine Box* and *Dance the Night Away* reissue), Sub Pop, 1997.

Sources

Books

The Trouser Press Guide to '90s Rock, Fireside, 1997.

Periodicals

New Musical Express, June 15, 1996, p. 47.
Newsweek, April 29, 1996, p. 80.
Option, July/August 1996, p. 129.
Rolling Stone, December 26, 1996, p. 45.

Union-News (Northampton, MA), June 15, 1995.
White Bread (fanzine), 1995.

Online

http://www.subpop.com/bands/scud
http://www.shmooze.net/pwcasual/exclaim/cur/scudboy.htm
http://www.iuma.com/Warner/images/bio.gif

Additional information was provided by Sub Pop Records publicity materials, 1997.

—*John F. Packel*

Simple Minds

Rock band

Over the course of the last 20 years, Simple Minds' story has been a study of the whims of music fans and the winds of musical fate. Employing a sound that has evolved from moody and atmospheric to anthemic, the Scottish rock band has ridden a career rollercoaster that has combined international success and virtual anonymity in America. This was followed by a series of surprise hit singles in the U.S. before a return to relative obscurity there.

Through it all have been singer Jim Kerr and guitarist Charlie Burchill. The pair came from working-class families and grew up together in in Glasgow, Scotland. As Burchill recalled in a 1986 interview in *Rolling Stone,* "Even before we were really close friends, me and Jim, we'd say hello and talk for five minutes, then we'd see each other at school. Gradually, it got to the stage where we'd walk and talk about music."

Thus, it was probably no surprise to those who knew them when the two childhood pals teamed up in their late teens with drummer Brian McGee to form the punk outfit Johnny and the Self-Abusers around 1977. "Glasgow is so industrial, and there are only two ways of escaping the banality of an upbringing like that: football and music," Burchill was quoted as saying in a 1991 *Guitar Player* article. "Jim and I were very fortunate with our upbringing—it was working-class, but not any sort of rags-to-riches crap. When we were about 14, we both hitchhiked around Europe, and that's

when we committed ourselves to doing something together musically. It had something to do with the fact that we realized that we could travel—it all comes back to a desire to escape Glasgow." Johnny and the Self-Abusers, a precursor to Simple Minds, reportedly disbanded the day their single (reports vary as to whether it was entitled "Souls and Sinners" or "Saints and Sinners") was released on the Chiswick label.

Simple Start for Simple Minds

The band re-formed the following year under the moniker Simple Minds, with a lineup that consisted of Kerr, Burchill, McGee, second guitarist Duncan Barnwell, bass player Derek Forbes, and Michael "Mick" McNeil on keyboards. In short order, the band signed with the Edinburgh-based Zoom record label and in 1979 recorded *Life in a Day,* an album whose sound a number of critics likened to Roxy Music. A modest hit in the United Kingdom, Simple Minds recorded *Life in a Day* without Barnwell, who had been booted from the band prior to recording. As observed in *The Trouser Press Record Guide,* Simple Minds' debut touched "lightly on several forms, including pop, psychedelia, and an adventurous tense/terse style they explored on subsequent albums."

Subsequent albums followed in rapid succession, with four records released over a period of three years. Despite the short time span, the band demonstrated a surprisingly marked evolution with the atmospheric Eurodisco of *Empires and Dance* in 1980. "I Travel," a single from that album, became a club staple in London. The four records were condensed into a single compilation, *Themes for Great Cities,* for American release in 1981 on Stiff.

McGee, for whom the rigors of touring proved to be too much, subsequently left the band. Simple Minds enlisted former Skids drummer Kenny Hyslop and session musician Mel Gaynor for their next album *New Gold Dream,* in 1982. Gaynor soon became McGee's permanent replacement. *New Gold Dream* marked the beginning of what *Rolling Stone* writer Mark Coleman said was "the shimmering, effervescent sound that's automatically associated with them now."

Enlisting the aid of producer Steve Lillywhite, who has worked with bands such as U2, the band began making inroads in America with *Sparkle in the Rain,* which contained the singles "Waterfront" and "Up on the Catwalk." The band toured the States in support of the album as an opening act for the Pretenders, whose lead singer, Chrissie Hynde, married Kerr in New

For the Record . . .

Members include **Charlie Burchill** (born November 27, 1959, in Glasgow, Scotland), guitar, keyboards; **Jim Kerr** (born July 9, 1959, in Glasgow, Scotland; married Chrissie Hynde [lead singer for The Pretenders], 1984; marriage ended, 1988; married Patsy Kensit [an actor], 1992; marriage ended, 1996; children: [with Hynde] Yasmin), vocals.

Former members include **Duncan Barnwell** (bandmember, 1978), guitar; **Tony Donald**, bass; **Derek Forbes** (born June 22, 1956; left band, 1985), bass; **Mel Gaynor** (born May 29, 1959; bandmember, 1981), drums; **John Giblin** (joined band, 1985), bass; **Sue Hadjopulos** (bandmember, 1985), percussions; **Kenny Hyslop** (born February 14, 1951, in Strathclyde, Scotland; bandmember, 1981), drums; **Michael** "Mick" **MacNeil** (born July 20, 1958; bandmember, 1979-91), synthesizers; **Brian McGee** (bandmember, 1978-81), drums; **Mike Ogletree** (bandmember, 1982), drums.

Formed in 1978 in Glasgow; released debut album *Life in A Day* in 1979 on Edinburgh-based Zoom label; condensed first four albums into compilation *Themes for Great Cities* for American release in 1981 on Stiff; signed with Virgin for *Sons and Fascination/Sister Feelings Call* in 1981; scored No. 1 hit in America with "(Don't You) Forget about Me," theme from the 1985 John Hughes movie *The Breakfast Club;* performed at 1988 birthday concert for Nelson Mandela; released greatest hits album, *Glittering Prize: Simple Minds '81-'92,* in 1993; dropped from A&M and released *Good News from the Next World* on Virgin in 1995.

Addresses: *Record company*—Virgin, 30 West 21st Street, New York, NY 11019.

seeing their singles and albums rocket up the charts. That is, until the band agreed—reluctantly—to record a Ken Forsey and Steve Schiff-penned song called "Don't You (Forget about Me)" for the soundtrack to the 1985 John Hughes high school angst-film *The Breakfast Club.* The movie's theme song, it would go on to not only become the band's first bona fide hit in the States, but also its biggest, eventually topping the *Billboard* pop charts.

It was a song that the band would retain mixed feelings about. As Kerr told Brett Atwood in a 1995 *Billboard* magazine interview, "We did the song at the time because we thought it would help our relations with the record company. We weren't getting along too well with them, so we reluctantly did it. We never thought it would be so successful. In fact, we felt a bit of guilt because we didn't write it."

A Reluctant Shift

The song also marked what many critics and fans perceived to be a shift in the band's sound. Although Simple Minds did not include "Don't You (Forget about Me)" on its next album, *Once upon a Time* in 1985, a number of critics contended that the album's more bombastic, arena-friendly approach was evidence of the "Americanization" of the band's music. The selection of Jimmy Iovine (Bruce Springsteen) and Bob Clearmountain (Hall and Oates) to produce only reinforced the notion that Simple Minds was consciously vying for a wider American audience. In any case, *Once upon a Time* was a huge hit in the U.S. and abroad, selling more than 500,000 copies in the United States alone and generating three Top 40 hits, including the top 10 single "Alive and Kicking." For the first time, Simple Minds had become a stadium band in America, much like U2, to whom they have frequently been compared. That level of commercial success in the U.S. was relatively short-lived, however.

Music Takes a Political Turn

Simple Minds' music became increasingly politicized in the late-1980s, with the band donating the proceeds of several concerts to the human rights organization Amnesty International. They also played a large role in the 1988 birthday concert for then-imprisoned South African freedom crusader Nelson Mandela. "Whether it's violence in Northern Ireland or crack dealers in New York, we're writing for the person who sees nothing in either side but every day has this on his doorstep and has to get on with his life," Kerr said of the band's

York's Central Park in June, 1984. Still, in spite of the tour and the fact that the album generated several hits in the United Kingdom, the band could only achieve cult status in the United States. The disappointed band took a year-long break at this point, during which Kerr and Hynde, back in Scotland, welcomed a baby daughter, Yasmin, with Hynde.

For almost the first decade of its career, Simple Minds enjoyed a hugely successful streak in Europe that was not matched in America, selling out stadiums and choice of lyrical content in a 1989 interview in *Stereo Review.*

Though no one denied that the band's heart was in the right place, the music Simple Minds produced during this period did not fare quite so well. *Street Fighting Years,* a 1989 release that contained songs such as "Belfast Child," "Mandela Day," and a cover of Peter Gabriel's "Biko" (about the slain South African rights leader Stephen Biko), was dubbed "an unfortunate example of politicized rock at its most simple-minded" by *Rolling Stone*'s Coleman. While the album sold more than three million copies worldwide, it failed to generate much interest in America. The band's failure to tour in the States in support of the album—the result of exhaustion after near-constant worldwide touring over the last decade—did not help that album's fortunes.

New Decade Marks New Era

By 1991, the only original Simple Minds members left were childhood pals Kerr and Burchill, who had traditionally written the band's songs, with Kerr adding lyrics to Burchill's music. The return to basics was reflected in the band's next album.

With the album *Real Life,* which the band recorded in Amsterdam in 1991, Simple Minds focused once more on more personal themes. "See the Lights," a single from that album, became a modest Top 40 hit in the United States, but fared even better on alternative and album rock charts. As Kerr told Steve Hochman in a 1991 interview in the *Los Angeles Times,* "It was, 'OK, we've gotten a lot of stuff off our chests.' I don't think we've turned our back on [the larger issues] and I think it's something we'll go over again in the future." *Real Life* failed to return the band to prominence, however, prompting a three-year hiatus after the band returned from the road. During the break, Kerr, whose marriage with Hynde reportedly ended amicably in early 1988, married actress Patsy Kensit (formerly of the band Eighth Wonder) in early 1992. The break also enabled Kerr and Burchill to focus on their songwriting.

In 1993, Simple Minds released *Glittering Prize,* a greatest hits album—and its last record for A&M. The band switched to Virgin for its American releases, although its international records had already been released by Virgin since 1979.

The band's next album, recorded in 1995, revealed yet another transformation. *Good News from the Next World* found Simple Minds largely favoring the guitar instead of the keyboards. In an interesting twist, the album also reunited the band with producer Forsey. As Kerr told Mike Joyce of the *Washington Post,* when the band recorded "Don't You (Forget about Me)," "we only worked with Keith for a couple of days and, not to be disrespectful, but we thought he was kind of a pop guy and we wanted to draw from a deeper well.... When he got in touch with us, we asked him to work on one song, and it sparked a great alliance." The album earned mixed reviews—although Kara Manning of *Rolling Stone* praised "Simple Minds' uniquely sonic explosion—brazenly heavy-handed, but always exciting." Still, *Good News* demonstrated that, even if Simple Minds could no longer fill stadiums in the United States, the band was determined to soldier on. As Michael Parrish, music director of radio station WDRE in Long Island, New York, told Brett Atwood of *Billboard,* "They have changed from where they were in the past, and I think that there is a new generation of listeners ready to accept them."

Selected discography

Life in a Day, Zoom, 1979, (reissue) Virgin, 1987.
Real to Real Cacophony, Zoom, 1980.
Empires and Dance, Zoom, 1980.
Sons and Fascination/Sister Feelings Call, Virgin, U.K., 1981.
New Gold Dream (81-82-83-84), A & M, 1982.
Themes for Great Cities, Stiff, 1982.
Celebration, Virgin, 1982.
Sparkle in the Rain, A & M, 1984.
Once Upon a Time, A & M, 1985.
Simple Minds Live: In the City of Lights, A & M, 1987.
Street Fighting Years, A & M, 1989.
Real Life, A & M, 1991.
Glittering Prize: Simple Minds '81-'92, A & M, 1993.
Good News from the Next World, Virgin, 1995.

Sources

Books

Buckley, Jonathan, and Mark Ellingham, eds., *Rock: The Rough Guide,* Rough Guides, 1996.
Clark, Donald, ed., *The Penguin Encyclopedia of Popular Music,* Viking, 1989.
DeCurtis, Anthony, James Henke and Holly George-Warren, ed., *The Rolling Stone Album Guide,* Random House, 1992.
Elrewine, Michael, executive ed., *All Music Guide to Rock,* second edition, Miller Freeman Books, 1997.
Hardy, Phil, and Dave Laing, *The Faber Companion to 20th Century Music,* Faber and Faber, 1990.

Larkin, Colin, *The Guiness Encyclopedia of Popular Music,* Stockton Press, 1995.

1996 People Entertainment Almanac, Cader Books/Little, Brown and Company, 1995.

Robbins, Ira A., ed., *The Trouser Press Record Guide,* fourth edition, Macmillan Publishing Company, 1991.

Romanowski, Patricia, and Holly George-Warren, eds., *The New Rolling Stone Encyclopedia of Rock and Roll,* Fireside, 1995.

Stambler, Irwin, ed., *Encyclopedia of Pop, Rock and Soul,* St. Martin's Press, 1989.

Periodicals

Billboard, April 6, 1991; May 25, 1991; January 7, 1995.

Entertainment Weekly, February 19, 1993; February 10, 1995; February 17, 1995.

Guitar Player, November 1991.

Los Angeles Times, June 8, 1991.

New York Times, March 4, 1995.

People, April 16, 1984; December 9, 1985; October 23, 1989; March 13, 1995.

Rolling Stone, November 21, 1985; June 19, 1986; July 13, 1989; March 9, 1995.

Stereo Review, November 1989.

Washington Post, February 24, 1995.

—K. Michelle Moran

Son Volt

Alternative country, rock band

Born from the ashes of the critically-loved Uncle Tupelo, Son Volt's emergence in 1995 was one of the most closely watched of the year, as rock critics and alt-country fans alike tried to determine if Jay Farrar, one of that band's two leaders, could continue to craft winning, weary songs without songwriting partner Jeff Tweedy. The answer, apparently, was yes. While Tweedy went on to form the more lighthearted Wilco, the solemn-voiced Farrar carried the darker torch in the form of Son Volt and laid to rest any concerns about whether or not he could pen songs on his own, winning over critics and fans alike while managing to stay true to his rural roots.

The seeds from which Son Volt would eventually spring were sown in Farrar's childhood. The youngest of four boys (the others being John, Wade and Dade), Farrar grew up primarily in Belleville, Illinois, a town almost a half an hour away from St. Louis. Although his father worked on a dredge boat, Farrar did not see his family as traditionally working-class. His father collected old cars and instruments, so like his siblings, Farrar

Photograph by David Atlas. © David Atlas. Reproduced by permission.

developed an early fascination with music, learning to play guitar at age eleven. His mother, who owned a used bookstore where Farrar worked by day, taught him how to play. "It was a good environment to grow up in," he was quoted in a 1997 interview in *Option.* "Both of my parents had an appreciation for music, and a willingness to pass on what they knew."

Finding small-town farm life stifling, he saw music as a way to escape. Along with older brother Wade, and high school friends Tweedy and Mike Heidorn, Farrar got his start as a high schooler in the Primitives, a primarily 1960s cover band. Although initially compelled by the punk rock bands they saw perform at shows in St. Louis, the teens soon found fresher inspiration in plaintive classics by country artists like Hank Williams and George Jones.

Wade Farrar's departure from the band around 1987 to join the Army was an event that precipitated the birth of Uncle Tupelo, a band that would blend the twin influences of country and punk. The band became cult favorites and released three country-flavored rock albums on the independent label Rockville (to which they were signed in 1989) before they were signed to Warner Brothers' Sire division in 1993. For financial reasons, Heidorn left the band before it recorded for Sire.

Ironically, by the time Uncle Tupelo's major label debut, *Anodyne,* was released by Sire in 1993, the band was

on the verge of dissolution. Uncle Tupelo officially called it quits the following year, citing the usual creative differences. As producer Brian Paulson, who worked on that album as well as the debuts of Tupelo splinter groups Wilco and Son Volt, told Steve Appleford of the *Los Angeles Times* in 1996, "The tension on *Anodyne* is kind of apparent, as far as I'm concerned. Stylistically, it starts to diverge quite a bit."

In the wake of the break-up, Farrar relocated for a period to New Orleans, reportedly the site of his family's only vacation. There, he focused on penning songs that would become the basis of Son Volt's debut album.

A Bright Beginning

Naming itself in honor of the legendary bluesman Son House, Son Volt formed in 1995 and reunited Farrar and Heidorn, who was then doing production work for a local newspaper. The formation of the band, with Farrar at the head, forced the notoriously shy and reticent songwriter more into the spotlight than he had been as a member of Uncle Tupelo. He would rather speak through his music.

With their own backgrounds in rootsy rock and country, the Boquist brothers, who grew up in the tiny Minnesota farming town of Rosemount before moving to Minneapolis, were logical choices to round out the group. Since the 1980s, the brothers had singly or jointly performed with bands like the Jayhawks, the Replacements, and Soul Asylum. Jim Boquist, who met Farrar in the early 1990s while playing bass for Joe Henry during an Uncle Tupelo tour, had remained in touch with Farrar over the years. Thus, when Farrar needed to assemble additional musicians to record post-Uncle Tupelo songs, he turned to Jim, and then Dave Boquist as well.

Studio Work Produces Solid Recordings

Work on Son Volt's first album started with the recording of demos in Illinois. The band then headed to Minnesota for recording sessions for *Trace* for Warner Bros., the label with which Farrar still had a record contract. The long drives from his home in New Orleans to see the Boquists in Minneapolis and Heidorn in St. Louis inspired Farrar to write songs like "Tear Stained Eye" for *Trace.* As Karen Schoemer observed in a 1995 article in *Newsweek,* as the songwriter traveled "up and down the country, tracing a vertical line along the Mississippi River, Farrar's head filled up with images of aimlessness and wandering, highways and dead ends, neon signs and late-night radio stations. Like any good writer, he filtered them all into his work."

Following its much-anticipated release in 1995, *Trace* garnered a host of glowing accolades from the music press and landed in a number of critics' year-end Top Ten picks. In a review that appeared in the *Detroit News* in 1995, Eric Fiedler of the Associated Press called *Trace* "magnificent" and "mesmerizing." Similarly, Jeff Gordinier wrote in *Entertainment Weekly* that the band turned "heartland rust into gold" on its first album. "Borrowing from country and lazy, early-'70s Southern California country rock, Son Volt creates music that is at once open to the possibilities of the next vista and suffused with a weary traveler's melancholy," music critic Tom Moon wrote in the *Philadelphia Enquirer.*

Time Well Spent

After spending two years together in the studio and on the road, the members of Son Volt noted that their second album, 1997's *Straightaways,* came more naturally to them. The album re-teamed the band with producer Brian Paulson, who also produced *Trace.* "Brian Paulson deserves a lot of credit," Dave Boquist was quoted in *Option.* "Like in photography, you try to get a good negative. I think that's what he tries to do—get the most unadulterated, good sound, so that he doesn't have to fine-tune too much." Among the songs on *Straightaways* is the ballad "Been Set Free," a song written in response to Uncle Tupelo's "Lilli Schull." Where "Lilli Schull" was written from the perspective of a contrite man imprisoned for the murder of his wife, "Been Set Free," with initial lyrics written by Farrar's wife, tells a similar tale from the woman's perspective.

Although not quite as well-received as *Trace, Straightaways* also earned a host of favorable reviews. In a piece for the *Wall Street Journal,* Jim Fusilli wrote that the band "delivers stark, weary ballads with teary-eyed sincerity that's undeniably charming, and uptempo rockers with a natural, unassuming power." Striving, as *Rolling Stone* critic Rob O'Connor put it, "for a more intimate back-porch vibe" than *Trace, Straightaways* "is Son Volt rocking at their most forlorn."

Selected discography

Trace, Warner Bros. Records, 1995.
Straightaways, Warner Bros. Records, 1997.
(With others) *VH1 Crossroads,* Atlantic, 1996.

Sources

Books

Buckley, Jonathan, and Mark Ellingham, eds., *Rock: The Rough Guide,* Rough Guides, 1996.
DeCurtis, Anthony, James Henke and Holly George-Warren, eds., *The Rolling Stone Album Guide,* Random House, 1992.
Elrewine, Michael, executive ed., *All Music Guide to Rock,* second edition, Miller Freeman Books, 1997.
Larkin, Colin, *The Guiness Encyclopedia of Popular Music,* Stockton Press, 1995.
Romanowski, Patricia, and Holly George-Warren, eds., *The New Rolling Stone Encyclopedia of Rock and Roll,* Fireside, 1995.

Periodicals

Chicago Tribune, April 18, 1997; August 8, 1997.
Detroit Free Press, April 20, 1997.
Detroit News, November 25, 1995; September 25, 1997.
Entertainment Weekly, November 10, 1995; October 11, 1996; April 25, 1997.
Interview, October 1996.
Los Angeles Times, December 6, 1995; March 17, 1996; April 27, 1997.
Metro Times (Detroit), September 24, 1997.
Newsweek, October 2, 1995.
New York Times, October 30, 1995.
Option, May/June 1997.
People, May 12, 1997.
Philadelphia Enquirer, September 24, 1995.
Rolling Stone, April 17, 1997.
Time Out New York, April 24, 1997.
Tribe Inside, June 1997.
Wall Street Journal, July 18, 1997.

Additional information was provided by Warner Bros. Records publicity materials.

—K. Michelle Moran

Soul Coughing

Alternative pop band

Photograph by Ken Settle. © Ken Settle. Reproduced by permission.

Most artists borrow from their predecessors, and those most diverse in their inspiration are dubbed "eclectic." Those bold enough to incorporate such far-flung styles as Soul Coughing does are deemed "eccentric." That label, among others more and less flattering, has greeted the band that dares to combine rock, jazz, hip-hop, R&B, funk, spoken word, and recorded samples of everything from blues man Howlin' Wolf and reggae band Toots & the Maytals, to assorted elephant sounds, slowed down voices, and unidentifiable squeals. "Everything is possible," drummer Yuval Gabay told SonicNet, a website featuring music news and broadcasts. "It's not about style or genre—we'll try an idea and experiment with any sound." Emerging from the New York City club scene in 1992 with little more than a commitment to finding out what comes after rock music, the band became a quick success in the alternative and college music scene. From 1994 to 1997 they released two critically acclaimed albums, toured the United States and Europe on the Lollapalooza and H.O.R.D.E. tours, and appeared in a number of mass culture outlets like the *Late Night with Conan O'Brien,* HBO, *The X Files,* and the *Howard Stern Show.*

As the group's wordsmith, performance front man and all-around cultural commentator, Michael Doughty is clearly Soul Coughing's central presence. Known as "M. Doughty," or most often just "Doughty," the artist's early life was that of the "Army brat." He experienced cultures as different as Leavenworth, Kansas and Belgium before his family settled in West Point, New York, where his father taught military history. Before Soul Coughing became a staple of New York alternative music clubs like the Wetlands and Irving Plaza, Doughty counted Greenwich Village's Knitting Factory as his primary source of employment. In addition to penning music reviews for the weekly *New York Press,* he was a six-dollar-an-hour doorman at the nightclub that hosted a range of alternative and experimental acts and served as a sort of social club for struggling musicians. Here Doughty met keyboardist Mark De Gli Antoni, who was pursuing a master's degree in composition at the Mannes Conservatory of Music and playing with Knitting Factory regulars like jazz saxophonist John Zorn. Israeli-born drummer Gabay and upright bass player Sebastian Steinberg were recruited soon after.

Having been in numerous groups that had run the gamut from 60s-heavy improvisational jam bands to hardcore punk outfits, Doughty was looking for something new. "I was buying a lot of rock records and none of them appealed to me," he told Stephen Rodrick in *Details.* "I turned entirely to hip-hop. I wanted something that reflected A Tribe Called Quest, but I'm not an M.C. I was trying to do a James Brown thing, with myself talking over something, and the music just became one animal." True to the band's later fluid, improvisational style, their first sessions were rooted in little more than that common desire for novelty, and little preparation went into their first show. Securing a two o'clock a.m. time slot at the Knitting Factory, Doughty assembled the group to play for an uninspiring 17 people. However, the group continued to coalesce around a distinctive jazzy-rock sound, the late night shows became more and more popular, eventually evolving into crowded Friday night parties at CB's Gallery, the sister club to the famous CBGB's in New York's East Village.

Amazed Themselves with Major Label Debut

Within a year this buzz had produced a recording contract with the Warner Brothers subsidiary, Slash Records. This was not a typical trajectory for an alternative band, which usually start out on smaller, independent labels like Sub Pop or Matador, or even with self-financed recordings. The band marveled at the speed of their acceptance by the music industry. "By the time I joined this band, I'd had a bellyful of chasing record contracts," bassist Sebastian Steinberg told *Rolling Stone*'s David Sprague in 1996. "So when we started getting [record label] offers, I couldn't believe it." Instead of testing the market with a less expensive EP, as many labels do with a new alternative rock act, Slash released the first Soul Coughing album, *Ruby Vroom,* in 1994. Critical acclaim followed, including a four-star rating from *Rolling Stone* and an "A" from *Entertainment Weekly.* The release also sold well for its category—over 70,000 copies by mid-1996, according to SoundScan data.

The band's name, which is slang for heavy vomiting, apparently came from a poem Doughty wrote about Neil Young. The members liked the sound of it and the name stuck. Writing for America Online's music reviews, Smith Galtney compared the name to the Beatles' 1965 album, *Rubber Soul,* citing John Lennon's word play on the incongruity between the white musicians and the soul music feel they were trying to achieve.

Soul Coughing's unique sound has to be heard—or better yet witnessed—to be fathomed, but *Rolling Stone*'s review of *Ruby Vroom* called the band "hiphop, spoken word, dance hall, Manhattan's avantgarde scene, Ken Nordine and straight jazz without being any one of them or even a hyphenated combination." What one might expect to sound like a hodgepodge of dissonant styles is in fact brought under one roof. Writing in *Details,* Stephen Rodrick called them an art-rock band and compared their ability to meld a wide variety of musical influences to that of 1980s eclectipop stars the Talking Heads: "Soul Coughing appropriate a collection of disparate postmodern sounds— from hip-hop to synth-pop—and they do it cleverly enough to get overeducated white kids up and dancing."

The band kept a lot of kids dancing, touring almost constantly in the U.S. and Europe with bands like Girls Against Boys, The Dave Matthews Band and Jeff Buckley. Their second album, *Irresistible Bliss,* released in July of 1996, revealed a move in the direction of mainstream pop music, sticking closer to the three-minute standard than in the first record. But in doing so Soul Coughing sacrificed none of its trademark bizarreness. Rating the album a seven (out of ten), A *New Musical Express* writer said this of the band's sophomore effort: "There's enough cool cat invention, liquidated guitars and squirming pop hooks ... to stun a small elk at 500 paces.... What happens after rock? Indefinable bliss." Two singles were released from the album, the jaunty "Soft Serve" and the fat-bass-thrusting "Super Bon Bon." Both had chart success, with the former reaching number two in alternative radio rotation (behind mega-stars U2) and the latter reaching number 30 on Modern Rock Tracks.

Doughty's album lyrics and live vocal improvisations inspire more than the usual fan club devotion to what a band is trying to say. The lyrics have been referred to as everything from "abstract art rants and bleatings of trash-culture poetry" in *Details* to "spoken word ramblings" in the *New York Observer* and are inevitably linked to the Beat poets, a comparison clearly irksome to Doughty. "The Beats must have been the best marketers in history, since anyone who mentions poetry is called a Beat," he quipped to *Rolling Stone* in 1996. "What about Whitman?" But nevertheless the similarities are there in refrains such as, "Collapse, unload it; pop pop, I must accumulate," from "Collapse," a song on *Irresistible Bliss* about rampant consumerism. Other choice lyrics include those in *Ruby Vroom*'s "True Dreams of Wichita:" "Brooklyn like a sea in the asphalt stalks/Push out dead air from a parking garage/Where you stand with the keys and your cool hat of silence/Where you grip your love like a driver's license."

In a posting to the Soul Coughing message board on America Online, Doughty described his methodology : "When I'm hashing out the lyrics, I'm thinking, 'Ooh, nice word. Pretty word. Mm, word tastes nice, I like.' So it's mostly a sound thing, a musicality thing." He added that if a fan should mishear a lyric and interpret it differently, that person should bring it to his attention so he can use the new version in a live performance. This is evidence of the band's close connection to its fans and the way it draws inspiration from them. "This band lives to play live," Doughty told SonicNet. "We lose our minds sitting at home." *Village Voice* rock critic Robert Christgau, writing an America Online review of *Irresistible Bliss,* described this aspect of the band: "Live, with Doughty's frenetically rectilinear hands invoking the music's shifting techtonics, it has so much action you can watch it bounce. And then there are the words. Doughty makes them swing, rock, move."

Brought Weirdness to Middle America

This ability to make words move brought even wider success to Soul Coughing in 1997. In April they appeared in a number of scenes of an HBO show called *Reverb* and in June were guests on the *Howard Stern Show,* serving up an in-studio rendition of "Super Bon Bon" at Howard's request.

The band's songs also appeared on a number of mass market soundtracks, *Songs in the Key of X: Music from the X-Files,* whose creator, Chris Carter reportedly called the group one of his favorites. After playing on the second stage of the Lollapalooza tour in 1996, the band joined the H.O.R.D.E. tour in August of 1997,

sharing a bill with Neil Young & Crazy Horse, Beck, Morphine and others. The New York City show was broadcast live on the Internet on SonicNet, one of the first concert broadcasts in that new medium. In fact, the group was already well-versed in using the Internet to communicate with their audience, having posted tour diaries on America Online as far back as 1994, and actively promoting their web site and email address on their albums.

The end of 1997 saw Doughty living in London between shows and taking in the city's club scene, particularly the new "drum'n'bass" offshoot of hip-hop music. Doughty told *Billboard*'s Bradley Bambarger that some of what he was absorbing from the cutting edge British music was bound to find its way on there: "I can't promise how, of course. It might just end up sounding like Led Zeppelin's take on reggae." This wouldn't be out of step with the band's signature eclecticism, but at the same time Soul Coughing is about more than just musical and lyrical experimentation and raucous live performance. There's a good deal of pain and vulnerability thrown into the mix, too, as seen by these lyrics from "Super Bon Bon:" "And by/The phone/I live/In fear/Sheer chance/Will draw/You in/to here." Speaking in typically expressive metaphor, Doughty summed up the group's embrace of incongruity, telling SonicNet, "I see Soul Coughing as this sort of V.U. meter with Heartbreak on the left, and Nonsense on the right. The needle twitches constantly from one side to the other."

Selected discography

Ruby Vroom (includes "True Dreams of Wichita" and "Sugar Free Jazz"), Slash/Warner Bros., 1994.
Sugar Free Jazz (remix CD with bonus tracks), Slash/ Warner Bros., 1995.
Irresistible Bliss (includes "Super Bon Bon" and "Soft Serve"), Slash/Warner Bros., 1996.
(Contributor) *Blue in the Face* (soundtrack), Luaka Bop/ Warner Bros, 1996.
(Contributor) *Songs in the Key of X: Music from the X-Files,* Warner Bros., 1996.
(Contributor) *Batman & Robin* (soundtrack), Warner Bros., 1997.
(Contributor) *Spawn* (soundtrack), Epic, 1997.

Sources

Books

The Trouser Press Guide to '90s Rock, Fireside, 1997.

Periodicals

Billboard, February 1, 1997. p. 71.
Details, November 1996; July 1997.
Entertainment Weekly, September 16, 1994, p. 121.
Los Angeles Times, February 17, 1997.
New Musical Express, May 25, 1996, p. 53.
New York Observer, 1996.
People, July 22, 1996, p. 24.
Rolling Stone, December 15, 1994, p.96; May 30, 1996, p. 96.
Spin, August 1996, p. 112.
USA Today, December 26, 1996.

Online

http://www.soulcoughing.com
http://www.sonicnet.com/altaccess
http://www.addict.com/issues/2.08
http://www.mcs.net/~brow/soulcough
America Online Rock Music Reviews

Additional information was provided by Shore Fire Media publicity materials, 1997.

—*John F. Packel*

The Specials

Ska pop band

Relating the band's genesis to Glenn Burn-Silver of the *Boulder Planet* nearly twenty years later, Specials bassist Horace Panter explained: "People had had enough of punk. The Sex Pistols were history. The Clash was seduced by the Yankee dollar. There were just too many bad punk acts around." Brandishing a ska sound and style that harkened back to the early 1960s, The Specials were clearly a product of the 1977 punk explosion in England. The revolution consisted of young music fans rejecting the extended instrumentals and elaborate performances of quintessentially 1970s bands like Led Zeppelin, Yes, and Pink Floyd in favor of stripped-down, three-chord, rough pop tunes, often with a liberal political or social message. "The sound was tied closely to the ideology of our time," Specials guitarist Lyndval Golding told *Billboard*'s Carrie Bell in a 1997 article about the resurgence of ska. "You used your music to get your message across to kids. Music is a vice, but you can use it to educate."

The group's influence is seen both by the trail it blazed for other ska bands like Madness, The Selecter, and The English Beat, and by the rankings its first two seminal albums were accorded by music critics—*The Specials* at number 25 on the *New Musical Express'* greatest albums of the 1970s, and *More Specials* at number 68 on *Rolling Stone*'s top picks for the 1980s. Bought at the price of a frenetic pace and significant group tension, this success was concentrated in a few short years as The Specials disbanded in 1981 and then reformed with various line-ups off and on through 1997.

The Specials were founded in England's industrial Coventry and originally called themselves the Automatics. After a dispute with another band of the same name, they changed to The Special AKA the Automatics, which was shortened to The Special AKA—or simply The Specials, as the band was known from 1978 on. The group was led by Jerry Dammers on keyboards, Golding on guitar, and Horace Panter on bass.

In 1978, one of punk rock's leading figures, Joe Strummer, invited The Specials to open for his band, The Clash, on its "On Parole" tour of the United Kingdom. At that point The Specials were still experimenting with their sound, playing a mix of Clash-like punk songs alternating with much slower reggae, which punk music fans favored for its message of political protest. Finding that the different tempos didn't work together, the band settled on ska, a Jamaican precursor to reggae popularized in England in the early 1960s by "mods"—young, urban devotees of bands like the Who and the Kinks and their R&B inspirations. "There is a spiritual connection between punk and reggae," Panter told writer Burn-Silver. "Both were rebel music when they started. That fact that we (the band) all liked reggae and punk helped. We thought, 'Wouldn't it be great if there was something that filled the gap?' It turns out that there was something—ska. Ska was different, and it still had energy and attitude."

Led Ska Revival by Forming 2-Tone Records

Energy and attitude would be in large supply over the next two whirlwind years of The Specials' career. Filling out the band's sound, the founding triumvirate added drummer John Bradbury, guitarist Roddy Byers, and singers Terry Hall and Neville Staples—the latter having been promoted from his duties as a roadie. Trombonist Rico Rodriguez joined in 1979. Displaying characteristic attention to style and control, as well as the do-it-yourself ethic of the punk movement, Dammers hatched the idea of starting the band's own record label. Like the great record labels behind many previous movements in pop music, such as Chess with Blues and Motown with R&B, Dammers wanted 2-Tone Records to be the sponsor of a ska explosion. And to a great extent it was, signing major names of second-wave ska, like Madness, The Selecter, and The English Beat. The first wave of ska had been sixties Jamaican artists like the Skatalites, Prince Buster, and Desmond Dekker, and the third came in the 1990s with bands like Bim Skala Bim and The Toasters, as well as the

For the Record . . .

Members include **Mark Adams** (bandmember, 1994—), keyboards; Adam Birch (bandmember, 1994—), horns; **Roddy Byers** (founding member), guitar; **Lynval Golding** (founding member; born July 7, 1952, in Jamaica), guitar; **Aitch Hyatt** (bandmember, 1994—), drums; **Horace Panter** (founding member), bass; **John Read** (bandmember, 1994—), trumpet; **Neville Staples** (founding member; born April 11, 1956, in Jamaica), vocals, percussion.

Former members include **Jerry Dammers** (born Gerald Dankin May 22, 1954, in India; bandmember, 1977-81), keyboards; **John Bradbury** (bandmember, 1979-81), drums; **Terry Hall** (born March 19, 1959, in Coventry, England; bandmember, 1978-81), vocals; **Rico Rodriguez** (born October 17, 1934; bandmember, 1979), trombone; **Siverton** (bandmember, 1977-78), drums.

Group formed in Coventry, England in 1977; invited to open for The Clash on United Kingdom tour, 1978; recorded self-financed single, "Gangsters," formed 2-Tone Records (distributed by Chrysalis), released first LP, *The Specials,* and signed The Selector and Madness to 2-Tone, 1979; toured U.S., Japan, and Belgium, saw *Special AKA Live* EP hit number one on U.K. charts, and released *More Specials,* 1980; released *Dance Craze* (movie) and number one U.K. single, "Ghost Town," then disbanded to form The Special AKA, Fun Boy Three, General Public, and The Special Beat, 1981; partially reformed to release *In the Studio* and "Nelson Mandela," 1984; hosted 70th birthday celebration concert for Nelson Mandela, 1988; released *The Singles Collection,* 1991; reformed (minus Dammers) to release *Today's Specials,* 1996; recorded *Payback Time* released in 1998.

Addresses: *Record company*—Way Cool Music, P.O. Box 100, Sunset Beach, CA, 90742. *Website*—Official Specials site: www.waycoolmusic.com/artists/thespecials/

ska-influenced No Doubt, Rancid, and Mighty Mighty Bosstones.

The Selecter, in fact, was born as the name given to an instrumental written by Dammers's friend Noel Davies

to occupy the B-side of The Specials' first single, "Gangsters." Recorded in early 1979 with borrowed money, the single ended up making it to number six on the U.K. charts. On the basis of this recording and a black and white (two-tone) logo of a stylishly dressed man Dammers had concocted, London label Rough Trade Records pressed 5,000 copies of "Gangsters," and the American label Chrysalis signed on to distribute the fledgling 2-Tone Records' releases.

Though lacking regular offices, a staff, or even a phone, 2-Tone was chartered as a corporation with each member of The Specials as a director. By November the first LP, *The Specials,* produced by Elvis Costello, was on its way to number four on the U.K. charts, followed by its single, "A Message to You Rudy," which hit number ten. Early the next year *Rolling Stone*'s Mick Brown reported on the 2-Tone phenomenon saying, "The Specials' story is one of those remarkable collusions of enterprise, timing and luck that rarely occurs in rock." And he quoted Panter explaining the group's motivation: "We'd had so many managers, and prospective managers, so many promises, and it had all fallen through. So we thought if we wanted to get anything done, we were going to have to do it ourselves."

The Specials began 1980 with a six-week tour of the U.S. and released a live EP, *The Special AKA Live,* which hit number one in the U.K. Two more top-ten singles were released that year—"Rat Race" and "Stereotype"—bringing to five the number of top-ten U.K. hits and seven the number of 2-Tone songs selling at least 250,000 copies. The group returned to the road in June, touring Japan and Belgium. The end of the year saw another full-length release, *More Specials.* Though it contained a number of songs in the ska tradition of the first album, like "Do Nothing" and "Man at C&A," the majority were of a slower, less hectic style that Dammers referred to as "lounge" music.

The following year, 1981, started off on a bad note as Dammers and Hall were fined for inciting violence and using threatening words after a fight broke out at a raucous concert. Soon after, 2-Tone expanded its influence, releasing the movie *Dance Craze* with an accompanying album featuring the music of The Specials, The Selecter, Madness, and Bad Manners. February 1981 also saw the group release "Ghost Town," the million-selling single decrying the state of race relations and urban poverty in Britain. The song proved hauntingly prophetic, as race riots broke out in economically depressed areas like Brixton and Liverpool that summer. Guitarist Golding himself was the victim of an attack that left him with 27 stitches. Seeking to quell the disturbances and fearing "Ghost Town" a negative influence, the single was banned by the BBC.

Splintered into Numerous Offshoots

With "Ghost Town" topping sales charts in the country and The Specials at their most popular ever, the group succumbed to the strains of a hectic touring and recording schedule, growing musical differences, and probably also Dammers' insistence on control. The group disbanded, splintering off into shifting alliances in successive recording projects. Staples, Hall, and Golding formed Fun Boy Three, which recorded two albums, had five hits, and split up in 1993. Panter teamed up with Ranking Roger from the 2-Tone band The English Beat and formed the equally successful General Public, which recorded two albums (Panter only appeared on the first) and scored with hits like "Tenderness" and a cover of Elvis Presley's song "Suspicious Minds" before evolving into Fine Young Cannibals. The Special Beat was a Specials/English Beat hybrid including Staples, Panter, and Roger, which toured the U.S. and released a live album, Special Beat Live, in 1992. And not to be left out, guitarist Byers formed the short-lived Roddy Radiation and the Tearjerkers, and drummer Bradbury formed the similarly eponymous J.B.'s Allstars.

Dammers, apparently hurt by the defections, continued his musical evolution toward even more benign forms of pop music which he compared to Muzak, resurrecting the old "The Special AKA" moniker to do so. Occasionally joined by Panter, Byers, and Bradbury, this vestige of The Specials released In the Studio: The Special AKA, as well as a few singles from 1982 to 1984—most notably "Free Nelson Mandela." Dammers also organized a 70th birthday concert celebration in 1988 for the jailed South African leader featuring Dire Straits, Whitney Houston, Stevie Wonder, and others. Dammers involved himself in other causes, too, like the 1985 compilation album, Starvation, benefitting Ethiopian famine relief and featuring The Special AKA, UB40, and General Public. Dammers also oversaw the release of a Specials greatest hits album, The Singles Collection, which entered the U.K. charts at number ten in 1991.

Reformed and Began Comeback

The seeds for a Specials rebirth were sown in 1994 when London-based Trojan Records convinced Panter, Byers, Staples, and Golding to back first-wave ska legend Desmond Dekker on an album that became Kings of Ska by Desmond Dekker and The Specials. The release's success in Japan led to a tour there, followed by a seven-week stint in the U.S. in the fall, both featuring selections from the group's old material. This experience energized the members to consider recording another album. "We were asked to put out an album but didn't have any new material," Panter told Burn-Silver of the Boulder Planet. "Someone suggested that we do an album of covers. We all sat round and had a big argument.... The Specials were always about bringing disparate influences together, and some of the ideas were pretty wild." Today's Specials, released on UB40 singer Ali Campbell's Kuff Records, included reggae covers like Bob Marley's "Hypocrite" and Toots and the Maytals' "Pressure Drop," as well as jazzman Paul Desmond's "Take Five," and pop songs like Neil Diamond's "A Little Bit Me, A Little Bit You." "Pressure Drop" was later included in the 1996 John Cusack film, Grosse Pointe Blank and its soundtrack.

This Dammers-less reunion led to the reformed Specials (joined by former Selecter drummer Aitch Hyatt, keyboardist Mark Adams, trombonist Adam Birch and trumpeter John Read) signing with MCA-distributed Way Cool Music in 1997. Ironically, Specials drummer Bradbury was at the same time playing with a recently reformed Selecter. A brief U.S. tour that summer, as well as some dates in South America, brought the band to the recording studio in the fall, where they began work on Payback Time. Released in early 1998, the band hoped that the record, as well as the current popularity of ska-influenced bands like Mighty Mighty Bosstones and No Doubt, would lead to a resurgence of their popularity. Applauding this revival of ska, Panter nevertheless gave word that he, for one, was prepared to hold it to the high standards of the past. "I have this fear that ska is becoming 'Revenge of the Nerd' music," he told Burn-Silver. "It's like, 'Let's dress silly and do a funny dance.' The Specials always had a sharp, stylish attitude. I think it is important to always have a certain style, rather than no real style at all."

Selected discography

The Specials, 2-Tone/Chrysalis, 1979.
The Special AKA Live EP, 2-Tone/Chrysalis, 1980.
More Specials, 2-Tone/Chrysalis, 1980.
(Contributor) Dance Craze (soundtrack), 2-Tone/Chrysalis, 1981.
The Singles Collection, 2-Tone/Chrysalis, 1991
Too Much Too Young Live (recorded in 1979), Receiver, 1992.
Kings of Ska by Desmond Dekker and The Specials, Trojan, 1994.

(Contributor) *Grosse Pointe Blank* (soundtrack), 1996.
Today's Specials, Kuff/Virgin, 1996.
Payback Time, Way Cool Music/MCA, 1998.

Sources

Periodicals

Billboard, October 18, 1997.
Boulder Planet, July 23, 1997.
Progressive, August 1996, p. 15.
Rolling Stone, March 6, 1980, p. 24; October 2, 1997.
Time, April 7, 1980, p. 75.
Washington Post, May 29, 1996.

Online

www.ecsel.psu.edu/~wsiddall/2tone.html
www.geocities.com/SunsetStrip/6339/whatska.html
www.sonicnet.com/sonicore/chat/bios/biospecials.html
www.waycoolmusic.com/artists/thespecials

Additional information was provided by Way Cool Music publicity materials, 1997.

—John F. Packel

The
Spinners

Motown-style soul quintet

The five young men who would become the Spinners started making doo-wop music together in 1957, under the name The Domingos, while attending Ferndale High School near Detroit. The Spinners never reached the heights attained by other Motown artists during the label's heyday in the 1960s, but the group continued to tour and record, releasing a string of hits in the 1970s. "The Spinners distinguished themselves with memorable melodies, rich harmonies, and a musical delivery full of spirit and feeling," according to the *African American Encyclopedia*. Despite changes in personnel and recording companies, the Spinners continued to turn out soul-oriented records into the 1990s.

The lively, soulful quintet had a polished nightclub act and a new name by 1961, when singer/producer Harvey Fuqua discovered them. Fuqua began recording The Spinners music on Tri-Phi Records, a small Detroit label he founded with his wife Gwen, sister of future Motown Music mogul Berry Gordy. The group's first single, "What Girls Are Made for," reached No. 27 on the pop charts and cracked the R&B Top 10. Some sources

AP/Wide World Photos, Inc. Reproduced by permission.

For the Record . . .

Members were **G.C. Cameron,** replaced Robert Smith in 1968; **George W. Dixon,** lead and tenor vocals; **Edgar Edwards** replaced George Dixon in 1962; **John Edwards** replaced Phillipe Wynn in 1977; **Henry Fambrough,** baritone vocals, (born May 10, 1935, in Detroit, MI); **Billy Henderson,** tenor-baritone vocals, (born August 9, 1939, in Detroit, MI); **Pervis Jackson,** bass vocals, (born May 16); **Robert Smith,** lead and tenor vocals, (born April 10, 1937, in Detroit, MI); **Philippe Wynne** (born April 3, 1941, in Cincinatti, and died July 14, 1984, in Oakland, CA) replaced G.C. Cameron in 1972.

Formed in Detroit, Michigan, 1957; released first single, "What Girls Are For," 1961; released two career retrospectives, early 1990s; released *A One of a Kind Love Affair: The Anthology* on Atlantic, 1991; released *The Very Best of the Spinners* on Rhino, 1993.

say Fuqua, who had been a member of the Moonglows alongside Marvin Gaye, sung lead on the Spinners debut. *Rolling Stone* refuted that, however, saying that lead vocalist Bobby Smith simply borrowed Fuqua's singing style for the song. The Spinners followed "What Girls Are Made for" with a series of singles, but none of them made a splash.

Overlooked at Motown

In 1963, Tri Phi merged with Motown and the Spinners transferred to the larger label, but it was not a fortuitous move. At Motown, the fivesome languished, lost in the crowd, overshadowed by Motown stars such as The Supremes, Smokey Robinson, Aretha Franklin and Marvin Gaye. At times, the Spinners sang back-up on their label-mates records, including Shorty Long's "Here Comes the Judge" in 1968 and Junior Walker's "What Does It Take to Win Your Love" in 1969. Other times, members of the group served as chauffeurs.

Although they were not considered a major act by Motown management, the Spinners crafted a handful of hits for the label: "I'll Always Love You," which reached No. 8 on the R&B chart in 1965; "Truly Yours" in 1966; and 1970's "It's a Shame," which was written and produced by Stevie Wonder. "It's a Shame"

reached No. 4 on the R&B chart and cracked the pop Top 20 in both the United States and the United Kingdom.

Changing Lineups and Fortunes

The Spinners original lineup featured Smith, George Dixon, Billy Henderson, Henry Fambrough and Pervis Jackson. The first in a series of personnel changes occurred in the early 1960s, when Edgar Chico Edwards replaced Dixon. In 1968 Smith left the group and lead vocals were handed off to G.C. Cameron. Cameron spent four years with The Spinners before being replaced by the charismatic Philippe Wynne in 1972. After leading the Spinners through its most successful period ever, Wynne left the group in 1977 to launch a solo career. The venture, however, proved dismal. Wynne's solo debut album, *Starting All Over,* fared poorly; although he later began performing with George Clinton's Parliament-Funkadelic. Wynne recorded the album *Jammin'* on Clinton's Uncle Jam label and achieved a minor hit in 1983 with the song "Wait Til Tomorrow." He died of a heart attack on July 13, 1984, after collapsing onstage at Ivey's, a nightclub in Oakland, California. The soulful singer was 43 years old.

The Spinners' fortunes changed in 1972, when the group left Motown for Atlantic Records at the urging of Aretha Franklin. At Atlantic, the Spinners teamed with writer/producer Thom Bell, who was known for his work with the doo-wop group the Stylistics. G.C. Cameron chose not to leave Motown, however, and Wynne, who previously had worked with Catfish and Bootsy Collins, replaced him. Wynne's "expressive falsetto lent an air of distinctiveness to an already crafted harmony sound and ... the Spinners completed a series of exemplary singles which set a benchmark for 70's sophisticated soul," according to the 1984 version of the *Rolling Stone Encyclopedia of Rock & Roll.* The "quintet deftly pursued a sweet, orchestrated sound which nonetheless avoided the sterile trappings of several contemporaries."

Top of the charts

In the next seven years, the Spinners' brand of soul and dance music racked up five gold albums. The group reached the R&B Top 20 more than a dozen times and the No. 1 spot with six million-selling singles. Hits included "Could It Be I'm Falling In Love" in 1972, "One of a Kind Love Affair" in 1973, "I'm Coming Home" in 1974, "They Just Can't Stop It (The Games People

Play)" in 1975, "The Rubberband Man," in 1976, and "If You Wanna Do a Dance" in 1978. In 1974 the Spinners and Dionne Warwick collaborated on the single "Then Came You," which hit No. 1 on the pop chart a first for both of them. The Spinners were second only to the O'Jays as the era's most popular black vocal group and achieved immense popularity in the United Kingdom, where they went by the Detroit Spinners to avoid confusion with the British folk group called the Spinners.

After Wynne's departure he was replaced by John Edwards, and it took the Spinners nearly three years to return to the top of the charts. The 1979 medley coupling a remake of the Four Seasons' "Working My Way Back to You" with "Forgive Me Girl," was a huge hit, reaching No. 1 in the United Kingdom and No. 2 in the United States. It was followed by another medley, "Cupid" and "I've Loved You for a Long Time" which broached the Top 10 on both sides of the Atlantic the following year. Bell stopped working with the Spinners and the group's success waned in the 1980s. While several singles reached the R&B charts, none cracked the Top 20.

A Spinners anthology released in 1992 called *A One of a Kind Love Affair* was well-received. "The great black vocal groups of the '70s were no less great for using a cliched dance beat," reviewer Ira Robbins wrote in *Entertainment Weekly*. "Hearing the Spinners now, it's painfully obvious how incidental a dance beat is to their magnificent delivery of American pop standards like 'Mighty Love,' 'I'll Be Around,' and 'Could It Be I'm Falling in Love'.... The combination of rich voices, uplifting lyrics, and lush production makes these songs a lasting, soul-satisfying pleasure."

Selected discography

Albums

The Original Spinners, Motown, 1967.
Second Time Around, V.I.P., 1970.
Best, Motown, 1973.
The Spinners, Atlantic, 1973.
Mighty Love, Atlantic, 1974.

New and Improved, Atlantic, 1974.
Pick of the Litter, Atlantic, 1975.
Live, Atlantic, 1975.
Happiness is Being with the Spinners, Atlantic, 1976.
Yesterday, Today and Tomorrow, Atlantic, 1977.
8, Atlantic, 1977.
From Here to Eternally, Atlantic, 1979.
Dancin' and Lovin', Atlantic, 1979.
Love Trippin', Atlantic, 1980.
Labor of Love, Atlantic, 1981.
Can't Shake This Feelin', Atlantic, 1981.
Grand Slam, Atlantic, 1983.
Cross Fire, Atlantic, 1984.
Lovin Feelings, Mirage, 1985.
Down to Business, Volt, 1989.

Compilations

Smash Hits, Atlantic, 1977.
The Best of The Spinners, Atlantic, 1978.
Superstar Series, Volume 9, Motown, 1981.
One of a Kind Love Affair: The Anthology, Atlantic, 1991.
The Very Best of The Spinners, Rhino, 1993.

Sources

Books

Helander, Brock, ed., *The Rock Who's Who*, second edition, 1997.
Hitchcock, H. Wiley and Stanley Sadie, eds., *The New Grove Dictionary of American Music*, Vol. 4, 1987.
Larkin, Colin, ed., *The Guinness Encyclopedia of Popular Music*, Vol. 1, 1993.
Romanowski, Patricia and Holly George-Warren, eds., *The Rolling Stone Encyclopedia of Rock & Roll*, 1996.
Williams, Michael W., ed., *The African American Encyclopedia*, Vol. 5, 1994.

Periodicals

Entertainment Weekly, January 31, 1992.
Playboy, April 1992.
Rolling Stone, August 30, 1984.

—Dave Wilkins

Igor Stravinsky

Composer

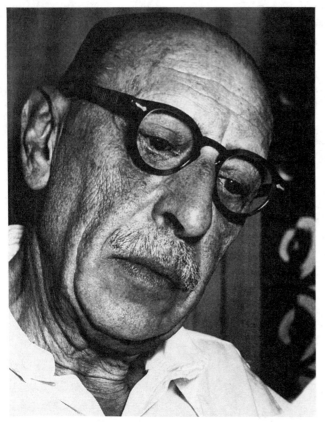

Few composers have made such dramatic breaks from the status quo in classical music as Igor Stravinsky did in the twentieth century. As Harold C. Schonberg remarked in *The Lives of the Great Composers,* "What Stravinsky represented, among many other things, was a compete rupture with Romanticism." Long considered the leader of the musical avant garde, Stravinsky developed his reputation by putting his own musical label on the classical styles of the past. His shift to Neo-classicism after World War I resulted in a series of compositions hallmarked by simplicity and restraint that were often critically praised but not favored by the public.

Stravinsky stressed that music was notes and nothing more, and that composition should be an expression of form and logic rather than passion. While his so-called "intellectual" scores often didn't strike a chord with audiences, his colleagues generally regarded him as one of the best musical technicians of his time. He also had a tremendous influence on other composers who followed him, although he had little interest in discussing his own music.

As the son of a renowned singer at the Imperial Opera in Russia, Stravinsky was surrounded by classical music while growing up. He began taking piano lessons at the age of nine, and also studied composition as a child. Trips to the ballet and opera were commonplace for the young Stravinsky, but his early training did not reveal any significant talent, nor did his compositions foreshadow his musical explorations of the future. As a teenager he became more interested in improvisation and began dabbling in composition.

A key influence of Stravinsky's early work was the famous Russian composer Nikolai Rimsky-Korsakov, whom Stravinsky met around 1900. When Stravinsky's father died in 1902, Rimsky-Korsakov became the young man's substitute father and musical mentor as he continued with studies at law school. Stravinsky became the composer's private student in 1903 and continued in this capacity until Rimsky-Korsakov's death in 1908. One of his first big compositions, the *Symphony in E-flat Major* in 1907, clearly showed the influences of Rimsky-Korsakov's style. Other early influences on Stravinsky's work were Scriabin, Tchaikovsky, Debussy, and Dukas.

Serge Diaghilev, who had recently established his Ballet Russe in Paris, attended a 1908 performance of Stravinsky's *Fireworks* in St. Petersburg. He was so impressed by Stravinsky's work that he asked the composer to write the music for a ballet based on the Russian fairy tale of the Fire Bird. Stravinsky agreed

Born Igor Fyodorovich Stravinsky, June 17, 1882, in Oranienbaum, Russia; died April 6, 1971, in New York, NY; son of Fyodor Stravinsky (opera singer) and Anna (Kholodovsky) Stravinsky; one of four children; married Katerina Nossenko, 1906 (died 1939); children: Fyodor, Ludmila, Svyatoslav, Sulema, Milena, Nicholas, and Katherine; married Vera de Bossett, 1940.

Studied piano and composition as a child; began taking private lessons with Nikolai Rimsky-Korsakov while attending law school, 1903; composed first major work, *Symphony in E-flat Major,* 1907; wrote *Firebird* for Ballet Russe, Paris, France, 1908; created major furor with *The Rite of Spring,* 1913; made first public appearance as a conductor, 1915; composed series of Neo-classical works that featured polytonal features; became known as leader of avant-garde music, 1920s; made first tour of U.S., 1925; began composing more religious works, starting with *Symphony of Psalms,* 1930; toured South America with son Sulima, a professional pianist, 1936; moved to Hollywood, CA, 1939; gave series of lectures at Harvard University as Elliot Norton Chair, Cambridge, MA, 1940; served as guest conductor with numerous American Symphony Orchestras, including the Boston Symphony Orchestra and the New York Philharmonic; had major worldwide success with *The Rake's Progress,* an opera, 1951; compared scores for a number of ballets choreographed by George Balanchine; developed partnership with conductor Robert Craft; experimented with serialism, late 1950s; composed *Elegy for J.F.K.* following President Kennedy's assassination, 1964; completed last major composition, *Requiem Canticles,* 1966; moved to New York, NY, 1969; died at the age of 88 in New York, NY, and was buried in Venice, Italy, 1971.

Awards: Gold Medal, Royal Philharmonic Society, 1954; U.S. State Department Medal, 1962.

and became famous overnight as a result of his *Firebird,* which backed choreography by Vaslav Nijinsky and received rave notices in France. Despite six decades of composing to follow, the *Firebird* would remain Stravinsky's most popular work. He followed this with 1911's *Petrushka,* which, according to Schonberg, "solidified Stravinsky's position as the coming man of European music." Quite daring for its time, this work featured a section that had two unrelated harmonies converging.

Nothing Stravinsky had done before prepared the pubic for his legendary next work, *Le Sacre du Printemps* (The Rite of Spring), which was also choreographed by Nijinsky. In his discussion of the work, *New York Times* music critic Paul Griffiths wrote, "By means of syncopation and rapid changes of metre Stravinsky did away with the regular pulse which had governed almost all Western music since the Renaissance." Most shocking about this ballet was its reception at its premiere, where members of the audience jeered and booed during the performance. Schonberg explained the response by writing, "Hardly anybody in the audience was prepared for a score of such dissonance and ferocity, such complexity and such rhythmic oddity." In a single stroke, Stravinsky had thrown out the time-honored standards of harmony and melody and created a new set of musical values.

A Change of Style

Prevented from returning to his native land due to World War I, Stravinsky and his family moved to Switzerland. After the Bolshevik revolution in Russia, he lived in France and soon encountered financial trouble, as funds had been cut off from Russia. Money problems forced Stravinsky to curtail his composing time by working more often as a performing musician and conductor. At this point he began composing a different type of music, focusing on concise works for small groups of instruments rather than majestic scores for large orchestras. One of these was a folk-tale piece composed in 1918 called *Histoire du Soldat,* which was an early example of musical theater. Based on a Russian tale about a deserting soldier, the piece used the services of a narrator, two actors, a dancer, and seven instrumentalists, while featuring a ragtime number and a chorale. Other notable Neo-classical works that he composed around this time include the *Symphonies of Wind Instruments* in 1921, a one-act opera entitled *Mavra* in 1922, and the cantata *Les Noces (The Wedding)* in 1923. Up to this time many of his pieces still drew heavily on the folk tales of Russia, but eventually his music left that heritage behind.

With his music after 1920 labeled as abstract and cosmopolitan, Stravinsky never again had the impact on audiences that he did with his Russian ballets. This was no surprise to him; he did not expect his anti-sentimental works to cater to the general public. By now his music was much more controlled and featured a strict economy of composition and little bombast. This approach was considerably evident in his oratorio called *Oedipus Rex,* composed in 1927. His *Violin Concerto* in the early 1930s was also an example of traditional musical forms put through Stravinsky's ultra-modern filter. His evolution during this period created two schools of thought among critics, one side admiring his newly found simplicity and restraint, the other yearning for the urgency and energy of his previous composition. The composer made his thoughts quite clear in his 1930 autobiography: "I consider that music is, by its very nature, powerless to express anything at all.... The phenomenon of music is given to us with the sole purpose of establishing an order in things."

In the 1930s Stravinsky was devoting much of his attention to religious works. He wrote a *Symphony of Psalms* for chorus and orchestra in 1930, and his late 1930s *Symphony in C* was, according to him, written to honor God's glory. During this decade he also found himself more in demand in the United States. He had visited America in 1925 and conducted the New York Philharmonic Orchestra, and in 1935 he returned there to conduct a number of major American orchestras.

Tragedy struck the Stravinsky family in the late 1930s. The death of his daughter of tuberculosis in 1938 was followed the next year by the death of his wife. The composer then lost his mother three months later. As World War II began to gain steam in Europe, he moved to the United States, which remained his home for the rest of his life. After settling in Hollywood in 1939, he received a number of requests to compose music for films, but little became of them. His most significant work during his first decade in the U.S. was the very dynamic *Symphony in Three Movements* completed in 1945. He also composed his *Mass* for chorus and woodwinds in 1948 for use in church services.

Lost Status in Avant Garde

In the U.S. Stravinsky reconnected with the Russian-born choreographer George Balanchine, with whom Stravinsky had worked previously in Europe. They formed a successful partnership in ballets, including 1948's *Orpheus.* Stravinsky's greatest post-World War II success was an opera collaboration with W.H. Auden and Chester Kallman entitled *The Rake's Progress,* which premiered in 1951 and gained international popularity. By this time Stravinsky had lost his position as leader of the avant garde, being upstaged by the rising popularity of Austro-Hungarian Arnold Schoenberg's 12-tone techniques and the school of serialism (a musical style whereby a series of different notes is used as the basis of a whole composition). For many years he had condemned serialism, but then had a change of tune in the 1950s due partly to increasing exposure to younger European composers resulting from the European premier of *The Rake's Progress.* He was also urged to explore serialism by his friend Robert Craft, an American conductor who had a major influence on Stravinsky in his later years. Stravinsky dabbled with serial elements in a ballet score for *Agon,* commissioned by Lincoln Kirstein and Balanchine in 1957. Other serial works included *Threni* in 1958 and *Movements for Piano and Orchestra* in 1959. Some critics attacked the composer's embracing of serialism as just a stunt to regain his status in the avant-garde world, but few of Stravinsky's works in this vein have had any staying power in the musical repertory.

In 1962 Stravinsky returned to Russia for the first time in half a century, giving a series of concerts in Moscow and Leningrad. His visit helped eliminate restrictions against the playing of his work in the Soviet Union. Many of Stravinsky's compositions in the 1960s were elegies or sacred music, among them the *Elegy for J.F.K.* in 1964. He wrote his last major composition, the serialism-influenced *Requiem Canticles,* in 1966, most likely with consideration of his own approaching death.

The Winter of a Legend

By 1967 Stravinsky's health was deteriorating rapidly, and that year he conducted his last public performance, of the *Pulcinella Suite,* in Toronto, Canada. In 1968, he and his second wife moved to New York City from Hollywood, then spent three months in 1970 at Evian on Lake Geneva in Switzerland. Stravinsky died at his home in New York City the following year. Soon after his death scandal broke out regarding books he had co-written with Craft when Lillian Libman, Stravinsky's personal representative, claimed that many of the details conveyed about the composer's life were fraudulent. Bernard Holland noted in the *New York Times* that Stravinsky "rearranged past events, experienced memory lapses (convenient or otherwise) or just plain lied."

Although he experienced many changes during his more than 65 years as a composer, Stravinsky maintained a commitment to precision and directness. As was noted about the composer in the *New Grove Dictionary of Music and Musicians,* "His life was a varied one, and his music too went through several changes, often startling at the time but revealing an inner consistency when viewed with hindsight."

Selected compositions

Tarantella, 1898.
Symphony in E-flat Major, Opus 1, 1907.
L'Oiseau de Feu (The Firebird) (ballet), 1910.
Le Sacre du Printemps (The Rite of Spring) (ballet), 1913.
Histoire du Soldat (A Soldier'sTale), 1918.
Mavra (an opera), 1922.
Oedipus Rex, 1927.
Jeu de Cartes (ballet), 1936.
Four Norwegian Moods, 1942.
The Rake's Progress (opera), 1951.
In Memoriam Dylan Thomas, 1954.
Agon (ballet), 1957.
Elegy for J.F.K., 1964.
Requiem Canticles, 1966.

Selected writings

Stravinsky: An Autobiography, Simon & Schuster, 1936.
Poetics of Muse, Harvard University Press, 1942.

Sources

Books

Arnold, Denis, ed., *The New Oxford Companion to Music, Volume 2,* Oxford University Press, 1983, pp. 1757–1760.
Sadie, Stanley, ed., *The New Grove Dictionary of Music and Musicians, Volume 18,* Macmillan, 1980, pp. 240–265.
Schonberg, Harold C., *The Lives of the Great Composers, Revised Edition,* W.W. Norton, pp. 484–506.
Stravinsky, Igor, *Stravinsky: An Autobiography,* Simon & Schuster, 1936.
Stravinsky, Igor, *Poetics of Muse,* Harvard University Press, 1942.
Taruskin, Richard, *Stravinsky and the Russian Traditions: A Biography of the Works Through "Mavra,"* University of California Press, 1996.

Periodicals

New York Times, October 7, 1996, p. C15.
New York Times Book Review, August 4, 1996, p. 10.

—Ed Decker

Jule Styne

Composer

Achieving great success as a composer for musicals during Broadway's heyday, Jule Styne claimed to have written 2,000 songs and had some 200 hits during a songwriting career that lasted over 50 years. He was known for being a great collaborator who could tailor his music perfectly for different scenes and for the vocal abilities of particular singers. "A master of plugging holes, he could sit down at the piano and come up with a song for any dramatic situation at the proverbial drop of a hat," noted Stephen Holden in the *New York Times* in 1994, soon after the composer's death.

Styne was one of the last survivors of the great American songwriters for the musical theater that included Cole Porter, Rodgers and Hammerstein, George and Ira Gershwin, and Irving Berlin. Although he wrote songs for a number of movies, he much preferred composing for the stage where the music was more of an integral part of the story. While he didn't expand the frontiers of the musical, Styne struck a chord with audiences with his catchy melodies and dramatic numbers that often brought the house down. "Although his style is traditional, and shows little harmonic or melodic experimentation, his best songs have melodies that often take unexpected turns toward the end," noted Gerald Bordman of Styne in the *New Grove Dictionary of American Music*. "Styne's best songs have reflective, sometimes romantic lyrics, with slow melodies based on repetition of short, distinctive phrases," added Deane L. Root in the *New Grove Dictionary of Music*.

Styne often claimed that the lyrics were more important than the music, and he was generous in giving credit to his collaborators and singers for making his songs popular. "You write as well as you write with," he remarked to the *New York Times*. He was a tireless workhorse in the composing arena who never let his ego get in the way of his craftsmanship. As he was quoted saying in *The Guinness Encyclopedia of Popular Music,* "I believe in perspiration—not inspiration."

Some of Styne's musicals sparked the careers of some of Broadway's most famous female talents. He helped launch the careers of Carol Channing (in 1949's *Gentlemen Prefer Blondes*) and Barbra Streisand (in 1964's *Funny Girl*), and provided memorable showcases for the talents of Mary Martin, Ethel Merman, and Judy Holliday. He also provided Frank Sinatra with a number of his early hits in the 1940s, among them "Some Other Time," "I Fall in Love Too Easily," and "Time After Time." One of Styne's greatest successes was *Gypsy,* which starred Merman in it's premiere in 1959 and featured the classic Broadway show-stopper "Everything's Coming Up Roses." Other classics hat he composed included "Three Coins in the Fountain," "Saturday Night (Is

For the Record . . .

Born Julius Kerwin Stein, December 31, 1905, in London, England; died September 20, 1994, in New York, NY; son of Isadore and Anna Kertman Stein; married Ethel Rubenstein, 1927 (divorced, 1952); married Margaret Ann Bissett Brown, 1962; children: Stanley, Norton (with Rubenstein); Nicholas, Katherine (with Brown). *Education:* Chicago College of Music; Northwestern University.

Moved from England to Chicago, IL, 1913; debuted as solo pianist with Chicago Symphony Orchestra, 1914; granted scholarship to the Chicago College of Music, 1914; played piano at burlesque houses and composed first songs while in high school; toured with Edgar Benson's Orchestra; wrote first hit song, "Sunday," with Ned Miller, Chester Conn, and Bennie Kreuger, 1926; began playing piano with Ben Pollack's band, late 1920s; changed name to Jule Styne; became vocal coach for Broadway entertainer Harry Richman; moved to Hollywood and worked as vocal coach at 20th Century Fox, 1920s; formed own ensemble, 1931; wrote songs for low-budget films, late 1930s—early 1940s; hired by Republic Studios and wrote songs for Gene Autry and Roy Rogers; wrote war-time hits "I Don't Want to Walk Without You" and "I Said No" with Frank Loesser, 1942; began long-time partnership with lyricist Sammy Cahn; created score for *High Button Shoes,* 1947; worked with Betty Comden, Adolph Green, Leo Robin, E.Y. "Yip" Harburg, and Bob Hilliard; wrote score for *Gypsy* with Stephen Sondheim, 1959; scored *Funny Girl* with Bob Merrill, 1964; composed scores for *Hallelujah, Baby!,* 1967, and *Sugar,* 1972; composed music for television and ballet; wrote his final score, for *The Red Shoes,* 1993; died of heart failure at age 88, 1994.

Awards: Academy Award, Best Song ("Three Coins in the Fountain"), with Sammy Cahn, 1954; Songwriters Hall of Fame; Theater Hall of Fame; John F. Kennedy Center for the Performing Arts honor for cultural contributions to the nation, 1990; New Dramatists Lifetime Achievement Award, 1992.

the Loneliest Night of the Week)," "Diamonds Are a Girl's Best Friends," and "People."

Julius Kerwin Stein began his musical career with a dramatic flourish at the age of three when he was living in the Bethnal Green of east London, where his parents ran a butter and egg store. While he and his family were watching a performance of the Scottish entertainer Harry Lauder, the young Stein jumped on the stage and sang a song. Lauder recommended that the Steins buy their son a piano, but they rented one instead to save money, and arranged for their son to take lessons.

By the time the Stein family moved to Chicago in 1913, Julius was a very accomplished pianist. He debuted as a soloist with the Chicago Symphony Orchestra at age nine, and soon was performing with the Detroit Symphony Orchestra as well. Studies in harmony and composition followed after he was awarded a scholarship to the Chicago College of Music in 1914. Despite his obvious talent, a career in classical music was deemed impossible for him by the time he was in high school because his hands were too small to cover the necessary spans.

As a teenager Stein began frequenting jazz clubs and developed a love for the music he heard there. He began playing piano in burlesque houses and composed his first two songs while still in high school, a pair of ditties called "The Guy in the Polka-Dot Tie" and "The Moth and the Flame." Around this time he also developed an enduring addiction to gambling, after betting on the horses at a racetrack for the first time. Following graduation he tickled the ivories in various nightclubs and with a number of combos, as well as toured with Edgar Benson's Orchestra. His parents were not pleased with the shift in his musical interests. "My father wouldn't like the success I've had as a songwriter," he was quoted as saying in the *New York Times.* "He said he never paid for me to be a composer. He paid for me to be a pianist."

"Sunday" Brings Success

Success as a songwriter came to Stein with his catchy "Sunday," which he co-wrote in 1927 with Ned Miller, Chester Conn, and Bennie Kreuger. This hit earned him a spot with the well-established Chicago band of Ben Pollack, whose members at various times included Benny Goodman, Glenn Miller, and Charlie Spivak. Around this time Stein rechristened himself Jule Styne, to make his name sound less Jewish, at the suggestion of an executive at the Music Corporation of America.

Styne continued to play piano in jazz groups and dance bands, and formed his own combo in 1931. He honed his ability as a composer and arranger as his band played at Chicago night clubs and speakeasies. Before long Styne ended up in New York City, where he became a vocal coach for the Broadway entertainer Harry Richman. This connection helped him get a job in Hollywood as a vocal coach at the 20th Century Fox film studio, where he worked with Shirley Temple, Alice Faye, and Constance Bennett, among others. He got his first taste of film composing as a writer of songs for low-budget movies such as *Hold That Co-Ed* in 1938. After making a move to Republic Studios, he wrote songs for the singing cowboys Gene Autry and Roy Rogers, while also providing music for forgettable films such as *Hit Parade of 1941, Melody Ranch, Rookies on Parade,* and *Angels With Broken Wings.*

Achieved Great Success With Cahn

Teaming up with Frank Loesser while on loan out to Paramount, Styne composed two songs for1941's *Sweater Girl* that became big hits during World War II: "I Don't Want to Walk Without You" and "I Said No," the former of which recorded by vocalist Helen Forrest with Harry James and His Orchestra. Meanwhile, back at Republic, Styne began the most successful partnership of his career when he began collaborating with lyricist Sammy Cahn. With Cahn he struck gold in the 1940s with songs such as "I've Heard That Song Before," "Saturday Night (Is the Loneliest Night of the Week)", "Let It Snow! Let It Snow! Let It Snow!," and "I'm in Love." He also had success writing songs with lyricists Herb Magidson and Walter Bishop. Sinatra helped build his following by singing Styne tunes in various movies in the 1940s, including "Some Other Time" in *Step Lively,* "Fall in Love Too Easily" in *Anchors Aweigh,* and "Time After Time" in *It Happened in Brooklyn.*

An Oscar for Styne

Despite his success as a composer for songs showcased in film—he won an Oscar for 1954's "Three Coins in the Fountain" and was nominated seven other times—Styne never liked writing music for the movies. According to the *New York Times,* he once said, "I don't like a director telling me what song goes where." He found his true love as a composer for stage musicals after World War II, scoring over 20 of them before his death. But success did not come immediately to Styne on Broadway. His and Cahn's first attempt, *Glad to See You,* never made it to New York after its brief run out of town. However, the show included their "Guess I'll Hang My Tears Out to Dry," which became a long-time standard on the cabaret circuit. The duo hit their stride in 1947 with their score for *High Button Shoes,* a musical starring Phil Silvers and Nanette Fabray that

became a big hit and ran for 727 performances. Two years later Styne struck gold on stage again with *Gentlemen Prefer Blondes,* which made Carol Channing a major star and became a popular film version in 1953 starring Marilyn Monroe and Jane Russell.

In 1951 Styne teamed up with the lyricists Betty Comden and Adolph Green for *Two on the Aisle,* a revue that featured Bert Lahr and Dolores Gray. The partnership proved a lasting one, and the threesome worked together often over the next decade, ranging from the stage musical *Bells Are Ringing* in 1956 to the film score for *What a Way to Go!* in 1964. During the 1950s Styne also worked with Leo Robin, E.Y. "Yip" Harburg, and Bob Hilliard. He put on a producer's hat on occasion, co-producing a revival for *Pal Joey* in 1952 and *Mr. Wonderful* in 1956. Styne reached what many consider his peak in 1959 with *Gypsy,* whose lyrics were penned by the young Stephen Sondheim. Featuring Styne's "Everything's Coming Up Roses"—his personal favorite among his songs, according to the *New York Times*—*Gypsy* was based on the memoirs of the stripper Gypsy Rose Lee, which dealt with her days on the vaudeville circuit as her domineering mother tried to force her into becoming a star. The musical became one of Ethel Merman's biggest triumphs on Broadway, and it was later made into a film with Rosalind Russell in the title role.

Provided Showcase for Streisand

Five years later Styne had another great triumph with *Funny Girl,* a musical about the life of Fanny Brice with the new superstar Barbra Streisand. According to Kurt Gänzl in *The Blackwell Guide to the Musical Theatre on Record,* the songs created by Styne and lyricist Bob Merrill for the show "helped lift the piece right to the forefront of that favourite type of Broadway musical,the vehicle for a larger-than-life female start, which Styne had already served so well in *Gypsy*." Although the Hollywood version of *Funny Girl* released in 1968 was much acclaimed, Styne had nothing good to say about the film versions of his musical or any other musical. "The movies destroyed every musical they ever made from the stage," he said in the *New York Times.*

Funny Girl turned out be somewhat of a creative finale for Styne, and his musicals that followed had little impact. Minimal runs were tallied for his *Hallelujah Baby!* in 1967, *Darling of the Day* in 1968, *Look to the Lilies* in 1970, and *Sugar* in 1972. He maintained a high visibility during the 1960s and 1970s despite his advancing age, and often performed his own songs on television or for industry showcases. He also made the rounds at nightclubs on a regular basis so he could hear singers belt out songs from the "good old days."

Still active at his piano well into his eighties, Styne worked on his last musical, *The Red Shoes,* in 1993. The show was a major flop, closing after only three days. He died the next year, six weeks after having open-heart surgery, at the age of 88. At the time he had been involved in a revival of *Gentlemen Prefer Blondes* being planned for the Goodspeed Opera House in Connecticut. "Born three years after Richard Rodgers and seven years after George Gershwin, he was the last great American songwriter to hark from the era when great American songwriters seemed to give unified voice to an entire nation," remarked Frank Rich of Styne in the *New York Times* after the composer's death in 1994.

Selected stage musical scores

High Button Shoes, 1947
Gentlemen Prefer Blondes, 1949.
Peter Pan, 1954.
Bells Are Ringing, 1956.
Gypsy, 1959.
Do Re Mi, 1960.
Funny Girl, 1964.

Selected film scores

Sweater Girl, 1942.
Anchors Aweigh, 1945.
It Happened in Brooklyn, 1947.

My Sister Eileen, 1955.
What a Way to Go, 1963.

Sources

Books

Gänzl, Kurt, *The Blackwell Guide to the Musical Theatre on Record,* Blackwell, 1990, pp. 391–392.
Hitchcock, H. Wiley, and Stanley Sadie, editors, *The New Grove Dictionary of American Music,* Macmillan, 1986, p. 328.
Larkin, Colin, editor, *The Guinness Encyclopedia of Popular Music, Volume 5,* Guinness Publishing, 1995, p. 4011–4012.
Sadie, Stanley, editor, *The New Grove Dictionary of Music and Musicians,* Macmillan, 1980, p. 321.
Slonimsky, Nicolas, reviser, *Baker's Biographical Dictionary of Musicians, Eighth Edition,* Schirmer Books, 1992, p. 1817.
Taylor, Theodore, *Jule,* Random House, 1979.

Periodicals

Billboard, October 1, 1994, p. 3; March 18, 1995, p. 42.
New York Times, September 21, 1994, Section 1, p. 1; September 25, 1994, Section 4, p. 17; October 2, 1994, Section 2, p. 6;
New Yorker, October 3, 1994, p. 47
U.S. News & World Report, October 3, 1994, p. 20.
Vogue, December 1993, p. 132.

—*Ed Decker*

Tool

Rock band

Created around the idea of *lachrymology*, or the "study of crying," Tool became both a symbol of success in the music world and a tribute to the concept of channeling negative energy toward positive means. With early hits such as "Sober" and "Prison Sex," the band propelled its mission to use the intellectual and musical influences of its members to inspire its own listeners. Ted Drozdowski wrote in a review of Tool in *Rolling Stone*: "Their songs about the living hell that humans create connect with the seething frustrations of an audience who have seen the cynicism of their parents' generation devour the fruits of opportunity."

Unlike the flood of bands who targeted the angry youth of the 1990s, Tool set out to stimulate thought, rather than simply complain about the state of the world. "Evolution didn't stop with us getting thumbs," singer Maynard James Keenan told Jon Wiederhorn in *Rolling Stone*. "There are a lot of metaphysical, spiritual, and emotional changes going on right now, and we're just trying to reflect that."

Photograph by Ken Settle. © Ken Settle. Reproduced by permission.

For the Record . . .

Members include **Danny Carey** (born Daniel Edwin Carey, May 10, 1961, in Paola, KS,), drums; **Justin Chancellor** (replaced Paul D'Amour; born Justin Gunnar Walte Chancellor, November 19, 1972), bass; **Paul D'Amour** (born Paul M. D'Amour, June 8, 1968, in Spokane, WA,); **Adam Jones** (born Adam Thomas Jones, January 15, 1965, in Libertyville, IL) guitar; **Maynard James Keenan** (born James H. Keenan, April 17, 1964 in Ravenna, OH), vocals.

Band formed in Los Angeles, California, and signed to Zoo Entertainment/BMG, 1991; released debut EP *Opiate*, 1992; released debut LP, *Undertow*, 1993; bassist Paul D'Amour replaced by Justin Chancellor, 1995; released *Ænima*, 1996.

Awards: Grammy Award, Best Metal Performance, for "Aenema"' 1998.

Addresses: *Record company*—BMG Records, 6363 Sunset Blvd., Los Angeles, CA 90028.

From Tool's inception, they drew inspiration from authors and philosophers, as well as their own personal experiences. The group referenced concepts and themes from writers such as Joseph Campbell, Aleister Crowley, William Gibson, Carl Jung, and Ronald P. Vincent. In fact, it was the latter who inspired the concept of the band from the beginning. Guitarist Adam Jones read Vincent's book *A Joyful Guide to Lachrymology* after he moved from Illinois to Los Angeles. He had been working as a sculptor and special effects designer for film, working on movies like *Jurassic Park*, *Terminator 2*, and *Predator 2*. Vincent's ideas about feeding off of pain and using its energy in a positive way sparked Jones' desire to bring musicians together to direct their own frustrations into art. "The philosophy of that book is basically using your pain to a profit, rather than letting it drag you down," drummer Danny Carey told Scott Schalin in *BAM*. "A lot of people who can't master that art end up jumping off buildings."

Philosophy Sculpted Early Years

In 1991 Jones met Carey through their mutual friend, Rage Against the Machine guitarist Tom Morello. He also met bass player Paul D'Amour through the movie industry. At the time, singer Maynard James Keenan lived upstairs from Carey. When they all got together, they took Jones' idea and gave it a life in a group they called Toolshed, later simplified to Tool.

All four members of Tool moved to Los Angeles from different areas of the United States. Keenan was born near Akron, Ohio, an only child in a Baptist family. His mother died when he was just eleven years old. Before moving to L.A., he lived in Michigan, New Jersey, New York, Oklahoma, Kansas, Texas, and Massachusetts, and had served three years in the Army.

Danny Carey was the only member of Tool to have played music full-time before the band's formation. He was the drummer for an L.A. band called Pigmy Love Circus in the late 1980s and early 1990s, and he played in a band called Green Jelly. Even after joining Tool, Carey played in another band on the side, called Zaum. When he joined Tool, they hadn't developed a success strategy, nor had they planned the rapid launch they received.

"It began as a self-satisfying thing for us," Carey told Schalin. "Our music was a release and a vehicle to get out whatever tensions we were feeling at that time." "When we started the band, we all had our own jobs," Jones said to Edward Fruchtman in *Circus*. "We did this as a side project. We never intended to get signed. It was all about the music—music that inspires and music that creates thought."

Sharpened Popularity Through Performances

Before the end of Tool's first year together, they had signed a record contract with Zoo Entertainment, distributed by BMG Records. (The label later changed its name to Freeworld.) In 1992, Tool released an EP titled *Opiate* to introduce their loud, aggressive sound. "Everyone thought we were a hard metal band," Adam Jones recalled to Chuck Crisfulli in *Guitar Player*, "but our tastes run through Joni Mitchell, King Crimson, Depeche Mode, and country [music]. We're not a metal band, rock band, or a country band. We're Tool."

By July of that same year, they had the opening slot on a tour with the Rollins Band. Then, the following year, they released their debut full-length disc, *Undertow*. The first single, "Sober," began getting exposure on several regional music video shows across the country. Adam Jones had designed the video using stop-motion camera techniques with claymation. Soon, the video became a hit on MTV.

In May of 1993, Tool began its U.S. tour, opening for bands such as Rage Against the Machine, Living Colour, and Fishbone. By the summer, they had landed a slot on the second stage of the Lollapalooza tour. Midway through the tour, they moved up to the opening band on the main stage.

Changed Parts Smoothly

Tool began receiving more and more exposure and critical acclaim. David Browne wrote in *Entertainment Weekly*, "What put this L.A. band a notch above the rest are better songs (with actual verses, choruses, and hooks—check out the terrific 'Prison Sex') and the hints of vulnerability in Maynard James Keenan's voice."

The next single and video, "Prison Sex," was also designed by Jones in the same claymation style. The notoriety they received on the Lollapalooza tour and the popularity of their music videos, launched Tool's *Undertow* to platinum sales status before the end of 1994. The following year, the group's progress was slightly interrupted by the departure of bassist Paul D'Amour. The foursome had already started recording their next record, when D'Amour decided to move on to form his own band called Lusk.

However, Tool didn't waste much time. Bass player Justin Chancellor, whose previous band Peach had performed with Tool in Europe, soon filled the empty position. He jumped right into the studio, and Tool's next LP, *Ænima* was released in 1996. It debuted at number two on *Billboard*'s album chart, and went platinum within the year. The album, which included the single "Stinkfist," was co-produced by Dave Bottril, who had previously worked with artists such as King Crimson and Peter Gabriel. Adam Jones continued to express his visual artistic talent on the 3-D "multi-image" packaging for the disc.

Strengthened Hard-Edged Messages

Some reviews commented that *Ænima* had an even harder edge than Tool's previous releases. "Dense and looming, *Ænima* spirals through a bleak landscape of metallic rhythms and industrial textures, mutating at will like a sadistic demon from an H.R. Giger sketchbook," Jon Wiederhorn wrote in *Rolling Stone*. "One of the goals of the record, among a lot of things, was to make it obvious to all the materialistic idiots that energy is primary and the illusion of matter is secondary," Danny Carey told Carl Hammerschmidt in *Hot Metal*.

By the summer of 1996, Tool had returned to the Lollapalooza tour, this time as its co-headliner. They performed on the bill with Korn, Tricky, Snoop Doggy Dogg, Orbital, and James. Chancellor, their new bass player, fit in without missing a beat. His fresh approach to the ideas of Tool gave him a unique perspective of the group. He described his impressions to Edward Fruchtman in *Circus*. "I've never come across or been a part of a collection of souls so diverse in character and belief that possess the ability to mutually accommodate those differences and evolve them into positive creativity."

Even through all of the recognition and success, Tool stayed true to their original mission inspired by Ronald P. Vincent. After the platinum records and headlining tours, they still included a reading list of their favorite recently read books in their fan club mailing list, and they have said that they want the band to serve as a "tool" to understanding the concepts and benefits of lachrymology.

Selected discography

Opiate, Zoo Entertainment/BMG, 1992.
Undertow, Freeworld/BMG, 1993.
Ænima, Freeworld/BMG, 1996.

Sources

Periodicals

Billboard, September 11, 1993.
Circus, August 1997.
Entertainment Weekly, May 28, 1993; October 4, 1996.
Guitar Player, September 1993.
Hot Metal, Summer 1997.
Rolling Stone, April 7, 1994; November 28, 1996; December 26, 1996-January 9, 1997; August 7, 1997.

Online

http://www.hypermall.com/~willp/tool
http://toolshed.down.net

—*Sonya Shelton*

Treadmill Trackstar

Rock quartet

The Columbia, SC rock/pop quartet Treadmill Track star was one of the first two bands signed to Breaking Records, a Columbia-based imprint founded by the band Hootie and the Blowfish in early 1997 and a subsidiary of Atlantic Records. Like Hootie and the Blowfish—another Columbia-based band—Treadmill Trackstar also favors a strident guitar sound and a melodic catchiness in their music. However, Treadmill Trackstar features something most rock bands do not: a cellist. The addition of a cello defines their music to a great extent, adds a more pensive sound to pop and alternative rock, and sets Treadmill Trackstar apart from other bands.

Georgia-born Angelo Gianni was bitten by the music bug at an early age, playing in rock bands as a teen. Gianni was raised in Connecticut but when it came time to go to college, he returned to the South. During his time at University of South Carolina Film School, Gianni met drummer Tony Lee. Together they formed a band called Root Cellar, playing the usual college hangouts—coffeehouses and clubs. In 1993 they

Photograph by Craig Cameron Olson. Breaking Records. Reproduced by permission.

For the Record . . .

Members include **John Furr**, guitar; **Angelo Gianni**, songwriter, lead vocals; **Chris Grigg**, bass; **Tony Lee**, drums; **Katie Hamilton**, cello; Former members include, **Heidi Brown**, cello.

Treadmill Trackstar, based in Columbia, SC, were one of the first two bands signed to Breaking Records, a Columbia-based imprint founded by the band Hootie and the Blowfish in early 1997 and affiliated with Atlantic Records; the band evolved in 1994 from Angelo Gianni's desire to release a CD; released their debut album, *Excessive Use of the Passive Voice,* on Raging Rose Records in 1995; released first album *Only This* for Breaking Records in 1997; opened for Hootie and the Blowfish, Matthew Sweet, and Dillon Fence in 1996.

Addresses: *Record company*—Breaking Records/Atlantic Records, 75 Rockefeller Plaza New York, NY 10019. *Website*—www.treadmilltrackstar.com/index.htm

disbanded, Lee moved to Los Angeles to pursue a career in film editing, while Gianni remained in South Carolina and tried (unsuccessfully) to form a new band. After a short period of playing on his own, Gianni coaxed Lee from California and Treadmill Trackstar evolved in 1994. Treadmill Trackstar released their debut album, *Excessive Use of the Passive Voice,* on the Columbia-based Raging Rose Records in 1995. When the album was recorded, the band didn't really exist: Gianni simply asked some musician friends to help him record the album in the studio.

The various musicians on *Excessive Use of the Passive Voice* included Dan Cook from the band Lay Quiet Awhile, John Furr from Blightobody, Todd Garland, Tony Lee, and original cellist Heidi Brown. Gianni decided he needed a band to promote the record and to tour, so he played acoustic gigs with Heidi Brown at local venues while searching for his future bandmates. He placed advertisements in four cities, and the result was that he met bassist Chris Grigg. The remainder of the band then fit easily into place.

When describing the band's sound, Brian McCollum of the *Detroit Free Press* appropriately wrote, "Treadmill takes the acoustic sound, steps on the distortion pedal, pushes a warm cello to the front of the mix, and sets the energy knob just a hair below 'full blown'. The result is a colorful gush of grassroots pop."

Excessive Use of the Passive Voice includes an eighty-page companion book of poems and short stories for order which, at first glance, seemed to have little to do with the album's lyrics, yet all of the material was tied together in a philosophical way. Angelo Gianni told Dave Lucas of the *Free Times,* "The way I was thinking about it was I may only get to make one CD my whole life, so we better put as much stuff on there as we can."

The album also included spoken-word poetry and fictional tales after the music, and additional story material was inserted in the liner notes. Gianni also read Bob Mould's "Too Far Down" near the close of the album. Treadmill Trackstar plans to incorporate film at their future live performances, and to utilize visual themes that could accompany their harmonies or lyrics.

Gianni told Lucas, "Almost everything I write has got to do with ... futility, sort of, and feeling trapped in situations." *Excessive Use of the Passive Voice* opens with thirty seconds of silence, and then the album begins with the sound of Gianni croaking the lyrics to "Singing in the Rain" as if on his deathbed. The album's songs range from loose and raucous to sublimely delicate and slightly despondent. The band's first album featured cellist Heidi Brown, but she grew tired of the band's excessive touring and decided to replace herself with her longtime high school friend, cellist Katie Hamilton, who had never played in a rock band before. Brown's departure was announced just weeks before the band was slated to record its first album for Atlantic's Breaking Records in January of 1997.

Songs like "Virgin S. and the Mechanic" clearly set Treadmill Trackstar apart from the pop and alternative rock fray by highlighting memorable, intelligent lyrics that seem to linger long after the song has ended. "Pale Bright Sun," for example, on *Excessive Use of the Passive Voice* contains all of the trappings of solid pop sensibility and thorough musical craftsmanship.

Treadmill Trackstar thanked Charleston's hard-edged rock band Muthafist in their CD's liner notes, which was a clear nod of thanks for their musical inspiration; other musical influences include Bob Dylan's songwriting and lyrics, and the rollicking, driving musical sound of the Stone Temple Pilots.

Treadmill Trackstar is, to a remarkable degree, a diligent touring band with a thirst for the road. After their debut album was released, band members became veritable touring machines similar to Jack Kerouac's

"On the Road" character, Dean Moriarity, covering more than 90,000 miles in a nonstop tour in 1996. The band covered the south and much of the midwest and even needed to replace their first truck. While touring, band members often lived on a meager five dollars a day, subsided mainly on fast food, watched television in their truck, slept in basements, and even slept on pool tables. Yet the experience, which would seem grinding to many others, was viewed as a great adventure by Treadmill Trackstar. The band opened for Hootie and the Blowfish, Matthew Sweet, and Dillon Fence while on tour.

After touring, Gianni told *The State*'s Michael Miller, "I've only been apart from my bandmates for five days this month, and sometimes it gets hard to deal with the same people for hours and hours a day for weeks at a time. But we've learned to deal with that, and I think we're a closer-knit unit than we've ever been." Treadmill Trackstar released *Only This*, their first album for the Breaking Records label, in the fall of 1997. Based upon the band's history and dedication, it was worth the wait. The album contains songs that reflect Treadmill Trackstar's emotional range. According to Thom Owens' *All Music Guide* website review, *Only This* is "a record that's melodic and often enchanting."

With their major label debut in circulation, Treadmill Trackstar is becoming a more widely recognized band. Constant touring and their participation in the R.O.A.R. tour in the summer of 1997 brought their music to new audiences. Treadmill Trackstar has also opened for more mainstream artists and bands, including Hootie and the Blowfish, Matthew Sweet, and Edwin McCain.

This extensive touring and constant motion would tire the average person, but not the members of Treadmill Trackstar. They give no indication of slowing their pace. In his interview with Dave Lucas, Angelo Gianni summed it up: "It's just fun traveling and playing new places."

Selected discography

Excessive Use of the Passive Voice, Raging Rose Records, 1995.
Only This, Breaking Records/Atlantic Records, 1997.

Sources

Periodicals

Billboard, August 24, 1996.
Break (Tallahassee, FL), November 1995.
The State (Columbia, SC), December 4, 1996.
The Sun News (Myrtle Beach, SC), December 4, 1996.
Free Times (Columbia, SC), July 1996.

Online

http//205.186.189.2/cg/amg.exe.sql=A315452
members.aol.com/ragingrose/Treadmill/Press.html
www.penduluminc.com/mm/treadmill.htm
www.treadmilltrackstar.com/index.htm

—B. Kimberly Taylor

Jen Trynin

Rock singer, songwriter, guitarist

Unlike some artists, Jen Trynin's first glimpse of fame was overwhelming and disconcerting. Up to that point, she had been perfectly content playing her smart and funny songs in Boston's music clubs, working a couple part-time jobs, and operating a small desktop publishing business out of her apartment. Then she put out her first record, *Cockamamie,* a collection critics described as hard-edged, quick-witted garage rock which deftly balanced tenderness and a sardonic attitude. This debut led to a contract with a major record label, promotional appearances, and a tour. "The weirdest thing was just losing my entire life as I had known it before," Trynin told Robin Vaughan of the *Boston Herald.* "(Before signing a record contract) I would stay up all night doing desktop publishing stuff, drinking beer and writing songs—and I loved it."

That all changed in 1994, however, after Trynin released *Cockamamie* on her own label, called Squint Records, and the big record companies came calling. She ultimately signed a lucrative deal with Warner Bros., which re-released *Cockamamie* and sent Trynin on the road to promote it. She quit her jobs, left her friends and her home, and swapped the solitude she cherished for a chaotic lifestyle and a stream of one-night appearances and long van trips. *Cockamamie* received good reviews and spawned the modest hit "Better Than Nothing," but radio play was minimal and sales were weak. As a result, pressure mounted for Trynin. "When you think, 'Oh, I'm going to get a record

deal, I'm going to travel the country,' you don't think of all the incredible pressure that other people are putting on you because so many people's livelihoods depend on your success," she was quoted in the *Boston Globe.* "I was going around the country for months with these guys in a van and I kept asking myself, 'What am I doing?' Then the record wasn't doing all that well, Warner Brothers was going through some trouble, my management was going through trouble, everything was just falling apart, and I had given up my whole life for this."

When Trynin returned to the home she shares with her boyfriend and producer, Mike Denneen, she spent a few months in seclusion and regained her bearings. She ultimately emerged from the experience "scarred but smarter ... armed with both knowledge and experience, two commodities she earned the hard way," Michael Saunders wrote in the *Globe.* "I learned a whole lot," Trynin confessed to Vaughn. "Not just about the music business, but about myself and what I really want. I was kind of surprised by what I want, because it's not what I thought it was."

Trynin's second album for Warner Bros., 1997's *Gun Shy Trigger Happy,* revealed a softer, yet stronger performer. "Both the music and the musician appear to have arrived at a more soulful place," Vaughan wrote. "The floating, funky arrangements suggest the feel-good grooves of Marvin Gaye and Stevie Wonder more than the boys-school rock rhythms of *Cockamamie.* And a breathy, feminine singing voice has replaced Trynin's old growl." On the other hand, Trynin did not abandon her fatalistic humor and biting, acerbic lyrics on the new record. On the song "Bore Me," for example, she croons to an ex-lover who wants to remain friends: "Oh baby, bore me just a little more."

Meanwhile, she handled the requisite promotional appearances and touring with more balance and perspective the second time around. While on the road, Trynin decided that she would ensure a daily dose of solitude by driving her own car, stay fit by running each day, and maintain other elements of "real life." "I just feel more relaxed," she told Saunders. "Now that I've been through it, I can understand that I won't have three interviews a day for the rest of my life. It just happens at certain times. That's OK, I can handle that. And, OK, you travel sometimes, but sometimes you're home. And I know that when this record cycle ends, I can take a year off if I want and be by myself again."

If the reviews for *Gun Shy Trigger Happy* are any indication, that cycle will last longer and be more intense than it was the first time. *Billboard* praised the

For the Record . . .

Began career performing songs in the Boston folk music scene; released debut album, *Cockamamie* on her own label, Squint Records, 1994; signed with Warner Bros. Records, which re-released *Cockamamie*, 1995; released sophomore effort, *Gun Shy Trigger Happy*, 1997.

Addresses: *Record company*—Warner Bros., 3300 Warner Blvd., Burbank, CA 91505-4694.

album as "strikingly lovely," while *Rolling Stone* said it "achieves a perfect balance between wry chutzpah and forthright tenderness."*People* called it dazzling and one of the best discs of 1997, featuring "Trynin's hypnotic vocals, gritty guitar playing, and grown-up lyrics about faltering relationships and lost innocence—with the kind of mixed emotions her album title cleverly captures." And the *Minneapolis Star-Tribune* concluded, "*Gun Shy Trigger Happy* is loaded with hooks and crackles with raw energy, thanks to the sensitive production of Mike Denneen. Most important is the singer-guitarist's emotional purity, which resonates with heartbreak, resignation, and warped wit."

Trynin wrote the songs on *Gun Shy Trigger Happy* in her living room on an acoustic guitar and recorded them with drummer Chris Foley and bass player Ed Valauskas. They are evenly divided between guitar-driven numbers and quieter, introspective ones. "In addition to moodier pieces like 'Go Ahead' and 'I

Resign,' they turned out savvy pop-rockers like 'Love Letter' and 'Bore Me,' bristling with drum loops and guitar spasms," Andy Seiler wrote in *USA Today*. "Trynin's music, however fraught with romantic quandaries, sparkles with clean hooks and rare intelligence." *Stereo Review*, meanwhile, suggested that the disc projects a confident songwriter who's just getting started—an assessment that's hard to argue with. "It took me a while to get my feet back on the ground and enjoy playing music again," Trynin told the *Boston Globe*. "I'm not capable to living in the regular world. I played in little clubs, I waitressed, I had no money for eight years. I just wanna write and make music—and I still am. I'm used to being an underdog ... (but) I'm not feeling all the weirdness, the emotional willies, anymore."

Selected discography

Cockamamie, Warner Bros., 1995.
Gun Shy Trigger Happy, Warner Bros., 1997.

Sources

Billboard, August 23, 1997, p. 92.
Boston Globe, August 15, 1996; September 19, 1997.
Boston Herald, September 18, 1997.
Entertainment Weekly, August 15, 1997, p. 72.
Minneapolis Star-Tribune, September 7, 1997.
People, September 22, 1997, p. 30.
Rolling Stone, August 21, 1997, p. 112.
Stereo Review, October 1997, p. 92.
USA Today, August 23, 1997, p. D1.

—*Dave Wilkins*

Tsunami

Alternative rock band

Tsunami is an Arlington, Virginia, based band fronted by the razor-sharp smarts of Jenny Toomey and Kristin Thomson, who also boast musical talent in such excess that they moonlight in other bands. Furthermore, Toomey and Thomson run their own label, Simple Machines, dedicated to providing welcoming business turf for fledgling indie bands. That label is also home of the Tsunami catalog, which includes a staggering number of singles in near-collectible sleeve designs. "Tsunami come across like a kind of teen gang," wrote *Melody Maker*'s Sharon O'Connell. "It's their autonomy, their spirit and their drive, and the way they celebrate the raw and the very ordinary; the way it is when you're very young and every feeling is new each time you feel it."

Tsunami was formed inside the suburban Washington, DC house that Toomey and Thomson shared with John Pamer in the last months of 1990. Toomey had been in a band called Geek, where she met Andrew Webster, and she talked him into moving to the area so they could form a band with Pamer and Thomson; their goal was to play a New Year's Eve 1990 party. Toomey and Thomson were no newcomers to the music scene, having already formed the Simple Machines label with the help of their friend Ian MacKaye, head of the famed DC label Dischord. By February of 1991, they took their fledgling band on the road.

During 1991, Tsunami came into being as a band with some difficult tours and a well-packaged single or two.

Touring was a strictly low-budget affair, with the band and gear loaded into a sometimes unreliable Isuzu Trooper, playing college towns across the country. Their worst show ever, Toomey told *ViVidzine*'s Juliette Morris, was at a college in Ohio—not at a bar, but at "some really bad fraternity-type of party *and* it was `Mom's Night,' which meant that everywhere we looked, we saw mothers with their arms around their staggering, drunk children." A bad sound system, and a sound man who mistakenly thought Toomey was making fun of him and began lousing up everything during their performance completed the farce. Their first single, released in the spring of 1991, was "Headringer," followed by that summer's "Genius of Crack."

Tsunami recorded and toured with pals Velocity Girl, and also recorded split singles with them, such as 1992's SubPop release "Left Behind." Another track from 1992 sums up the unique attitude with which Toomey and Thomson hurtle through the male-dominated world of indie rock: "Punk Means Cuddle" calls for a nicer, less belligerent attitude among their college-radio bands and fans. Toomey used to be active in the riot-grrl movement, but came to some realizations about what Tsunami call the "loadhog" phenomenon, and even wrote a song about it. "Loadhogs are people who martyr themselves for the cause," Toomey told *Melody Maker*'s Sally Margaret Joy. "People who would rather do the work for you than teach you how to do it yourself." In the song, Toomey explained, she "was trying to explore the delicate problem of how work is delegated."

In early 1993 a national promoter phoned and asked them if they might be interested in playing on that summer's Lollapalooza tour. Originally, they assumed it was a prank call. Their six shows on a side stage shared with other acts such as Sebadoh and Thurston Moore dovetailed nicely with the release of their first full-length record, *Deep End*. Later that year Tsunami recorded their follow-up, *The Heart's Tremolo,* in Chicago and it was released in 1994. Like all of their Tsunami issues, the two albums boasted beautifully designed covers; one single, from the previous year, "Diner," featured the menu from their favorite low-budget restaurant.

This irreverence infects much of what Tsunami does. They once undertook a microphone relay race from their office to a club, taped it, and played it live during a show. Yet they also donate money to non-profit organizations and are quite serious about the seemingly insurmountable wall between feminist ideology and alternative music. "I believe that women will never be accepted in punk rock, and that is why Tsunami walks the line between pop and punk," Toomey told *Melody*

Maker. Band members still had their day jobs in 1993: Toomey worked as a bookkeeper for an anti-nuclear organization, while Thomson worked in a food co-op— but continued to run the Simple Machines label. Its office was at their house—"so we wake up, put on our clothes, and start work," Thomson told Joy in *Melody Maker.* "We have no free time at all.... [L]uckily, there are no pubs near where we live."

The members of Tsunami were busy throughout 1993 and 1994. They had a friend in England, John Loder, who owns a studio, and began traversing back and forth to do recordings. They toured with the bands Rodan and Eggs, and, when asked how England responds to Tsunami, Toomey told *ViVidzine* that the music press there is quite fickle—"It's depending on what bands are popular at the moment, you could be everyone's darlings or everyone could hate you. It's such a small country, and they start these weird little trends a lot." Sharon O'Connell reviewed a live show for *Melody Maker* and lauded it: "They bang and strum, leaving slight spaces before they storm in to mess things up."

Tsunami completed two American tours in 1994 in addition to more dates in England, but time became more unmanageable with Pamer still in college and living elsewhere. During their get-togethers, the band was forced "to write and record real fast, so we're very goal-oriented," Toomey told *Melody Maker's* Joy. Toomey also explained to *ViVidzine* that her bandmate "has had a hard time on tour," she said of Thomson, "because she's a good workaholic and it's been hard for her to get in the van, because there's no desk in there."

Though the band has managed to issue a full-length record annually, it is their singles that fuel the Tsunami wave. In 1994 they released "Be Like That," as well as a split CD with Rodan and Eggs from their U.K. tour entitled "Cowed by the Blah Blah." After releasing *World Tour and Other Destinations* in 1995—containing 22 singles previously released and difficult to find— the band went on hiatus so Pamer could finish his degree. Toomey and Thomson continued to run the label and work with other bands. Toomey moonlighted in Liquorice, signed to England's 4AD label. Thomson married and began spending time in Philadelphia with her husband, Brian Dilworth, of the band the Gelcaps and head of the Compulsiv record label. Webster began a career as a documentary filmmaker. Yet after Pamer graduated in 1996, he remained in Massachusetts and made clear his intention to live in New York, not Virginia.

The break seemed to have changed everyone. "When we stopped playing, I was exhausted," Toomey told *Magnet's* Cyndi Elliott. "It was because we didn't want to play. I've always thought that a band benefits from not having to be a band all the time. We always held day jobs and did other things. That's one of the reasons we were able to stay a band for so long. When you are forced to play because you have to pay rent, you lose quality control and a lot of the joy of it." In a decision made with some trepidation, they hired another drummer, Luther Gray. Formerly an intern at Simple Machines, Gray has a jazz background and brought a new rhythmic dimension to their music. It fit in perfectly with their maturation as a band, with Toomey and Thomson writing more melodic and less strident songs, which was evident on their 1997 release *A Brilliant Mistake.* Many of Tsunami's friends from the Chicago music scene contributed as well, including members of the Coctails and Poi Dog Pondering, and Rob Christiansen from Liquorice, who played bass on half the record.

Despite her work with Liquorice and Tsunami, Toomey admits to being insecure about her songwriting abilities: "Very rarely I'll have something I think I should write," she told *Magnet.* "Except e-mails and purchase orders." Both Toomey and Thomson are confident about their business acumen, however. They claim anyone can begin a label, and have even written a booklet on how to do it, "but we don't talk about ambition in it," Toomey told Joy in the *Melody Maker* interview. Referring to the observation that substance abuse sometimes prevents creative types from accomplishing things, Toomey noted that "You can't give people energy and enthusiasm." Sometimes other labels or bands call the Simple Machines offices and ask to have their radio-station mailing list, for instance, and Toomey and Thomson must refuse. Notes Toomey: "The only reason those stations play us is because of our track record with them.... You have to find the addresses of the stations you like and send them nice letters—just like we had to."

Selected discography

Singles; on Simple Machines unless otherwise noted

"Headringer," 1991.
"Genius of Crack," Homestead, 1991.
"Left Behind" (split single with Velocity Girl; on SubPop), 1992.
"Punk Means Cuddle," C/Z, 1992.
"Beautiful; Arlington VA," 1992.

"Season's Greetings" (split single with Velocity Girl), 1992.
"Diner," 1993.
"Matchbook," 1993.
"Be Like That," 1994.
"Cowed by the Blah Blah" (split CD with Rodan and Eggs), 1994.
"She Cracked" (split single with Superchunk; on Huggy Bear Records), 1995.
"Poodle/Old City," 1997.

LPs; on Simple Machines

Deep End, 1993.
(Contributor) *The Machines 1990-1993*, 1993.
The Heart's Tremolo, 1994.
World Tour and Other Destinations, 1995.
A Brilliant Mistake, 1997.

Sources

Melody Maker, January 30, 1993, p. 16; February 20, 1993, pp. 36-37; June 3, 1995, p. 37.
ViVidzine, December 1994.

—Carol Brennan

Tuxedomoon

Experimental rock band

Tuxedomoon was an art-rock ensemble whose vividly experimental musical efforts set the stage for a host of transcontinental musical subgenres. The group itself was similarly cosmopolitan, forming in San Francisco in the late 1970s but decamping in Europe a few years later. This act helped foster a cult-like following for the band and their records. Influenced by sources as diverse as skeletal new-wave, Frank Zappa, and Dadaism, Tuxedomoon took form as multimedia art experience that combined music, dance, visual art, and film; its revolving-door roster of musicians played instruments that ranged from synthesizers and electric guitar to piano and clarinet. As pioneers in experimental music, Tuxedomoon laid the groundwork for what became the industrial dance music phenomenon later in the decade.

Tuxedomoon's beginnings can be traced back to an electronic-music class at San Francisco City College in 1976, in which Blaine Reininger and Steven Brown were both enrolled. Reininger was trained in classical music—he had studied the violin since childhood—but in 1965 had also formed his first rock band, the Tycoons, at the age of eleven. He received a degree in music from the University of Southern Colorado and moved to the Bay Area shortly thereafter. His musical influences were panoramic—from jazz to classical to the synthesizer-based new wave music then gaining ground, and he would soon meld all of these into Tuxedomoon. As a solo musician Reininger had just obtained a performance date at a San Francisco coffeehouse as "Tuxedomoon"; when his electronic-music class held a concert showcasing the students' compositions in May of 1977, he was impressed by Steven Brown's piece and invited him to play at the coffeehouse.

Their first performance, billing themselves the "Tuxedomoon New Music Ensemble," took place on June 14, 1977. Reininger and Brown soon added several more members to what they conceived as not just a band, but a multimedia performance experience with visual art and elements of theater. Brown belonged to a radical theater group called the Angels of Light, and several of his colleagues moonlighted as early Tuxedomoon members. They included synthesizer genius Tom Tadlock, Gregory Cruikshank, and vocalist Victoria Lowe; Lowe brought modernist puppet-theater master Winston Tong into the fold. Most of these early members left the band, but some came back during the 1980s; other musicians who would drift in and out of Tuxedomoon over the years included drummer Paul Zahl and guitarist Michael Belfer. Around 1978 the Tuxedomoon nucleus of Reininger and Brown was joined by an underground radio personality who called himself Peter Carcinogenic and renamed himself once again (his actual surname was Dachert) "Peter Principle" for his new career as a musician.

The Deaf Club Gigs

From the start, Tuxedomoon was a phenomenon—first in San Francisco from their performances in galleries, and the staging of their own multimedia installations with artist friends—and soon finding approval among avant-garde and experimental-music enthusiasts on the East Coast and Europe. Their first single, "Pinheads on the Move/Joeboy the Electronic Ghost," released in 1978, was reviewed in Andy Warhol's *Interview* magazine. By this time the band had signed with Time Release Records, but from the start became embroiled in legal battles with its owner. The "Joeboy" moniker Tuxedomoon adopted reflected their love of the absurd and a penchant for incorporating Dada-type elements into their work: it was taken from a graffiti tagger common to San Francisco's Chinatown at the time; they named their production company after it. Tuxedomoon were also regulars on the stage of the Deaf Club, an ideal punk rock/avant-garde venue, since it was set up as a bar for the hearing-impaired where drinks could be ordered in sign language.

Success for Tuxedomoon seemed certain, especially after they opened for Devo in early 1978. Yet the highly-opinionated, certifiably brainy collective seemed doomed from the start. Several members left—Tadlock and Tong among them—taking much of the musical gear and Reininger and Brown fell into financial difficulties. When a local San Francisco label, Ralph Records (home of fellow art-rockers the Residents) invited Tuxedomoon to contribute their version of the Tony Bennett song, "I Left My Heart in San Francisco" for a compilation, their submission featured Reininger at a pay phone trying to apply for welfare; he then gives his last half-dollar to a blind street musician who performs the tune on harmonica.

Between 1978 and 1980 the Tuxedomoon recorded output consisted of singles—"Stranger" and "What Use" among them—and the EPs *Tuxedomoon* and *Scream with a View*. Tuxedomoon did manage to extricate themselves from their Time Release contract and signed with the Ralph label, on which their first full-length record was issued in early 1980, *Half-Mute*. About half of the tracks were instrumental, and show-

cased the standard Tuxedomoon meanderings of drum machine, organ, saxophone, and bass guitar. Electronic-music godfather Brian Eno was in the audience at their record release party, but reportedly was unimpressed. Another bit of bad timing occurred when Tuxedomoon were slated to open for Joy Division, but lead singer Ian Curtis committed suicide and Joy Division disbanded.

Reception Abroad

Tuxedomoon did manage to book a tour anyway, and found that audiences in London and Paris "got" it. Reininger and Brown and Principle decided to leave the United States for good, and after touring England and doing some recording in Italy, finally settled at an artists' commune in the Dutch city of Rotterdam. They released several works, such as the EP *Ninotchka* and the LP *Desire*—and found appreciative fans in Brussels, where they sojourned for a time to compose and record music for a ballet that found its way to vinyl as 1982's *Divine* LP. In Rotterdam the members of Tuxedomoon lived in an old water tower, but one day Reininger was hit by car in Amsterdam before a performance and spent time in wheelchair; their landlord, who was also suspicious of the special dispensation they received from the state as "artists," evicted them.

By this point Tong had returned, and continued to be a part-time member of Tuxedomoon; he was responsible for bringing Bruce Geduldig into the ever-changing line-up. Geduldig was an experimental filmmaker and musician who would work with the band for years to come, shooting films to accompany their aural releases and providing images to project overhead for their live performances. By 1982 Tuxedomoon were living permanently in Brussels, and had released the EPs *Suite en Sous-Sol* and *Time to Lose*. Over the next three years the group became involved in an ambitious opera project in Italy, *The Ghost Sonata,* and Reininger, Brown, and Tong each began or pursued solo projects. Reininger officially "left" the band for a time in 1983, but continued to be involved in Tuxedomoon recordings; horn player Lars van Lieshout joined around this time. Meanwhile, Tuxedomoon performances became more elaborate affairs, ideally held at European film festivals or in spectacular outdoor settings.

"Perfect *Film Noir* Soundscapes"

The year 1985 saw the release of *Holy Wars* on the CramBoy label, a subsidiary of Brussels' Crammed Records set up just for Tuxedomoon issues. Critics declared the band a sellout, however, for it marked a new direction with far more accessible songs. A *Melody Maker* review by Martin Aston praised such tracks as "Bonjour Tristesse and "St. John" as "haunting messages of disarray and dislocation." Aston also lauded the "wonderful ensemble playing" and "perfect *film noir* soundscapes." Tuxedomoon founder Steven Brown defended the record and responded to the negative comments a year later in *Musician:* "If this is commercial, then that's great because somebody's changed and it hasn't been us."

By 1985 Tong had officially left the band to pursue a solo career. The 1986 Tuxedomoon LP *Ship of Fools* marked the appearance of Ivan Georgiev into the line-up, but actual recordings and tours slowed down as members spent more time pursuing individual projects. The last official Tuxedomoon studio recording was 1987's *You,* but that same year the original trio of Reininger, Brown, and Principle got together for a birthday dinner on June 14, ten years to the day of their inaugural San Francisco performance. They decided to regroup for a reunion tour, and played several successful dates across Europe and even went to Japan. The following year Tuxedomoon played dates in Holland and Italy with the Georgiev-Van Lieshout axis, who had not been present on the previous year's reunion tour.

The year 1988 had also seen the release of *Pinheads on the Move,* which showcased the early Tuxedomoon years prior to 1980. "These early records perfectly illustrate the subterranean channels between street rhetoric and the performance-art/sound-lab culture," wrote Paul Oldfield in *Melody Maker.* CramBoy continued to re-release early Tuxedomoon records on CD from the first half-decade, often with bonus tracks that had never made it to full-length vinyl. These included the comprehensive, career-long compilation *Solve et Coagula,* 1989's *Ten Years in One Night,* and the final version of the aborted Italian opera project, *The Ghost Sonata (Les Temps Moderne),* in 1991. This final release, which had started in 1982 as music to accompany their own deaths, was termed "as ambient as a knife in your back" by *Melody Maker*'s Dave Simpson.

Though Tuxedomoon has perhaps permanently disbanded, all members continue to be active in the performing arts. Reininger is a solo artist, composes music for television and film, and acts in the short films of Nicholas Triandafyllidis. Tong went on to work with Cabaret Voltaire, Principle lives in New York City and produces industrial bands, and Brown is a resident of Mexico City whose projects include collaborations with Vini Reilly of Durutti Column. Van Lieshout and Gedulgig still live in Europe and have worked with Bel Canto and Colin Newman, formerly of Wire.

Selected discography

Singles

"Pinheads on the Move/Joeboy (The Electronic Ghost)," Tidal Wave, 1978.
"Stranger/Love/No Hope," Time Release, 1978.
"What Use/Crash," Ralph, 1980.
"Dark Companion/59 to 1 Remix," Ralph, 1980.
"Egypt/Une Nuit au Fond de la Frayere," Sordide Sentimental, 1981.
"Soma/H.T.E.," Soundwork, 1984.

EPs

Tuxedomoon, Tuxedomoon Records, 1978.
Scream with a View, Tuxedomoon Records, 1979.
Ninotchka/Again, Les Disques du Crepuscule, 1982.
Time to Lose, Les Disques du Crepuscule, 1982.
Suite en Sous-Sol, Italian Records, 1982.

Albums

Half-Mute, Ralph Records, 1980, CD re-issue, CramBoy, 1984.
Desire, Ralph Records, 1981, CD re-issue, CramBoy, 1985.
Divine, CramBoy, 1982.
Holy Wars, CramBoy, 1985.
Ship of Fools, CramBoy, 1986.
You, CramBoy, 1987.
Pinheads on the Move, CramBoy, 1988.
Ten Years in One Night, CramBoy, 1989.
The Ghost Sonata (Les Temps Moderne), CramBoy, 1991, re-issue, 1997.

Other

"I Left My Heart in San Francisco" appeared on the 1978 Ralph Records release *Subterranean Modern.*

Sources

Melody Maker, July 13, 1985, p. 28; July 5, 1986, p. 28; May 7, 1988, p. 39; March 30, 1991, p. 33;
Musician, April, 1986.

Additional information for this profile was provided by Internet websites devoted to Tuxedomoon.

—*Carol Brennan*

Vangelis

Composer

Known around the world for his award-winning soundtrack to the film *Chariots of Fire*, Vangelis has been classified under a variety of genres, including New Age. He's composed a lifetime of music for ballet and film, as well as released a number of international solo records. Born and raised in Greece, Vangelis has also lived in Paris and London, where he has his own studio called Nemo Studios, near London's Marble Arch.

Vangelis was born Evangelos Odessey Papathanassiou in Greece in 1943. Although he began playing piano at four years old, he has never been able to read or write music on paper. When he was six, his parents enrolled him in an Athens music school. Soon, he performed his first concert of his own compositions.

Despite his love for music, Vangelis despised being schooled in the art. "When the teachers asked me to play something, I would pretend that I was reading it and play from memory," Vangelis told Joe Klien in *Life*. "I didn't fool them, but I didn't care." The young boy

AP/Wide World Photos, Inc. Reproduced by permission.

knew his teachers could help him become a musician, but they could not teach him how to be creative.

When Vangelis was 14 years old, he received an organ, which he painted gold, and fell in love with the electronic sound. In the 1960s, he looked forward to playing the first synthesizers, but was disappointed at their crudeness. Vangelis performed in the popular Greek pop band called Formynx when he was a teenager. He had changed his name to Vangelis—meaning "angel that brings good news"—as a derivative of his first name. Formynx was the first pop group to surface in Greece and quickly gained a large following. "It was very fortunate that I tasted success early with Formynx — playing in front of 10,000 people in stadiums, all the hysteria," Vangelis told Kurt Loder in *Rolling Stone*. "It was great fun, but I wasn't interested in that."

In 1967, Vangelis left Formynx and Greece after a right-wing military coup occurred in his homeland. He moved to Paris, where he formed the band Aphrodite's Child, with Demis Roussos and Loukas Sideras. The group released the album *Rain and Tears* and the double-album *666* in France, before they broke up in 1970. Instead of moving onto another band, Vangelis began scoring music for French television documentaries. He also composed the soundtrack for the French film *L'Apocalypse des Animaux* for director Frederic Rossif.

Vangelis released his first solo album *Dragon* in 1971 on Phillips Records. In 1974, he moved to London,

England, to work with the rock band Yes. Rumors began circulating that Vangelis would replace former Yes keyboardist Rick Wakeman. However, after he rehearsed with the band for a few weeks, Vangelis determined that his musical direction was not in line with the rest of the group. But he did continue a long friendship with singer Jon Anderson.

The following year, Vangelis created his own recording studio, called Nemo Studios, near London's Marble Arch. He often referred to it as his laboratory. The first album he recorded there was *Heaven and Hell* released on RCA Records. Music from the album was later used in Carl Sagan's *Cosmos* television series.

Ignited Success with *Chariots*

In 1981, Vangelis made his mark in the world of music with the soundtrack for a film about the 1924 Olympics, called *Chariots of Fire*. It became the fastest-selling LP and single in the United States at the time, and quickly topped the *Billboard* charts. Irv Cohn wrote in *Stereo Review*, "The music is very much Vangelis' style, yet it is perfectly suited to the action and atmosphere of the film, with gorgeous pastoral melodies that capture the feel of England between the wars."

Vangelis had composed the popular theme for the movie using a group of synthesizers in a single room, and completed it in one afternoon. "I saw the beginning of the film, the athletes running by the ocean," Vangelis recalled in *Life*. "It was so healthy and joyous, all that oxygen ... and *exhilaration*." For his effort, the composer won an Academy Award the following year for "Best Original Score." When the award was presented, Vangelis was fast asleep in London. He discovered that he had won when a friend in Los Angeles called to congratulate him. "Over the phone, I could hear the television and a big party in the background," Vangelis later told Jereme Jones in *People*. "This incredible thing was going on and *I* was in bed."

His success with *Chariots of Fire* stimulated many other movie soundtracks over the years, including *Missing, Blade Runner, The Bounty* and *1492: The Conquest of Paradise*. Almost any reference made to Vangelis after 1981 mentioned *Chariots of Fire* and often compared it to his later works. In 1982, he released a compilation of his previous work on *The Unknown Man*, released on RCA. He also continued to produce his own solo albums, as well as working with other artists.

Vangelis teamed up with his friend Jon Anderson for a series of records beginning in 1983. The duo released

The Friends of Mr. Cairo and *Private Collection* within the same year. The latter album included a 23-minute track called "Horizon." Meanwhile, *Chariots of Fire*'s popularity held on strong; it was used as the theme for the 1984 Olympic Games in Sarajevo.

Vangelis released *Soil Festivities* on Polygram during the same year. He derived his inspiration for the collection from the life processes taking place on the earth's surface. "I work like a bridge between nature and what comes out through my fingers," Vangelis told Jones in *People*.

In 1985, Vangelis expanded into another musical venue, composing music for ballet. He wrote the music for *Frankenstein* and *Beauty and the Beast*. London's Royal Ballet performed both pieces between 1985 and 1987 at Covent Garden.

Returned to Solo Experiments

Vangelis entered the next decade with a more modern style. He recorded and released *The City* in 1990, which he composed and produced in a hotel room in Rome. He used the music from the disc to describe the feel of an urban day from morning until night. Jon Andrews wrote in a review for *Down Beat*, "Ingenious and full of hooks, *The City* recalls some of Vangelis' best work ... so it's easy to forgive a little bombast or a few gimmicks."

Vangelis spent most of the 1990s experimenting in his studio and traveling around the world, although he rarely performed in concert or granted interviews. He continued to release his solo work, such as 1995's *Voices* and *Oceanic* in 1997. He also played a special performance for the opening ceremonies at the Sixth IAAF World Championships in Athletics in Athens, Greece, in 1997.

From the very beginning, Vangelis showed little concern for his popularity or success as an artist. Instead, he concentrated on creative expression. "All I try to do is let people know what I think through my music," Vangelis stated in the liner notes of his 1981 *Greatest Hits*. "I just bring the music to you, and it's up to you to do what you want with it."

Selected discography

Albums

Dragon, Phillips Records, 1971.
Earth, Phillips Records, 1973.
Heaven and Hell, RCA Records, 1975.
China, RCA Records, 1979.
Chariots of Fire (soundtrack), Polygram Records, 1981.
Greatest Hits, 1981.
Blade Runner (soundtrack), 1982.
Missing (soundtrack), 1982.
To the Unknown Man, RCA Records, 1982.
The Friends of Mr. Cairo, Polygram Records, 1983.
Private Collection, Polygram Records, 1983.
The Bounty (soundtrack), 1984.
Soil Festivities, Polygram Records, 1984.
The City, Atlantic Records, 1990.
1492: The Conquest of Paradise (soundtrack), 1992.
Voices, East/West Records, 1995.
Oceanic, Atlantic Records, 1997.

Sources

Periodicals

Commonweal, November 20, 1992.
Down Beat, February 1992.
High Fidelity, August 1983.
Library Journal, May 1, 1983.
Life, July 1982.
New Yorker, July 12, 1982; June 11, 1984.
People, April 19, 1982.
Playboy, January 1983.
Rolling Stone, May 13, 1982.
Stereo Review, March 1982; January 1983; December 1983; June 1985.

Online

http://bau2.uibk.ac.at/perki/artist
http://www.athens-97.gr/gbr/vangelis
http://www.il.fontys.nl/~lodewks/introduc

—Sonya Shelton

Diane
Warren

Songwriter

Diane Warren is one of the most prolific, successful, and sought-after pop music composers in history. During the 1980s and 1990s, hundreds of performers recorded her music. She has penned more than 75 Top 10 hits for such artists as Michael Bolton, Celine Dion, Toni Braxton, and LeAnn Rimes, and crafted No. 1 hits in France, Australia, Holland, Germany, and England. Her independent publishing company, Realsongs, controls the rights to more than 600 Warren compositions, and her songs have been used in more than 50 movies, ranging from *Up Close and Personal* and *The Preacher's Wife* to *Caddyshack II* and *Karate Kid III*. She has been nominated for Grammy Awards, Academy Awards, and Golden Globe Awards. She was the first songwriter ever to log seven hits, each performed by a different singer, on the *Billboard* Hot 100 Singles chart. She is the only female composer to be named ASCAP's Writer of the Year three times. By one estimate, Warren has been responsible for the sale of more than 125 million records. Her songs have been important to the careers of a diverse list of artists including Joe Cocker, Roy Orbison, Whitney Houston, Tina Turner, Wynonna, Trisha Yearwood, Meat Loaf, Cher, and the infamous lip-synching duo Milli Vanilli. "Diane takes everyday situations and turns them into hit songs," producer David Foster said on the Realsongs website. "When I've recorded her songs, there's always some little magical turn that really heightens the song for me. Part of what makes her so good is sheer hard work. Without a doubt, she is the hardest working songwriter I've ever met."

Warren's obsession with songwriting began when she was a child, after her father, an insurance salesman, brought her a guitar from Tijuana, Mexico. "I took lessons, and the teacher told my parents I was tone deaf," Warren recalled to Cynthia Sanz of *People*. "I just didn't want to do the goddamn scales. I wanted to make up my own little songs.... I think I willed myself into being a songwriter. I was in love with the idea when I was 11. I got serious about it when I was 14, writing three songs a day." As a teenager, Warren sent countless demo tapes to music producers—and received countless rejections. Her breakthrough came in 1982, when Laura Branigan recorded her song "Solitaire." Three years later, Warren wrote "Rhythm of the Night," which De-Barge took to No. 3 on the pop charts and No. 1 on the adult contemporary charts. "'Rhythm of the Night' ... changed my life," Warren stated in a chat with Back-stage Pass. "People started returning my calls." In 1985, she founded Realsongs to publish and market her material. It became a Top 10 music publishing company and the most successful female-owned and operated business in the music industry, racking up more No. 1 singles than any other music publisher. "For me, it's always about improving and achieving more," Warren told Terri Horak of *Billboard*. "I am way beyond a workaholic. It hasn't changed since I was 14.... If anything, I work even harder now."

Warren's hard work and intensity are legendary in the entertainment business—Cher calls her "totally nuts," and Michael Bolton has said that the writer obsesses and slaves over her songs. As a result, Warren readily acknowledges, she has virtually no social life. "She spends so much time at her cluttered Hollywood office," Sanz wrote in *People*, "that a recent weekend at home in the hills above Sherman Oaks, California, left her perplexed." "I didn't know what to do," Warren told Sanz. "I tried watching TV, but I hate TV. I thought about drinking a beer, but I don't really drink. I wanted to relax, but I never relax and didn't know how. Finally, after a couple hours, I realized the thing I really wanted to do was write. So I said to hell with relaxing and went to my office."

"In the background"

Warren follows no particular pattern or method when she's writing. "Ideas and titles just pop in my head," she was quoted in *People*. "I've written songs on Kotex, lyrics on the palm of my hand. If I don't have a tape recorder, I'll call home and sing into my answering machine.... I try to write something that I love, something emotional with great melodies and lyrics that can really touch people. Something that isn't trendy, that will last

For the Record . . .

Born in Van Nuys, CA.

Began writing songs at age eleven; Laura Branigan sang Warren's first recorded song, "Solitaire," 1982; wrote "Rhythm of the Night" for the band DeBarge, which hit No. 1 on adult contemporary charts, 1985; founded independent publishing company, Realsongs, 1985; has written Top 10 songs for artists such as Belinda Carlisle, Barbra Streisand, Michael Bolton, Celine Dion, Gloria Estefan, and Trisha Yearwood, 1983-1997; reached top songwriter on *Billboard*'s Hot 100 and Hot R&B Singles charts, 1997.

Awards: ASCAP, Songwriter of the Year, 1990, 1991, 1993; *Billboard,* Singles Publisher of the Year, 1990; *Billboard,* Writer of the Year, 1990 and 1993; LA Music Awards, Songwriter of the Year, 1991; *Billboard,* Top 10 Publishing Company, 1991-1994; ASCAP, Voice of Music Award, 1995; National Academy of Songwriters, Songwriter of the Year, 1996; Grammy Award, Best Song Written Specifically for a Motion Picture or Television, "Because You Loved Me," performed by Celine Dion for *Up Close and Personal,* 1996; American Songwriter, Songwriter of the Year and Publisher of the Year, 1996; International Achievement in the Arts Award, Distinguished Achievement in Songwriting, 1997; *Billboard* Award, No. 1 Songwriter in pop and R&B, 1997.

Addresses: *Publishing company—Realsongs, on the Internet at http://www.realsongs.com.; phone:* (213) 462-1709.

through the ages. The best ones are the ones that make me cry when I'm writing them." That artistic sensitivity seems a bit odd coming from a woman who is rarely openly emotional, but is instead cynical and armed with a cutting sense of humor. "People that know me don't really understand how someone like me writes the songs I do," Warren told *Billboard's* Carrie Borzillo. "I don't know where it comes from because in real life I'm very cynical and sarcastic, so it's like this strange dichotomy."

It's often difficult for Warren to give up her compositions to the artists who will record them. "I have to keep in mind that it's not my record," she told Borzillo. "I'm just here to help them with their vision. It's hard because I write and I really nit-pick and I'm really precise, and you have to give (the artist) some freedom of artistic expression, because it's like a suit, It has to fit right.... A lot of times people will really change a song, change my lyrics, change chords, change melody, and it kind of pisses me off." On the other hand, Warren says she has never been tempted to record her own songs; she prefers to remain in the background where she can enjoy her privacy. She also disregards the suggestion that her work is overly sentimental and unhip, or that pop music is a demeaning style in which to work. "I love pop," she proclaimed to Neville Farmer of the Country Music Association. "Great soul is pop. Motown is pop. I'm in love with the concept of the three-and-a-half-minute song."

Warren has also been an active and generous supporter of the National Academy of Songwriters, AIDS Project Los Angeles, People for the Ethical Treatment of Animals (PETA), the Simon Wiesenthal Center Museum of Tolerance, and other causes. In the end, she says, gets the most satisfaction from reaching a listener. "When I was a kid, the songs I heard on the radio affected me in a deep way," she stated in the Backstage Pass interview. "I hope mine are doing the same thing to other people. If I can speak to someone's heart and soul, then I'll have come up with a pretty good song."

Sources

Periodicals

Billboard, April 22, 1995, p. 58; May 24, 1997, p. 45.
People, July 22, 1991, p. 61.
Stereo Review, March 1994, p. 96.

Online

http://bspaa.com/Artist/DianeWarren/warren2.html
http://www.dotmusic.co.uk/MWtalentwarren.html
http://www.realsongs.com

—Dave Wilkins

Don Was

Producer, composer, bassist

Veteran music producer Don Was has made a singular name for himself as one of the top producers in the music industry. Although he began his career as a co-founder, along with "brother" David Was (born David Weiss), of Was (Not Was), an eclectic and nontraditional band that combined soul, funk, R&B, and rock/dance influences with satiric, often bizarre lyrics, Was is today better known for his ability to attend to the diverse needs and aims of musicians in a wide variety of genres, including Bonnie Raitt, the B52s, and Bob Seger. In a 1994 *People* article, Was attributes his abilities as a producer to the blend of rock, R&B, and country music he heard growing up in Detroit. Al Teller, chairman of MCA Records, which backed Was's imprint Karambolage Records in the mid-1990s, described Was to Steve Pond of the *New York Times* as "the real deal. He has an eclectic ear and perspective, and he can communicate well with a broad assortment of artists. Also, he works from the heart. He doesn't make calculated commercial decisions. He keeps to what is truly important, which in today's music business is often forgotten."

Born Donald Fagenson in 1952, Was grew up in and around Detroit, Michigan. With his friend David Weiss, who later became his "brother" David Was when the pair founded Was (Not Was), Fagenson grew up listening to Motown music and Detroit rock of the 1960s. Acts as diverse as funk frontrunner George Clinton and the hard-rockers MC5 played regular concerts at their high school in Oak Park, a suburb of Detroit. Fagenson and Weiss grew up in a suburban middle-class Jewish neighborhood and developed offbeat tastes from a young age. The pair began writing songs in the basement of Weiss's parents' home, in a room they called the "Humor Prison." "[David] wore a Colonel Sanders mask and I wore a President Kennedy mask," Fagenson told Michael Goldberg in *Rolling Stone*. "This was because it was tough to reject the other one's ideas and look him in the eyes at the same time." The pair also published a humor magazine, led a neighborhood comedy troupe, and once staged a show at their high school entitled "You Have Just Wasted Your Money." Weiss's mother told Goldberg: "Everyone thought they were strange, including their parents. They were always weird. Both of those kids marched to a different drummer."

Both Fagenson and Weiss attended the University of Michigan, and Weiss went on to Los Angeles, where he became a jazz critic for the *Herald Examiner*. Fagenson remained in Detroit, where he variously worked as a record producer and studio musician, and played gigs with local bands. Was (Not Was)—the name originated with a word game of Fagenson's young son—was created when Fagenson, nearly broke, called Weiss for help, and the two decided to make a recording. With

Born Donald Fagenson, 1952, in Detroit, MI; son of Harriet and Bill Fagenson (both teachers); grew up in Oak Park, MI; married in 1972 (divorced); remarried in early 1980s; children: two.

With David Was (born David Weiss, flautist and lyricist), formed band Was (Not Was) in 1980 (disbanded, 1993; other band members included Sweet Pea Atkinson, vocalist, and Sir Harry Bowens, vocalist); coproduced Sweet Pea Atkinson's *Don't Walk Away,* Christina's *Sleep It Off,* and Bob Dylan's *Under the Red Sky;* achieved the status of a top-rate music producer by reviving or updating the careers of many artists, including Bonnie Raitt, the B52s, and Iggy Pop, early 1990s; fomed label, Karambolage Records, 1994; produced recordings for Dion, David Crosby, Leonard Cohen, Elton John, Ozzy Osbourne, Paula Abdul, Bob Seger Willie Neson, Brian Wilson, the Rolling Stones, 1990—; directed *Not Made for These Times,* a music documentary about Beach Boys' founder Brian Wilson, 1995; teamed with L.A.-based film production, distribution, and financing firm Lakeshore Entertainment to buy a controlling interest in the Seattle-based independent label Will Records, 1997.

Addresses: *Office*—Will Records, 1122 East Pike St. #511, Seattle, WA 98122.

money borrowed from Weiss's parents, they recruited "Sweet Pea" Atkinson and "Sir Harry" Bowens, two African-American Detroit singers, and recorded "Wheel Me Out" in a Detroit studio (the song also featured a rap vocal supplied by Weiss's mother). The single was released by Ze Records in New York, and gained Was (Not Was) enough positive recognition in Great Britain and the United States for the project to continue. Was and Was began a long-distance songwriting collaboration between California and Michigan, with Weiss supplying lyrics to Fagenson over the phone or through the mail.

Was (Is)

Was described the intent of Was (Not Was) to Andrea Sachs in *Time:* "We would like to sound like the Motown revue on acid." According to Christopher Connelly in *Rolling Stone,* the brothers' debut album, *Was (Not Was)*—released by Ze in 1981—displayed "a lively fusion of jokey lyrics and hard-edged white-boy funk." Two years later, *Born to Laugh at Tornadoes* was acquired by Geffen Records and initiated an ongoing Was (Not Was) tradition of including appearances by unlikely guest vocalists. On this album, rocker Marshall Crenshaw sings the mournful pop standard "Feelings" and jazz scat legend Mel Torme recounts in "Zaz Turns Blue" a situation in which a lover is nearly strangled. Connelly called *Tornadoes* "a superb example of what smart rock & roll can be: tuneful, toe tapping, refreshingly irreverent." Although critical response was positive, the album found only a limited listening audience and sold a mere 50,000 copies. Geffen Records, in what Don Was says was not a racist move but reflective of the "reality of the music business," put pressure on the group to—as he told Sachs—"get rid of the black guys" and make the band more marketable as a one-color group. Was (Not Was) staunchly refused, and soon found themselves looking for another record company.

Was (Not Was) produced no more recordings for five years. During the interim, Don Was became a prominent record producer, handling the board for Bonnie Raitt's Grammy-winning album *Nick of Time,* among many other mainstream pop records. *Nick of Time* resurrected the 20-year career of Bonnie Raitt, sold three-million copies, won the singer four grammy awards, and garnered for Was a growing reputation as a producer able to resurrect and modernize previously outmoded careers. Bonnie Raitt commented on Was's laid-back and sympathetic approach to production: "He's totally unneurotic, completely amenable to any suggestion, and he does not let his ego get involved in any decision." Was commented to Pond: "Ideally an artist needs someone who understands their vision of where they want to go with a record. Because once they get involved in the process, they lose their objectivity…. And once you lose your objectivity, you need a producer to suggest things that you would have suggested if you had that distance from it."

Finding their contract with Geffen purchased by an English label, Fontana, Was (Not Was) returned in 1988 with *What up, Dog?,* which featured the hits "Spy in the House of Love" and "Walk the Dinosaur." These tracks became Top Ten hits in Europe, and the album was later released in the United States under the Chrysalis label. The same two cuts became top hits on *Billboard*'s dance charts. Among the album's guest vocalists was Frank Sinatra, Jr. singing "Wedding Vows in Las Vegas." Steve Dougherty and Jim McFarlin noted in *People* that "laughs flood most of the grooves, and such titles as "Out Come the Freaks" and "Dad, I'm in Jail" extend—most often with a dance-happy beat—the Wasmological view that life is a terrifying absurdity."

The group's next album, *Are You OK?*, continued to display their knack for the absurd, yet also demonstrated the ability of Was and Was to write more straightforward songs. Despite critical approval, *Are You OK?* failed to attain the commercial success of *What up, Dog?* Following the album's release, Don Was continued to pursue his production career, which began to increase tensions between him and David. In 1993, Was (Not Was) officially parted ways. Don Was commented on breakup of Was (Not Was) to Pond in 1994: "For the past couple of years, my collaborations with David have been uninspired. It was our own fault. There was a time when we made some very specific decisions. We went for hit singles.... [The] lack of commitment to our vision destroyed it and took the joy out of it." Was added: "In the end, Spinal Tap is the truth. You set out to conquer the world, and eventually the two principles in every band turn on each other." Prior to the break-up of Was (Not Was), Was had expressed a related pessimism about the 1980s music scene that may have contributed to the band's demise. In a 1990 *Rolling Stone* article, Was described the decade as being "most prominent for the death of music as an audio experience. With the importance of video and the use of songs in movie soundtracks, if you can't associate a song with a seminaked chick or a car chase or some real cool violence, there's no way to appreciate it anymore....We're really making music as a way of advertising films on MTV."

Productive Alternative to Commercialism

Despite his anti-commercial stance in the 1980s, Was became one of the top producers in the music industry over the next decade based on his principles. In 1989, the same year he produced Bonnie Raitt's *Nick of Time,* Was co-produced (with Nile Rodgers) the B-52's multi-platinum comeback album, *Cosmic Thing.* In 1991, Was helped Raitt to maintain her critical and commercial success with a follow-up, *Luck of the Draw.* According to David Gates and Andrew Murr, Was's repeat performance established his reputation as "a bankable producer." Other artists soon sought out Was to revive their reputations among the young, hip set, including Bob Dylan, Bob Seger, Iggy Pop, and Paula Abdul. Was's strength as a producer, according to Seger as quoted in a 1992 *Newsweek* article, is that "he's very true to the music itself" and does not "put something on your record just to fit some formula." Was commented to *Rolling Stone* on his philosophy: "I wouldn't take a gig if I had to figure out how to embellish it. I only want to

work with people who have an existing point of view and an ability to express it. I should just be there to channel it. Like in photography, turning on all the lights and pointing right in someone's face."

In 1992, Was again joined Nile Rodgers to co-produce the B-52's *Good Stuff* on Reprise. The album scored a major hit with "Hot Pants Explosion" and was generally praised as seamless, despite the temporary absence of the band's co-founder, Cindy Wilson. With Robbie Robertson and Jeff Lyne, formerly of The Band and Electric Light Orchestra, respectively, Was produced Roy Orbison's posthumous album *King of Hearts* the same year.

Over the next two years, Was embarked on a variety of projects that established him as one of the most visible and eclectic pop producers of his day, according to Steve Pond in the *New York Times*. In 1994, with the backing of MCA Records, he launched his own independent label, Karambolage Records; worked on Raitt's next album, *Longing in Their Hearts;* put together, and performed in, an all-star band of alternative musicians to record covers for *Backbeat*—a documentary about the early days of the Beatles—including R.E.M.'s Mike Mills, Sonic Youth's Thurston Moore, and Soul Asylum's Dave Pirner; and produced the MCA album *Rhythm, Country, and Blues,* featuring 11 genre-bending duets by such soul and country music artists as the Pointer Sisters and Clint Black, Lyle Lovett and the Reverend Al Green, Vince Gill and Gladys Knight, Aaron Neville and Trisha Yearwood, and Sam Moore and the late Conway Twitty.

In late 1994, Was helped the Rolling Stones record *Voodoo Lounge,* which many reviewers praised for Was's ability to update the Stones' quintessential, trademark style. In 1995, what began as an unplugged studio project as the band prepared for the concluding European leg of its *Voodoo Lounge* tour turned into a huge live-taping party. The end result was *Paradiso,* a live album co-produced by Was, Mick Jagger, and Keith Richards and composed of cuts from two shows at the Paradiso Club in Amerstam. According to Was, the project is intended to "capture the tremendous energy and power the Stones have developed over the past 30 years."

Foray into Film

In 1995, Was made his first foray into film production when he directed *Not Made for These Times,* a documentary about the life and career of Beach Boys' singer/songwriter Brian Wilson. The film, which focuses on Wilson's composing and producing talents while only briefly referring to the troubled musician's problems with friends, drugs, and mental illness, featured an assemblage of twenty years of footage, with Wilson performing such songs as "Caroline No," "Warmth of the Sun," and "Do It Again" (the latter delivered with the help of his daughters). Was explained to Melinda Newman in *Billboard* how the movie came about: "I had become friendly with Brian, and we started doing a few gigs. We did a pediatric AIDS benefit, and he dug deep into the song "Love & Mercy"; it was just one of the most remarkable performances I ever heard." Was added: "It was so different from his public image of a drug burnout or someone catatonic propped up by a greedy psychiatrist. That was when I decided to make the movie."

The film initially premiered at the 1995 Sundance Film Festival in Utah and aired on the Disney channel, earning Emmy and cable ACE Award nominations following the Disney broadcast. Janet Maslin in the *New York Times* labeled the film "fascinating" in that it illuminates Wilson's music and makes interesting and accessible a sense of his genius, while Jason Cohen in *Rolling Stone* found the documentary both affectionate and informative. However, Verlyn Klinkenborg in the *New York Times* deemed *Not Made for These Times* "a disappointing and unhappy film, made sadder for its glibness. It wants to praise Brian Wilson, but it actually buries him—under dime-store psychology, and the inane accolades of David Crosby and Graham Nash."

Was released an accompanying soundtrack to *Not Made for These Times* on his Karambolage imprint in August of 1995. Was's ownership of the increasingly successful label ended his relationship with MCA Records in 1996, presumably due to a fear that the bigger rival would lose musicians to the younger upstart. In 1997, Was teamed up with the Los Angeles-based film production, distribution, and financing firm Lakeshore Entertainment to buy a controlling interest in the Seattle-based independent label Will Records. With Lakeshore, Was conspired to release soundtrack albums from films produced by Lakeshore as well as the label's existing artists. Was stated to Chris Morris in *Billboard:* "I think it's got a better chance than most of these start-up labels because, wow, what a great roster they've got…. They've signed some great groups, and they've got great taste." Acts include Sage, Katies Dimples, and Lucky Me.

In late 1997 Was produced the score for Francis Ford Coppola's film *The Rainmaker.* New projects for Was include developing a dramatic film about a fictional R&B label of the 1960s for Lakeshore, as a solo album on Verve that will reflect both his musical and cinematic talents. Set for release in February 1998 is *Forever is a Long, Long Time,* which Was described to Morris as "a collection of Hank Williams songs turned inside-out." Guests include Merle Haggard, Herbie Hancock, Terence Blanchard, and Harvey Mason. The album will be issued as an enhanced CD that includes a short film directed by Was and produced by Coppola.

Selected discography

With Was (Not Was)

"Wheel Me Out" (single), Ze/Antilles, 1980.
Was (Not Was), Ze/Island, 1981.
Born to Laugh at Tornadoes, Ze/Geffen, 1983.
What up, Dog? (includes "Spy in the House of Love" and "Walk the Dinosaur"), Chrysalis, 1988.
Are You OK? (includes "Papa Was a Rolling Stone"), Chrysalis, 1990.

Sources

Books

All Music Guide, Volume 1 , No. 1, 1993.

Periodicals

Billboard, August 5, 1995; March 1, 1997.
Boston, October, 1990.
Creem, January ,1984; July, 1984.
High Fidelity, April, 1984.
Melody Maker, May 12, 1990.
Musician, November, 1983.
Newsweek, August 20, 1990; December 28, 1992.
New York Times, March 27, 1994; August 16, 1995; August 27, 1995.
People, December 12, 1988; July 11, 1994.
Rolling Stone, October 13, 1983; December 18, 1983; October 6, 1988; November 17, 1988; May 17, 1990; June 14, 1990; September 6,1990; November 15, 1990; August 8, 1991; July 9-23, 1992; August 11, 1994; May 4, 1995; July 13-27, 1995; September 19, 1996.
Stereo Review, February, 1984; June, 1989; October, 1991.
Time, January 30, 1989.
Vogue, March, 1994.

—Sean Pollock

Karyn White

Singer, songwriter

AP/Wide World Photos, Inc. Reproduced by permission.

The title of White's hit single, "Superwoman," seems to describe her life. Karyn White has gone from a back-up vocalist with local bands, to a rhythm and blues/pop singer and song writer of international acclaim, producing albums which went gold and double platinum. To this successful singing, song writing, and touring career add marriage to Terry Lewis, the co-producer of many of her hits, and three children. In addition to balancing her singing career, marriage, and family, White along with husband, Terry Lewis, also finds time to share herself with needy children across the country. White and Lewis frequently visit facilities like the Hale House, in New York City, where people suffering from AIDS and recovering addicts live. She provides support to residents, and has been known to sing lullabies to the tiniest of the residents of Hale House. Not only does White have talent, beauty, and a silken smooth voice, she has a "heart of gold."

Karyn White was born Karyn Lay Vonne White on October 14, 1965 in Los Angeles, California. Her parents, Clarence and Vivian White, were both musicians. Her father played the trumpet and her mother was the director of and sang in the church choir. In her youth, White also sang in the choir. At the tender age of five years old, White won first place in a talent and beauty contest in Culver City, California for her rendition of "Somewhere over the Rainbow." In high school White was a cheerleader, but quit the squad because she felt yelling was damaging her voice. When White was 18 years old, she wrote the song "Automatic Passion," which Stephanie Mills recorded.

White fronted the L.A. band Legacy for a short time, and in 1984 she toured with rhythm and blues singer, O'Bryan. She also did session work with other well known artists including the Commodores, Ray Parker, Jr., Shanice Wilson, Bobby Brown, Sheena Easton, and Julio Iglesias. Two years later, in 1986, she was the featured vocalist for Jeff Lorber's dance hit single "The Facts of Love." This exposure proved to be her big break, and it was through her relationship with Lorber that Warner Brothers signed her as a solo recording artist.

White's self-titled debut album was released in 1988 and sold double platinum. The success of this album was stimulated by the recognition several of her singles received internationally. These included "The Way You Love Me," "Love Saw It," and the tune that has become recognized as White's trademark song, "Superwoman." Throughout the album, White's ability to project realism and depth of feeling into the rhythm and blues tunes is apparent. The songs on this album all reverberate with emotional nuances. White shapes the songs to her stylist needs. On the album's first hit single, "The

For the Record . . .

Born Karyn Lay Vonne White, October 14, 1965 in Los Angeles, CA; daughter of Clarence (a trumpeter) and Vivian (a choir director) White; married Terry Lewis (a producer); children: Ashley, Chloe, Tre.

Participated in numerous beauty pageants and talent shows as a teenager; sang with band Legacy; toured as backup singer with rhythm and blues vocalist O'Bryan in 1984; sang on Jeff Lorber's "Facts of Love" (1986); signed with Warner Brothers Records and released debut album, *Karyn White,* (1988), *Ritual of Love,* (1991), *Make Him Do Right,* (1994), and *Sweet and Sensual,* (1995); featured on the Disney album, *Rock-a-Bye Baby,* (1996).

Addresses: *Record company*—Warner Bros. Records, 3300 Warner Blvd., Burbank, CA 91505. *Agent*—Jeff Frasco, William Morris Agency, 151 El Camino Dr., Beverly Hills, CA 90212. *Fan Club*—Karyn White Fan Club, 9016 Wilshire Blvd., P.O. Box 321, Beverly Hills, CA 90211. *Correspondence*—Kings Kid Entertainment, 1800 North Vine St., Suite 300, Hollywood, CA 90028.

Way You Love Me," she displays her ability to interject "breathy cries, a short string of 'oh's,' even a bit of scat," according to a review in the *New Yorker,* around and within the available space created between co-producers L.A. Reid's and Babyface's synthesized strings and drums.

White's hit single, "Superwoman," begins tenderly and affectionately, and soon turns to remorse. This song has been called "the women's national anthem." It's the grieving of a smart, 1980's career woman who in addition to managing her professional life, tries to satisfy her spouse. She is unappreciated by her man, and is tired of trying to make him happy. The success that hit single "Superwoman" brought White was repeated in 1991 when three other superwomen of soul, Gladys Knight, Patti LaBelle, and Dionne Warwick re-released the tune on Knight's *Good Woman* album. The song ends with the refrain, "Boy, I am only human," repeating over and over like an incantation.

The only possible disappointment on White's debut album, is the slightly feigned, "One Wish," which was described by one reviewer from the *New Yorker* as "one of those unbearable upbeat peace-all-over-the-world tunes that established stars like to include as finales to show that they're, you know, really nice guys." At least this one reviewer felt that on the basis of the rest of the album, this gesturing was unnecessary.

Fell in Love

Three years later, in 1991, White's second album, *Ritual of Love,* was released by Warner Brothers. *Ritual of Love* sold gold-plus. The release followed her extended touring throughout the country and across the globe. White co-wrote ten of the songs from this album as well as co-producing some of the tracks with Jimmy Jam and Terry Lewis, and an executive from Warner Brothers, Benny Medina. The majority of tunes were produced by Jam and Lewis, but the album also featured tracks produced by Michael J. Powell, Laney Stewart, Christopher Troy, and Zack Harmon.

The single, "Romantic," became a number one hit, and very popular rhythm and blues number. Producing *Ritual of Love,* was also important for White personally because it was during production of this album that she first met her future husband, Terry Lewis. White told an interviewer at Warner online that upon release of her second album, "I was in love and feeling great. I wanted an album that reflected all the facets of a romantic relationship."

In 1992, after White became Lewis' wife and stepmother to his two children from a previous marriage, she took some time off from performing. White felt it was important to spend time with her new family, and it was during that year that White and Lewis' daughter, Ashley was born. Also during that period she continued to co-write songs that other artists recorded. These included the rhythm and blues hit single, "Till You Come to Me," which was recorded on Rachelle Ferrell's debut album, and the 1993 cut released on Johnny Gill's second album under the Motown label, "I Know Where I Stand." White also toured in Japan during the summer of 1993, and sang background vocals for the 1994 release of Gladys Knight's, *Just for You.*

Trusted Her Own Instincts

While White sang the lamentation of the "Superwoman," in her music, in her own life she strove to maintain a balance between work and her personal life. She felt it was very important to keep the two separate, particularly since she and husband, Lewis, worked together in producing her third album, *Make Him Do Right.* White spoke about the essence of her new album with Warner online, "The basis for this album was simple: it was about trusting my 'gut' feelings. ... about doing what was natural." In the title track, "Make Him Do Right," White recoils from the themes of the unappreciated woman, as in "Superwoman," and here demands self-respect for women in relationships. The lyrics encourage women to be alone rather than subject themselves to mistreatment.

The majority of the tunes on *Make Him Do Right* were produced by husband, Terry Lewis, with his partner Jimmy Jam. White also worked with Kenny "Babyface" Edmonds on two cuts, "Here Comes the Pain," and "Can I Stay with You." White feels that this album is different from her previous albums, because she focused more on allowing her own personal style to come through. The ballads on *Make Him Do Right,* display White's ability to project clear, articulate, and heartfelt personal expression through her lyrics.

In 1996, White was featured on a collection of lullabies released by Walt Disney Records, called *Rock-a-Bye Baby: Soft Hits for Little Rockers.* This collection also featured Toni Childs and The Wild Colonials, and was produced by Grammy nominees Michael Becker and Harold J. Kleiner. Disney's first release in this genre, the company sought to produce something different from the current music available for young children. White performed a heartfelt rendition of the Frank Sinatra hit, "Dream," and also a calming rendering of the song, "Baby Baby," by South African Grammy winner, Lebo M., which has also been sung by Amy Grant.

When not performing or recording, one of White's favorite pastimes is simply to be at home. She also would welcome an opportunity to showcase her dancing or acting skills, and would embrace a chance to perform on Broadway. As she told an interviewer at *Ebony* magazine, "Performing to a live audience is what really gets me going. To be able to reach so many people at one time."

Selected discography

Karyn White, (includes "The Way You Love Me," "Love Saw It," "Superwoman," and "One Wish"), Warner Bros., 1988.
Ritual of Love, (includes "Romantic"),Warner Bros., 1991.
Make Him Do Right, (includes "Make Him Do Right," "Here Comes the Pain," and "Can I Stay With You"), Warner Bros., 1994.
Sweet and Sensual, Warner Bros., 1995.
(With others) *Rock-a-Bye Baby,* (includes "Dream," and "Baby Baby"), Walt Disney Records, 1996.

Sources

Books

Romanowski, Patricia; George-Warren, Holly; editors. *The New Rolling Stone Encyclopedia of Rock and Roll,* Fireside, 1995.

Periodicals

Ebony, September 1989, p.152-54.
Jet, November 7, 1994, p. 60; January 2, 1995, p.15.
New Yorker, March 20, 1989, p. 83.

Online

http://cdnow.com/
http://home.pi.net/~prism/karynw.htm
http://www.cduniverse.com/programs/
http://www.disney.com/DisneyRecords/_RockaBye.html
http://www.geocities.com/SunsetStrip/4879/cs000009.htm
http://www.iuma.com/Warner/html/White,_Karyn-bio.html
http://www.streetsound.com/interviews/intkarynwhite.html
http://www.tunes.com/tunes-cgi2/tunes/person_frame/24417/0/0/76

—Debra Reilly

Dar Williams

Singer, songwriter

In the short time since her first album was released in 1995, Dar Williams has established herself as one of the most promising young songwriters of the modern folk era. Her intimate, introspective songs, lyrical wit and wisdom, three-octave vocal range and consistent artistic growth have charmed critics and attracted a growing base of fans. "She has the craft heart to make the folky basics ring true again," the *New York Times* wrote. "(H)er songs reach beyond modest ambitions; they glow with compassion and intelligence." *Billboard* put Williams on its cover to illustrate an article on the modern folk resurgence, and *Stereo Review* labeled her the Great Folk Hope. "Williams' songs—spare, pleasing melodies in which she transcends the vocal range from smoky lows to falsetto highs—exert a subtle undertow," Lyndon Stambler wrote in *People.* "They typically have word images within images. Each time you listen ... you hear something different in her shades and patterns." Williams, for her part, had this to say about all the attention and adoration: "I'm probably getting a little more hype than I'm worth."

Williams is routinely compared with female folkies such as Joni Mitchell, Joan Baez, Emmylous Harris and Suzanne Vega and she acknowledges that her musical influences include artists like The Mamas and the Papas, Simon & Garfunkel, and Bob Dylan. "What's in my blood is the folk music of the '60s," she told Amy Stephens of *The Cincinnati Post.* "Songs where you can still hear the human voice." Williams is perfectly com-fortable being associated with the decidedly unhip folk music genre. According to Williams: "In a fast-moving, split-second MTV world ... (folk-music audiences) pay attention and sit still." That is not to say, however, that her music is mired in the past. Far from it. Williams' songs—like those of her folk-influenced peers Shawn Colvin, Patty Larkin and Ani Difranco—build a thoroughly contemporary musical structure upon a traditional foundation.

Williams devotees—dubbed "Dar-heads"—have taken their obsession to the Internet's music chat rooms in unexpected numbers and with unusual fervor. Spreading the word about Williams via cyberspace, they "discuss and dissect all things Dar, from her guitar tunings and humor to her lyrics and live shows," J. Freedom du Lac wrote in *The Sacramento Bee.* In the process, the Dar-heads have wedded the rusticity of folk with the electron-speed and cutting-edge wonder of the Internet.

Persistence Pays Off

In college, Williams studied religion and theater; she performed in the Boston folk scene in the early 1990s. Unfortunately, she also suffered from clinical depression during her college years. In late 1992, she settled in western Massachusetts. In her early years as a performer, she self-released albums called *I Have No Story, All My Heroes are Dead,* and, in 1993, *The Honesty Room,* which was recorded in a tiny basement studio in Belchertown, Massachusetts. That same year, she compiled *The Tofu Tollbooth,* "a sort of traveler's guide to the country's natural foods outlets," John Jesitus wrote in *Backbeat.* Williams created the book, Jesitus said, at a time when "she felt fairly certain that her music would never support her full-time."

The Honesty Room, however, created a buzz in the folk music world and brought Williams a management deal, a booking agent, a showcase spot at the 1994 Newport Folk Festival, and a contract with indie record label Razor & Tie. The sparsely arranged record was re-released natioanlly in 1995 and garnered radio play on many adult/alternative album stations for the single "When I Was a Boy." Promoting the record kept Williams on the tour circuit for more than 200 nights in 1995. Her audiences grew—with help from rave reviews, her photo on the cover of *Billboard*, and the nurturing hand of Joan Baez. The folk icon recorded one of Williams' compositions on her album *Ring Them Bells* and took the fledgling songstress with her on tour in the United States and Europe. Although Williams had been told that opening acts are often mistreated on tours, she

For the Record . . .

Started performing in the Boston/Cambridge folk scene, early 1990s; moved to western Massachusetts, 1992; released *Honesty Room* and signed with Razor & Tie Records, 1993; performed at the Newport Folk Festival, 1994; Razor & Tie rereleased *Honesty Room*, 1995; released *Mortal City*, 1996, and *End of the Summer*, 1997; toured with music legend Joan Baez, and played several dates on the heralded Lilith Tour, 1997.

Addresses: *Website*—razrntie@aol.com.

claimed that her collaboration with Baez was a very positive experience.

Williams recorded her second album, 1996's *Mortal City*, in her bedroom. The album contains a theme of displacement; it speaks of wanting to find a home and describes the journeys people take to find a place where they feel they can belong. *Mortal City* also showed the evolution of Williams' musical vision, expanding on the acoustic guitar-and-voice delivery that dominated *The Honesty Room*. On the second record, the arrangements were more complex and the sound was fleshed out with cello, fiddle, mandolin, dobro, and electric guitar. In addition, Williams added other voices to the mix, singing with John Prine, Cliff Eberhardt, The Nields, and Lucy Kaplansky, who used to work with Shawn Colvin. The song "Cool as I Am"—built around the repeated, haunting refrain "I will not be afraid of women"—received solid radio play. *Billboard* called *Mortal City* a "palatable album of introspective, often witty tunes (that) present an intimate portrait of a maturing artist."

The End of Summer is Just the Beginning

Williams' popularity and musical experimentation both continued to grow with the release of 1997's *End of the Summer*, which features a full band, backup singers, and a more of an electric sound. Some critics suggested that the release was a calculated bid to break into the pop music mainstream—but most raved. "Folkies may fight it, but as Dar Williams goes more and more electric, her music is getting increasingly intriguing," music critic Kevin O'Hare wrote. "Firmly established as one of the leading ligths on the new folk movement, (Williams) offers plenty of poetic wonder while revealing considerable musical growth on her exceptional third album.... She lets her musical inhibitions fly frequently here, on tracks like the fiesta-flavored 'Party Generation,' hot-rocking 'Teenager, Kick Our Butts,' and a marvelous cover of the Kinks' 'Better Things'." In an interview with *Billboard*, Williams acknowledged that she had pushed in new directions on *End of the Summer*. "I know this was more of a pop/rock album," she said. "I could have done the same thing (as on the first two albums) and I'm nervous people will think I've sold out. But I'm trying to be true to my muse."

Selected discography

The Honesty Room, Razor & Tie, 1995.
Mortal City, Razor & Tie, 1996.
End of the Summer, Razor & Tie, 1997.

Sources

Billboard, January 13, 1995; July 5, 1997
Boston Globe, September 19, 1997.
Boston Herald, July 5, 1996; August 1, 1997.
Cincinnati Post, October 12, 1995; February 22, 1996; October 24, 1996.
Minneapolis Star Tribune, February 20, 1996; October 3, 1997.
Patriot Ledger (Quincy, MA), February 2, 1996; February 16, 1996.
People, March 25, 1996; August 25, 1997.
Philadelphia Inquirer, July 18, 1997.
Sacramento Bee, April 28, 1996.
Stereo Review, April 1996.
Union-News (Springfield, MA), July 13, 1997.

Additional information was provided by Razor & Tie press materials

—*Dave Wilkins*

Dwight Yoakam

Singer, songwriter

AP/Wide World Photos. Reproduced by permission.

Critically and popularly acclaimed country singer Dwight Yoakam has not only continued to prove himself as a recording artist, he has also made a name for himself as an actor, earning rave reviews for his roles in such films as the Academy Award-winning *Sling Blade*, released in 1996. Upon receiving *Premiere* magazine's Premiere Performance Award (in recognition of his "breakthrough performance" in *Sling Blade*) in October 1996, Yoakam remarked: "Acting is a different form of creative expression for me than performing music. In acting, I'm able to actually escape myself using the character as a vehicle for exploring emotions I might not otherwise confront, whereas with music, I feel as though I go deeper inside myself in articulating emotions that are almost exclusively an outgrowth of my personal experiences." Yoakam's 1997 release of his eighth album, *Under the Covers*, which features cover versions of songs originally recorded by such diverse artists as The Clash and Johnny Horton, drew praise from critics who expressed appreciation for the singer's artistic inventiveness and mastery of a wide range of musical styles.

Yoakam was born on October 23, 1956, in Pikeville, Kentucky, but the family moved to Columbus, Ohio, when Dwight was very young. Yoakam first showed an interest in playing the guitar at the age of two, and quickly taught himself to play along with Hank Williams records. He composed his first song at the age of eight, but, as he told *People*'s Pam Lambert, because he "didn't think [he] was doing it right, because it came so easily," Yoakam did not write another song until much later. He worked as a singer in night clubs while attending Ohio State University, but after two years he left for Nashville, Tennessee, in search of a career in country music. Unable to get his career started while living in Nashville, Yoakam decided to try his luck in Los Angeles, where he moved in 1978. In Los Angeles, Yoakam worked as a truck driver and on a loading dock while struggling to find a niche for himself among the popular country music artists of the time. These artists had a modern sound that was a far cry from his traditional, down-home variety of country music. Finally in 1986 he landed a recording contract with Reprise and released his debut album, *Guitars, Cadillacs, Etc. Etc.*, which was well-received by critics and country music fans alike.

After making a splash with *Guitars, Cadillacs, Etc. Etc.*, Yoakam released four more albums in the next four years—1987's *Hillbilly Deluxe*, 1988's *Buenas Noches from a Lonely Room*, 1989's *Just Lookin' for a Hit*, and 1990's *If There Was a Way*—and managed to keep his loyal fans of his traditional country music satisfied. His first album quickly went platinum, and the next four

Born October 23, 1956, in Pikeville, KY; son of David (a gas station owner) and Ruth (a keypunch operator) Yoakam. *Education:* Attended Ohio State University.

Singer and songwriter, 1974—. Performer in West Coast night clubs and bars, c. 1970-78; worked as a truck driver, beginning in 1978; recording artist with Reprise, 1986—; has appeared as an actor in films, including *Red Rock West,* 1992, *The Little Death,* 1995, *Painted Hero,* 1996, *Sling Blade,* 1996, and *The Newton Boys,* 1998; actor in television programs, including the movies *Roswell,* 1994, and *Don't Look Back,* 1996, and as a guest star on the series *Ellen,* 1997; has appeared as an actor on stage, in *Southern Rapture,* MET Theatre, Los Angeles, 1993; has toured with The Babylonian Cowboys (a backup band), and has appeared with singer and musician Buck Owens.

Awards: American Academy of Country Music Award, best new male vocalist, 1987; Grammy Award, best country vocal performance, male, 1993, for "Ain't That Lonely Yet"; Premiere Performance Award (for outstanding breakthrough performances in film), 1996, for portrayal of Doyle Hargraves in *Sling Blade;* has received numerous Grammy Award nominations.

Addresses: *Record company*—Reprise, 75 Rockefeller Plaza, New York, NY 10019.

country or pop star on the radio. Songs such as "A Thousand Miles from Nowhere" and "King of Fools" were especially lauded, and Yoakam himself, in an article by *People* contributor Tony Scherman, characterized the type of music he plays as "country rock," but asserted: "I'll never quit playing country music, or at least acknowledging it, always, as the cornerstone of what I am." In a review in *Maclean's,* Nicholas Jennings declared that on *This Time* Yoakam's "songwriting ... ranks among the best in country music," and that even though the artist deviates from his previous traditional country music style, his "plaintive vocals make every song convincing."

He Can Really Sing

Despite his busy schedule as an actor on stage and screen, in 1995 Yoakam managed to release *Dwight Live,* which, as the name suggests, consisted of versions of songs that were recorded live during concert performances, and *Gone,* an album on which Yoakam continued the trend he had started with *This Time,* performing songs that blended a variety of music styles and influences. Both albums were well regarded by critics and were popular with fans. Tony Scherman, writing in *Entertainment Weekly,* called *Dwight Live* "the most satisfying country record of the half year," applauded Yoakam's vocal abilities, declaring "the boy can flat-out sing," and praised the singer's unwavering power to "bar[e] his soul" in every song. *Guitar Player*'s Art Thompson also offered a glowing review of the live album, and advised his readers that "[t]his is the music of dented pickup trucks and funky bars, not the silly tight-Wranglers scene that dominates today's `young country.'" Reviews of *Gone* were largely positive, but some critics asserted, as Alanna Nash did in her *Entertainment Weekly* assessment, that in incorporating all of the different types of music on the album, some of the heart of Yoakam's music was lost. As Nash termed it, "he's so busy getting the synthesis right that he forgot the soul." Scherman, this time writing for *People,* offered a different appraisal, proclaiming that Yoakam alone "has the grit and individuality once common currency in" country music, and that on *Gone* the singer "pushes his voice into places it has never been" with spectacular results.

In 1996 Yoakam earned rave reviews for his potrayal of the abusive, alcoholic Doyle in the film *Sling Blade.* Regarding his performance, most critics and moviegoers expressed sentiments similar to *Entertainment Weekly* contributor Owen Gleiberman's assertion that in the film "Yoakam ... gives a shattering performance, lending Doyle the redneck varmint authentic shades

went gold; Dwight Yoakam was clearly a major country music star. Still, there were fans and critics who expressed a desire for the singer to expand his musical horizons, abandon his characteristic honky-tonk, rural sound, and adopt a more sophisticated, rock-driven, contemporary country music sound. Yoakam's response to this request was his 1993 album, *This Time,* with which he succeeded, according to *Entertainment Weekly*'s Alanna Nash, in "pull[ing] off a near miracle: Staying stone country for his core following, and turning progressive enough for radio, without alienating either audience."

This Time received high praise from critics, who applauded Yoakam's ability to blend rock, pop, and country music without compromising any of the musical influences and without sounding like every other of self-loathing and cowardice." Although he expressed interest in acting, and following his performance in *Sling Blade*, he received offers to appear in many more films, Yoakam maintained his dedication to music, and in 1997, he released *Under the Covers,* an album on which he offered listeners creative alternative versions of songs made popular by other artists. The album features such songs as "Train in Vain," by the punk rock band The Clash, reworked and presented in a style that often differs considerably from the original; The Clash's original pop rock style and vocals are replaced by what critic Graham Weekly, in his review broadcast on WVIA-FM and published on the internet, called "a style somewhere between bluegrass and Cajun." Critical response to the album was mixed, with some critics praising Yoakam's creativity, daring, and range, and other critics characterizing the work as overdone. *People*'s Amy Linden, who while admitting that initially the new versions are interesting and enjoyable to listen to, remarked that "eventually the production razzle-dazzle and sudden leaps of genre get tiresome." *Entertainment Weekly*'s Jeremy Helligar, however, was enthusiastic about *Under the Covers,* and concluded that Yoakam's performance on the album was "[i]nspired as hell and absolutely out of control." This critic's opinion seems to be shared by a great many others, judging from the media attention placed on Yoakam, who has continued to provide the public with fresh, innovative performances as an actor, singer, and songwriter.

Selected discography

Guitars, Cadillacs, Etc. Etc. (includes "Honky Tonk Man," "Miner's Prayer," and "Guitars, Cadillacs"), Reprise, 1986.
Hillbilly Deluxe (includes "Please, Please, Baby," "Little Ways," and "This Drinkin' Will Kill Me"), Reprise, 1987.
Buenas Noches from a Lonely Room (includes "I Got You," "Hold on to God," and "I Sang Dixie"), Reprise, 1988.

Just Lookin' for a Hit, Reprise, 1989.
If There Was a Way (includes "Turn It On, Turn It Up, Turn Me Loose," "It Only Hurts When I Cry," and "Since I Started Drinking Again"), Reprise, 1990.
This Time (includes "Ain't That Lonely Yet" and "Fast As You"), Reprise, 1993.
Dwight Live, Reprise, 1995.
Gone (includes "Sorry You Asked?," "Gone (That'll Be Me)," and "Heart of Stone"), Reprise, 1995.
Under the Covers, Reprise, 1997.

Sources

Periodicals

Entertainment Weekly, April 2, 1993, p. 51; May 26, 1995, p. 86; November 3, 1995, p. 66; December 6, 1996, p. 48; July 25, 1997, p. 73.
Guitar Player, September, 1995, p. 119.
Los Angeles Magazine, May, 1993, p. 165.
Maclean's, April 26, 1993, p. 44.
People, March 29, 1993, p. 19; April 26, 1993, p. 46; November 27, 1995, p. 22; August 4, 1997, p. 23.

Online

Dwightsite, http://dwightsite.com/pr/sbpr.html.
Dwight Yoakam Fact Sheet, http://www.msopr.com/mso/dyoakamfact.html.
Dwight Yoakam's homepage, http://www.wbr.com/nashville/dwightyoakam/cmp.
George Graham Weekly Album Review, broadcast August 6, 1997 on WVIA-FM, http://george.scranton.com/yoakam.html.

—*Lynn M. Spampinato*

Cumulative Indexes

Cumulative Subject Index

Volume numbers appear in **bold**.

Ashton, Susan **17**
Champion, Eric **21**
Chapman, Steven Curtis **15**
dc Talk **18**
Duncan, Bryan **19**
Eskelin, Ian **19**
Grant, Amy **7**
Jars of Clay **20**
King's X **7**
Paris, Twila **16**
Patti, Sandi **7**
Petra **3**
Point of Grace **21**
Smith, Michael W. **11**
Stryper **2**
Waters, Ethel **11**

Clarinet
Adams, John **8**
Bechet, Sidney **17**
Braxton, Anthony **12**
Dorsey, Jimmy
  See Dorsey Brothers, The
Fountain, Pete **7**
Goodman, Benny **4**
Herman, Woody **12**
Shaw, Artie **8**

Classical
Anderson, Marian **8**
Arrau, Claudio **1**
Baker, Janet **14**
Bernstein, Leonard **2**
Boyd, Liona **7**
Bream, Julian **9**
Britten, Benjamin **15**
Bronfman, Yefim **6**
Canadian Brass, The **4**
Carter, Ron **14**
Casals, Pablo **9**
Chang, Sarah **7**
Clayderman, Richard **1**
Cliburn, Van **13**
Copland, Aaron **2**
Davis, Anthony **17**
Davis, Chip **4**
Fiedler, Arthur **6**
Galway, James **3**
Gingold, Josef **6**
Gould, Glenn **9**
Gould, Morton **16**
Hampson, Thomas **12**
Harrell, Lynn **3**
Hayes, Roland **13**
Hendricks, Barbara **10**
Herrmann, Bernard **14**
Hinderas, Natalie **12**
Horne, Marilyn **9**
Horowitz, Vladimir **1**
Jarrett, Keith **1**
Kennedy, Nigel **8**
Kissin, Evgeny **6**
Kronos Quartet **5**
Kunzel, Erich **17**
Lemper, Ute **14**

Levine, James **8**
Liberace **9**
Ma, Yo-Yo **2**
Marsalis, Wynton **6**
Masur, Kurt **11**
McNair, Sylvia **15**
McPartland, Marian **15**
Mehta, Zubin **11**
Menuhin, Yehudi **11**
Midori **7**
Nyman, Michael **15**
Ott, David **2**
Parkening, Christopher **7**
Perahia, Murray **10**
Perlman, Itzhak **2**
Phillips, Harvey **3**
Rampal, Jean-Pierre **6**
Rostropovich, Mstislav **17**
Rota, Nino **13**
Rubinstein, Arthur **11**
Salerno-Sonnenberg, Nadja **3**
Salonen, Esa-Pekka **16**
Schickele, Peter **5**
Schuman, William **10**
Segovia, Andres **6**
Shankar, Ravi **9**
Solti, Georg **13**
Stern, Isaac **7**
Sutherland, Joan **13**
Takemitsu, Toru **6**
Toscanini, Arturo **14**
Upshaw, Dawn **9**
von Karajan, Herbert **1**
Weill, Kurt **12**
Wilson, Ransom **5**
Yamashita, Kazuhito **4**
York, Andrew **15**
Zukerman, Pinchas **4**

Composers
Adams, John **8**
Allen, Geri **10**
Alpert, Herb **11**
Anka, Paul **2**
Atkins, Chet **5**
Bacharach, Burt **20**
  Earlier sketch in CM **1**
Badalamenti, Angelo **17**
Beiderbecke, Bix **16**
Benson, George **9**
Berlin, Irving **8**
Bernstein, Leonard **2**
Blackman, Cindy **15**
Bley, Carla **8**
Bley, Paul **14**
Braxton, Anthony **12**
Britten, Benjamin **15**
Brubeck, Dave **8**
Burrell, Kenny **11**
Byrne, David **8**
  Also see Talking Heads
Cage, John **8**
Cale, John **9**
Casals, Pablo **9**
Clarke, Stanley **3**

Coleman, Ornette **5**
Cooder, Ry **2**
Cooney, Rory **6**
Copeland, Stewart **14**
  Also see Police, The **20**
Copland, Aaron **2**
Crouch, Andraé **9**
Curtis, King **17**
Davis, Anthony **17**
Davis, Chip **4**
Davis, Miles **1**
de Grassi, Alex **6**
Dorsey, Thomas A. **11**
Elfman, Danny **9**
Ellington, Duke **2**
Eno, Brian **8**
Enya **6**
Esquivel, Juan **17**
Evans, Bill **17**
Evans, Gil **17**
Fahey, John **17**
Foster, David **13**
Frisell, Bill **15**
Frith, Fred **19**
Galás, Diamanda **16**
Gillespie, Dizzy **6**
Glass, Philip **1**
Golson, Benny **21**
Gould, Glenn **9**
Gould, Morton **16**
Green, Benny **17**
Grusin, Dave **7**
Guaraldi, Vince **3**
Hamlisch, Marvin **1**
Hammer, Jan **21**
Hancock, Herbie **8**
Handy, W. C. **7**
Hargrove, Roy **15**
Harris, Eddie **15**
Hartke, Stephen **5**
Henderson, Fletcher **16**
Herrmann, Bernard **14**
Hunter, Alberta **7**
Isham, Mark **14**
Jacquet, Illinois **17**
Jarre, Jean-Michel **2**
Jarrett, Keith **1**
Johnson, James P. **16**
Jones, Hank **15**
Jones, Quincy **20**
  Earlier sketch in CM **2**
Joplin, Scott **10**
Jordan, Stanley **1**
Kenny G **14**
Kenton, Stan **21**
Kern, Jerome **13**
Kitaro **1**
Kottke, Leo **13**
Lateef, Yusef **16**
Lee, Peggy **8**
Legg, Adrian **17**
Lewis, Ramsey **14**
Lincoln, Abbey **9**
Lloyd Webber, Andrew **6**
Loesser, Frank **19**

Cruz, Celia **10**
de Lucia, Paco **1**
DeMent, Iris **13**
Donovan **9**
Dr. John **7**
Drake, Nick **17**
Dylan, Bob **3**
Elliot, Cass **5**
Enya **6**
Estefan, Gloria **15**
  Earlier sketch in CM **2**
Fahey, John **17**
Feliciano, José **10**
Galway, James **3**
Germano, Lisa **18**
Gilmore, Jimmie Dale **11**
Gipsy Kings, The **8**
Gorka, John **18**
Griffith, Nanci **3**
Grisman, David **17**
Guthrie, Arlo **6**
Guthrie, Woody **2**
Hakmoun, Hassan **15**
Hardin, Tim **18**
Harding, John Wesley **6**
Hartford, John **1**
Havens, Richie **11**
Henry, Joe **18**
Hinojosa, Tish **13**
Ian and Sylvia **18**
Iglesias, Julio **20**
  Earlier sketch in CM **2**
Indigo Girls **20**
  Earlier sketch in CM **3**
Ives, Burl **12**
Khan, Nusrat Fateh Ali **13**
Kingston Trio, The **9**
Klezmatics, The **18**
Kottke, Leo **13**
Kuti, Fela **7**
Ladysmith Black Mambazo **1**
Larkin, Patty **9**
Lavin, Christine **6**
Leadbelly **6**
Lightfoot, Gordon **3**
Los Lobos **2**
Makeba, Miriam **8**
Mamas and the Papas **21**
Masekela, Hugh **7**
McLean, Don **7**
Melanie **12**
Mitchell, Joni **17**
  Earlier sketch in CM **2**
Moffatt, Katy **18**
Morrison, Van **3**
Morrissey, Bill **12**
Nascimento, Milton **6**
N'Dour, Youssou **6**
Near, Holly **1**
Ochs, Phil **7**
O'Connor, Sinead **3**
Odetta **7**
Parsons, Gram **7**
  Also see Byrds, The
Paxton, Tom **5**

Pentangle **18**
Peter, Paul & Mary **4**
Pogues, The **6**
Prine, John **7**
Proclaimers, The **13**
Redpath, Jean **1**
Ritchie, Jean, **4**
Roches, The **18**
Rodgers, Jimmie **3**
Sainte-Marie, Buffy **11**
Santana, Carlos **1**
Seeger, Pete **4**
  Also see Weavers, The
Selena **16**
Shankar, Ravi **9**
Simon, Paul **16**
  Earlier sketch in CM **1**
Snow, Pheobe **4**
Steeleye Span **19**
Story, The **13**
Sweet Honey in the Rock **1**
Taj Mahal **6**
Thompson, Richard **7**
Tikaram, Tanita **9**
Toure, Ali Farka **18**
Van Ronk, Dave **12**
Van Zandt, Townes **13**
Vega, Suzanne **3**
Wainwright III, Loudon **11**
Walker, Jerry Jeff **13**
Watson, Doc **2**
Weavers, The **8**
Whitman, Slim **19**

French Horn
Ohanian, David
  See Canadian Brass, The

Funk
Bambaataa, Afrika **13**
Brand New Heavies, The **14**
Brown, James **2**
Burdon, Eric **14**
  Also see War
Clinton, George **7**
Collins, Bootsy **8**
Fishbone **7**
Gang of Four **8**
Jackson, Janet **16**
  Earlier sketch in CM **3**
Khan, Chaka **19**
  Earlier sketch in CM **9**
Mayfield, Curtis **8**
Meters, The **14**
Ohio Players **16**
Parker, Maceo **7**
Prince **14**
  Earlier sketch in CM **1**
Red Hot Chili Peppers, The **7**
Stone, Sly **8**
Toussaint, Allen **11**
Worrell, Bernie **11**

Funky
Front 242 **19**

Jamiroquai **21**
Wu-Tang Clan **19**

Fusion
Anderson, Ray **7**
Beck, Jeff **4**
  Also see Yardbirds, The
Clarke, Stanley **3**
Coleman, Ornette **5**
Corea, Chick **6**
Davis, Miles **1**
Fishbone **7**
Hancock, Herbie **8**
Harris, Eddie **15**
Johnson, Eric **19**
Lewis, Ramsey **14**
Mahavishnu Orchestra **19**
McLaughlin, John **12**
Metheny, Pat **2**
O'Connor, Mark **1**
Ponty, Jean-Luc **8**
Reid, Vernon **2**
Ritenour, Lee **7**
Shorter, Wayne **5**
Summers, Andy **3**
  Also see Police, The
Washington, Grover, Jr. **5**

Gospel
Anderson, Marian **8**
Baylor, Helen **20**
Boone, Pat **13**
Brown, James **2**
Caesar, Shirley **17**
Carter Family, The **3**
Charles, Ray **1**
Cleveland, James **1**
Cooke, Sam **1**
  Also see Soul Stirrers, The
Crouch, Andraé **9**
Dorsey, Thomas A. **11**
Five Blind Boys of Alabama **12**
Ford, Tennessee Ernie **3**
Franklin, Aretha **17**
  Earlier sketch in CM **2**
Green, Al **9**
Hawkins, Tramaine **17**
Houston, Cissy **6**
Jackson, Mahalia **8**
Kee, John P. **15**
Knight, Gladys **1**
Little Richard **1**
Louvin Brothers, The **12**
Mighty Clouds of Joy, The **17**
Oak Ridge Boys, The **7**
Paris, Twila **16**
Pickett, Wilson **10**
Presley, Elvis **1**
Redding, Otis **5**
Reese, Della **13**
Robbins, Marty **9**
Smith, Michael W. **11**
Soul Stirrers, The **11**
Sounds of Blackness **13**
Staples, Mavis **13**

Perry, Joe
  See Aerosmith
Petty, Tom **9**
Phair, Liz **14**
Phillips, Sam **12**
Prince **14**
  Earlier sketch in CM **1**
Raitt, Bonnie **3**
Ray, Amy
  See Indigo Girls
Redbone, Leon **19**
Reed, Jimmy **15**
Reid, Vernon **2**
  Also see Living Colour
Reinhardt, Django **7**
Richards, Keith **11**
  Also see Rolling Stones, The
Richman, Jonathan **12**
Ritenour, Lee **7**
Robbins, Marty **9**
Robertson, Robbie **2**
Robillard, Duke **2**
Rodgers, Nile **8**
Rush, Otis **12**
Saliers, Emily
  See Indigo Girls
Santana, Carlos **19**
Santana, Carlos **1**
Satriani, Joe **4**
Scofield, John **7**
Segovia, Andres **6**
Sharrock, Sonny **15**
Shines, Johnny **14**
Simon, Paul **16**
  Earlier sketch in CM **1**
Skaggs, Ricky **5**
Slash
  See Guns n' Roses
Springsteen, Bruce **6**
Stewart, Dave
  See Eurythmics
Stills, Stephen **5**
Stuart, Marty **9**
Summers, Andy **3**
  Also see Police, The
Taylor, Mick
  See Rolling Stones, The
Thielemans, Toots **13**
Thompson, Richard **7**
Tippin, Aaron **12**
Toure, Ali Farka **18**
Townshend, Pete **1**
Travis, Merle **14**
Trynin, Jen **21**
Tubb, Ernest **4**
Ulmer, James Blood **13**
Vai, Steve **5**
Van Halen, Edward
  See Van Halen
Van Ronk, Dave **12**
Vaughan, Jimmie
  See Fabulous Thunderbirds, The
Vaughan, Stevie Ray **1**
Wagoner, Porter **13**

Waits, Tom **12**
  Earlier sketch in CM **1**
Walker, Jerry Jeff **13**
Walker, T-Bone **5**
Walsh, Joe **5**
  Also see Eagles, The
Wariner, Steve **18**
Watson, Doc **2**
Weir, Bob
  See Grateful Dead, The
Weller, Paul **14**
White, Lari **15**
Whitfield, Mark **18**
Whitley, Chris **16**
Whittaker, Hudson **20**
Wilson, Nancy
  See Heart
Winston, George **9**
Winter, Johnny **5**
Wiseman, Mac **19**
Wray, Link **17**
Yamashita, Kazuhito **4**
Yarrow, Peter
  See Peter, Paul & Mary
Yoakam, Dwight **21**
Young, Angus
  See AC/DC
Young, Malcolm
  See AC/DC
York, Andrew **15**
Young, Neil **15**
  Earlier sketch in CM **2**
Zappa, Frank **17**
  Earlier sketch in CM **1**

Harmonica
Dylan, Bob **3**
Guthrie, Woody **2**
Horton, Walter **19**
Lewis, Huey **9**
Little Walter **14**
McClinton, Delbert **14**
Musselwhite, Charlie **13**
Reed, Jimmy **15**
Thielemans, Toots **13**
Waters, Muddy **4**
Wells, Junior **17**
Williamson, Sonny Boy **9**
Wilson, Kim
  See Fabulous Thunderbirds, The
Wonder, Stevie **17**
  Earlier sketch in CM **2**
Young, Neil **15**
  Earlier sketch in CM **2**

Heavy Metal
AC/DC **4**
Aerosmith **3**
Alice in Chains **10**
Anthrax **11**
Black Sabbath **9**
Blue Oyster Cult **16**
Cinderella **16**
Circle Jerks **17**
Danzig **7**

Deep Purple **11**
Def Leppard **3**
Dokken **16**
Faith No More **7**
Fishbone **7**
Ford, Lita **9**
Guns n' Roses **2**
Iron Maiden **10**
Judas Priest **10**
King's X **7**
Led Zeppelin **1**
L7 **12**
Megadeth **9**
Melvins **21**
Metallica **7**
Mötley Crüe **1**
Motörhead **10**
Nugent, Ted **2**
Osbourne, Ozzy **3**
Pantera **13**
Petra **3**
Queensryche **8**
Reid, Vernon **2**
  Also see Living Colour
Reznor, Trent **13**
Roth, David Lee **1**
  Also see Van Halen
Sepultura **12**
Skinny Puppy **17**
Slayer **10**
Soundgarden **6**
Spinal Tap **8**
Stryper **2**
Suicidal Tendencies **15**
Tool **21**
Warrant **17**
Whitesnake **5**
White Zombie **17**

Humor
Borge, Victor **19**
Coasters, The **5**
Jones, Spike **5**
Lehrer, Tom **7**
Pearl, Minnie **3**
Russell, Mark **6**
Sandler, Adam **19**
Schickele, Peter **5**
Shaffer, Paul **13**
Spinal Tap **8**
Stevens, Ray **7**
Yankovic, "Weird Al" **7**

Inventors
Fender, Leo **10**
Harris, Eddie **15**
Paul, Les **2**
Scholz, Tom
  See Boston
Teagarden, Jack **10**
Theremin, Leon **19**

Jazz
Adderly, Cannonball **15**
Allen, Geri **10**

Price, Leontyne **6**
Sills, Beverly **5**
Solti, Georg **13**
Sutherland, Joan **13**
Te Kanawa, Kiri **2**
Toscanini, Arturo **14**
Upshaw, Dawn **9**
von Karajan, Herbert **1**
Weill, Kurt **12**
Zimmerman, Udo **5**

Percussion
Aronoff, Kenny **21**
Baker, Ginger **16**
  Also see Cream
Blackman, Cindy **15**
Blakey, Art **11**
Bonham, John
  See Led Zeppelin
Burton, Gary **10**
Collins, Phil **20**
  Earlier sketch in CM **2**
  Also see Genesis
Copeland, Stewart **14**
  Also see Police, The
DeJohnette, Jack **7**
Densmore, John
  See Doors, The
Dunbar, Aynsley
  See Jefferson Starship
  Also see Journey
          Also see Whitesnake
Dunbar, Sly
  See Sly and Robbie
Fleetwood, Mick
  See Fleetwood Mac
Hampton, Lionel **6**
Hart, Mickey
  See Grateful Dead, The
Henley, Don **3**
Jones, Elvin **9**
Jones, Kenny
  See Who, The
Jones, Philly Joe **16**
Jones, Spike **5**
Kreutzman, Bill
  See Grateful Dead, The
Krupa, Gene **13**
Mason, Nick
  See Pink Floyd
Moon, Keith
  See Who, The
Mo', Keb' **21**
N'Dour, Youssou **6**
Otis, Johnny **16**
Palmer, Carl
  See Emerson, Lake & Palmer/Powell
Palmieri, Eddie **15**
Peart, Neil
  See Rush
Powell, Cozy
  See Emerson, Lake & Palmer/Powell
Puente, Tito **14**
Rich, Buddy **13**
Roach, Max **12**

Sheila E. **3**
Starr, Ringo **10**
  Also see Beatles, The
Walden, Narada Michael **14**
Watts, Charlie
  See Rolling Stones, The
Webb, Chick **14**

Piano
Allen, Geri **10**
Allison, Mose **17**
Amos, Tori **12**
Arrau, Claudio **1**
Bacharach, Burt **20**
  Earlier sketch in CM **1**
Ball, Marcia **15**
Basie, Count **2**
Berlin, Irving **8**
Blake, Eubie **19**
Bley, Carla **8**
Bley, Paul **14**
Borge, Victor **19**
Britten, Benjamin **15**
Bronfman, Yefim **6**
Brubeck, Dave **8**
Bush, Kate **4**
Charles, Ray **1**
Clayderman, Richard **1**
Cleveland, James **1**
Cliburn, Van **13**
Cole, Nat King **3**
Collins, Judy **4**
Collins, Phil **20**
  Earlier sketch in CM **2**
    Also see Genesis
Connick, Harry, Jr. **4**
Crouch, Andraé **9**
DeJohnette, Jack **7**
Domino, Fats **2**
Dr. John **7**
Dupree, Champion Jack **12**
Esquivel, Juan **17**
Ellington, Duke **2**
Evans, Bill **17**
Evans, Gil **17**
Feinstein, Michael **6**
Ferrell, Rachelle **17**
Flack, Roberta **5**
Flanagan, Tommy **16**
Frey, Glenn **3**
Galás, Diamanda **16**
Glass, Philip **1**
Gould, Glenn **9**
Green, Benny **17**
Grusin, Dave **7**
Guaraldi, Vince **3**
Hamlisch, Marvin **1**
Hancock, Herbie **8**
Helfgott, David **19**
Henderson, Fletcher **16**
Hinderas, Natalie **12**
Hines, Earl "Fatha" **12**
Horn, Shirley **7**
Hornsby, Bruce **3**
Horowitz, Vladimir **1**

Jackson, Joe **4**
Jarrett, Keith **1**
Joel, Billy **12**
  Earlier sketch in CM **2**
John, Elton **20**
  Earlier sketch in CM **3**
Johnson, James P. **16**
Jones, Hank **15**
Joplin, Scott **10**
Kenton, Stan **21**
Kissin, Evgeny **6**
Levine, James **8**
Lewis, Jerry Lee **2**
Lewis, Ramsey **14**
Liberace **9**
Little Richard **1**
Manilow, Barry **2**
Marsalis, Ellis **13**
McDonald, Michael
  See Doobie Brothers, The
McPartland, Marian **15**
McRae, Carmen **9**
McVie, Christine
  See Fleetwood Mac
Milsap, Ronnie **2**
Mingus, Charles **9**
Monk, Thelonious **6**
Morton, Jelly Roll **7**
Newman, Randy **4**
Nero, Peter **19**
Palmieri, Eddie **15**
Perahia, Murray **10**
Peterson, Oscar **11**
Post, Mike **21**
Powell, Bud **15**
Pratt, Awadagin **19**
Previn, André **15**
Professor Longhair **6**
Puente, Tito **14**
Pullen, Don **16**
Rich, Charlie **3**
Roberts, Marcus **6**
Rubinstein, Arthur **11**
Russell, Mark **6**
Schickele, Peter **5**
Sedaka, Neil **4**
Shaffer, Paul **13**
Solal, Martial **4**
Solti, Georg **13**
Spann, Otis **18**
Story, Liz **2**
Strayhorn, Billy **13**
Sunnyland Slim **16**
Sykes, Roosevelt **20**
Tatum, Art **17**
Taylor, Billy **13**
Taylor, Cecil **9**
Tyner, McCoy **7**
Vangelis **21**
Waits, Tom **12**
  Earlier sketch in **1**
Waller, Fats **7**
Weston, Randy **15**
Wilson, Cassandra **12**
Winston, George **9**

Winwood, Steve **2**
  Also see Spencer Davis Group
  Also see Traffic
Wonder, Stevie **17**
  Earlier sketch in CM **2**
Wright, Rick
  See Pink Floyd
Young, La Monte **16**

Piccolo
Galway, James **3**

Pop
Abba **12**
Abdul, Paula **3**
Adam Ant **13**
Adams, Bryan **20**
  Earlier sketch in CM **2**
Adams, Oleta **17**
All-4-One **17**
Alpert, Herb **11**
America **16**
Amos, Tori **12**
Andrews Sisters, The **9**
Arden, Jann **21**
Arena, Tina **21**
Armatrading, Joan **4**
Arnold, Eddy **10**
Astley, Rick **5**
Atkins, Chet **5**
Avalon, Frankie **5**
Bacharach, Burt **20**
  Earlier sketch in CM **1**
Backstreet Boys **21**
Bailey, Pearl **5**
Basia **5**
Beach Boys, The **1**
Beatles, The **2**
Beaver Brown Band, The **3**
Bee Gees, The **3**
Belly **16**
Bennett, Tony **16**
  Earlier sketch in CM **2**
Benson, George **9**
Benton, Brook **7**
B-52's, The **4**
Better Than Ezra **19**
Blige, Mary J. **15**
Blondie **14**
Blood, Sweat and Tears **7**
Blue Rodeo **18**
BoDeans, The **20**
  Earlier sketch in CM **3**
Bolton, Michael **4**
Boo Radleys, The **21**
Boone, Pat **13**
Boston **11**
Bowie, David **1**
Boyz II Men **15**
Bragg, Billy **7**
Branigan, Laura **2**
Braxton, Toni **17**
Brickell, Edie **3**
Brooks, Garth **8**
Brown, Bobby **4**

Browne, Jackson **3**
Bryson, Peabo **11**
Buckingham, Lindsey **8**
  Also see Fleetwood Mac
Buckley, Tim **14**
Buffett, Jimmy **4**
Burdon, Eric **14**
  Also see War
Cabaret Voltaire **18**
Campbell, Glen **2**
Campbell, Tevin **13**
Cardigans **19**
Carey, Mariah **20**
  Earlier sketch in CM **6**
Carlisle, Belinda **8**
Carnes, Kim **4**
Carpenters, The **13**
Case, Peter **13**
Chandra, Sheila **16**
Chapin, Harry **6**
Chapman, Tracy **20**
  Earlier sketch in CM **4**
Charlatans, The **13**
Charles, Ray **1**
Checker, Chubby **7**
Cher **1**
Cherry, Neneh **4**
Chicago **3**
Chilton, Alex **10**
Clapton, Eric **11**
  Earlier sketch in CM **1**
  Also see Cream
  Also see Yardbirds, The
Clayderman, Richard **1**
Clooney, Rosemary **9**
Coasters, The **5**
Cocker, Joe **4**
Cocteau Twins, The **12**
Cole, Lloyd **9**
Cole, Natalie **21**
Cole, Natalie **1**
Cole, Nat King **3**
Cole, Paula **20**
Collins, Judy **4**
Collins, Phil **20**
  Earlier sketch in CM **2**
  Also see Genesis
Colvin, Shawn **11**
Como, Perry **14**
Connick, Harry, Jr. **4**
Cooke, Sam **1**
  Also see Soul Stirrers, The
Cope, Julian **16**
Costello, Elvis **12**
  Earlier sketch in CM **2**
Cranberries, The **14**
Crash Test Dummies **14**
Crenshaw, Marshall **5**
Croce, Jim **3**
Crosby, David **3**
  Also see Byrds, The
Crow, Sheryl **18**
Crowded House **12**
Cure, The **20**
  Earlier sketch in CM **3**

Daltrey, Roger **3**
  Also see Who, The
D'Arby, Terence Trent **3**
Darin, Bobby **4**
Dave Clark Five, The **12**
Davies, Ray **5**
Davis, Sammy, Jr. **4**
Davis, Skeeter **15**
Dayne, Taylor **4**
DeBarge, El **14**
Del Amitri **18**
Del Rubio Triplets **21**
Denver, John **1**
Depeche Mode **5**
Des'ree **15**
Devo **13**
Diamond, Neil **1**
Dion **4**
Dion, Céline **12**
Doc Pomus **14**
Donovan **9**
Doobie Brothers, The **3**
Doors, The **4**
Duran Duran **4**
Dylan, Bob **3**
Eagles, The **3**
Earth, Wind and Fire **12**
Easton, Sheena **2**
Edmonds, Kenneth "Babyface" **12**
Electric Light Orchestra **7**
Elfman, Danny **9**
Elliot, Cass **5**
Enigma **14**
En Vogue **10**
Estefan, Gloria **15**
  Earlier sketch in CM **2**
Eurythmics **6**
Everly Brothers, The **2**
Everything But The Girl **15**
Exposé **4**
Fabian **5**
Feliciano, José **10**
Ferguson, Maynard **7**
Ferry, Bryan **1**
Fiedler, Arthur **6**
Fisher, Eddie **12**
Fitzgerald, Ella **1**
Flack, Roberta **5**
Fleetwood Mac **5**
Fogelberg, Dan **4**
Fordham, Julia **15**
Foster, David **13**
Four Tops, The **11**
Fox, Samantha **3**
Frampton, Peter **3**
Francis, Connie **10**
Franklin, Aretha **17**
  Earlier sketch in CM **2**
Frey, Glenn **3**
  Also see Eagles, The
Garfunkel, Art **4**
Gaye, Marvin **4**
Gayle, Crystal **1**
Geldof, Bob **9**
Genesis **4**

Post, Mike **21**
Prince **14**
  Earlier sketch in CM **1**
Riley, Teddy **14**
Robertson, Robbie **2**
Rodgers, Nile **8**
Rubin, Rick **9**
Rundgren, Todd **11**
Shocklee, Hank **15**
Simmons, Russell **7**
Skaggs, Ricky **5**
Spector, Phil **4**
Sure!, Al B. **13**
Sweat, Keith **13**
Swing, DeVante
  See Jodeci
Too $hort **16**
Toussaint, Allen **11**
Tricky **18**
Vandross, Luther **2**
Vasquez, Junior **16**
Vig, Butch **17**
Walden, Narada Michael **14**
Was, Don **21**
Wexler, Jerry **15**
Whelan, Bill **20**
Willner, Hal **10**
Wilson, Brian
  See Beach Boys, The
Winbush, Angela **15**

Promoters
Clark, Dick **2**
Geldof, Bob **9**
Graham, Bill **10**
Hay, George D. **3**
Simmons, Russell **7**

Ragtime
Johnson, James P. **16**
Joplin, Scott **10**

Rap
Anthony, Marc **19**
Arrested Development **14**
Austin, Dallas **16**
Bambaataa, Afrika **13**
Basehead **11**
Beastie Boys, The **8**
Biz Markie **10**
Black Sheep **15**
Bone Thugs-N-Harmony **18**
Busta Rhymes **18**
Campbell, Luther **10**
Cherry, Neneh **4**
Combs, Sean "Puffy" **16**
Coolio **19**
Cypress Hill **11**
Das EFX **14**
De La Soul **7**
Digable Planets **15**
Digital Underground **9**
DJ Jazzy Jeff and the Fresh Prince **5**
Dr. Dre **15**
  Also see N.W.A.

Eazy-E **13**
  Also see N.W.A.
EPMD **10**
Eric B. and Rakim **9**
Franti, Michael **16**
Fugees, The **17**
Gang Starr **13**
Geto Boys, The **11**
Grandmaster Flash **14**
Hammer, M.C. **5**
Heavy D **10**
House of Pain **14**
Ice Cube **10**
Ice-T **7**
Jackson, Millie **14**
Kane, Big Daddy **7**
Kid 'n Play **5**
Knight, Suge **15**
Kool Moe Dee **9**
Kris Kross **11**
KRS-One **8**
L.L. Cool J. **5**
Last Poets **21**
MC Breed **17**
MC Lyte **8**
MC 900 Ft. Jesus **16**
MC Serch **10**
Nas **19**
Naughty by Nature **11**
N.W.A. **6**
Notorious B.I.G. **20**
Pharcyde, The **17**
P.M. Dawn **11**
Public Enemy **4**
Queen Latifah **6**
Rage Against the Machine **18**
Riley, Teddy **14**
Rubin, Rick **9**
Run-D.M.C. **4**
Salt-N-Pepa **6**
Scott-Heron, Gil **13**
Shaggy **19**
Shanté **10**
Shocklee, Hank **15**
Simmons, Russell **7**
Sir Mix-A-Lot **14**
Snoop Doggy Dogg **17**
Spearhead **19**
Special Ed **16**
Sure!, Al B. **13**
TLC **15**
Tone-L c **3**
Too $hort **16**
Tribe Called Quest, A **8**
2Pac **17**
Tricky **18**
US3 **18**
Vanilla Ice **6**
Wu-Tang Clan **19**
Young M.C. **4**
Yo Yo **9**

Record Company Executives
Ackerman, Will **3**
Alpert, Herb **11**

Brown, Tony **14**
Busby, Jheryl **9**
Combs, Sean "Puffy" **16**
Davis, Chip **4**
Davis, Clive **14**
Ertegun, Ahmet **10**
Foster, David **13**
Gabriel, Peter **16**
  Earlier sketch in CM **2**
  Also see Genesis
Geffen, David **8**
Gordy, Berry, Jr. **6**
Hammond, John **6**
Harley, Bill **7**
Harrell, Andre **16**
Jam, Jimmy, and Terry Lewis **11**
Knight, Suge **15**
Koppelman, Charles **14**
Krasnow, Bob **15**
LiPuma, Tommy **18**
Madonna **16**
  Earlier sketch in CM **4**
Marley, Rita **10**
Martin, George **6**
Mayfield, Curtis **8**
Mercer, Johnny **13**
Miller, Mitch **11**
Mingus, Charles **9**
Near, Holly **1**
Ostin, Mo **17**
Penner, Fred **10**
Phillips, Sam **5**
Reznor, Trent **13**
Rhone, Sylvia **13**
Robinson, Smokey **1**
Rubin, Rick **9**
Simmons, Russell **7**
Spector, Phil **4**
Teller, Al **15**
Too $hort **16**
Wexler, Jerry **15**

Reggae
Bad Brains **16**
Black Uhuru **12**
Burning Spear **15**
Cliff, Jimmy **8**
Dube, Lucky **17**
Inner Circle **15**
Israel Vibration **21**
Marley, Bob **3**
Marley, Rita **10**
Marley, Ziggy **3**
Mystic Revealers **16**
Skatalites, The **18**
Sly and Robbie **13**
Steel Pulse **14**
Third World **13**
Tosh, Peter **3**
UB40 **4**
Wailer, Bunny **11**

Rhythm and Blues/Soul
Aaliyah **21**
Abdul, Paula **3**

Adams, Oleta **17**
Alexander, Arthur **14**
All-4-One **17**
Austin, Dallas **16**
Ballard, Hank **17**
Baker, Anita **9**
Ball, Marcia **15**
Basehead **11**
Belle, Regina **6**
Berry, Chuck **1**
Bland, Bobby "Blue" **12**
Blessid Union of Souls **20**
Blige, Mary J. **15**
Blues Brothers, The **3**
Bolton, Michael **4**
Boyz II Men **15**
Brandy **19**
Braxton, Toni **17**
Brown, James **16**
 Earlier sketch in CM **2**
Brown, Ruth **13**
Brownstone **21**
Bryson, Peabo **11**
Burdon, Eric **14**
 Also see War
Busby, Jheryl **9**
C + C Music Factory **16**
Campbell, Tevin **13**
Carey, Mariah **20**
 Earlier sketch in CM **6**
Charles, Ray **1**
Cole, Natalie **21**
 Earlier sketch in CM **1**
Cooke, Sam **1**
 Also see Soul Stirrers, The
Cropper, Steve **12**
Curtis, King **17**
D'Angelo **20**
D'Arby, Terence Trent **3**
DeBarge, El **14**
Des'ree **15**
Dibango, Manu **14**
Diddley, Bo **3**
Domino, Fats **2**
Dr. John **7**
Earth, Wind and Fire **12**
Edmonds, Kenneth "Babyface" **12**
En Vogue **10**
Evora, Cesaria **19**
Fabulous Thunderbirds, The **1**
Four Tops, The **11**
Fox, Samantha **3**
Franklin, Aretha **17**
 Earlier sketch in CM **2**
Gaye, Marvin **4**
Gill, Johnny **20**
Gordy, Berry, Jr. **6**
Green, Al **9**
Hall & Oates **6**
Hayes, Isaac **12**
Holland-Dozier-Holland **5**
Incognito **16**
Ingram, James **11**
Isley Brothers, The **8**
Jackson, Freddie **3**

Jackson, Janet **3**
Jackson, Michael **17**
 Earlier sketch in CM **1**
 Also see Jacksons, The
Jackson, Millie **14**
Jacksons, The **7**
Jam, Jimmy, and Terry Lewis **11**
James, Etta **6**
Jodeci **13**
Jones, Booker T. **8**
Jones, Grace **9**
Jones, Quincy **20**
 Earlier sketch CM **2**
Jordan, Louis **11**
Kelly, R. **19**
Khan, Chaka **19**
Khan, Chaka **19**
 Earlier sketch CM **9**
King, Ben E. **7**
Knight, Gladys **1**
Kool & the Gang **13**
LaBelle, Patti **8**
Los Lobos **2**
Mayfield, Curtis **8**
Medley, Bill **3**
Meters, The **14**
Milli Vanilli **4**
Mills, Stephanie **21**
Mo', Keb' **21**
Moore, Chante **21**
Moore, Melba **7**
Morrison, Van **3**
Ndegéocello, Me'Shell **18**
Neville, Aaron **5**
 Also see Neville Brothers, The
Neville Brothers, The **4**
Ocean, Billy **4**
Ohio Players **16**
O'Jays, The **13**
Otis, Johnny **16**
Pendergrass, Teddy **3**
Peniston, CeCe **15**
Pickett, Wilson **10**
Pointer Sisters, The **9**
Priest, Maxi **20**
Prince **14**
 Earlier sketch in CM **1**
Rawls, Lou **19**
Redding, Otis **5**
Reese, Della **13**
Reeves, Martha **4**
Richie, Lionel **2**
Riley, Teddy **14**
Robinson, Smokey **1**
Ross, Diana **6**
 Also see Supremes, The
Ruffin, David **6**
 Also see Temptations, The
Sam and Dave **8**
Scaggs, Boz **12**
Secada, Jon **13**
Shanice **14**
Shirelles, The **11**
Shocklee, Hank **15**
Sledge, Percy **15**

Soul II Soul **17**
Spinners , The **21**
Stansfield, Lisa **9**
Staples, Mavis **13**
Staples, Pops **11**
Stewart, Rod **20**
 Earlier sketch in CM **2**
Stone, Sly **8**
Subdudes, The **18**
Supremes, The **6**
 Also see Ross, Diana
Sure!, Al B. **13**
Sweat, Keith **13**
SWV **14**
Temptations, The **3**
Third World **13**
Thomas, Irma **16**
TLC **15**
Thornton, Big Mama **18**
Tony! Toni! Toné! **12**
Toussaint, Allen **11**
Turner, Tina **1**
Vandross, Luther **2**
Was (Not Was) **6**
Waters, Crystal **15**
Watley, Jody **9**
Wexler, Jerry **15**
White, Karyn **21**
Williams, Deniece **1**
Williams, Vanessa **10**
Wilson, Jackie **3**
Winans, The **12**
Winbush, Angela **15**
Womack, Bobby **5**
Wonder, Stevie **17**
 Earlier sketch in CM **2**

Rock
311 **20**
AC/DC **4**
Adam Ant **13**
Adams, Bryan **20**
 Earlier sketch in CM **2**
Aerosmith **3**
Afghan Whigs **17**
Albini, Steve **15**
Alexander, Arthur **14**
Alice in Chains **10**
Allman Brothers, The **6**
Alvin, Dave **17**
America **16**
American Music Club **15**
Anthrax **11**
Archers of Loaf **21**
Babes in Toyland **16**
Bad Brains **16**
Baker, Ginger **16**
 Also see Cream
Ballard, Hank **17**
Band, The **9**
Barenaked Ladies **18**
Barlow, Lou **20**
Basehead **11**
Beach Boys, The **1**
Beastie Boys, The **8**

Harper, Ben **17**
Harrison, George **2**
  Also see Beatles, The
Harry, Deborah **4**
  Also see Blondie
Harvey, Polly Jean **11**
Hatfield, Juliana **12**
  Also see Lemonheads, The
Healey, Jeff **4**
Helmet **15**
Hendrix, Jimi **2**
Henley, Don **3**
  Also see Eagles, The
Henry, Joe **18**
Hiatt, John **8**
Hole **14**
Holland-Dozier-Holland **5**
Hooters **20**
Hootie and the Blowfish **18**
Idol, Billy **3**
INXS **21**
 Earlier sketch in CM **2**
Iron Maiden **10**
Isaak, Chris **6**
Jackson, Joe **4**
Jagger, Mick **7**
  Also see Rolling Stones, The
Jane's Addiction **6**
Jars of Clay **20**
Jayhawks, The **15**
Jefferson Airplane **5**
Jesus Lizard **19**
Jesus and Mary Chain, The **10**
Jethro Tull **8**
Jett, Joan **3**
Joel, Billy **12**
 Earlier sketch in CM **2**
Johansen, David **7**
John, Elton **20**
 Earlier sketch in CM **3**
Jon Spencer Blues Explosion **18**
Joplin, Janis **3**
Journey **21**
Joy Division **19**
Judas Priest **10**
KMFDM **18**
Kennedy, Nigel **8**
Kidjo, Anjelique **17**
King Crimson **17**
Kinks, The **15**
Kiss **5**
Knopfler, Mark **3**
Korn **20**
Kravitz, Lenny **5**
Landreth, Sonny **16**
Led Zeppelin **1**
Leiber and Stoller **14**
Lemonheads, The **12**
Lennon, John **9**
  Also see Beatles, The
Lennon, Julian **2**
Lindley, David **2**
Little Feat **4**
Little Texas **14**

Live **14**
Living Colour **7**
Loggins, Kenny **20**
 Earlier sketch in CM **3**
Los Lobos **2**
Love Spit Love **21**
Love and Rockets **15**
L7 **12**
Luna **18**
Luscious Jackson **19**
Lush **13**
Lydon, John **9**
  Also see Sex Pistols, The
Lynne, Jeff **5**
Lynyrd Skynyrd **9**
MacIsaac, Ashley **21**
Madder Rose **17**
Marilyn Manson **18**
Martin, George **6**
Marx, Richard **3**
McCartney, Paul **4**
  Also see Beatles, The
McClinton, Delbert **14**
MC5, The **9**
McKee, Maria **11**
McMurtry, James **10**
Meat Loaf **12**
Meat Puppets, The **13**
Megadeth **9**
Mekons, The **15**
Mellencamp, John **20**
 Earlier sketch in CM **2**
Metallica **7**
Midnight Oil **11**
Mighty Mighty Bosstones **20**
Mike & the Mechanics **17**
Miller, Steve **2**
Ministry **10**
Moby Grape **12**
Money, Eddie **16**
Moody Blues, The **18**
Morphine **16**
Morrison, Jim **3**
  Also see Doors, The
Morrison, Van **3**
Mötley Crüe **1**
Motörhead **10**
Mould, Bob **10**
Mudhoney **16**
Muldaur, Maria **18**
Myles, Alannah **4**
Nelson, Rick **2**
New York Dolls **20**
Newman, Randy **4**
Nicks, Stevie **2**
  Also see Fleetwood Mac
Nirvana **8**
NRBQ **12**
Nugent, Ted **2**
Oasis **16**
Ocasek, Ric **5**
O'Connor, Sinead **3**
Offspring **19**
Ono, Yoko **11**

Orbison, Roy **2**
Osbourne, Ozzy **3**
Page, Jimmy **4**
  Also see Led Zeppelin
  Also see Yardbirds, The
Palmer, Robert **2**
Pantera **13**
Parker, Graham **10**
Parker, Maceo **7**
Parsons, Alan **12**
Parsons, Gram **7**
  Also see Byrds, The
Pavement **14**
Pearl Jam **12**
Pere Ubu **17**
Perkins, Carl **9**
Petty, Tom **9**
Phillips, Sam **5**
Phish **13**
Pigface **19**
Pink Floyd **2**
Pixies, The **21**
Plant, Robert **2**
  Also see Led Zeppelin
Pogues, The **6**
Poi Dog Pondering **17**
Poison **11**
Police, The **20**
Pop, Iggy **1**
Presley, Elvis **1**
Pretenders, The **8**
Primal Scream **14**
Primus **11**
Prince **14**
 Earlier sketch in CM **1**
Prine, John **7**
Proclaimers, The **13**
Pulp **18**
Queen **6**
Queensryche **8**
Rage Against the Machine **18**
Raitt, Bonnie **3**
Ramones, The **9**
Red Hot Chili Peppers, The **7**
Redd Kross **20**
Reed, Lou **16**
 Earlier sketch in CM **1**
  Also see Velvet Underground, The
Reid, Vernon **2**
  Also see Living Colour
R.E.M. **5**
Replacements, The **7**
Residents, The **14**
Reverend Horton Heat **19**
Reznor, Trent **13**
Richards, Keith **11**
  Also see Rolling Stones, The
Richman, Jonathan **12**
Robertson, Robbie **2**
Rolling Stones, The **3**
Rollins, Henry **11**
Roth, David Lee **1**
  Also see Van Halen
Rubin, Rick **9**

Henderson, Joe **14**
Herman, Woody **12**
Jacquet, Illinois **17**
James, Boney **21**
Kenny G **14**
Kirk, Rahsaan Roland **6**
Koz, Dave **19**
Lateef, Yusef **16**
Lopez, Israel "Cachao" **14**
Lovano, Joe **13**
Marsalis, Branford **10**
Morgan, Frank **9**
Mulligan, Gerry **16**
Najee **21**
Osby, Greg **21**
Parker, Charlie **5**
Parker, Maceo **7**
Pepper, Art **18**
Redman, Joshua **12**
Rollins, Sonny **7**
Sanborn, David **1**
Sanders, Pharoah **16**
Shorter, Wayne **5**
Threadgill, Henry **9**
Washington, Grover, Jr. **5**
Winter, Paul **10**
Young, La Monte **16**
Young, Lester **14**
Zorn, John **15**

Sintir
Hakmoun, Hassan **15**

Songwriters
Acuff, Roy **2**
Adams, Bryan **20**
 Earlier sketch in CM **2**
Albini, Steve **15**
Alexander, Arthur **14**
Allen, Peter **11**
Allison, Mose **17**
Alpert, Herb **11**
Alvin, Dave **17**
Amos, Tori **12**
Anderson, Ian
 See Jethro Tull
Anderson, John **5**
Anka, Paul **2**
Armatrading, Joan **4**
Astbury, Ian
 See Cult, The
Atkins, Chet **5**
Autry, Gene **12**
Bacharach, Burt **20**
 Earlier sketch in CM **1**
Baez, Joan **1**
Baker, Anita **9**
Balin, Marty
 See Jefferson Airplane
Barlow, Lou **20**
Barrett, (Roger) Syd
 See Pink Floyd
Basie, Count **2**
Becker, Walter
 See Steely Dan

Beckley, Gerry
 See America
Belew, Adrian **5**
Benton, Brook **7**
Berg, Matraca **16**
Berlin, Irving **8**
Berry, Chuck **1**
Bjork **16**
 Also see Sugarcubes, The
Black, Clint **5**
Black, Frank **14**
Blades, Ruben **2**
Blige, Mary J. **15**
Bloom, Luka **14**
Bono
 See U2
Brady, Paul **8**
Bragg, Billy **7**
Brickell, Edie **3**
Brooke, Jonatha
 See Story, The
Brooks, Garth **8**
Brown, Bobby **4**
Brown, James **16**
 Earlier sketch in CM **2**
Brown, Junior **15**
Brown, Marty **14**
Browne, Jackson **3**
Buck, Peter
 See R.E.M.
Buck, Robert
 See 10,000 Maniacs
Buckingham, Lindsey **8**
 Also see Fleetwood Mac
Buckley, Tim **14**
Buffett, Jimmy **4**
Bunnell, Dewey
 See America
Burdon, Eric **14**
 Also see War
Burnett, T Bone **13**
Burning Spear **15**
Bush, Kate **4**
Byrne, David **8**
 Also see Talking Heads
Cahn, Sammy **11**
Cale, J. J. **16**
Cale, John **9**
Calloway, Cab **6**
Captain Beefheart **10**
Carpenter, Mary-Chapin **6**
Carter, Carlene **8**
Cash, Johnny **17**
 Earlier sketch in CM **1**
Cash, Rosanne **2**
Cetera, Peter
 See Chicago
Chandra, Sheila **16**
Chapin, Harry **6**
Chapman, Steven Curtis **15**
Chapman, Tracy **4**
Charles, Ray **1**
Chenier, C. J. **15**
Childs, Toni **2**
Chilton, Alex **10**

Clapton, Eric **11**
 Earlier sketch in CM **1**
 Also see Cream
 Also see Yardbirds, The
Clark, Guy **17**
Clements, Vassar **18**
Cleveland, James **1**
Clinton, George **7**
Cockburn, Bruce **8**
Cohen, Leonard **3**
Cole, Lloyd **9**
Cole, Nat King **3**
Collins, Albert **4**
Collins, Judy **4**
Collins, Phil **2**
 Also see Genesis
Cooder, Ry **2**
Cooke, Sam **1**
 Also see Soul Stirrers, The
Collie, Mark **15**
Cooper, Alice **8**
Cope, Julian **16**
Corgan, Billy
 See Smashing Pumpkins
Costello, Elvis **12**
 Earlier sketch in CM **2**
Cotten, Elizabeth **16**
Crenshaw, Marshall **5**
Croce, Jim **3**
Crofts, Dash
 See Seals & Crofts
Cropper, Steve **12**
Crosby, David **3**
 Also see Byrds, The
Crow, Sheryl **18**
Crowe, J. D. **5**
Crowell, Rodney **8**
Daniels, Charlie **6**
Davies, Ray **5**
 Also see Kinks, the
DeBarge, El **14**
DeMent, Iris **13**
Denver, John **1**
Des'ree **15**
Diamond, Neil **1**
Diddley, Bo **3**
Difford, Chris
 See Squeeze
DiFranco, Ani **17**
Dion **4**
Dixon, Willie **10**
Doc Pomus **14**
Domino, Fats **2**
Donelly, Tanya
 See Belly
 Also see Throwing Muses
Donovan **9**
Dorsey, Thomas A. **11**
Doucet, Michael **8**
Dozier, Lamont
 See Holland-Dozier-Holland
Drake, Nick **17**
Dube, Lucky **17**
Duffy, Billy
 See Cult, The

Lavin, Christine **6**
LeDoux, Chris **12**
Lee, Peggy **8**
Lehrer, Tom **7**
Leiber and Stoller **14**
Lennon, John **9**
 Also see Beatles, The
Lennon, Julian **2**
Lewis, Huey **9**
Lightfoot, Gordon **3**
Little Richard **1**
Llanas, Sammy
 See BoDeans, The
L.L. Cool J **5**
Loggins, Kenny **20**
 Earlier sketch in CM **3**
Love, Courtney
 See Hole
Love, Laura **20**
Loveless, Patty **5**
Lovett, Lyle **5**
Lowe, Nick **6**
Lydon, John **9**
 Also see Sex Pistols, The
Lynn, Loretta **2**
Lynne, Jeff **5**
Lynne, Shelby **5**
Lynott, Phil
 See Thin Lizzy
MacColl, Kirsty **12**
MacDonald, Barbara
 See Timbuk 3
MacDonald, Pat
 See Timbuk 3
Madonna **16**
 Earlier sketch in CM **4**
Manilow, Barry **2**
Manzarek, Ray
 See Doors, The
Marley, Bob **3**
Marley, Ziggy **3**
Marx, Richard **3**
Mattea, Kathy **5**
May, Brian
 See Queen
Mayfield, Curtis **8**
MC Breed **17**
McCartney, Paul **4**
 Also see Beatles, The
McClinton, Delbert **14**
McCoury, Del **15**
McDonald, Michael
 See Doobie Brothers, The
McGuinn, Roger
 See Byrds, The
McLachlan, Sarah **12**
McLean, Don **7**
McLennan, Grant **21**
McMurtry, James **10**
MC 900 Ft. Jesus **16**
McTell, Blind Willie **17**
McVie, Christine
 See Fleetwood Mac
Medley, Bill **3**

Melanie **12**
Mellencamp, John **20**
 Earlier sketch in CM **2**
Mercer, Johnny **13**
Merchant, Natalie
 See 10,000 Maniacs
Mercury, Freddie
 See Queen
Michael, George **9**
Miller, Roger **4**
Miller, Steve **2**
Milsap, Ronnie **2**
Mitchell, Joni **17**
 Earlier sketch in CM **2**
Moffatt, Katy **18**
Morrison, Jim **3**
Morrison, Van **3**
Morrissey **10**
Morrissey, Bill **12**
Morton, Jelly Roll **7**
Mould, Bob **10**
Moyet, Alison **12**
Nascimento, Milton **6**
Ndegéocello, Me'Shell **18**
Near, Holly **1**
Nelson, Rick **2**
Nelson, Willie **11**
 Earlier sketch in CM **1**
Nesmith, Mike
 See Monkees, The
Neville, Art
 See Neville Brothers, The
Newman, Randy **4**
Newmann, Kurt
 See BoDeans, The
Nicks, Stevie **2**
Nilsson **10**
Nugent, Ted **2**
Nyro, Laura **12**
Oates, John
 See Hall & Oates
Ocasek, Ric **5**
Ocean, Billy **4**
Ochs, Phil **7**
O'Connor, Sinead **3**
Odetta **7**
Orbison, Roy **2**
Osbourne, Ozzy **3**
Oslin, K. T. **3**
Owens, Buck **2**
Page, Jimmy **4**
 See Led Zeppelin
 Also see Yardbirds, The
Palmer, Robert **2**
Paris, Twila **16**
Parks, Van Dyke **17**
Parnell, Lee Roy **15**
Parker, Graham **10**
Parsons, Gram **7**
 Also see Byrds, The
Parton, Dolly **2**
Paul, Les **2**
Paxton, Tom **5**
Peniston, CeCe **15**

Penn, Michael **4**
Perez, Louie
 See Los Lobos
Perkins, Carl **9**
Perry, Joe
 See Aerosmith
Petty, Tom **9**
Phair, Liz **14**
Phillips, Sam **12**
Pickett, Wilson **10**
Pierson, Kate
 See B-52's, The
Plant, Robert **2**
 Also see Led Zeppelin
Pop, Iggy **1**
Porter, Cole **10**
Prince **14**
 Earlier sketch in CM **1**
Prine, John **7**
Professor Longhair **6**
Rabbitt, Eddie **5**
Reid, Charlie
 See Proclaimers, The
Reid, Craig
 See Proclaimers, The
Reid, Vernon **2**
 Also see Living Colour
Rich, Charlie **3**
Richards, Keith **11**
 Also see Rolling Stones, The
Richey, Kim **20**
Richie, Lionel **2**
Richman, Jonathan **12**
Riley, Teddy **14**
Ritchie, Jean **4**
Robbins, Marty **9**
Roberts, Brad
 See Crash Test Dummies
Robertson, Robbie **2**
Robillard, Duke **2**
Robinson, Smokey **1**
Rodgers, Jimmie **3**
Rodgers, Richard **9**
Roland, Ed
 See Collective Soul
Roth, David Lee **1**
 Also see Van Halen
Russell, Mark **6**
Rutherford, Mike
 See Genesis
Sade **2**
Sager, Carole Bayer **5**
Saliers, Emily
 See Indigo Girls
Sandman, Mark
 See Morphine
Satriani, Joe **4**
Scaggs, Boz **12**
Schneider, Fred III
 See B-52's, The
Scott-Heron, Gil **13**
Scruggs, Earl **3**
Seal **14**
Seals, Dan **9**

Hirt, Al **5**
Isham, Mark **14**
James, Harry **11**
Jones, Quincy **20**
 Earlier sketch in CM **2**
Jones, Thad **19**
Loughnane, Lee **3**
Marsalis, Wynton **20**
 Earlier sketch in CM **6**
Masekela, Hugh **7**
Mighty Mighty Bosstones **20**
Mills, Fred
 See Canadian Brass, The
Oliver, King **15**
Rodney, Red **14**
Romm, Ronald
 See Canadian Brass, The
Sandoval, Arturo **15**
Severinsen, Doc **1**

Tuba
Daellenbach, Charles
 See Canadian Brass, The
Phillips, Harvey **3**

Vibraphone
Burton, Gary **10**
Hampton, Lionel **6**

Jackson, Milt **15**
Norvo, Red **12**

Viola
Dutt, Hank
 See Kronos Quartet
Jones, Michael
 See Kronos Quartet
Killian, Tim
 See Kronos Quartet
Menuhin, Yehudi **11**
Zukerman, Pinchas **4**

Violin
Acuff, Roy **2**
Anderson, Laurie **1**
Bell, Joshua **21**
Bromberg, David **18**
Bush, Sam
 See New Grass Revival, The
Chang, Sarah **7**
Clements, Vassar **18**
Coleman, Ornette **5**
Daniels, Charlie **6**
Doucet, Michael **8**
Germano, Lisa **18**
Gingold, Josef **6**
Grappelli, Stephane **10**

Gray, Ella
 See Kronos Quartet
Harrington, David
 See Kronos Quartet
Hartford, John **1**
Hidalgo, David
 See Los Lobos
Kennedy, Nigel **8**
Krauss, Alison **10**
Lamb, Barbara **19**
Lewis, Roy
 See Kronos Quartet
Marriner, Neville **7**
Menuhin, Yehudi **11**
Midori **7**
O'Connor, Mark **1**
Perlman, Itzhak **2**
Ponty, Jean-Luc **8**
Salerno-Sonnenberg, Nadja **3**
Shallenberger, James
 See Kronos Quartet
Sherba, John
 See Kronos Quartet
Skaggs, Ricky **5**
Stern, Isaac **7**
Whiteman, Paul **17**
Wills, Bob **6**
Zukerman, Pinchas **4**

Cumulative Musicians Index

Volume numbers appear in **bold**.

Aaliyah **21**
Abba **12**
Abbott, Jacqueline
 See Beautiful South
Abbott, Jude
 See Chumbawamba
Abbruzzese, Dave
Abdul, Paula **3**
Abong, Fred
 See Belly
Abrahams, Mick
 See Jethro Tull
Abrantes, Fernando
 See Kraftwerk
AC/DC **4**
Ackerman, Will **3**
Acland, Christopher
 See Lush
Acuff, Roy **2**
Acuna, Alejandro
 See Weather Report
Adam Ant **13**
Adamendes, Elaine
 See Throwing Muses
Adams, Bryan **20**
 Earlier sketch in CM **2**
Adams, Clifford
 See Kool & the Gang
Adams, Craig
 See Cult, The
Adams, Donn
 See NRBQ
Adams, John **8**
Adams, Mark
 See Specials, The
Adams, Oleta **17**
Adams, Terry
 See NRBQ
Adcock, Eddie
 See Country Gentleman, The
Adderly, Cannonball **15**
Adderly, Julian
 See Adderly, Cannonball
Adé, King Sunny **18**
Adler, Steven
 See Guns n' Roses
Aerosmith **3**
Afghan Whigs **17**
Afonso, Marie
 See Zap Mama
AFX
 See Aphex Twin
Ajile
 See Arrested Development

Akingbola, Sola
 See Jamiroquai
Alabama **21**
 Earlier sketch in CM **1**
Albarn, Damon
 See Blur
Albert, Nate
 See Mighty Mighty Bosstones
Alberti, Dorona
 See KMFDM
Albini, Steve **15**
Albuquerque, Michael de
 See Electric Light Orchestra
Alexakis, Art
 See Everclear
Alexander, Arthur **14**
Alexander, Tim
 See Asleep at the Wheel
Alexander, Tim "Herb"
 See Primus
Ali
 See Tribe Called Quest, A
Alice in Chains **10**
Allcock, Martin
 See Jethro Tull
Allen, April
 See C + C Music Factory
Allen, Dave
 See Gang of Four
Allen, Debbie **8**
Allen, Duane
 See Oak Ridge Boys, The
Allen, Geri **10**
Allen, Johnny Ray
 See Subdudes, The
Allen, Papa Dee
 See War
Allen, Peter **11**
Allen, Red
 See Osborne Brothers, The
Allen, Rick
 See Def Leppard
Allen, Ross
 See Mekons, The
All-4-One **17**
Allison, Luther **21**
Allison, Mose **17**
Allman, Duane
 See Allman Brothers, The
Allman, Gregg
 See Allman Brothers, The
Allman Brothers, The **6**
Allsup, Michael Rand
 See Three Dog Night

Alpert, Herb **11**
Alphonso, Roland
 See Skatalites, The
Alston, Andy
 See Del Amitri
Alston, Shirley
 See Shirelles, The
Altan **18**
Alvin, Dave **17**
 Also see X
Am, Svet
 See KMFDM
Amedee, Steve
 See Subdudes, The
Ament, Jeff
 See Pearl Jam
America **16**
American Music Club **15**
Amos, Tori **12**
Anastasio, Trey
 See Phish
Anderson, Al
 See NRBQ
Anderson, Andy
 See Cure, The
Anderson, Brett
 See Suede
Anderson, Cleave
 See Blue Rodeo
Anderson, Emma
 See Lush
Anderson, Gladstone
 See Skatalites, The
Anderson, Ian
 See Jethro Tull
Anderson, John **5**
Anderson, Jon
 See Yes
Anderson, Laurie **1**
Anderson, Marian **8**
Anderson, Pamela
 See Incognito
Anderson, Ray **7**
Anderson, Signe
 See Jefferson Airplane
Andersson, Benny
 See Abba
Andrews, Barry
 See XTC
Andrews, Julie **4**
Andrews, Laverne
 See Andrews Sisters, The
Andrews, Maxene
 See Andrews Sisters, The

Barnes, Micah
　See Nylons, The
Barnwell, Duncan
　See Simple Minds
Barnwell, Ysaye Maria
　See Sweet Honey in the Rock
Barr, Ralph
　See Nitty Gritty Dirt Band, The
Barre, Martin
　See Jethro Tull
Barrere, Paul
　See Little Feat
Barrett, Dicky
　See Mighty Mighty Bosstones
Barrett, (Roger) Syd
　See Pink Floyd
Barron, Christopher
　See Spin Doctors
Bartels, Joanie 13
Bartholomew, Simon
　See Brand New Heavies, The
Bartoli, Cecilia 12
Barton, Lou Ann
　See Fabulous Thunderbirds, The
Bartos, Karl
　See Kraftwerk
Basehead 11
Basher, Mick
　See X
Basia 5
Basie, Count 2
Bass, Colin
　See Camel
Bass, Colin
　See Chumbawamba
Batchelor, Kevin
　See Steel Pulse
Batel, Beate
　See Einstürzende Neubauten
Battin, Skip
　See Byrds, The
Battle, Kathleen 6
Bauer, Judah
　See Jon Spencer Blues Explosion
Baumann, Peter
　See Tangerine Dream
Bautista, Roland
　See Earth, Wind and Fire
Baxter, Jeff
　See Doobie Brothers, The
Bayer Sager, Carole
　See Sager, Carole Bayer
Baylor, Helen 20
Baynton-Power, David
　See James
Bazilian, Eric
　See Hooters
Beach Boys, The 1
Beale, Michael
　See Earth, Wind and Fire
Beard, Frank
　See ZZ Top
Beasley, Paul
　See Mighty Clouds of Joy, The

Beastie Boys, The 8
Beatles, The 2
Beauford, Carter
　See Dave Matthews Band
Beautiful South 19
Beaver Brown Band, The 3
Bechet, Sidney 17
Beck, Jeff 4
　Also see Yardbirds, The
Beck, William
　See Ohio Players
Beck 18
Becker, Walter
　See Steely Dan
Beckford, Theophilus
　See Skatalites, The
Beckley, Gerry
　See America
Bee Gees, The 3
Beers, Garry Gary
　See INXS
Behler, Chuck
　See Megadeth
Beiderbecke, Bix 16
Belafonte, Harry 8
Belew, Adrian 5
　Also see King Crimson
Belfield, Dennis
　See Three Dog Night
Bell, Andy
　See Erasure
Bell, Brian
　See Weezer
Bell, Derek
　See Chieftains, The
Bell, Eric
　See Thin Lizzy
Bell, Jayn
　See Sounds ofBlackness
Bell, Joshua 21
Bell, Melissa
　See Soul II Soul
Bell, Ronald
　See Kool & the Gang
Bell, Taj
　See Charm Farm
Belladonna, Joey
　See Anthrax
Bellamy, David
　See Bellamy Brothers, The
Bellamy, Howard
　See Bellamy Brothers, The
Bellamy Brothers, The 13
Belle, Regina 6
Bello, Frank
　See Anthrax
Belly 16
Belushi, John
　See Blues Brothers, The
Benante, Charlie
　See Anthrax
Benatar, Pat 8
Benedict, Scott
　See Pere Ubu

Ben Folds Five 20
Benitez, Jellybean 15
Bennett, Tony 16
　Earlier sketch in CM 2
Bennett-Nesby, Ann
　See Sounds ofBlackness
Benson, George 9
Benson, Ray
　See Asleep at the Wheel
Benson, Renaldo "Obie"
　See Four Tops, The
Bentley, John
　See Squeeze
Benton, Brook 7
Bentyne, Cheryl
　See Manhattan Transfer, The
Berenyi, Miki
　See Lush
Berg, Matraca 16
Berigan, Bunny 2
Berlin, Irving 8
Berlin, Steve
　See Los Lobos
Bernstein, Leonard 2
Berry, Bill
　See R.E.M.
Berry, Chuck 1
Berry, John 17
Berry, Robert
　See Emerson, Lake & Palmer/Powell
Best, Nathaniel
　See O'Jays, The
Best, Pete
　See Beatles, The
Bettencourt, Nuno
　See Extreme
Better Than Ezra 19
Bettie Serveert 17
Betts, Dicky
　See Allman Brothers, The
Bevan, Bev
　SeeBlack Sabbath
　Also see Electric Light Orchestra
B-52's, The 4
Bezozi, Alan
　See Dog's Eye View
Biafra, Jello 18
Big Audio Dynamite 18
Big Head Todd and the Monsters 20
Big Mike
　See GetoBoys, The
Big Money Odis
　See Digital Underground
Bin Hassan, Umar
　See Last Poets
Bingham, John
　See Fishbone
Binks, Les
　See Judas Priest
Biondo, George
　See Steppenwolf
Birchfield, Benny
　See Osborne Brothers, The
Bird
　See Parker, Charlie

Brookes, Jon
 See Charlatans, The
Brooks, Baba
 See Skatalites, The
Brooks, Garth **8**
Brooks, Leon Eric "Kix"
 See Brooks & Dunn
Brooks & Dunn **12**
Broonzy, Big Bill **13**
Brotherdale, Steve
 See Joy Division
 Also see Smithereens, The
Broudie, Ian
 See Lightning Seeds
Brown, Bobby **4**
Brown, Clarence "Gatemouth" **11**
Brown, Donny
 See Verve Pipe, The
Brown, Duncan
 See Stereolab
Brown, George
 See Kool & the Gang
Brown, Harold
 See War
Brown, Heidi
 See Treadmill Trackstar
Brown, Ian
 See Stone Roses, The
Brown, James **16**
 Earlier sketch in CM **2**
Brown, Jimmy
 See UB40
Brown, Junior **15**
Brown, Marty **14**
Brown, Mick
 See Dokken
Brown, Norman
 See Mills Brothers, The
Brown, Ray **21**
Brown, Ruth **13**
Brown, Selwyn "Bumbo"
 See Steel Pulse
Brown, Steven
 See Tuxedomoon
Brown, Tim
 See Boo Radleys, The
Brown, Tony **14**
Browne, Jackson **3**
 Also see Nitty Gritty Dirt Band, The
Brownstein, Carrie
 See Sleater-Kinney
Brownstone **21**
Brubeck, Dave **8**
Bruce, Dustan
 See Chumbawamba
Bruce, Jack
 See Cream
Bruford, Bill
 See King Crimson
 Also see Yes
Bruster, Thomas
 See Soul Stirrers, The
Bryan, David
 See Bon Jovi
Bryan, Karl

See Skatalites, The
Bryan, Mark
 See Hootie and the Blowfish
Bryant, Elbridge
 See Temptations, The
Bryson, Bill
 See Desert Rose Band, The
Bryson, David
 See Counting Crows
Bryson, Peabo **11**
Buchanan, Wallis
 See Jamiroquai
Buchholz, Francis
 See Scorpions, The
Buchignani, Paul
 See Afghan Whigs
Buck, Mike
 See Fabulous Thunderbirds, The
Buck, Peter
 See R.E.M.
Buck, Robert
 See 10,000 Maniacs
Buckingham, Lindsey **8**
 Also see Fleetwood Mac
Buckley, Betty **16**
 Earlier sketch in CM **1**
Buckley, Tim **14**
Buckwheat Zydeco **6**
Budgie
 See Siouxsie and the Banshees
Buerstatte, Phil
 See White Zombie
Buffalo Tom **18**
Buffett, Jimmy **4**
Bulgarian State Female Vocal Choir, The
 10
Bulgarian State Radio and Television
 Female Vocal Choir, The
 See Bulgarian State Female Vocal Choir,
 The
Bulgin, Lascelle
 See Israel Vibration
Bumbry, Grace **13**
Bumpus, Cornelius
 See Doobie Brothers, The
Bunker, Clive
 See Jethro Tull
Bunnell, Dewey
 See America
Bunskoeke, Herman
 See Bettie Serveert
Burch, Curtis
 See New Grass Revival, The
Burchill, Charlie
 See Simple Minds
Burden, Ian
 See Human League, The
Burdon, Eric **14**
 Also see War
Burgess, Paul
 See Camel
Burgess, Tim
 See Charlatans, The
Burke, Clem
 See Blondie

Burnett, Carol **6**
Burnett, T Bone **13**
Burnette, Billy
 See Fleetwood Mac
Burnham, Hugo
 See Gang of Four
Burning Spear **15**
Burns, Bob
 See Lynyrd Skynyrd
Burns, Karl
 See Fall, The
Burr, Clive
 See Iron Maiden
Burrell, Kenny **11**
Burrell
 See King Crimson
Burton, Cliff
 See Metallica
Burton, Gary **10**
Burton, Tim
 See Mighty Mighty Bosstones
Busby, Jheryl **9**
Bush **18**
Bush, Dave
 See Fall, The
Bush, John
 See Anthrax
Bush, Kate **4**
Bush, Sam
 See New Grass Revival, The
Bushwick, Bill
 See Geto Boys, The
Busta Rhymes **18**
Butler, Bernard
 See Suede
Butler, Richard
 See Love Spit Love
Butler, Terry "Geezer"
 See Black Sabbath
Butler, Tim
 See Love Spit Love
Butterfly
 See Digable Planets
Butthole Surfers **16**
Buzzcocks, The **9**
Byers, Roddy
 See Specials, The
Byrds, The **8**
Byrne, David **8**
 Also see Talking Heads
Byrne, Dermot
 See Altan
Byrom, Larry
 See Steppenwolf
Byron, David
 See Uriah Heep
Byron, Lord T.
 See Lords of Acid
C + C Music Factory **16**
Cabaret Voltaire **18**
Cachao
 See Lopez, Israel "Cachao"
Caesar, Shirley **17**
Cafferty, John
 See Beaver Brown Band, The

Chevalier, Maurice **6**
Chevron, Phillip
  See Pogues, The
Chicago **3**
Chieftains, The **7**
Childress, Ross
  See Collective Soul
Childs, Toni **2**
Chilton, Alex **10**
Chimes, Terry
  See Clash, The
Chopmaster J
  See Digital Underground
Christ, John
  See Danzig
Christian, Charlie **11**
Christina, Fran
  See Fabulous Thunderbirds, The
  Also see Roomful of Blues
Chuck D
  See Public Enemy
Chumbawamba **21**
Chung, Mark
  See Einstürzende Neubauten
Church, Kevin
  See Country Gentlemen, The
Church, The **14**
Cieka, Rob
  See Boo Radleys, The
Cinderella **16**
Cinelu, Mino
  See Weather Report
Circle Jerks, The **17**
Clapton, Eric **11**
  Earlier sketch in CM **1**
  Also see Cream
  Also see Yardbirds, The
Clark, Dave
  See Dave Clark Five, The
Clark, Dick **2**
Clark, Gene
  See Byrds, The
Clark, Guy **17**
Clark, Keith
  See Circle Jerks, The
Clark, Mike
  See Suicidal Tendencies
Clark, Roy **1**
Clark, Steve
  See Def Leppard
Clark, Terri **19**
Clark, Tony
  See Blessid Union of Souls
Clarke, "Fast" Eddie
  See Motörhead
Clarke, Michael
  See Byrds, The
Clarke, Stanley **3**
Clarke, Vince
  See Depeche Mode
  Also see Erasure
Clarke, William
  See Third World
Clash, The **4**

Clayderman, Richard **1**
Claypool, Les
  See Primus
Clayton, Adam
  See U2
Clayton, Sam
  See Little Feat
Clayton-Thomas, David
  SeeBlood, Sweat and Tears
Cleaves, Jessica
  See Earth, Wind and Fire
Clegg, Johnny **8**
Clements, Vassar **18**
Clemons, Clarence **7**
Cleveland, James **1**
Cliburn, Van **13**
Cliff, Jimmy **8**
Clifford, Douglas Ray
  See Creedence Clearwater Revival
Cline, Nels
  See Geraldine Fibbers
Cline, Patsy **5**
Clinton, George **7**
Clivilles, Robert
  See C + C Music Factory
Clooney, Rosemary **9**
Coasters, The **5**
Cobain, Kurt
  See Nirvana
Cobham, Billy
  See Mahavishnu Orchestra
Cochran, Bobby
  See Steppenwolf
Cockburn, Bruce **8**
Cocker, Jarvis
  See Pulp
Cocker, Joe **4**
Cocking, William "Willigan"
  See Mystic Revealers
Coco the Electronic Monkey Wizard
  See Man or Astroman?
Cocteau Twins, The **12**
Codenys, Patrick
  See Front 242
Codling, Neil
  See Suede
Coe, David Allan **4**
Coffey, Jeff
  See Butthole Surfers
Coffie, Calton
  See Inner Circle
Cohen, Jeremy
  See Turtle Island String Quartet
Cohen, Leonard **3**
Cohen, Porky
  See Roomful of Blues
Colbourn, Chris
  See Buffalo Tom
Cole, David
  See C + C Music Factory
Cole, Holly **18**
Cole, Lloyd **9**
Cole, Natalie **21**
  Earlier sketch in CM **1**

Cole, Nat King **3**
Cole, Paula **20**
Cole, Ralph
  See Nylons, The
Coleman, Ornette **5**
Collective Soul **16**
Colley, Dana
  See Morphine
Collie, Mark **15**
Collin, Phil
  See Def Leppard
Collins, Albert **19**
  Earlier sketch in CM **4**
Collins, Allen
  See Lynyrd Skynyrd
Collins, Bootsy **8**
Collins, Judy **4**
Collins, Mark
  See Charlatans, The
Collins, Mel
  See Camel
Collins, Mel
  See King Crimson
Collins, Phil **20**
  Earlier sketch in CM **2**
  Also see Genesis
Collins, Rob
  See Charlatans, The
Collins, William
  See Collins, Bootsy
Colomby, Bobby
  See Blood, Sweat and Tears
Colt, Johnny
  See Black Crowes, The
Coltrane, John **4**
Colvin, Shawn **11**
Combs, Sean "Puffy" **16**
Comess, Aaron
  See Spin Doctors
Como, Perry **14**
Conneff, Kevin
  See Chieftains, The
Connelly, Chris
  See KMFDM
Connick, Harry, Jr. **4**
Connors, Marc
  See Nylons, The
Conti, Neil
  See Prefab Sprout
Conway, Billy
  See Morphine
Conway, Gerry
  See Pentangle
Cooder, Ry **2**
Cook, Jeffrey Alan
  See Alabama
Cook, Paul
  See Sex Pistols, The
Cook, Stuart
  See Creedence Clearwater Revival
Cook, Wayne
  See Steppenwolf
Cooke, Sam **1**
  Also see Soul Stirrers, The

Danzig **7**
Danzig, Glenn
  See Danzig
D'Arby, Terence Trent **3**
Darin, Bobby **4**
Darling, Eric
  See Weavers, The
Darriau, Matt
  See Klezmatics, The
Darvill, Benjamin
  See Crash Test Dummies
Das EFX **14**
Daugherty, Jay Dee
  See Church, The
Daulne, Marie
  See Zap Mama
Dave, Doggy
  See Lords of Acid
Dave Clark Five, The **12**
Dave Matthews Band **18**
Davenport, N'Dea
  See Brand New Heavies, The
Davidson, Lenny
  See Dave Clark Five, The
Davies, Dave
  See Kinks, The
Davies, Ray **5**
  Also see Kinks, The
Davies, Saul
  See James
Davis, Anthony **17**
Davis, Chip **4**
Davis, Clive **14**
Davis, Jonathan
  See Korn
Davis, Linda **21**
Davis, Michael
  See MC5, The
Davis, Miles **1**
Davis, Reverend Gary **18**
Davis, Sammy, Jr. **4**
Davis, Skeeter **15**
Davis, Spencer
  See Spencer Davis Group
Davis, Steve
  See Mystic Revealers
Davis, Zelma
  See C + C Music Factory
Dawdy, Cheryl
  See Chenille Sisters, The
Dayne, Taylor **4**
dc Talk **18**
de Albuquerque, Michael
  See Electric Light Orchestra
Deacon, John
  See Queen
Dead Can Dance **16**
Deakin, Paul
  See Mavericks, The
Deal, Kelley
  See Breeders
Deal, Kim
  See Breeders
  Also see Pixies, The
Dean, Billy **19**

DeBarge, El **14**
de Coster, Jean Paul
  See 2 Unlimited
Dee, Mikkey
  See Dokken
  Also see Motörhead
Deee-lite **9**
Deep Forest **18**
Deep Purple **11**
Def Leppard **3**
DeGarmo, Chris
  See Queensryche
de Grassi, Alex **6**
Deily, Ben
  See Lemonheads, The
DeJohnette, Jack **7**
Del Rubio Triplets **21**
Delaet, Nathalie
  See Lords of Acid
De La Soul **7**
DeLeo, Dean
  See Stone Temple Pilots
DeLeo, Robert
  See Stone Temple Pilots
De La Luna, Shai
  See Lords of Acid
de la Rocha, Zack
  See Rage Against the Machine
DeLorenzo, Victor
  See Violent Femmes
Del Amitri **18**
Del Mar, Candy
  See Cramps, The
Delp, Brad
  See Boston
de Lucia, Paco **1**
DeMent, Iris **13**
Demeski, Stanley
  See Luna
De Meyer, Jean-Luc
  See Front 242
Demos, Greg
  See GuidedBy Voices
Dempsey, Michael
  See Cure, The
Dennis, Garth
  See Black Uhuru
Denison, Duane
  See Jesus Lizard
Densmore, John
  See Doors, The
Dent, Cedric
  See Take 6
Denton, Sandy
  See Salt-N-Pepa
Denver, John **1**
De Oliveria, Laudir
  See Chicago
Depeche Mode **5**
Derosier, Michael
  See Heart
de Prume, Ivan
  See White Zombie
Desaulniers, Stephen
  See Scud Mountain Boys

Desert Rose Band, The **4**
Des'ree **15**
DeVille, C. C.
  See Poison
Deschamps, Kim
  See Blue Rodeo
Destri, Jimmy
  See Blondie
Deupree, Jerome
  See Morphine
Deutrom, Mark
  See Melvins
Devo **13**
Devoto, Howard
  See Buzzcocks, The
DeWitt, Lew C.
  See Statler Brothers, The
de Young, Joyce
  See Andrews Sisters, The
Dexter X
  See Man or Astroman?
Diagram, Andy
  See James
Diamond "Dimebag" Darrell
  See Pantera
Diamond, Mike
  See Beastie Boys, The
Diamond, Neil **1**
Diamond Rio **11**
Di'anno, Paul
  See Iron Maiden
Dibango, Manu **14**
Dickens, Little Jimmy **7**
Dickerson, B.B.
  See War
Dickinson, Paul Bruce
  See Iron Maiden
Dickinson, Rob
  See Catherine Wheel
Diddley, Bo **3**
Diffie, Joe **10**
Difford, Chris
  See Squeeze
DiFranco, Ani **17**
Digable Planets **15**
Diggle, Steve
  SeeBuzzcocks, The
Digital Underground **9**
DiMant, Leor
  See House of Pain
Di Meola, Al **12**
DiMucci, Dion
  See Dion
DiNizo, Pat
  See Smithereens, The
Dilworth, Joe
  See Stereolab
Dinning, Dean
  See Toad the Wet Sprocket
Dinosaur Jr. **10**
Dio, Ronnie James
  See Black Sabbath
Dion **4**
Dion, Céline **12**

Edmonton, Jerry
  See Steppenwolf
Edwards, Dennis
  See Temptations, The
Edwards, Edgar
  See Spinners, The
Edwards, Gordon
  See Kinks, The
Edwards, John
  See Spinners , The
Edwards, Johnny
  See Foreigner
Edwards, Leroy "Lion"
  See Mystic Revealers
Edwards, Mike
  See Electric Light Orchestra
Edwards, Nokie
  See Ventures, The
Ehran
  See Lords of Acid
Einheit
  See Einstürzende Neubauten
Einheit, F.M.
  See KMFDM
Einstürzende Neubauten 13
Eitzel, Mark
  See American Music Club
Eklund, Greg
  See Everclear
El-Hadi, Sulieman
  See Last Poets
Eldon, Thór
  See Sugarcubes, The
Eldridge, Ben
  See Seldom Scene, The
Eldridge, Roy 9
  Also see McKinney's Cotton Pickers
Electric Light Orchestra 7
Elfman, Danny 9
Elias, Manny
  See Tears for Fears
Ellefson, Dave
  See Megadeth
Ellington, Duke 2
Elliot, Cass 5
Elliot, Joe
  See Def Leppard
Elliott, Cass
  See Mamas and the Papas
Elliott, Dennis
  See Foreigner
Elliott, Doug
  See Odds
Ellis, Bobby
  See Skatalites, The
Ellis, Herb 18
Ellis, Terry
  See En Vogue
ELO
  See Electric Light Orchestra
Ely, John
  See Asleep at the Wheel
Ely, Vince
  See Cure, The

Emerson, Bill
  See Country Gentlemen, The
Emerson, Keith
  See Emerson, Lake & Palmer/Powell
Emerson, Lake & Palmer/Powell 5
Emery, Jill
  See Hole
Emmanuel, Tommy 21
English Beat, The 9
Enigma 14
Eno, Brian 8
Enos, Bob
  See Roomful of Blues
Enright, Pat
  See Nashville Bluegrass Band
Entwistle, John
  See Who, The
En Vogue 10
Enya 6
EPMD 10
Erasure 11
EricB.
  See Eric B. and Rakim
Eric B. and Rakim 9
Erickson, Roky 16
Erlandson, Eric
  See Hole
Erskine, Peter
  See Weather Report
Ertegun, Ahmet 10
Esch, En
  See KMFDM
Escovedo, Alejandro 18
Eshe, Montsho
  See Arrested Development
Eskelin, Ian 19
Esquivel, Juan 17
Estefan, Gloria 15
  Earlier sketch in CM 2
Estrada, Roy
  See Little Feat
Etheridge, Melissa 16
  Earlier sketch in CM 4
Eurythmics 6
Evan, John
  See Jethro Tull
Evans, Bill 17
Evans, Dick
  See U2
Evans, Gil 17
Evans, Mark
  See AC/DC
Evans, Shane
  See Collective Soul
Everclear 18
Everlast
  See House of Pain
Everly, Don
  See Everly Brothers, The
Everly, Phil
  See Everly Brothers, The
Everly Brothers, The 2
Everman, Jason
  See Soundgarden

Everything But The Girl 15
Evora, Cesaria 19
Ewen, Alvin
  See Steel Pulse
Exkano, Paul
  See Five Blind Boys of Alabama
Exposé 4
Extreme 10
Ezell, Ralph
  See Shenandoah
Fabian 5
Fabulous Thunderbirds, The 1
Fadden, Jimmie
  See Nitty Gritty DirtBand, The
Fagan, Don
  See Steely Dan
Fahey, John 17
Faithfull, Marianne 14
Faith No More 7
Fakir, Abdul "Duke"
  See Four Tops, The
Falconer, Earl
  See UB40
Fall, The 12
Fallon, David
  See Chieftains, The
Fältskog, Agnetha
  See Abba
Fambrough, Henry
  See Spinners, The
Farley, J. J.
  See Soul Stirrers, The
Farndon, Pete
  See Pretenders, The
Farrar, Jay
  See Son Volt
Farrell, Perry
  See Jane's Addiction
Farris, Dionne
  See Arrested Development
Farris, Tim
  See Israel Vibration
Farriss, Andrew
  See INXS
Farriss, Jon
  See INXS
Farriss, Tim
  See INXS
Fay, Johnny
  See Tragically Hip, The
Fay, Martin
  See Chieftains, The
Fearnley, James
  See Pogues, The
Fehlmann, Thomas
  See Orb, The
Feinstein, Michael 6
Fela
  See Kuti, Fela
Felber, Dean
  See Hootie and the Blowfish
Felder, Don
  See Eagles, The
Feldman, Eric Drew
  See Pere Ubu

Gadler, Frank
Gagliardi, Ed
  See Foreigner
Gahan, Dave
  See Depeche Mode
Gaines, Steve
  See Lynyrd Skynyrd
Gaines, Timothy
  See Stryper
Galea, Darren
  See Jamiroquai
Galás, Diamanda **16**
Gale, Melvyn
  See Electric Light Orchestra
Gallagher, Liam
  See Oasis
Gallagher, Noel
  See Oasis
Gallup, Simon
  See Cure, The
Galore, Lady
  See Lords of Acid
Galway, James **3**
Gambill, Roger
  See Kingston Trio, The
Gamble, Cheryl "Coko"
  See SWV
Gane, Tim
  See Stereolab
Gang of Four **8**
Gang Starr **13**
Gano, Gordon
  See Violent Femmes
Garcia, Dean
  See Curve
Garcia, Jerry **4**
  Also see Grateful Dead, The
Garcia, Leddie
  See Poi Dog Pondering
Gardner, Carl
  See Coasters, The
Gardner, Suzi
  See L7
Garfunkel, Art **4**
Garland, Judy **6**
Garrett, Peter
  See Midnight Oil
Garrett, Scott
  See Cult, The
Garvey, Steve
  See Buzzcocks, The
Gaskill, Jerry
  See King's X
Gatton, Danny **16**
Gaudreau, Jimmy
  See Country Gentlemen, The
Gaugh, "Bud" Floyd, IV
  See Sublime
Gavurin, David
  See Sundays, The
Gaye, Marvin **4**
Gaynor, Mel
  See Simple Minds
Gayol, Rafael "Danny"
  See BoDeans

Gayle, Crystal **1**
Geary, Paul
  See Extreme
Gee, Rosco
  See Traffic
Geffen, David **8**
Geldof, Bob **9**
Genesis **4**
Gentling, Matt
  See Archers of Loaf
Gentry, Teddy Wayne
  See Alabama
George, Lowell
  See Little Feat
George, Rocky
  See Suicidal Tendencies
Georges, Bernard
  See Throwing Muses
Georgiev, Ivan
  See Tuxedomoon
Geraldine Fibbers **21**
Germano, Lisa **18**
Gerrard, Lisa
  See Dead Can Dance
Gershwin, George and Ira **11**
GetoBoys, The **11**
Getz, Stan **12**
Giammalvo, Chris
  See Madder Rose
Gianni, Angelo
  See Treadmill Trackstar
Gibb, Barry
  See Bee Gees, The
Gibb, Maurice
  See Bee Gees, The
Gibb, Robin
  See Bee Gees, The
Gibbons, Billy
  See ZZ Top
Gibbons, Ian
  See Kinks, The
Giblin, John
  See Simple Minds
Gibson, Debbie **1**
Gibson, Wilf
  See Electric Light Orchestra
Gifford, Katharine
  See Stereolab
Gifford, Peter
  See Midnight Oil
Gift, Roland **3**
Gilbert, Gillian
  See New Order
Gilbert, Nicole Nicci
  See Brownstone
Gilbert, Ronnie
  See Weavers, The
Gilbert, Simon
  See Suede
Giles, Michael
  See King Crimson
Gilkyson, Tony
  See X
Gill, Andy
  See Gang of Four

Gill, Janis
  See Sweethearts of the Rodeo
Gill, Johnny **20**
Gill, Pete
  See Motörhead
Gill, Vince **7**
Gillan, Ian
  See Deep Purple
Gillespie, Bobby
  See Primal Scream
Gillespie, Dizzy **6**
Gilley, Mickey **7**
Gillian, Ian
  See Black Sabbath
Gillies, Ben
  See Silverchair
Gillingham, Charles
  See Counting Crows
Gilmore, Jimmie Dale **11**
Gilmour, David
  See Pink Floyd
Gin Blossoms **18**
Gingold, Josef **6**
Gioia
  See Exposé
Gipsy Kings, The **8**
Gittleman, Joe
  See Mighty Mighty Bosstones
Glass, Philip **1**
Glasscock, John
  See Jethro Tull
Glennie, Jim
  See James
Glitter, Gary **19**
Glover, Corey
  See Living Colour
Glover, Roger
  See Deep Purple
Gobel, Robert
  See Kool & the Gang
Godchaux, Donna
  See Grateful Dead, The
Godchaux, Keith
  See Grateful Dead, The
Goettel, Dwayne Rudolf
  See Skinny Puppy
Gogin, Toni
  See Sleater-Kinney
Golden, William Lee
  See Oak Ridge Boys, The
Golding, Lynval
  See Specials, The
Goldsmith, William
  See Foo Fighters
Goldstein, Jerry
  See War
Golson, Benny **21**
Goo Goo Dolls, The **16**
Gooden, Ramone Pee Wee
  See Digital Underground
Goodman, Benny **4**
Goodman, Jerry
  See Mahavishnu Orchestra
Goodridge, Robin
  See Bush

Haley, Mark
  See Kinks, The
Halford, Rob
  See Judas Priest
Hall, Daryl
  See Hall & Oates
Hall, Lance
  See Inner Circle
Hall, Randall
  See Lynyrd Skynyrd
Hall, Terry
  See Specials, The
Hall, Tom T. **4**
Hall, Tony
  See Neville Brothers, The
Hall & Oates **6**
Halliday, Toni
  See Curve
Hamer, Harry
  See Chumbawamba
Hamilton, Frank
  See Weavers, The
Hamilton, Katie
  See Treadmill Trackstar
Hamilton, Milton
  See Third World
Hamilton, Page
  See Helmet
Hamilton, Tom
  See Aerosmith
Hamlisch, Marvin **1**
Hammer, Jan **21**
  Also see Mahavishnu Orchestra
Hammer, M.C. **5**
Hammerstein, Oscar
  See Rodgers, Richard
Hammett, Kirk
  See Metallica
Hammon, Ron
  See War
Hammond, John **6**
Hammond-Hammond, Jeffrey
  See Jethro Tull
Hampson, Sharon
  See Sharon, Lois & Bram
Hampson, Thomas **12**
Hampton, Lionel **6**
Hancock, Herbie **8**
Handy, W. C. **7**
Hanley, Steve
  See Fall, The
Hanna, Jeff
  See Nitty Gritty Dirt Band, The
Hanneman, Jeff
  See Slayer
Hannon, Frank
  See Tesla
Hannan, Patrick
  See Sundays, The
Hansen, Mary
  See Stereolab
Hanson **20**
Hanson, Isaac
  See Hanson

Hanson, Taylor
  See Hanson
Hanson, Zachary
  See Hanson
Hardcastle, Paul **20**
Hardin, Eddie
  See Spencer Davis Group
Hardin, Tim **18**
Harding, John Wesley **6**
Hardson, Tre "Slimkid"
  See Pharcyde, The
Hargrove, Kornell
  See Poi Dog Pondering
Hargrove, Roy **15**
Harley, Bill **7**
Harper, Ben **17**
Harper, Raymond
  See Skatalites, The
Harrell, Andre **16**
Harrell, Lynn **3**
Harrington, Carrie
  See Sounds of Blackness
Harrington, David
  See Kronos Quartet
Harris, Addie "Micki"
  See Shirelles, The
Harris, Damon Otis
  See Temptations, The
Harris, Eddie **15**
Harris, Emmylou **4**
Harris, Evelyn
  See Sweet Honey in the Rock
Harris, Gerard
  See Kool & the Gang
Harris, James
  See Echobelly
Harris, Lee
  See Talk Talk
Harris, Mary
  See Spearhead
Harris, R. H.
  See Soul Stirrers, The
Harris, Steve
  See Iron Maiden
Harrison, George **2**
  Also see Beatles, The
Harrison, Jerry
  See Talking Heads
Harrison, Nigel
  See Blondie
Harrison, Richard
  See Stereolab
Harry, Deborah **4**
  Also see Blondie
Hart, Lorenz
  See Rodgers, Richard
Hart, Mark
  See Crowded House
Hart, Mickey
  See Grateful Dead, The
Hart, Tim
  See Steeleye Span
Hartford, John **1**
Hartke, Stephen **5**

Hartley, Matthieu
  See Cure, The
Hartman, Bob
  See Petra
Hartman, John
  See Doobie Brothers, The
Hartnoll, Paul
  See Orbital
Hartnoll, Phil
  See Orbital
Harvey, Bernard "Touter"
  See Inner Circle
Harvey, Philip "Daddae"
  See Soul II Soul
Harvey, Polly Jean **11**
Harvie, Iain
  See Del Amitri
Harwood, Justin
  See Luna
Haseltine, Dan
  See Jars of Clay
Hashian
  See Boston
Haskell, Gordon
  See King Crimson
Haskins, Kevin
  See Love and Rockets
Haslinger, Paul
  See Tangerine Dream
Hassan, Norman
  See UB40
Hatfield, Juliana **12**
  Also see Lemonheads, The
Hauser, Tim
  See Manhattan Transfer, The
Havens, Richie **11**
Hawes, Dave
  See Catherine Wheel
Hawkes, Greg
  See Cars, The
Hawkins, Coleman **11**
Hawkins, Erskine **19**
Hawkins, Nick
  See Big Audio Dynamite
Hawkins, Roger
  See Traffic
Hawkins, Screamin' Jay **8**
Hawkins, Sophie B. **21**
Hawkins, Taylor
  See Foo Fighters
Hawkins, Tramaine **17**
Hay, George D. **3**
Hayes, Isaac **10**
Hayes, Roland **13**
Haynes, Gibby
  See Butthole Surfers
Haynes, Warren
  See Allman Brothers, The
Hays, Lee
  See Weavers, The
Hayward, David Justin
  See Moody Blues, The
Hayward, Richard
  See Little Feat

Horton, Walter **19**
Hossack, Michael
　See Doobie Brothers, The
House, Son **11**
House of Pain **14**
Houston, Cissy **6**
Houston, Whitney **8**
Howard, Harlan **15**
Howe, Steve
　See Yes
Howell, Porter
　See Little Texas
Howlin' Wolf **6**
H.R.
　See Bad Brains
Hubbard, Greg "Hobie"
　See Sawyer Brown
Hubbard, Preston
　See Fabulous Thunderbirds, The
　Also see Roomful of Blues
Huber, Connie
　See Chenille Sisters, The
Hudson, Earl
　See Bad Brains
Hudson, Garth
　See Band, The
Huffman, Doug
　See Boston
Hughes, Bruce
　See Cracker
Hughes, Glenn
　See Black Sabbath
Hughes, Glenn
　See Village People, The
Hughes, Leon
　See Coasters, The
Human League, The **17**
Humes, Helen **19**
Humperdinck, Engelbert **19**
Humphreys, Paul
　See Orchestral Manoeuvres in the Dark
Hunt, Darryl
　See Pogues, The
Hunter, Alberta **7**
Hunter, Mark
　See James
Hunter, Shepherd "Ben"
　See Soundgarden
Hurley, George
　See fIREHOSE
Hurst, Ron
　See Steppenwolf
Hutchence, Michael
　See INXS
Hutchings, Ashley
　See Steeleye Span
Huth, Todd
　See Primus
Hyatt, Aitch
　See Specials, The
Hyman, Rob
　See Hooters
Hyslop, Kenny
　See Simple Minds

Hütter, Ralf
　See Kraftwerk
Hutton, Danny
　See Three Dog Night
Huxley, Rick
　See Dave Clark Five, The
Hyman, Jerry
　See Blood, Sweat and Tears
Hynde, Chrissie
　See Pretenders, The
Ian, Janis **5**
Ian, Scott
　See Anthrax
Ian and Sylvia **18**
Ibbotson, Jimmy
　See Nitty Gritty Dirt Band, The
Ibold, Mark
　See Pavement
Ice Cube **10**
　Also see N.W.A
Ice-T **7**
Idol, Billy **3**
Iglesias, Julio **20**
　Earlier sketch in CM **2**
Iha, James
　See Smashing Pumpkins
Incognito **16**
Indigo Girls **20**
　Earlier sketch in CM **3**
Inez, Mike
　See Alice in Chains
Infante, Frank
　See Blondie
Ingram, James **11**
Inner Circle **15**
Innes, Andrew
　See Primal Scream
Innis, Dave
　See Restless Heart
Interior, Lux
　See Cramps, The
INXS **21**
　Earlier sketch in CM **2**
Iommi, Tony
　See Black Sa bbath
Iron Maiden **10**
Irons, Jack
　See Red Hot Chili Peppers, The
Isaak, Chris **6**
Isham, Mark **14**
Isles, Bill
　See O'Jays, The
Isley, Ernie
　See Isley Brothers, The
Isley, Marvin
　See Isley Brothers, The
Isley, O'Kelly, Jr.
　See Isley Brothers, The
Isley, Ronald
　See Isley Brothers, The
Isley, Rudolph
　See Isley Brothers, The
Isley Brothers, The **8**
Israel Vibration **21**

Ives, Burl **12**
Ivey, Michael
　See Basehead
J.
　See White Zombie
J, David
　See Love and Rockets
Jabs, Matthias
　See Scorpions, The
Jackson, Alan **7**
Jackson, Eddie
　See Queensryche
Jackson, Freddie **3**
Jackson, Jackie
　See Jacksons, The
Jackson, Janet **16**
　Earlier sketch in CM **3**
Jackson, Jermaine
　See Jacksons, The
Jackson, Joe **4**
Jackson, Karen
　See Supremes, The
Jackson, Mahalia **8**
Jackson, Marlon
　See Jacksons, The
Jackson, Michael **17**
　Earlier sketch in CM **1**
　Also see Jacksons, The
Jackson, Millie **14**
Jackson, Milt **15**
Jackson, Pervis
　See Spinners , The
Jackson, Randy
　See Jacksons, The
Jackson, Tito
　See Jacksons, The
Jackson 5, The
　See Jacksons, The
Jacksons, The **7**
Jacobs, Jeff
　See Foreigner
Jacobs, Walter
　See Little Walter
Jacox, Martin
　See Soul Stirrers, The
Jacquet, Illinois **17**
Jade 4U
　See Lords of Acid
Jaffee, Rami
　See Wallflowers, The
Jagger, Mick **7**
　Also see Rolling Stones, The
Jairo T.
　See Sepultura
Jalal
　See Last Poets
Jam, Jimmy
　See Jam, Jimmy, and Terry Lewis
Jam, Jimmy, and Terry Lewis **11**
Jam Master Jay
　See Run-D.M.C.
James **12**
James, Alex
　See Blur

Jones, Thad **19**
Jones, Tom **11**
Jones, Will "Dub"
　See Coasters, The
Joplin, Janis **3**
Joplin, Scott **10**
Jordan, Lonnie
　See War
Jordan, Louis **11**
Jordan, Stanley **1**
Jorgensor, John
　See Desert Rose Band, The
Joseph-I, Israel
　See Bad Brains
Jourgensen, Al
　See Ministry
Journey **21**
Joyce, Mike
　See Buzzcocks, The
　Also see Smiths, The
Joy Division **19**
Judas Priest **10**
Judd, Naomi
　See Judds, The
Judd, Wynonna
　See Judds, The
　Also see Wynonna
Judds, The **2**
Juhlin, Dag
　See Poi Dog Pondering
Jukebox
　See Geto Boys, The
Jungle DJ "Towa" Towa
　See Deee-lite
Jurado, Jeanette
　See Exposé
Kabongo, Sabine
　See Zap Mama
Kahlil, Aisha
　See Sweet Honey in the Rock
Kain, Gylan
　See Last Poets
Kakoulli, Harry
　See Squeeze
Kalligan, Dick
　See Blood, Sweat and Tears
Kaminski, Mik
　See Electric Light Orchestra
Kamomiya, Ryo
　See Pizzicato Five
Kanal, Tony
　See No Doubt
Kanawa, Kiri Te
　See Te Kanawa, Kiri
Kane, Arthur
　See New York Dolls
Kane, Big Daddy **7**
Kane, Nick
　See Mavericks, The
Kannberg, Scott
　See Pavement
Kanter, Paul
　See Jefferson Airplane
Karajan, Herbert von
　See von Karajan, Herbert

Kath, Terry
　See Chicago
Kato, Nash
　See Urge Overkill
Katz, Simon
　See Jamiroquai
Katz, Steve
　See Blood, Sweat and Tears
Kaukonen, Jorma
　See Jefferson Airplane
Kavanagh, Chris
　See Big Audio Dynamite
Kay, Jason
　See Jamiroquai
Kay, John
　See Steppenwolf
Kaye, Tony
　See Yes
Kay Gee
　See Naughty by Nature
K-Ci
　See Jodeci
Kean, Martin
　See Stereolab
Keane, Sean
　See Chieftains, The
Kee, John P. **15**
Keelor, Greg
　See Blue Rodeo
Keenan, Maynard James
　See Tool
Keifer, Tom
　See Cinderella
Keitaro
　See Pizzicato Five
Keith, Jeff
　See Tesla
Keith, Toby **17**
Kelly, Charlotte
　See Soul II Soul
Kelly, Kevin
　See Byrds, The
Kelly, Rashaan
　See US3
Kemp, Rick
　See Steeleye Span
Kendrick, David
　See Devo
Kendricks, Eddie
　See Temptations, The
Kennedy, Delious
　See All-4-One
Kennedy, Frankie
　See Altan
Kennedy, Nigel **8**
Kenner, Doris
　See Shirelles, The
Kenny G **14**
Kenton, Stan **21**
Kentucky Headhunters, The **5**
Kern, Jerome **13**
Kerr, Jim
　See Simple Minds
Kershaw, Sammy **15**
Ketchum, Hal **14**

Key, Cevin
　See Skinny Puppy
Keyser, Alex
　See Echobelly
Khan, Chaka **19**
　Earlier sketch in CM **9**
Khan, Nusrat Fateh Ali **13**
Khan, Praga
　See Lords of Acid
Kibble, Mark
　See Take 6
Kibby, Walter
　See Fishbone
Kick, Johnny
　See Madder Rose
Kid 'n Play **5**
Kidjo, Anjelique **17**
Kiedis, Anthony
　See Red Hot Chili Peppers, The
Kilbey, Steve
　See Church, The
Killian, Tim
　See Kronos Quartet
Kimball, Jennifer
　See Story, The
Kimball, Jim
　See Jesus Lizard
Kimble, Paul
　See Grant Lee Buffalo
Kincaid, Jan
　See Brand New Heavies, The
Kinchla, Chan
　See Blues Traveler
King, Albert **2**
King, B.B. **1**
King, Andy
　See Hooters
King, Ben E. **7**
King, Bob
　See Soul Stirrers, The
King, Carole **6**
King, Ed
　See Lynyrd Skynyrd
King, Freddy **17**
King, Jon
　See Gang of Four
King, Kerry
　See Slayer
King, Philip
　See Lush
King Ad-Rock
　See BeastieBoys, The
King Crimson **17**
Kingston Trio, The **9**
King's X **7**
Kinks, The **15**
Kinney, Sean
　See Alice in Chains
Kirk, Rahsaan Roland **6**
Kirk, Richard H.
　See Cabaret Voltaire
Kirkwood, Cris
　See Meat Puppets, The
Kirkwood, Curt
　See Meat Puppets, The

Lee, Geddy
  See Rush
Lee, Peggy **8**
Lee, Pete
  See Gwar
Lee, Sara
  See Gang of Four
Lee, Tommy
  See Mötley Crüe
Lee, Tony
  See Treadmill Trackstar
Leeb, Bill
  See Front Line Assembly
Leen, Bill
  See Gin Blossoms
Leese, Howard
  See Heart
Legg, Adrian **17**
Lehrer, Tom **7**
Leiber, Jerry
  See Leiber and Stoller
Leiber and Stoller **14**
Lemmy
  See Motörhead
Lemonheads, The **12**
Le Mystère des VoixBulgares
  See Bulgarian State Female Vocal Choir,
  The
Lemper, Ute **14**
Lenear, Kevin
  See Mighty Mighty Bosstones
Lenners, Rudy
  See Scorpions, The
Lennon, John **9**
  Also see Beatles, The
Lennon, Julian **2**
Lennox, Annie **18**
  Also see Eurythmics
Leonard, Glenn
  See Temptations, The
Lerner, Alan Jay
  See Lerner and Loewe
Lerner and Loewe **13**
Lesh, Phil
  See Grateful Dead, The
Lessard, Stefan
  See Dave Matthews Band
Levene, Keith
  See Clash, The
Levert, Eddie
  See O'Jays, The
Levin, Tony
  See King Crimson
Levine, James **8**
Levy, Andrew
  See Brand New Heavies, The
Levy, Ron
  See Roomful of Blues
Lewis, Huey **9**
Lewis, Ian
  See Inner Circle
Lewis, Jerry Lee **2**
Lewis, Marcia
  See Soul II Soul

Lewis, Otis
  See Fabulous Thunderbirds, The
Lewis, Peter
  See Moby Grape
Lewis, Ramsey **14**
Lewis, Roger
  See Inner Circle
Lewis, Roy
  See Kronos Quartet
Lewis, Samuel K.
  See Five Blind Boys of Alabama
Lewis, Terry
  See Jam, Jimmy, and Terry Lewis
Lhote, Morgan
  See Stereolab
Li Puma, Tommy **18**
Libbea, Gene
  See Nashville Bluegrass Band
Liberace **9**
Licht, David
  See Klezmatics, The
Lifeson, Alex
  See Rush
Lightfoot, Gordon **3**
Lightning Seeds **21**
Ligon, Willie Joe
  See Mighty Clouds of Joy, The
Liles, Brent
  See Social Distortion
Lilienstein, Lois
  See Sharon, Lois & Bram
Lilker, Dan
  See Anthrax
Lilley, John
  See Hooters
Lillywhite, Steve **13**
Lincoln, Abbey **9**
Lindley, David **2**
Linna, Miriam
  See Cramps, The
Linnell, John
  See They Might Be Giants
Lipsius, Fred
  See Blood, Sweat and Tears
Little, Keith
  See Country Gentlemen, The
Little Feat **4**
Little Richard **1**
Little Texas **14**
Little Walter **14**
Littrell, Brian
  See Backstreet Boys
Live **14**
Living Colour **7**
Llanas, Sam
  See BoDeans
Llanas, Sammy
  See BoDeans, The
L.L. Cool J. **5**
Lloyd, Richard
  See Television
Lloyd Webber, Andrew **6**
Lockwood, Robert, Jr. **10**
Lodge, John

  See Moody Blues, The
Loewe, Frederick
  See Lerner and Loewe
Loggins, Kenny **20**
Loggins, Kenny **3**
Lombardo, Dave
  See Slayer
London, Frank
  See Klezmatics, The
Lopes, Lisa "Left Eye"
  See TLC
Lopez, Israel "Cachao" **14**
Lord, Jon
  See Deep Purple
Lords of Acid **20**
Lorson, Mary
  See Madder Rose
Los Lobos **2**
Los Reyes
  See Gipsy Kings, The
Loughnane, Lee
  See Chicago
Louison, Steve
  See Massive Attack
Louris, Gary
  See Jayhawks, The
Louvin, Charlie
  See Louvin Brothers, The
Louvin, Ira
  See Louvin Brothers, The
Louvin Brothers, The **12**
Lovano, Joe **13**
Love, Courtney
  See Hole
Love, Gerry
  See Teenage Fanclub
Love, Laura **20**
Love, Mike
  See Beach Boys, The
Love and Rockets **15**
Loveless, Patty **21**
  Earlier sketch in CM **5**
Lovering, David
  See Cracker
  Also see Pixies, The
Love Spit Love **21**
Lovett, Lyle **5**
Lowe, Chris
  See Pet Shop Boys
Lowe, Nick **6**
Lowell, Charlie
  See Jars of Clay
Lowery, David
  See Cracker
Lozano, Conrad
  See Los Lobos
L7 **12**
Luccketta, Troy
  See Tesla
Lucia, Paco de
  See de Lucia, Paco
Luciano, Felipe
  See Last Poets
Luke
  See Campbell, Luther

Mavericks, The **15**
Maxwell, Charmayne
　See Brownstone
Maxwell, Tom
　See Squirrel Nut Zippers
May, Brian
　See Queen
Mayall, John **7**
Mayfield, Curtis **8**
Mays, Odeen, Jr.
　See Kool & the Gang
Mazelle, Kym
　See Soul II Soul
Mazibuko, Abednigo
　See LadysmithBlack Mambazo
Mazibuko, Albert
　See LadysmithBlack Mambazo
Mazzola, Joey
　See Sponge
Mazzy Star **17**
MCA
　See Yauch, Adam
McAloon, Martin
　See Prefab Sprout
McAloon, Paddy
　See Prefab Sprout
McArthur, Keith
　See Spearhead
McBrain, Nicko
　See Iron Maiden
MCBreed **17**
McBride, Christian **17**
McBride, Martina **14**
McCabe, Nick
　See Verve, The
McCall, Renee
　See Sounds of Blackness
McCarrick, Martin
　See Siouxsie and the Banshees
McCarroll, Tony
　See Oasis
McCartney, Paul **4**
　Also see Beatles, The
McCarty, Jim
　See Yardbirds, The
MC Clever
　See Digital Underground
McCary, Michael S.
　See Boyz II Men
McClinton, Delbert **14**
McCluskey, Andy
　See Orchestral Manoeuvres in the Dark
McCollum, Rick
　See Afghan Whigs
McConnell, Page
　See Phish
McCook, Tommy
　See Skatalites, The
McCoury, Del **15**
McCowin, Michael
　See Mighty Clouds of Joy, The
McCoy, Neal **15**
McCracken, Chet
　See Doobie Brothers, The

McCready, Mike
　See Pearl Jam
McCulloch, Andrew
　See King Crimson
McDaniels, Darryl "D"
　See Run-D.M.C.
McDermott, Brian
　See Del Amitri
McDonald, Barbara Kooyman
　See Timbuk 3
McDonald, Ian
　See Foreigner
　Also see King Crimson
McDonald, Jeff
　See Redd Kross
McDonald, Michael
　See Doobie Brothers, The
McDonald, Pat
　See Timbuk 3
McDonald, Steven
　See Redd Kross
McDorman, Joe
　See Statler Brothers, The
McDowell, Hugh
　See Electric Light Orchestra
McDowell, Mississippi Fred **16**
McEntire, Reba **11**
MC Eric
　See Technotronic
McEuen, John
　See Nitty Gritty Dirt Band, The
McFarlane, Elaine
　See Mamas and the Papas
McFee, John
　See Doobie Brothers, The
McFerrin, Bobby **3**
MC5, The **9**
McGee, Brian
　See Simple Minds
McGee, Jerry
　See Ventures, The
McGeoch, John
　See Siouxsie and theBanshees
McGinley, Raymond
　See Teenage Fanclub
McGraw, Tim **17**
McGuigan, Paul
　See Oasis
McGuinn, Jim
　See McGuinn, Roger
McGuinn, Roger
　See Byrds, The
M.C. Hammer
　See Hammer, M.C.
McGuire, Mike
　See Shenandoah
McIntosh, Robbie
　See Pretenders, The
McIntyre, Joe
　See New Kids on the Block
McJohn, Goldy
　See Steppenwolf
McKagan, Duff
　See Guns n' Roses

McKay, Al
　See Earth, Wind and Fire
McKay, John
　See Siouxsie and the Banshees
McKean, Michael
　See Spinal Tap
McKee, Maria **11**
McKeehan, Toby
　See dc Talk
McKenzie, Derrick
　See Jamiroquai
McKenzie, Scott
　See Mamas and the Papas
McKernarn, Ron "Pigpen"
　See Grateful Dead, The
McKinney, William
　See McKinney's Cotton Pickers
McKinney's Cotton Pickers **16**
McKnight, Claude V. III
　See Take 6
McLachlan, Sarah **12**
McLaughlin, John **12**
　Also see Mahavishnu Orchestra
McLean, A. J.
　See Backstreet Boys
McLean, Don **7**
McLennan, Grant **21**
McLeod, Rory
　See Roomful of Blues
MC Lyte **8**
McLoughlin, Jon
　See Del Amitri
McMeel, Mickey
　See Three Dog Night
McMurtry, James **10**
McNabb , Travis
　See Better Than Ezra
McNair, Sylvia **15**
McNeilly, Mac
　See Jesus Lizard
MC 900 Ft. Jesus **16**
McPartland, Marian **15**
McQuillar, Shawn
　See Kool & the Gang
McRae, Carmen **9**
M.C. Ren
　See N.W.A.
McReynolds, Jesse
　See McReynolds, Jim and Jesse
McReynolds, Jim
　See McReynolds, Jim and Jesse
McReynolds, Jim and Jesse **12**
MC Serch **10**
McShane, Ronnie
　See Chieftains, The
McShee, Jacqui
　See Pentangle
McTell, Blind Willie **17**
McVie, Christine
　See Fleetwood Mac
McVie, John
　See Fleetwood Mac
Mdletshe, Geophrey
　See Ladysmith Black Mambazo

Nico
  See Velvet Underground, The
Nicolette
  See Massive Attack
Nielsen, Rick
  See Cheap Trick
Nilija, Robert
  See Last Poets
Nilsson **10**
Nilsson, Harry
  See Nilsson
Nirvana **8**
Nisbett, Steve "Grizzly"
  See Steel Pulse
Nitty Gritty Dirt Band, The **6**
Nobacon, Danbert
  See Chumbawamba
Nocentelli, Leo
  See Meters, The
No Doubt **20**
Nolan, Jerry
  See New York Dolls
Nomiya, Maki
  See Pizzicato Five
Noone, Peter
  See Herman's Hermits
Norica, Sugar Ray
  See Roomful of Blues
Norman, Jessye **7**
Norman, Jimmy
  See Coasters, The
Northey, Craig
  See Odds
Norum, John
  See Dokken
Norvo, Red **12**
Notorious B.I.G. **20**
Novoselic, Chris
  See Nirvana
Nowell, Bradley James
  See Sublime
NRBQ **12**
Nugent, Ted **2**
Nunn, Bobby
  See Coasters, The
N.W.A. **6**
Nutter, Alice
  See Chumbawamba
Nylons, The **18**
Nyman, Michael **15**
Nyolo, Sally
  See Zap Mama
Nyro, Laura **12**
Oakes, Richard
  See Suede
Oakey, Philip
  See Human League, The
Oakley, Berry
  See Allman Brothers, The
Oak Ridge Boys, The **7**
Oasis **16**
Oates, John
  See Hall & Oates
O'Brien, Derek
  See Social Distortion

O'Brien, Dwayne
  See Little Texas
O'Bryant, Alan
  See Nashville Bluegrass Band
Ocasek, Ric **5**
  Also see Cars, The
Ocean, Billy **4**
Oceans, Lucky
  See Asleep at the Wheel
Ochs, Phil **7**
O'Connell, Chris
  See Asleep at the Wheel
O'Connor, Billy
  See Blondie
O'Connor, Daniel
  See House of Pain
O'Connor, Mark **1**
O'Connor, Sinead **3**
O'Day, Anita **21**
Odds **20**
Odetta **7**
O'Donnell, Roger
  See Cure, The
Odmark, Matt
  See Jars of Clay
Ogletree, Mike
  See Simple Minds
Ogre, Nivek
  See Skinny Puppy
O'Hagan, Sean
  See Stereolab
Ohanian, David
  See Canadian Brass, The
O'Hare, Brendan
  See Teenage Fanclub
Ohio Players **16**
O'Jays, The **13**
Oje, Baba
  See Arrested Development
Olafsson, Bragi
  See Sugarcubes, The
Olander, Jimmy
  See Diamond Rio
Oldfield, Mike **18**
Olds, Brent
  See Poi Dog Pondering
Oliver, Joe
  See Oliver, King
Oliver, King **15**
Olson, Jeff
  See Village People, The
Olson, Mark
  See Jayhawks, The
Olsson, Nigel
  See Spencer Davis Group
Onassis, Blackie
  See Urge Overkill
Ono, Yoko **11**
Orb, The **18**
Orbison, Roy **2**
O'Reagan, Tim
  See Jayhawks, The
O'Riordan, Cait
  See Pogues, The

O'Riordan, Dolores
  See Cranberries, The
Orbital **20**
Orchestral Manoeuvres in the Dark **21**
Orff, Carl **21**
Orlando, Tony **15**
Örn, Einar
  See Sugarcubes, The
Örnolfsdottir, Margret
  See Sugarcubes, The
Orr, Benjamin
  See Cars, The
Orr, Casey
  See Gwar
Orrall, Frank
  See Poi Dog Pondering
Orzabal, Roland
  See Tears for Fears
Osborne, Bob
  See Osborne Brothers, The
Osborne, Buzz
  See Melvins
Osborne, Sonny
  See Osborne Brothers, The
Osborne Brothers, The **8**
Osbourne, Ozzy **3**
  Also see Black Sabbath
Osby, Greg **21**
Oskar, Lee
  See War
Oslin, K. T. **3**
Osman, Mat
  See Suede
Osmond, Donny **3**
Ostin, Mo **17**
Otis, Johnny **16**
Ott, David **2**
Outler, Jimmy
  See Soul Stirrers, The
Owen, Randy Yueull
  See Alabama
Owens, Buck **2**
Owens, Ricky
  See Temptations, The
Oyewole, Abiodun
  See Last Poets
Page, Jimmy **4**
  Also see Led Zeppelin
  Also see Yardbirds, The
Page, Patti **11**
Page, Steven
  See Barenaked Ladies
Paice, Ian
  See Deep Purple
Palmer, Carl
  See Emerson, Lake & Palmer/Powell
Palmer, David
  See Jethro Tull
Palmer, Jeff **20**
Palmer, Robert **2**
Palmer-Jones, Robert
  See King Crimson
Palmieri, Eddie **15**
Paluzzi, Jimmy
  See Sponge

Pamer, John
See Tsunami
Pankow, James
See Chicago
Panter, Horace
See Specials, The
Pantera **13**
Papach, Leyna
See Geraldine Fibbers
Parazaider, Walter
See Chicago
Paris, Twila **16**
Park, Cary
See Boy Howdy
Park, Larry
See Boy Howdy
Parkening, Christopher **7**
Parker, Charlie **5**
Parker, Graham **10**
Parker, Kris
See KRS-One
Parker, Maceo **7**
Parks, Van Dyke **17**
Parnell, Lee Roy **15**
Parsons, Alan **12**
Parsons, Dave
See Bush
Parsons, Gene
See Byrds, The
Parsons, Gram **7**
Also see Byrds, The
Parsons, Tony
See Iron Maiden
Parton, Dolly **2**
Partridge, Andy
See XTC
Pasemaster, Mase
See De La Soul
Pass, Joe **15**
Pastorius, Jaco
See Weather Report
Paterson, Alex
See Orb, The
Patinkin, Mandy **20**
Earlier sketch CM **3**
Patti, Sandi **7**
Patton, Charley **11**
Patton, Mike
See Faith No More
Paul, Alan
See Manhattan Transfer, The
Paul, Les **2**
Paul, Vinnie
See Pantera
Paul III, Henry
See BlackHawk
Paulo, Jr.
See Sepultura
Pavarotti, Luciano **20**
Earlier sketch in CM **1**
Pavement **14**
Paxton, Tom **5**
Payne, Bill
See Little Feat
Payne, Scherrie
See Supremes, The

Payton, Denis
See Dave Clark Five, The
Payton, Lawrence
See Four Tops, The
Pearl, Minnie **3**
Pearl Jam **12**
Pearson, Dan
See American Music Club
Peart, Neil
See Rush
Pedersen, Herb
See Desert Rose Band, The
Peduzzi, Larry
See Roomful of Blues
Peek, Dan
See America
Peeler, Ben
See Mavericks, The
Pegg, Dave
See Jethro Tull
Pegrum, Nigel
See Steeleye Span
Pence, Jeff
See Blessid Union of Souls
Pendergrass, Teddy **3**
Pengilly, Kirk
See INXS
Peniston, CeCe **15**
Penn, Michael **4**
Penner, Fred **10**
Pentangle **18**
Pepper, Art **18**
Perahia, Murray **10**
Pere Ubu **17**
Peretz, Jesse
See Lemonheads, The
Perez, Louie
See Los Lobos
Perkins, Carl **9**
Perkins, John
See XTC
Perkins, Percell
See Five Blind Boys of Alabama
Perkins, Steve
See Jane's Addiction
Perlman, Itzhak **2**
Perlman, Marc
See Jayhawks, The
Pernice, Joe
See Scud Mountain Boys
Perry, Brendan
See Dead Can Dance
Perry, Doane
See Jethro Tull
Perry, Joe
See Aerosmith
Perry, Steve
See Journey
Persson, Nina
See Cardigans
Peter, Paul & Mary **4**
Peters, Bernadette **7**
Peters, Dan
See Mudhoney
Peters, Joey
See Grant Lee Buffalo

Petersen, Chris
See Front Line Assembly
Peterson, Oscar **11**
Petersson, Tom
See Cheap Trick
Petra **3**
Pet Shop Boys **5**
Petty, Tom **9**
Pfaff, Kristen
See Hole
Phair, Liz **14**
Phantom, Slim Jim
See Stray Cats, The
Pharcyde, The **17**
Phelps, Doug
See Kentucky Headhunters, The
Phelps, Ricky Lee
See Kentucky Headhunters, The
Phife
See Tribe Called Quest, A
Phil, Gary
See Boston
Philips, Anthony
See Genesis
Phillips, Chris
See Squirrel Nut Zippers
Phillips, Chynna
See Wilson Phillips
Phillips, Glenn
See Toad the Wet Sprocket
Phillips, Grant Lee
See Grant LeeBuffalo
Phillips, Harvey **3**
Phillips, John
See Mamas and the Papas
Phillips, Mackenzie
See Mamas and the Papas
Phillips, Michelle
See Mamas and the Papas
Phillips, Sam **5**
Phillips, Sam **12**
Phillips, Shelley
See Point of Grace
Phillips, Simon
See Judas Priest
Phish **13**
Phungula, Inos
See Ladysmith Black Mambazo
Piaf, Edith **8**
Piazzolla, Astor **18**
Picciotto, Joe
See Fugazi
Piccolo, Greg
See Roomful of Blues
Pickering, Michael
See M People
Pickett, Wilson **10**
Pierce, Marvin "Merv"
See Ohio Players
Pierce, Webb **15**
Pierson, Kate
SeeB-52's, The
Pilatus, Rob
See Milli Vanilli
Pilson, Jeff
See Dokken

Redd Kross **20**
Reddy, Helen **9**
Red Hot Chili Peppers, The **7**
Redman, Don
  See McKinney's Cotton Pickers
Redman, Joshua **12**
Redpath, Jean **1**
Reece, Chris
  See Social Distortion
Reed, Jimmy **15**
Reed, Lou **16**
 Earlier sketch in CM **1**
  Also see Velvet Underground, The
Reese, Della **13**
Reeves, Dianne **16**
Reeves, Jim **10**
Reeves, Martha **4**
Reich, Steve **8**
Reid, Charlie
  See Proclaimers, The
Reid, Christopher
  See Kid 'n Play
Reid, Craig
  See Proclaimers, The
Reid, Delroy "Junior"
 See Black Uhuru
Reid, Don
  See Statler Brothers, The
Reid, Ellen Lorraine
  See Crash Test Dummies
Reid, Harold
  See Statler Brothers, The
Reid, Janet
  See Black Uhuru
Reid, Jim
  See Jesus and Mary Chain, The
Reid, Vernon **2**
  Also see Living Colour
Reid, William
  See Jesus and Mary Chain, The
Reifman, William
  See KMFDM
Reinhardt, Django **7**
Reitzell, Brian
  See Redd Kross
Relf, Keith
  See Yardbirds, The
R.E.M. **5**
Renbourn, John
  See Pentangle
Reno, Ronnie
  See Osborne Brothers, The
Replacements, The **7**
Republica **20**
Residents, The **14**
Restless Heart **12**
Revell, Adrian
  See Jamiroquai
Rex
  See Pantera
Reyes, Andre
  See Gipsy Kings, The
Reyes, Canut
  See Gipsy Kings, The

Reyes, Nicolas
  See Gipsy Kings, The
Reynolds, Nick
  See Kingston Trio, The
Reynolds, Robert
  See Mavericks, The
Reynolds, Sheldon
  See Earth, Wind and Fire
Reznor, Trent **13**
Rhodes, Nick
  See Duran Duran
Rhodes, Philip
  See Gin Blossoms
Rhodes, Todd
  See McKinney's Cotton Pickers
Rhone, Sylvia **13**
Rich, Buddy **13**
Rich, Charlie **3**
Richard, Cliff **14**
Richard, Zachary **9**
Richards, Keith **11**
  Also see Rolling Stones, The
Richardson, Kevin
  See Backstreet Boys
Richey, Kim **20**
Richie, Lionel **2**
Richling, Greg
  See Wallflowers, The
Richman, Jonathan **12**
Rieckermann, Ralph
  See Scorpions, The
Rieflin, William
  See Ministry
Riley, Teddy **14**
Riley, Timothy Christian
  See Tony! Toni! Toné!
Rippon, Steve
  See Lush
Ritchie, Brian
  See Violent Femmes
Ritchie, Jean **4**
Ritenour, Lee **7**
Roach, Max **12**
Roback, David
  See Mazzy Star
Robbins, Charles David
  See BlackHawk
Robbins, Marty **9**
Roberts, Brad
  See Crash Test Dummies
Roberts, Brad
  See Gwar
Roberts, Dan
  See Crash Test Dummies
Roberts, Ken
  See Charm Farm
Roberts, Marcus **6**
Robertson, Brian
  See Motörhead
  Also see Thin Lizzy
Robertson, Ed
  See Barenaked Ladies
Robertson, Robbie **2**
  Also seeBand, The

Robeson, Paul **8**
Robillard, Duke **2**
  Also see Roomful of Blues
Robinson, Arnold
  See Nylons, The
Robinson, Chris
  See Black Crowes, The
Robinson, David
  See Cars, The
Robinson, Dawn
  See En Vogue
Robinson, R.B.
  See Soul Stirrers, The
Robinson, Rich
  See Black Crowes, The
Robinson, Romye "BootyBrown"
  See Pharcyde, The
Robinson, Smokey **1**
Roche, Maggie
  See Roches, The
Roche, Suzzy
  See Roches, The
Roche, Terre
  See Roches, The
Roches, The **18**
Rockenfield, Scott
  See Queensryche
Rocker, Lee
  See Stray Cats, The
Rockett, Rikki
  See Poison
Rockin' Dopsie **10**
Rodford, Jim
  See Kinks, The
Rodgers, Jimmie **3**
Rodgers, Nile **8**
Rodgers, Richard **9**
Rodney, Red **14**
Rodriguez, Rico
  See Skatalites, The
  Also see Specials, The
Rodriguez, Sal
  See War
Roe, Marty
  See Diamond Rio
Roeder, Klaus
  See Kraftwerk
Roeser, Donald
  See Blue Oyster Cult
Roeser, Eddie "King"
  See Urge Overkill
Rogers, Kenny **1**
Rogers, Norm
  See Jayhawks, The
Rogers, Roy **9**
Rogers, Willie
  See Soul Stirrers, The
Roland, Dean
  See Collective Soul
Roland, Ed
  See Collective Soul
Rolie, Gregg
  See Journey
Rolling Stones, The **3**

Scherpenzeel, Ton
  See Camel
Schickele, Peter **5**
Schlitt, John
  See Petra
Schloss, Zander
  See Circle Jerks, The
Schmelling, Johannes
  See Tangerine Dream
Schmit, Timothy B.
  See Eagles, The
Schmoovy Schmoove
  See Digital Underground
Schneider, Florian
  See Kraftwerk
Schneider, Fred III
  See B-52's, The
Schnitzler, Conrad
  See Tangerine Dream
Scholten, Jim
  See Sawyer Brown
Scholz, Tom
  See Boston
Schon, Neal
  See Journey
Schrody, Erik
  See House of Pain
Schroyder, Steve
  See Tangerine Dream
Schulman, Mark
  See Foreigner
Schulze, Klaus
  See Tangerine Dream
Schuman, William **10**
Schuur, Diane **6**
Scofield, John **7**
Scorpions, The **12**
Scott, Ronald Belford "Bon"
  See AC/DC
Scott, George
  See Five Blind Boys of Alabama
Scott, Howard
  See War
Scott, Jimmy **14**
Scott, Sherry
  See Earth, Wind and Fire
Scott-Heron, Gil **13**
Scruggs, Earl **3**
Schulz, Guenter
  See KMFDM
Scud Mountain Boys **21**
Seal **14**
Seales, Jim
  See Shenandoah
Seals, Brady
  See Little Texas
Seals, Dan **9**
Seals, Jim
  See Seals & Crofts
Seals & Crofts **3**
Sears, Pete
  See Jefferson Starship
Secada, Jon **13**
Sedaka, Neil **4**

Seeger, Pete **4**
  Also see Weavers, The
Seger, Bob **15**
Segovia, Andres **6**
Seldom Scene, The **4**
Selena **16**
Sen Dog
  See Cypress Hill
Senior, Milton
  See McKinney's Cotton Pickers
Senior, Russell
  See Pulp
Sensi
  See Soul II Soul
Sepultura **12**
Seraphine, Daniel
  See Chicago
Sermon, Erick
  See EPMD
Setzer, Brian
  See Stray Cats, The
Severin, Steven
  See Siouxsie and the Banshees
Severinsen, Doc **1**
Sex Pistols, The **5**
Sexton, Chad
  See 311
Seymour, Neil
  See Crowded House
Shabalala, Ben
  See Ladysmith Black Mambazo
Shabalala, Headman
  See Ladysmith Black Mambazo
Shabalala, Jockey
  See Ladysmith Black Mambazo
Shabalala, Joseph
  See Ladysmith Black Mambazo
Shaffer, Paul **13**
Shakespeare, Robbie
  See Sly and Robbie
Shakur, Tupac
  See 2Pac
Shallenberger, James
  See Kronos Quartet
Shane, Bob
  See Kingston Trio, The
Shanice **14**
Shankar, Ravi **9**
Shannon, Del **10**
Shanté **10**
Shapiro, Jim
  See Veruca Salt
Shapps, Andre
  SeeBig Audio Dynamite
Sharon, Lois & Bram **6**
Sharpe, Matt
  See Weezer
Sharrock, Chris
  See Lightning Seeds
Sharrock, Sonny **15**
Shaw, Artie **8**
Shaw, Martin
  See Jamiroquai
Shea, Tom

See Scud Mountain Boys
Shearer, Harry
  See Spinal Tap
Sheehan, Bobby
  See Blues Traveler
Sheehan, Fran
  See Boston
Sheila E. **3**
Shelley, Peter
  See Buzzcocks, The
Shelley, Steve
  See Sonic Youth
Shenandoah **17**
Sherba, John
  See Kronos Quartet
Sherman, Jack
  See Red Hot Chili Peppers, The
Shines, Johnny **14**
Shirelles, The **11**
Shocked, Michelle **4**
Shock G
  See Digital Underground
Shocklee, Hank **15**
Shogren, Dave
  See Doobie Brothers, The
Shonen Knife **13**
Shontz, Bill
  See Rosenshontz
Shorter, Wayne **5**
  Also see Weather Report
Shovell
  See M People
Shudder to Think **20**
Siberry, Jane **6**
Sice
  See Boo Radleys, The
Siegal, Janis
  See Manhattan Transfer, The
Sikes, C. David
  See Boston
Sills, Beverly **5**
Silva, Kenny Jo
  See Beaver Brown Band, The
Silverchair **20**
Simien, Terrance **12**
Simmons, Gene
  See Kiss
Simmons, Joe "Run"
  See Run-D.M.C.
Simmons, Patrick
  See Doobie Brothers, The
Simmons, Russell **7**
Simmons, Trinna
  See Spearhead
Simon, Carly **4**
Simon, Paul **16**
  Earlier sketch in CM **1**
Simone, Nina **11**
Simonon, Paul
  See Clash, The
Simons, Ed
  See Chemical Brothers
Simins, Russell
  See Jon Spencer Blues Explosion

Spinal Tap **8**
Spin Doctors **14**
Spinners , The **21**
Spitz, Dan
  See Anthrax
Spitz, Dave
  See Black Sabbath
Sponge **18**
Spring, Keith
  See NRBQ
Springfield, Dusty **20**
Springfield, Rick **9**
Springsteen, Bruce **6**
Sproule, Daithi
  See Altan
Sprout, Tobin
  See Guided By Voices
Squeeze **5**
Squire, Chris
  See Yes
Squire, John
  See Stone Roses, The
Squires, Rob
  See Big Head Todd and the Monsters
Squirrel Nut Zippers **20**
Stacey, Peter "Spider"
  See Pogues, The
Staley, Layne
  See Alice in Chains
Staley, Tom
  See NRBQ
Stanier, John
  See Helmet
Stanley, Ian
  See Tears for Fears
Stanley, Paul
  See Kiss
Stanley, Ralph **5**
Stansfield, Lisa **9**
Staples, Mavis **13**
Staples, Neville
  See Specials, The
Staples, Pops **11**
Starcrunch
  See Man or Astroman?
Starling, John
  See Seldom Scene, The
Starr, Mike
  See Alice in Chains
Starr, Ringo **10**
  Also see Beatles, The
Starship
  See Jefferson Airplane
Statler Brothers, The **8**
Stead, David
  See Beautiful South
Steele, Billy
  See Sounds of Blackness
Steele, David
  See English Beat, The
Steel Pulse **14**
Steele, Jeffrey
  See Boy Howdy
Steely Dan **5**
Stefani, Gwen

  See No Doubt
Steier, Rick
  See Warrant
Stein, Chris
  See Blondie
Steinberg, Sebastian
  See Soul Coughing
Stephenson, Van Wesley
  See BlackHawk
Steppenwolf **20**
Sterban, Richard
  See Oak Ridge Boys, The
Stereolab **18**
Sterling, Lester
  See Skatalites, The
Stern, Isaac **7**
Stevens, Cat **3**
Stevens, Ray **7**
Stevens, Roger
  See Blind Melon
Stevenson, Don
  See Moby Grape
Steward, Pat
  See Odds
Stewart, Dave
  See Eurythmics
Stewart, Derrick "Fatlip"
  See Pharcyde, The
Stewart, Ian
  See Rolling Stones, The
Stewart, Jamie
  See Cult, The
Stewart, John
  See Kingston Trio, The
Stewart, Larry
  See Restless Heart
Stewart, Rod **20**
  Earlier sketch in CM **2**
Stewart, Tyler
  See Barenaked Ladies
Stewart, William
  See Third World
Stewart, Winston "Metal"
  See Mystic Revealers
Stills, Stephen **5**
Sting **19**
  Earlier sketch in CM **2**
  Also see Police, The
Stinson, Bob
  See Replacements, The
Stinson, Tommy
  See Replacements, The
Stipe, Michael
  See R.E.M.
Stockman, Shawn
  See Boyz II Men
Stoller, Mike
  See Leiber and Stoller
Stoltz, Brian
  See Neville Brothers, The
Stonadge, Gary
  See Big Audio Dynamite
Stone, Curtis
  See Highway 101
Stone, Doug **10**

Stone Roses, The **16**
Stone, Sly **8**
Stone Temple Pilots **14**
Stookey, Paul
  See Peter, Paul & Mary
Story, Liz **2**
Story, The **13**
Stradlin, Izzy
  See Guns n' Roses
Strain, Sammy
  See O'Jays, The
Strait, George **5**
Stratton, Dennis
  See Iron Maiden
Stravinsky, Igor **21**
Straw, Syd **18**
Stray Cats, The **11**
Strayhorn, Billy **13**
Street, Richard
  See Temptations, The
Streisand, Barbra **2**
Strickland, Keith
  See B-52's, The
Strummer, Joe
  See Clash, The
Stryper **2**
Stuart, Marty **9**
Stuart, Peter
  See Dog's Eye View
Stubbs, Levi
  See Four Tops, The
Styne, Jule **21**
Subdudes, The **18**
Sublime **19**
Such, Alec Jon
  See Bon Jovi
Suede **20**
Sugarcubes, The **10**
Suicidal Tendencies **15**
Sulley, Suzanne
  See Human League, The
Summer, Donna **12**
Summer, Mark
  See Turtle Island String Quartet
Summers, Andy **3**
  Also see Police, The
Sumner, Bernard
  See Joy Division
  Also see New Order
Sundays, The **20**
Sun Ra **5**
Sunnyland Slim **16**
Super DJ Dmitry
  See Deee-lite
Supremes, The **6**
Sure!, AlB. **13**
Sutcliffe, Stu
  See Beatles, The
Sutherland, Joan **13**
Svenigsson, Magnus
  See Cardigans
Svensson, Peter
  See Cardigans
Svigals, Alicia
  See Klezmatics, The

Toad the Wet Sprocket **13**
Toback, Jeremy
  See Brad
Todd, Andy
  See Republica
Tolhurst, Laurence
  See Cure, The
Tolland, Bryan
  See Del Amitri
Toller, Dan
  See Allman Brothers, The
Tone-L c **3**
Tony K
  See Roomful of Blues
Tony! Toni! Toné! **12**
Too $hort **16**
Toohey, Dan
  See Guided By Voices
Took, Steve Peregrine
  See T. Rex
Tool **21**
Toomey, Jenny
  See Tsunami
Topham, Anthony "Top"
  See Yardbirds, The
Tork, Peter
  See Monkees, The
Torme, Mel **4**
Torres, Hector "Tico"
  See Bon Jovi
Toscanini, Arturo **14**
Tosh, Peter **3**
Toure, Ali Farka **18**
Tourish, Ciaran
  See Altan
Toussaint, Allen **11**
Townes, Jeffery
  See DJ Jazzy Jeff and the Fresh Prince
Townshend, Pete **1**
  Also see Who, The
Tragically Hip, The **18**
Travers, Brian
  See UB40
Travers, Mary
  See Peter, Paul & Mary
Travis, Merle **14**
Travis, Randy **9**
Treach
  See Naughty by Nature
T. Rex **11**
Treadmill Trackstar **21**
Tribe Called Quest, A **8**
Tricky
  See Massive Attack
Tricky **18**
Tritt, Travis **7**
Trotter, Kera
  See C + C Music Factory
Trucks, Butch
  See Allman Brothers, The
Trugoy the Dove
  See De La Soul
Trujillo, Robert
  See Suicidal Tendencies

Truman, Dan
  See Diamond Rio
Trynin, Jen **21**
Tsunami **21**
Tubb, Ernest **4**
Tubridy, Michael
  See Chieftans, The
Tucker, Corin
  See Sleater-Kinney
Tucker, Moe
  See Velvet Underground, The
Tucker, Sophie **12**
Tucker, Tanya **3**
Tufnel, Nigel
  See Spinal Tap
Tull, Bruce
  See Scud Mountain Boys
Turbin, Neil
  See Anthrax
Turgon, Bruce
  See Foreigner
Turner, Big Joe **13**
Turner, Erik
  See Warrant
Turner, Joe Lynn
  See Deep Purple
Turner, Steve
  See Mudhoney
Turner, Tina **1**
Turpin, Will
  See Collective Soul
Turtle Island String Quartet **9**
Tutton, Bill
  See Geraldine Fibbers
Tutuska, George
  See Goo Goo Dolls, The
Tuxedomoon **21**
Twain, Shania **17**
Twitty, Conway **6**
2 Unlimited **18**
23, Richard
  See Front 242
2Pac **17**
  Also see Digital Underground
Tyagi, Paul
  See Del Amitri
Tyler, Steve
  See Aerosmith
Tyner, McCoy **7**
Tyner, Rob
  See MC5, The
Tyson, Ian
  See Ian and Sylvia
Tyson, Ron
  See Temptations, The
UB40 **4**
US3 **18**
Ulmer, James Blood **13**
Ulrich, Lars
  See Metallica
Ulvaeus, Björn
  See Abba
Um Romao, Dom
  See Weather Report

Unruh, N. U.
  See Einstürzende Neubauten
Uosikkinen, David
  See Hooters
Upshaw, Dawn **9**
Urge Overkill **17**
U2 **12**
  Earlier sketch in CM **2**
Vachon, Chris
  See Roomful of Blues
Vai, Steve **5**
  Also see Whitesnake
Valentine, Gary
  See Blondie
Valentine, Rae
  See War
Valenzuela, Jesse
  See Gin Blossoms
Valli, Frankie **10**
Valory, Ross
  See Journey
van Dijk, Carol
  See Bettie Serveert
Van Gelder, Nick
  See Jamiroquai
Van Hook, Peter
  See Mike & the Mechanics
Vandenburg, Adrian
  See Whitesnake
Vander Ark, Brad
  See Verve Pipe, The
Vander Ark, Brian
  See Verve Pipe, The
Vandross, Luther **2**
Van Halen **8**
Van Halen, Alex
  See Van Halen
Van Halen, Edward
  See Van Halen
Vanilla Ice **6**
Van Ronk, Dave **12**
Van Shelton, Ricky **5**
Van Vliet, Don
  See Captain Beefheart
Van Zandt, Townes **13**
Van Zant, Johnny
  See Lynyrd Skynyrd
Van Zant, Ronnie
  See Lynyrd Skynyrd
Vasquez, Junior **16**
Vaughan, Jimmie
  See Fabulous Thunderbirds, The
Vaughan, Sarah **2**
Vaughan, Stevie Ray **1**
Vedder, Eddie
  See Pearl Jam
Vega, Suzanne **3**
Velvet Underground, The **7**
Ventures, The **19**
Verlaine, Tom
  See Television
Verta-Ray, Matt
  See Madder Rose
Veruca Salt **20**

Weston
  See Orb, The
Weston, Randy **15**
Wetton, John
  See King Crimson
Wexler, Jerry **15**
Weymouth, Tina
  See Talking Heads
Whalen, Katharine
  See Squirrel Nut Zippers
Wheat, Brian
  See Tesla
Wheeler, Audrey
  See C + C Music Factory
Wheeler, Caron
  See Soul II Soul
Wheeler, Harriet
  See Sundays, The
Wheeler, Robert
  See Pere Ubu
Whelan, Bill **20**
Whelan, Gavan
  See James
Whitaker, Rodney **20**
White, Alan
  See Oasis
White, Alan
  See Yes
White, Barry **6**
White, Billy
White, Dennis
  See Charm Farm
  See Dokken
White, Clarence
  See Byrds, The
White, Dave
  See Warrant
White, Freddie
  See Earth, Wind and Fire
White, Lari **15**
White, Mark
  See Mekons, The
White, Mark
  See Spin Doctors
White, Maurice
  See Earth, Wind and Fire
White, Ralph
  See Bad Livers, The
White, Roland
  See Nashville Bluegrass Band
White, Verdine
  See Earth, Wind and Fire
White Zombie **17**
Whitehead, Donald
  See Earth, Wind and Fire
Whiteman, Paul **17**
Whitesnake **5**
Whitfield, Mark **18**
Whitford, Brad
  See Aerosmith
Whitley, Chris **16**
Whitley, Keith **7**
Whittaker, Hudson **20**
Whitwam, Barry
  See Herman's Hermits

Who, The **3**
Widenhouse, Je
  See Squirrel Nut Zippers
Wiggins, Dwayne
  See Tony! Toni! Toné!
Wiggins, Raphael
  See Tony! Toni! Toné!
Wiggs, Josephine
  See Breeders
Wikso, Ron
  See Foreigner
Wilborn, Dave
  See McKinney's Cotton Pickers
Wilburn, Ishmael
  See Weather Report
Wilcox, Imani
  See Pharcyde, The
Wilde, Phil
  See 2 Unlimited
Wilder, Alan
  See Depeche Mode
Wilk, Brad
  See Rage Against the Machine
Wilkeson, Leon
  See Lynyrd Skynyrd
Wilkinson, Geoff
  See US3
Wilkinson, Keith
  See Squeeze
Williams, Andy **2**
Williams, Boris
  See Cure, The
Williams, Cliff
  See AC/DC
Williams, Dana
  See Diamond Rio
Williams, Deniece **1**
Williams, Don **4**
Williams, Fred
  See C + C Music Factory
Williams, Hank, Jr. **1**
Williams, Hank, Sr. **4**
Williams, James "Diamond"
  See Ohio Players
Williams, Joe **11**
Williams, John **9**
Williams, Lamar
  See Allman Brothers, The
Williams, Lucinda **10**
Williams, Marion **15**
Williams, Otis
  See Temptations, The
Williams, Paul **5**
  See Temptations, The
Williams, Phillard
  See Earth, Wind and Fire
Williams, Vanessa **10**
Williams, Victoria **17**
Williams, Walter
  See O'Jays, The
Williams, Wilbert
  See Mighty Clouds of Joy, The
Williamson, Sonny Boy **9**
Willie D.
  See Geto Boys, The

Willis, Clarence "Chet"
  See Ohio Players
Willis, Kelly **12**
Willis, Larry
  See Blood, Sweat and Tears
Willis, Pete
  See Def Leppard
Willis, Rick
  See Foreigner
Willis, Victor
  See Village People, The
Willner, Hal **10**
Wills, Bob **6**
Wills, Aaron (P-Nut)
  See 311
Willson-Piper, Marty
  See Church, The
Wilmot, Billy "Mystic"
  See Mystic Revealers
Wilson, Anne
  See Heart
Wilson, Brian
  See Beach Boys, The
Wilson, Carl
  See Beach Boys, The
Wilson, Carnie
  See Wilson Phillips
Wilson, Cassandra **12**
Wilson, Chris
  See Love Spit Love
Wilson, Cindy
  See B-52's, The
Wilson, Don
  See Ventures, The
Wilson, Dennis
  See Beach Boys, The
Wilson, Eric
  See Sublime
Wilson, Jackie **3**
Wilson, Kim
  See Fabulous Thunderbirds, The
Wilson, Mary
  See Supremes, The
Wilson, Nancy **14**
  See Heart
Wilson, Patrick
  See Weezer
Wilson, Ransom **5**
Wilson, Ricky
  See B-52's, The
Wilson, Robin
  See Gin Blossoms
Wilson, Shanice
  See Shanice
Wilson, Wendy
  See Wilson Phillips
Wilson Phillips **5**
Wilton, Michael
  See Queensryche
Wimpfheimer, Jimmy
  See Roomful of Blues
Winans, Carvin
  See Winans, The
Winans, Marvin
  See Winans, The

The Seasonal Hearth

The

Seasonal Hearth

THE WOMAN AT HOME IN EARLY AMERICA

by Adelaide Hechtlinger
illustrated by Margaret Geiger

THE OVERLOOK PRESS
WOODSTOCK, NEW YORK

First edition 1977
Published by
The Overlook Press
Lewis Hollow Road
Woodstock, New York 12498
Copyright © 1977 Adelaide Hechtlinger

ISBN 0-87951-052-8
Library of Congress
Catalog Card Number: 75-27290

Designed by Elizabeth Woll
Illustrated by Margaret Geiger

Printed in the United States of America

Contents

SPRING

SUMMER

AUTUMN

INTRODUCTION

In the seventeenth and eighteenth centuries, American eating was limited by the manner of cooking and the food itself. Nothing was wasted; the grease skimmed from the top of the pot or dripping from the roast eventually was used to make soap or candles.

In the nineteenth century, cooking had changed. Gravies of all sorts were now used, and the ever-popular puddings became very complex. Responsible was the invention of the cooking stove, which radically altered the style of cooking and eating. Many different types of stoves were invented and perfected, and this plus several of the other inventions of the century such as the icebox changed the lot of the housewife. The various cleaning devices and cooking accessories now available also changed the manner of living for the first time in hundreds of years.

From the first starving years of the early settlements, the American housewife has managed quite well in feeding her family. She used ingenuity and determination to take the new foods she found here and turn them into tempting dishes ranging from baked beans to apple pie. The pioneer women cooked everything from Buffalo tongue to Beaver tail. They baked bread in front of fires or in makeshift stoves. They became experts at creating corn bread, pumpkin soup, and hasty puddings.

Those housewives who came from other countries besides England adapted their native dishes to the food found here. All of them were busy from morning to night just taking care of their own little households, food, clothing, and accessories for living. Their quiet determination in the home gave their menfolk the strength and courage to build in this new land. Perhaps the fact that the women stood so firmly behind their men gave the latter the confidence and impetus needed to rebel against the Mother country—England—and strike out on their own.

Although cooking is much more appealing in our day than in the days of our grandmothers and their grandmothers' era, I wonder what the Early American housewife would think if by some miracle she were able to visit with us for a short time today.

The range of recipes today is so wide that meals need never be routine, yet it is positively amazing to think of the meals that these earlier American housewives turned out with just the fireplace and, perhaps, if they were fortunate, a wall oven.

Our markets offer a wide variety of foods, especially of fruits and vegetables, which are easily and quickly shipped to us from all parts of the world. But we must remember that our forefathers were so happy to have food in the early days of their settling here that they complained very little, if at all, about the sameness of their fare.

Just stop to think about the various things we do today that were completely unknown even a hundred years ago. We can cook without a fire, on a piece of what seems to be furniture, with no obvious means of heat. We have microwave ovens that take just minutes to prepare a meal from "scratch." Our freezers keep our food fresh for months. We have frozen TV dinners for the person in a hurry, who wants a meal and has no time to cook. We also must not overlook our powdered eggs, milk, and other dehydrated foods, our instant liquid breakfasts, cake mixes, soup mixes, and dozens of other convenience foods.

Our Early American housewife did have what was called "portable soup," to which water was added to make a soup, as well as dried corn and dried beef which could be used on journeys. Her meat was fresh only when something was slaughtered, else the beef or pork had to be smoked or pickled. She did have lots of fresh fowl of all sorts and fresh fish, but again we must remember the sameness of her menus.

In this book I shall attempt to give a very brief history of the American housewife from 1607 to 1910. Each section of the country had its own customs and mannerisms and I have tried to give the reader a picture of what the role of the housewife was in a particular area.

I personally own many old cookbooks, home-remedy books, magazines, and almanacs which I have culled over to extract parts that I think will be of interest to the reader.

A.H.
Island Park, N.Y.
July 4, 1976

Winter

JANUARY, FEBRUARY, MARCH

THE EARLY AMERICAN HOUSEWIFE

Although there was some leisure for the men in the early days of America, even so much as a rainy day or one in the middle of the winter, which kept them indoors, it was the women who least of all knew the luxury of leisure. A common proverb ran, "Man works from sun to sun, but woman's work is never done." This was literally true. The Early American housewife was responsible for the care, clothing, and feeding of her family, whatever her social status. If she had servants, she had to direct them, see that they did their work properly, show them how to do certain things, look after them when they were ill, and maintain a watchful eye at all times.

If she did not have servants, as was the case with most of the women in the early settlements, she had even less leisure. Not only did she have to bear and care for the children, but she also had to cook and wash for the whole family without the benefit of any labor-saving devices such as we have today. She not only had to make garments for the entire family, including the men, but she also had to spin the thread and weave the yarn into the cloth for these garments.

She also had to knit socks and stockings. Her hands could never be idle, and she could not even afford the luxury of nodding quietly in the chimney corner. If she did, some duty was being neglected. She did not have time to worry about amusements, though she did manage at times to find pleasure in such communal activities as quilting parties. Pleasure in the colonial period, both for women and men, frequently had to be found in some essential activity.

Colonial appetites were hearty, and there were no prepared mixes to satisfy them quickly and easily. Even sausages had to be made "from the ground up." She cooked over an open fire and so was constantly burning herself at the fire and with the hot pots. Since cooking space was limited, she often baked for several days in advance (remember, there was no bakery around the corner, or supermarket). She planted and tended her own herb garden, and if she was fortunate, the menfolk in the family took care of her kitchen garden, where she planted special foods needed for cooking. She did her own soap-making, candle-making, and preserving, too.

It was not an easy life; no wonder the life expectancy was so short, considering that she gave birth and immediately went back to taking care of the rest of the family.

EARLY DAYS IN NEW ENGLAND

At Plymouth in 1620 there was first a temporary shelter or camp, then a common house. The settlers at first lived in "smoaky homes" dug into the hillsides, with roofs of bark and walls of sod. But it was not long before they built themselves simple frame houses. In the beginning, the village was surrounded by a stockade. Later, each house had its own, inside of which there was room for a "prety garden plote."

The one-room structure of 1620 was built around a fireplace. It held only the bare necessities—it was many years before the colonies could think of physical comfort. At first the occupants had to do without windows, the only light being provided by the open fire, or a few tallow candles. Next, small latticed windows, with panes of oiled paper or linen, made their appearance. Some settlers brought glass with them, usually in the form of heavy, greenish, diamond-shaped panes.

The chimneys of the early structures were built on the ground, resting on a foundation set into the dirt. A Puritan family never knew when it might not be disturbed by a long-nosed fire warden peeking into the fireplace for "foul chimney hears," for the old chimneys often caught fire. Of the thirty-two buildings in Plymouth, seven burned down in one winter. In Boston during the first winter, there was a fire every week.

But it was not until the latter part of the century that the colonists began to build the houses customarily associated with seventeenth-century New England. There were the stark, rectangular garrison houses, with the second story jutting out a little over the first. There also were the pleasant, rambling frame houses, with windows of all different sizes, placed anywhere, hit or miss; floors of different heights; and walls of varying thickness. The shingled roofs often sloped from the top of the second story in front, to near the ground in back. Other houses had gambrel roofs with gables at the end.

The single room, found at first, was a small, low-ceilinged room that contained little more than a few benches; two or three four-legged stools; a settle by the fire; perhaps a plain deal table and a simple frame bedstead or jack bed in the corner.

The English four-poster bed was really a little house, designed to protect the occupant from drafts when the bed draperies were drawn. The same might be said of the Puritan settle. The high back and side pieces served as a protection against the wind that blew through the cracks between the timbers of those primitive homes.

Tables for eating purposes were improvised by laying rough boards across trestles. Blocks of wood about a foot square, hollowed in the middle, served as plates,

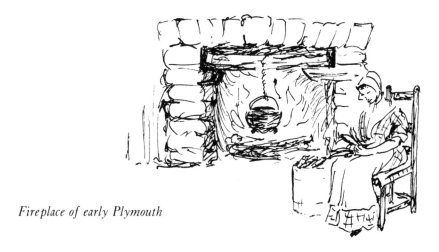

Fireplace of early Plymouth

a man and his wife, or a couple of children, often sharing the same one. These plates were called trenchers.

Because the same room was used for cooking, eating, living, and sleeping, the first real tables—known as "tuckaways"—were narrow, with wide leaves, so they could be tucked away in a corner, or trestle tables fitted with draw pins.

The most important part of the room was the kitchen with its big fireplace—known as "chimneys"—sometimes as much as eight or ten feet in width. Whole animals could be roasted in such a fireplace. A hard wood bar crossed the flue, and from it hung the pots and kettles for cooking, for making cheese, for boiling soap and dipping candles. Inside the fireplace was a bench to sit on during the cold winter evenings. The flickering firelight was reflected in the brightly shined copper and brass and pewter ware which hung along the walls. Ladles, skimmers, spoons, colanders, and candlesticks were made of brass and iron and pewter.

The only light besides that of the open fire came from a few tallow candles, rushlights of reeds, or rushes, dipped in tallow, and long pieces of resinous pitch pine stuck between the hearth glads. Known as candlewood sets, these gave off a bright flare and a good deal of smoke.

"Betty lamps" were also used—small iron saucers filled with oil, with a handle at one end, and a nose or spout for the wick to lie in. These lamps dated back to the days of Pompeii and Athens.

FOOD IN EARLY NEW ENGLAND

The first winter was the hardest. In addition to being terrified by the roar of "lyons" and by wolves "who sat upon their tayles and grinned at them," the Pilgrims watched their scanty store of provisions shrink to almost nothing. By spring, half the members of the little colony were dead. The chance of survival of the others depended on the harvest, and when it came in, the rejoicing was great. For three days the settlers feasted on wild turkeys, geese, and eels and lobsters from the bay.

Flocks of wild pigeons darkened the sky, and lobsters were found in the bay that weighed from sixteen to twenty-five pounds and measured five to six feet from claw tip to claw tip.

Corn inevitably furnished the bulk of the settlers' fare, cooked Indian fashion, made into johnny cake, and hasty pudding—cornmeal mush and milk. It also provided bread in the form of "bannock"—cornmeal spread on a board and baked in front of the fires. Mixed with rye meal and baked in the brick oven along with the beans, it became the "Boston brown bread" of ever-popular fame.

In addition to corn, boiled meats and vegetables and stews predominated in the diet of the seventeenth-century New Englander. And the brick oven, in addition to beans, was used for the baking of peas, Indian puddings, pies, cakes, and sometimes meat and potatoes. Pumpkins with the seeds taken out through a hole in the stem were filled with milk and baked—and the empty shells were later used either to hold yarn and other housewifely items or as jack-o'-lanterns. Bean porridge was cooked in bulk and used over a period of time, hence the line in the old rhyme: "Bean porridge in the pot, nine days old." Cider came to be considered a necessity; a thoughtful husband would stipulate in his will that his widow was to be furnished with several—sometimes as many as eight—barrels a year.

Even in the Massachusetts Bay colony there were no stores for fifteen years; potatoes were not introduced for half a century; and though apple trees were planted, it was a long time before they bore fruit. Roger Clap of Dorchester wrote in his diary: "It was not accounted a strange thing in those days to drink water, and to eat Samp or Homine without Butter or Milk. Indeed it would have been a strange thing to see a piece of Roast Beef . . . though it was not long before there was a Roast Goat."

There was no lack of game and fish in these early days to help round out the diet.

NEW ENGLAND, 1720–1775

The houses became larger, often with four rooms to a floor for a two-story house, a stair hall or a large hall running through from front to back. These houses were of Georgian style. There was much woodwork on both the exterior and interior, although the houses retained their plain clapboard exteriors.

The furniture went from the simple and merely useful to the more elaborate and decorative. This was mostly true of the large towns and cities, however, for in the country plain homemade furniture continued to be the rule. During the long winter evenings, some of the men turned carpenter.

What people ate did not change essentially from one century to the other, but there was more variety. People ate beef, veal, mutton, lamb, pork, and chicken. There was butter, milk, and cheese. Gardens were green with vegetables, orchards luscious with fruit. There was much game and all kinds of fish.

The country folk and common fold had to content themselves with a fare of salted meat, fish, beans, and pudding. The "New England boiled dinner" of salted meat and cabbage, and perhaps one other vegetable, served as one dish, usually in a wooden trencher, was already in existence. During the winter, people ate pumpkins that had been baked in the ashes of the open fire.

An observer wrote of the Boston women in 1740: "They are not much esteemed now that will not treat high and gossip about. Tea has now become the darling of our women. Almost every little tradesman's wife must sit sipping tea for an hour or more in the morning, and maybe again in the afternoon, and nothing will please them to sip it out of but china ware, if they can get it. They talk of bestowing thirty or forty shillings upon a tea equipage, as they call it. There is the silver spoons, the silver tongs, and many other trinkets that I cannot name." Although tea was the common drink until the Revolution, coffee equaled it in popularity after that.

Preparing a meal in early Boston

COOKING IN NEW ENGLAND

All cooking was done in and over the fire. The first pole on which the pots and kettles hung was made of wood and called the lug pole. Wood was considered a failure, however, when, after the pole had charred to a point of weakness, it let the meal down into the embers. So iron was then substituted and a Yankee invention brought about the "crane," thus called because it suspended from the side wall in such a manner that it could be swung out into the room. Various-length hooks were used to hold the pots, from those of six inches to some fifteen inches. A trammel was a hook which could be lengthened or shortened to accommodate the height of the fire and the size of the kettle. This was made of two pieces of iron, the end of one having a hook which set into the other which had notches. This arrangement was copied in wood and used for holding a candle, the whole suspended near the fireplace. In those first fireplaces, the pots and kettles stood on legs, raising them above the hot embers. If they swung on the crane, they had flat bottoms. Much later, kettles had an extension which set into the stove hole.

SETTING THE TABLE

A letter written by one of the first settlers of Plymouth to a friend in Scrooby, England.

Dear Hannah:

I often ask myself what you of Scrooby would say could you see us at dinner. We have no table, and boards are very scarce and dear in price here in this village of ours, therefore father carefully saved the top of one of our packing boxes, while nearly all in the settlement did much the same, and these we call table boards.

When it is time to serve the meal, mother and I lay this board across two short logs; but we cover it with the linen brought from the old home, and none in the plantation, not even the governor himself, has better, as you well know.

I would we had more dishes; but they are costly, as even you at home know. Yet our table looks very inviting when it is spread for a feast, such as when guests come.

We have three trencher bowls, and another larger one in which all the food is placed. Then, in addition to the wooden cups we brought from home, there are many vessels of gourds that we have raised in the garden, and father has fashioned a mold for making spoons, so that now our pewter ware, when grown old with service, can be melted down into the spoons until we have a goodly abundance of them.

It is said, although I have not myself seen it, that a table implement called a fork is in the possession of Master Brewster, having been brought over from England. It is of iron, having two sharp points made to hold the food.

I cannot understand why any should need such a tool while they have their own cleanly fingers, and napkins of linen on which to wipe them. Perhaps father was right when he said that we who are come into this world for the single reason of worshipping God as we please, are too much bound up in the vanities of life, and father says he knows of no more vain thing than an iron tool with which to hold one's food.

I have seen at Master Bradford's home two bottles made of glass, and they are exceedingly beautiful; but so frail that I should scarce dare to wash them, for it would be a great disaster to break so valuable a vessel.

Ruth

SERVING THE FOOD IN NEW ENGLAND

Very simple folk sometimes put the cooking pot on the table and the whole family ate directly from it; but most people ladled the food onto the wooden trenchers and ate from them. A few families owned big pewter chargers on which they brought the food to the table.

Clean linen napkins were needed for every meal, because people ate with their fingers. If the nature of the food was such that fingers could not handle it, it was eaten with a spoon. If meat needed to be cut, you took your own knife out of its sheath and cut it. Spoons were made of wood, of horn, and of pewter. Silver spoons were unknown here until after 1650. Pewter is easily melted, so when spoons broke or wore out, they could be recast in a gunmetal mold.

Along with the trenchers and spoons, there were wooden noggins and tankards for milk, if the family owned a cow, and for beer whether there was a cow or not. There were pewter mugs for drinking, and some made of boiled leather, called "black jacks"—black for their color, jack from their material. Boiled leather was generally known as jacked leather; jack boots got their name the same way. Black jacks were sewn together with waxed linen thread and rimmed with pewter, copper, or silver.

When the meal ended, a basket called a voider was passed around the table and everything that had been used, including the napkins, was put into it to be taken away and washed.

Dining table of early Plymouth

Lob! Lob!! Lob!!! Lobsters!!!!
Who will buy my lobsters? Yesterday
These were down in Boston Bay.
Come, little maiden, buy one! Buy
And you may suck his claws all dry.

From A Quaint Old Picture Book

Higginson in his *New England Plantation* in 1630 realized how great the natural resources of the new country were when he said:

"Our Governor hath store of green pease growing in his garden as good as ever I eat in England. This country aboundeth naturally with store of roots of great variety and good to eat. Our turnips, parsnips and carrots are here both bigger and sweeter than is ordinarily to be found in England. Here are also store of pumpions, cowcumbers, and other things of that nature which I know not. Also, divers pot-herbs grow abundantly among the grass, as strawberries, penny-royal, winter savoury, sorrel, brooklime, liverwort, carvel and watercresses; also leeks and onions are ordinary and divers physical herbs. Here are also abundance of other sweet herbs whose names we know not. . . . Excellent vines are here up and down in the woods. Also mulberries, plums, raspberries, currants, chestnuts, filberts, walnuts, smallnuts, hurtleberries, and haws of whitethorn."

HIGGINSON ON FISH

"The abundance of sea-fish are almost beyond believing. . . . I saw great store of whales and grampuses, and such abundance of mackerels that it would astonish one to behold; likewise codfish, abundance on the coast and in their season plentifully taken. There is a fish called a bass, a most sweet and wholesome fish as ever I did eat; it is altogether as good as our fresh salmon, and besides bass we take plenty of scate and thornback, and abundance of lobsters. For my own part I was soon cloyed with them, and they were so great and fat and luscious. Also here is abundance of herring, turbot, sturgeon, cusks, haddock, mullets, eels, crabs, muscles, and oysters."

New England Plantation

COOKING UTENSILS

There was quite an array of cooking and roasting utensils for the big fireplace, first brought from the old countries and later made by the local blacksmiths.

The kettles were of many sizes and shapes, and pots vied with them in boasting of variety. Kettles have straight sides and no covers, while pots have bulging sides and covers. Brass and copper kettles were highly prized, coming as they did from across the water, while the lowly iron kettle was often used in trade with the Indians. The first iron kettle, rightly a pot, made in the new country was fashioned on a mold made by Joseph Jenks of Lynn in 1646.

Skillets were iron cooking utensils, standing on legs, with a protruding handle, and there were many sizes and often variety as to depth. The long handle of the fry pan measured three feet so that the housewife might stand away from the hot embers as she prepared dinner. Short-handled pans were called spiders, and aside from those, there were flat griddles which either hung on the crane by a hoop handle or stood on three legs. Gridirons were stands with gratings on legs. They were both round and square, and some even had a revolving head so that the food might be exposed to the fire on all sides. The long-legged stand was the trivet, and this was used to hold food to keep it warm after it had been prepared. Generally it had a handle for lifting it.

FOR AN OINTMENT TO CAUSE HAIR TO GROW

Take of boar's grease two ounces, ashes of burnt bees, ashes of southernwood, juice of white lily-root, oil of sweet almonds, of each one drachm; six drachms of pure musk; and according to art make an ointment of these; and the day before the full moon shave the place, anointing it every day with this ointment; it will cause hair to grow where you will have it. Oil of sweet almonds, or spirit of vinegar, is very good to rub the head with, if the hair grows thin.

The Complete Housewife, E. Smith, 1766

HASTY PUDDING

Puddings were a favorite New England food in the seventeenth and eighteenth centuries. They were easy for a housewife to make for a large gathering, the ingredients usually were at hand, they were an unpretentious way to satisfy a hankering for sweets, and they were economical. All these reasons made them ideal to Abigail Adams, who served puddings frequently. Least pretentious of any, and eaten in all homes, was hasty pudding, which is nothing more than boiled cornmeal mush served hot with maple sugar and butter. Here is a description of how to eat hasty pudding:

The hasty pudding being spread out equally on a plate, while hot, an excavation is made in the middle of it with a spoon, into which excavation a piece of butter as large as a nutmeg is put, and upon it a spoonful of brown sugar . . . The butter, being soon heated by the heat of the pudding, mixes with the sugar and forms a sauce, which, being confined in the excavation, occupies the middle of the plate. Thus for the array—now for the battle! Dip each spoonful in the sauce, before it is carried to the mouth, care being had in taking it up to begin on the outside, and near the brim of the plate, and to approach the center by gradual advances, in order not to demolish too soon the excavation which forms the reservoir of sauce.

THE FIRST AMERICAN BROOMS

During the winter, on the long, cold evenings when the family sat around the fireplace, the boys of the family made birch brooms for the household and earned spending money by making them for the country stores, from whence they were sent to the large cities, especially Boston, where there was a constant demand for them.

These earliest brooms made in America were simply slender birch saplings with the ends splintered. First, all the bark was removed from a sapling about six feet long and about two inches in diameter, then the wide end was splintered up about one foot, the hard core removed, and the splintered ends tied down tightly near the top with a length of hemp. About one foot, two inches above this tied section, more flat slivers were cut down from the opposite direction, leaving about a two-inch uncut ring between the two sets of splinters. The second bunch of splinters was folded over the first and bound securely. The rest of the sapling was shaped and smoothed to form a handle.

Tiny brooms similarly made were used for whisking eggs and whipping cream, slightly larger ones for cleaning pots and pans and for sweeping the ashes from the brick bake oven, and very large ones for heavy-duty sweeping, such as a barn floor. More bristly brooms were made by cutting and binding only the first section of slivers.

"Wing dusters," made from the wings of turkeys, geese, or chickens, were used as stove and hearth brushes. If the housekeeper was not careful, the cat managed to chew them up.

FOR SHORTNESS OF BREATH

Take two quarts of elder-berry juice when very ripe, put one quart in a pipkin to boil, and as it consumes, put in the rest by a little at a time; boil it to a balsam; it will take five or six hours in boiling. Take a little of it night and morning, or any time.

The Complete Housewife, E. Smith, 1766

MORE ABOUT COOKING UTENSILS

A busy utensil was the iron toaster for bread or cheese. The waffle iron was a pincher-shaped contrivance with a long handle.

Every fireplace had a Dutch oven, or fire pan. This was a shallow kettle with three legs, a cover, and a hoop handle. The cover had a rim which held the embers when the kettle was placed in the fire. This was a bake oven and was a result of the first principle of putting food directly in the embers to cook.

There were other tools and utensils at the fireside, such as the kettle-tilter, various spit turners, jack racks, and many forks, skimmers, and ladles for handling the meat cooking in the big pots.

CLAM PIE

1 pie shell, with crust to cover; 2 cups hard clams, chopped fine; ¼ cup clam liquor; 1 tablespoon butter, melted; ½ cup cracker crumbs; 1 egg, well beaten; 1 cup milk; salt and pepper.

Clean the clams and strain the liquor, saving ¼ cup of the liquor. Combine all of the ingredients, season with salt and pepper and pour into a deep pie shell. Cover with upper crust, seal all around and pierce top crust with fork. Bake in a moderate oven [350°F.] for about one hour. Serve very hot with mashed potatoes.

An Old Cape Cod Recipe

PORTSMOUTH, NEW HAMPSHIRE, 1750

James Birket visited Portsmouth, New Hampshire, in 1750, at which time it probably had a population of about 4,000. He described his visit thusly:

"The Town of Portsmouth is Scituated upon Piscataway river about 3 miles from the sea upon a Moderate rising ground, not only from the river, but also from the Adjacent country to the Parade or Center thereof; where 4 Principal streets meet in the nature of a + there are pretty Streight and regular through which you have a prospect of the country on every side; . . .

The houses that are of Modern Architecture are large and Exceeding neat this Sort is generally 3 Story high & well Sashed and Glazed with the best glass the rooms are well plastered and many Wainscoted or hung with painted paper from England the outside Clapboarded very neatly and are very warm. . . .

. . . The better sort of People here live very well and Genteel, They have no fixt market but the Country people come to town as it suits them with such of the Commoditys as they have for Sale by which the town is pretty well Supply'd with Beefe, Mutton, veal and other Butcher's Meat; they have plenty of large Hoggs and very fat bacon, they have also abundance of good fish of diferent Kinds, And abundance of Garden Culture as Beans, Peas, Carrots, Parnsips, Turnips, Radishes, Onions, Cabages, Colliflowers, Asparagus, English or whats commonly called Irish Potatoes also the Sweet Potatoe, Obtains almost all over North America, More so to southward, They have also Apples, Pears, Plumbs, Cherries, & Peaches in Abundance They have also Apricots & Nectrines from England, but do not Observe they had given any of them the Advantage of awall, there's likewise Goosberrys Currant Ditto Rasberries, Strawberries, Huckleberries Water & Muskmellions, Squashes and Sundry Other kinds of fruits roots &c &c There common drink is Cyder which they have in great Plenty, and New England rum And also a new rum from the West Indies, But People of fortune (especially the Marsh's) have very good rum and Madeira wine in their homes, Indeed the wine most commonly Drunk here is from the Canaries & Western Islands—called Oidonia, tis of a pale collor tastes harsh and is inclined to looke thick."

NEW ENGLAND HOME IN THE 1790'S

"The kitchen was large, fully twenty feet square, with a fireplace six feet wide and four feet deep. On one side it looked out upon the garden, the squashes and cucumbers climbing up and forming festoons over the door. The kitchen was in fact the most comfortable room in the house, cool in summer and perfumed with the breath of the garden and orchard; in the winter, with its roaring blaze of hickory, it was a cosy resort, defying the bitterest blasts of the season. . . . The cellar, extending under the whole house . . . was by no means the least important part of the house. In the autumn it contained barrels of beef and pork, barrels of cider, bins of potatoes, turnips, beets, carrots and cabbages. The garret, which was of huge dimensions, at the same time displayed a labyrinth of dried pumpkins, peaches, and apples, hung in festoons upon the rafters, amid bunches of summer savory, boneset, fennel and other herbs—the floor being occupied by heaps of wool, flax, tow and the like. . . ."

New England house and barn

AMERICAN COOKBOOKS

The first American cookbook was printed in Williamsburg, Virginia, in 1742. It was Eliza Smith's *The Compleat Housewife*. However, it was the most popular cookbook in England and there was nothing American about it. There were several printings after that.

The first cookbook published in Boston was Susannah Carter's *The Frugal Housewife* in 1772, and that, too, was British. Another English cookbook was *The New Art of Cookery* by Richard Briggs, printed in Philadelphia in 1792.

Since cookbooks were not actually in demand in young America, there was no cookbook written here until 1796. This was *American Cookery* and its author was Amelia Simmons, who called herself "An American Orphan." This cookbook introduced American dishes such as Indian pudding, Indian slapjack, and johnny cake. Since there were not enough American recipes to fill the book, she also included standard English recipes for meats, puddings, and vegetables.

After *American Cookery* came what can be called a rash of American cookbooks, such as *New England Cookery* in 1808 and an American version of an English cookbook in 1823 called *The Experienced American Housekeeper*, which contained just a few American recipes.

The first truly successful author of American cookbooks was Eliza Leslie, who started out in 1828 with a small volume called *Seventy-Five Receipts for Pastry, Cakes, and Sweetmeats*. From that she went on to *Domestic French Cookery, New Receipts for Cooking*, and finally, *Miss Leslie's New Cookery*. Although she had some English and French recipes, she included many that were purely American.

In 1824, the first of the regional cookbooks appeared with Mrs. Mary Randolph's *The Virginia Housewife*, to be followed by *The Carolina Housewife* in 1847 and *The Philadelphia Housewife* in 1855.

Meanwhile, many other cookbooks appeared and became popular. These served as springboards for the writers to project their views on thrift, morals, improved diet, and the evils of drunkenness. Mrs. Lydia Child in *The American Frugal Housewife* in 1835 extolled the value of thrift. Catherine Beecher, noted educator, was a supporter of the temperance movement and held out against tea, coffee, and certain types of food as well as alcohol.

Miss Beecher's Domestic Receipt Book made concessions when the author did fry some foods in lard and added wine to certain puddings, but on the whole she emphasized wholesome cooking and used many types of fruit. Catherine Beecher and her sister, Harriet Beecher Stowe, combined their talents and produced *The Housekeeper's Manual*, although Catherine had done a number of books prior to that on her own, and they also co-authored several other cookbooks.

Domestic Science became a part of the American school studies and Catherine Beecher was responsible for that. Also, special cooking schools were opened to teach the housewife the whys and wherefores of good and wise shopping and cooking.

Eventually there were many involved in the cooking schools, such as Maria Parloa in Boston who was then followed by Mary J. Lincoln and the most famous of all of the Boston cooking school heads, Fannie Merritt Farmer.

Sarah Rorer was a teacher of cooking in Philadelphia and was one of the first to publish a book with only vegetarian recipes.

Of all the cookbooks published prior to 1900, those by Fannie Merritt Farmer are still used today, as is *The Settlement Cook Book* by Mrs. Simon Kander, which was a schoolbook in the beginning in 1901 and today is one of the standbys in cookbooks.

VERY POPULAR COOKBOOKS, 1766 - 1910

The Complete Housewife, Eliza Smith, 1766

The Domestic Encyclopedia—Three Volumes, A.F.M. Willich, 1821

The Cook's Oracle, 1825

The Whole Art of Confectionary, 1831

The Cook's Own Book, 1832

The American Frugal Housewife, Mrs. Lydia Child, 1835

Directions for Cookery, Miss Eliza Leslie, 1837

The Good Housekeeper, Sarah Josepha Hale, 1839

The American Economical Housekeeper, Mrs. E.A. Howland, 1845

Mackenzie's Five Thousand Receipts, 1848

The Modern Housewife, Alexis Soyer, 1849

Receipt Book, Mrs. Putnam, 1849

American Lady's System of Cookery, Mrs. T.J. Crowen, 1850

Ladies Indispensable Assistant, 1851

The New Household Receipt Book, Sarah Josepha Hale, 1853

The Practical Housekeeper, Mrs. Ellet, 1857

Miss Beecher's Domestic Receipt Book, 1858

The Young Housekeeper's Friend, Mrs. Cornelius, 1859

The Virginia Housewife, Mrs. Mary Randolph, 1860

Dr. Chase's Recipes or Information for Everybody, A.W. Chase, M.D., 1866

American Woman's Home, Catherine E. Beecher and Harriet Beecher Stowe, 1869

Buckeye Cook Book, 1875

All Around the House, Mrs. H.W. Beecher, 1878

Housekeeping in Old Virginia, Marian Cabell Tyree, 1879

The Book of Household Management, Mrs. Isabella Beeton, 1880

Mary J. Lincoln's Boston Cook Book, 1883

Cookery for Beginners, Marion Harland, 1884

Breakfast, Luncheon and Tea, Marion Harland, 1887

Miss Parloa's Kitchen Companion, 1887

Boston Cook Book, Fannie Farmer, 1896

Mrs. Rorer's Cook Book, 1898

The Settlement Cook Book, Mrs. Simon Kander, 1901

Complete Cook Book, Marion Harland, 1903

Ladies' Home Cook Book, Julia MacNair Wright, 1903

What to Have for Dinner, Fannie Farmer, 1905

Queen of the Household, Mrs. M.W. Ellsworth, 1906

Mrs. Curtis's Cook Book, 1908

Aunt Babette's Cook Book, 1910

THE SOLITARY ORPHAN

It must ever remain a check upon the poor solitary orphan, that while those females that have parents, or brothers, or riches to defend their indiscretions, that the orphan must depend solely upon character. How immensely important therefore, that every action, every word, every thought, be regulated by the strictest purity, and that every movement meet the approbation of the good and wise.

American Cookery by Amelia Simmons, 1796

INDIAN SLAPJACK

One quart milk, one pint Indian meal, four eggs, four spoons of flour, little salt, beat together, baked on griddles, or fry in a dry pan, or baked in a pan which has been rubbed with suet, lard or butter.

American Cookery by Amelia Simmons, 1796

THE NEW HOUSEHOLD RECEIPT BOOK,
Sarah Josepha Hale, 1853

Sarah Josepha Hale was well-known as the editor of *Godey's Lady's Book*, but she also wrote several cookbooks which contained household hints.

In this one she said: "In the economy and well-being of a family, personal and individual improvement should be sedulously kept in view. It is not enough that the woman understands the art of cookery and of managing her house: she must also take care of herself; of children; of all who will be dependent on her for direction, for health, for happiness. . . ."

One of her topics for discussion was CORPULENCE: "Those who are afflicted with corpulence should not allow themselves above six hours' sleep in the twenty-four. They should take as much exercise as possible, and avoid cream, malt liquors and soups—at least until they have succeeded in reducing their bulk. Salt provisions are good, having a tendency to promote perspiration and carry off fat. Soda water is also beneficial. *Receipt*: Take Castile soap, in the form of pills or electuary, of from one to four drachms dissolved in a quarter of a pint of soft water, when going to bed. But let not our lovely girls abuse their constitutions by drinking vinegar for this purpose, for consumption has often been produced by that habit."

MISS LESLIE'S NEW COOKERY, 1858

By the time this, the last of Eliza Leslie's cookbooks, appeared, her original 75 recipes mentioned earlier had expanded to a thousand. Along with the recipes, she now included timely advice:

"No man (or woman either) ought to be incapable of distinguishing bad eatables from good ones. Yet, I have heard some few ladies boast of that incapacity as something meritorious, and declare that they considered the quality, the preparation, and even the taste of food, as things entirely beneath the attention of a rational being; their own minds being always occupied with objects of far greater importance.

"Let no man marry such a woman. If indifferent to her own food, he will find her still more indifferent to his. . . .

"Let all housekeepers remember that there is no possibility of producing nice dishes without a liberal allowance of good ingredients. . . .

"A sufficiency of wholesome and well-prepared food is absolutely necessary to the preservation of health and strength, both of body and mind. . . For those who possess the means of living well, it is false (and sometimes fatal) economy to live badly; particularly when there is a lavish expenditure in fine clothes, fine furniture, and other ostentations, only excusable when *not* purchased at the expense of health and comfort."

EGG PLANTS, STUFFED

Parboil them to take off their bitterness. Then slit each one down the side and extract the seeds. Have ready a stuffing made of grated bread-crumbs, butter, minced sweet herbs, salt, pepper, nutmeg, and beaten yolk of egg. Fill with it the cavity from whence you took the seeds, and bake the egg plants in a Dutch Oven. Serve them up with a made gravy poured into the dish.

Miss Leslie's New Cookery, 1858

Author's note: A nice tomato sauce would be delicious. Use your favorite bread stuffing.

INDIAN CAKE OR BANNOCK

Is sweet and cheap food. One quart of sifted meal, two great spoonfuls of molasses, two teaspoonfuls of salt, a bit of shortening half as big as a hen's egg, stirred together. Make it pretty moist with scalding water, put it in a well greased pan and bake it brown on both sides before a quick fire. A little stewed pumpkin scalded with milk improves the cake. Bannock split and dipped in butter makes very nice toast.

The Pocumtuc Housewife, 1805

HOW TO HEAT THE OVEN

Some people consider it economical to heat Ovens with fagots, brush and light stuff. Hard wood heats it quicker and hotter. Take four foot wood split fine, and pile it criss-cross so as to nearly fill the oven, and keep putting in. A Roaring fire for an hour or more is usually enough. The top and sides will at first be covered with black soot. See that it is all burned off. Rake the coals over the bottom of the Oven and let them lie a minute. Then sweep it out clean. If you can hold your hand inside while you count forty, it is about right for flour bread; to count twenty is right for Rye and Indian. If it is too hot, wet an old broom two or three times and turn it around near the top of the oven till it dries; this prevents pies and cakes from scorching on top. When you go into a new house, heat your oven two or three times to get it seasoned before you use it.

Bake the Brown bread first, then flour bread and Pies, then Cake or puddings, and last Custards. After everything else is out put in a pan of apples. Next morning they will be deliciously baked. A pot of Beans can be baking back side, out of the way of the Rest.

If bread runs short before baking day comes, light cakes can be baked in the bake Kettle or the tin Baker. Draw out a solid mass of coals, set the bake-kettle over it, put in your biscuit, put on the lid, and cover it with a thick layer of coals.

The Pocumtuc Housewife, 1805

Baking in fireplace oven

THE STOVE

The convenience of the stove for cooking had more influence on its eventual popularity than all other factors combined. Food was said to be better cooked in a fireplace, but the operation was slow and much labor was required to prepare a meal. The first attempt at a closed fireplace was made by Cardinal Polignac of France in 1708. Holland invented the plain box-stove with a single door, a single hole in the top, and a small smoke pipe. Both styles saved valuable fuel but were not popular with the people.

Ben Franklin made many suggestions on the topic of stoves. In 1745, he invented an enclosed fireplace in which the current of flame and air passed through air boxes in the sides. Thus, most of the heat was saved and passed into the room. The stove had a damper and would have been airtight except that castings were not made to fit tightly.

In 1771, Franklin invented a stove for bituminous coal. It had a downward draft and consumed its own smoke. From 1785 to 1795, Count Rumford, an American, devised many improvements. He invented the cooking range and the ventilating ovens that were used in New York and Boston. These were first used from around 1798–1800.

Until 1835, the stoves were made at bog-iron and blast furnaces. The plates were cast directly from the iron in the smelting furnaces.

The first furnace to cast stoves from pig iron was built in New York by Jordan L. Mott. He had been making self-feeding coal stoves since 1827, and anthracite coal stoves since 1833. In 1835, Mott bought some of the immense refuse or tailings in the Schuylkill coalyards and screened them for nut and pea coal for his stoves. He sold this coal to the owners of his stoves. His success encouraged others to begin the manufacture of stoves, and plants were started in Albany and Providence.

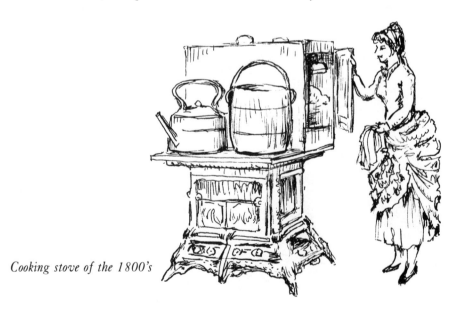

Cooking stove of the 1800's

Dr. Eliphalet Nott of the Union College began experimenting and developed the gas burner and other stoves. He was the president of the college, but he never reaped a reward for his many contributions to the stove industry.

With better transportation, cooking stoves were shipped and sold around the country. The early patterns were ten-plate oval stoves with the oven above the fire and a stove collar over it. The saddlebag design came next, with the oven in the center of the stove and the stovepipe and collar over it. By 1881, nearly a thousand patents had been issued on stoves.

In that same year, there were two hundred and twenty firms manufacturing all types of stoves. They were made with two, four, six, and eight holes for kettles. Some had fixed boilers and some had double ovens. Stove producers were indebted to the county fairs, which popularized and advertised the newest model of stove.

OF EATING

Accustom your palate to what is most usual; he that delights in rarities must often feed displeased, and lie at the pleasure of a dear market; common food nourishes best; delicacies please most; the sound stomach prefers neither; what is any man the worse for the last year's plain diet, or what now the better for last year's feasting?

An Astronomical Diary, or Almanack, for the Year of Christian Era, 1795,
Daniel Sewall, Portsmouth, N.H.

WINTER

Winter was the time to stay indoors and try to keep warm. Lots of baking was done in order to keep the kitchen warm.

Often the children of the family went to another town to attend school, since the local school was a one-room affair. In order to get a little more of an education, the children attended an academy in a neighboring village.

The housewife would cook the food and send it to or with the children so that it would be more reasonable to keep them in school. Also, the children preferred the food from home. Each weekend the family would be together, and the children would take the food for the following week with them late Sunday evening or very early Monday morning.

While the older children were away at school in the neighboring village, the younger children went to school locally, and the rural schoolteacher lived in one of the local households.

The winter was the time for the housewife to get her weaving, spinning, and other indoor chores done. Meanwhile, she was planning her spring activities; what herbs she would plant, and what plants and flowers she would put in the garden to pretty things up.

HINTS AND MAXIMS

If you chance to occupy the important position of a cook, remember that cleanliness is the first, second, and third requirement in point of importance, to be observed.

Keep your flour-box, sugar, salt, and spices always covered, that dust and insects may not get in.

Never put onion or cheese on the same dish with anything else, and never cut anything else with the knife you use for them. Keep a particular pitcher for beer or buttermilk, or you may chance to put milk or water into the remains.

Keep your tin and copper vessels as sweet and clean as glass or china. The saucepans are of far more consequence than tumblers or teacups. If glasses be dirty, those who drink from them are disgusted; but if saucepans be foul, they may chance to be poisoned. Many have died from this cause. The sort of rust which forms in copper vessels not kept clean is a deadly poison. If a housekeeper is careful, she will look into all her saucepans at least once a week, to see if they are well cleaned, or want tinning.

Let the dinner be served quite hot, and have the plates as hot as you can handle them. Cold plates spoil the finest joint of meat; and it is very easy to have plates hot. At breakfast and tea it will be your fault if the tea is not good. It is a very common fault in cooks, as soon as the teakettle boils, to set it on one side where the water cools a little, so that it is not *quite* boiling when poured on the tea.

The true economy of housekeeping is simply the art of gathering up all the fragments, so that nothing be lost. I mean fragments of *time*, as well as materials. Nothing should be thrown away so long as it is possible to make any use of it, however trifly that use may be; and whatever be the size of a family, every member should be employed either in earning or saving money.

Few know how to keep the flavor of sweet marjoram, the best of all herbs for broth and stuffing. It should be gathered in bud or blossom and dried in a tin kitchen at a moderate distance from the fire; when dry it should be rubbed, sifted, and corked up in a bottle.

Herbs should be kept from the air. Herb tea, to do any good, should be made very strong. Herbs must be gathered while in blossom. Those who have a little ground will do well to raise the most useful herbs; apothecaries make large profits on them.

Cut lemon and orange peel, when fresh, into a bottle kept full of brandy. This brandy gives a delicious flavor to pies, cakes, &c. Roseleaves may be preserved in brandy. Peach leaves steeped in it make an excellent seasoning for custards and puddings.

Potatoes boiled and mashed hot, are good in shortcakes and puddings; they save flour and shortening.

Let there be a place for every article, and when not in use let every article be in its place.

The Practical Housekeeper, Mrs. Ellet, 1857

PRESERVATION OF WINTER APPLES

Apples keep best in low temperatures, and may be well preserved in an ice-house. An English journal recommends the use of dry pit sand for preserving pears and apples. Glazed earthen jars are to be provided, and the sand to be thoroughly dried. A layer of sand an inch thick is then placed in the bottom of the jar; above this a layer of fruit, to be covered with a layer of sand an inch thick; then lay a second stratum of fruit, covering again with an inch of sand. An inch and a half of sand may be placed over the uppermost row of fruit. The jar is now to be closed, and placed in a dry situation, as cool as possible, but entirely free from frost. Some assert that apples may be kept in casks through the winter, in a chamber or garret, by being merely covered with linen cloths.

Farmer's Almanack, 1830, Robert B. Thomas

FOR AN OBSTINATE COUGH

Take a half pound of the best honey, and squeeze the juice of four lemons upon it; mix them well together, and add a small portion of sugar candy. A teaspoonful may be taken every time the cough is troublesome, and in a short time a cure will be effected.

The Housekeeper's Book, 1838

ODDS AND ENDS

There are certain odds and ends, where every housekeeper will gain much by having a regular time to attend to them. Let this time be the last Saturday forenoon in every month, or any other time more agreeable, let there be a regular fixed time once a month, in which the housekeeper will check rooms, closets, cellars, etc. to make certain that all is in order.

Miss Beecher's Domestic Receipt Book, 1846

TO REMEDY THE CREAKING OF A DOOR: Rub a piece of soap on its hinges, and it will be instantly silenced.

TO CLEAN PAPERED WALLS: Moisten with water a clean large cloth; gently wipe off the dust from the paper. Stale bread rubbed on will answer the purpose.

TO TAKE IRON STAINS OUT OF MARBLE: Mix equal quantities of spirit of vitriol and lemon-juice, shake it well, wet the spots, and in a few minutes rub with a soften linen till they are gone.

The American Practical Cookery Books, 1859

KITCHEN FURNITURE—1800

The kitchen floor should be covered with an oil cloth. Carpets, or bits of carpet, are not so good, because of the grease and filth that must accumulate in them, and the labor of sweeping, shaking, and cleansing them. Nothing is cleansed so easily as an oil cloth, and it is much better than a painted floor, because it can be removed to be painted.

If the cook is troubled with cold feet in winter, small bits of carpeting can be laid where she sits and stands the most. Otherwise they had better be kept out of the kitchen.

There should always be a clock in the kitchen, as indispensable to success in cooking, and regularity of meals.

Two tables, a large one for cooking, and a small one for meals, should be provided.

There should be tin boxes made with tight lapping covers, and of three sizes. In the largest put two kinds of sugar, and starch. In the medium size keep tea and coffee, table salt and ginger. In the smallest size keep cream of tartar, indigo, mustard, sweet herbs, and spices. In Junk bottles, keep a supply of vinegar, molasses and catsup.

Miss Beecher's Domestic Receipt Book, 1846

VICTORIAN KITCHEN

The Victorian kitchen was a bright, warm, and cozy room with a pleasant window or two, plants on the window sill, and an easy chair with a work basket nearby for sewing, mending, and darning materials. The curtains were either white muslin or a gay print.

The walls were painted or calcimined, while the floor usually had a linoleum on it since this was easier to care for than a plain wooden floor.

The kitchen sink was of iron, soapstone, wood, granite, or crockery, depending upon the means and preferences of the housekeeper. The stove burned hard or soft coal, wood, or cobs; it cooked the food, heated the water, boiled the laundry. In the winter the stove heated the room to a cozy warmth, while it made the same room uncomfortably hot in the summer.

The kitchen table was wood, plain or painted. Sometimes a piece of linoleum matching that on the floor was shaped into a durable table covering. Small rag rugs by the stove and sink made a comfortable spot for the cook or dishwasher to stand on. These rugs were either bought from a door-to-door salesman or made by the woman of the house.

Most kitchens had a pantry next to it. This was a small room provided with a table or table-shelf that could be raised or lowered as necessary and shelves and drawers for storing supplies. The shelves were either open or concealed behind doors that were solid wood or had curtained glass panels. The flour barrel and sugar bucket were also stored in the pantry.

On one side of the pantry there were hooks on the walls for aprons and towels. The broom, mop, carpet beater, pails, dust pans, feather duster, and other cleaning equipment were also kept here, as were oil and wicks for the oil lamps and a handy small stepladder.

Kitchen sink of the 1880's

Scrubbing the floor

THE CARE OF THE KITCHEN

If parents wish their daughters to grow up with good domestic habits, they should have, as one means of securing this result, a neat and cheerful kitchen. . . .

A sink should be scalded out every day, and occasionally with hot lye. On nails, over the sink, should be hung three good dishcloths, hemmed, and furnished with loops; one for dishes not greasy, one for greasy dishes, and one for washing greasy pots and kettles. These should be put in the wash every week. The lady who insists upon this will not be annoyed by having her dishes washed with dark, musty and greasy rags, as is too frequently the case.

American Woman's Home, Beecher and Stowe, 1869

BAKING BREAD

It used to be said that Sunday was go-to-meeting day, Monday was washday, Tuesday was ironing day, Wednesday was mending day, Thursday was get-together day, Friday was cleaning day, and Saturday was baking day. This schedule was followed religiously by most of the housewives after the Civil War.

Baking a week's supply of bread was a regular chore on Saturday for every housewife or some other female in the household. It did not stop with bread or rolls. Our housewife also baked a pie or two and at least one cake and maybe some doughnuts.

THE GENERAL STORE

The smaller towns could not support separate grocery, meat, fruit, hardware, and notions stores, so they had their general stores. These handled food, housewares, hardware, farm supplies—almost anything you might think of. If the general store was out of a particular size or brand that you wanted, you either took a substitute, waited for a new shipment to come in, or got back in your wagon or buggy and drove to the next town to get what you wanted.

Usually the general store was also the post office and general meeting place for the area. There were cracker barrels to sit around on inclement days and checkerboards where one could while away the hours with a friend or with the owner. Or one could gossip about crops or about the antics of the local residents.

FASHIONABLE ROUTS

"How strange it is," said a lady, "that fashionable parties should be called routs! Why routs formerly signified the death of an army and when the soldiers were all put to flight or to the sword they were said to be routed." "This title has some propriety too," said a clergyman. "For all these meetings whole families are frequently ROUTED OUT OF HOUSE AND HOME."

The New England Almanac, 1836, Anson Allen

CABBAGE JELLY

A tasty little dish, and by some persons esteemed more wholesome than cabbage simply boiled. Boil cabbage in the usual way, and squeeze in a colander till perfectly dry. Then chop small; add a little butter, pepper, and salt. Press the whole very closely into an earthenware mould, and bake one hour, either in a side oven or in front of the fire; when done, turn it out.

Godey's Lady's Book and Magazine, 1861

MORE ABOUT KITCHENS

"A man knows—or thinks he does—just what he needs in his study or library. . . . But a woman who practically understands what it is to do the work, or daily

Churning butter

arrange for others to do, naturally realizes more truly than a man can do, that, in building a kitchen, whenever beauty and utility are not compatible, utility must be the major, and beauty the minor, consideration.

"To be sure, we see no reason why a particular apartment cannot be made tasteful and attractive, yet perfectly convenient. . . .

"Much time is wasted, and not half the efficient labor performed, for lack of more attention to the architectural design of many of our kitchens. Some are so small that one cannot but feel 'cribbed, cabined and confined,' just to step inside of them. In others, one is bewildered and lost in the great "SAHARAS" which are called kitchens—a wilderness, where everything is lost, and nothing can be found; . . .

". . . . a long table, fitted so closely to the sink that no water can drip between is much needed. It is better to have it permanently fastened to the wall, and made as wide as the sink—a kind of long, wide shelf or table on which to clean vegetables, dress meat, poultry, game, etc., and, by being thus made of easy access to hot and cold water, it saves time and many steps. . . ."

All Around the House, H.W. Beecher, 1878

ALMANACS

The origins of the modern almanac go well back into the eighteenth century, when the annual publication of each volume was a significant event in the life of colonial America. Almost every household had need of the information contained in its pages in order to plan the planting of crops, care for the ill, educate the young, and take care of dozens of household chores. The pages also served as handy places, for those who could write, to jot down personal information, recipes, cures, and agricultural data.

In many a colonial household where the Bible and Psalmbook formed the sole standing library, the almanac was the only other book that crossed the threshold.

In the latter part of the nineteenth century, almanacs were issued by various companies to advertise their products. They often contained the basic material found in the old almanacs and in addition contained recipes, games, songs, etc., for the edification of the entire family.

CONVENIENT KITCHENS
MAKE PATIENT HOUSEWIVES

Three large windows are desirable, and for a spacious kitchen, four will make work more comfortable.

A range, or cooking-stove, should never be placed opposite a door or window if it can be avoided; for sunlight or wind, striking across them, will deaden either coal or wood fires, and thus prevent the oven from baking evenly.

Some kind of ventilator is important over the range or stove, by which steam and all disagreeable odors can be carried off without pervading the whole house.

It is more convenient to have the sink on the left side of the range; but, whichever side it is placed, it should be as near the window as possible, to secure plenty of light.

All Around the House, H.W. Beecher, 1878

THE DINING ROOM

Let your breakfasts be of wholesome and substantial food. The system needs nourishment in the morning after the long, unbroken fast of the night. The practice of taking only a cup of tea or coffee, or chocolate with hot biscuits, and possibly pie

The dumbwaiter—1870's

or doughnuts, gives a very poor foundation for the morning's labor, which is and should be the hard labor of the day. The morning meal should be taken as soon as possible after rising.

The midday and evening meal may vary with the occupations and habits of the family; but a regular hour for eating should be observed, whether the more substantial meal come at noon or night; and if at night sufficient time should be allowed for digestion to be completed before sleeping. A supper of cold bread and cake or pie is neither appetizing nor satisfying for those who have been hard at work throughout the day.

Boston Cook Book, Mary J. Lincoln, 1883

FOOD FOR THE URBAN FAMILY—1800'S

Fresh foods had to be purchased in quantity when they became available and then immediately processed so as to remain fresh. Often the entire family was pressed into kitchen duty.

Fruits and vegetables arrived in the kitchen in sacks or baskets from local gardens and farms.

Out-of-season foods would arrive in the kitchen in smaller quantities, if at all, only as they could be purchased in the general store. These foods usually included oranges, grapes, raisins, pineapples, bananas.

Flour, cornmeal, and other grains were bought by the barrel or the fifty-pound sack and then transferred to kitchen canisters as needed.

Sugar came in large cones or loaves, sometimes two or three feet high, weighing anywhere from twelve to fifty-five pounds. The housewife hung them from the ceiling by cords and put a netting over the cone to discourage flies. To prepare the sugar for use, the housewife knocked a chunk from the cone with a hammer or cut off a piece with "sugar cutters" and pounded it into granules.

Salt arrived in the kitchen in large blocks, and of course peppercorns, nutmeg, cloves, and cinnamon had to be ground as needed.

Ale and cider came in large stoppered jugs. These were the most popular drinks prior to the Civil War, when the men were introduced to coffee as regular fare and it soon became the national beverage.

The housewife bought the coffee beans green, so she roasted them first in a special home coffee roaster and then ground the coffee in a coffee mill when needed.

Chickens, turkeys, and ducks came to the kitchen trussed up but alive and had to be processed by the housewife before being used. The same was true of fish, which may not have been alive but which had to be scaled, shelled, and prepared at sink or counter.

The only way a family could be certain of having meat on the table was to buy it in quantity when available and "put down" a supply in the cellar after smoking and pickling the parts. They also made their own sausages.

In many homes dairy products also involved the entire family since, to be assured of a regular supply, families usually kept a cow or two that had to be fed, milked, the cream separated, butter churned, and cheese made.

With all that the housewife had to do just to keep her family fed, it was no wonder that she had little leisure time.

"The well-fed family, especially when that family is not 'eating up its margins,' is usually the cheery, comfortable, amiable family, and any physician can speedily expound the close connection between good morals and good digestion."

POTATO PIE

Scald one quart of milk, grate in four large potatoes while the milk is hot; when cold add four eggs well beaten, and four ounces of butter; spice and sweeten to taste; lay in paste. Bake half an hour.

Mrs. Winslow's Domestic Receipt Book, 1871
Brown's Bronchial Troches for Coughs and Colds

FRIED CABBAGE

Chop cold boiled cabbage fine and drain very dry, add two well beaten eggs, three tablespoonfuls of cream, one of melted butter, salt and pepper. Heat all in a buttered frying pan, stir until smoking hot. Then let it stand long enough to brown slightly on the bottom. Turn upside down on a platter and serve.

Ransom's Family Receipt Book, D. Ransom & Son, Buffalo, N.Y.

Bloomville, O., Jan. 31, 1900

D. Ransom Son & Co.

On the 1st of April next, I will have sold Ransom's Hive Syrup and Tolu for 23 years. Of a family of five boys, the youngest of whom graduates this summer, every one has been carried through Croup on this medicine. Have found Physicians here honest enough to send such cases to Drug Stores for this remedy.

F. A. Chatfield
Ransom's Family Receipt Book, D. Ransom & Son, Buffalo, N.Y.

A GOOD RECIPE

Here is a receipt which I once read, and always remember it because of its goodness. I sent it that others may try it.

Take a gill of forbearance
A pinch of submission
Twelve ounces of patience
A handful of grace
Mix well with the milk of the best human kindness.

Household, January 1876

TO KEEP PIANO KEYS CLEAN AND WHITE

Dampen a piece of muslin with alcohol, and with it rub the keys. If this does not remove the stains, use a piece of cotton flannel wet with cologne water. The keys can also be bleached white by laying over the keys cotton flannel cloths that have been saturated with a solution of oxalic acid.

Marion Harland's Complete Cook Book, 1903

A musical evening

In no department of industry has the last century brought greater changes than in the department of housekeeping. Then, the housekeeper was at the head of, and the principal worker in a manufacturing plant in which was made nearly everything used by the family. . . .

Today all this is changed. While food has still to undergo some measure of preparation within the household, and while there are still a sufficiency of duties for the housekeeper, the work has been greatly simplified and made easier by the invention of many labor-saving devices, appliances, and processes.

The New England Cook Book, 1905

RUM PUDDING

Take 19 eggs (yolks and whites beaten separately), 1 pint of sweet cream, ½ pound sugar, ½ pint rum and 1½ ounces gelatine; stir the yolks of the eggs and sugar to a cream, add the cream and rum, put this in a tin pail and set in a vessel of hot water; keep stirring with an egg beater until just about to boil; then quickly remove from the fire; have gelatine soaked in a little cold water, add it to the cream and mix well; when cold add the beaten whites of the eggs, pour into a mould and set on ice; in serving turn out and send fruit sauce to table with it.

Desserts and Salads, 1907

KITCHEN FURNITURE—1900

The kitchen of 1900 was a huge and often severely plain room with a large table used as a family gathering place. The table also served as a work area for preparing the daily meals, a handy place for after-school snacks, a desk for doing homework, and a place to gather for family discussions.

A washstand stood close by the back door. On it were a pitcher or pail of water, a washbasin, and a hand towel to be used by anyone who came into the house from outside chores.

The kitchen stove was wood-burning, and next to it was a built-in water reservoir. It was the responsibility of the boys in the family to keep the woodbin and water reservoir filled at all times.

There was a pie safe with perforated tin doors that held all the baked goods that had been prepared on the previous bake-day.

In city homes and homes that had an icehouse, there was an icebox for keeping milk, butter, and other perishable foods. Usually the farm kitchen had no icebox but there was a well house or spring house to serve the purpose.

Kitchen cabinets were free-standing and had flour and coffee bins built in above the work counter along with built-in sifters and grinders. The space beneath the counter contained storage bins for potatoes and other dry storage vegetables.

KITCHEN UTENSILS—1900

Since the kitchen was large and used constantly, there usually was a small rocking chair and sewing drawer in it so that mending might be done while the baking was in progress. Butter-churning was also done in the kitchen, so this equipment was kept handy there.

Storage vessels ranging from small butter crocks through milk jars of assorted sizes to huge pickle and kraut crocks were of pottery or stoneware, while mixing bowls of all sizes were of woodenware or stoneware. Dishpans, coffee pots, pie pans, and other baking pans were usually of graniteware. In fact, most of the cookware was of graniteware, except for the cast-iron beanpots and frying pans.

Butter molds and various types of mashers and mallets were made of wood, with the most important item in the kitchen being a set of stirring spoons of all sizes. No self-respecting housewife used a metal spoon, since it was said that metal spoiled the taste of the food and could contaminate it.

There was a glass-front cabinet filled with "company" china, glassware, and silver, used only for special occasions. The everyday table was set with the cheaper ironstone dishes and a form of metal alloy tableware.

The kitchen was well stocked with labor- and time-saving gadgets—for this was the age of gadgetry. Graters and grinders ranged from the tiny metal nutmeg grater to the heavy iron sausage grinder. Potato ricers and graters did double duty, helping to prepare horseradish and relishes as well as finely ground infant and invalid foods.

The iron sausage grinder was clamped to a table top and kept in constant use during the butchering season.

Apple peelers and cherry seeders also clamped to the table top, and not a kitchen was without these utensils. Also needed were iron ice tongs and stove lid lifters, and a long iron poker for the kitchen stove.

Some of these may seem like useless gadgets to us today, but they certainly were of the utmost importance to the housewife in 1900. Perhaps some of the utensils used today will appear obsolete in seventy-five years.

HANDIWORK

The long winter months were an opportune time for the women of the family to concentrate on their handiwork. Little girls were taught to knit as soon as their hands could hold the needles. Sometimes girls four years of age could knit stockings. Boys had to knit their own suspenders. All the stockings and mittens for the family, and coarse socks and mittens for sale, were made in large numbers. Much fine knitting was done, with many intricate and elaborate stitches. Those known as the "herringbone" and "fox and geese" were great favorites.

An elaborate and much-admired form of knitting was the bead bag and purse which were made with great variety and ingenuity. Beautiful bags were knitted to match wedding gowns. Knitted purses were given as gifts to husband and lover.

Netting was another decorative work. Netted fringes for edging the coverlets, curtains, tests, and valences were made of cotton thread or twine, while silk or cotton netting was used to trim sacks and petticoats.

Small fishing nets were also netted, but of twine.

Prior to the Revolution there was a boarding school kept in Philadelphia by a Mrs. Sarah Wilson, who advertised thusly:

"Young ladies may be educated in genteel manner, and pains taken to teach them in regard to their behavior, on reasonable terms. They may be taught all sorts fine needlework, viz., working on catgut or flowering muslin, sattin stitch, quince stitch, tent stitch, cross-stitch, open work, tambour, embroidering curtains or chairs, writing and cyphering. Likewise waxwork in all its several branches, never as yet particularly taught here; also how to take profiles in wax, to make wax flowers and fruits and pinbaskets."

NEW YEAR'S DAY CALLS

The custom of paying New Year's calls originated in New York, where the Dutch held open house on New Year's Day and served cherry bounce, olykoeks steeped in rum, cookies, and honey cakes. Gradually the custom spread throughout the country, and General Washington on the first New Year's Day after his inauguration held an open house and continued to do so while he was President.

However, eventually it became so popular that those who intended to receive company listed in the newspapers the hours they would be receiving. It soon got out of hand as strangers went from house to house for a glass of punch and a bit of a meal. The public announcements were dropped, and open house was just for invited friends.

THE FOOT WARMER

The foot warmer in its various forms was an indispensable item of family equipment since it was used to keep warm in church and in sleighs and carriages in

One-horse shay

winter. Some took the form of metal boxes and cylinders into which live coals could be placed; others were heated stones with handles and wrapped in blankets, and some consisted merely of woolen bags into which the feet could be inserted.

However, the most popular was a long-handled, covered pan containing hot coals, which was inserted between the sheets of a bed on cold nights. Thus cold feet were eliminated for at least a few minutes upon retiring in an unheated bedroom.

FASTNACHTS

These Pennsylvania Dutch doughnuts were served traditionally on Fastnacht Day (Shrove Tuesday), a last sweet before the Lenten season began.

THE WEEKLY BATH: *Diary of An Early American Housewife*

February 10, 1772—Although it was one of the coldest days of this winter, I would not let the children go without their personal ablutions this week. Personal cleanliness is a duty and with the coming of Sabbath must be carried out.

TAKING A BATH

From the beginning of the New Englander's Sabbath, at sunset on Saturday evening, the housewife must have found that portion of sacred time anything but a rest period. The Saturday evening meal was hastened so that the dishes might be washed on secular time. However, personal washings were held to be of religious importance, since personal cleanliness was considered a religious duty.

The conscientious scrubbing of each member of the family began with the youngest and concluded with the oldest member of the household.

There were no special rooms for bathing. Hot water could only be procured by heating in great iron pots over the open fire, and the tubs used for baths were, in general, the same that were used for the washing of clothes. However, there were some tubs made for bathing purposes only. These were of cedar and large enough for a tall man to lie in at full length. As there were no particular rooms for bathing, the tubs were usually left in the damp cellars through the week, that they might not become dry enough to leak.

If a fire was not kept in the best room throughout the week, one would be lighted there every Saturday during the cold weather and maintained until late on Sunday night. This left the fires in the kitchens free for the servants, and those in the living rooms, for the family. If there were no servants, often the kitchen would be the improvised bathroom for the entire family.

If the best room was used, the carpets, if any, were protected and the tubs were set, each one shielded from view on all sides, save that nearest the fire, by heavy woolen coverlets or blankets hung over clotheshorses. With the fireplaces being generally large, as many as three or four or even more such curtained cabinets might be made in front of each fire. As much cold water as was desired was poured into the tub and was then brought to the required temperature by the addition of boiling water from the great iron or brass kettles.

Carrying out the water that had been used by each bather and emptying the tubs at a little distance from the house was hard work, and usually the strongest servants and members of the family were assigned this task.

Nothing but a case of severe illness was allowed to excuse any inmate of a self-respecting household from taking the weekly Saturday night bath.

Original Saturday night bath

SOAP AND THE SKIN

Since the soap was of home manufacture and very harsh in quality, as little of it as possible was used on the body. Those who were careful of their complexions rarely used any soap about their faces, but instead softened the water by using a very little lye made from the ashes of hard woods. Rose-water made by the housewife and various unguents also made by her were then applied to heal the smart. In warm weather, buttermilk was considered excellent for the complexion, and in severe winter weather, cider brandy was used by some, while an ointment of mutton tallow and lard was used by others.

SLEIGH RIDING IN NEW YORK

"Their diversion in winter is riding in sleighs about three miles out of town, where they have houses of entertainment at a place called the Bowery; and some go to friends' houses, who handsomely treat them. I believe we mett fifty or sixty sleighs one day; they fly with great swiftness, and some are so furious that they turn out for none except a loaded cart."

Madame Knight's Visit To New York, 1704

THE TURKEY

The origin of the name "turkey" has been variously explained but one of the most reasonable explanations is that it comes from the Indian name *turkee*, for the bird.

Benjamin Franklin once wrote his daughter, Sarah, that he wished the Bald Eagle was not the bird of our land but that "the turkey is a much more respectable bird, and withal a true original Native of America."

TO ROAST A GOOSE

Take a little sage, and a small onion chopped small, some pepper and salt, and a bit of butter; mix these together, and put it into the belly of the goose. Then spit it, singe it with a bit of white paper, dredge it with a little flour, and baste it with butter. When it is done, which may be known by the legs being tender, take it up, and pour through it two glasses of red wine, and serve it up in the same dish, and apple-sauce in a bason.

The Complete Housewife, E. Smith, 1766

BUILDING THE FIRE: *A Letter from Ruth*

Dear Hannah:

The greatest trouble we have, or did have during our first winter here, was in building the fire, for the wood, having just been cut in the forest, is green, and the fire very like to desert it unless we keep a close watch. Neither mother nor I can strike a spark with flint and steel as ably as can many women in the village; therefore, when as happened four or five times, we lost our fire, one of us take a strip of green bark or a shovel, and borrowed from whosoever of our neighbors had the brightest blaze, enough of the coals to set our own hearth warm again.

Some of the housewives more skilled in the use of firearms than my mother or myself, kindle a blaze by flashing a little powder in the pan of a gun, allowing the flame to strike upon tinder, and thus be carried to shavings of dry wood. It is a speedy way of getting fire but one needs to be well used to the method, else the fingers or the face will get more of the heat than does the tinder. Father cautions us against such practice, declaring that he will not allow his weapons to remain unloaded simply for kitchen use when at any moment the need may arise for a ready bullet.

Ruth

Carrying the fire scoop

THE FARMER'S CHOICE

Our ancestors lived on bread and broth,
And woo'd their healthy wives in home-spun cloth;
Our mothers, nurtur'd to the nodding reel,
Gave all their daughters lessons on the wheel.
Though spinning did not much reduce the waist,
It made their food much sweeter to the taste:
They plied with honest zeal the mop and broom,
And drove the shuttle through the noisy loom.
They never once complained as we do now—
"We have no girls to cook, or milk the cow;"
Each mother taught her red-cheeked son and daughter
To bake and brew, and draw a pail of water:
No damsel shunn'd the wash-tub, broom, or pail,
To keep unsoil'd a long grown finger-nail.
They sought no gaudy dress, no wasp-like form,
But ate to live, and work'd to keep them warm;
No idle youth—no tight lac'd mincing fair,
Became a living corpse for want of air!
No fidgits, faintings, fits or frightful blues;
No painful corns from wearing Chinese shoes.

Troy Almanac for 1839, Robert Wasson

SOUP

Nothing can be easier than to make a good soup if one only knows how and has the will to do it; and if one will, it is easy to know how. Considerations of economy and healthfulness make it the duty of every housekeeper to thoroughly inform herself on the few essential points in soup-making. When these are learned it will be as simple as any other duty. . . .

Soups are made with meat, fish, and vegetables, with water or milk; seasoned or flavored with any or every kind of vegetable, sweet herbs, spices, curry powder, catchups, aromatic sauces, and with some kind of fruit. They are served thin and clear, thickened with vegetables or cereals, and with or without meat.

Buckeye Cook Book, 1875

A FISH TIDBIT

Take what is left of boiled or baked fresh fish, remove the bones and skin, and warm it in hot milk enough to moisten. Turn it out on a platter. Poach three or four eggs, lay them on the fish. Mix one tablespoon of chopped parsley, a few grains of cayenne, a little salt, with two tablespoons of butter melted. Pour this evenly over the eggs, and serve at once and very hot.

The American Kitchen Magazine, 1892

TRAVEL ON THE FARM

Throughout the months when there was no snow on the ground, the horse was used to pull some sort of vehicle on wheels. But in the winter, a sleigh was used since it was much easier for a horse or a team to pull a vehicle on runners. The sleigh was used instead of the buggy and carriage, and the sled replaced the farm wagon. For rides in the sleigh, the farm family was usually equipped with a lap robe, earmuffs, wool mittens, and heavy scarfs, not to mention high boots and a foot warmer.

SLEIGH RIDING: *Diary of An Early American Housewife*

February 26, 1772—Priscilla told me that she went on a sleigh riding party while she was in Boston. It reminded me of the time that I was visiting my uncle Silas

Green in Boston when I was a young girl. Joshua was also visiting some of his cousins in Boston and one day a party of young people gathered to go on a sleigh party. It was a wonderful day.

SLEIGHING PARTIES

Sleighing parties came comparatively later to the New England colonies than they did elsewhere. Sleighing had been a great thing in New York in 1704 when Madame Knight of Boston had visited that city.

Several years later, sleighing parties were begun in Boston and a young British officer, Alexander Macraby, wrote to his brother: "You can never have had a party in a sligh or slidge. I had a very clever one a few days ago. Seven slighs with two ladies and two men in each proceeded by fiddlers on horseback set out together upon a snow of about a foot deep on the roads to a public house, a few miles from town where we danced, sung, romped, and ate and drank and kicked away care from morning till night, and finished our frolic in two or three side boxes at the play. You can have no idea of the state of the pulse seated with a pretty woman mid-deep in straw, your body armed with furs and flannels, clear air, bright sunshine, spotless sky, horses galloping, every feeling turned to joy and jollity."

However, not everyone approved of sleighing parties, as we learn from a letter written by Hannah Thompson to John Mifflin in 1786: "This Slaying match Mr. Houston of Houston St gave his Daughters, Dear Papa, Dear Papa, do go us a slaying—he at last consented, told them to get ready and dress themselves warm, which they accordingly did and came running. We are ready papa. He ordered the Servants to have some burnt wine against they came back. He desir'd them to step upstairs with him before they went. As soon as they got in an Attick chamber, he threw up all the windows and seated them in two old Arm Chairs and began to whip and Chirrup with all the Spirit of a Slaying Party. And after he kept them long enough to be sufficiently cold he took them down and call'd for the Mulled Wine and they were very glad to set close to the Fire and leave Slaying for those who were too warm."

MIXED SPICE FOR RICH CAKES AND PLUM PUDDINGS

½ teaspoonful each of cloves and allspice
1 teaspoonful each of mace and grated nutmeg
3 teaspoonfuls of cinnamon

THE PERSON

Cleanliness, absolute purity of person is the first requisite in the appearance of a gentleman or lady. Not only should the face and hands be kept clean, but the whole skin should be subjected to frequent ablutions. Better wear coarse clothes with a clean skin, than silk stockings drawn over dirty feet. Let the whole skin be kept pure and sweet, the teeth and nails and hair, clean; and the last two of medium length, and naturally cut. Nothing deforms a man more than bad hair-cutting, and unnatural deformity in wearing it. Abstain from all eccentricities. Take a medium between nature and fashion, which is perhaps the best rule in regard to dress and appearance that can be given.

Ladies Indispensable Assistant, 1851

TO RAISE HYACINTHS IN WINTER

When they are put into the glasses or earth, set them into a dark closet until they sprout. If they are in glasses, do not let the water touch the bulb, by an inch. When the roots have shot down to the water, fill the glass, put in a piece of charcoal, and set them in the sun.

The Young Housekeeper's Friend, 1859

HOUSECLEANING

The latter part of the 1800's was a period in which inventors tackled all the basic housecleaning problems. The housewife was still doing most of the work by hand. She untacked the carpets, hung them out on the line, and beat them with a wicker carpet beater. Dragging along a bucket of soapy water, she got down on her knees and applied the scrubbing brush to the floor. Then she got down again and applied wax.

Carpet sweepers appeared quite early in the 1900's. The simplest models just rolled a stiff rotary brush over the carpet. Later on they contained agitators or polished metal bars that would turn the brush and help loosen the dirt in the rug. Then came a form of vacuum cleaner in which the housewife created the vacuum by means of a hand pump.

HEATING THE HOUSE

From the earliest time, most houses relied upon the open fireplace to heat the room. If they were fortunate, the bedrooms had fireplaces, else our Early Americans slept in an ice-cold room. The fireplaces were cozy and cheerful, but they used an enormous amount of wood, and most of the heat went up the chimney.

The Dutch and Swedish immigrants brought to America six-plate stoves which brought the fire out into the room to radiate heat in all directions instead of just from the front. In 1744, Benjamin Franklin developed what became known as the Franklin stove and that was the beginning of America's great stove-manufacturing industry.

POTATO SOUP

Potato soup is suitable for a cold day. Make it in the following manner: get as many beef or ham bones as you can, and smash them into fragments. Add a little bit of lean ham to give flavor. Boil the bone and ham for two hours and a half at least. The bone of a roast beef is excellent. Strain off the liquor carefully, empty the bones and debris of the ham, restore the liquor to the pot, and place again on the fire. Having selected, wash and pare some nice potatoes, cut them into small pieces and boil them in the stock till they melt away. An onion or two may also be boiled among the bones to help the flavor. I do not like thick potato soup, and I usually strain it through a hair sieve, after doing so placing it again on the fire, seasoning it with pepper and salt to taste. A stick of celery boiled with the bones is an improvement. Make only the quantity required for the day, as potato soup is best when it is newly made.

Compendium of Cookery and Reliable Recipes, 1890

MENUS FOR THE WINTER MONTHS

JANUARY

MONDAY. *Breakfast*—Milk toast, rolls, broiled steak, fried apples. *Dinner*—Roast duck, apple sauce, beef stew, mashed turnips, baked sweet potatoes, celery, plum pudding with sauce, fruit cake, oranges. *Supper*—Light biscuit, cold meat, whipped cream with preserves, sliced beef.

TUESDAY. *Breakfast*—Waffles, broiled fish, fried raw potatoes. *Dinner*—Tomato soup, salmi of duck, roasted potatoes, cabbage salad, canned pease, celery sauce, pumpkin pie. *Supper*—Toasted muffins, cold tongue, tea rusk, baked apples.

WEDNESDAY. *Breakfast*—Griddle cakes, pig's feet souse, baked potatoes. *Dinner*—

Boiled bacon with cabbage, potatoes, turnips, carrots, onion sauce, chicken pie, bread pudding with sauce. *Supper*—Biscuit, cold bacon shaved, bread and milk, sponge cake and jelly.

THURSDAY. *Breakfast*—Hot rolls, corned beef hash, potato cakes. *Dinner*—Escaloped turkey, baked potatoes, pickled beets, cottage pudding, cake. *Supper*—Cold rolls, frizzled dried beef, hot buns, fried apples.

FRIDAY. *Breakfast*—Graham gems, broiled mutton, fried potatoes. *Dinner*—Turkey soup, roast beef with potatoes, stewed tomatoes, celery, rice pudding, mince pie. *Supper*—Cold buns, sliced beef, Indian pudding (corn mush) and milk, sponge cake, sauce.

SATURDAY. *Breakfast*—Steamed toast, fried mush and maple syrup, fried liver and bacon. *Dinner*—Meat pie with chili sauce, mashed turnips, stewed corn, apple dumplings with sauce. *Supper*—Tea rolls, sardines with sliced lemon, rusk, jelly.

SUNDAY. *Breakfast*—Buckwheat cakes, croquette of sausage meat, breakfast hominy. *Dinner*—Roast turkey, mashed potatoes, lima beans, cranberry sauce, celery, mince pie, ambrosia cake. *Supper*—Cold biscuit, sliced turkey, cranberry jelly, eggless cake, apple sauce.

FEBRUARY

MONDAY. *Breakfast*—Corn pone, ham and eggs, potatoes *a la Lyonnaise*. *Dinner*—Whole boiled potatoes and carrots, baked heart, stewed tomatoes, ginger puddings, fruit sauce. *Supper*—Toasted pone, cold heart sliced, plain bread, quince preserves with whipped cream.

TUESDAY. *Breakfast*—Buckwheat cakes, broiled sausage, chipped potatoes, toast. *Dinner*—Celery soup, roast mutton, mashed potatoes, baked macaroni, celery, currant jelly, chocolate blanc mange, peach pie. *Supper*—Cold mutton sliced, currant jelly, buttered toast, rusk, stewed apples.

WEDNESDAY. *Breakfast*—Graham bread, broiled bacon, fried potatoes. *Dinner*—Boiled corned beef with horse-radish sauce, boiled potatoes and turnips, slaw, hot apple pie with whipped cream, oranges and cake. *Supper*—Toasted Graham bread, cold corned beef sliced, grape jelly, hot buns, cake.

THURSDAY. *Breakfast*—Broiled fish, corn batter cakes, potato rissoles. *Dinner*—Roast beef with potatoes, tomatoes, canned beans, celery sauce, tapioca cream, cake. *Supper*—Cold roast beef, drop biscuit, floating island, tea cakes.

FRIDAY. *Breakfast*—Broiled oysters on toast, tomato sauce, flannel cakes with honey or maple syrup. *Dinner*—White soup, baked or boiled fish if fresh, or fricassee, if canned, mashed potatoes, fried parsnips, cabbage salad *a la mayonnaise*, apple dumplings with sauce. *Supper*—Dried beef shaved and warmed up in butter, hot corn mush with milk, canned fruit and light cakes.

SATURDAY. *Breakfast*—Broiled mutton chops, toast, rolls, scrambled eggs. *Dinner*—Beef soup, boiled potatoes, boiled ham, cabbage, parsnips, mixed pickles, cottage pudding with sauce, pie. *Supper*—Light biscuit, cold ham shaved, apple croutes, plain rice with sugar and cream.

SUNDAY. *Breakfast*—Sally Lunn, ham balls, fried raw potatoes. *Dinner*—Oyster soup, roast duck, baked potatoes, mashed turnips, cranberry sauce, celery, mince pie, oranges, iced cakes. *Supper*—Cold Sally Lunn, cold duck, dried apple sauce, cakes.

MARCH

MONDAY. *Breakfast*—Griddle cakes, chicken croquettes, potatoes, escaloped eggs. *Dinner*—Soup, boiled beef's tongue dressed with sauce piquante, stewed potatoes, boiled onions, pudding. *Supper*—Cold biscuit, shaved tongue, orange sauce, cake.

TUESDAY. *Breakfast*—Buttered toast, pork chops broiled, stewed potatoes. *Dinner*—Tomato soup, pigeon pie, creamed potatoes, canned corn or beans, pickles, steamed pudding with sauce, almonds, raisins. *Supper*—Graham biscuit, cold meat, apple fritters with sugar, sponge cake.

WEDNESDAY. *Breakfast*—Griddle cakes, broiled mutton chops, potatoes. *Dinner*—Beef soup, broiled steak, boiled potatoes, salsify, oyster salad, sweet pickles, transparent pudding, cream puffs, oranges. *Supper*—Plain bread, sardines with lemon, light coffee cake or sweet buns and jam.

THURSDAY. *Breakfast*—Graham bread, broiled fish, potatoes. *Dinner*—Corned beef boiled with turnips or parsnips, canned corn, boiled onions, horse-radish sauce, cocoanut pie. *Supper*—Toasted Graham bread, cold beef shaved, warm rusk and jelly.

FRIDAY. *Breakfast*—Corn batter cakes, broiled bacon, boiled eggs, or omelette souffle. *Dinner*—Veal broth, baked or boiled fish or steaks of halibut, mashed potatoes, stewed carrots, onion sauce, eggless ice cream, apples and nuts. *Supper*—Pates of fish, plain bread, toasted rusk, sweet omelette and sauce.

SATURDAY. *Breakfast*—Bread puffs, fried liver, boiled eggs, potatoes. *Dinner*—Bean soup, escaloped oysters, tomatoes, pickled beets, kiss pudding with sauce, pie. *Supper*—French rolls, cold tongue, bread fritters, cake and canned fruit.

SUNDAY. *Breakfast*—Baked beans with pork and Boston brown bread, omelette. *Dinner*—Roast turkey, potatoes, canned corn, plum jelly, Charlotte russe, sponge cake and jelly. *Supper*—Cold turkey, cranberry jelly, canned fruit, jam and cake.

Queen of the Household, 1906

HOLIDAY MENUS

LINCOLN'S BIRTHDAY DINNER

Cherry stone clams, cream of squash soup, croutons, celery, olives, oyster pie, brown bread sandwiches, baked ham, candied sweet potatoes, corn pudding, Virginia apples, spiced grapes, soda biscuits, molasses pie, Stilton cheese with salt biscuits, coffee.

VALENTINE DINNER

Lobster cocktails, cream of tomato soup in cups, roasted squab chickens, potato hearts, peas with pimiento, savory beet salad, raspberry sherbet, cocoanut frosted cake, coffee.

WASHINGTON'S BIRTHDAY SUPPER

Chicken bouillon, whipped cream, cold roast turkey, scalloped oysters, vegetable salad, pickles, jelly, soda biscuits, cherry pie with vanilla ice cream, coffee.

ST. PATRICK'S DAY SUPPER

Lobster salad in green pepper cases, bread and butter sandwiches, peppermint ice cream, coffee.

Modern Priscilla Cook Book, 1909

Spring

APRIL, MAY, JUNE

EARLY DAYS IN NEW AMSTERDAM

The very first comers among the Dutch settlers must, like the New England pioneers and all others, have lived in huts of rough, or at best, squared logs; but instead of being treated with biting neglect as the colonies from England were, the Dutch received every possible aid and comfort from the government of their motherland, and stores and supplies of all sorts were sent out to them as rapidly as possible and with a liberal hand, so that they were supplied with the comforts of those days sooner than their neighbors.

Even had the English so desired, they could not have given to their colonies as many comforts as could the Dutch, for the latter were far in advance in all the peaceful and domestic arts. In addition to the help which they received from the homeland, the Dutch were fortunate in being most advantageously placed for acting as "middle-men" between Holland and native American tribes, and thus they rapidly accumulated property; hence their dwellings speedily became seats of comfort, or even of luxury, as these terms were then used.

The early houses in New Amsterdam were usually a story and a half high, with the gable end fronting the street. On the first floor were low-ceilinged rooms, the most important being the kitchen and parlor. The half-story had bedrooms, and a large attic above them. The parlor was frequently furnished with a bed and used also as a guest room. The walls and furniture were kept scrupulously clean, and the floor was adorned with figures made in the sand that covered it. The attic and cellar were also important parts of the home. The attic was used as a place for drying clothes in the winter. In it there was also a kind of smokehouse, in which were hung hams, bacon, and other kinds of meat after it had been cured. The cellar was used as a storeroom for potatoes, turnips, apples, parsnips, beets, firkins of butter, barrels of salt pork, tubs of hams, and many other food supplies.

Before the front door there was a little porch called a "stoop," a word which comes from the Dutch *stoep*. From these stoops came the idea for porches and verandas. On warm evenings it was the custom for everyone to sit on the stoop, and the street had a lively appearance with all the vivacious front-door parties laughing and singing, and visiting one another.

There were no sidewalks, nor was there a street-cleaning department in the town administration. But every Friday the year round, the streets had to be cleaned by the householders and the refuse thrown into the river. Each resident cleaned only that part of the street which lay in front of his house.

The street lighting was done by the citizens. One householder in every seven hung out a lantern before his residence, and six of his nearest neighbors shared with him the expense of keeping the light burning.

VISIT TO NEW YORK: *Diary of An Early American Housewife*

April 10, 1772—We have just returned from a visit to New York City where we visited with some friends of ours, the Beekmans. They live in a house that had been built about one hundred years ago and it combines both Dutch and English ideas.

When the house was built land was very cheap, even more so than today, and the house was built on a large scale. In the center of the house there rose a great chimney-stack of stone, having four immense fireplaces, each striding across the corner of a wide, low-ceiled, broad-windowed room about twenty-two feet square. On either side, beyond the four rooms thus grouped around the chimney-stack, were two others of about equal dimensions, each having its own fireplace, for two more chimneys rose, one in each gable-end of the house.

The exterior walls of the upper stories were covered by overlapping cedar shingles, clipped at the corners to produce an octagonal effect. In front and at the gable-ends the second stories projected a little beyond the lower. At the rear there was but one story, the long roof sloping from the peak by a slightly inward-curving sweep till it terminated over the low, comfortable-looking stoep, upon which opened the rear windows and doors of the first floor.

All the first-floor rooms were handsomely wainscoted, and these, as well as the heavy ceiling beams, were cased and painted white. Each fireplace was surrounded by borders of tiles, all illustrating scriptural or naval scenes.

Walls of the best rooms were hung with a very substantial sort of paper, pictured with sprawling landscapes in which windmills, square-rigged boats, and very chunky cows figured prominently. According to the customs of the local people, the bedrooms were always washed with lime.

On the second floor there were six rooms across the front extending to the center of the house. The rest was left unceiled—a big open garret with square windows at each end and dormers along the sides of the roof, which sloped from the peak to the floor. In this great garret flax-hatcheling, wool-carding, and weaving went on almost without cessation, save in the very coldest weather, when the looms were abandoned.

The diamond-paned and leaded window-sashes had originally been brought from Holland when the house was first built and are very clear even today.

Of course, I must mention the door, which is different than ours. I was told that this is a typical Dutch door. The door is in two sections. The upper, in fair weather, was left open to admit light and air; the lower was kept closed to prevent stray pigs and other animals from coming into the house.

DUTCH FURNITURE

The furniture of the Dutch reflected their solid home- and comfort-loving temperaments. There were large, heavy beds, huge chests, and substantial chairs of dark wood which were sometimes elaborately carved and ornamented. There were dressers for the proud display of well-polished silver, pewter, glass, and china, most of which was never taken off the shelf.

A favorite type of bed in the early days was a closet-like bunk built into the wall, with two doors which were kept closed when the bed was not in use. Inside was a large feather bed, with a smaller one above it, and in between these two layers, like the filling in a sandwich, lay the sleeper himself. The Dutch were hospitable, and the family sitting room often boasted an auxiliary bunk for guests. There might also be a pile of skins and rugs close to the fire, known as a "Kermis bed," because at festival time the house overflowed with visitors.

Probably the most important article of furniture in the early Dutch home was the great cupboard or universal hold-all known as the "Kas." Their moldings and cornices were not infrequently heavily carved, and some had elaborate marquetry depicting familiar scenes. Others were painted. Often there were secret drawers tucked away behind the regular drawers and shelves, and the lock might be concealed by a carved piece of wood which could be swung aside. So large was the key that it "seemed more fitted to unlock a fortress than a marriage-chest." But then, these valued cupboards, stocked with household linen patiently gathered together by the women of the family over the long years, constituted an important part of the dowry.

Trader or farmer, the Dutchman's ideal was to convert the fruits of his industry into a quantity of handsome objects that bore eloquent, if mute, witness to his success and to his social standing. The shelves of the dresser were crammed with handsome pewter, fine glass, Delftware and china, and silver beakers, candlesticks, and spoons polished to the dazzling point. Typical also was the wooden spoon rack, or *lepel-bortie*, with narrow shelves containing holes into which the spoons were inserted.

When the family gathered around the kitchen table, the plainest of wooden ware and pewter was used, the china making its appearance only for some special occasion, such as a tea party. Tea was a luxury, to be taken in sips from a tiny cup, alternating with nibbles at a piece of sugar loaf laid beside each plate.

CLEANLINESS

In addition to having a dresser of beautiful things which were rarely taken out, the Dutchman had a "best room" into which persons were rarely invited. But let no one imagine that the dust was allowed to accumulate there; with typical Dutch thoroughness, it was given a good cleaning once a week.

One thing is certain: in an uncleanly age, the Dutch were the cleanest people in the world. Outside of clothes brushes and hair brushes, inventories mention scrubbing brushes, dish brushes, floor brushes, rake brushes, whitening brushes, painting brushes, hearth hair brushes with brass and wooden handles, chamber brooms, hearth brooms, "Bermudian brooms with sticks," not to mention washing tubs, pails, rain water casks, sticks to hang clothes on, smoothing irons, and wicker baskets. One family owned fifty-six brushes and twenty-four pounds of soap.

ADVERTISEMENT: 1733

This is to give Notice, That Richard Noble, living in Wall Street, next Door to Abraham Van Horn's, Esq; in the City of New York, makes White-Wash Brushes, and mends all Sorts of other Brushes, at reasonable Rate: He also gives ready Money for good Hog-Bristles, at the following Rate, viz. For clean'd comb'd, and five Inches in Length, one Shilling per Pound, and for uncomb'd, six Pence.

MILADY'S DRESS

The patroon's lady or any other well-to-do woman of the colony might wear a satin or velvet gown trimmed with gold braid, a pointed bodice with full slashed sleeves showing white undersleeve, and a lace collar or stiff ruff. She also wore a long linen over-dress, open down the front to show the dress beneath. It was tied at the elbows with bands of ribbon. Later it evolved into a loose knee-length jacket, trimmed with fur.

Women of lesser degree than the patroon's wife wore as many petticoats as she, and over them a full skirt gathered at the waist. They wore little waistcoats with tight, elbow-length sleeves, and a demure folded white kerchief over their shoulders.

Their fine lace, linen, or cambric caps were worn over a metal headband, trimmed with metal ornaments sometimes consisting of spirals or rosettes.

The young bride wore all the petticoats she had—they were part of her dowry and indicated the wealth of her family. Her bridal gown—that precious memento which was carefully stowed away after the wedding and handed down from mother to daughter—was of silver set with precious stones, provided her family could afford it. Otherwise it was made of cardboard, covered with gold and silver silk.

Apron and cap were indispensable to the Dutch woman's wardrobe. One New Amsterdam dame had one purple apron and four blue ones, and twenty-three cambric and linen caps.

The usual costume of peasant women and house servants consisted of short woolen petticoats with loose red or blue jackets of coarse linen, long white aprons of coarse homespun, white kerchiefs about the shoulders, and close-fitting white caps.

MADAME KNIGHT'S VISIT TO NEW YORK: 1704

"The English go very fashionable in their dress. But the Dutch, especially the middling sort, differ from our women, in their habitt go loose, wear French muches which are like a Capp and headband in one, leavin their ears bare, which are sett out with jewells of a large size and many in number; and their fingers hopp'd with rings, some with large stones in them of many Coullers, as were their pendants in their ears, which you should see very old women wear as well as Young."

A BRIDE'S DOWRY

No bride went to her new home without a large dowry. The family began to lay aside linens as soon as the child was born, and it was considered essential that a young

woman be amply endowed with these worldly goods. At first thought it would seem that this custom developed from financial and social reasons. But when one reads deeper into the history of those first years, one finds that the large linen dowry was a personal necessity. Washing was done only twice a year, preceding summer and winter, and the necessity of enough linens to last the season was most essential. Later, washing was performed three and finally four times a year. With no conveniences, with the crudest of implements, and with heavy homespun linens and blankets, one can well see why these household goods went through the process of being cleaned so infrequently.

TABLE FURNISHINGS

The Dutch had appointments for the table similar to those of the people of New England, but much more silver was used since the Dutch of that period were more affluent than the pilgrims. However, pewter was universally possessed in the New Netherlands. Brass candlesticks were in great demand. Judging from the prevalence and the amount of pewter, brass, and copper listed in the old documents, the homes of the Dutch residents must have been filled with brightly shining metal articles for domestic use.

During this century, Delft potteries reached the height of their activities, and collecting this type of porcelain became a craze with the Dutch. The inventories of New Amsterdam prove that the colonists shared this luxurious taste with their relatives back in Holland. The Dutch were using more china quite a while before the New Englanders.

THE DUTCH LARDER

The Dutch were very fortunate. Their land was rich and fertile. The rye was tall, as was the barley and wheat. In fact, all the crops grew well. The Dutch readily took to the native corn, since they were fond of all cereal food.

Indian corn became a staple with the Dutch, too. Samp and samp porridge were soon their favorite dishes. Samp is Indian corn pounded to a coarsely ground powder in a mortar. Samp porridge usually boiled for a week at a time. Pork or beef and various root vegetables were added to the samp porridge, and it was then cooked slowly for at least three days. At the end of that time, it could be taken out of the pot in one chunk. Suppawn was another favorite made of thick cornmeal and milk porridge.

The river was full of fish. Lobsters, five to six feet in length, were in the bay.

Crabs were large, and there also were foot-long oysters. The shad caught in the Hudson River was dried and salted. This was the result of shad being so plentiful and so cheap.

Plenty of game was to be had; passenger pigeons, wild turkeys, and venison could be bought for pennies. There also was an ample supply of partridges, wild ducks, white swans, grey geese, and pelicans.

The Dutch ate much cheese which they grated, stating that it enhanced the flavor of the food. They also had butter on their bread, which the English did not. The housewife could buy her bread in public bakeries.

There were plenty of vegetables, such as chibbals, peas, artichokes, carrots, lettuce, beets, parsnips, and radishes; pumpkins and squashes were not as widely used as in New England. There also were a variety of melons. The Dutch, in fact, are believed to be the fathers of cole slaw, shredded cabbage with vinegar and oil.

Domestic swine gave the Dutch many varied and appetizing foods, such as headcheese, while there were similar dishes made of lean meat stewed in tripe. All sorts of sausages were made from the swine.

The Dutch also used an open fire for cooking. The smoke rose into a projecting canopy that was a little lower than the ceiling but led directly into the chimney. With the Dutch penchant for concealing things, it is not surprising to learn that the canopy was covered with a ruffled, linen valence which was changed every Sunday. The utensils were the same long-handled iron ones used all over, but the Dutch also had special long-handled utensils to bake their beloved waffles and other "Baker's Meats."

The "Baker's Meats" were all sorts of cakes and breads. The bakers had to use just weights and good materials. They were ordered to bake twice a week and to charge certain prices, such as 14 stuvyers for a double coarse loaf of eight pounds, with smaller loaves at proportionate prices. Bakers were not permitted to sell sweet cakes unless they had coarse bread for sale. There were "pye-women" as well as bakers.

The Dutch were partial to various types of doughnuts and crullers fried in deep fat. Their *olijkoeck* was a doughnut of apples, citron, and raisins. Tea cakes were called "izer-cookies," since they were baked in long-handled irons called "izers" or wafer irons which had the initials of the owner impressed in the metal and thus on the cakes. These wafer irons were usually wedding presents with the initials of the bride and groom intertwined. There also were many other cakes made of chopped pork with spices, almonds, currants, raisins, and flavored with brandy.

There were many apple trees, and cider soon rivaled domestic use of the beer of the Fatherland. It was used during the winter, and in summer made a good drink diluted and sweetened and flavored with nutmeg. There also was an abundance of peaches, plums, and cherries.

Cans of buttermilk or good beer, brewed by the patroon, washed down a breakfast of suppawn and rye bread and grated cheese and sausage or headcheese.

The Dutch did not use as much rum as the English, but at any transaction, private or public, there was a drink. If either party to a contract did not sign the contract, he had to furnish half a barrel of beer or a gallon of rum to assuage the pangs of disappointment.

Much beer, wine, and brandy was drunk daily. Workmen building a house were supplied with liquor to keep them contented, and the cost of the liquor was often figured into the cost of the house. When a Dutchman married, he laid in a "pipe" of Madeira. This wine was broached at his wedding feast, and for the christening of his first son. What was left of the 126-gallon pipe was finally finished by his friends at his funeral.

JAMAICA, LONG ISLAND

"Such an abundant of strawberries is in June that the fields and woods are dyed red; which the country people perceiving, instantly arm themselves with bottles of wine, cream and sugar, and instead of a coat of Mail every one take a Female upon his Horse behind him, and so rushing violently into the fields, never leave till they have disrobed them of their red colors and turned them into the old habit."

A Briefe Description of New York, Daniel Denton, 1670

WAFFLE FROLIC

"We had the wafel-frolic at Miss Walton's talked of before your departure. The feast as usual was preceded by cards, and the company so numerous that they filled two tables; after a few games, a magnificent supper appeared in grand order and decorum, but for my own part, I was not a little grieved that so luxurious a feast should come under the name of a wafel-frolic, because if this be the case I must expect but a few wafel-frolics for the future; the frolic was closed with *ten sunburnt virgins lately come from Columbus's Newfoundland,* besides a play of my own invention which I have not room enough to describe at present. However, kissing constitutes a great part of its entertainment."

Description of Wafel-Frolic, William Livingston, 1744

NEW AMSTERDAM HOUSEKEEPING

Soon after daybreak the family arose, sometimes even before the bells of the city rang, for early rising was the custom. The first to get up, as a rule, was the head of the house, who would go downstairs in his dressing gown and slippers, with nightcap on, open the door and shutters, look at the weather, and call the servant. While she lighted the fire and got things ready for breakfast, the rest of the family would get up. The maid set the table, shook up the pillows in the chairs, heated the foot warmer for the mistress, and placed the Bible before the master's chair. The family now came downstairs, washed, combed, and dressed, and took their places at the table. The servant also took her place at the end of the board. Then the father stood up and led the family in prayer, after which breakfast was eaten. After the meal and at the end of the reading of a chapter from the Bible which was done during the meal, all stood up, sang the hymn, and the father said grace.

Bread, butter, and cheese always appeared upon the table, but many families included pastries of venison and meat. Fried fish was a favorite dish at breakfast.

Burghers (who lived in the towns) seldom ate two relishes at once. Butter and cheese on a "piece" of bread was considered a wicked extravagance. With the bread, milk was drunk, and sometimes a small beer. Coffee did not make its appearance until the end of the seventeenth century.

After breakfast, everybody went her or his way—the husband to his office or his business, the boys to their offices, shops, or schools; but the girls usually helped their mother and the servant with the housework. The husband and wife attended to their special duties and hardly met except at meals or at night. Before going to market, the mistress saw that the kitchen was put in order, cooking utensils scoured, brasses polished, and floors scoured.

The mistress worked along with the servant, and after the house was in order, she in a simple dress and with a headcloth folded over her head would go to market, accompanied by the servant with the basket.

Although the Dutch housewife was a very clever cook and superintendent of the kitchen, for great occasions she called in the help of the baker, who was also a confectioner.

Toward noon the tablecloth was spread on the table. Prayers were again said at the meal. A large pewter dish with boiled food was served. Seldom were more than two or three dishes served at the noonday meal. The first cooked dish was generally "potage," made of brown and green peas, mashed with butter, ginger, and celery, or some bean dish; the second course was fish, and the third, meat or chicken.

A couple of hours after the noonday meal, the family gathered again to eat the "piece" of bread cut by the father of the house, with either cold or warm beer or water. Later, cake, fruit, and tea were added to this, as well as coffee or chocolate when available.

At the stroke of nine the maid came to spread the table. The supper was very simple, and consisted in most houses of bread, butter, and cheese; but some people had *gekookte pot* (a cooked meal), consisting of three courses. Grace was said before and after the meal. At ten o'clock, all would retire.

ADVERTISEMENT

To be sold, a good New House, with a Kitchin, and Store-House, and a good Stable, and a Lot of Ground Containing in the Front and Rear about 83 Foot in Length, about 125 Foot lying within 50 Yards of New-York Ferry, Landing on the high Road on Long Island very convenient to keep a Shop.

Whoever Inclines to Purchase the same may apply to Daniel Boutecou now living on the Premises, and agree on Reasonable Terms.

New York Gazette, June 26, 1730

MORE ABOUT NEW YORK:
Diary of An Early American Housewife

April 11, 1772—I shall now continue to write about our trip to New York City.

While we were with the Beekmans, they took us to visit their Aunt Aletta who lived in the country about 5 miles outside of the city. Since it was not easy to go into the city and visit the markets as the Beekmans did, Aunt Aletta supervised everything needed for household consumption. She and her daughters supervised the cleaning of the house and other labors around. They did not personally scrub the uncarpeted floors or tend the fires, or hatchel the flax, or card the wool, or weave the cloth, or make the soap, or chop the sausage meat, or dip the candles, or wash the linen, but they knew exactly what had to be done.

Aunt Aletta kept flocks of hens, geese, and ducks. There were no public bakeries out in the country, so she made her own bread, which was delicious to eat, especially warm.

She used leaven, which is a lump of the latest baking buried in flour and kept in a cool, dry place until needed for the next baking. Numberless were the accidents which might happen to this. A degree too cold or a trifle too damp, and the leaven would not rise, so the bread was heavy; or a degree too hot, and the leaven would ferment, and so the bread was sour. If the sponge stood too short or too long a time, or its temperature was not just right, again there was trouble. If the big brick oven was under-heated, the well-made loaves would over-rise and sour before they were sufficiently baked, or they might be removed too quickly from the oven, and the half-baked dough would fall into flat and solid masses. If the oven was over-heated, the loaves would again be heavy, for the crust would form before the bread had had time to take its last rising in the oven as it should.

Aunt Aletta superintended every step of the way, and when the bread was baked, they were full, round loaves of a brown so light as to be almost golden. I would like to bake bread so good.

Making lye for soap

MAKING SOAP: *A Letter from Ruth*

Dear Hannah:

It seems strange that some industrious person, who is not overly fine in feelings or in habits, does not take it upon himself to make soap for sale. Verily it would be better that a family like ours buy a quart of soap whenever it is needed, than for the whole house to be turned topsy-turvy because of the dirty work.

I wonder if there are in this country any girls so fortunate as not to have been obliged to learn how to make soap. I know of none in Boston, although it may be possible that in Salem, where are some lately come over from England, live those who still know the luxury of hard soap, such as can be bought in London.

For those fortunate ones I will set down how my mother and I make a barrel of soap, for once we are forced to get about the task, we contrive to make up as large a quantity as possible.

First, as you well know, we save all the grease which cannot be used in cooking, and is not needed for candles, until we have four and twenty pounds of such stuff as the fat of meat, scraps of suet, and drippings of wild turkey or wild geese, which last is not pleasant to use in food, and not fit for candles.

Well, when we have saved four and twenty pounds of this kind of grease, and set aside six bushels of ashes from what is known as hard wood, such as oak, maple, or birch, we "set the leach."

I suppose every family in Boston has a leach-barrel, which is a stout cask, perhaps one that has held pickled pork or pickled beef, and has in it at the very bottom a hole where is set a wooden spigot.

This barrel is placed upon some sort of platform built to raise it sufficiently high from the ground, so that a small tub or bucket may be put under the spigot. Then it is filled with ashes, and water poured into the top, which, of course, trickles down until it runs, or, as some say, is leached, out through the spigot, into the bucket, or whatsoever you have put there to receive it.

While running slowly through the ashes, it becomes what is called lye, and upon the making of this lye depends the quality of the soap.

Now, of course, as the water is poured upon the contents of the barrel, the ashes settle down; as fast as this comes to pass, yet more ashes are added and more water thrown in, until one has leached the entire six bushels, when the lye should be strong enough, as mother's receipt for soap-making has it, to "bear up an egg, or a potato, so that you can see a portion of it on the surface as big as a ninepence."

If the lye is not of sufficient strength to stand this test, it must be ladled out and poured over the ashes again, until finally, as will surely be the case, it has become strong enough.

The next turn in the work is to build a fire out of doors somewhere, because to make your soap in the house would be a most disagreeable undertaking. One needs a great pot, which should hold as much as one-third of a barrel, and into this is poured half of the grease and half of the lye, to be kept boiling until it has become soap.

Now just when that point has been reached I cannot say, because of not having a sufficient experience; but mother is a master hand at this dirty labor, and always has great success with it.

Of course, when one kettle-full has been boiled down, the remainder of the lye and the remainder of the grease is put in, and worked in the same manner as before.

It is possible, and we shall do so when time can be spent in making luxuries, to get soap from the tallow of bayberry plants. I have already said that we stew out a kind of vegetable tallow from bayberries with which to make candles, and this same grease, when boiled with lye as if you were making a soft soap, can be cooked so stiff that when poured into molds, it will form little hard cakes that are particularly convenient for the cleansing of one's hands.

There can be no question but that bayberry soap will whiten and soften the skin better than does soft soap; but the labor of making it is so disagreeable that I had rather my hands were tough and rough, than purchase a delicate skin at such an expense.

Ruth

AN OLD CAPE COD RECIPE FOR PREPARING HADDOCK

You cut the innards out, 'an you cut the head off and that's all. You don't never bone 'em nor split 'em.

FOOD IN BROOKLYN

"Then was thrown upon the fire, to be roasted, a pail full of Gowanes oysters which are the best in the country. They are fully as good as those of England, better than those we eat in Falmouth. I had to try some of them raw. They are large and full, some of them no less than a foot long. Others are young and small. In consequence of the great quantities of them everybody keeps the shells for the burning of lime. They pickle the oysters in small casks and send them to Barbados. We have for supper a roasted haunch of venison which he had bought for three guilders and half of a sea want, that is fifteen stivers of Dutch money (fifteen cents), and which weighed thirty pounds. The meat was exceedingly tender and good and also quite fat. It had a slight aromatic flavor. We were also served with wild turkey, which was also fat and of good flavor, and a wild goose, but that was rather dry. We saw here lying in a heap a whole hill of watermelons which were as large as pumpkins."

Diaries of Labadist Missionaries, 1679

WASHING CLOTHES

The first method of washing clothes was at a nearby brook, with a stone for the washboard and a wooden club for a beater. However, in the colonies there was a wash tub in the dooryard, water heated in kettles over fires often built outdoors, and wooden washboards on which to rub.

THE WASH TUBS: *A Letter from Ruth*

Dear Hannah:

It was during this third winter that the cooper spent three days in our home, making for mother two tubs which are fair to look upon, and of such size that we are no longer troubled on washdays by being forced to throw away the soapy water in order to rinse the clothes which have already been cleansed. You may think this strange to hear me speak thus of the waste of soapy water, because you in Scrooby have of soap an abundance, while here in this new land we are put to great stress through lack of it.

It would not be so ill if all the housewives would make a generous quantity, but there are some among us who are not so industrious as others, and dislike the labor of making soap. They fail to provide sufficient for themselves, but depend upon borrowing, thus spending the stores of those who have looked ahead for the needs of the future.

Ruth

MAPLE-SUGARING TIME:
Diary of An Early American Housewife

April 16, 1772—Josh and the boys are making sugar. They are spending the next five days in the maple woods back of our house and hope to get enough sugar to last us for the year. Perhaps there will be enough sugar to sell in Boston. If the weather holds as nicely as it is at this time, we might have some of our neighbors join the men in finishing the process of making the sugar. We have not had a party for some time now. It will be good to see the neighbors again now that the winter is ending. This winter was not good; there was too much snow to get around visiting.

Making maple sugar

MAPLE-SUGARING TIME IN NEW ENGLAND

The end of the long, cold, harsh winter was hailed with the maple-sugaring, especially in Vermont, New Hampshire, and New York. The art of making maple sugar was learned by the settlers from the Indians.

In the 1700's, many inland families used no sugar but that which they made themselves from the sap of the maple. Every farmer in the districts where these trees flourished wished to have his "sugar orchard and sugaring-off." This was as much a part of the agricultural year as plowing or haymaking. On the coast, cane sugar was imported from the West Indies, but this was, of course, more expensive to the farmer than that which he could extract from his own trees.

In the northern colonies, harvesting of the sugar was begun in February or March. The maple trees were generally a few miles from the homestead, and among the trees was a cabin and a sugar house. The entire family or else the father and the sons often lived in the cabin while the sugaring went on. The best weather for sugaring was frosty nights, a westerly wind, and clear thawing days. Thawing days started the sap flowing.

The first spouts were made of sumach or elder with the pith turned out. A notch was cut in the trunk of the tree at a convenient height from the ground, usually four or five feet, and the running sap was guided by setting in the notch a semicircular basswood spout cut and set with a special tool called a tapping-gauge. In earlier days the trees were "boxed," that is, a great gash was cut across the side and scooped out and down to gather the sap. This often proved fatal to the trees and was abandoned. A trough about three feet long was placed under the end of the spout. These troughs were made deep enough to hold about ten quarts.

In later years a hole was bored in the tree with an auger, and sap buckets were used instead of troughs. The sap bucket had one protruding stave in which there was a hole so that the bucket might hang on the spout, also called the spile. The children would keep watch of the running sap, and when the buckets were full, they poured the sap into the carrying buckets.

The carrying buckets had two protruding staves, each with a hole through which a stick was run to serve as a handle. To carry these buckets, one used a shoulder yoke. Oxen were used to pull the sleds on which the buckets were placed if the sugar house was a distance from the trees and if there was still a deep snow on the ground.

Dry wood had to be gathered for the fires. It was hard work to keep them constantly supplied, so wood was often cut a year in advance. Under the huge kettles the fires were kept burning day and night for three days. Someone had to constantly watch the kettles, so shifts of watchers were formed. Although little stirring was needed, the sap was closely watched and the fires not allowed to go out. A scoop was used to stir the sugar when necessary.

The syrup was then skimmed, strained through woolen cloths, boiled again, and strained again. Each time that the process was repeated, the syrup became clearer. The number of times that it was strained depended upon the clarity of the syrup wanted.

The first run of the sap made the purest and whitest sugar, so this was made into cake form for selling by putting partitions between the large forms and placing elaborate patterns on the cakes of sugar to be sold. The sugar used by the family was usually left in large cakes to be stored in the attic or shed chamber.

The second run was darker and used only for soft sugar. After being boiled down and strained, this was poured into covered tubs near the bottom of which was a hole with a wooden stopper or plug. As the sugar hardened, a sugar molasses, called maple molasses, was drawn off and used as sweetening in cooking. The soft sugar was also kept in the attic or shed, tightly covered and the plug tight so that no ants or other tiny insects could get into the tub.

Many families lived on the proceeds of the sugar sales, since a fifty-year-old tree yielded about five pounds of sugar a year.

The sugar-making season was always greeted with delight by the boys of the household, who found in this work in the woods a wonderful outlet for the love of wild life. If the camp was near enough to the farmhouse to have visitors, the last afternoon and evening in camp was turned into a country frolic. Great sledloads of girls came out to taste the new sugar, to drop it into the snow to candy, and to have an evening of fun. The farmers also took turns inviting their neighbors to a "sugaring-off." It was said that the sugar season of New England did more to encourage marriage than almost any other industrial phenomenon in nature.

SCALLOP FRY

8 pieces bacon; 36 bay scallops; 2 eggs; 2 tablespoons water; ½ cup bread crumbs; salt; pepper; 4 sprigs of parsley; 1 lemon, sliced.

Fry bacon, drain on paper towels and cut into 1-inch squares. Reserve bacon fat in fry pan. Cut a slit in each scallop and insert 1 or 2 pieces of bacon in each slit. Beat eggs slightly with water. Roll scallops in bread crumbs, then dip into egg mixture, then again in crumbs. Heat bacon fat. Fry scallops in hot fat and season with salt and pepper to taste. Serve with parsley and lemon slices.

From An Old Long Island Favorite

WE HAVE COWS: *A Letter from Ruth*

Dear Hannah:

Can you imagine how I feasted when for the first time in four years I had milk to drink, and butter and cheese to eat?

You must not believe that we drank milk freely, as do you at Scrooby, for there are many people in Plymouth, all of whom had been hungering for it even as had I. Father claimed that each must have a certain share, therefore it is a great feast day with us when we have a large spoonful on our pudding, or to drink.

A beautiful churn was made for mother; but many a long month passed before we would get cream enough to make butter, so eager were our people for the milk. Now, however, when there are seventeen cows in this town of ours, we not only have butter on extra occasions; but twice each year mother makes a cheese.

Ruth

QUILTING: *Diary of An Early American Housewife*

April 28, 1772—Invited to a quilting party at Martha Worthington's. This will be the first time I have been away from the farm since the blizzard last month. I have many pieces to be exchanged for other cotton goods. However, I have been doing some samplers and Susan, although only 7, has made two this winter.

QUILT-MAKING IN THE COLONIES

Quilt-making during this time period was most important. The quilt was in the beginning a strictly utilitarian article, born of the necessity of providing warm cover for beds, and hangings for doors and windows that were not sufficiently set to keep out the cold of a New England winter.

Warm clothing and coverings were needed when going out on a cold winter's day, and the New England woman made quilted clothing, such as hoods, capes, and waistcoats for men, as well as quilted "petti-skirts" or underskirts.

The feminine love of color, the longing for decoration, as well as pride in the skill of needlecraft found an outlet in quilt-piecing. All the fragments and bits of stuff which were necessarily cut out in the shaping of garments helped to make the patchwork a satisfaction to the woman.

Nearly all the quilts made in America prior to 1750 were pieced quilts, and most of the quilts in New England were of woolen garments and pieces. Many of the quilts of that period were square, as the beds were wider than those of the present day.

Many were made of four blocks measuring thirty-five inches square to which was added an eighteen-inch border, making the finished quilt 108 inches square.

Although fabrics had been hard to obtain at first, with the expansion of trade calicoes, silks, and velvets were available from the Indies, England, and France. These cloths were extremely expensive, and after cutting enough material for clothing, the scraps were used to make quilts and their ornamentation.

Quilting not only provided warm coverings for beds in poorly heated homes but also filled a social need. Neighbors could be invited to a "quilting bee," and such affairs were gala events. They usually ended with supper and dancing—the men arriving when the quilting was finished.

ADVERTISEMENT

Elizabeth Boyd gives notice that she will as usual graft Pieces in knit Jackets and Breeches not to be discern'd, also to graft and foot Stockings, and Gentlemens Gloves, mittens or Muttatees made of old Stockings, or runs them in the Heels. She likewise makes Childrens Stockings out of Old Ones.

New York Gazette, April 1, 1751

RANDOM NOTE FROM A NEW YORK NEWSPAPER

Moses Slaughter, Stay Maker from London, has brought with him a Parcel of extraordinary good and Fashionable Stays of his own making, of several Sizes and Prices. The Work of them he will warrant to be good, and for Shape, inferiour to none that are made.

He lodges at present at the house of William Bradford, next Door but one to the Treasurer's near the Fly Market, where he is ready to suit those that want, with extraordinary good Stays. Or he is ready to wait upon any Lady's or Gentlewomen that please to send for him to their Houses. If any desire to be informed of the Work he has done, let them enquire of Mrs. Elliston in the Broad-Street, or of Mrs. Nichols in the Broadway, who have had his work.

SPRING IN THE FOREST

Spring in the forest provided the colonists with an assortment of wild berries, such as huckleberries, whortleberries, cranberries, gooseberries, raspberries, blackberries, boxberries, gingerberries, checkerberries, blueberries, and strawberries. The freshly picked fruits were eaten much as they are today, with cream and sugar, or baked into pies. One particularly popular fresh berry dish was a baked pudding of fresh cranberries, flour, and molasses. The cranberry was unknown in Europe before the settlement of the colonies, and early settlers named the plants bearberries, because eastern bears so frequently ate the fruit.

The settlers found that the fresh food season was short, and so most berries were sugared or otherwise preserved for future use. Berries were dried, pounded into a hard paste, and then cut into squares which were chewed like candy. The fruits were boiled with syrup or sugar to produce marmalades and jellies.

Wild elderberries, mulberries, and grapes were used for wines, and other alcoholic drinks were produced from pears, peaches, currants, and shrub roots. Wild plums were preserved to be used in the Christmas puddings.

COURTSHIP AND MARRIAGE IN NEW AMSTERDAM

Two festivals were particularly honored among the Dutch—the christening and the wedding. Parents began to provide for the future from the very birth of the child, and betrothals sometimes took place while the babies were lying in the cradle. Gold coins and medals were accumulated for dowry, silver and jewels were collected, and coffers and chests filled with linen; and as she grew up, the maiden spun and collected her linen, and made a lace collar and cuffs, her bridal gift to her future husband.

This custom of infant betrothal was naturally most prevalent among the upper classes, where wealthy alliances were of importance for political or business reasons; but in the family of the average burgher, considerable latitude of choice was allowed, and as long as the prospective bride, or groom, was not absolutely objectionable to the parents on either side, the course of true love ran fairly smoothly.

The binding nature of the betrothal in the eyes of the law is evident from many entries in the records. The offense of breaking the engagement after the publication of the banns was a very serious one. Parental consent was necessary for the publication of the banns, and to render the marriage legal.

Once married, it was impossible for husband or wife to have the bonds of matrimony broken except on the ground of unfaithfulness. Even a separation was difficult to obtain except for persistent cruelty. If one did divorce, the offending party could not remarry without permission from the authorities.

It was the custom among the wealthier classes, after formal consent had been given, to invite all relations and friends to the betrothal, where the contract was signed in the presence of a notary.

The days preceding the wedding were spent in festivity and general merry-making. The homes of both bride and groom were beautifully decorated during the period between the betrothal and wedding ceremonies, and nearly every day a dinner was given in honor of the couple by relatives and friends. These "banns dinners" were returned by the bride and groom's "antenuptial dinner." The bride also received in state. She sat on a sort of throne while friends and relations came with congratulations and wedding gifts.

The procession to the wedding ceremony and the elaborate dinner that followed were held only by the wealthier Dutch. Poorer people were often married in numbers on the appointed day, and went on foot, sometimes preceded by the strewers, who continually strewed flowers and greens from a basket. So accompanied by a crowd of people they would walk to the church and back again.

MARGARET PHILIPSE

A merchant princess from whom many New Yorkers are descended was Margaret Hardenbrook, who married, in 1658, Rudolphus De Vries, an extensive trader of New Amsterdam, and after his death became the wife of Frederick Philipse. During her widowhood, Mrs. De Vries undertook the management of her husband's estate, which is said to have been a practice not uncommon in New Amsterdam, and was early known as a woman trader going to Holland repeatedly in her own ship as supercargo, and buying and trading in her own name. After her second marriage, Mrs. Philipse continued to manage her estate; through her thrift and enterprise, as well as his own industry, Mr. Philipse soon came to be the richest man in the colony, trading extensively with the Five Nations at Albany, and sending ships to both the East and West Indies. From this marriage was descended Mary Philipse, whose chief claim to distinction now rests upon the tradition that she was an early love of Colonel George Washington.

A CHRISTENING AND A DINNER: *A Letter from Ruth*

Dear Hannah:
The other day, we girls had a most delightful time, for there was a baby baptized in the house where are held the meetings, and one of the gentlefolks who came here with Master Higginson was to give a dinner because of his young son's having lived to be christened.
To both these festivals, Sarah and I were bidden. The christening was attended to first, as a matter of course, and, because of his so lately arrived from England, Master Winthrop was called upon to speak to the people, which he did at great length. Although the baby, in stiff dress and mittens of linen, with his cap of cotton wadded thickly with wool, must have been

very uncomfortable because of the heat, he made but little outcry during all this ceremony, or even when Master Higginson prayed a very long time.

We were not above two hours in the meetinghouse, and then went to the home of Mistress White, getting there just as she came down from the loft with her young son in her arms.

Mother was quite shocked because of the baby's having nothing in his hands, and, while she is not given to placing undue weight in beliefs which savor of heathenism, declares that she never knew any good to come of taking a child up or down in the house without having first placed silver or gold between his fingers.

Of course it is not so venturesome to bring a child downstairs empty-handed; but to take him back for the first time without something of value in his little fist, is the same as saying that he will never rise in the world to the fathering of wealth.

The dinner was much enjoyed by both Sarah and me, even though the baby, who seemed to be frightened because of seeing so many strange faces, cried a goodly part of the time.

We had wild turkey roasted, and it was as pleasing a morsel as ever I put in my mouth. Then there was a huge pie of deer meat, with baked and fried fish in abundance, and lobsters so large that there was not a trencher bowl on the board big enough to hold a whole one. We had whitpot, yokhegg, suquash, and many other Indian dishes, the making of which I shall tell you about soon.

Ruth

CHEESE TOAST

Take a slice of good, rich, old cheese, cut it up into small pieces, put it into a tin or iron stew-pot, and to one cup of milk add 3 eggs; beat eggs and milk together and pour on to the cheese; set it on the stove, and when it begins to simmer stir briskly until it forms a thick curdle, then pour over the toast and carry to table.

Boston Cultivator, May 17, 1873

NEW YORK IN THE PRE-REVOLUTIONARY PERIOD, 1765-1775

The city of New York at this period was, in politics, in culture, and in social display, the capital. The Governor resided here and the General Assembly met here. The British Commander-in-Chief and the only garrison in the colonies for some years after the close of the French War added the peculiar influences which gather about military quarters.

For the high gentry, the English officials, and those of the colony in particular who had country estates in the neighborhood of New York, racing was the chief delight.

Cockfighting was a more aristocratic pastime. Good fighting cocks were advertised in the New York papers, as were cock-gaffs of silver and steel, and the sign of the Fighting-Cocks hung next door to the Exchange Coffee House.

Fox-hunting was a favorite pastime in the colony. There were foxes on this island, but the less broken grounds of Long Island afforded better running, and by permission each year three days' sport was had on the Flatland plains, the hunters meeting at daybreak during the autumn racing season.

Good living was the rule, not the exception, in this colony. Nowhere on this continent, nor perhaps on any other, was there such a profusion of native and imported products to delight the inner man as in the New York province. The dinner hour was from one to three and tea at nightfall was what today would be called "high tea." A supper invariably followed at a tavern or coffee house.

In the costume of the period the ladies wore stiff-laced bodices, skirts with deep panniers, hooped petticoats of considerable width, high-heeled colored shoes, and, later, slippers of dainty satin or white dressed kid. They carried fans of the latest pattern. Materials were rich and heavy brocades in bunches of gold and silver of the large English pattern. By day they were simple as Cinderella at the chimney-corner.

COOKING

Despite elaborate chimney systems for numerous types of ovens, baking never became the most common method of cooking. Hashes, ragouts, and the traditional boiled dinner that could be slowly stewed were undoubtedly the most widely accepted dishes, primarily because of their relative ease of preparation.

Cooking was simply another chore for the early housewife, who had scores of other daily tasks to complete while dinner was in the making. Combinations of chopped meat and vegetables could simmer unattended in the pot for several hours, during which time she attended to her other jobs.

Slow boiling was also ideal for cooking porridges, which were often mixed after supper and allowed to cook at low temperatures throughout the night. Many wild meats, which tended to be tough, also needed a long period of cooking or stewing to make them edible.

SHEEP-SHEARING: *Diary of An Early American Housewife*

June 2, 1772—The sheep are being washed today so that they can be sheared next week.

SHEEP-SHEARING

The sheep were usually washed on a fine morning in June. The sheep-shearing, which followed a few days after the washing, had its interests, too, especially for the younger members of the family. The sheep were driven home and placed in a stable; the barn floor was nicely swept. Then the poor animal, trembling with fright, was brought out and made to assume an awkward sitting posture, where, with its back toward and between the knees of the shearer, it was ready to be sheared. The shearer then parted the wool under the neck and his nimble shears worked their way close to the skin and beneath the matted wool which soon began to fall around the shoulders of the sheep. After the neck was done, the sheep was laid on its side, and soon the fleece was removed in one piece. The sheep was now so small that it did not seem to be the same animal of minutes before.

A TROUSSEAU

Great simplicity characterized many colonial weddings, but, yielding to the sweet and wholesome instinct that has always led parents to rejoice and make merry over their children's settling for life, the colonists gradually surrounded their weddings with more ceremony and gaiety. In families where large fortunes were acquired, a handsome trousseau was usually prepared for the bride. Before the

The Bride—1880's

marriage of his daughter to Nathaniel Sparhawk, Sir William Pepperell wrote to England for an outfit which included:

"Silk to make a woman a full suit of clothes, the ground to be white padusoy and flowered with all sorts of coulers suitable for a young woman—another of white water *Taby* and *Gold Lace* for trimming of it; twelve yards of Green Padusoy; thirteen yards of Lace, for a woman's head dress, 2 inches wide, as can be bought for 13 s. per yard; a handsome Fan, with a leather mounting, as good as can be bought for about 20 shillings; 2 pair silk shoes, and cloggs a size bigger than ye shoe."

FLEECE: *Diary of An Early American Housewife*

June 10, 1772—The sheep have all been sheared and now it is necessary that Mother and I work on the fleece so that we might have some material ready for our heavy clothing.

PREPARATION OF THE FLEECE

Fleece had to be opened with care and have all pitched and tarred locks, daglocks, brand, and felting cut out. These cuttings were not wasted, but were spun

Spinning

into coarse yarn. The white locks were carefully tossed and separated and tied into net bags with tallies to be dyed.

After the dyeing, the next process was carding into small fleecy rolls, which were now ready for spinning.

All these processes were tedious and required much skill on the part of the workers. It was a task that was not looked forward to but had to be done in order to have warm clothing for the cold New England winters.

A BABY BOY: *Diary of An Early American Housewife*

June 15, 1772—A baby boy was born to Dorothy Mullins this morning. It is a nice big boy and let us pray that he makes it to manhood. Dorothy has not been very lucky with her sons. She gave birth to six of them and only this new one is alive; the others died very young before they were two years of age. However, she does have her three lovely girls who are a great help to her.

Rocking baby

THE BIRTH OF A BABY

Babies were born at home, in a room commonly called "the borning room" since births were so frequent. The delivery became something of a social event, with all the participants female unless the infant proved to be a boy. Midwives were always called, but, nonetheless, the neighboring women would gather to help and to hover over the mother while they kept the males at a distance.

Once the child was born, the new mother could relax for a while since there was so much help. Friends dropped in with small presents for the mother, usually pincushions. Whether or not the child was christened, his first gift of value was a christening blanket of fine cloth, often quilted and sometimes embroidered. The cradle was usually a hand-me-down unless it was the first child and the father had just fashioned one for his first-born.

There were many manuals on ways of raising children, but most of them were long on moral advice and short on practical suggestions. Farm children, once they got past the first two critical years when weaning, teething, scarlet fever and diptheria took a fearful toll, were generally healthy.

By the time the child was weaned, about two years of age, he usually sat at the family table and ate what the adults ate. The fare usually consisted of meat twice a day, vegetables of all sorts, as well as fruit and berries, pastry in abundance, homemade bread, pies and puddings. Babies drank milk, but once they were old enough to be seated at the table with the adults, they, too, had either apple cider, beer, or tea.

TO ROAST A TONGUE

Take a Tongue well powdered boyl it put it stuck well with Cloves then Roast it and for the Sauce take Clarrett Crumbs of bread Sinomon & sugar boyl it then put it into the dish under the Tongue Serve it up.

Isabella Ashfield, *Her Book*, April 1, 1724

HOUSE-CLEANING *by Francis Hopkinson* (1785)

When a young couple are about to enter on the matrimonial state, a never failing article in the marriage treaty is, that the lady shall have and enjoy the free and unmolested exercise of the rights of white-washing, with all its ceremonials, privileges, and appurtenances. You will wonder what this privilege of white-washing is. I will endeavour to give you an idea of the ceremony, as I have seen it performed.

There is no season of the year in which the lady may not, if she pleases, claim her privilege; but the latter end of May is generally fixed upon for the purpose. The attentive husband may judge by certain prognostics, when the storm is nigh at hand. If the lady grows uncommonly fretful, finds fault with the servants, is discontented with the children, and complains much of the nastiness of everything about her: these are symptoms which ought not to be neglected, yet they sometimes go off without any further effect. But if, when the husband rises in the morning, he should observe in the yard, a wheelbarrow, with a quantity of lime in it, or should see certain buckets filled with a solution of lime in water, there is no time for hesitation. He immediately locks up the apartment or closet where his papers, and private property are kept, and putting the key in his pocket, betakes himself to flight. A husband, however beloved, becomes a perfect nuisance during this season of feminine rage. His authority is superseded, his commission suspended, and the very scullion who cleans the brasses in the kitchen becomes of more importance than him. He has nothing for it but to abdicate, for a time, and run from an evil which he can neither prevent nor modify.

The husband gone, the ceremony begins. The walls are stripped of their furniture—paintings, prints, and looking-glasses lie in huddled heaps about the floors: the curtains are torn from their testers, the beds crammed into windows, chairs and tables, bedsteads and cradles crowd the yard; and the garden fence bends beneath the weight of carpets, blankets, cloth cloaks, old coats, under-petticoats, and ragged breeches.

The ceremony completed, and the house thoroughly evacuated, the next operation is to smear the walls and ceilings with brushes, dipped in a solution of lime called white-wash; to pour buckets of water over every floor, and scratch all the partitions and wainscoats with hard brushes, charged with soft soap and stone-cutter's sand.

The windows by no means escape the general deluge. A servant scrambles out upon the penthouse, at the risk of her neck, and with a mug in her hand, and a bucket within reach, dashes innumerable gallons of water against the glass panes, to the great annoyance of passengers in the street.

I have been told that an action at law was once brought against one of these water nymphs, by a person who had a new suit of clothes spoiled by this operation: but after long argument it was determined, that no damages could be awarded; inasmuch as the defendant was in the exercise of a legal right, and not answerable for the consequences. And so the poor gentleman was doubly non-suited; for he lost both his suit of clothes and his suit at law.

These smearings and scratchings, these washings and dashings, being duly performed, the next ceremonial is to cleanse and replace the distracted furniture. You may have seen a house-raising, or a ship-launch—recollect, if you can, the hurry, bustle, confusion, and noise of such a scene, and you will have some idea of this cleansing match. The misfortunate is, that the sole object is to make things clean. It matters not how many useful, ornamental, or valuable articles suffer mutilation or death under the operation. A mahogany chair and a carved frame undergo the same discipline: they are to be made clean at all events; but their preservation is not worthy of attention. For instance: a fine large engraving is laid flat upon the floor; a number of smaller prints are piled upon it, until the superincumbent weight cracks the lower glass—but this is of no importance. A valuable picture is placed leaning against the sharp corner of a table; others are made to lean against that, till the pressure of the whole forces the corner of the table through the canvas of the first. The frame and glass of a fine print are to be cleaned; the spirit and oil used on this occasion are suffered to leak through and deface the engraving—no matter! If the glass is clean and the frame shines it is sufficient—the rest is not worthy of consideration. An able arithmetician hath made a calculation, founded on long experience, and proved that the losses and destruction incident to two white-washings are equal to one removal and three removals equal to one fire.

This cleansing frolic over, matters begin to resume their pristine appearance; the storm abates, and all would be well again: but it is impossible that so great a convulsion in so small a community should pass over without producing some consequences. For two or three weeks after the operation, the family are usually afflicted with sore eyes, sore throats, or severe colds, occasioned by exhalations from wet floors and damp walls.

LIFE IN THE YOUNG REPUBLIC—THE EARLY 1800'S

CLOTHING: About 1795 a change took place in the fashionable dress of women. Instead of the rich, heavy brocades and damasks, soft, clinging muslin, gauze, or similar materials were used. Skirts were narrower and shorter, reaching only to the ankles. The bodice was very short and had a low neck. Sometimes a gauze or muslin handkerchief was draped over the shoulders. These gowns were either sleeveless or had short puff sleeves, sometimes with long sleeves attached to the puffs.

When it was warm outdoors, women wore long scarves reaching to the feet, and long cloaks when it was cold. Slippers, for indoors and out, were light and had no heels.

The hair was dressed in loose curls, either hanging about the shoulders or caught up with ribbons or combs. Sometimes it was lightly powdered. Hats were very large and were tied under the chin; turbans were popular. Older women wore caps.

FOOD: Food was distinguished by its abundance rather than by its quality. Corn, most often in the form of corn bread, or "rye and Injun," which was the bread made of mixed corn and rye, was still the chief staple of the American diet. Except among the well-to-do, salt pork was the staple meat; in many parts of the country it was served three times a day. In those days there was no way of preserving meat except by salting or smoking. Hogs were plentiful and cost nothing to care for, since they could be allowed to run loose and pick up their own food. A hog slaughtered by the farmer could be salted and eaten by the family before it spoiled.

There was always an abundance of potatoes, squash, turnips and beans, but some of the vegetables familiar today, such as cauliflower, rhubarb, and eggplant, were unknown. The tomato was grown for ornamental purposes only, as it was thought to be poisonous. It was called the "love apple." Fruit was abundant but inferior in quality to that of today. Pears, peaches, plums, and cherries were dried for winter consumption; apples were made into cider. Strawberries and raspberries grew wild. Exotic fruits like oranges and bananas were found only on the tables of the wealthy.

In New England, especially among the common people, the three daily meals were very much alike. At each of them pea and bean porridge, salt pork, cornmeal with milk, and perhaps dried or salted fish appeared practically every day in the year. Of course, the menu of the New England merchant or banker showed a greater variety of tasty dishes.

The Southern gentleman, with numerous slaves to grow, cook and serve his food, paid more attention to what appeared on his table, which groaned under a burden of various kinds of soups; turkey, ham, chicken, bacon, beef, mutton; sweet potatoes prepared two or three different ways; hot bread and hot biscuits, muffins and corn bread; jellies, relishes, and pastries; wines and liquors.

North or South, there were still few stoves; food was usually prepared in the open fireplace.

SPRING

Every season of the year had its own tasks and triumphs for our American housewife. The only thing that changed the weekly routine of work—in fact life itself—was the coming of a new season.

Spring was a period in which life came back into the trees, the snow was melting away, animals were being born, such as the spring lambs and sheep. This was the time of the year when the housewife dug up the horseradish root, picked the dandelion greens, brewed spring tonic, and opened the windows and started the annual spring housecleaning after a winter of being shut indoors. Seeds were put into a cold frame. Visiting started up again with friends coming over, while the village seamstress would pull in to stay a week or so and help get all the children fixed up. This was also the calling time of the peddler, the scissors grinder, and the tramp. But above all, the two big occasions were (1) the making of maple sugar, and (2) arrival of the seed catalog.

The making of the maple sugar was a big event which, as described earlier, almost always ended with a sugaring-off party and maple syrup being poured over dishes of snow.

After 1800, spring also heralded the arrival of the Shakers, a religious sect. The Shakers made trips through the farm country peddling seeds and their well-built hickory and maple splint-bottom chairs. Shaker seed was considered the best in America, and its salesmen went from place to place selling it.

However, in the late 1800's, the seed catalog for mail order buying began to replace the Shakers'.

FARMER'S ALMANAC, 1840

LOVE-MAKING

Most worthy of admiration,
After a long consideration
And serious meditation,
Of the great reputation
You have in this region;
I have a strong inclination
To become your relation.
I am now making preparation
To remove my habitation
To a more convenient situation,
To pay you adoration,
By more frequent visitation.
If this kind of oblation
Be but worthy of observation,
It will be an obligation
Beyond all moderation.
Believe me in every station
From generation to generation.

Yours, &c.

THE LADY'S ANSWER

I received your adoration,
With much delineration,
And some consternation,
At the seeming infatuation
That seized your imagination,
When you made such a declaration,
On so slender a foundation;
But on examination,
Supposed it done from ostentation.
To display an education
Or rather multiplication
Or words of the same termination,
Though with great variation
And different signification,
Which, without disputation,
May deserve commendation;
And I think imitation
A sufficient gratification.

Yours, &c., Jane

SPINACH TARTS

Scald some spinach in boiling water, and then drain it quite dry; chop it, and stew it in some butter and cream, with a very little salt, some sugar, some bits of citron, and a very little orange-flower water. Put it into a very fine puff paste, and let it be baked in a moderate hot oven.

The Whole Art of Confectionary, 1831

THE SEAMSTRESS

Before the Civil War and even shortly after, most clothing was made either by a housewife, a grandmother, a spinster daughter, or an individual called a needle-woman, modiste, semptress, or seamstress. Known today as a dressmaker, she either went to the customer's home with her needles, pins, threads, thimbles, scissors, beeswax, and tape measure and did her work in a spare bedroom or parlor, or else she had a small shop to which customers brought their materials and had their fittings.

MOTHER'S ADVICE TO HER DAUGHTER ON THE DAY OF HER MARRIAGE

Now Polly, as you are about to leave us, a few words seem appropriate to the occasion. Although I regret the separation, yet I am pleased that your prospects are good. You must not think that all before you are Elysian fields. Toil, care, and troubles are the companions of frail human nature. Old connexions will be dissolved by distance, by time, and death. New ones are formed. Everything pertaining to this life is on the change.

A well cultivated mind, united with a pleasant, easy disposition, is the greatest accomplishment in a lady. I have endeavored, from the first to the present moment, to bring you up in such a manner as to form you for future usefulness in society. Woman was never made merely to see and be seen; but to fill an important space in the great chain in nature, planned and formed by the Almighty Parent of the universe. You have been educated in the habits of industry, frugality, economy, and neatness, and in these you have not disappointed me.

It is for the man to provide, and for the wife to take care and see that everything within her circle of movements is done in order and season; therefore let method and order be considered important. A place for everything and everything in its time and place, are good family mottos.

Farmer's Almanack, 1842, Robert B. Thomas

FRICANDEAU WITH SPINACH

Neatly trim a nice piece of fillet or cushion of veal. Place in a large stew-pan a layer of slices of bacon, then some carrots and onions, cut in slices, with a bundle of sweet herbs, pepper, salt, and spices to taste; lay the piece of veal in the middle, and moisten with about a pint of stock. Let the meat stew gently for three or four hours, basting the top occasionally. Then strain off the gravy, put it into a small saucepan, skim off superfluous fat, add to it a little butter, mixed smooth with a small quantity of flour, and let the gravy reduce nearly to a glaze; pour it over the meat, the top of which should be previously browned with a salamander if necessary, and serve with a border of spinach.

Godey's Lady's Book and Magazine, 1862

BEEF SANDERS

Mince cold beef small with onions, add pepper and salt, and a little gravy; put into a pie-dish until about three parts full. Then fill up with mashed potatoes. Bake in the oven or before the fire until done a light brown. Mutton may be dressed in the same way.

Peterson's Magazine, March 1866

LOVE

We distinguish four seasons in love. First comes love before betrothal, or spring; then comes the summer, more ardent, and fiercer, which lasts from our betrothal to the altar; the third, the richly laden, soft, dream autumn, the honey-moon; and after it the winter, bright, clear winter—when you take shelter by your fireside from the cold world without, and find comfort and pleasure there. In each season the beauties seem supremely beautiful, and add to life all its sweetness.

Farmer's Almanac, 1869, Samuel Hart Wright

EASTER CAKES

One pound flour, nine ounces of butter, five ounces currants, five ounces white sugar, the yolks of three and white of two eggs, cinnamon and nutmeg to flavor. Bake as flat biscuits in a moderate oven.

New England Fireside, September 1880

HOUSECLEANING

The following remark we consider worth fifty dollars in any family, in city or country, and we commend it to all housekeepers, old and young: "The best way to clean a house, is to keep it clean by a daily attention to small things, and never allow it to get into such a state of dirtiness and disorder as to require great and periodical cleanings, which turn comfort out of doors."

The Old Farmer's Almanack, 1855, Robert B. Thomas

Polishing the andirons

SPRING HOUSECLEANING

In all households there are certain periods in which the comfort of the family is subordinate to the good of the cause. One of these periods has arrived. Certain housekeepers take work, as some children do the measles, "hard." Others go through with a vast amount without allowing the machinery to be visible.

There is no need of turning everything upside down at once. Clean little by little, finishing one room before beginning another, even if it is more convenient to have all the carpets taken up at the same time.

Do not be afraid to give away or sell cast off clothing for which you have no need. Too much trash is carefully hoarded each year, on the chance that "it may come in handy some day," and old clothing is stored away in drawers and boxes to become a nest in which moths may breed, which ought to have been given away.

Household, April 1884

FOR THE COMPLEXION

If ladies use anything, the following are the best and most harmless: Blanch one-fourth pound best Jordan's almonds, slip off the skin, mash in a mortar, and rub together with the best white soap for fifteen minutes, adding gradually one quart of rose-water; or clean fresh rain-water may be used. When the mixture looks like milk, strain through fine muslin. Apply after washing with a soft rag. To white the skin and remove freckles and tan, bathe three times a day in a preparation of three quarts of alcohol, two ounces cologne, and one of borax, in proportion of two tea-spoons mixture to two table-spoons of soft water.

Ladies' Home Cook Book, 1896

HEAVE OFFERING

A Quaker invited a tradesman to dine with him, whom he treated with an excellent dinner, a bottle of wine, and a pipe of tobacco. His guest, after drinking pretty freely, became extremely rude to his host, insomuch that the Quaker's patience was at length exhausted, and he rose up and addressed him in the following words—"Friend, I have given this meat offering and drink offering, and burnt offering, and for thy misconduct, I will give thee a heave offering" and immediately threw him into the street out of the parlor window.

New Jersey Almanac, 1832, David Young

HOPPING JOHN

It is said in the South that without a dish of Hopping John, which is a combination of rice and black-eyed peas and bacon, on New Year's Day, a year of bad luck will follow. The name may have been derived from a custom that children must hop once around the table before the dish is served.

DUTCH OVEN

The Dutch oven was another place for baking bread. This was the shallow, three-legged kettle with a bail handle and a cover with a rim. Placed in the embers and covered over with them, it baked in the same slow way as the brick oven.

Baking in embers was the earliest and only way known to primitive people. The Dutch oven was one of the first kettles and appeared before the brick oven was added to the open fireplace.

Early Dutch oven

A NEW OVEN: *A Letter from Ruth*

Dear Hannah:
I must tell you how we happen to have an oven, when there has been only the big fire-

place in which to cook our food. Mistress White and Mistress Tilley each brought from Leyden, in Holland, what some people call a "roasting kitchen," and you can think of nothing more convenient. It is made of thin iron like unto a box, the front of which is open, and the back rounded as is a log. It is near to a yard long, and stands so high as to take all the heat from the fire which would otherwise be thrown out into the room. In it we put our bread, pumpkins, or meat and set it in front of and close against a roaring fire. The back or rounded part is then heaped high with hot ashes or live embers, and that which is inside must of necessity be cooked. At the very top of the oven is a small door which can be opened for the cook to look inside, and one may see just how the food is getting on without disturbing the embers.

We often borrow of Mistress Tilley hers, and father has promised to send by the first ship that comes to this harbor for one that shall be our very own.

Ruth

BUNDLING

Early marriage was encouraged and there was a tolerance of premarital intimacy in the early days of the colonies.

Whether the Dutch or the English invented bundling nobody seems quite certain, but by the late eighteenth century, it was an accepted part of courtship in New England and the middle colonies.

In warm months, lovers could walk off into the woods or meet in the barn or the spring house, but on cold or stormy nights they could be together only indoors—and it was pretty crowded around the fireplace. As a result of a genuine wish to hasten the courtship, an invitation might have been given to the young man to stay and share the girl's bed; it was usually the only place where the boy could have slept, and the center board kept for such occasions theoretically discouraged close intimacy.

One obvious advantage was that the parents knew where the girl was and who was with her, whether or not the center board remained in place. If the bride was pregnant at her wedding, the ceremony sanctified it and, besides, bearing children was a woman's duty.

In colonies where bundling was not a practice, "natural children" were quite numerous.

A BRIDE IN NEW YORK, 1800

My head is almost turned, and yet I am very happy. I am enraptured with New York. You cannot imagine anything half so beautiful as Broadway, and I am sure you would say I was more romantic than ever, if I should attempt to describe the Battery, —the fine water prospect,—you can have no idea how refreshing in a warm evening. The gardens we have not yet visited; indeed, we have so many delightful things to see 'twill take me forever. My husband declares he takes as much pleasure in showing them to me as I do in seeing them; you would believe it if you saw him.

I went shopping yesterday, and 'tis a fact that the little white satin Quaker bonnets, cap-crowns, lined with pink or blue or white, are the most fashionable that are worn. But I'll not have one, for if any of my old acquaintance should meet me in the street, they would laugh: I would if I were they.

I have been to two of the Columbia gardens, near the Battery, a most romantic place, it is enclosed in a circular form and has little rooms and boxes all around, with chairs and tables, these full of company; the trees are all hung with lamps, twinkling through the branches; in the centre is a pretty little building with a fountain playing continually, and the rays of the lamps on the drops of water gave it a cool sparkling appearance that was delightful. This little building, which has a kind of canopy and pillars all around the garden, had festoons of colored lamps, that at a distance looked like large brilliant stars seen through the branches; and placed all around were marble busts, beautiful little figures of Diana, Cupid and Venus, which by the glimmering of the lamps, partly concealed by the foliage, give you an idea of enchantment.

As we strolled through the trees, we passed a box that Miss Watts was in. She called to us, and we went in, and had a charming refreshing glass of ice cream, which has chilled me ever since. They have a fine orchestra and have concerts here sometimes.

We went on toward the Battery. This is a large promenade by the shore of the North River: there are rows and clusters of trees in every part, and a large walk along the shore, almost over the water, gives you such a fresh delightful air, that every evening in summer it is crowded with company. Here, too, they have music playing in boats on the water of a moonlight night.

I am in raptures, as you may imagine, and if I had not grown sober before I came to this wonderful place, it would have turned my head.

Reprinted from an Old Valentine Manual

ODD SCRAPS FOR THE ECONOMICAL

If you would avoid waste in your family, attend to the following rules, and do not despise them because they appear so unimportant: 'many a little makes a mickle.'

Look to the grease-pot, and see that nothing is there which might have served to nourish your own family, or a poorer one.

As far as is possible, have bits of bread eaten up before they become hard. Spread those that are not eaten, and let them dry, to be pounded for puddings, or soaked for brewis. Brewis is made of crusts and dry pieces of bread, soaked a good while in hot milk, mashed up, and salted, and buttered like toast.

Make your own bread and cake. Some people think it is just as cheap to buy of the baker and confectioner; but it is not half as cheap. True, it is more convenient; and therefore the rich are justifiable in employing them; but those who are under the necessity of being economical should make convenience a secondary object. In the first place, confectioners make their cake richer than people of moderate income can afford to make it; in the next place you may just as well employ your own time, as to pay them for theirs.

Indian meal and rye meal are in danger of fermenting in summer; particularly Indian. They should be kept in a cool place, and stirred open to the air, once in a while. A large stone, put in the middle of a barrel of meal, is a good thing to keep it cool.

Spots in furniture may usually be cleansed by rubbing them quick and hard, with a flannel wet with the same thing which took out the color; if rum, wet the cloth with rum, &c. The very best restorative for defaced varnished furniture, is rotten-stone pulverized, and rubbed on with linseed oil.

New iron should be very gradually heated at first. After it has become inured to the heat, it is not as likely to crack.

If you happen to live in a house which has marble fire-places, never wash them with suds; this destroys the polish, in time. They should be dusted; the spots taken off with a nice oiled cloth, and then rubbed dry with a soft rag.

If you wish to preserve fine teeth, always clean them thoroughly after you have eaten your last meal at night.

Keep a bag for odd pieces of tape and strings; they will come in use. Keep a bag or box for old buttons, so that you may know where to go when you want one.

Use hard soap to wash your clothes, and soft to wash your floors. Soft soap is so slippery, that it wastes a good deal in washing clothes.

The American Frugal Housewife, 1844

MENUS FOR SPRING EATING

APRIL

MONDAY. *Breakfast*—Rolls, veal chops, fried raw potatoes. *Dinner*—Rice soup, roast beef, turnips, potatoes, tomato sauce, pickled oysters, baked custard pie. *Supper*—Cold rolls, omelette, cold beef sliced, cake and jam.

TUESDAY. *Breakfast*—Muffins, fried liver, fried potatoes. *Dinner*—Mutton soup, mutton garnished with eggs, pickles, creamed potatoes, canned tomatoes, bread pudding with sauce. *Supper*—Toasted muffins, sliced mutton, sponge cake and jelly.

WEDNESDAY. *Breakfast*—Flannel cakes, minced mutton or broiled chops, breakfast potatoes. *Dinner*—Roast pork, apple sauce, mashed potatoes, fried parsnips, lettuce, lemon pudding, jelly cake. *Supper*—Yankee dried beef, soda biscuit and honey, floating island.

THURSDAY. *Breakfast*—Sally Lunn, veal cutlets, potato cakes. *Dinner*—Baked stuffed heart, potatoes, turnips, canned corn, pickled eggs, cup custard, peach tapioca pudding. *Supper*—Light biscuit, cold sliced heart, bread fritters with sugar, cake and sauce.

FRIDAY. *Breakfast*—French rolls, broiled fish if salt, fried, if fresh, fried raw potatoes, tomato sauce. *Dinner*—Soup, baked or boiled fresh fish, mashed potatoes, canned peas or beans, lettuce, onions, English pudding, jelly tarts. *Supper*—Cold rolls, bologna sausage sliced, steamed crackers, cake and preserved fruit.

SATURDAY. *Breakfast*—Batter cakes, broiled chops, scrambled eggs, potato rissoles. *Dinner*—Bean soup, broiled beefsteak, spinach, potatoes, pickled beets, pudding with sauce, oranges and cake. *Supper*—Toasted bread, cold tongue sliced, hot buns and marmalade.

SUNDAY. *Breakfast*—Baked beans and Boston brown bread, omelette with parsley. *Dinner*—Vermicelli soup, baked shad or croquettes of canned lobster, broiled squabs or pigeon pie, mashed potatoes, turnips, asparagus, spring cresses, dressed lettuce, grape jelly, custard pie. *Supper*—Plain bread, canned salmon, cold buns, jelly, sponge cake.

MAY

MONDAY. *Breakfast*—Gems, dry toast, potato cakes, broiled beefsteak. *Dinner*—Roast of mutton with potatoes, canned tomatoes, rhubarb sauce, baked custards, fruit cake. *Supper*—Cold biscuit, sliced mutton, currant jelly, sweet buns, cream.

TUESDAY. *Breakfast*—Corn cakes, fried pickled tripe, scrambled eggs, potatoes. *Dinner*—Boiled beef with soup, whole potatoes, asparagus with eggs, cocoanut pudding, jelly. *Supper*—Plain bread, cold beef, toasted buns with strawberry jam or canned fruit, cake.

WEDNESDAY. *Breakfast*—Dropped eggs on toast, broiled ham, potatoes. *Dinner*—Boiled tongue with Chili sauce, fricasseed potatoes, cresses, boiled asparagus, ice-cream, sponge cake. *Supper*—Tea biscuits, shaved tongue, sago jelly, lady cake.

THURSDAY. *Breakfast*—Graham bread, fried mutton chops, fried raw potatoes. *Dinner*—Asparagus soup, roast of veal with potatoes, stewed onions, pickled beets, cake, orange float. *Supper*—Toasted Graham bread, sliced veal, tea rusk, lemon jelly.

FRIDAY. *Breakfast*—Muffins, broiled beefsteak, poached eggs, chipped potatoes. *Dinner*—Baked or boiled fish (if large, or fried small fish), boiled potatoes in jackets, lettuce salad, custard pie. *Supper*—Toasted muffins, cold rusk with strawberries, or marmalade, cake.

SATURDAY. *Breakfast*—Bread puffs with maple syrup, fricasseed potatoes, croquettes of fish. *Dinner*—Boiled leg of mutton, mint sauce, asparagus, boiled macaroni, potatoes, bread pudding. *Supper*—Cold rolls, cold mutton sliced, plain boiled rice with cream and sugar.

SUNDAY. *Breakfast*—Rice waffles, mutton croquettes, boiled eggs, fried raw potatoes. *Dinner*—Soup, roast beef, clam pie, new potatoes, tomatoes, dressed lettuce, young beets, strawberry cream and snow custard, coffee and macaroons. *Supper*—Light rolls, cold beef, cake and jelly, or strawberries.

JUNE

MONDAY. *Breakfast*—Oranges, French rolls, broiled liver, scrambled eggs. *Dinner*—Roast beef, mashed potatoes, beets, salmon salad, boiled rice with cream. *Supper*—Plain bread, Graham bread, bologna sausage, rusk with berries.

TUESDAY. *Breakfast*—Rice cakes, lamb chops, boiled eggs, fried potatoes. *Dinner*—

Boiled beef's tongue (fresh) served with Chili sauce, baked potatoes, young beets, lettuce dressed, raspberry cream, cake. *Supper*—Rolls, sliced beef's tongue, cheese, toasted rusk, berries.

WEDNESDAY. *Breakfast*—Graham gems, muffins, beefsteak, potato cakes. *Dinner*—Soup of stock boiled yesterday with tongue, chicken pie, mashed potatoes and turnips, spinach, lettuce, cream fritters with sauce. *Supper*—Toasted muffins, cold chicken pie, cake and strawberries.

THURSDAY. *Breakfast*—Sally Lunn, veal cutlets, potatoes, radishes. *Dinner*—Ragout of lamb, mashed potatoes, asparagus, lettuce, lemon pudding, pie. *Supper*—Rolls, bread, cold sliced lamb, sliced tomatoes, Swiss cakes, berries.

FRIDAY. *Breakfast*—Rolls, breakfast stew, potatoes or tomatoes. *Dinner*—Soup, fresh fish fried or baked, mashed potatoes, asparagus, beet salad, rice pudding with sauce and cake, oranges. *Supper*—Cold rolls, dried beef chipped, custard cake with fruit or berries.

SATURDAY. *Breakfast*—Graham gems, croquettes of fish or breaded veal cutlets, potatoes, escaloped eggs. *Dinner*—Ham boiled with greens, potatoes, beets, young onions, Eglantine pudding, Italian cream. *Supper*—Toasted gems, cold ham, oatmeal with cream, cake and jelly.

SUNDAY. *Breakfast*—Light rolls, broiled beefsteak, sliced tomatoes, omelets. *Dinner*—Vegetable soup, baked chicken, mashed potatoes, green pease, pickled beets, Bavarian cream with strawberries. *Supper*—Cold rolls, cold chicken, toast with jelly, fruit.

Queen of the Household, 1906

MENUS FOR PEOPLE OF LIMITED MEANS

Sunday's Dinner: Roast beef, potatoes, greens, and yorkshire pudding.
Monday's Dinner: Hashed beef, potatoes, and bread pudding.
Tuesday's Dinner: Broiled beef and bones, vegetables, apple pudding.
Wednesday's Dinner: Fish, if cheap, chops, vegetables, pancakes.
Thursday's Dinner: Boiled pork, pea pudding, greens, rice pudding.
Friday's Dinner: Pea soup, remains of pork, and baked batter pudding.
Saturday's Dinner: Stewed steak with suet dumpling, and rice in a mould with sauce.

The Practical Housekeeper, Mrs. Ellet, 1857

Author's note: Imagine a family of limited means trying to tackle the above.

MENUS FOR THE HOLIDAYS

LENTEN DINNER

Clam and corn soup, bread rings, egg and pimento tamales, baked stuffed haddock, hollandaise sauce, French fried potatoes, boiled Brussels Sprouts, apple and chestnut salad, danish custard, crackers, cheese, coffee.

EASTER BREAKFAST

Strawberry and rhubarb cup, fried chicken, Julienne potatoes, fresh asparagus, hollandaise sauce, tomato and pineapple salad, hot biscuits, sponge cake baskets filled with caramel flavored whipped cream, coffee.

EASTER DINNER

Chicken soup, bread rings, broiled trout, roast spring lamb, mint sauce, new potatoes, boiled green peas, dressed lettuce, cheese eggs, lemon ice, currant wafers, boiled salted almonds, bonbons, coffee.

What to Have for Dinner, Fannie Farmer, 1905

Summer

JULY, AUGUST, SEPTEMBER

THE QUAKERS

The Quakers broke away from the Church of England because they felt that all men were equal before God and that no man could set himself above his fellowmen. This meant that they would not take off their hats even to the King. They felt no need for the sacraments of Communion and Baptism, and these beliefs outraged almost everyone.

William Penn, the son of a prominent admiral of the Royal Navy, was converted to this belief in 1667, and his father was both shocked and angry when he heard the news of his conversion, for the Quakers at this time were one of the most disliked religious groups in England. But Penn went his own way. His father finally forgave him and left him a large inheritance.

Part of Penn's inheritance was a debt that Charles II had owed his father. In place of the money, the King in 1681 gave Penn a charter granting him full ownership, thus making him proprietor, of a huge grant of land in the New World. On this land Penn founded a colony to which the King gave the name Pennsylvania. As a proprietor, Penn had power over this proprietary colony almost as great as the King's power over the Royal colonies.

Pennsylvania had no coastline. Penn solved this problem in 1682 by asking for, and receiving, another grant of land to the south, on the west bank of Delaware Bay. This new land, later called Delaware, was for many years referred to as "the lower counties." Until the Revolutionary War, both grants remained in the hands of the Penn family, which governed them as Separate Colonies.

Penn settled Philadelphia first with the Quakers. Philadelphia was planned according to Quaker principles, with each man having space and freedom, and no man's house being larger than his neighbor's. However, by the middle of the eighteenth century, Philadelphia was the largest city in the English colonies, and much of the simplicity and soberness of the Quaker town was forgotten.

The first Quaker colonists dug themselves caves in the river bank where

Philadelphia was to be. As the town grew, it was laid out in neat rectangular blocks. The early Quaker dwelling usually had four rooms and an attic, with perhaps a separate kitchen out back. It was built of brick with painted woodwork. The windows were some of the first sash windows in America that slid up and down.

The Quaker was by preference a town dweller and was usually engaged in business or in some other distinctly town occupation. A description of Philadelphia: "There were many drab-coated men, and there were elderly women, in gowns of drab or gray, with white silk shawls and black silver-covered cardboard bonnets. Here and there a man or woman was in gayer colors or wore buckles, and some had silver buttons; but these were rare."

THE HOUSEHOLD AND FOOD IN PHILADELPHIA

The women who were at the head of the old Philadelphia homes were usually good housewives, for in that day more attention was paid to educating a girl in housework and homemaking than in studies at school. It was considered to be of far

Main room of an 18th-century Pennsylvania house

greater value for a young girl to know how to spin, knit, sew, and cook than that she should be familiar with literature or be able to scan a line of Latin verse. The average mother took great pride in having her floor spotless, in making the clothing for her children as well as for her husband, and in collecting china, brass, pewter, or possibly silver for her pantry shelves.

The ordinary kitchen was apt to contain some modest supply of furnishings such as that sold in 1760 to Thomas Potts, owner of the house in which Washington later made his headquarters at Valley Forge: "A large copper sauce pann; a small dome, 8 shillings; a pair of Brass Candlesticks, 15 shillings; a pair of Rose Blanketts, 46 shillings; 6 china bowls, 23 shillings 6 pence; a pr. of Snuffers, 2 shillings 6 pence; 2 Brush, 2 shillings 9 pence; a pr. Iron Candlesticks, 2 shillings; 2 China bowles, 5 shillings; 3 saucers, 2 shillings 3 pence; a Looking Glass, 54 shillings; a dozen Knives and Forks, 7 shillings; 6 yards of Drapery, 11 shillings; a dozen Plates, 32 shillings; 6 hardkettle porringers, 15 shillings; a dozen spoons, 6 shillings; a trunk, 18 shillings; a cotton Counterpane, 57 shillings; ½ dozen Chairs, 40 shillings; 3 galls. of Spirit, 22 shillings; 3 silver spoons, 66 shillings 10 pence; a Bedsted, 40 shillings; Fire shovel and Tongs, 10 shillings."

The cleanliness of Philadelphia homemakers is shown by this excerpt from a magazine article of the early 1800's: "There is another cherished custom peculiar to the city of Philadelphia and nearly allied to the former. I mean that of washing the pavement before the doorway every Saturday evening. I at first took this to be a regulation of the police, but, on further enquiry, find it to be a religious rite in which the numerous sectarians of the city profoundly agree.

"The ceremony begins about sunset, and continues till about ten or eleven at night. It is very difficult for a stranger to walk the streets on these evenings. He runs a continual risk of having a bucket of water thrown against his legs, but a Philadelphia born is so accustomed to this danger that he avoids it with surprising dexterity. It is from this circumstance that a Philadelphian is known anywhere by his gait."

The Quakers got on extremely well with the Indians and soon learned to use Indian corn and cornmeal in their cookery, as well as elk, venison, wild turkey, passenger pigeons, and water-fowl, all of which were plentiful in the region.

The opportunities in Philadelphia to enjoy the pleasures of the table were soon unlimited. Farm, garden, and dairy products, vegetables, poultry, beef, and muttons were produced in immense quantity and variety and of excellent quality. Madeira obtained in trade with Spain was the popular drink even at the taverns. Various forms of punch and rum were common, but the modern light wines and champagne were not then in vogue.

The Quakers were known to have had gout. Food in great quantity and variety seems to have been placed on the table at the same time with little regard to formal courses. Beef, poultry, and mutton would all be served at one dinner. Fruit and nuts were also placed on the table in great quantities, as were puddings and desserts, of which there were many. Dinners were usually served in the afternoon.

Chastellux, a Frenchman who visited the country and then wrote about its people and customs, complained that the breakfasts were very heavy. Loins of veal, legs of mutton, and other substantial dishes at an early hour in the morning were rather staggering to a Frenchman who was accustomed to a cup of coffee and a roll. One of these breakfasts lasted an hour and a half, according to him.

In 1786, a quiet family meal consisted of roast turkey, mashed potatoes, whipped syllabubs, oyster pie, boiled leg of pork, bread pudding, and tarts, to be followed by an "early dish of tea for the old folks."

GULIA PENN

William Penn's first wife, Gulia, kept a handwritten book of family recipes which had been handed down from her mother and grandmother. In 1702, a manuscript copy of them was made and brought to America for use in the Penn household.

TOO MAKE A PUDING IN MUTTEN: Take grated bread, yeolks of eggs Rosted hard and sliced very fine, corants, parsly, time, Rosmary shreed youre herbs very fine, put a Litell sugar Cloves mace put all these together between the skin and the flesh of the mutton and so Rost it with the meat.

TOO MAKE A COLLWORT OR CABIDGE PUDING: Take a pound of beefe and ½ pound of suett shred them small season them with peper salt nutmegs sweet herbs work it up with some yeolks of eggs, boyle it in a Collwort or Cabidge Leafe when it is boyled putt in sum butter and eat it—

TRIP TO PHILADELPHIA MARKETS

"You may be Supply'd with every Necessary of Life throut the whole year, but Extraordinary Good and reasonably Cheap, and it is allow'd by Foreigners to be the best of its bigness in the known World, and undoubtedly the largest in America; I got to the place by 7; and had no small satisfaction in seeing the pretty Creatures, the Young Ladies, traversing the place from Stall to Stall, where they could make the best Market, some with their Maids behind them with a Basket to carry home the Purchase. Others that were designed to buy but trifles, as a little fresh Butter, a Dish of Green Peas, or the like, had Good Nature and Humility enough to be their own Porter."

William Black, 1744

JOHN ADAMS ON FOOD IN PHILADELPHIA: 1787

(Of the home of Miers Fisher, a young Quaker lawyer.)

"This plain Friend, with his plain but pretty wife with her Thees and Thous, had provided us a costly entertainment; ducks, hams, chickens, beef, pie, tarts, creams, custard, jellies, fools, trifles, floating islands, beer, porter, punch, wine, etc."

(Of the home of Chief Justice Chews.)

"About four o'clock we were called to dinner. Turtle and every other thing, flummer, jellies, sweetmeats of twenty sorts, trifles, whipped sillabubs, floating islands, fools, etc., with a dessert of fruits, raisins, almonds, pears, peaches.

"A most sinful feast again! everything which could delight the eye or allure the taste; curds and creams, jellies, sweetmeats of various sorts, twenty kinds of tarts, fools, trifles, floating islands, whipped sillabubs, etc., Parmesan cheese, punch, wine, porter, beer."

THE HOLY EXPERIMENT

Pennsylvania, which Penn liked to call the "Holy Experiment," attracted many settlers. One of Penn's first acts was to write and publish in English, French, Dutch, and German a pamphlet describing the colony he proposed to build. In the pamphlet he invited honest, hard-working settlers to come, promising them religious toleration, representative government, and cheap land. To every settler who would establish his home and family in the colony, Penn offered 500 acres of free land, with the right to buy additional land at one shilling an acre.

The Welsh Quakers came to Philadelphia and its surrounding area. There were Germans from the Palatinate, and the Scotch-Irish, each settling in a different section of the area.

THE SCOTCH-IRISH

This group came to Pennsylvania early in the eighteenth century and eventually spread throughout the colonies. They were primarily spinners and weavers by trade. They did not have the Quaker calm or German thrift. They took any land they wished and dared anyone to move them. They were independent and belligerent, ready to fight anyone, any place, for any reason.

They did little farming at first in the frontier homes that they established in the Allegheny Mountains.

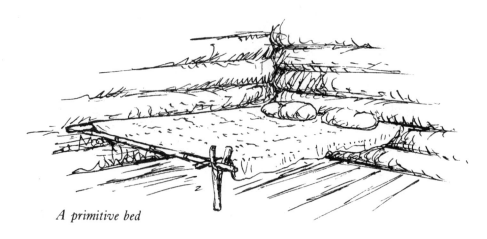

A primitive bed

In the daily life of the Scotch-Irish there were just four things essential—the rifle, the backwoods axe, the fort or blockhouse, and the trail, later to become a road connecting them with their source of supplies and their markets back East and following their spearhead farther and farther on toward the Ohio and the West.

Their homes were grouped around "forts" built where three or four cabins were close together and where a good spring could be enclosed. The forts were nothing more than log fences with one or more blockhouses. Their entire cabin was built of logs, the floor of half-logs with their flat sides upwards. The puncheons also made the tops of the tables and benches. When a cabin was to be built, the neighbors gathered and within three days the house was up and furnished. Before the family moved in, there was a housewarming, which was a dance lasting all night long.

The Scotch-Irish settler lived by hunting, and bought only such things as salt and iron. He scratched out a living by making whiskey, collecting pelts, and making alum from the burning of wood, leaching the ashes, and boiling down the residue.

However, soon every cabin had a truck garden which the wife and children took care of. Later a small field of grain brought real bread to the table. From the first

Clearing the land

settling they had potatoes, pumpkins, beans, and corn, and soon a cow and a few pigs gave them milk and pork. So the table afforded them a diet of "hog and hominy," johnny cake, corn pone, and mush and milk within a short time. Supper usually consisted of mush and milk. When milk was in short supply, mush was eaten with sweetened water, molasses, bear's oil, or the gravy of fried meat. The standard fare for every log-rolling, house-raising, harvest day, or whenever the neighbors got together, was a pot pie!

With so many trees about, the dishes were mostly woodenware. Utensils of gourds and squashes were made. They had neither tea, coffee, nor china at first.

SCRAPPLE

Scrapple was invented by the Mennonites, who were sometimes called the German Quakers. They spread out into the wilderness surrounding Philadelphia, which they soon transformed into farmlands. Scrapple was the wedding of German sausage skills and American Indian corn meal.

THE MORAVIANS

The Moravians also came from Germany and believed in peace not only with others but also among themselves. The Moravian settlements were as truly church settlements as were those of the Puritans in New England.

They settled in the area of Pennsylvania known later as the city of Bethlehem. Their first buildings were the church buildings, with the Bell House, completed in 1745, as the center.

Moravians were music-loving people, and Bethlehem had the first symphony orchestra in America.

At harvest time, the men mowed the oats, while the women pulled the flax.

Education became one of their first interests once they were settled. They were also interested in the care of their sick, and established one of the first hospitals, in 1742.

During the Revolutionary War, practically the entire town became a hospital, since the Continental Army was in the vicinity from December 3, 1776 to March 27, 1777, and then from September 17, 1777 to April 14, 1778.

PENNSYLVANIA DUTCH

In the early days of the eighteenth century, nearly all the first settlers in eastern Pennsylvania came from the Palatinate in Germany. They selected pieces of land, built log houses, and began to clear and cultivate the soil. Though these good people came from Germany, they came to be known as "Dutch." These same people developed a language—a mixture of their mother tongue in the Old World and that spoken in their new homeland, America—which came to be known as Pennsylvania Dutch.

They were the best farmers in the colonies, but, since they had been so poor in Germany, many of them mortgaged their own labor and that of their children to pay for passage across the ocean.

In those early days, the Germans sacrificed not only luxury but comfort in order to gain profit. Their barns were usually larger and finer than their homes. The German houses were generally built of logs, although some were half timber, framed and braced with hewn beams, and the spaces filled with brick. By the middle of the 1700's, their houses were made of thick fieldstone, built into the sides of a hill and over a spring so that the cellar could be used as a milk-cooling room.

Although they were simple people, once they prospered, the interiors of their houses were often quite elaborately finished. The kitchen was the main room of the house, and many fine things were to be found there. Where a stairway led to a second story, the staircase often had such carved bannisters that one might expect to see it in a mansion instead of a farmer's dwelling.

Many of them decorated their houses by painting flowers and decorations on the window shutters. The rose and the tulip were their traditional emblems and were painted on chests, benches, and even on some dishes.

THE KLOSTER OF THE SEVENTH-DAY BAPTISTS

Many sects of Germans came to Pennsylvania, among whom was a group headed by Johann Conrad Beissel. He founded a sort of farm community at Ephrata, Lancaster County. It was a community growing up among "the hands," without a family unit as the nucleus. The people believed in the spiritual superiority of celibacy.

Although they were extremists, they were excellent farmers, and their buildings were extremely well built. They lived very simply and dressed very simply, the men in shirt, trousers, and vest under a long gown to which was attached a pointed cowl or hood. The women wore shirts and narrow skirts with a long gown covering all, to which was attached a rounded cowl or hood.

They supplied most of the paper, and did some of the best printing, in colonial America. They had a bookbindery which was the largest and best in all the colonies.

PENNSYLVANIA DUTCH AND GOOD FOOD

In anything pertaining to food, the Pennsylvania Dutch were inventive. To bring home more game, they designed a longer, more accurate rifle. The first American cookstove was cast at Mary Ann Furnace in 1765. They also made a long-handled waffle iron, imprinting a tulip design, for use on the open hearth. Instead of diamonds, young men gave their sweethearts handsomely carved rolling pins as engagement presents.

Many of their early stoves were decorated with biblical scenes that are today called "The Bible in Iron." And Henry William Stiegel, the glassmaker, was Pennsylvania Dutch. The Conestoga wagon is another of their inventions which was originally used to transport their produce to fairs and farmers' markets.

Christopher Ludwick, a baker, was commissioned to be baker general of the Continental Army, while the famous Philadelphia Pepper Pot is supposed to be another delicacy invented by a German at Valley Forge in answer to General Washington's plea for some good food.

In the early days, the housewives had brought with them the recipes of the traditionally famous German cooks. Life was hard, and at first the land yielded but little return. There were few roads, and towns were far apart. It was not always possible to secure the prescribed ingredients, and it became necessary to develop new recipes to utilize the plainer foods in the creation of tasty dishes. Necessity was again the mother of invention, and these good women became famous for their fine cooking. The Pennsylvania Dutch created the colored Easter egg, shoofly pie, and apple butter.

HAM WITH GREEN STRING BEANS *(Speck und Beans)*

3 pounds smoked ham, water, 1 quart green string beans; 5 medium-sized potatoes; salt and pepper.

Cover the piece of ham with cold water and set over a low flame to cook for three hours. Add water from time to time during the cooking in order to have at least one quart of broth at all times. Wash and clean the string beans, break into small pieces and add to the ham. Continue cooking about 25 minutes. Pare and quarter the potatoes; add to the beans and ham and cook about 25 or 30 minutes, or until beans and potatoes are tender. About 15 minutes before serving, add salt and pepper to taste. Serve hot, providing vinegar for those who like the dish strongly flavored.

MOULDASHA *(Parsley Pie)*

Mash and season with butter and salt half a dozen boiled white potatoes, add a little grated onion and chopped parsley. Sift together in a bowl 1 cup of flour, 1 teaspoon baking powder and a little salt. Add one egg and a small quantity of milk if not enough liquid to mix into a soft dough. Roll out like pie crust, handling as little as possible. Cut into small squares, fill with the potato mixture, turn opposite corners over and pinch together all around like small three-cornered pies. Drop the small triangular pieces into boiling salted water a few minutes, or until they rise to top; then skim out and brown them in a pan containing a tablespoon each of butter and lard. Stale bread crumbs, browned in butter, may be sprinkled over these pies when served. Serve hot.

MORE ABOUT PENNSYLVANIA DUTCH FOOD

The Pennsylvania Dutch believed in "plain and plenty" food, and so they had all sorts of pot-roasted meats and stews as well as plenty of chicken, especially as chicken pot pie.

Many of their dishes are still eaten today, such as sauerbraten, Boova shenkel (beef stew with potato dumplings), noodles, and dumplings, which form a substantial part of many of their dishes.

Dried apples were used for all sorts of pies and other desserts.

The early Pennsylvania Dutch settlers built huge outdoor ovens of stone. The interiors of these ovens were sometimes seven feet wide and could accommodate five or six loaves of bread, seven or eight pies, half a dozen crumb cakes, and several batches of cookies all at one time.

Corn was an important crop, and the housewife dried it for use throughout the winter months. To dry it, the kernels were cut from the ripe ears and dried in a very slow oven, or out of doors in the sun on a cloth-covered screen suspended from wooden posts.

The Germans brought the art of pretzel-making to the New World. It is said that the shape of the twisted pretzel symbolizes the position of the arms crossed in prayer, and that pretzels date back to the time of the Crusades.

Raisin pie was known as "funeral pie," since it was traditionally served along with a nourishing meal to mourners who had come a long distance to attend a funeral.

Christmas dinner always had roast duck or goose as its main dish.

The Pennsylvania Dutch had many superstitions and one is that at a company or holiday meal there must be exactly "seven sweets and seven sours" on the table. The Pennsylvania Dutch housewife did not dream of asking her family, much less guests, to sit down to a table that didn't have at least the "seven sweets and seven sours" on it. Rhubarb jam, rhubarb marmalade, lemon honey, cherry relish, pear marmalade, and quince marmalade were some of the more unusual "sweets," although all sorts of preserves were served. As for the "sours," they included such dishes as green tomato relish, cucumber relish, onion, pepper, pickle relish, and vegetable catsup, as well as all the other relishes.

A FRONTIER WEDDING

In the first years of the settlement of the frontier, a wedding engaged the attention of a whole neighborhood and was anticipated by young and old alike. The wedding was almost the only gathering held in this area that was not accompanied by the labor of reaping, log rolling, building a cabin, or planning some sort of campaign.

The groom and his attendants assembled at the house of his father early in the day, since he had to reach the home of his bride before noon, which was the usual time for celebrating the nuptials.

The men were dressed in mocassins, leather breeches, leggings and linsey hunting shirts, all homemade. The ladies were dressed in linsey petticoats and linsey or linen gowns, coarse shoes, stockings, handkerchiefs, and buckskin gloves.

The party marched off to the bride's house, and when it was about a mile from her home, two young men would single out to run for the whiskey bottle; the worse the path, the more logs, brush, and deep hollows, the better. The start was announced by an Indian yell. The first who reached the door was presented with the prize, which he returned to the company. He then gave the bottle first to the groom and his attendants and then to each pair in the succession to the rear of the line, saving the rest for himself.

The ceremony of the marriage preceded the dinner, which was a substantial backwoods feast of beef, pork, fowls, and sometimes venison and bear meat roasted and boiled, with plenty of potatoes, cabbage, and other vegetables. If there were not enough plates and knives, fingers did very nicely.

After dinner there was dancing which generally lasted till the following morning, with refreshments throughout the night. About nine o'clock a deputation of young ladies stole off the bride and put her to bed; this was followed by a deputation of young men stealing off the groom and placing him snugly by the side of his bride. All the while, the dancing went on. During the night, food and drink were sent up to the bride and groom which they were compelled to eat and drink.

The feasting and dancing often lasted for several days, at the end of which the whole company was so exhausted with lack of sleep that several days of rest were needed to return them to their ordinary daily chores.

FARMER'S HOUSEWIFE

The main entrance to her farmhouse was the kitchen door, since no housewife in her right mind would allow farm mud and grasses to be tracked into her parlor.

The kitchen of the 1700's

The children generally made use of the shed door so that they could leave their dirty shoes there. The kitchen usually was filled with aromas—the pleasant ones of baking bread or gingerbread, bubbling stew, or roasting meat; mundane ones of wax melting for candle-making, apple slices and herbs drying before the fire, coffee beans roasting, or sausage being stuffed; or the unpleasant ones of the dyepot and its indigo mixture, the products of slaughtering, or milk souring for cheese-making.

Cooking was done at the large fireplace, where pots and kettles, toaster, waffle iron, oven peel, tin roaster, and all the other cooking paraphernalia were stored. On the mantel were pressing irons, candle molds, lamps, and other gear. The big table was used for both work and dining, and might have been set with a hand-loomed linen cloth, blue Staffordshire ware, white napery, and bone-handled knives and forks.

The cupboard contained all the necessary kitchen equipment. Beyond it on one side was the buttery, where much food preparation took place. Here the housewife churned her butter, pressed and cared for her cheeses, kneaded her dough, put up her preserves, and filled her pie shells and bean pot.

There was a long ell-room between kitchen and shed where equipment not in daily use was stored. There might be spare pots and kettles to be used for extra mouths to feed, wool and flax waiting to be spun and dyed.

The parlor beyond the kitchen was never used except for weddings and funerals. The room usually had stencilled walls, a rag carpet, and gay curtains. There also was a desk, chest, and sewing table rarely used.

The housewife had her bedroom on the downstairs floor, while the children slept up on the second floor. Under her bedstead was a trundle bed where the current toddler slept while the infant was in a cradle by the side of the bed.

A FARMER'S DAINTY DISH

Peel and slice thin potatoes and onions (five potatoes to one small onion); take half a pound of sweet pork (in thin slices) to a pound of beef, mutton, or veal; cut the meat in small pieces; take some nice bread dough and shorten a little; line the bottom of the stewpan with slices of pork, then a layer of meat, potatoes and onions, dust over a little pepper and cover with a layer of crust; repeat this until the stewpot is full. The size of the pot will depend on the number in the family. Pour in sufficient water to cover and finish with crust. Let it simmer until meat, vegetables, etc., are done, but do not let it boil hard. Serve hot. This we are assured by one who knows is a dish fit to set before a king.

The Successful Housekeeper, 1885

In 1686, James Harrison, a Quaker minister, praised the new land: "The Peach-Trees are much broken down with the weight of Fruit this Year . . . Rasberries, Goosberries, Currans, Quinces, Roses, Walnuts and Figs grow well . . . Our Barn, Porch and Shed, are full of Corn this year."

FARM WIVES—THEIR DAY

Farm wives before 1820 rose long before dawn to begin their day's chores. They were married at twenty or earlier and produced large families. They had no leisure and often died young.

At this time, the housewife had no cookstove, so in the morning she had to revive the fire on the kitchen hearth and prepare a breakfast of cornmeal mush, bread or toast, and a hot drink. Occasionally there was a bit of bacon or sausage for the adults, leftover potatoes fried up, or doughnuts. In some families there was pie.

After breakfast she cleared up and got her dinner under way. If she had spare time, she might weave linen for sheets or some cloth for clothing.

The noon meal was a boiled dinner—salted beef or pork boiled with potatoes, carrots, turnips, onions, and whatever else she chose to put into the pot. There was cider for drinking, and gingerbread, apple pie, or a baked Indian pudding for dessert.

She then cleaned up again and either worked in her garden in the summer or at her loom or wheel or ironing in the winter. Her evening meal served at five or six o'clock was simpler. The evening was spent in supervising the children and then back again to the things that had to be done for the house and family.

When finally in bed after her prayers, it seemed as if she had just fallen asleep when the daily round began again.

APPLE BUTTER

Apple butter has always been associated with the Pennsylvania Dutch, and it has a special meaning for one particular group, the Schwenkfelders. Every September this group holds a Thanksgiving service. In July 1734, they left Germany for America, and they finally anchored on September 21, 1734, near New Castle. There they obtained their first fresh water in weeks out of the river, while the captain rowed over and brought back a supply of apples from the shore. This was their first meal of fresh food, along with some rolls that the Schwenkfelders had, and their traditional Thanksgiving, water, bread, butter, and apple butter, commemorates that fact each year.

Making apple butter

THE HOUSEWIFE'S WORK WEEK

MONDAY: Monday was washday. Everyone would rise early and, before the sun was up, carry the water in and build up a fire. The water would be put into the boiler to boil while breakfast was being prepared. After that the women of the family would get to the clothes and would continue for the next five or six hours. Usually by noontime the clothes were being dried either on lines or over the bushes, and our housewife would now attend to the noon meal and then get back to the clothes, folding each item and putting it away either to iron or in storage.

TUESDAY: Tuesday was ironing day, and with the type of equipment at hand, ironing for the average family was an all-day, morning-to-night affair. The oldest girls in the family helped their mother, each one working at her own ironing board.

WEDNESDAY: Wednesday was usually known as mending or sewing day. If there were new clothes to cut out and put together by basting or on the small hand-operated sewing machine, this would be one of the days to do it. Also, all the mending was supposed to be done on this day.

Women made their own clothing and the clothing for the family unless they were more affluent and could afford the services of a seamstress, one who either stayed at the house for a while or one to whom the housewife went with her material and ideas. Men's clothing was usually handled by a local or itinerant tailor.

Women and girls also made their own stockings or later on bought cotton stocking by the yard and cut it off in sections and sewed a toe on it.

The small pieces of cloth left over from sewing were used to make quilts.

THURSDAY: Thursday was odd-job day. This was the day that our housewife might do her gardening in the summer or sharpen knives or do quilting. Whatever task that she could not categorize into another day was done on Thursday, so that often this day was one in which lots of little jobs were done. It could be a most tiring day.

FRIDAY: Friday was cleaning day for the entire house. Although wash was done on Monday, linen was changed on Friday since the beds were supposed to be thoroughly cleaned and brushed on that day.

Friday was the day that the broom and dustpan were in constant use. Rugs were not beaten unless it was spring and spring-cleaning was under way. Spring-cleaning meant everything, including curtains and rugs and other dust-catchers which were divested of their accumulated dust.

SATURDAY: Saturday was baking and bath day. The children were home from school and helped with the baking and watched the process so that nothing would burn. Baking was often done for the following week and consisted of bread, cakes, pies, cookies, beans, and meats. Cooking and baking was done for Sunday since no one worked on Sunday. It was a day of rest.

On Saturday afternoon and evening there would be bath time. The children took their baths as soon as baking was over, and after an early supper, they went to bed. The adults took their baths after supper and then went to bed.

SUNDAY: Sunday was church day. Everyone went to church. It was a religious obligation and at the same time it was a day to catch up on all local news and gossip. For the housewife it was a day of pleasure and rest from her hard work. One week was gone and the other was first thing tomorrow. Sunday was her day of peace and quiet.

FRESH AIR AND HEALTH

Very many persons, especially ladies, have a horror, in winter, of going out-of-doors for fear of taking cold. If it is a little damp, or a little windy, or a little cold, they wait, and wait; meanwhile, weeks and even months pass away, and they never, during the whole time, breathe a single breath of pure air. The result is they become so enfeebled that their constitutions have no power of resistance; the least thing in the world gives them a cold, even going from one room to another; and before they know it, they have a cold all the time, and this is nothing more or less than incipient consumption. Whereas, if an opposite practice had been followed of going out for an hour or two every day, regardless of the weather, except actually falling rain, a very different result would have taken place.

Peterson's Magazine, 1875

KIND OF WIFE

Hannah More says, that when a man of sense comes to marry, it is a companion whom he wants, and not an artist. It is not merely a creature who can paint, play, dress and dance; it is a being who can comfort and console him.

The Old Farmer's Almanac, 1858, Robert B. Thomas

TO FRESHEN BAKED GOODS

Doughnuts and cookies, as well as crackers, can be freshened by heating them thoroughly in a moderate oven, after which they should be cooled in a dry place before serving.

Household, 1869

NO MARRIAGE LICENSES

"As no Licenses for Marriage could be obtained since the first of November for Want of Stamped paper, we can assure the Publick several Genteel Couples were publish'd in the different Churches of this City last Week; and we hear that the young Ladies of this place are determined to Join Hands with none but such as will to the utmost endeavour to abolish the Custom of marrying with License which Amounts to many Hundred per annum which might be saved."

New York Gazette and Postbody, December 6, 1709

A FARMER'S BREAKFAST

For those of our readers who live in the city and wondered about the breakfast eaten by a farmer, here is a menu sent to us by one of our readers along with various recipes for the breakfast. No doubt you will enjoy it.

Buckwheat cakes	Coffee	Fried Mush
Potatoes	Ham and Eggs	Apple Sauce
Graham Gems	Maple Syrup	Doughnuts

Household, 1884

A HOUSEHOLD ABC

As soon as you are up, shake blankets and sheet;
Better be without shoes than sit with wet feet;
Children, if healthy, are active, not still;
Damp sheets and damp clothes will both make you ill;
Eat slowly, and always chew your food well;
Freshen the air in the house where you dwell;
Garments must never be made to be tight;
Homes will be healthy if airy and light;
If you wish to be well, as you do, I've no doubt,
Just open the windows before you go out;
Keep your rooms always neat, and tidy, and clean;
Let dust on the furniture never be seen;
Much illness is caused by the want of pure air,
Now to open your windows be ever your care;
Old rags and old rubbish should never be kept
People should see that their floors are well swept;
Quick movements in children are healthy and right;
Remember the young cannot thrive without light;
See that the cistern is clean to the brim;
Take care that your dress is all tidy and trim;
Use your nose to find out if there be a bad drain,
Very sad are the fevers that come in its train;
Walk as much as you can without feeling fatigue—
Xerxes could walk full many a league;
Your health is your wealth, which your wisdom must keep;
Zeal will help a good cause, and the good you will reap.

Peterson's Magazine, June 1888

A frontier kitchen

THE OLD EAGLE COFFEE HOUSE AT CONCORD, N.H.

Author's note: This was a famous country inn, noted for its food in the mid-1800's.

In this kitchen the mistress of the house reigned supreme. Working *with* her, not *under* her (for we write of the days when *help* was hired, not *servants*), were a meat cook, one who attended to the vegetables, a "kitchen colonel," kitchen boy, and a little girl who made herself generally useful. There were others, but these are the ones we know most about. The mistress herself made all the pies, cake, and most of the puddings, in a room adjoining the kitchen, and on great occasions she would be up at four in the morning to make at least a hundred pies. The "kitchen colonel's" duties must have been arduous with all the wood to bring for the fireplace and oven, and the latter to clean out every time it was heated. The kitchen boy was expected to scour the knives, blacken the boots of the guests, and to trim and fill the whale oil lamps used in lighting all the rooms.

What were some of the dishes which made our old tavern famous? Meats roasted in tin kitchens before the fireplace—in the common size tin kitchens for ordinary occasions, but when preparations were made for a great feast in "double-decked" ones, as they were called. Meats cooked in this way were never surpassed, each kind retaining its own flavor. Vegetables of all kinds boiled over the fireplace in kettles suspended from the crane; pies (famous ones too); the rich old-fashioned cakes; little cheese cakes; bread and Indian puddings; and those who washed the dishes remember well the great number of custard cups to be washed when "June Court" was in session; so cup custards must have been a favorite dainty with those who came to make the laws.

Potatoes were at first served plain, but the mistress, going away for a visit, came back with a new and wonderful rule for preparing them, and afterwards mashed potatoes were also served. Another time it was a new recipe for puddings, "packed puddings" she called them, thick slices of bread, buttered, packed into the deep brown earthen pudding pots with alternate layers of apples, spices, and sugar, covered and baked in the brick oven until they were red and delicious. One of the duties of the useful little girl was to beat the butter and sugar together in a broad earthen milk pan, for the sauce to serve with these puddings; then to mould it in a little old china cup kept for that purpose, and after turning the balls out on small saucers, to mark them with a knife to somewhat resemble a pineapple, and to finish by grating nutmeg over them. Another of her duties was to line all the pans used in baking sponge cake with a thick paste of ryemeal and water. When the cake was baked it came out of the paste without a crust, soft and delicious. The pound cake was so light that those who ate it could not believe it was pound cake, so tradition says. All the eggs were beaten in a tall earthen jar with a beater which resembled a bunch of wires fastened to a handle.

For Saturday dinner boiled salt codfish was served, as a special dish. It made its reappearance Sunday morning in fish hash, beefsteak being also served on that morning. For dinner on Sunday there would be brown bread, beans, and Indian puddings. These would be prepared the day before and put into the brick oven by four o'clock on Sunday morning. Poor kitchen colonel! No Sunday morning nap for him. Sunday nights for supper hot biscuits and "flapjacks" were the chief substantials. The "flapjacks" were made as large as a plate, buttered and sugared while warm, piled on top of one another, and served in wedge-shaped pieces, cut from the pile.

Georgia L. Green, in Concord Monitor.
American Kitchen, September 19, 1882

MAPLE BISCUIT

2 cups flour; ½ teaspoon salt; 4 teaspoons Rumford Baking Powder; 2 tablespoons shortening; about ¾ cup milk or milk and water, mixed; softened shortening; crushed maple sugar.

Sift together the flour, salt and baking powder; cut or rub in the shortening until the fat is thoroughly blended with the flour, then mix to a very soft dough with the liquid, having this as cold as possible. After mixing, divide into two portions and roll out each not over a half an inch thick, keeping the shape of the dough as square as possible. Brush over one portion with softened shortening, spread thickly with crushed maple sugar, cover with the second portion of dough and cut into squares that they may be no left-over fragments for re-rolling. Bake in a quick oven [450° F] twelve to fifteen minutes.

The Rumford Cook Book, Fannie Merrit Farmer

SAUERKRAUT

Sauerkraut is a Pennsylvania Dutch staple. It is so popular that it is said that when General Lee captured Chambersburg on his way to Gettysburg, one of the first things he demanded for his army was twenty-five barrels of sauerkraut.

HOMEMADE RECEIPT BOOK

Have at hand a blank book in which to paste or copy valuable recipes. Cover this with white oilcloth neatly pasted on. Have a special part of this book or a separate book for menus. This will help to solve the problem of what to have for dinner.

Household Discoveries, 1905

A REAL OVEN: *A Letter from Ruth*

Dear Hannah:

Father brought in the vessel as many bricks as would serve to make an oven by the side of our fireplace, and thus it was that we were the first family here who could bake bread or roast meats as do people in England.

This oven is built on one side of the fireplace, with a hole near the top for the smoke to go through. It has a door of real iron, with an ash pit below so that we may save the ashes for soap-making without storing them in another place.

At first the oven was kept busily at work for the benefit of our neighbors, being heated each day, but for our own needs it is used once a week. Inside a great fire of dried wood is kindled and kept burning from morning until noon, when it has thoroughly heated the bricks. Then the coals and ashes are swept out, the chimney draught is closed, and the oven filled with whatsoever we have to cook. A portion of our bread is baked in the two pans which mother owns, but the rest of it we lay on green leaves, and it is cooked quite as well, although one is forced to scrape a few cinders from the bottom of the loaf.

Ruth

THE ARRIVAL OF THE GERMANS

When the ships have landed at Philadelphia after their long voyage, no one is permitted to leave them except those who pay for their passage or can give good security; the others, who cannot pay, must remain on board the ships till they are purchased, and are released from the ships by their purchasers. The sick always fare the worst, for the healthy are naturally preferred and purchased first; and so the sick and wretched must often remain on board in front of the city for 2 or 3 weeks, and frequently die, whereas many a one, if he could pay his debt and were permitted to leave the ship immediately, might recover and remain alive.

Journey to Pennsylvania, 1750

GODEY'S LADY'S BOOK

It has been said that the era of the American magazine began with *Godey's Lady's Book,* which was founded in 1830 and ran almost to the end of the nineteenth century.

Godey's, like the happy little man, Louis A. Godey, who owned it and like Mrs. Sarah Josepha Hale, the feminist from Boston, who edited it from 1837 to 1877, was marvelous. It may not have been as academic a magazine as *North American Review* or as brilliant as the magazine *Graham's,* or as readable as the *Knickerbocker Magazine,* but the popular *Godey's Lady's Book* under the militant Sarah Josepha Hale had more real influence on American life than any other magazine of the same period.

Godey's was directed entirely to the woman and as a result it affected the manners, morals, tastes, fashions, homes, and diets of generations of Americans. It did much to form the American woman's idea of what she was like, how she should act, and how she should insist that she be treated. It had no interest in political or intellectual subjects.

It is said that Sarah Josepha Hale wrote the American classic:

> Mary had a little lamb;
> Its fleece was white as snow;
> And everywhere that Mary went
> The lamb was sure to go.

This great woman's magazine of the mid-century captured its audience through its superbly detailed engravings of long-gowned and gusseted ladies, whose carefully tinted regalia made them suitable for framing as well as imitation. Along with the patterns for these dresses went a regular ration of sentimental fiction in which the main concern was whether the heroine was marrying beneath or above her station. Much of the verse and more of the fiction reads like drivel today, but they must have been adored in their day, for *Godey's* claimed a circulation of 25,000 in 1839—which might well mean 100,000 readers since the magazine was passed around to friends, neighbors and relatives—and the magazine reached a circulation of 100,000 before the Civil War.

Besides fashions, fictions, and feminine verse, *Godey's* published recipes, embroidery patterns and instructions, beauty and health hints, and elaborate illustrations called "embellishments."

Every issue also contained complete plans and illustrations for a model cottage, together with the prices of materials needed in its construction.

Mrs. Hale was a determined individual and campaigned for the recognition of women writers. Before that time many women writers used masculine pseudonyms or initials. She had them boldly sign their names. She introduced Harriet Beecher Stowe when still an unknown writer. Mrs. Hale believed in educational opportunities and physical exercises for women and argued for national recognition of Thanksgiving Day until President Abraham Lincoln proclaimed it on October 20, 1863.

Sarah Josepha Hale gave up the editorship of *Godey's* two years before her death, and Louis A. Godey died in 1878, but *Godey's Lady's Book* continued until 1898, when it finally vanished.

PETERSON'S MAGAZINE

The other popular woman's magazine of the 1800's was *Peterson's Magazine*, founded in January 1842 as *Ladies National Magazine*. It was founded by Charles J. Peterson and George R. Graham of *Graham's Magazine* to cut into the rising circulation of *Godey's Lady's Book*.

It had the same features as *Godey's* but was a slimmer edition since it was one dollar cheaper per year. It, too, had the colored fashion plates and mezzotints. By the Civil War, it had surpassed *Godey's Lady's Book* in circulation.

By 1870, the magazine had serials, monthly departments of fancywork, recipes, etc., including some music. The stories were very much alike: virtue in poverty, a broken heart, the dangers of frivolity.

However, there was some humor injected into the magazine with Marietta Holley's stories of "Josiah Allen's Wife."

Charles Peterson died in 1887 and his widow took over, but the magazine gradually went downhill and by 1895 it was out of existence. Yet this magazine together with *Godey's Lady's Book* influenced the women of America and indirectly the entire country in the mid-1800's.

TO PRESERVE EGGS

It is only necessary to close the pores of the shell. This may be done by varnishing, or by dipping in melted suet, and then packing them in salt with the small end downward.

Mrs. Rorer's Philadelphia Cook Book, 1886

FARMING VILLAGES, 1750

Not far from the coast, and particularly in New England, New Jersey, and Pennsylvania, there were many small farming villages of fifty or a hundred families, with a church or meetinghouse, a school, and several shops. The villagers might go to a cobbler to have their shoes made, to a blacksmith to have their wagons fixed, to a doctor for medical attention, or to a general store to buy sugar, spices, or English fabrics for dresses. Traveling barbers also came to the villages to cut hair and pull teeth. Everything else was performed by the householder.

To pay for these services, the farmers of the village and the surrounding territory hauled their surplus tobacco, grain, cattle, and hogs to the nearest seaboard or river-port town. There they sold their products.

Before they returned home, the farmers often stopped to make purchases in the shops displaying goods from England. Thus the settlers who lived in areas where it was possible to market their surplus produce were able to live better than their more isolated fellows.

Washing clothes—1880's

THE WELL-TO-DO FAMILY

As families began to prosper, the houses were built with better accommodations. In the course of time there was a pantry, a buttery, a milk room, a shed, a shed chamber, and an attic. The first appearance of these homes came at the end of the eighteenth century, but it was not for another hundred years that it was a general thing to see.

The pantry was added to the one-room house as the first necessity, and every kitchen had its pantry, whether it was large or small.

The buttery served as an overflow of the pantry. Originally this room was used as a storeroom for provisions but eventually it held everything not found in the pantry, such as sap pail, butter boxes, butter tubs, the molasses keg, salt barrels, and the various cereals.

The third room added was the milk room where were found the butter churn, the cheese press, the racks for the buckets, and the cheese closet.

PERSPIRATION

The unpleasant odor produced by perspiration may be removed by putting a spoonful of spirits of ammonia in a basin of water and bathing in this. This is especially good for bathing the feet.

Sense in the Kitchen, 1881

GRANITEWARE

Graniteware was found in almost every American kitchen at the turn of the century. Essentially these are metal pieces with a coating of glass or enamel that has been fused onto the metal surface.

The term "graniteware" is in a sense wrong because the ware has no connection with the material granite except, in some cases, for a similarity in appearance. Although the enameled surface is very hard, it is also, unfortunately, brittle, so that it is easily chipped.

This nineteenth-century innovation was popularized by the Philadelphia Centennial Exposition of 1876. Here, many people were shown the sanitary advantages of glass combined with the strength of metal; compared to the older cast iron, copper, brass, and crockery utensils, it was more healthful and easier to handle and to care for. If it had lacked these qualities, its beauty alone would probably have made it popular.

In the 1890's the work of Charles Martin Hall with aluminum replaced graniteware with aluminum ware.

FOOD FOR THOUGHT

From the first cookbook published in 1742 at Williamsburg, Virginia, up to the newest published in our day, there have been so many that an entire book would be needed just to list them all.

GADGETS

The nineteenth-century inventor concentrated his efforts on the various household problems. As a result, he came up with gadgetry galore for food processing,

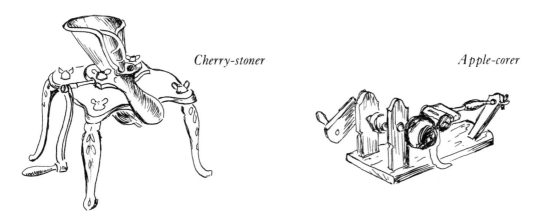

Cherry-stoner   *Apple-corer*

internal communications, baby care, household chores, and pest control. However, all or most of the gadgets were "woman-powered," and so few of them are recognizable to us today.

There were all manner of parers, graters, beaters, home canners, etc. No matter what job was to be done in the home, there was a gadget to make it "easier." But the poor housewife had to use all her energy in working these "conveniences," so as soon as electric power came into existence, many of the gadgets just disappeared from the shelves of the general or hardware store and became items for the collector of today to ferret out.

SPICED SALT FOR SOUPS AND STUFFINGS

> 4 ounces of salt
> 2 ounces of celery salt
> 1 ounce each of white pepper and ground thyme
> 1 ounce each of marjoram and summer savory
> ½ ounce of sage
> 1 saltspoonful of cayenne pepper
> ½ teaspoonful each of cloves, allspice, and mace.
> Mix, sift, and keep closely covered.

New Household Receipt Book, Sarah Josepha Hale, 1853

NEW KINDS OF FOOD: *A Letter from Ruth*

Dear Hannah:
Often my mother prepared nassaump, which is nothing but corn beaten into small pieces and boiled until soft, after which it is eaten hot, or cold, with milk or butter.

I wrote to you about nookick and save for the flavor lent to it by the roasting, I can see no difference between nookick and the meal made from the ground corn.

Mother makes a mixture of oatmeal, milk, sugar, and spice, which is much to my taste, although father declares it is not unlike oatmeal porridge such as is eaten in some parts of England; but it hardly seems to me possible, because of one's not putting sugar and spice into porridge.

We often have bread made of pumpkins boiled soft, and mixed with the meal from Indian corn, and this father much prefers to the bread of rye with the meal of corn, but the manner of cooking pumpkins most to my liking is to cut them into small pieces, when they are ripe, and stew during one whole day upon a gentle fire, adding fresh bits of pumpkin as the mass softens. If this be steamed enough, it will look much like baked apples, and, dressed with a little vinegar and ginger, is to me a most tempting rarity. But we do not often have it upon the table because of so much labor being needed to prepare it.

Yokhegg is a pudding of which I am exceedingly fond, and yet it is made of meal from the same Indian corn that supplies the people hereabout with so much of their food. It is boiled in milk and chocolate, sweetened to suit one's taste after being put on the table, and while to English people, who are not accustomed to all the uses which we make of this wheat, it may not sound especially inviting, it most truly is a toothsome dainty.

The cost of setting one's table here is not great as compared with that in England, for we may get a quart of milk by paying a penny, or a dozen fat pigeons, in the season, for three pence, while father has more than once bought wild turkeys, to the weight of thirty pounds, for two shillings, and wild geese are worth but eight pence.

Ruth

APPLE SAUCE OMELET (BAKED)

Beat the yolks of seven eggs light, sift into them five spoonfuls of powdered sugar and a cupful and a half of sweetened apple sauce. Beat long and hard, stir in the stiffened whites, beat for a minute longer and turn into a greased pudding dish. Bake, serve at once with whipped cream. It is also good served with a hot sauce made by the following recipe.

Into a pint of boiling water stir a half-cupful of sugar, and when this dissolves add a teaspoonful of butter, the juice and the grated rind of a lemon and the stiffened white of an egg. Beat for a minute over the fire, but do not let the sauce boil.

Marion Harland's Complete Cook Book, 1903

Churning butter—1890's

BISCUITS

The Marquis de Chastellux, traveling through North America in the early 1780's, wrote of a meal he had at the Bullion Tavern in Basking Ridge, New Jersey: "Our supper was very good; only bread was lacking; but inquiring of us what sort we wanted, in an hour's time they served us what we had asked for. This speed will appear less extraordinary, if one knows that in America little cakes, which are easily kneaded and baked in half an hour, often take the place of bread. Possibly one might tire of them, but I always found them to my taste whenever I met with them."

CRACKNELS

Two cups of rich milk, four tablespoonfuls of butter and a gill of yeast, a teaspoonful of salt; mix warm, add flour enough to make a light dough. When dough is ready, roll thin and cut in long pieces three inches wide, prick well with a fork and bake in a slow oven. They are to be mixed rather hard and rolled very thin, like soda crackers.

The White House Cook Book, 1887

THE SCHOOLMASTER 'BOARDING ROUND'

Extract from the Journal of a Vermont Schoolmaster.

Monday.—Went to board at Mr. B—'s, had a baked goose for dinner; supposed from its size, the thickness of its skin, and other venerable appearances, to have one of the first settlers of Vermont—made a slight impression on the patriarch's breast. *Supper*—cold goose and potatoes; family consisting of man, good wife, daughter Peggy, four boys, Pompey the dog, and a brace of cats, fire built in the square room about 9 o'clock, and a pile of wood laid by the fire place; saw Peggy scratch her fingers, and couldn't take the hint—felt squeamish about the stomach, and talked about going to bed; Peggy looked sullen, and put out the fire in the square room; went to bed, and dreamed of having eaten a quantity of stone wall.

Tuesday.—Cold gander for breakfast, swamp tea and some nutcakes; the latter some consolation. *Dinner*—The legs, &c. of the gander done up warm, one nearly dispatched. *Supper*—The other leg, &c. cold; went to bed as Peggy was carrying the fire to the square room, dreamed I was a mad turtle, and got on my back and could not get over again.

Wednesday—Cold gander for breakfast; complained of sickness, and could eat nothing. *Dinner*—Wings, &c. of the gander warmed up; did my best to destroy them for fear they should be left for supper, did not succeed; dreaded supper all the afternoon. *Supper*—Hot Indian Johnny cakes, and no goose; felt greatly relieved, thought I had got clear of the gander, and went to bed for a good night's rest; disappointed; very cold night, and couldn't keep warm in bed; got up, and stopped the broken windows with my coat and vest; no use; froze the tip of my nose a little before morning.

Thursday—Breakfast; cold gander again! felt very much discouraged to see the gander not half gone; went a visiting for dinner and supper; slept abroad and had pleasant dreams.

Friday—Breakfast abroad. Dinner at Mr. B—'s; cold gander and hot potatoes; last very good; eat three, and went to school quite contented. *Supper*—Cold gander, and no potatoes; bread heavy and dry; had the head ache and couldn't eat; Peggy much concerned; had a fire built in the square room and thought she and I had better sit there out of the noise; went to bed early; Peggy thought too much sleep bad for the head ache.

Saturday—Breakfast, cold gander, and hot Indian Johnny-cake; did very well; glad to come off so. *Dinner*—Cold gander again; didn't keep school this afternoon; weighed, and found I had lost six pounds the past week; grew alarmed; had a talk with Mr. B. who concluded I had boarded out his share; made no objection—bid the family and gander 'good bye,' and went to Mr. C's.

Farmer's Almanac, 1845

Ordering from the grocer

FOOD, 1860–1900

Although the city man was beginning to acquire a taste for new foods, outside of the city the frying pan was still the most used kitchen pan. Isolated in winter, the farmer tried to make up in warmth on the inside what he lacked on the outside by stuffing himself with poultry and game. Then in the spring he trekked off to the village druggist for the spring dose of sulphur 'n' molasses.

After 1870, with the refrigerator cars now in operation, food was brought from other places, not all locally. From factories came canned tomatoes and milk, canned corn and beef, canned peas and beans, canned tuna and sardines. Forerunners of a long line of packaged cereals, Quaker Oats and Wheatena took the place of the traditional cornmeal mush at breakfast.

Meanwhile there was a surge of immigration from the European countries and each of the immigrants brought their native dishes. While German sauerkraut and the white potato had been familiar for many years, the Italians contributed spaghetti, the Hungarians, goulash.

Appliances—the steam cooker, the double boiler, the Dover egg beater, the gas toaster, the asbestos stove mat, the cake tin with removable bottom—invaded the kitchen in such bewildering variety that the housekeeper had to learn cooking all over again. Schools were organized throughout the country for just this purpose. Another revolution occurred in the nineties with the introduction of light, non-poisonous, heat-conductible, and easily handled aluminum ware.

HOUSEHOLD CONVENIENCE: *A Letter from Ruth*

Dear Hannah:

Do you know what a Betty lamp is? We have two in our house, which were brought over by Captain Pierce as a gift for my mother.

You, who have more or less trouble with your rushlights, cannot fancy how luxurious it is to have one of these Betty lamps, which cost in care no more than is required to fill them with grease or oil.

Fearing lest you may not know what these lamps are, which Sarah's mother says should be called brown-Bettys, I will do my best to set down here such a description as shall bring them before you.

The two which we have are made of brass; but we were told that they are also to be found in pewter or in iron.

These are round, and very much the shape of half an apple, save that they have a nose an inch or two long, which sticks out from one side. The body of the bowl is filled with tallow or grease, and the wick, or a piece of twisted cloth, is threaded into the nose, with one end hanging out to be lighted.

Ours hang by chains from the ceiling, and the light which they give is certainly equal to, if not stronger than, that of a wax candle; but they are not so clean, because if the wick be ever so little too long, the lamps send forth a great smoke.

Father says he has seen a Phoebe lamp, which is much like our Betty lamps, save that it has a small cup underneath the nose to catch the dripping grease, and that I think would be a great improvement, if indeed it is possible to improve upon so useful an article of household furniture as this.

Speaking of our Betty lamps reminds me that Sarah's mother had sent over to her a set of cob irons, which are something after the fashion of andirons, or fire dogs, save that they are also intended to hold the spit and the dripping pan. She has also a pair of "creepers," which are small andirons, and which she sometimes uses with the cob irons.

The andirons which we brought from England are much too fine to be used in this fireplace, which is filled with pothooks, trammels, hakes, and other cooking utensils.

They were a wedding present to my mother, and are in what we call "sets of three," meaning that on each side of the fireplace are three andirons; one to hold the heavy logs that are at the bottom of the fire, another raised still higher to bear the weight of the smaller sticks, and a third for much the same purpose as the second; or, perhaps, to make up more of an ornamentation, for they are of iron and brass, and are exceedingly beautiful to look upon.

Ruth

FOOD FOR THE VEGETARIAN

The subject of vegetarianism is coming more and more to the front, and is no longer treated with ridicule by thoughtful people. Fifty years ago the vegetarian required courage to face the attitude of contemptuous incredulity attached to his peculiar mode of living, but we of to-day have grown broader in our opinions and less ready to condemn our neighbors because they differ in theories or methods of living from ourselves . . .

To be a vegetarian means the abjuring of all flesh that has given up its life for food. The use of eggs and milk is allowed, and inconsistent as it seems, fish is sometimes eaten . . . Milk and eggs are called animal products. Their use does not require the taking of life. Strictly speaking they are not vegetable foods and a considerable number of vegetarians exclude them. On the other hand a few include oysters and some, fish with milk and eggs . . .

The vegetarian needs to know how to combine food so that the body will be nourished without the use of meat. Fruit and nuts should largely enter into a menu that excludes flesh . . . Peas, beans and lentils are also especially nourishing. It is said that the Pyramids of Egypt were built by men who could have had little else to sustain them than lentils.

The Delineator, June 1883

MAGAZINES

In the twenty years following the Civil War, 9,000 different magazines were printed; yet in no single year were there more than 3,300 in existence. However, in 1900 there were about 5,500 magazines, many of which were magazines slanted to the woman. In fact, about half a dozen periodicals had passed the 500,000 circulation mark by 1900 and of these *Comfort, Ladies' Home Journal,* and *Hearthstone* were the leaders.

JUICE PIE

Two cups of fruit juice, one cup of sugar, let come to a boil, stir in two tablespoons of cornstarch dissolved in a little juice, boil from three to five minutes, set off the fire, add a lump of butter the size of an egg, one half teaspoon of Buckeye cinnamon, one half teaspoon of vanilla, yolks of two eggs. Bake with one crust, using the two whipped whites for frosting.

Cherry City Cook Book, 1898

HUNGER IS THE BEST SAUCE

As a rule a person who has a good appetite has good health. But how many there are who enjoy nothing they eat, and sit down to meals only as an unpleasant duty. Nature's antidotes for this condition are so happily combined in Hood's Sarsaparilla that it soon restores good digestion, creates an appetite, and renovates and vitalizes the blood so that the beneficial effect of good food is imparted to the whole body. Truly hunger is the best sauce, and Hood's Sarsaparilla induces hunger.

Good Bread, published by C. I. Hood & Co
Proprietors of Hood's Sarsaparilla

BREAKFAST

Breakfast may be made the pleasantest meal of the day. In some families it is so; it ought to be in all. The table should be made attractive in appearance; luncheons and dinners should not alone absorb all attention and ornamentation . . .

As to what should be eaten, that must be left to the tastes of each family, modified, of course, by the season. But as a rule, there should be fruit, in some shape, at least. An old proverb says that fruit in the morning is golden, but in the evening is lead. A dish of it ought always to be on the table in the morning, so that we may at any rate have the chance of indulging in the gold. In summer, fresh fruit is attainable by everyone; in the winter stewed fruit should replace the fresh . . . Some people indulge in different sorts of breakfast cakes and hot breads, although they are generally unhealthy and indigestible. Why not be content with good crisp toast? or, if dry toast be objected to, do not make it dry. New rolls, if quite cold, are not so unwholesome as hot bread and cakes. Bread a day old, or brown bread, are far better than the smoking rolls, etc., one so often sees. We often hear people wondering why they have dyspepsia, after they have eaten enough hot rolls, at breakfast, to kill anything, but an ostrich. Of course, if you take a good deal of exercise, you may eat even hot cakes with impunity. But sedentary people cannot indulge in these dishes without dyspepsia.

Peterson's Magazine, January 1865

EVERYONE HAS ARRIVED

For a family gathering, the housewife would usually prepare a week or two in advance. Fruitcakes and tins of puddings were prepared, pies of every kind baked. The turkeys were taken from the fattening pen, butchered, stuffed, and roasted, and whole hams were studded with cloves, maple sugar-glazed, and baked. When the family got together for Thanksgiving or Christmas, it was not just for the day. Travel was hard, and once one arrived at his destination he made a long visit.

The housewife also had to prepare for a crowd on threshing day, when all the neighbors came to help in the field and the women helped in the kitchen. Every farmer cooperated with his neighbor. There was a holiday atmosphere and a square dance and refreshments served at the day's end.

Barn raisings, house raisings—practically any type of help was cooperative, and mountains of food were prepared with the workers and the guests. Neighbors were neighbors and always ready and willing to cooperate with one another. "Love thy neighbor" was in effect.

GRINDING CORN: *A Letter from Ruth*

Dear Hannah:

When I heard Squanto telling father that corn must be ground, I said to myself that we were not like to know how it might taste, for there is not a single mill in this land; but Squanto first cut a large tree down, leaving the stump a full yard in weight. Then by building a fire in the stump, scraping away with a sharp rock the wood as fast as it was charred, he made a hollow like unto a hole, and so deep that one might put in half a bushel of this turkie wheat.

From another portion of the tree, he shaped a block of wood to fit exactly the hole in the stump, and this he fastened to the top of a young slender tree, when even we children knew that he had made a mortar and pestle, although an exceedingly rude one.

We had only to pull down the heavy block with all our strength upon the corn, thus bruising and crushing it, when the natural spring of the young tree would pull it up again. In this way did we grind our Guinny wheat until it was powdered so fine that it might be cooked in a few moments.

Ruth

CORN ON THE COB

When Fredrika Breme visited America in 1850, she was amazed when she saw: "Some people take the whole stem and gnaw out with their teeth: two gentlemen do so who sit opposite myself at the table, and whom we call 'the sharks,' because of their remarkable ability in gobbling up large and often double portions of everything which comes to table, and it really troubles me to see how their wide mouths ravenously grind up the beautiful, white, pearly maize ears."

TO DRY PEACHES

Take the fairest and ripest peaches, pare them into fair water; take their weight in double refined sugar. Of one half make a very thin syrup; then put in your peaches, boiling them till they look clear, then split and stone them.

Boil them till they are very tender, lay them a-draining, take the other half of the sugar and boil it almost to a candy. Then put in your peaches and let them lie all night. Then lay them on a glass, and set them in a stove till they are dry. If they are sugar'd too much wipe them with a wet cloth a little; let the first syrup be very thin, a quart of water to a pound of sugar.

The Frugal Housewife, 1772

HERB DYES OF THE 1700'S

The housewife did her own dyeing of cloth and therefore used whatever she had at hand.

Blue, in all shades, was the favorite color, and was dyed with indigo. So great was the demand for this dyestuff that indigo-peddlers traveled over the countryside selling it.

Madder, cochineal, and dogwood dyed beautiful reds. The bark of red oak or hickory made very pretty shades of brown and yellow. Various flowers growing on the farm could be used for dyes. The flower of the goldenrod, when pressed of its juice, mixed with indigo, and added to alum, made a beautiful green. The juice of the pokeberry boiled with alum made crimson dye, and a violet juice from the petals of the iris, or "flower-de-luce," that blossomed in June meadows, gave a delicate light purple tinge to white wool.

The bark of the sassafras was used for dyeing yellow or orange color, and the flowers and leaves of the balsam, also. Fustic and copperas gave yellow dyes. A good black was obtained by boiling woolen cloth with a quantity of the leaves of the common field sorrel, then boiling again with logwood and copperas.

Elderberry was also used for blue, while parsley made a lovely shade of green, and hop-stalks dyed the wool brown.

TIN UTENSILS

When tin found its way into the homes, there was another array of cooking utensils. There was a tin bird roaster and a tin apple roaster. The bird roaster was an upright support holding six hooks, onto which bobwhites were hung by their breasts. The bottom part of this small roaster, ten inches wide and eight inches high, was shaped like a pan into which the juices ran. The apple roaster was made with two shelves, holding four apples each. This stood before the fire, resting on one support at the back and two small front feet. A biscuit oven was made in sizes to accommodate various sizes of family. It was in two parts, one hinged to the other, so that the biscuits might be watched as they baked in front of the hot embers. A sheet of tin held the biscuits, resting on supports at the sides of the lower part of the oven. Small biscuit ovens were made of one piece.

EARLY HERBS

As the early ships from Europe landed along the Atlantic Coast, colonists brought their cherished seeds and plants with them because of the "vertues" attributed to them in Old World medicine and cooking. The people believed that many plants indicated their usefulness to health by some particular sign, such as color, texture, or shape.

Herbals published in England before 1650 formed the basis for "Physick" during the following century. In America, the early colonists used their gardens to furnish both food and remedies.

Many secrets bubbled in colonial kitchen pots. A good cook knew her fruits, vegetables, and herbs—and interesting things to do with them. She prepared teas, wines, or remedies ("Simples") as easily as a meal.

Herbs were gathered as follows: flowers in summer; leaves and bark in spring;

and roots in spring and fall. To dry the herbs, the colonists hung them from the rafters of the kitchen in bundles.

The small colonial herb garden was cultivated carefully as a kitchen necessity. Herbs, fresh or dried, were used in daily cooking to improve flavor, and because it was believed that herbs aided in digestion and health. A colonial woman often established her reputation as a homemaker by her knowledge of the flavoring magic of herbs as well as their medicinal value.

When a colonial hostess served a "dish of tea," she brewed it carefully in a non-metal pot, allowing 1 teaspoon dried herb to a cup of boiling water. It was steeped until as strong as desired, then served with honey or lemon. Long before the Boston Tea Party, certain teas were thought to have mildly medicinal values and could refresh, quieten, or warm the blood on a cold day.

While colonial cooks knew nothing about vitamins, or nutrition as we know it today, they knew what foods were considered necessary to maintain good health. Children were told to eat a certain food because it was a specialty food for a certain part of the body.

Although nuts and seeds were used from Biblical times, in 1608 a Virginia colonist wrote home to London of the strange uses the Indians made of the simple seeds and nuts gathered in the woods and fields. He said that the Indians used acorns to furnish a sweet oil which they kept in gourds to anoint their "heades and joynts."

It was believed that spices had almost magical powers for preserving foods and meat, stimulating the body, and protecting against illness. When the colonists came to America, spices were still being used as antiseptics, pain killers, and stimulants. Cooks used spices to flavor foods, and also believed that they added protection against gas, colic, and poor digestion.

HONEY

Honey could be gathered wild in the forests and used as a sweetener, but the supply was limited and the long hours of searching needed to find a single comb could be spent on other tasks.

GLASS

Glass was made in the colonies of silica (sand) and two alkaline bases, either soda (found in salt water) or potash (leached from wood ashes) and lime (found in oyster shells). There was much and varied need for glass in the form of beads, window glass, bottles, and other utensils. The Wistars of Philadelphia were good businessmen and the first American glass manufacturers to make flint glass. They had competition from Henry William Stiegel, mentioned earlier, who arrived in Philadelphia from Rotterdam on August 31, 1750.

SEVERAL SAUCES FOR ROAST HENS

Take beer, salt, the yolks of three hard eggs minced small, grated bread, three or four spoonfuls of gravy; and being almost boiled, put in the juice of two or three oranges, slices of a lemon and orange, with lemon peel shred small.

Beaten butter with juice of lemon or orange, white or claret wine.

Gravy and claret wine boiled with a piece of onion, nutmeg, and salt; serve it with slices of oranges or lemons, or the juice in the sauce.

Or with oyster liquor, an anchovy or two, nutmeg, and gravy, and rub the dish with a clove of garlic.

Take the yolks of hard eggs and lemon peel, mince them very small, and stew them in white wine, salt, and the gravy of the fowl.

The Accomplisht Cook, 1678

TO STEW PEARS

Pare six pears, and either quarter them or do them whole; they make a pretty dish with one whole, the rest cut in quarters, and the cores taken out. Lay them in a deep earthen pot, with a few cloves, a piece of lemon peel, a gill of red wine, and a quarter of a pound of fine sugar.

If the pears are very large, they will take half a pound of sugar, and a half a pint of red wine; cover them close with brown paper, and bake them till they are done enough.

Serve them up hot or cold, just as you like them, and they will be very good with water in the place of wine.

The Frugal Housewife, 1772

TO POT LOBSTERS

Take a dozen of large lobsters; take out all the meat of their tails and claws after they are boiled; then season them with pepper, salt, cloves, mace, and nutmeg, all finely beaten and mixed together; then take a pot, put therein a layer of fresh butter, upon which put a layer of lobster, and then strew over some seasonings, and repeat the same till your pot is full, and your lobster all in; bake it about an hour and a half, then set it by two or three days, and it will be fit to eat. It will keep a month or more, if you pour from it the liquor when it comes out of the oven, and fill it up with clarified butter. Eat with vinegar.

The Complete Housewife, E. Smith, 1766

PLUM-POTTAGE

Take two gallons of strong broth; put to it two pounds of currants, two pounds of raisons of the Sun, half an ounce of Sweet Spice, a pound of Sugar, a quart of claret, a pint of Sack, the juice of three oranges and three lemons; thicken it with grated biskets, or rice flour with a pound of pruants.

Author's note: Pruants are prunes, Sweet Spice is cloves, mace, nutmeg, cinnamon, sugar, and salt.

Receipts of Pastry and Cookery, c. 1730

TO MAKE A CATCHUP TO KEEP SEVEN YEARS

Take two quarts of the oldest strong beer you can get, put to it one quart of red wine, three quarters of a pound of anchovies, three ounces of shalots peeled, half an ounce of mace, the same of nutmegs, a quarter of an ounce of cloves, three large races [roots] of ginger cut in slices. Boil all together over a moderate fire, till one third is wasted. The next day bottle it for use; it may be carried to the East Indies.

The Experienced English House-Keeper, 1778

MUSTARD OF DIJON, OR FRENCH MUSTARD

The seed being cleansed, stamp it in a mortar with vinegar and honey. Then take eight ounces of seed, two ounces of cinnamon, two of honey, and vinegar as much as will serve good mustard not too thick. And keep it close covered in little oyster-barrels.

The Accomplisht Cook, 1678

CORN PUDDING

The Early American housewife was particularly ingenious at inventing variations for what became a standard table item—corn pudding. The six most common recipes all involved meal and liquid, which were mixed in differing proportions and cooked various lengths of time. The most popular concoctions were:

Hasty pudding, a quickly cooled gruel of cornmeal boiled in almost equal parts with milk or water. Hasty pudding was also called loblolly.

Indian pudding, a slightly more liquid version of hasty pudding which was boiled in a bag containing various spices.

Suppawn, a thick mixture of cornmeal and milk, eaten either hot or cold from the pot, or allowed to cool. Then it could also be sliced and fried in deep fat.

Mush, a watery type of suppawn eaten with sweetened fruit or molasses.

Samp porridge, an Indian goulash featuring cornmeal cooked for a minimum of three days with meats and vegetables. After the prolonged simmering, this mixture became so thick that it could be removed from the pot in one solid chunk.

HOME REMEDIES

Descriptions of popular household remedies of the seventeenth century are to be found in a volume entitled *The Queen's Closet Opened, or The Pearl Of Practice,* published in 1656. For example, "Bruise a handfull of aniseeds, and steep them in Red Rose Water. Make it up in little bags, and bind one of them to each nostril, and it will cause sleep."

Again, to cure deafness, "Take Garden Daisie roots, and make juice thereof. Lay the worst side of the head low upon the bolster, and drop three or four drops thereof into the better ear. This do three or four days together."

SALADS

Mixed greens and vegetable salads, topped with oil and vinegar dressings, were well known to the colonists. Wild greens, such as leeks, pigweed, cowslip, cress, milkweed, ferns, purslane, swamp cabbage, and the leaves of the pokeberry bush, were often eaten raw in what was then called "sallet." In some cases, these were supplemented with radishes, violets, sorrel, sunflowers, spinach, savory, wild rhubarb, mushrooms, endive, and turnip greens. Beet tops, dandelions, and lettuce were all important salad greens. Cucumbers, believed valuable in unstopping the liver, were also used in salads.

FASHIONS IN PHILADELPHIA *by Dolly Madison* (1791)

And now, my dear Anna, we will have done with judges and juries, courts, both martial and partial, and we will speak a little about Philadelphia and the fashions, the beaux, Congress, and the weather. Do I not make a fine jumble of them? What would Harper or beau Dawson say were they to know it, ha, ha,—mind you laugh here with me. Philadelphia never was known to be so lively at this season as at present; for an accurate account of the amusements, I refer you to my letter to your sister Mary.

I went yesterday to see a doll, which has come from England, dressed to show us the fashions, and I saw besides a great quantity of millinery. Very long trains are worn, and they are festooned up with loops of bobbin and small covered buttons, the same as the dress; you are not confined to any number of festoons, but put them according to your fancy, and you cannot imagine what a beautiful effect it has. There is also a robe which is plaited very far back, open and ruffled down the sides, without a train, even with the petticoat. The hats are quite a different shape from what they used to be: they have no slope in the crown, scarce any rim, and are turned up at each side, and worn very much on the side of the head. Several of them are made of chipped wood, commonly known as cane hats; they are all lined: one that has come for Mrs. Bingham is lined with white, and trimmed with broad purple ribbon, put round in large puffs, with a bow on the left side. The bonnets are all open on the top, through which the hair is passed, either up or down as you fancy, but latterly they wear it more up than down; it is quite out of fashion to frizz or curl the hair, as it is worn perfectly straight. Earrings, too, are very fashionable. The waists are worn two inches longer than they used to be, and there is no such thing as long sleeves. They are worn half way above the elbow, either drawn or plaited in various ways, according to fancy; they do not wear ruffles at all, and as for elbows, Anna, ours would be alabaster, compared to some of the ladies who follow the fashion; black or a colored ribbon is pinned round the bare arm, between the elbow and the sleeve. Some new-fashioned slippers for ladies have come made of various colored kid or morocco, with small silver clasps sewed on; they are very handsome, and make the feet look remarkably small and neat. Everybody thinks the millinery last received the most tasty seen for a long time.

All our beaux are well; the amiable Chevalier is perfectly recovered, and handsomer than ever. You can have no idea, my dear girl, what pleasant times I have; there is the charming Chevalier, the divine Santana, the jolly Vicar, the witty and agreeable Fatio, the black-eyed Lord Henry, the soft, love-making Count, the giggling, foolish Duke, and sometimes the modest, good Meclare, who are at our house every day. We have fine riding parties and musical frolics.

Traveling in style

SUMMERTIME IN THE LATE 1800'S

Summertime was a time for heavy work if one lived on a farm. There was planting, haying, harvesting, and threshing. Fruit was gathered and preserved, while the vegetables were also preserved for use in the coming winter.

However, it was also the time for visiting, family reunions, and home picnics. There were country fairs to be visited, and the farm wife looked forward to exhibiting her quilts and pies and preserves. Perhaps she would get a ribbon for one of her exhibitions.

BAKED BEETS

Beets retain their sugary delicate flavor to perfection if they are baked instead of boiled. Turn them frequently while in the oven, using a knife, as the fork allows the juice to run out. When done, remove the skin and serve with butter, salt and pepper on the slices.

Ladies' Home Cook Book, 1885

FEMALE PHYSICIANS

A very influential Boston paper submits the following opinions, as those now popular in New England:—

That the medical profession is hereafter to consist of women as well as men, is no longer a matter of doubt, judging from the strong setting of public sentiment in this direction. The preference for females in some departments of practice is becoming so general, we understand that the few who are educated are overtasked with labor, and many incompetent women are prompted to advertise themselves, and, for the want of those better qualified, they are employed. To prevent the evils from this source, it is important that the Female Medical College in this city, designed to accommodate the whole of New England, should be placed in a condition to afford a thorough scientific and practical education to a sufficient number of suitable females.

Godey's Lady's Book and Magazine, 1853

MADEMOISELLE HAZARD,—This young lady succeeds her mother, lately deceased, in the tuition of dancing, at the corner of Twelfth and Chestnut Streets, Sime's Building. We cheerfully recommend her as one well versed in the art, and worthy of the support of Philadelphians, with whom her mother was so deservedly a favorite.

Godey's Lady's Book and Magazine, 1853

FISH A L'ORLY

Bone, skin and cut the fish in pieces; beat two eggs and a pinch of salt together and dip each piece of fish in it; roll in browned bread crumbs; fry in hot fat; turn the sauce on a platter and lay the fish in it. The sauce is made by putting half a can of tomatoes in a saucepan with a little onion, two or three stalks of parsley, thyme, one bay leaf, one clove, six pepper corns and salt; reduce, by boiling, one-third; strain gently through a collender, and return to the fire with half a spoonful of butter, a little water and flour mixed smoothly.

Everyday's Need, 1873

CLAMS

First catch your clams,—along the ebbing edges
Of saline coves you'll find the precious wedges,

With backs up, lurking in the sandy bottom;
Pull in your iron rake, and lo! you've got 'em.
Take thirty large ones, put a basin under,
Add water, (three quarts) to the native liquor,
Bring to a boil (and, by the way, the quicker
It boils the better, if you do it cutely).
Now add the clams, chopped up and minded minutely,
Allow a longer boil of just three minutes,
And while it bubbles quickly stir within its
Tumultuous depths, where still the mollusks mutter,
Four tablespoons of flour and four of butter,
A pint of milk, some pepper to your notion,—
And clams need salting, although born of ocean.
Remove from fire (if much boiled they will suffer,—
You'll find that Indian-rubber isn't tougher);
After 'tis off, add three fresh eggs well beaten,
Stir once more, and it's ready to be eaten.
Fruit of the wave! Oh, dainty and delicious!
Food for the gods! Ambrosia for Apicius!
Worthy to thrill the soul of sea-born Venus,
Or titillate the palate of Silenus!

The Household Friend, 1879

HOUSES, 1825–1860

What had been beautiful when applied to religious architecture became grotesque when applied to houses. Householders, decorators, and most architects attempted to make up for lack of imagination in style and design by lavishness of decoration. A bare spot was not to be endured. Pointed gables, towers, and oriel windows broke the outline of roof and facade. Bay windows were supported by heavy decorative brackets. Hollow brick walls, often painted a dark brown, were adorned with elaborate stone trimmings on the slightest provocation. Behind the flamboyant curves of cast-iron ornaments gleamed small, diamond-paned casement windows.

Inside, softwood floors were entirely covered with carpets in brightly flowered patterns. There was a fireplace in every room. Flowered paper covered the walls to within two or three feet of the floor. A stained or gilded wood molding separated the wallpaper from the plain strip beneath, which was painted a uniform color. Thick satins, draped to the jambs and crowned with festooned lambrequins, did their best to shut out light and air.

LETTER FROM MARTHA WASHINGTON TO HER SISTER

Mt. Vernon, Aug. 28, 1762

My Dear Nancy,—I had the pleasure to receive your kind letter of the 25 of July just as I was setting out on a visit to Mr. Washington in Westmoreland where I spent a weak very agreably I carried my little Patt with me and left Jackey at home for a trial to see how well I could stay without him though we are gone but wone fortnight I was quite impatient to get home. If I at aney time heard the doggs barke or a noise, out I though thair was a person sent for me. . .

We are daly expect[ing] the kind laydes of Maryland to visit us. I must begg you will not lett the fright you had given you prevent you comeing to see me again—If i could leave my children in as good Care as you can I would never let Mr. W. . .n come down without me— Please to give my love to Miss Judy and your little babys and make my best compliments to Mr. Bassett and Mrs. Dawson.

I am with sincere regard

dear sister
Yours most affectionately
MARTHA WASHINGTON

Roasting meat—colonial days

ROASTING

Roasting was a third method of fireplace cooking, but one usually reserved for cuts of domestic stock or the most tender sections of game animals.

Andirons, or fire dogs, were equipped with special notches for supporting the spit on which meats were skewered for roasting. If andirons were lacking, the meat was wrapped in a rope sling and hung from the lug pole. Using either method, the meat was turned periodically to assure even cooking, and a pan was placed just below the roast to catch the drippings for use in basting or in flavoring other dishes.

Children were often assigned the job of turning the spit, but more elaborate roasting mechanisms were devised as the country became more advanced technologically.

With time, less cumbersome methods of roasting were introduced in America. Many homes used portable metal ovens called roasting kitchens. These were shaped like rectangular boxes but were open on the side that was placed before the fire. Smaller versions of this appliance were used to prepare any small game or bird.

A SALMON PYE

Take a convenient piece of fresh Salmon, 2 quarts of Shrimps or prawns, & ye like quantity of Oysters, Half a Quarter of an ounce of whole Mace, ye like of Beatton Pepper, & 4 Anchovies, Spread Your pye Bottom with a good piece of Butter, then lay in your Salmon, first Laid 3 or 4 hours in white Wine, then Strane your Seasoning upon it, lay good store of Butter on ye Topp then cover it & Bake it.

Manuscript of 18th Century at Tryon Palace, New Bern, N.C.

MISS BEECHER'S DOMESTIC RECEIPT BOOK, 1846

The temperance movement was founded in this country in the early years of the century and by the 1830's had attracted more than a million members. Some cookbooks stumped for the cause and Catherine Beecher, noted educator, was one of the most effective members of the temperance movement.

However, she held out for temperance in everything, not only alcohol, but tea, coffee, and food in general. She objected to fried foods, especially fried in animal oils. She was also materialistic, though, and realized that a cookbook without "receipts" for rich dishes would not be a best-seller; therefore, she did have some in the book, such as veal cutlets and fried mush.

TO PICKLE MUSHROOMS

Take your mushrooms as soon as they come in; cut the stalks off and throw your mushrooms into water and salt as you do them; then rub them with a piece of flannel, and as you do them, throw them into another vessel of salt and water, and when all is done, put some salt and water on the fire, and when it is scalding hot, put in your mushrooms, and let them stay in as long as you think will boil an egg; but first put them in a sieve, and let them drain from the hot water, and be sure to take them out of the hot water immediately, or they will wrinkle and look yellow. Let them stand in the cold water till next morning, then take them out, and put them into fresh water and salt, and change them every day for three or four days together; then wipe them very dry, and put them into distilled vinegar; the spice must be distilled in the vinegar.

The Complete Housewife, E. Smith, 1766

KEEPING FOOD FRESH

In the early days, the householder spent a lot of his time and energy just trying to keep food fresh.

If he was an early settler in his area, his first concern was to locate as near as possible to a cold, flowing spring, at which he built a "spring house," a low building with a stone trough running through it. The housewife was then able to set her bowls of milk and cream, and crocks of butter and cheese near or in its shaded icy water.

However, not every settler was lucky enough to have a stream on his property, but he did have a well, and it was the well that was used for refrigeration. The spoilables were put into a large bucket, or into a wooden frame with shelves, which was lowered into the well on a rope slung over a pulley until it hung just over the water level, where the air was quite cold.

The luckiest man of all was one who lived on land near a lake, pond or river that froze deeply in the winter. He built an ice house, a wooden building with double walls between which he stuffed sawdust for insulation. In the middle of the winter, he cut blocks of ice from the water and lugged it back to the ice house for use the following summer. Usually the ice-cutting was a community affair.

HOW TO BATHE PLANTS

Large-leaved plants, either the smooth- or the hairy-leaved, may be easily bathed in the windows where they stand, if the pots are too heavy to be removed, or if for any other reason it may seem best.

A soft cloth or sponge, well wet in slightly warm water, may be used to gently wipe off the upper and under sides of each leaf and wash down each stem. But a soft brush, similar to the hair brushes for babies, is better, especially for rough- or fuzzy-leaved plants.

If the leaf is corrugated it is yet more necessary that each depression be reached.

Household, 1875

FLAX: *A Letter from Ruth*

Dear Hannah:

It would be strange indeed if I failed to set down anything concerning the flax which we spin, because save for it we would have had nothing of linen except what could be brought from England.

Flax is sown early in the spring, and when the plants are three or four inches long, we girls are obliged to weed them, and in doing so are forced to go barefooted, because of the stalks being very tender and therefore easily broken down.

I do not believe there is a child in town who fails to go into the flax fields, because of its being such work as can be done by young people better than by older ones, who are heavier and more likely to injure the plants.

I have said that we are obliged to go barefooted, but where there is a heavy growth of thistles, as is often the case, we girls wear two or three pairs of woolen stockings to protect our feet.

If there is any wind, we must perforce work facing it, so that such of the plants as may by accident have been trodden down, may be blown back into place by the breeze.

Wearying labor it is indeed, this weeding of the flax, and yet those who come into the new

Breaking the flax

Weeding the flax

world, as have we, must not complain at whatsoever is set them to do, for unless much time is expended, crops cannot be raised, and we children of Boston need only to be reminded of the famine, when we are inclined to laziness, in order to set us in motion.

Of course you know that flax is a pretty plant, with a sweet, drooping, blue flower, and it ripens about the first of July, when it is pulled up by the roots and laid carefully out to dry, much as if one were making hay. This sort of work is always done by the men and boys, and during two or three days they are forced to turn the flax again and again, so that the sun may come upon every part of it.

I despair of trying to tell anyone who has never seen flax prepared, how much and how many different kinds of labor are necessary, before it can be woven into the beautiful linen of which our mothers are so proud.

First it must be rippled. The ripple comb is made of stout teeth, either wood or iron, set on a pouch, and the stalks of the flax are pulled through it to break off the seeds, which fall into a cloth that has been spread to catch them, so they may be sown for the next year's harvest.

Of course this kind of work is always done in the fields, and the stalks are then tied in bundles, which are called "bates," and stacked up something after the shape of a tent, being high in the middle and broadened out at the bottom.

After the flax has been exposed to the weather long enough to be perfectly dry, then water must be sprinkled over it to rot the leaves and such portions of the stalks that are not used.

Then comes that part of the work which only strong men can perform, called breaking the flax, to get from the center of the stalks the hard, wood-like "bun," which is of no value. This is done with a machine made of wood, as if you were to set three or four broad knives on a bench, at a certain distance apart, with as many more on a lever to come from above, fitting *closely between the lower blades. The upper part of the machine is pulled down with force upon the flax, so that every portion of it is broken.*

After this comes the scutching, or swingling, which is done by chopping with dull knives on a block of wood to take out the small pieces of bark which may still be sticking to the fiber.

Now that which remains is made up into bundles, and pounded again to clear it yet more thoroughly of what is of no value, after which it is hackled, and the fineness of the flax depends upon the number of times it has been hackled, which means pulling it through a quantity of iron teeth driven into a board.

After all this preparation has been done, then comes the spinning, which is, of course, the work of the women and girls. I am proud to say that I could spin a skein of thread in one day, before I was thirteen years old, and you must know that this is no mean work for a girl, since it is reckoned that the best of spinners can do no more than two skeins.

Of course the skeins must be bleached, otherwise the cloth made from them would look as if woven of tow. This portion of the work mother is always very careful to look after herself.

The skeins must stay in warm water for at least four days, and be wrung out dry every hour or two, when the water is to be changed. Then they are washed in a brook or river until there is no longer any dust or dirt remaining, after which they are bricked, which is the same as if I had said bleached, with ashes and hot water, over and over again, afterward left to remain in clear water a full week.

Then comes more rinsing, beating, washing, drying, and winding on bobbins, so that it may be handy for the loom.

The chief men in Boston made a law that all boys and girls be taught to spin flax, and a certain sum of money was set aside to be given those who made the best linen that had been raised, spun, and woven within the town.

I am told that in some villages nearabout, the men who make the laws have ordered that every family shall spin so many pounds of flax each year, or pay a very large amount of money as a fine for neglecting to do so.

Ruth

Bleaching the flax

GARDENING FOR LADIES

Make up your beds early in the morning; sew buttons on your husband's shirts; do not rake up any grievances; protect the young and tender branches of your family; plant a smile of good temper in your face, and root out all angry feelings, and expect a good crop of happiness.

The Old Farmer's Almanac, 1862, Robert B. Thomas

Charles Joseph Latrobe in 1836 said: "No where is the stomach of the traveller or visitor put in such constant peril as among the cake-inventive housewives and daughters of New England. Such is the universal attention paid to this particular branch of epicurism in these states, that I greatly suspect that some of the Pilgrim Fathers must have come over to the country with Cookery Book under one arm and the Bible under the other."

CHEESE-MAKING: *Diary of An Early American Housewife*

August 5th, 1772—This is a good time to begin making our cheese. We are now waiting for some of the vegetables to ripen before preserving them for the winter. I hope that we shall have enough cheese to sell some to Abner Smith at the corners.

CHEESE-MAKING

Butter was not made during the hot summer months of July and August, but during these months the cheese was made, and the task was a hard one, requiring daily attention.

The first step was to prepare the rennet, or runnet. The stomach of a young calf which had never taken anything but milk was used. It was washed, turned, and washed again and put into a strong brine. When well salted, it was taken out and stretched over a stick to dry. It was then cut into small pieces and placed in jars or a bag called a "cheeselep." The liquid obtained was poured into the milk or cream, standing in tubs, and then stirred with wooden paddles. Coagulation took place and the curds which hardened had to be cut several times. The following morning the curds were put into the cheese drainer.

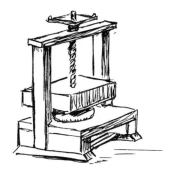

The cheese press

The drainer was placed on a rack or tongs, also called a cheese ladder, which rested on a tub. Cheesecloth was laid in the drainer and the mixture poured in, filling the drainer. The whey then drained through and was given to the pigs, while the curds were tied in the cloth and hung up to drain thoroughly. This mass again had to be cut with a curd knife made of wood, or run through a curd breaker, which was a box-shaped grinder with wooden teeth. This broken mass was then put into a wooden bowl, salted, and worked again, and thus made ready for the cheese press.

The purpose of the cheese press was to press and drain the curds of all the whey. There were many kinds. The press generally consisted of two uprights placed on a "floor" which was called the cheese board. The cheese board had a circular groove in it with a snout in front. As the top and bottom were pushed together, the balance of the whey was forced down the snout into a tub.

The following morning the cheese was taken out to be pressed. The cheesecloth was taken off and the cheese pared with a wooden knife and made smooth. It was then buttered, and a band of cloth, an inch wider than the cheese, was wrapped around it, lapping over fully four inches. The top and bottom were left exposed so that as the cheese was cured it could be turned and buttered every day. This last process took two weeks, the cheese having been put into the cheese closet. The air could come in and the flies kept out of the cheese because the front had cheesecloth.

Dutch cheese was made by crumbling cottage cheese and working in butter, salt, and chopped sage. Formed into pans, it was set to ripen. Cottage cheese was eaten with molasses on bread, like the Yankee combination of pork and molasses.

Cheese was often made with juices, which gave it different flavors, adding also to its appearance. Sage cheese was a common variety and was made by adding the juice of sage leaves or the leaves themselves, chopped fine. Other flavors were made from various herbs and herb teas, and from teas made by boiling young, green corn husks or spinach, which gave a fine green color. Pigweed water was used to color the cheese green without giving it any taste.

ICEBOXES

The first primitive refrigerator was patented in 1834 by Jacob Perkins, although at that time there were many large storehouses for ice throughout the country. No matter how well the housewife covered the ice in her cellar pantry, it melted very quickly. So she hailed the invention of the icebox, designed to make the ice last longer.

The first refrigerators were little more than lined boxes which held ice. The manufacturers also made refrigerators that looked like sideboards or lowboys.

The German Revolution of 1848 sent many German emigrants to the United States, and many of them were butchers who settled in and around Cincinnati, which had developed into a significant meat-packing area. Besides bringing with them the frankfurter, the weiner, and the hamburger, they also became involved with the process of refrigeration for train cars with blocks of ice. The first practical refrigerator car was built in the 1860's with ice bunkers lined with lead. From these cars the first models of home iceboxes emerged and rapidly found acceptance among homeowners.

Early home models were priced as low as $2.75 for a chest model to $56.00 for a large upright model.

After 1870 the ice was not always natural, since artificial ice was now being made in ice plants.

With the coming of the icebox, the milkman emerged as an important part of food delivery. The housewife also found that she could buy and store a greater variety of fresh foods and foods out of season.

FRYING

Frying was not one of the daily cooking techniques in most homes prior to 1850. A primary reason was the basically dangerous nature of open hearth cooking. Skillets with handles up to three feet in length were needed to reach into the fire if the housewife was to stand in a safe position on the hearth.

Frying pans could be set on long-legged trivets, but the action of turning the food without upsetting the skillet required a steady hand. This problem was solved to some degree by the manufacture of spiders, special skillets with legs attached to the bottom of the pan which were specifically used for frying over an open fire.

Splattering fat or flammable grease into the fire was an additional hazard in frying, as were the long-handled wooden spoons or turning spatulas that could catch fire at any moment. Finally, frying required much closer attention than other cooking methods, a distinct drawback for the harried colonial cook.

COOKBOOKS AND COOKSTOVES

After 1850, the compilers of cookbooks generally assumed that a woman who would buy a cookbook would be using a wood range that was economical in its fuel consumption and easy—well, relatively—to clean.

However, many good cooks believed that the cookstove worsened the American cuisine. Mrs. Harriet Beecher Stowe put into words what others felt when she wrote that "an open fireplace is an altar of patriotism. Would our Revolutionary fathers have gone barefooted and bleeding over snow to defend air-tight stoves and cooking ranges? I trow not. It was the memory of the great open kitchen-fire . . . its roaring, hilarious voice of invitation, its dancing tongues of flame, that called to them through the snows of that dreadful winter. . . ."

TRAINING DAY: *A Letter from Ruth*

Dear Hannah:

I must tell you of our Training Day and I am setting down what happened on that particular day, because of its being the largest and most exciting training ever held in Boston, so everyone says.

Sarah believes Training Day should come oftener than four times a year, so that we young people may get some idea of what gay life is in the old countries, where they make festivals of Christmas, and other Saint Days. It does truly seem as if we might see our soldiers perform quite often, for it is a most inspiring spectacle, and especially was it on last Training Day, when, so father says, there were upwards of seven hundred men marching back and forth across the Common in a manner which at times was really terrifying, because of their fierce appearance when fully armed.

Imagine, if you can, a row of booths along the Common, in which are for sale ground nuts, packages of nookick, sweet cakes, pumpkin bread roasted brown and spread with maple syrup, together with dainties of all kinds lately brought over from England.

Between these booths and the water are many tents, which have been set up so that the people of quality may entertain their friends therein with toothsome food and sweet waters.

The middle of the Common, and a long space at either end, is kept clear of idle ones, so that the soldiers may exercise at arms, and these do not appear until the on-lookers are in their places. Then we hear a flourish of trumpets, the rolling of drums, and from the direction of the Neck comes our army, a mighty array of seven hundred or more men, all armed and equipped as the law directs.

When this vast body of warlike men have marched into the vacant space, they are drawn up in line, there is another flourish of trumpets, together with the rolling of drums, and a prayer is offered by Master Cotton.

On this day, moved by the sight of the great throng, the prayer was long and fervent, whereat some of the younger soldiers, having not the fear of God in their hearts, pulled long faces, one to another, or shifted about uneasily on their feet, as if weary with long standing, and I trembled lest the Governor, seeing such levity, might rebuke them openly, which would be a great disgrace at such a time.

After the prayer, the soldiers began to march here and there in many ways until one's eyes were confused with watching them, and then came the volleys, as the men shot straight over the heads of the people; but father says one need not fear such warlike work, for there were no bullets in the guns. However, I could not but shudder when so many guns were fired at one time, while the smoke of powder in the air was most painful to the eyes.

After the soldiers had marched back and forth in the most ferocious manner possible until noon, they were allowed a time for rest, and then it was that those who set up tents entertained their friends at table with stores upon stores of dainties of every kind.

Ruth

CANNING

Summertime was canning time—and a busy time for the housewife until she had the cellar filled with hundreds of jars full of fruits and vegetables. There were steamer cookers and pressure cookers invented and marketed as early as 1870, but most of the steamer cookers were ineffectual, while the pressure cookers were dangerous.

Therefore the housewife resorted to boilers of all sizes that could hold up to eighteen jars at a time. These came equipped with a metal rack to hold the jars a little above the bottom surface. Vegetables were usually precooked for a short time and packed in jars sterilized by boiling. The hot jars were sealed and placed on the rack in the boiler and covered with water to about two inches below the top; they were then boiled for as long as three or four hours.

Fruits did not require a water bath. Once the fruits were boiled in a sugar and water syrup they were placed in sterilized jars and the jars were sealed and set aside to cool.

However, the problem then as now was getting the jar to be perfectly airtight after filling. A little air in the jar and that was the end of the food in that jar.

HOUSEKEEPING

I love the good old-fashioned word
    "Housekeeping"—whatsoe-er they say;
There is another we have heard
    To take the place of it to-day.

It is a word that's long and dry,
    But everywhere they're preaching it;

Bathroom—1890's

Co-operation is the cry,
    It may be hard to practice yet.

Might we not call it *Coop*-eration,
    And each construct herself a tub,
Diogenes our mediation,
    And rest from all the fret and rub?

Ah, we are all of us to blame,
    For we are faint, and out of heart;
The homely ways we put to shame,
    And everyday we shirk our part.

The little cares that make the sum,
    Of our accustomed days and hours,
If we are faithful when they come,
    Will sweeten life like humble flowers.

So let us learn to live aright,
    To guide our homes with grace and power;
Then shall we grow in depth and height,
    And ripen for the coming hour.

by Martha Perry Lowe, *American Kitchen Magazine*, July 1889

ICE CREAM FREEZER

Ice cream used to be made only in the home, in an ice cream freezer that consisted of a wooden tub containing a metal can equipped with a crank and a paddle that were turned by hand. The freezing was accomplished with the aid of crushed ice, rock salt, and plenty of muscle. But muscle power was not lacking, as the reward for turning the crank was the privilege of licking the paddle after the job was done.

The variety of flavors was limited to vanilla, chocolate, fresh peach, and fresh strawberry.

DAMPNESS IN THE CLOSET

Place a bowl of quicklime in a damp pantry, cupboard, or closet. This not only removes dampness but kills all odors.

Household Discoveries, 1903

CHINA: *Diary of An Early American Housewife*

August 10, 1772—I have ordered some dishes which Captain Abner will bring back to me when he returns from his latest trip.

CHINAWARE

There was no china in common use on the table, and even little was owned by persons of wealth, throughout the seventeenth century, either in England or America. It was not until the late 1700's that china became a common table commodity and began to crowd out pewter. The sudden and tremendous spurt in East Indian commerce, along with the vast cargoes of Chinese pottery and porcelain brought to American ports, had given rise to ample china for every housewife. The first china used for general tableware was the handleless tea cup as tea became a necessity in the more affluent homes.

At first, china was not universally accepted because it broke so easily and dulled the edge of the knife as compared with woodenware.

Americans appreciated good china whether Oriental or European in origin and it was not uncommon to send special orders to be completed on an individual basis. Often monograms or armorial bearings on each piece were requested.

A very popular pattern then and still popular today was the Willow Pattern, which was designed by Thomas Turner in England in 1772 from a design of Chinese antiquity. The pattern caught on immediately and has been made ever since.

A GOOD BISQUE OF LOBSTER

Chop one pound of lobster meat very fine, melt two ounces of butter, adding three tablespoonfuls of sifted flour; when smooth add one pint of rich stock or soup; when boiled up add the lobster meat, one tablespoonful of fresh butter, one pint of cream, salt, pepper and mace to taste.

Culinary Helps and Hints,
Ladies' Home Journal, 1892

EXPERIENCE TALKS: EGGS

Eggs, in an emergency, will stamp or seal letters. Will seal the paper jelly-glass cover. Will render corrosive sublimate harmless, if half a dozen be given after an emetic. Will soothe a burn, if several applications of the white be put on to exclude the air. Will not permit a plaster to blister, if the mustard be mixed with egg instead of water. Will remove a fishbone from the throat, if the white be beaten and given at once.

Household, 1877

HOME MEDICINE

In an era when doctors, trained nurses, and well-equipped hospitals were still relatively scarce, childbearing and the treatment of sickness typically took place in the home. An ailing member of the family was bundled up in bed in the guest room or, in winter, on a daybed in the living room, and home remedies were applied: hot and cold compresses, immersion of the feet in hot water, drinking of special teas and herb brews—remedies that had not changed much for centuries. It was an age when the editor of a leading women's magazine could claim that dizziness, unsettled nerves, and female disorders could be cured by sleeping with the head of the bed northward.

The housewife would use one of the many patent medicines advertised in her magazines with complete confidence in its remedial powers. Only when home and patent remedies had failed was the doctor summoned, and his arrival was a signal for concern. Neighbors brought prepared food, with offers to attend the ailing one, and with the inevitable morsels of advice and recountings of personal experiences, most of them bad.

WHAT A YOUNG GIRL DOES AT HOME:
A Letter from Ruth

Dear Hannah:

Living here, if we do not know how to make what is needed, then we must go without, because one cannot well afford to spend the time, nor the money, required to send to London for whatever may be desired, and wait until it shall be brought across the sea.

I wonder if it would interest any of you to know what Sarah and I are obliged to do in our homes during each working day of the week?

I can remember a time when we were put to it to perform certain tasks within six days, and have set down that which we did.

It was on a Monday that Sarah and I hackled fifty pounds of flax, and tired we were when the day had come to an end. On Tuesday we carded tow, and on Wednesday each spun a skein of linen thread. On Thursday we did the same stint, and on Friday made brooms of guiney wheat straw. On Saturday we spun twine out of the coarser part of flax, which is called tow.

All this we did in a single week, in addition to helping our mothers about the house, and had no idea that we were working overly hard.

And now about tow: When flax has been prepared to that stage where it is to be hackled, the fibers pulled out by the comb are yet further divided into cobweb-like threads, and laid carefully one above the other as straight as may be. To these a certain yellow substance sticks, which we call tow, and this can be spun into coarse stuff for aprons and mats, or into twine, which, by the way, is not very strong.

It would surprise you, when working flax, to see how small a bulk may be reduced. What seems like an enormous stack, before being made ready for spinning, is lessened to such extent that you may readily take it in both hands, and then comes the next surprise, when you see how much cloth can be woven out of so small an amount of threads.

As for myself, I am not any too fond of working amid the flax, save when it comes to spinning; but such labor is the greatest pleasure as compared with soap-making, which is to my mind the most disagreeable and slovenly of all the housewife's duties.

Ruth

FROZEN COFFEE

Put one quart of cream in a bowl; add a pint of granulated sugar and half pint of cold, black coffee, very strong; whip until a stiff froth, then pour into a freezer and pack in salted ice; let stand two hours. Serve in little glass cups.

The Woman's Magazine, June 1903

THE WOMAN WHO LAUGHS

For a good, everyday household angel, give us the woman who laughs. Her biscuits may not be always just right, and she may occasionally burn her bread, and forget to replace dislocated buttons; but, for solid comfort all day and every day, she is a very paragon. The trick of always seeing the bright side, or, if the matter has no bright side, of shining up the dark one, is a very important faculty; one of the things no woman should be without. We are not all born with the sunshine in our hearts, as the Irish prettily phrase it; but we can cultivate a cheerful sense of humor, if we only try.

The Old Farmer's Almanac, 1889, Robert B. Thomas

DR. KING'S NEW DISCOVERY

William H. Mullen of 255 Wabash Avenue, Chicago, has no desire to stand as close to the awful brink of death as he had to before he was induced by a friend to try that marvelous cure, Dr. King's New Discovery. Mr. Mullen says that for a long time he suffered intensely from a very serious bronchial and lung trouble. He had tried six physicians, but without avail. They all gave him up. Then he followed his friend's advice and commenced to use Dr. King's New Discovery. After taking five bottles he was entirely cured, and felt as well as he ever did. He says he owes his life to this greatest of all cures.

Dr. King's Guide to Health and Family Cook Book, 1890

KEROSENE LAMPS

One of the daily chores for the farm boy and girl was taking care of the kerosene lamps—filling them with kerosene, trimming the wicks, and cleaning the glass chimneys. Kerosene lamps were widely used before electricity.

Some of the lamps were quite ornate, and many have been saved and converted to electricity for use today. In larger homes there was a chandelier or a large kerosene lamp hanging from the ceiling.

Child's carriage—1880's

A RECIPE FOR A WIFE

As much of beauty as preserves affection,
As much of cheerfulness as spurns detection,
Of modest deference as claims protection,
Yet stored with sense, with reason and reflection.
And every passion held in due subjection,
Just faults enough to keep her from perfection;
Find this, my friend, and then make your selection.

The Old Farmer's Almanac, 1858, Robert B. Thomas

BOILED FOWL WITH OYSTERS

Ingredients: One young fowl, three dozen oysters, the yolks of two eggs, quarter pint of cream.

Mode: Truss a young fowl as for boiling; fill the inside with oysters which have been bearded and washed in their own liquor; secure the end of the fowl, put it into a jar and plunge the jar into a saucepan of boiling water. Keep it boiling for one hour and a half, or rather longer, then with the gravy that has flowed from the oysters and fowl, of which there will be a good quantity, stir in the cream and yolks of the eggs, add a few oysters scalded in their liquor; let the sauce get quite hot, but do not allow it to boil; pour some of it over the fowl, and send the remainder to table in a tureen.

A blade of pounded mace added to the sauce, with the cream and eggs, will be found an improvement.

Time: One hour and a half. Sufficient for three or four persons.

Godey's Lady's Book and Magazine, 1861

Feeding the fowl

TO CLEAN BRUSHES

The best way in which to clean hairbrushes is with spirits of ammonia as its effect is immediate. No rubbing is required, and cold water can be used just as successfully as warm. Take a tablespoonful of ammonia to a quart of water, dip the hair part of the brush without wetting the ivory, and in a moment the grease is removed; then rinse in cold water, shake well, and dry in the air, but not in the sun. Soda and soap soften the bristles and invariably turn the ivory yellow.

Ladies' Home Cook Book, 1890

TO MAKE THE TEETH WHITE

A mixture of honey with the purest charcoal will prove an admirable cleanser.

MacKenzie's Five Thousand Receipts, 1848

THE TONGUE

A white fur on the tongue attends simple fever and inflammation. Yellowish of the tongue attends a derangement of the liver, and is common to bilious and typhus fevers. A tongue vividly red on the tip and edges, or down the centre, or over the whole surface, attends inflammation of the mucuous membrane of the stomach or bowels. A white velvety tongue attends mental disease. A tongue red at the lips, become brown, dry and glazed attends typhus fever.

Arts Revealed, 1859

FRIED ASPARAGUS

Wash and scrape the asparagus, cover with boiling water and let it stand five minutes; drain and dry on a soft towel. Sprinkle well with salt and pepper. Beat an egg until very light, add to it a half cup of milk and sufficient flour to make a thin batter, add a half teaspoonful of salt and beat the batter until smooth. Dip the asparagus one piece at a time into this batter, and drop at once into hot fat, and fry until a golden brown. When done, drain on brown paper and serve hot.

Hot Weather Dishes, 1888

CANNED BANANAS

Grate rind of four lemons into their juice and let soak over night. Boil two cups sugar and two cups water to a syrup. Add the lemon juice strained and one dozen bananas peeled and cut in pieces three-fourths of an inch long. Cook until of a semi-transparent appearance. Put into self-sealing glass jars which have been scalded.

For immediate use make half the above quantity, lift the fruit carefully into a glass fruit dish, boil the syrup very thick and pour over them. It will jelly when cold.

For variety substitute for the juice of each lemon one tablespoonful of cider jelly which is made by boiling cider fresh from the press without sugar until it jellies.

American Kitchen Magazine, 1872

EMBROIDERY: *Diary of An Early American Housewife*

August 25, 1772—I have asked Joshua to bring me some patterns to embroider when he next goes to Boston. Mrs. Allen who is located near the Old North Meetinghouse has put notices into the Boston Gazette about the new patterns she has. I would like some patterns of animals since I see boats whenever I look out of my window. Tomorrow I will finish embroidering the flowers on my new stockings. I am making a cap for Joshua to wear on his head at night when it gets so cold in the winter.

EMBROIDERY

Crewel work was a big thing at that time, as was needlepoint. Wools for needlepoint and crewels were known as worsted. The *Boston News Letter* of April 28, 1743, advertises: "Shaded crewels, blue, red, and other colours of Worsteds." At about the same time, another advertisement read: "Imported white thread and white chapple needles."

Although patterns could be bought ready-made, as seen in the advertisement of Mrs. Condy in the *Boston News Letter:* "All sorts of beautiful figures on Canvas, for Tent Stitch," others advertised at the same time that they made "All sorts of Drawing for Embroider." There were also advertisements from women who wanted to give instruction in the art of embroidery "and other Works proper for young Ladies." The tent stitch was usually the first stitch taught to very young girls as they attended the Dame Schools.

Silk stockings which were worn by the wealthier were frequently more costly than the attire on their backs and were elaborately embroidered on the instep in florals in silk. Nightcaps were also very elaborately made of silk and embroidered with flowers and gold lace effects.

BAKING BREAD

Although it was cheaper to buy bread than to make it (the fuel for the stove cost more than the flour at the end of the nineteenth century), most American housewives

still preferred to make their own loaves. It was a time-consuming process, as indicated by a warning from a popular cookbook, *Practical Housekeeping* (1883): "Knead for from forty-five minutes to one hour . . . Any pause in the process injures the bread."

REFRIGERATORS

A refrigerator should be examined daily and kept thoroughly clean. If a suitable brush cannot be had, a long stiff wire with a bit of cloth on the end should be used to clean the drain pipe. Pour boiling washing-soda water through it every other day; and do not forget to wash off the slime that adheres to the water pan. Fish, onions, cheese, any strong vegetables, lemons, or meat not perfectly sweet, should not be kept in the same icebox with milk or butter.

Boston Cook Book, 1883

THE ICE WAGON

One of the most frequently seen vehicles on the street in the summertime was the ice wagon. Pulled by one or more horses, it delivered blocks of ice to stores and homes. The ice wagon was usually driven by a husky individual, who also had to cut and weigh the ice and carry it, by means of ice tongs, to the icebox. To keep from freezing his shoulder and getting himself wringing wet, the iceman placed a leather blanket over the shoulder on which he carried the ice.

To simplify the process of delivering ice to city homes, each home had a card with large numbers, visible from the street, telling the iceman how many pounds of ice was wanted on that particular day. If the card did not appear in the usual window, the iceman drove on, assuming no ice was wanted.

Usually the same driver delivered coal in winter.

FOOD: 1825–1860

Although people in the growing Republic lived frugally, as we can see from the cookbooks of the era, they did not deny themselves the joys of a good table. The English writer Harriet Martineau, who traveled in the United States in 1834, described an average breakfast as consisting of a pie dish full of buttered toast, hot biscuits and coffee, beefsteak, apple sauce, hot potatoes, cheese, butter, and two large dishes of eggs. No true New Englander denied himself the joys of pie at breakfast.

The entire family sat down for breakfast at seven o'clock. Dinner was served at noon except on festive occasions and consisted of chops, steaks, or roast, with potatoes, green corn, and peas, finished off with pudding, pie, and coffee. In wealthy homes the principal dish might be home-raised chicken and a Virginia ham, preceded by okra soup and followed by orange fritters to the accompaniment of wine, champagne, liqueur, and coffee.

People were constantly eating and insisted upon meat three times a day to be followed by all sorts of snacks, especially fruit between meals.

In 1840 a man in Connecticut, Sylvester Graham, fell ill and blamed it on his bread. He tried unbolted bread and his health improved. As a result he became a vegetarian and a teetotaler and ate bread made only from the unbolted flour. This flour became known as Graham flour.

BAKING-POWDER AND COCOA CANS

One of these cans, with a few nail holes in each end, is a good soap shaker. This will utilize all the scraps of soap.

Household Discoveries, 1903

MONDAY: WASHDAY

Throughout the world the task of washing clothes has always been the woman's lot. Until the modern washing machines came into use, this was a back-breaking task which entailed long hours of carrying water to a tub after heating it in boilers, tea kettles, stove reservoirs, and even over the open outdoor fire.

When the water was hot, our housewife placed her tub on a wooden bench, filled it with hot water, placed a washboard in it, and reached for a bar of homemade lye soap.

White articles were always washed first, then the colored clothing was done. Each item was rubbed well with a bar of soap, treated to a good scrubbing on the washboard, and then tossed into one of the pots of boiling water. Here more soap was added and the clothes were stirred with a long wooden paddle or stick. After boiling, they were transferred by means of the stick to a pot of clean boiling water and finally to a wash tub filled with cold water. The clothes were then wrung out by hand and hung up to dry.

"Automatic" washtub—1880's

However, in the late 1800's a hand-operated wringer was devised to make the job easier, and a number of various types of washing machines came onto the market. These machines were sold primarily through mail order and ranged in price from about two to five dollars.

Washing clothes took from five to six hours, so the housewife had breakfast prepared earlier than usual.

TUESDAY: IRONING DAY

Our housewife of the 1800's did not save her ironing to do on a rainy day or on a day when she had some free time. She knew that as sure as Monday was Washing Day, Tuesday was Ironing Day, and ironing was not any simpler than was the washing the day before.

We know that at one time there were no irons, but that a smoothing board was used to get some of the wrinkles out of the clothes. However, somewhere along the line, the iron was invented. It was called the "sad iron." The iron was stuck into the hot ashes of the fireplace or, later on, put on the stove to heat; it was then used to smooth out a newly washed piece of clothing. There were several sizes and shapes kept hot and brought to the ironing board just short of scorching temperatures.

It has been said that women pushed the sad iron a mile or two in the course of doing the ironing on a Tuesday. When the iron grew too cold to remove wrinkles, it was exchanged for one fresh off the stove. At first the iron was of one piece with the handle, so that it was impossible to touch unless one used a pot holder of sorts. Eventually, however, came the removable handle of wood, which could be taken off one cool iron and placed into a new, hot one.

There was also a flatiron which contained a compartment into which live charcoal was placed. This type was handy when there was no stove or when the pressing was to be done at a distance from the stove.

These irons held their heat so well that it has been said that many a house burned down because the iron was left standing on the ironing board after the one who was doing the ironing walked away.

At first, ironing was done on the broad wooden kitchen table. Then an ironing board without legs was devised which was supported by the kitchen table at one end and a kitchen chair at the other. This was not too convenient, since it was not simple to slip anything over the board to iron.

There were all sizes of ironing boards to be used for various pieces of clothing. Each of the boards was padded with an old blanket or something similar tacked to it and covered with muslin.

It was a while before the folding ironing board came into use.

HINTS ON THE PRESERVING OF FRUIT

The first and most important thing to be attended to is the selection of the fruit. This, to insure the finest flavor, should have been gathered in the morning of a bright, sunny day; but as this is an advantage which none but the country housewife can be sure of, she who is not blessed with a rural home must take her chances in this particular. She should see, however, that the fruit is sound, perfectly clean and dry, and, as a general rule, thoroughly ripe. These are essentials which her own judgment will find but little difficulty in securing. If not used immediately the fruit should be kept in a cool, dark place until wanted. At the same time it is well to remember that the sooner it is boiled after gathering the better.

... Fruits vary much in the amount of acidity they contain, and it is this variation that regulates the amount of sugar that should be used. The preserving pan may be either an enameled one or made of brass or copper. If either of the latter metals, great care should be used to keep it bright and clean.

In selecting preserve jars have none but glass. They are far preferable, because they allow the examination of the preserves from time to time, a precaution which it is well to take during the first month or two, in order to discover whether they show any indication of fermentation or mould. If they do, they should be at once removed from the jars, and re-boiled.

In storing preserves, a dry, cool place should be selected, and one to which the fresh air can have access, for dampness will soon mould the fruit and heat cause it to ferment.

Jams and marmalades are similar in their character, and are prepared from the pulp of the fruits, and sometimes the proteins of the rinds, by boiling them with sugar. The chief difference between the marmalade and the jam is that the former is made from the firmer fruits, while the latter is prepared from that which is more juicy, such as the strawberry, raspberry, currant, etc.

A very important thing in the preserving of fruits in syrup is to have the latter of proper strength. Sugar, we know, ferments readily, but only when dissolved in a sufficient quantity of water. When the quantity is just sufficient to render it a strong syrup it will not ferment at all. The right degree of strength for the preserving of fruits, so that there may be neither fermentation nor crystallization, may be obtained by dissolving double refined sugar in water in the proportion of two parts of sugar to one of water, and boiling it a little. The degree thus obtained, which is the proper one for the preserving of fruits, is technically known as smooth. In preserving fruits whole it is necessary that this syrup should penetrate every portion of it, therefore, to aid this, the fruit should be blanched before it is boiled in the syrup.

Fruit jellies are made by so combining the juices of fruits with sugar by boiling that the product, when cold, becomes a quivering, translucent mass, the consistency of which is neither that of a solid or liquid. The jelly must be gratifying to the eye as well as the palate.

The Successful Housekeeper, 1885

THE HOME IN 1890

The home in this period was comfortably warm in the winter because of the use of wood- and coal-burning stoves.

Getting water from the well

The sewing machine—1890's

A typical parlor had a marble-top table, an organ in the corner, and an array of treasures on the mantle. It was a gay room for the holidays and guests, and a somber one in times of illness and death. It was also used as a visiting room for the minister.

The kitchen was the housewife's special room. The huge stove was there, with something always in the oven sending out an aroma.

The pantry had all sorts of round wooden boxes of spices, pails of lard, colorful boxes of oatmeal, red tins of coffee and tea, as well as all types of boxes, tins, and crocks for cookies.

Food was plentiful, either fresh from one's own garden and yard or else just delivered to one's back door from the local farm.

The pace was slower than today's in spite of all the work the housewife had to do; she seemed to enjoy her work, her house, and her family.

MENUS FOR SUMMER EATING

JULY

MONDAY. *Breakfast*—Griddle cakes, broiled ham, tomato omelette, radishes. *Dinner*—Baked lamb, green pease, baked potatoes, squash, rice custard, berries with cream. *Supper*—Biscuit, cold lamb sliced, cake, ripe currants with cream.

TUESDAY. *Breakfast*—Rice muffins, hash on toast, tomatoes. *Dinner*—Economical soup, stuffed fillet of veal, green pease, mashed potatoes, beet salad, blackberry pudding with sauce, cake. *Supper*—Buttered toast, cold sliced meat, blackberries with cream.

WEDNESDAY. *Breakfast*—Rolls, vegetable hash, broiled beefsteak, cottage cheese. *Dinner*—Mock (or real) turtle soup, baked heart, baked potatoes, stewed beans, chocolate pudding, cocoanut cake. *Supper*—Cold rolls, sliced heart, cottage puffs, berries.

THURSDAY. *Breakfast*—Cream toast, fried liver, dropped eggs, fricasseed potatoes. *Dinner*—Clam pie, boiled ham, mashed potatoes, string beans, lettuce, blackberry pie. *Supper*—Plain bread, dried beef frizzled, rice batter cakes with sugar, cake and berries.

FRIDAY. *Breakfast*—Muffins, broiled beefsteak, fried potatoes. *Dinner*—Soup, fish, fresh or canned, whole potatoes, pease, squash, lettuce, chocolate cream. *Supper*—Toasted muffins, cold pressed meat, corn meal mush with cream, cake and fruit.

SATURDAY. *Breakfast*—Plain bread, veal sweetbreads, fried mush, boiled eggs. *Dinner*—Boiled ham with potatoes, cabbage, string beans, warm gingerbread, pie. *Supper*—Dry toast, cold ham shaved, rusk, blackberries and cream.

SUNDAY. *Breakfast*—Vienna rolls, fried chicken with cream gravy, fried tomatoes, cottage cheese. *Dinner*—Barley soup, roast of beef with potatoes, stewed tomatoes, cucumber, wilted lettuce, charlotte russe. *Supper*—Cold rolls, sliced beef, blackberries, cake.

AUGUST

MONDAY. *Breakfast*—Dropped eggs on toast, roast beef warmed up with gravy, tomato omelette. *Dinner*—Baked lamb, creamed cabbage, stewed tomatoes, cream pudding. *Supper*—Buns, cold lamb sliced, preserve puffs, apple sauce.

TUESDAY. *Breakfast*—Plain bread, hash, stewed tomatoes. *Dinner*—Corn soup, beef *a la mode,* boiled potatoes, green corn pudding, sliced tomatoes, tapioca cream. *Supper*—Milk toast, cold pressed meat, chocolate custard.

WEDNESDAY. *Breakfast*—French rolls, broiled beefsteak, baked potatoes, cottage cheese. *Dinner*—Soup with chicken, celery, mashed potatoes, stewed beans, sliced cucumbers and onions, watermelon. *Supper*—Cold rolls, chicken salad, apple sauce, schmier kase.

THURSDAY. *Breakfast*—Cream toast, fried liver, potato cakes, stewed tomatoes. *Dinner*—Roast leg of mutton with potatoes, green corn, tomatoes, musk melon. *Supper*—Plain bread, dried beef with gravy, boiled rice with cream, berries.

FRIDAY. *Breakfast*—Rice cakes, waffles, mutton stew, fried potatoes. *Dinner*—Meat pie, young corn, boiled cauliflower, grapes, plain cake. *Supper*—Toast, cold pressed meat, Graham mush with cream, cake and berries.

SATURDAY. *Breakfast*—Bread, broiled bacon, Graham mush fried, boiled eggs. *Dinner*—Soup, boiled ham with potatoes, cabbage, string beans, lemon pie. *Supper*—Light biscuit, cold ham shaved, cake and peaches.

SUNDAY. *Breakfast*—Nutmeg melons, fried chicken with cream gravy, fried tomatoes, cottage cheese, fritters. *Dinner*—Soup, roast loin of veal, mashed potatoes, creamed cabbage, tomatoes, tapioca pudding, watermelon. *Supper*—Cold rolls, sliced veal, cake and fruit.

SEPTEMBER

MONDAY. *Breakfast*—Graham bread, rolls, fried liver, fried tomatoes. *Dinner*—Soup, roast beef, potatoes, green corn, fried egg plant, salad, watermelon. *Supper*—Toasted biscuit, cheese, cold beef, fruit.

TUESDAY. *Breakfast*—Buttered toast, hash, green corn, fried oysters. *Dinner*—Meat pie, potatoes, young turnips, stewed onions, pickled beets, apple dumplings with cream sauce, peach pie. *Supper*—Canned salmon, cold roast beef, biscuit and jam, cake.

WEDNESDAY. *Breakfast*—Hot muffins, broiled chicken, cucumbers. *Dinner*—Roast mutton, baked sweet potatoes, green corn, apple sauce, slaw, bread pudding with sauce. *Supper*—Toasted bread, sliced mutton, baked pears.

THURSDAY. *Breakfast*—Corn gems, rolls, stew of mutton, tomatoes. *Dinner*—Chicken pot pie, Lima beans, baked egg plant, peach meringue, lady cake. *Supper*—Pressed chicken, omelet, biscuit, baked sweet apples.

FRIDAY. *Breakfast*—Batter cakes, veal croquettes, fried apples, potatoes. *Dinner*—Soup, boiled or baked fish with potatoes, green corn, tomato slaw, peaches and cream, cake. *Supper*—Cold tongue, light biscuit, bread and iced milk, cake and fruit.

SATURDAY. *Breakfast*—Short cake, mutton chops, potatoes. *Dinner*—Soup, boiled leg of mutton, caper sauce, potatoes, squash, pickled beets, apple meringue, cake. *Supper*—Cold meat, warm rolls, grapes, cake.

SUNDAY. *Breakfast*—Rolls, breakfast stew, potatoes, stewed okra. *Dinner*—Broiled chicken, sweet potatoes, boiled cauliflower, plum sauce, cabbage salad, ice-cream, cake. *Supper*—Sliced veal, biscuit, floating island, baked pears.

Queen of the Household, 1906

FOURTH OF JULY COLLATION

Let the centre of the table be ornamented by a pyramid of evergreens or laurel, which may be made thus: make a stand or frame not less than three feet high, make a long wreath of the richest laurel or evergreens, and beginning at the top, wind it around the frame until the bottom is reached; at the summit, let there be a miniature

Early photography

flag of our country, or a small bust or statue of Washington, and at regular distances downward, small silk flags with the coat of arms and mottoes of each several State in the Union; or instead of the flags, take as many streamers of different shades of colored ribbons as there are States, or stars cut from gold or silver paper. The flags may be painted by ladies whose national feelings and talents inspire them to the work.—A cold boiled ham and cold roasted poultry may be placed on one end of the table, or at the middle of one side, and lobster and chicken salads at the sides or end, with bread and butter sandwiches and crackers and soda biscuits; such pastry, jelly tarts, jellies, floating island or blancmange and baskets of cut cake and maccaroons, as may be desired, may be distributed around the table; and syrup water and lemonade, with a fine bowl of temperance beverage and bottled soda, which will generally leave a more clear recollection, than wines, cordials, and champagne.

American Lady's System of Cookery, 1850

WARM WEATHER DINNER

Chicken soup, creamed sweetbreads, salmon loaf with frozen horseradish sauce, potatoes, boiled green peas, asparagus salad in lemon rings, vanilla ice cream in cantaloupe cases, oatmeal snaps.

What to Have for Dinner, Fannie Farmer, 1905

ITEMS OF ADVICE

If you keep an account of your stores, and the dates when they are bought, you can know exactly how fast they are used, and when they are wasted, or stolen.

Grate up dry cheese, and cheese crusts, moisten it with wine or brandy, and keep it in a jar for use. It is better than at first.

When you clean house, begin with the highest rooms, first, so that clean rooms be not soiled when done.

Repair house linen, turn sheets, and wash bedclothes in summer.

Buy your wood in August or September, when it usually is cheapest and plenty.

In cities, nothing is more pernicious to a housekeeper's health, than going up and down stairs, and a woman who has good taste and good sense, will not, for the sake of *show* keep two parlors on the ground floor and her nursery above and kitchen below. One of these parlors will be taken for her nursery and bedroom, even should all her acquaintance wonder how it can be, that a wife and mother should think her health and duties of more importance than two dark parlors shut up for company.

Do not begin housekeeping in the style in which you should end it, but begin on a plain and small scale, and increase your expenditures as your experience and means are increased.

Be determined to live within your income, and in such a style that you can secure time to improve your own mind, and impart some of your own advantages to others.

Eating too fast is unhealthful, because the food is not properly masticated, or mixed with the saliva, nor the stomach sufficient time to perform its office on the last portion swallowed before another enters.

Beef and mutton are improved by keeping as long as they remain sweet. If meat begins to taint, wash it and rub it with powdered charcoal and it removes the taint. Sometimes rubbing with salt will cure it.

A thick skin shows that the pork is old, and that it requires more time to boil.

It is best to fry in lard not salted, and this is better than butter. Mutton and beef suet are good for frying. When the lard seems hot, try it by throwing in a bit of bread. When taking up fried articles, drain off the fat on a wire sieve.

The best method of greasing a griddle is, to take a bit of salt pork, and rub over with a fork. This prevents adhesion, and yet does not allow the fat to soak into what is to be cooked.

The art of keeping a good table, consists, not in loading on a variety at each meal, but rather in securing a successive variety, a table neatly and tastefully set, and everything that is on it, cooked in the best manner.

Miss Beecher's Domestic Receipt Book, 1846

Autumn

OCTOBER, NOVEMBER, DECEMBER

EARLY DAYS IN VIRGINIA

When the little band of colonists landed on the banks of the James in 1607, their first thought was to protect themselves from what Captain John Smith called the "salvages." Within a month they had built a triangular enclosure of sturdy eight-foot poles, with half-moon-shaped bulwarks at each corner in which they mounted their four or five pieces of artillery. Without John Smith it is doubtful whether there would have been any settlement established in Virginia. He writes that four months after landing "we had no houses to cover us, Our Tents were rotten, and our cabins worse than nought."

The dampness of the Virginia climate was not for the houses of flimsy materials that had first been raised. For this reason, in 1611, Sir Thomas Dale built the new town of Henrico, near what is now Richmond, where he had kilns set up; thus the foundations and first-floor walls of some of the houses were built of brick.

Plenty of bricks were made, so that the authorities in January 1639 arbitrarily instructed Governor Wyatt "to require every land owner whose plantation was five hundred acres in extent (and proportionally for larger or lesser grants) to erect a dwelling house of brick, to be twenty-four feet in length, and fifteen feet in breadth, with a cellar attached." However, few heeded this law, so that there are few or no houses of wood still standing that were built in that period.

Tobacco was the main crop, and the planters became more and more affluent. As they did so the houses grew, but they still resembled the more modest English manor houses of Tudor days. The building formed a rectangle from twenty to forty feet in length on the long side, from fifteen to thirty on the short. At each end of the house was a big outside chimney of stone or logs-and-clay. The front door was in the middle of the long side, opening on a hall, or "Great Room," where the family lived and ate. The house was commonly of the two-story and dormer type, with about six rooms. The partitions were covered with a thick layer of dried mud, which had been "daubed and white limed, glazed and flowered." The steep-pitched roof was covered with cypress shingles and had attractive long dormer windows with sharp-peaked gables. Windows were glazed, with small panes set in lead, and were sometimes protected by shutters "which are made very pretty and convenient."

When his tobacco brought him a profit, the planter ordered many of his necessities and all of his luxuries from England, and only when it didn't arrive would he consent to take an interest in having things made at home. Often in debt, and often unable to afford travel, he found his chief distraction was his ungrudging hospitality to visitors.

At first there would be a long table for eating purposes in the Great Room, but it was little more than a few boards laid across trestles. Only the master of the house, or perhaps a distinguished guest, was entitled to use a chair, which was a heavy, impressive affair of paneled oak, with a solid wooden seat. Stools, and forms, as benches were then called, were the seats of everyday life.

By the late 1700's, a certain amount of comfort had begun to creep in. Besides the dining table there were small tables, some of which were known as "flap tables" since they had flaps, or leaves, which could be let down when the table was not in use.

SETTING THE TABLE IN THE EARLY SOUTH: 1700'S

In the early part of the century, the dining table boasted almost no china and no more than a tankard or two of silver. There were wooden trenchers, however, and the plates and dishes were made of pewter. Spoons, bowls, jugs, sugar pots, castors, and porringers were also made of pewter, as were the cups, flagons, tankards, and beakers. A pewterer at this time was a very important person. Wooden and pewter spoons were in common use, but knives and forks were rarely used.

In the latter part of the century, the wealthier planters bought more and more silver, not only because they liked it, but also because it was considered a safe investment. Forks and table knives were now in use. Spoons, dishes, plates, "hand wash bowls," tankards, candlesticks, and candle snuffers were all made of silver, and were often engraved with the arms of the owner.

The tablecloth for everyday use was of Holland linen, and, for special occasions, of damask. Napkins, often of excellent quality and beautifully embroidered, were plentiful. In fact, good linen was the pride of the Southern housewife.

FOOD IN THE EARLY SOUTH

"Virginia doth afford many excellent vegitables and living Creatures," wrote Captain Smith, and he sent home a coop of turkeys to prove it—the first ever seen

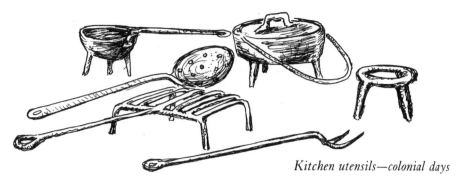

Kitchen utensils—colonial days

in England. And before him, Sir Walter Raleigh had declared the soil of the colonies to be "the most plentifull, sweete, fruitful, and wholesome of the world."

The waters also yielded food, and George Percy, Smith's companion, said of oysters: "I have seen some thirteen inches long," and continued, "The salvages used to boile oysters and mussels together and with the broath they make a good spoone meal, thickened with the flower of their wheat; and it is a great thrift and husbandry with them to hang oysters upon great strings, being shauled [shelled] and dried in the smoake, thereby to preserve them all the year."

Despite all this abundance, the following winter starvation set in, and many died before the ships came with provisions in the spring.

However, since the forest teemed with bear, deer, wild turkey, quail, pheasant, and partridge, and the marshes and bays were cloudy with canvasbacks, mallards, and redheads, the planters soon were no longer starving. They had plenty of fish and shellfish, as well as hogs that rooted in the woods. They learned how to plant corn for flour and to use Indian recipes.

Chickens are believed to have been introduced into the colonies at Jamestown about 1607, and by 1700 were so plentiful that they no longer were listed as valuable property.

THE SOUTH, 1765

Since tobacco growing required plenty of land, the planter's house was a long way from that of his neighbor and soon grew into a little village in itself. Some of the houses were extremely beautiful, with lawns, big trees, and gardens. The interior was a profusion of richly carved woodwork, with great stairways and beautiful furniture.

Since the climate was warm and there was plenty of help to carry the cooked food to the dining room, the kitchen became a little, separate house. Also near the "great house" would be a large dairy and a laundry. There were stables for the horses, pens and barns for the pigs and cattle, granaries for corn, and storehouses for tobacco.

With all the mouths to feed, the smokehouse had brick ovens for curing hams and bacon. There were no villages, so that each plantation had a blacksmith shop, a carpenter's shop, houses for spinning and weaving flax and hemp and for tanning leather for shoes. A malt house would complete the ensemble. The white indentured servants had cottages of their own, while the slaves had a little cluster of rudely built cabins.

DINING IN THE SOUTH, 1765

The napkins of the eighteenth century were nearly as big as a modern card-table cover and were customarily tied around the diner's neck to protect frills and furbelows. Forks appeared around the turn of the century, steel ones, with bone handles and only two tines. Their only purpose was to hold the meat down to be cut; to carry food to the mouth on a fork would have been bad manners. But that didn't last, and by 1750, finger-eating had become a taboo among the best people. Silver forks appeared then; they had three tines and were much smaller than a modern dinner fork. With silver forks came dinner knives. They had "pistol" handles, ending in a scroll. There were silver spoons, too, made with tapering "rat tails" on the backs of the bowls.

The big standing salt went out of fashion and the empty place in the center of the table was now filled with an elaborate silver epergne if one could afford it. It was ornamental and consisted of a central dish on a high stand, surrounded by three or four smaller dishes supported on arms attached to the pedestal. Fruit, flowers, or sweetmeats were put into the dishes. Silver candelabra were put on the table when needed, otherwise they stayed on the sideboard.

A few people began to use china plates for eating. These were imported from England and as rule were plain white "salt glaze" stuff, the glaze being produced by throwing pulverized salt into the kiln at a judicious moment.

In some of the plantation homes there was a separate dining room for the children, so that meals could be enjoyed in peace by adults and children alike. Dining was a fine art in Virginia, and the planters took great pride in setting their tables with more food than anyone could eat. Fruits and vegetables of every kind appeared on the table at a single meal, along with several different meats.

The colonists drank Sack Posset, which was made of sherry, ale, eggs, and milk dusted with nutmeg, and Syllabub, a frothy mixture of whipped cream and white wines. Then bourbon came into the picture, distilled from a corn mash, and the making of a mint julep became a ritual. One Virginia recipe called for cognac, Jamaica rum, port wine, and shaved ice, the drink topped by bruised mint leaves but no bourbon. In Kentucky, only bourbon was used for juleps.

Diamond-back terrapin was so plentiful in the early days that the kitchen help complained of having too much of it. Plentiful, too, were the shellfish, venison, bear steaks, and great hams.

In cool spring houses, cream, butter, and vegetables were kept chilled and fresh over the cold streams. Cellars were stocked with jars and crocks holding preserves, jams, and jellies of wild berries, peaches and pears. Cabbages, okra, carrots, kohlrabies, yams, and onions were packed in loose earth in the cellars throughout the winter.

Game, pork, and sausages hung over hickory smoke for weeks in stone houses built for that purpose. Game, pheasant, venison, beef, and muttons were seasoned by hanging in a dry place to age.

Lard and chicken fat and sweet country-churned butter were used lavishly in cooking.

They ate well in Virginia.

FOOD AND COOKING IN CHARLESTON

The records of early visitors to the province frequently refer to food. William Bartram, eighteenth-century botanist, told of the wild pigeons and of slaves hunting them by torchlight in the swampy section of southeastern Carolina. John F.D. Smyth, an English traveler, wrote of the wealthy widows of Edisto Island and suggested that the demise of their husbands was due partially to the rich food and drink in which they indulged.

Crabs and shrimp as well as oysters were abundant in the inlets and creeks of the Carolina coast, leading to a great variety of shrimp and crab dishes. "She-crabs" were preferred to "he-crabs" for soup because the eggs of the female added a special flavor. To make soup with "he-crabs," the cook crumbled hard-boiled egg yolk to simulate the eggs of the female. This was probably one of the rich soups that John F.D. Smyth wrote about.

Shrimp was eaten in all forms, including a paste made of ground shrimp with butter seasonings which was served at the breakfast table. The paste was so popular that it was eaten cold practically every day with hot buttered grits. Shrimp was also served sautéed in butter, and this was another popular breakfast dish.

Charleston used rice as a base for many of its dishes, such as purleaus (pilaus) of all kinds, hop-in-John (rice and peas), red rice, and rice wine. Many breads were made from rice flour.

Shrimp and rice croquettes were the Southern counterpart of New England codfish balls. There were other shrimp and rice dishes.

The African slaves introduced the planters to some exotic foods. The sesame seed was introduced into America by the Negro slaves in the late 1600's. In the South, sesame seeds are called benne seeds, and the Charlestonians used benne seeds to make cookies and a sort of benne brittle.

Calapash was a very common dish. It is turtle cooked in the shell. Many Charleston homes kept turtles in small "cooter" ponds covered with wire. The native yellow-bellied terrapin and the famous sea turtle were common dishes.

Some of the other local foods were: Pompey's head, tipsy pudding, jambalaya, panygetta, bogs, espetanga, corn bread, okra daube, ratifia pudding, and almond florentine.

Many forms of corn bread and corn dishes were part of the regular daily fare. Awenda was a hot bread made with hominy grits, corn meal, milk, eggs, and butter —no flour. It was of custard consistency. Carolina egg bread was a spoon bread made with many eggs separated and the white beaten to a stiff froth before being added to the batter. This caused the bread to rise high and puffy like a soufflé. It had to be eaten quickly, lest it fall.

CREOLE CUISINE

Creole cuisine, found in New Orleans, was a combination of the French and Spanish influence—the Spanish taste for strong seasoning of food combined with the French love for delicacies. The slaves of Louisiana had their share in refining the product, and likewise the Indians, who gathered roots and pungent herbs in the woods. No Creole kitchen was complete unless it had its iron pots, bay leaf, thyme, garlic, and cayenne pepper.

Louisianians had valuable natural resources which were a great asset in the preparation of food: partridge, snipe, quail, ducks, and rabbits; fresh- and salt-water fish of every description; numerous fruits, the outstanding being oranges and figs; many nuts, the most delicate being the pecan.

Creole menus could be very elaborate, with five to six courses. On occasion they were enriched by imported continental delicacies such as anchovies and brandied fruits. Creoles also imported, and drank, enormous quantities of wines which they bought in barrels at auction. Meals often included soups and stews composed of leftovers, for the Creole housewife threw nothing in the least edible away.

The Choctaw Indians were very friendly with the white men, and to them New Orleans is indebted for the filé, which is used in one of the best known Creole dishes—gumbo. The filé is made from dried sassafras leaves pounded to a powder. Gumbos of meats, poultry, or seafood were filling dishes and stretched a long way when unexpected guests were present.

The Mississippi River, Lake Ponchartrain, the Gulf of Mexico, the Mississippi Sound, and other nearby waterways furnished seafood of all flavors and varieties. Sheepshead, pompano, flounder, bluefish, silver and speckled trout as well as green trout and sacalit were taken from these waters. The protected bayous, coves, and small bays also furnished an inexhaustible supply of oysters as well as several varieties of shrimp and crab.

Madeline Hachard, the Ursuline nun, told of the magnificence of the fare that she found in 1727: "Buffalo, wild geese, deer, turkeys, rabbits, chickens, pheasant, partridge, quail; monstrous fish which I never knew in France" as well as other shellfish, and an array of fruits and vegetables, figs, watermelons, pecans, pumpkins. She also told how all drank chocolate and coffee with warm milk. Once she observed that though wild ducks were cheap and plentiful, "we scarcely buy any; we do not wish to pamper ourselves."

Removing the chaff from the wheat

THE FALL SEASON

In the fall of the year there were many jobs to be done. There was canning and food to be stored away for the coming cold weather. Apples were picked and either dried, stored away, or made into apple cider or apple butter. The housewife must dry the corn and get the potatoes, carrots, and beets into the root cellar.

The hogs were slaughtered and the sides of meat were smoked, pickled, and made into sausages and head cheese.

Because there were so few places to go, womenfolk would look forward from one fall to another to the fair. Like summer picnics, that and church were about all the recreation one had in the nineteenth century. Housewives would work the year through saving their money and building up their wardrobes for the County Fair. Exhibits were prepared for the various competitions and happy was the housewife who won a ribbon for it.

Finally, there was Thanksgiving and all its preparations, and then getting ready for Christmas.

AUTUMN FOOD

In the autumn, things had to be prepared for the winter. Fruits and berries were preserved in huge crocks or boiled into rich, spicy jams and marmalades. Apples were dried and strung up to be used the entire winter, while vast barrels of applesauce and apple butter were prepared. Meat and fish were salted down or smoked and packed into barrels. Cheese was pressed into flat wheels. Also, fancy pickles and relishes were made from such plants as nasturtium buds, green walnuts, barberries, marigolds, roses, violets, and peonies.

LIFE OF THE PLANTER'S WIFE

The mistress of a great house had to know every aspect of housekeeping. The training of servants required practical knowledge and skill. Few servants could read or write, and despite their vagaries cookbooks were a help in preparing very special dishes or some special fancy pudding. To teach the servant, the mistress had to be capable herself of making the dish.

Many housewives kept their own cookbooks and account books in order to have a smoothly run household.

Certain ingredients including sugar were expensive luxuries; to make preserves and jams over the open hearth meant lavish use of sugar, as they were made on a pound-to-pound basis. To prevent burning, scorching, or waste, the mistress of the household either made these luxuries herself or closely supervised the process.

The housewife also had to teach her daughters all domestic arts including the art

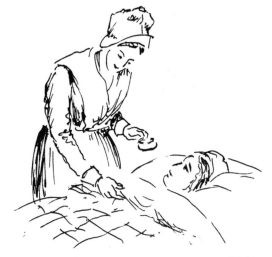

Taking care of the sick

of cookery and fine needlework against the time that they, too, would be running a large household.

There is an account of a day in the life of one of these wives which reads: "I would recall to you the picture of which I have often attempted to describe . . . . Of Aunt Helen, who was up by sunrise every day, making the rounds of the kitchen, the smokehouse, the dairy, the weaving room, and the garden, with a basket of keys on one arm, and of knitting on the other; whose busy fingers never stopped; and who, as the needles flew, would attend to every one of the domestic duties and give all the orders for the day, only returning to the house in time to preside at a bountiful breakfast table, then resuming her rounds to visit the sick, to give out work to the spinners and weavers, and those engaged in making clothes for the hands; prescribing for all the usual ailments of the young and old in the absence of the doctor, caring for her flowers, and then sitting down to her books and her music . . ."

Pounding the corn

CORN

The abundance, adaptability, and nourishing qualities of corn not only saved the colonists' lives, but altered many of their methods of living, especially their manner of cooking and their tastes in food.

If it had not been for the Indian corn, the history of the New England colonies might have read differently. The corn supplied what little food was available in the first winter, along with the fish from the sea, birds from the air, and wild animals. This corn had been buried with the Indian dead for their journey into other worlds.

Until Governor Bradford decided that "they should set corne every man for his owne particuler, furnishing a portion for public officers, fishermen, etc., who could not work, and in that regard trust to themselves," corn growing was unsuccessful.

In Virginia, the early settlers starved before all were convinced that corn was a better crop for settlers than silk or any of the many hoped-for products which might be valuable in one sense, but which could not be eaten.

Powhatan, the father of the Indian princess Pocahontas, was one of the first to "send some of his People that they may teach the English how to sow the Grain of his Country." Captain John Smith planted forty acres of corn. A succeeding governor of Virginia, Sir Thomas Dale, assigned small farms to each colonist and encouraged and enforced the growing of corn.

The Indians taught the colonists much more than the planting and raising of corn; they showed how to grind the corn and cook it in many palatable ways. The various foods which we use today made from Indian corn are all cooked just as the Indians cooked them at the time of the settlement of the country; and they are still called with Indian names, such as hominy, pone, suppawn, samp, and succotash.

HUSKING CORN: *Diary of An Early American Housewife*

October 8, 1772—John Lake is having a corn husking tomorrow. All the young people of the neighborhood should be there. I expect to have my new pink calico dress finished before the day is over so that I can wear it to the husking.

A CORN HUSKING

Indian corn matured much later than the small grains. But by late autumn, after a frost or two, the ears hung heavy and brown on the dry stalks. They were then pulled and taken to the corncribs, where they were stored in the husks. Later in the season, when the more pressing work was over, corn shuckings would take place in the evenings. Cider or persimmon beer and cakes and cookies would be provided and everybody would turn out to help shuck corn and enjoy the frolic.

A moonlight night in November was a favorite time. A great pile of unshucked corn would be stacked on the ground at some convenient place and a bonfire would be lighted at a safe distance. Then the huskers would set to work. Most of the corn was yellow or white, but an occasional red ear would turn up, a sign of good luck to the shucker who found it.

Boys and girls liked corn shuckings, which gave them a chance to have a party—and perhaps evade the curious eyes of their elders as they sought out the shadows out of sight of the bonfires.

PIES

Pies were a big item of food for the early settlers. It is hard to state when pies first appeared, but they must have been made when more thought could be given to the variety of food than in those first, more difficult days. The meat pie came first, used as a main dish, and the making of mince pies followed. At first, when meat from the farm animals was not obtainable, bear meat was a good substitute. Added to this were syrups and meat juices for liquids, dried fruit, and nuts, the whole seasoned highly with spices.

Pies made from fruits, squash, and pumpkins came in due time, and soon the pantry boasted of a continual row of pies. At Thanksgiving time many more pies were made than were to be used, and these were put away to "freeze" for the meals to come. They were called frozen pies and were stacked one on the other in the larder; sometimes there were as many as fifty.

A pie peel was a kitchen necessity in the days of brick ovens, to hold the pies as they were slid in or taken out. The pie peel had a short handle, whereas the bread peel had a long one.

THE FARMER'S WIFE

Some courteous angel guide my pen,
    While I describe a farmer's wife.
In her the poor do find a friend,
    To guide them through this life;
Before the king of day doth rise,
    To journey round the earth,
Before the stars fade from the skies,
    She quits her downy berth.
Then with a joyful, lovely song,
    She to her daily labor goes,
She never joins the idle throng,
    That seek their own repose.
Her mind is strong, and noble too,
    She judges all things right;
She hath her friends, a chosen few,
    And is to all polite;
She seeks not to adorn with gold,
    But looks upon the mind;
There nobler beauties doth behold,
    Than she in gold can find.

Farmer's Almanack, 1844, Robert B. Thomas

TO KEEP WEEVILS OUT OF WHEAT

Put the wheat in barrels, smooth it, and sprinkle a layer of salt over the top. Keep the barrels well covered by tying cloths over them. A sure preventive.

Housekeeping in Old Virginia, 1879

Reaping the harvest

HOW TO COOK WATER

I must tell you the old story of how the late Charles Delmonico used to talk about the hot water cure. He said the Delmonicos were the first to recommend it to the guests who complained of having no appetite. "Take a cup of hot water and lemon and you will feel better," was the formula adopted, and the cup of hot water and lemon in it take away the insipidity. For this anti-bilious remedy the caterers charged the price of a drink of their best liquors—twenty-five cents or more—and it certainly was a wiser way to spend small change than in alcohol.

"Few people know how to cook water," Charles used to affirm. "The secret is in putting good fresh water into a neat kettle, already quite warm, and setting the water to boiling quickly, and then taking it right off for use in tea, coffee or other drinks, before it is spoiled. To let it steam and simmer and evaporate until the good water is all in the atmosphere, and the lime and iron and dregs only left in the kettle—bah! That is what makes a great many people sick, and is worse than no water at all." Every lady who reads this valuable recipe of a great and careful cook should never forget how to cook water.

Household, 1871

ABOUT VIRGINIA WOMEN

"The Women are not (as reported) put into the ground to work, but occupie such domestique imployments and housewifery as in England, that is dressing victuals, righting up the house, milking, imployed about dayries, washing, sowing, etc., and both men and women have times of recreations, as much or more than in any part of the world, besides, yet some wenches that are nasty, beastly, and not fit to be imployed are put into the ground, for reason tell us, they must not at charge be transported, and then maintained for nothing."

John Hammond, 1656

ANNE FOSTER'S PARTY: *A Letter from Ruth*

Dear Hannah:

There were good friends of ours in England who believed that we had come into a wilderness where was to be found naught save savages and furious beasts, and it would have surprised them greatly, I believe, if they could have known how much of entertainment could already be found.

It was while we were waiting in Charlestown for our new home to be built, that Anne Foster, whose father is one of the tithing-men, invited all of us young girls to spend an evening with her, and we had much pleasure in playing both the whistle and thread the needle.

Anne was dressed in a yellow coat with black bib and apron, and she had black feathers on her head. She wore both garnet and jet beads, with a bracelet, and no less than four rings. There was a black collar around her neck, black mitts on her hands, and a striped tucker and ruffles. Her shoes were of silk, and one would have said that she was dressed for some evening entertainment in London.

Neither Sarah nor I wore our best, because of the candles here being made from a kind of tallow stewed out of bayberry plums, which give forth much smoke, and mother was afraid that it would soil our clothing. We were also told that because of there not being candles enough, some parts of the house would be lighted with candle-wood, which last is taken from the pitch of the pine tree, and fastened to the walls with nails. This wood gives forth a fairly good light; but there drops from it so much of a black, greasy substance, that whosoever by accident should stand beneath these flames would be in danger of receiving a most disagreeable shower.

This entertainment was not the only one which made for our pleasure while we remained in Charlestown. However, it seemed almost a sin for us to be thus light-hearted while so many were in dire distress.

Ruth

APPLES

Apples supplied the table in many ways. There were pies made from dried sliced apples, the apple butter and applesauce, as well as many barrels of cider for drinking, and the vinegar for cooking. To pare three hundred bushels of apples was a common occurrence, and this need brought about the apple-paring bees, which usually turned into occasions of festivity.

The first paring machines show great ingenuity. Wooden parers were used for many years until the patented machines of iron took their place. Those of iron eventually cored as well as pared.

After the apples were pared, there were two different ways of cutting them for dried apples. One way was to quarter them, remove the core, and then string them on a heavy thread two yards long with a big needle. Such strings were draped over tacks or hooks to dry. The other way was to core the apple and then slice it. These slices were placed on apple driers. When one half was dried, the other half was turned outside. A bushel of apples made seven pounds of dried apples, and these not only supplied the family but were often taken to town and exchanged for necessary commodities.

An old rule for apple butter reads: "10 gallons sweet cider, 3 pecks of cored and quartered apples—do a few at a time—cook slowly. Add 10 pounds of sugar, 5 ounces of cinnamon. Stir for 5 or 6 hours with a wooden paddle." Often, pumpkins were substituted for apples.

Applesauce was flavored with molasses, apple-molasses, maple sugar molasses, or cider.

Cider was the standard drink of all the early colonies, and inheriting barrels of cider in wills was as common as inheriting furniture or household supplies. Every family made its own cider, as apples were plentiful. Cider was used at the table and

The apple barrel

also taken to the fields in kegs, for water was not used much as a drink, perhaps because of the poor sanitation.

An old-time description of the old hand method of making cider was: Apple pomace was laid on a wooden slatted rack with layers of straw as a binder in between the layers of pomace. This was called a "cheese" when all set up. As the wooden screw pressed down on the "cheese" the juice was forced out while at the same time the pomace was squeezed out of the mass at the sides. This was cut down with a knife called a "cutting down" knife, having a long thin blade in an inverted position, on a short handle. The pomace was placed back on the top of the mass and another pressing took place. This was done two or three times, according to the amount of juice left in the pomace. The cider trickled out into buckets below the rack and the buckets were emptied into barrels. A bucket funnel was used, the size of an ordinary bucket, with a wooden funnel. This hand press produced about 2 gallons of cider to a bushel of apples.

After the cider was poured into barrels, the head was sealed. Near the bottom of the barrel was a bunghole, and in the early days this was sealed with a cluster of straw. This made a stopper and the straw was so deftly twisted that it was not only air-tight but moisture-tight and kept out all insects.

Vinegar was made from the inferior apple. Thus an orchard of apples provided raw fruit, apple butter, applesauce, cider for drinking, and vinegar for cooking and preserving.

THE CIDER PRESS

Almost every Northern farm had one or more apple trees, and many farmers either owned or borrowed a press with which to make cider for home consumption, if not for sale. The cider usually was consumed shortly after it was made, although the juice sometimes was allowed to harden until it developed an alcoholic content.

Making cider was one job that usually was not foisted off on the farm boy, as his elders preferred to do the work themselves so as to make sure that it was done right. The accidental inclusion of a rotten or wormy apple could alter the flavor of a whole batch of cider.

THE LARD KETTLE

Lard was made at butchering time, usually by the farm wife with the aid of any available male help. The process consisted of melting and rendering the fat of hogs over a hot wood fire, in a large iron kettle, usually out of doors. The kettle hung from a tripod and rested on the logs, or else was placed on a special fireplace built for that purpose.

PEDDLERS

In the days when most people lived on farms, often some miles from the nearest town, they obtained many of their everyday needs from peddlers, who brought the goods to them, instead of their having to take the time and trouble to go to town by horse and wagon or carriage, assuming they owned such equipment.

The old-time peddler transported his wares either in a trunk or knapsack that he carried on his back, in saddlebags if he rode a horse, or in a cart, wagon, or boat.

Peddlers sold almost every kind of movable commodity used by the public. They were most ingenious at condensing a maximum quantity of merchandise into a limited space, especially if they traveled on foot with their wares on their back or in a small wagon.

The foot peddler usually was obliged to confine himself to small, light items such as needles and pins, hooks and eyes, razors and razor strops, scissors, knives, etc.

Peddlers fortunate enough to have carts or wagons could handle heavier and bulkier goods ranging from Bibles, almanacs, and clocks to clothing, hardware, and housewares.

The country peddler

The peddler either was a self-employed individual or the employee of a small manufacturer, such as a maker of tinware. He obtained his stock from small producers in town, or it was taken in trade from farmers and their wives, who traded articles they made in their spare time for things they needed but could not make. Trades were more common than cash transactions.

Baking bread—1700's

BATTER BREAD

Break two eggs into a bowl. Beat to a stiff froth. Pour in one teacup of clabber or butter-milk, one of water, one of corn meal, one of flour, half teaspoonful of salt, a heaping teaspoonful of butter melted. Beat all well together. Have already heated on the stove or range, iron-clad muffin moulds (eight or ten in a group). Grease them well with a clean rag, dipped in lard. Fill each one nearly full with the batter, first sifting in half a teaspoonful of soda. Set in a hot oven and bake a nice brown. Oblong shapes are the nicest. If preferred sweet milk may be used instead of sour milk and water. In this case add another egg and dispense with the soda.

Housekeeping in Old Virginia, 1879

THE SMOKEHOUSE

The small building where carcasses of pork were cut up and smoked was called the smokehouse. It was an active place at butchering time, which was usually in early winter when the outside temperature was low.

The smokehouse sometimes could be recognized by a chimney, but often there was none because it was desirable to keep the smoke from escaping. As a result, you can still smell the hickory smoke in an old smokehouse that has not been used as such for many years.

DUKE OF CUMBERLAND'S PUDDING

Six ounces grated bread, six ounces of sultana raisins, six ounces finest beef-suet, six ounces apples, chopped fine, six ounces loaf-sugar, six eggs, a very little salt, the rind of a lemon grated; add lemon, orange, and citron-peel. Mix all well together, put it in a basin covered loosely with a floured cloth, boil it three hours and a half. Serve with wine sauce.

Peterson's Magazine, November 1866

WOMEN'S HEALTH

Women must have some light work to do if they desire to remain healthy is a truth becoming generally known, even among those who are sometimes described as "devotees of fashion." Medical men constantly prescribe this remedy for their lady patients; one eminent physician in New York frequently insists on his patients making up their own beds, and arranging their rooms in imitation of their housemaids . . . .

Peterson's Magazine, November 1866

A SIMPLE PILAU

Crack a knuckle of ham and boil for one hour in three quarts of water, adding one-half teaspoonful of mixed spices, and one large pinch of black pepper. Remove the bone and all bits of fat. Pick carefully and thoroughly; wash by rubbing between the hands through two waters a cup of best rice. Boil until the grains are nearly three times their original size. Strain through a colander until all the liquor is drained off; return to the saucepan, which place uncovered over a slow fire for ten minutes, stirring frequently with a fork. Five minutes before serving sprinkle two table-spoonfuls of cold water over the rice; cover tightly, and remove from the stove. In preparing plain rice, follow the above directions, using plain, salted water, and leaving out meat, spice and pepper.

Ladies' Home Journal, November 1892

COOKBOOKS IN VIRGINIA

The most popular English cookbooks in colonial Virginia were Mrs. Eliza Smith's *The Compleat Housewife,* as well as those by Mrs. Hannah Glasse, Mrs. Sarah Harrison, Mrs. Elizabeth Raffald, and Mrs. Martha Bradley. Several Virginians also had Robert May's *The Accomplisht Cook.*

Mrs. Smith's book was very popular in Williamsburg and sold well at the *Gazette* office, as did Mrs. Sarah Harrison's *The House-keeper's pocket-book, and Compleat Family Cook.*

Since there was an abundance and variety of food in colonial Virginia, the housewife needed but a few things from England, such as spices, oranges, lemons, raisins, and prunes, packaged sweetmeats, European wines, English beer, West Indian rum. She resorted to her English cookbooks for her menus.

The main meal was served at two or three o'clock in the afternoon, and her cookbooks dictated two courses and how the table should be set. The basic plan of the menu varied according to the number of guests, but the number of dishes in each course still had to be on the table. The table diagrams were followed carefully.

Breakfast at 8 or 9 o'clock featured a variety of hot breads and cold sliced meats or a hashed dish with a choice of milk, coffee, chocolate, or tea. Occasionally, tea was served between dinner and supper and included tea accompanied by bread and butter, hot buns or crumpets or muffins, and cake.

CHILBLAINS

Put the hands and feet once a week into hot water in which two or three handfuls of common salt have been thrown. This is a certain preventive as well as a cure.

Godey's Lady's Book and Magazine, December 1860

Cranberry-picking

CRANBERRIES

It is quite fitting that most of the cranberries which are made into sauce and eaten with turkey on Thanksgiving Day should come from New England, where the custom of serving cranberry sauce originated. The berry had existed in a wild state along New England shores long before the coming of the Pilgrims, who, because of the white blossom and stem which bore a fancied resemblance to the head and neck of a crane, called it the craneberry.

CHESTNUTTING: *Diary of An Early American Housewife*

October 23, 1772—We are going nutting in the woods tomorrow since the wind and the rain today make this the proper time. As early as July, we watched for the long plume-like blossoms, to know if the fruit were likely to be abundant. We welcome the frosts because they would open the burrs, and later in the season, the showers of wind and rain are our helpers to beat off the nuts and lay them at our feet.

PUMPION PYE

(Author's note: Pumpion is early spelling of pumpkin.)

Take a pound of Pumpion, and slice it; a handful of Thyme, a little Rosemary, sweet Marjoram stripped off the stalks, chop them small; then take Cinnamon, Nutmeg, Pepper, and a few Cloves, all beaten; also ten Eggs, and beat them all together, with as much Sugar as you shall think Sufficient. Then fry them like a pancake, and being fried, let them stand till they are cold. Then fill your Pye after this manner: Take Apples sliced thin round ways, and lay a layer of the pancake, and another of the Apples, with Currants between the layers. Be sure you put in a good amount of sweet Butter before you close it. When the Pye is baked, take six yolks of Eggs, some White-wine or verjuice, and make a caudle thereof, but not too thick; cut up the lid and put it in, and stir them well together, and so serve it up.

The Gentlewoman's Companion, 1673, Hannah Woolley

A CERTAIN CURE FOR A COMMON COLD (Indian Recipes)

Boil a common sized turnip and put it into a sauce, and pour upon it half a cup of molasses, and let it stand fifteen minutes; then turn off the syrup, at the same time squeezing the turnip so as to express its fluid. The syrup to be drank warm on going to bed.

Our Own Book of Every Day Wants, 1888

'PRACTICAL HOUSEKEEPING'

THE TASTE OF FISH may be removed very effectively from steel knives and forks by rubbing them with fresh orange or lemon peel.
TO MAKE MEATS TENDER—A spoonful of vinegar put into the water in which meats or fowls are boiled makes them tender.

Practical Housekeeping, 1883

Southern recipes were sprinkled through most American cookbooks, especially those printed in and around Philadelphia, but few cookbooks came from the pens of Southern writers. *The Virginia Housewife* by Mrs. Mary Randolph, printed in Washington, D.C., in 1824, and *The Carolina Housewife* (1847) by "A Lady of Charleston," were the most notable early examples of cookbooks that specialized in Southern foods.

The Colonial Williamsburg Foundation has in their Research Library a handwritten cookbook (c 1750). It contains medicinal recipes as well as food recipes. One of the recipes is:

LEMON BISKETTS: Take nine Eggs, the peels of two Lemmons—grated, one pound of double refin'd sugar, reserving a fourth part to Strew upon them when the pans are fill'd. Beat all two hours without intermission. Then add to it seven ounces of flower, put it in just as oven is ready. Butter & fill your pans but not full. Bake them a quarter of an Hour in a Quick Oven. Lay fine paper at the bottom of the Pans—to make 'em rise lighter.

THE CORN-SHELLER

Here was something that needed no skill but elbow grease. Shelling corn took a lot of time and energy when there were numerous young animals to be fed, and a boy's arm could get mighty tired.

The aim of the sheller was to remove the kernels of corn from the cob, making the corn easier for the cow or calf or chickens to eat.

THE CORN SHOCK

Modern mechanical means have doomed the corn shock that stood in the fields after harvest, an unmistakable sign that summer was gone and fall had arrived for sure. The corn shocks often stood there well into the winter, until hauled to the barnyard to serve as fodder for the livestock. The passing of the corn shocks heralded the end of the corn-husking bees and contests.

RECEIPT TO STOP BLEEDING, EVEN THE LARGEST BLOOD VESSELS

Take of Brandy or Common Spirits 2 oz. Castile Soap 2 drachms Potash 1 dram scrape the soap fine & dissolve in it the Brandy then add the potash mix it well together & keep it in a close phial, when you apply to let it be warmed & dip pieces of lint in & the blood will immediately congeal it operates by coagulating the blood considerable within a few applications may be necessary when the wound is deep or a limb cut off.

Handwritten book of Isabella Ashfield, 1720's

DINNER AT MOUNT VERNON

Dinner was served in three courses and on two tablecloths. One cloth was removed between each course, and the fruit, nuts and wines were served on the bare table. In the center of the table was an elegant epergne, and handsome platters containing meats and fish were symmetrically about the table—with a suitable assortment of vegetables and "corner dishes" of sauces, relishes, and preserves located at other appropriate spots. The dinner customarily concluded with toasts around the table.

HABIT

As habit can reconcile us to what is even disagreeable in itself, how much more will it enforce and improve whatever is pleasing, amiable, and praiseworthy.

The Maine Farmer's Almanac, 1849, Daniel Robinson

Philadelphia, Pa.
October 12, 1853

Dr. J.C. Ayer

My Dear Sir:
I think it but right to inform you that I have seen a most remarkable cure of Consumption by your Pectoral in this place. A beautiful young lady, nineteen years of age, was reduced to the

last stage of disease; her cough was most distressing, and the expectoration part blood, and part matter, mixed with large lumps like pieces of the lung. I used all the orthodox remedies without effect, and then had recourse to the Pectoral, which, to the indescribable joy of her family, has restored her to their arms perfectly well. It is not the custom for physicians to laud such preparation; but common justice demands this statement, and I shall always recommend the Cherry Pectoral in similar cases.

Yours respectfully,
JABEZ P. BURNET, M.D.

Ayer's American Almanac, 1861, Dr. J.C. Ayer & Co.

OMELETTE SOUP

Take half a pint of cream or milk, two ounces of flour, three eggs, and two ounces of melted butter, mix well together with cinnamon and salt; when well beaten, put a little butter or grease in the pan, and when it becomes hot and begins to smoke, put a large spoonful of the above mass into the pan, and turn it quickly, so that it runs all over the pan. When it looks brown on the lower side, and is dry on the outside, take it out and bake another in the same way, and continue to do so until the mixture is finished; when it is all baked, cut it into strips, lay the strips in the tureen, pour the bouillon over them, and serve with Parmesan cheese.

Carolina Housewife, 1847

COOKING PUMPKINS: *A Letter from Ruth*

Dear Hannah:

When the first pumpkins were ripe, Squanto showed us how to cook them, and most of us find the fruit an agreeable change from sweet puddings, parched corn, and fish.

This is the way Squanto cooked pumpkins. First he was careful to find one that was wholly ripe. In the top of the yellow globe he cut a small hole through which it was possible for him to take out the seeds, of which there are many. Then the whole pumpkin was put into the iron oven and baked until the pulp on the inside was soft, after which the shell could be broken open, and the meat of the fruit eaten with the sugar which we get from the trees.

Mistress Bradford invented the plan of mixing the baked pumpkin pulp with meal of the Indian corn, and made of the whole a queer looking bread, which some like exceeding well, but father says he is forced to shut his eyes while eating it.

Ruth

CRANBERRIES AND THEIR USES

Housekeepers should remember to cook cranberries in granite, agate-ware, or porcelain-lined dishes. They should not be allowed to stand in tin, iron or brass, the acid contained in them readily taking hold of these metals. In sweetening, it is best to use granulated sugar. There are a great variety of ways in which this fruit can be used.

CRANBERRY PIE: Line a pieplate with plain paste and fill it with uncooked cranberries; add half a cup of molasses and four table-spoonfuls of sugar, cover with an upper crust and bake thirty minutes in a hot oven.

Carrie May Ashton, *The Delineator*, November 1897

TO CHOOSE A TURKEY

If young it has a smooth black leg, with a short spur. The eyes full and bright, if fresh, and the feet supple and moist. If stale, the eyes will be sunk, and the feet dry.

The Good Housekeeper, 1839

APPLE MARMALADE

Take green fruit, sour, equal quantities of apples and sugar, cook the apples (a peck before they are cored) with a little water, and two lemons. When thoroughly cooked then sift, add sugar, boil fifteen minutes and can. This is delicious; much better than the ripe fruit, and it looks clearer, too. Common sour apples that are juicy, or crab apples, are the best for this. Try it.

Household, October 1884

APPLE CREAM

Five large apples, peeled and cored, and boiled until quite soft in a little water. Sweeten, and beat with them the whites of five eggs. Serve with cream poured around them.

The Ladies' World, October 1893

Early hand loom

WEAVING: *Diary of An Early American Housewife*

October 28, 1772 — I have been busy weaving some of the wool that we have ready. However, we are giving Daniel Worthington some of the wool to weave. He says that although he has much work from some of our neighbors, he will do ours first because we have been so kind to his family and gave them all the extra corn and apples that we did not need for our winter supply.

WEAVING

If a stranger came up to the front door of a home in the fall, he was certain to be greeted with a heavy "thwack-thwack" from within, a regular sound which would be readily recognized as coming from weaving on a hand loom. These looms were found in every house of any considerable size, usually in the ell part of the house or in the attic or shed loft used as a weaving room.

Many towns, however, had professional weavers, and they often took this chore away from the housewife, who had so many others. These weavers took in yarn and thread to weave on their looms at their own homes at so much a yard. Occasionally they worked in one's home.

Cloth that came from the loom was not ready to use until it was fulled underfoot or in fulling stocks, washed well in water, scratched and dressed with teazels, and tented. If cloth was to be dyed, it was done at this period and then allowed to shrink and dry.

WHAT AND HOW WE EAT: *A Letter from Ruth*

Dear Hannah:

And now, perhaps, you ask what we have to eat when the table is spread? Well, first, there is a pudding of Indian corn, or Turkie wheat, and this we have in the morning, at noon, and at night, save when there may be a scarcity of corn. For meats, now that our people are acquainted with the paths through the woods, we have in season plenty of deer meat, or the flesh of bears and of wild fowl, such as turkeys, ducks, and pigeons. Of course there are lobsters in abundance, and only those less thrifty people who do not put by stores sufficient for the morrow, live on such food as that.

Every Saturday we have a feast of codfish, whether alone or if there be company. It is said by some that I am pampered because my father allows me to be seated at the table with himself and my mother when they eat, instead of being obliged to stand, as do other children in the village when their elders are at meals.

Of course, we have not chairs; but the short lengths of tree trunks which father has cut to serve as stools are most comfortable even though it be impossible to do other than sit upright on them or there is danger of losing the stool. If one is careless, one can tumble backward.

Ruth

Preparing the menu

PORK APPLE PIE

Make your crust in the usual manner, spread it over a large deep plate, cut some slices of fat pork very thin, also some slices of apple; place a layer of apples, and then of pork, with a very little allspice, and pepper and sugar, between—three or four layers of each, with crust over the top. Bake one hour.

The American Economical Housekeeper and Family Receipt Book, 1845

STRIPPING GOOSE FEATHERS:
Diary of An Early American Housewife

November 2, 1772—I have enough goose feathers, so I invited some of our neighbors, the Porters, the Tates, the Mores, and several of Priscilla's friends to join us in a feather-stripping party. I promised Priscilla that I would not strip geese unless I had killed them first. I do not like the thought of goose-stripping either. It is cruel.

GOOSE–STRIPPING

Goose-stripping was cruel work. Several times a year the feathers were stripped from live birds. A stocking was pulled over the bird's head to prevent its biting. The strippers had to wear old clothes and tie covers over their hair, since the down flew everywhere.

Goose feather-stripping

"Automatic" spit

However, the more humane way to accumulate the feathers was by killing the geese first, in late summer or early fall. The geese were occasionally soaked to preserve them, but usually they were eaten as soon as they were slaughtered.

The housewife sorted the feathers carefully, separating the large feathers from the small ones. The small feathers were soft enough to be used as stuffing for feather beds. However, the large quills that had down on them were put into sacks and saved until a feather-stripping party was held some time later on in the year when it became colder. The down was then used as stuffing for soft cushions and quilts. The quills were used for pens.

All the men and women would sit at a long table in the center of the room, usually the kitchen. Open pillowcases were tacked to the edges of the table, and a man and a woman sat in front of each pillowcase. The woman would hold the basket for the discarded quills on her knees. Then each person would begin to strip down from the feathers as fast as possible. Each person held a feather by its tip with one hand and with the thumb and forefinger of the other hand stripped the soft down from the feather. Each couple raced to fill a pillowcase with down before it was time to stop work.

The young women stripped the feathers quickly, for their fingers were slender and nimble. Some of the men, however, had clumsy fingers that did not move fast. They told funny stories to make up for their slow work. Everyone laughed and talked so much that feather-stripping did not seem to be the hard, messy job it really was.

When the feathers and quills were cleared away, the workers usually ate a delicious supper of roast goose, venison, hot biscuits, and gingerbread. They drank gallons of cold sweet cider.

After the supper, the older folks usually went home, while the young people remained on to dance for many hours to the lively tunes of fiddlers. At last, the young people climbed into their sleighs and drove swiftly off into the night to the sound of sleigh bells and young laughter.

GOOSE, TO ROAST

Chop a few sage leaves and two onions very fine, mix them with a good lump of butter, a teaspoonful of pepper and two of salt, put it in the goose, then spit it, lay it down and dust it with flour; when it is thoroughly hot, baste it with nice lard; if it be a large one, it will require an hour and half, before a good clear fire; when it is enough, dredge and baste it, pull out the spit, and pour in a little boiling water.

Virginia Housewife, 1824

MAKING SPOONS OR DISHES: *A Letter from Ruth*

Clam-shell spoons

Dear Hannah:

I wish you might see how greatly I added to our store of spoons during the first year we were here in Plymouth. Sarah and I gathered from the shore clam shells that had been washed clean and white by the sea, and Squanto cut many smooth sticks, with a cleft in one end so that they might be pushed firmly on the shell, thus making a most beautiful spoon.

Sarah says that they are most to her liking, because it is not necessary to spend very much time each week polishing them, as we are forced to do with the pewter spoons.

We can use the large, flat clam shells to skim milk.

After the pumpkins had ripened, and when the gourds in the Indian village were hardened, we added to our store of bowls and cups until the kitchen was much the same as littered with them, and all formed of the pumpkin and gourd shells.

Out of the gourd shells we made what were really the most serviceable dippers, and even bottles, while in the pumpkin shell dishes we kept much of our supply of Indian corn.

Father gave me two of the most beautiful turkey wings, to be used as brushes, but they are so fine that mother has them hung on the wall as ornaments, and we sweep the hearth with smaller and less perfect wings from the birds or turkeys father also brought home.

This no doubt seems to you in Scrooby as a queer way to keep house.

Ruth

SOCIAL LIFE ON A VIRGINIA PLANTATION

Philip Fithian, a tutor for the Carter family, kept a Journal, and in one of the entries he describes a private ball that was given by Richard Lee, to which he had been invited:

Dancing the Roger de Coverly

". . . Next I was directed to the Dining Room to see young Mr. Lee; He introduced me to his Father—With them I conversed til Dinner, which came in at half after four. The Ladies dined first, when some Good Order was preserved; when they rose, each nimblest Fellow dined first—the Dinner was as elegant as could be well expected when so great an Assembly were to be kept for so long a time.—For Drink, there were several sorts of Wine, good Lemon Punch, Toddy, Cyder, Porter &c.—About Seven of the Ladies & Gentlemen began to dance in the Ball-room—first Minuets one Round; Second Giggs; third Reels; And last of all Country-Dances; tho' they struck several Marches occasionally—The music was a French-Horn and two Violins—The Ladies were Dressed Gay, and splendid, & when dancing, their Skirts & Brocades rustled and trailed behind them!— But all did not join in the Dance for there were parties in Rooms made up, some at Cards; some drinking for Pleasure. . . ."

Journal of Philip Vickers Fithian

A CHEAP AND QUICK PUDDING

Beat up four large eggs, add a pint of milk and a little salt, and stir in four large spoonfuls of flour, a little nutmeg and sugar to your taste. Beat it well and pour it into buttered teacups, filling them rather more than half full. They will bake in a stove or Dutch oven in fifteen minutes.

Confederate Receipt Book, 1863

CREOLE SOUP

¼ cup rice; ½ cup cut onion; 2 tablespoons bacon drippings; 2 cups tomatoes; 2 teaspoons salt; 1 teaspoon sugar; ⅛ teaspoon paprika; 1 tablespoon cut parsley.

Wash rice, add 3 cups boiling water and boil 30 minutes. Cook onions in pan with drippings until tender, but not brown. Add tomatoes and boil 10 minutes; rub through strainer into boiled rice and water; add seasoning and sprinkle with parsley. Add a little chopped green pepper if desired.

Royal Cook Book, Royal Baking Powder Co

Preparing a trousseau

MARRIAGE

Newlyweds, whatever their social status or the form of their wedding, began housekeeping at once; a honeymoon trip was extremely rare. Where there was money enough, the couple moved into a house built or bought for them; more commonly, they shared the home of one set of parents until they accumulated enough cash for a house of their own.

Most wives accepted their status of subordination to their husbands and with it the almost continuous pregnancies that aged them rapidly.

However, no marriage could be guaranteed as perfectly harmonious; especially with marriage at so early an age, incompatibility could develop, and often did.

One oddity of the times was that estrangement was announced in public, in the form of notices like this:

"Salem County, December 18, 1775

"I, Sarah Smith, School-mistress, the wife of William Smith, take this method to inform the public not to trust or credit the said Smith on my account, for I shall never pay any of his contractions; my living shall go no more after that rate as it did last March. . . I will not trust it that false man. I nine years have been his wife, tho' he for a widower doth pass, when he meets a suitable lass; for his wicked doings I never more can him abide, nor he never more shall lie by my side.

Sarah Smith"

MAKING CANDLES: *A Letter from Ruth*

Dear Hannah:

Squanto has shown us how we may get, at only the price of so much labor, that which looks like tallow, and of which mother has made well-shaped candles.

You must know that in this country there grows a bush which some call the tallow shrub; others claim it should be called the candleberry tree, while still others insist it is the bayberry bush.

This plant bears berries somewhat red, and speckled with white, as if you had thrown powdered clam shells on them.

I gathered near to twelve quarts last week, and mother put them in a large pot with water, which she stands over the fire, for as yet we cannot boast of an iron backbar to the fireplace, on which a heavy kettle may be hung with safety.

After these berries have been cooked a certain time, that which looks like fat is stewed out of them, and floats on the top of the water.

Mother skims it off into one of the four earthen vessels we brought from Scrooby, and when cold, it looks very much like tallow, save that it is of a greenish color. After being made into candles and burned, it gives off an odor which to some is unpleasant; but I think it very sweet to the nostrils.

I suppose you are wondering how it is we get the wicks for the candles, save at the expense and trouble of bringing them from England. Well, you must know that there is a plant which grows here plentifully, called milkweed. It has a silken down like unto silver in color, and we gather it in the late summer.

It is spun coarsely into wicks, and some of the more careful housewives dip them into

Making candles

saltpetre to insure better burning. Do you remember that poem of Master Tusser's which we learned in Scrooby?

> *Wife, make thine own candle,*
> *Spare penny to handle.*
> *Provide for thy tallow ere the frost cometh in,*
> *And make thine own candle ere winter begin.*

When·candle-making time comes, I wish there were others in this household besides me, for the work is hard and disagreeable, to say nothing of being very greasy, and I would gladly share it with sisters or brothers.

Mother's candle-rods are small willow shoots, and because of not having kitchen furniture in plenty, she hangs the half-dipped wicks across that famous wooden tub which we brought with us.

It is my task to hang six or eight of the milkweed wicks on the rod, taking good care that they shall be straight, which is not easy to accomplish, for silvery and soft though the down is when first gathered, it twists harshly, and of course, as everyone knows, there can be no bends or kinks in a properly made candle.

Mother dips perhaps eight of these wicks at a time into a pot of bayberry wax, and after they have been so treated six or eight times, they are of sufficient size, for our vegetable tallow sticks in greater mass than does that which comes from an animal.

A famous candle-maker is my mother, and I have know her to make as many as one hundred and fifty in a single day.

The candle box which was given to us is of great convenience, for since it has on the inside a hollow for each candle, there is little danger that any will be broken, and, besides, we may put therein the half-burned candles, for we cannot afford to waste even the tiniest scraps of tallow.

Ruth

WASHINGTON'S BREAKFAST

During his Southern tour in 1791, President George Washington drove up in his handsome white coach to the home of Colonel John Allen. President Washington was on his way to New Bern, North Carolina. The visit was unexpected, and when he asked whether he could have some breakfast, Mrs. Allen summoned all the help she could get and in little over an hour had a breakfast prepared which consisted of a young pig, a turkey, country ham, fried chicken, sausage, waffles, batter cakes, various styles of eggs, and hot soda biscuits.

The President sat down at the table, looked at all the food, and asked whether it would be possible to have only one hardboiled egg and a cup of coffee with a little rum in it.

BRISKET OF BEEF, BAKED

Bone a brisket of beef and make holes in it with a sharp knife about an inch apart; fill them alternately with fat bacon, parsley, and oysters, all chopped small and seasoned with pounded cloves and nutmeg, pepper, and salt; dredge it well with flour, lay it in a pan with a pint of red wine and a large spoonful of lemon pickle; bake it three hours; take the fat from the gravy and strain it. Serve it up garnished with green pickles.

Southern Cook Book, Gary & Dudley Hardware Co.

HOG KILLING: *Diary of An Early American Housewife*

November 14, 1772—There will be a hog killing on our farm tomorrow. Everything is ready for it.

HOG KILLING

Cold weather in early winter was the favorite time for hog killing, and the event became an occasion for cooperation and jollity, especially with small farmers who had no hired help.

No matter how small the farm, it always had a few pigs. They were easy to feed and maintain and provided the mainstay of the winter's provisions.

Outside, long before the first light of a crackling cold dawn, a huge iron kettle was filled with water and a roaring fire built under it that lighted up the farmstead. The water was boiling by sunrise.

The men took a sharp knife to the pigpen, and after the hog was hit over the head with an ax to stun it, its throat was cut. Some people were careful to catch the blood for blood puddings. Many a gentle wife sat in the kitchen with her hands over her ears until the slaughter was over and the carcasses had been hauled to the side of the fire.

The hog was then hoisted up and dipped into the great kettle of scalding water. Scalding was necessary to loosen the bristles which had to be scraped off. The bristles were saved for brushes. If the farmer did not own a hog-sized kettle, a barrel could be made to serve. Water in a barrel was heated by throwing hot stones into it.

The animal was then hung head down from the crotch of a tree, disemboweled, and halved. It was next taken into the kitchen where the women, usually helped by neighbors, waded into the business of processing it. The small intestines, emptied and scraped clean, could be used for stuffing sausages, or they could be eaten as "chitterlings." Not everyone liked chitterlings.

After the hog was cut up, the fat portions were tried into lard, and everybody chewed on the "craklin's" that floated to the top of the lard kettle. The back meat was chopped up for sausage, seasoned, and stuffed into skins (intestines) for smoking. Some of the sausage meat was kept out to be eaten fresh, and this was traditionally shared with all the neighbors.

Hams, shoulders, and bacon flanks went into a barrel of brine, "strong enough to float an egg," for corning, before they were smoked. Heads and feet were cooked at once, and the meat from them was mixed with vinegar and spices and made into head cheese and "souse." The livers were cooked, too, and chopped fine for "pudding" that might be stirred into cornmeal mush and cooked in pans as "scrapple." The last of the job was done by candlelight, and the final "redding up" of the kitchen was likely to be left for the next morning.

Often there would be a barter system among neighbors. They slaughtered by turn, exchanged with each other, and kept tallies of who owed what to whom. It reduced the number of animals any one man had to maintain.

Where the winters were cold enough, choice pieces could be frozen and packed with snow.

The housewives made a social event out of making the sausages, and smoking and salting the meat.

Making sausages

CORN AND BEANS

Corn and beans have long been intimately associated as articles of food. Boston baked beans and Boston brown bread are as inseparable now as they were in the early days; and in many families the baked Indian pudding, another form of serving this healthyful grain, is still considered the only pudding suitable to accompany a dinner of baked beans. All three were baked at the same time in the capacious brick oven, even in its own special shaped pot or pan, and subjected to the uniformly moderate heat quite impossible to secure in the modern range; who can say that each dish was not the better for such close companionship during the long hours between the finishing of Saturday's baking and the Sunday morning meal?

Bean porridge, another colonial dish, was not considered complete unless the meaty portions and leguminous liquid were held together by thickening with the starchy corn meal, then made still richer by the addition of hulled corn and eaten with brown bread. No wonder the men of those days could fell the trees and chop wood from sun to sun, through the long, cold winter, on a diet so rich in muscle-making and force-giving compounds.

In the succotash of Pilgrim fame, the meat might be simply salt pork or corned beef, or when one could afford it chickens would accompany the beef, and vegetables were added or not as the Pilgrim housewife preferred, but the hulled corn and stewed beans were indispensable, were what gave character to the dish, and doubtless were often the only ingredients of this nourishing food.

Corn and beans are among our most delicious and nourishing summer vegetables; they are wholesome when prepared properly, and may take the place of much of the heavy meat too often served freely as in winter.

Mary J. Lincoln's Boston Cook Book, 1883

WAYS OF COOKING INDIAN CORN: *A Letter from Ruth*

Dear Hannah:

I must tell you of a way to cook this Indian corn which Squanto showed father, and now we have it in all the houses when we are so fortunate as to have a supply of the wheat in our possession.

It is poured into the hot ashes of the fireplace, and allowed to remain there until every single wheat kernel has been roasted brown. Then it is sifted out of the ashes, beaten into a powder like meal, and mixed with snow in the winter, or water in the summer. Three spoonfuls a day is enough for a man who is on the march, or at work, so father says, and we children are given only two thirds as much.

Mother says it is especially of value because little labor is needed to prepare it; but neither Sarah nor I take kindly to the powder.

The Indians also steep the corn in hot water twelve hours before pounding it into a kind of coarse meal, when they make it into a pudding much as you would in Scrooby; but mother likes not the taste after it has been cooked before being pounded, thinking much of the fine flavor has been taken from it.

Sometimes we make a sweet pudding by mixing it with molasses and boiling it in a bag. It will keep thus for many days, and I once heard Captain Standish say that there were as many sweet puddings made in Plymouth every day as there were housewives.

Next fall we shall have bread made of barley and Indian corn meal, so father says, and I am hoping most fervantly that he may not be mistaken, for both Sarah and I are heartily tired of nookick, and of sweet pudding, which is not very sweet because we need to guard carefully our small store of molasses.

We girls often promise ourselves a great treat when a vessel comes out from England bringing butter, for we have had none that could be eaten since the first two weeks of the voyage in the MAYFLOWER.

Ruth

AUTUMN LEAVES

An exquisite transparency may be made by arranging pressed ferns, grasses, and autumn leaves on a pane of window glass, laying another pane of the same size over it, and binding the edges with ribbon, leaving the group imprisoned between. Use gum tragacanth in putting on the binding. It is well to secure a narrow strip of paper under the ribbon. The binding should be gummed all around the edge of the first pane and dried before the leaves, ferns, etc., are arranged; then it can be neatly folded over the second pane without difficulty.

To form the loop for hanging the transparency, paste a binding of galloon along the edge, leaving a two-inch loop free in the center, afterward to be pulled through a little slit in the final binding. These transparencies may either be hung before a window or, if preferred, secured against a pane in the sash.

Household, October 1887

THE POTATO HARVEST

One of the latest crops to be gathered is the store of potatoes which forms such an important part of the farmer's provision for himself and the rest of the world.

Latterly the poor potato has received more than its due share of condemnation. True, some household or some individuals are rather intemperate in the use of this vegetable, but that is its misfortune rather than its fault. We should pity its over-worked condition and try to induce people to allow it to rest while they experiment with other vegetables for a while. It is unfair to condemn even a vegetable unheard, and the potato has much in its favor when well grown and properly cooked.

The potato harvest may well be celebrated by a potato roast on these cool autumn evenings. This is an appropriate festival to combine with the Halloween orgies.

The room should be lighted with candles stuck in potatoes. An open fire is indispensable where the potatoes can be roasted in the ashes. Chestnuts and apples may be cooked over the same fire. The hot potatoes should be served on little wooden plates and eaten from their shells with cream and salt. Other suitable refreshments would be Saratoga chips or potato salad accompanied by toasted herring.

Fortunes or gifts may be distributed in cases made of potatoes well washed, cut in halves, and hollowed out and allowed to dry a little; then the folded paper or article is placed inside, the two halves placed together again and tied with a ribbon to hold them fast.

Where there is room a potato race would be in order. For a quieter entertainment let each one tell a story or give a quotation of which the potato is the central figure, like this from Gerard: "Likewise a foode, as also a meete for pleasure, being either rosted in the embers, or boiled and eaten with oile and vinegar, or dressed in anie other way by the hand of some cunning in cookerie."

American Kitchen Magazine, October 1892

MINCE MEAT

Four pounds solid meat without fat or bone, boil till tender, chop very fine, 1½ lbs suet chopped very fine.

To four bowls of chopped meat take one bowl of suet; to these five bowls add twelve or fourteen bowls of apples, chopped; then add eight lbs raisins, washed, chopped and stoned; four lbs currants, four tablespoons cloves, six tablespoons allspice, four lbs "C" sugar. Pack in jars, moisten with peach juice from pickled peaches. Add brandy to taste.

Home Queen Cook Book, 1905

MOCK MINCE MEAT

Take 1 cup sugar, 1 cup molasses, 1 cup raisins, 1 cup currants, 1 cup vinegar, 1 cup water, 1 grated nutmeg, 1 teaspoon cloves, 1 tablespoon cinnamon, butter the size of an egg, 1 cup powdered crackers. Heat on the stove before putting in tins. This will make six pies.

Home Queen Cook Book, 1905

CREOLE APPLES

Southern fried apples are thus prepared: Cut the apples into thick slices or into eighths. Roll each piece in beaten egg, to which a couple of spoonfuls of milk or water has been added, and then in crumbs, and lightly dredge them with flour. Fry them in plenty of butter until they are tender and a nice brown. Then arrange them on a hot platter. Pour into the frying pan a little milk and stir until it is boiling; then pour it over the apples, and they are ready to serve.

Housekeeper's Dept, *The Delineator*, October 1896

BONED TURKEY

With a sharp knife slit the skin down the back, and raising one side at a time with the fingers, separate the flesh from the bones with knife, until the wings and legs are reached. These unjoint from the body, and cutting through to the bone, turn back the flesh and remove from the bones. When bones are removed, the flesh may be re-shaped by stuffing. Some leave the legs and wings, as they are the most difficult to remove. Stuff with force-meat, made of cold lamb or veal and a little pork, chopped fine and seasoned with salt, pepper, sage, or savory, and the juice of one lemon; sew into shape, turn ends of wings under and press the legs close to the back, and tie all firmly so that the upper surface may be plump and smooth for the carver. Lard with two or three rows on the top, and bake thoroughly done, basting often with salt and water, and a little butter. This is a difficult dish to attempt. Carve across in slices and serve with tomato sauce.

Practical Housekeeping, 1881

KITCHEN OR OTHERWISE

. . . When your kitchen work is done we hope to rest and have a bit of change if only for a short time, and there is, in the very association of the kitchen, a weary workday feeling. . .In summer we may flee to the porch, the door-yard, under the shade tree, even to the barn, but let every working woman flee her kitchen if she would enjoy a respite from its cares. . . . Perhaps some women can rest as contentedly in their kitchens as elsewhere, and their tastes may incline them to prefer their work-room to any other; but for others this would be no rest, and actual burdens only made heavier because of self-imposed restrictions.

. . . When the country was new, necessity compelled living in narrow quarters, as it did spinning and weaving at home and weaving home-spun. As things advance, these matters change, yet now many, with unused rooms at their command, still cling to the old kitchen ways. It may be no concern of ours, only we would plead for the young folks, that they have a voice in the matter, and with mothers-in-law that they condemn not the new daughter who may enter their homes to just their own narrow ways of living.

Although the kitchen may not be the place where we would choose to pass all, or ever a great part of our time, yet kitchen work cannot be ignored, neither will it be despised if we sufficiently take into consideration the really important place which it holds in the economy of every dwelling.

The kitchen may be called the heart of the household, for out of it, literally, are the issues of material and physical life, and as the line has not yet been fully determined which divides the material and physical from the mental and spiritual life—one holds sway over the other continually—we may assume that the latter depends more or less upon the kitchen, or rather upon the cook in the kitchen, and that the human heart is affected for good or ill, as our bodies are well nourished with sufficient and wholesome food or otherwise.

The Household, October 1879

A SHAKER THANKSGIVING

The following glimpse into Shaker life is taken from a firsthand account of a Thanksgiving meal in a Shaker village in 1905:

The feasting really began with breakfast for, in addition to the regular fare, there were boiled rice with maple syrup and canned peaches or cherries. At ten o'clock everyone went to church except the cooks, whose presence in the kitchen was an absolute necessity; there was much to be done. During the service, the elder brother read the President's and then the Governor's Thanksgiving proclamation.

The deacons and trustees, whose responsibility was the community's property and money interests, gave an accounting of the year's temporal blessings. Hymns were sung.

Dinner was held at noon; here chicken substituted for the traditional turkey. These chickens had been selected and fattened for weeks before. So important was it that they should be cooked exactly right, if an inexperienced cook was on duty, a more skillful one was appointed for the day.

The menu was fricasseed chicken with cream gravy, boiled potatoes, baked hubbard squash, mashed turnips, ripe tomato pickle, mince and apple pies, homemade cheese, bread and butter, milk and tea. It was simple, hearty fare, but good.

PUMPKIN PIE?

New York chefs have been telling the newspaper reporters of that city that it is no longer necessary to have the genuine, old-fashioned yellow vegetable in order to make pumpkin pies that will delight the taste of the most experienced epicure. These knights of the stove and pan say that with a few yellow potatoes and a squash or two they can, by the judicious use of a few spices, build a pumpkin pie that can't be told from the genuine article—like mom used to make. Pumpkin pie is the favorite dessert in the winter's months, and perhaps the scarcity of the vegetable in the country's metropolis has led the professional cooks of that city to invent a substitute that passes muster with those busy New Yorkers, whose palates are naturally affected by the continual smoking of good, bad, and indifferent cigars, but the average country epicure is "from Missouri" and must "be shown" before he will believe that any substitute has been found for the succulent vegetable that furnishes the principal ingredient of the pumpkin pie that melts in the mouth and leaves a taste that lingers long, even after the after-dinner cigar or pipe has been smoked. There's only one pumpkin pie worthy of the name and fame—and that pie is not made from potatoes and squashes.

These are busy days in the average country and village kitchen, for winter weather makes sharp appetites and suitable dishes must be prepared to go with the back-bones, spare-ribs, and other evidences of "hog-killing" days that are found upon the table.

Woman's Farm Journal, November 1900

FOR THANKSGIVING

An eight-year-old lad was asked to write out what he considered a good dinner bill of fare and here it is:

FURST CORSE
Mince Pie

SEKOND CORSE
Pumpkin Pie and Terkey

THIRD CORSE
Lemon Pie, Terkey, Cranberries

FOURTH CORSE
Custard Pie, Apple Pie, Mince Pie,
Chocolate Cake, Ice Cream and
Plum Pudding

DESERT
Pie

American Kitchen Magazine, November 1896

THANKSGIVING IN EARLY AMERICA

We all know that Thanksgiving began in New England and was a celebration to give thanks for being alive after the first year of disease and famine. The first Thanksgiving was a festival of several days' length, during which time the Pilgrims and their Indian guests feasted in the open air on the meat, wild fowl, and deer that had been barbecued for the occasion.

The Puritans were opposed to the observance of Christmas, which they regarded as a Catholic custom, and during the colonial period, Christmas was, therefore, not a New England holiday except in Rhode Island. For the orthodox Puritan, Thanksgiving Day, or rather week, took the place of Christmas. While the practice of setting aside a day for thanksgiving did not originate with the Puritans, the New Englanders took up the custom at an early date and gave it a large place in their recreational life. Before the end of the seventeenth century the Thanksgiving season had become a regular annual holiday in Connecticut and Massachusetts. It lasted about a week and was the most important series of holidays that the Puritans had. It was not an especially religious celebration but a time of festivity, like the English yuletide. It is thought that Thursday was chosen as Thanksgiving Day because of its popularity as lecture day.

THANKSGIVING DAY, 1779

The following account of a Thanksgiving dinner in 1779 is given in a letter of Juliana Smith's, copied by her into her diary—a praiseworthy practice not uncommon when letters were written with care and might easily be lost in transmission. Juliana Smith was the daughter of the Reverand Cotton Mather Smith of Sharon, Connecticut.

This letter was addressed to its writer's "Dear Cousin Betsey." Who the latter may have been is not known, but it is assumed that she was the daughter of Reverand Smith's elder brother Dan.

After the usual number of apologies for delay in writing, Juliana proceeds:

"When Thanksgiving Day was approaching our dear Grandmother Smith, who is sometimes a little desponding of Spirit as you well know, did her best to persuade us that it would be for the better to make it a Day of Fasting & Prayer in view of the Wickedness of our Friends & the Vileness of our Enemies. *I am sure that you can hear Grandmother say that and see her shake her cap border. But indeed there was some occasion for her remarks, for our resistance to an* unjust Authority *has cost our beautiful Coast Towns very dear the last year & all of us have had much to suffer. But my dear Father brought her to a more proper frame of Mind, so that by the time the Day came she was ready to enjoy it almost as well as Grandmother Worthington did, & she, you will remember, always sees the bright side. In the meanwhile we had all of us been working hard to get all things in readiness to do honour to the Day.*

"This year it was Uncle Simeon's turn to have the dinner at his house, but of course we all helped them as they help us when it is our turn, & there is always enough for us all to do. All the baking of pies & cakes was done at our house & we had the big oven heated & filled twice each day for three days before it was all done. & everything was GOOD, *though we did have to do without some things that ought to be used. Neither Love nor Money could buy Raisins, but our good red cherries dried without the pits did almost as well & happily Uncle Simeon still had some spices in store. The tables were set in the Dining Hall and even that big room had no space to spare when we were all seated. The Servants had enough ado to get around the Tables & serve us all without over-setting things. There were our two Grandmothers side by side. They are always handsome old Ladies, but now, many thought, they were handsomer than ever, & happy they were to look around upon so many of their descendents. Uncle & Aunt Simeon presided at one Table, & Father & Mother at the other. Besides us five boys & girls there were two of the Gales & three Elmers, besides James Browne & Ephraim Cowles. We had them at our table because they could be best* supervised *there. Most of the students had gone to their own homes for the week, but Mr. Skiff & Mr.* ———[name illegible] *were too far away from their homes. They sat at Uncle Simeon's table & so did Uncle Paul & his family, five of them in all, & Cousins Phin & Poll. Then there were six of the Livingston family next door. They had never seen a Thanksgiving Dinner before, having been used to keep Christmas Day instead, as is the wont in New York Province. Then there were four Old Ladies who have no longer Homes or Children of their own & so came to us. They were invited by my Mother, but Uncle and Aunt Simeon wished it so.*

"Of course we could have no Roast Beef. None of us have tasted Beef this three years back as it all must go to the Army, & too little they get, poor fellows. But Nayquittymaw's Hunters were able to get us a fine red Deer, so that we had a good haunch of Venisson on each Table. These were balanced by huge Chines of Roast Pork at the other ends of the Tables. Then there was on one a big Roast Turkey & on the other a Goose, & two big Pigeon Pasties. Then there was an abundance of good Vegetables of all the old Sorts & one which I do not believe you have yet seen. Uncle Simeon had imported the Seede from England just before the War began & only this Year was there enough for Table use. It is called Sellery & you eat it without cooking. It is very good served with meats. Next year Uncle Simeon says he will be able to raise enough to give us all some. It has to be taken up, roots & all, & buried in earth in the cellar through the winter & only pulling up some when you want it to use.

"Our Mince Pies were good although we had to use dried Cherries as I told you, & the meat was shoulder of Venisson, instead of Beef. The Pumpkin Pies, Apple Tarts & big Indian Puddings lacked for nothing save Appetite by the time we had got round to them.

"Of course, we had no Wine. Uncle Simeon has still a cask or two, but it must all be saved for the sick, & indeed, for those who are well, good Cider is a sufficient Substitute. There was no Plumb Pudding, but a boiled Suet Pudding, stirred thick with dried Plumbs & Cherries, was called by the old Name & answered the purpose. All the other spice had been used in the Mince Pies, so for this Pudding we used a jar of West India preserved Ginger

Preparing the Thanksgiving dinner

which chanced to be left of the last shipment which Uncle Simeon had from there. We chopped the Ginger small and stirred it through with the Plumbs & Cherries. It was extraordinary good. The Day was bitter cold & when we got home from Meeting, which Father did not keep over long by reason of the cold, we were glad eno' of the fire in Uncle's Dining Hall, but by the time the dinner was one half over those of us who were on the fire side of one Table were forced to get up & carry our plates with us around to the far side of the other Table, while those who had sat there were as glad to bring their plates around the fire side to get warm. All but the Old Ladies who had a screen put behind their chairs.

"Uncle Simeon was in his best mood, and you know how good that is! He kept both Tables in a roar of laughter with his droll stories of the days when he was studying medicine in Edinborough, & afterwards he & Father & Uncle Paul joined in singing Hymns & Ballads. You know how fine their voices go together. Then we all sang a Hymn & afterwards my dear Father led us in prayer, remembering all Absent Friends before the Throne of Grace, & much I wished that my dear Betsey was here as one of us, as she has been of yore.

"We did not rise from the Table until it was quite dark, & then when the dishes had been cleared away we all got round the fire as close as we could, & cracked nuts, & sang songs & told stories. At least some told & others listened. You know nobody can exceed the two Grandmothers at telling tales of all the things they have seen themselves, & repeating those of the early years in New England, & even some in the Old England, which they heard in their youth from their Elders. My Father says it is a goodly custom to hand down all worthy deeds & traditions from Father to Son, as the Israelites were commanded to do about the Passover & as the Indians here have always done, because the Word that is spoken is remembered longer than the one that is written. . . .Brother Jack, who did not reach here until late on Wednesday though he had left College very early on Monday Morning & rose diligently considering the snow, brought an orange to each of the Grand-Mothers, but, Alas! they were frozen in his saddle bags. We soaked the frost out in cold water, but I guess they as n't as good as they should have been."

THANKSGIVING SEVENTY YEARS AGO
by Mrs. Henry Ward Beecher

Are the holidays of the present time as conducive to real enjoyment and happiness as the free-and-easy home celebrations of seventy or eighty years ago?

We do not believe they are. There may be more refinement—no, that is not the word, but style—now, but is there half the true, genuine pleasure and happiness for the young?

We look back three-quarters of a century, to a large, old-fashioned home in New England,—white, with green blinds, of course,—situated on one of the beautiful hills in Worcester County, Mass., where ten "merry lads and lassies" dwelt.

By the middle of November how we counted the day,—for Thanksgiving was close by,—and grandpa and grandma would spend the week there, for who could think of taking a troop of ten children to their pretty, quiet home; and certainly all must go, if any, for the family must not be divided on Thanksgiving Day!

So the dear old people would come to their son-in-law, "the doctor's" house, where there were many quiet places in which they could be undisturbed if the young, joyous, frolicsome children became tiresome.

We can hardly tell of the Thanksgiving entertainment with-out recalling the busy week spent in preparing for it, quite as full of pleasant memories as the day in prospect.

"The boys" took charge of slaughtering the turkeys, chickens and ducks, and picking and dressing them in an outbuilding,—not so remote as to prevent those engaged in the house from hearing the merry laughter over the work, and often responding, but without interrupting active labors in the house.

There was the meat to be cooked ready to be chopped for mince-pies, and the next day, apples and pumpkins to be made ready, and raisins to be picked over and stoned.

In the evening, the brothers helped to chop the meat, pare and chop the apples for the mince-pies, and while all old enough were at work, the grandparents told the stories of those earlier days, when all were compelled to fight the Indians, or seek protection from them in the forts, risking the loss and destruction of the little homes they had worked so hard to secure; or recounting their adventures connected with the Revolutionary war.

While listening to all these stories,—at that time of comparative recent date, —labor was pleasure, and the work progressed rapidly.

The morning before Thanksgiving Day, pies, bread and cake were baked in the two large brick ovens, after which one was re-heated to receive the bread-trough filled with brown-bread dough, and the plum and Indian suet pudding, dark with huckleberries. These were to remain until taken out hot for Thanksgiving dinner.

Meanwhile the poultry was made ready to be cooked on Thanksgiving Day.

For so large a family, breakfast must necessarily be bountiful, but nothing extra was prepared for that meal.

The dinner was to be all that abundant materials and the best skill could make it, and, therefore, the sensible parents would not venture to allow their large troop of growing children any extra indulgence in the way of food.

On Thanksgiving morning, the doctor, if not called off by patients, took the grandparents and the younger members of the family to church, leaving the workers free from interruption.

It is said "many hands make light work." However that may be, we know that while under the gentle mother's supervision everything must be done methodically and "on time," yet there was never a jollier time than the hours spent in preparing

Thanksgiving dinner, as we remember it, after we were old enough to lend a helping hand.

The brothers had charge of the two ovens, supplying fuel, and, when heated, clearing out the coals, ready to be filled with the chickens, ducks, and, of course, chicken-pie.

The turkeys in the large roaster, which no modern invention has ever equalled, were being roasted, not baked, before the great kitchen fire.

All is ready. The long table is spread, and hark! the carriage has turned up the lane, and the hungry occupants will soon be here.

The younger children rush in with merry voices, and then stand back surprised to see the tables set, not in the dining-room, but stretched through the long, wide hall, loaded with "costly piles of food." In a few minutes all are seated. Turkeys, ducks, chickens, baked, and always a huge chicken-pie, all varieties of vegetables, cranberry sauce, mince, pumpkin, apple and custard pies, plum pudding, Indian huckleberry suet pudding, tea, coffee, and the richest of cream, —all appeared in their appropriate order.

Rising from the table, when all were abundantly satisfied, they adjourned to the parlor for a little ceremony that was never omitted on Thanksgiving, and never repeated on any other day.

In the centre of the room stood a table on which was a very large bowl of milk punch, surrounded by tiny wine-glasses.

After telling us how much we had to be thankful for, what a blessing it was that we had enjoyed this day with no interruption or mishap, our father filled the little glasses from the punch-bowl, and with a smile and a kiss gave one to each of the children, and then all scattered to find such enjoyment as they chose till supper-time.

Supper! What could any one do with supper after sitting two hours and more at such a dinner, and eating to repletion?

Nevertheless, the table was spread temptingly, but not heartily complimented.

What little appetite there was left from dinner was reserved, certainly by the children, for a later entertainment in the evening, when all adjourned to the kitchen.

On the long table in the centre of the room was, first, a large glass bowl of lemonade,—and remember, in those early days, that was a luxury,—an abundance of such fruit as was in season, and a good supply of nuts and pop-corn. Now all were ready for fun. On the large stone hearth some cracked nuts, others popped corn over the large bed of coals, some of which was ground in a hand-mill, and served, in saucers, with rich cream to those who preferred, while the lemonade stood ready for all who wished.

While preparing and partaking of this repast, grandparents and parents entertained us all with a succession of stories. Then followed evening games in which the younger and, sometimes, the older members of the family took part.

This is a simple account of the Thanksgivings we remember, many, many years ago, a tame description of what used to seem to us—and does, even now—

more full of real pleasure and happiness than any other week could furnish in the whole year.

Household, November 1891

THE ROAST TURKEY

A gentleman in one of the eastern towns of Massachusetts, had a servant in his employ, who gave him not a little trouble on account of the complaints he made on the subject of his victuals. As is usual in many families, whatever remained from the table of the dining-room was placed upon that in the kitchen—the inmates of the latter fared in all respects as well as those of the former, with the exception of their being served last. The gentleman of whom we speak, took special pains that there should be no lack of provisions for the supply of all in his house, and was therefore at a loss to understand the grounds of the complaint thus made by his servant.

One day as he was passing through the kitchen, an opportunity presented itself for making some inquiries on the subject. While the other servants were partaking of their dinner with a keen relish, Sam, the disaffected servant, was tasting of it as reluctantly as if poison had been mixed with his food.

'How is it, Sam,' said the gentleman, 'that you are dissatisfied with your living—you fare the same as I do, and yet are not contented?'

'I know it,' said Sam, who was fresh from the country, 'but then I guess you are a little more fonder of corned beef than I be, to make a meal of it so often!'

'Corned-beef!' said the gentleman, 'I am indeed very partial to that dish, and am sorry that it is not equally agreeable to your taste—but since you are fastidious, tell me what dish of all others you would prefer, and you shall be entertained with it.'

'Why roast turkey, to be sure:' quoth Sam, 'I guess I aint seen nothing of that sort this many a day!'

'And you think, Sam, you would be contented to fare on roast turkey every day?'

'I guess, meister, if you'd only try me, you'd think so—nothing I relishes so hugely as roast turkey!'

'Well, then,' said the gentleman, 'to-morrow you shall be gratified—a turkey shall be roasted for your special benefit—no one but yourself shall partake of it, and you shall eat of no other meat till the turkey is gone.'

'By gumption!' exclaimed Sam, 'I agree to that willingly.'

The next morning the gentleman went into the market and purchased the largest and fattest turkey he could find, and sent it home with directions to be roasted and placed upon a separate table for Sam. In this he was strictly obeyed—the turkey was stuffed and roasted in the best style, and when Sam made his appearance at dinner, he found it smoking on the table which had been set for his sole occupation.

'By gauly now! if that aint curous though!' said Sam, drawing up a chair to the table, at the same time smacking his lips and feasting his eyes upon the scene before him. Forthwith he attacked the turkey in his own fashion, cutting a slice here and a slice there, just as inclination led him, without the slow and tedious operation of carving it, and having finished his dinner, he stretched himself out with the self-complacent air of an alderman. The next day the turkey was again served up as before, upon which, and upon which, alone, Sam made his dinner with apparent satisfaction. The third day, when the gobbler, shaved of his pinions and his exterior, was placed upon the table, Sam was not quite as prompt in commencing operations. Casting a wishful glance at his fellows, who were regaling themselves with a variety of dishes, Sam offered to exchange with them a portion of his turkey for a slice of beef, but to this proposition, having received instructions how to act in such an event, they all declined acceding, so that Sam was forced to make out his meal upon the cold carcass of the turkey.

The fourth day and the fifth came and departed, and found Sam still at work upon his turkey, more than two thirds of which was now consumed. He was by this time heartily sick of his bargain—pride prevented him from making complaint, while hunger compelled him to eat of what had become an object of disgust and loathing. At the end of a week's time, the turkey was reduced to a mere skeleton, and Sam was thanking his stars that he should soon see no more of it, when his master entered the kitchen and found him at his last meal.

'Well Sam,' said he, 'I see you've about finished the first turkey—it is high time for me to look out for another.'

'What, another!' echoed Sam, 'another turkey! you don't think a man can live on nothing but roast turkey, do you?'

'Certainly, I think you can—you cannot find fault with roast turkey—it is a dish of your own choosing.'

'I knows it—I knows it,' said Sam, 'but who would have thought of turkey to-day, and turkey to-morrow, and turkey next day, and turkey everyday—why, I'd as lief feed on corned beef at that rate, and a little liefser!'

'But, Sam, you are neither satisfied with living as I do, nor with living as you prefer yourself—neither with corned beef nor with roast turkey—what shall I do in such a case?'

'Oh! anything! I'll feed on roast cats—roast dogs—anything but roast turkey —I can't do that—don't make me eat another.'

'Well, then,' said the gentleman, 'if you think you can content yourself to fare as I do—to take pot luck when I take pot luck, and roast turkey when I do, and if you can do so without complaining, I consent that to-morrow you return to your old way of living.'

'Oh, yes, I consent to anything,' said Sam, 'anything but roast turkey.'

New Jersey Almanac, 1832

TWAS THE WEEK BEFORE THANKSGIVING

Especially associated with childhood on the old farm was the keeping of the annual Thanksgiving. It was one of the days we reckoned by, the dividing line between summer and winter, as well as the days of reunions and festivities. The season's work, as far as the land was concerned, was expected to be done before Thanksgiving; and indoors, house-cleaning with its vexations must be well out of the way.

The winter supply of apple-sauce must have been made ere this. The apples from the Mt. Warner orchard had been laid up, and a generous quantity of the juice had been boiled down to the consistency of thin molasses, with which to sweeten the sauce, for our forefathers were economical.

The old cider-mill, which had been all the season screeching its protest against the sacrilegious use of one of Nature's best gifts by turning it into brandy, had uttered its last groan, and stood with naked jaws and bending sweep, a ghastly spectacle, until another season should compel a renewal of its doleful cries. The apple-paring, with its array of tubs and baskets and knives and jolly faces before the bright kitchen fire, was completed, with the Hallowe'en games of counting the apple seeds, and throwing the paring over the head to see its transformation into the initials of some fair maiden.

The great day for the conversion of the apples into sauce had lately come and gone, for it must be delayed as long as possible, that it may not ferment and spoil. The stout crane that swung over the huge fireplace was loaded with one or more brass kettles filled with apples, sweet and sour in proper proportion, the former being put at the bottom because they required more time to cook. Sprinkled through the mass were a few quinces, if they were to be had, to give flavor, while over the whole was poured the pungent apple molasses which supplied the sweetening. The great danger was that the sauce should burn; and to prevent this, some housewives had clean straw prepared and laid at the bottom of the kettles, lest the apples should come in too near contact with the fire. It was an all-day process, but when completed an article was produced which was always in order for the table, and which, if slightly frozen, was enjoyed with a keener relish than the ice-cream of the restaurants of to-day.

Monday was devoted, of course, to the weekly washing, and nothing must interfere with that.

Tuesday was the great day for the making of pies, of which there were from thirty to fifty baked in the great oven that crackled and roared right merrily in anticipation of the rich medley that was being made ready for its capacious maw. Two kinds of apple pies, two of pumpkin, rice, and cranberry made out the standard list, to which additions were sometimes made. Then in our younger days we children each had a patty of his own. These were made in tins of various shapes, of which we had our choice, as well of the material of which our respective pies should be composed. The provident among us would put these aside until the good things were not quite so abundant.

Was not that a breath equal to the 'spicy breezes of Ceylon' that greeted us as the mouth of the oven was taken down, and the savor of its rich compounds penetrated every crevice of the old kitchen, like sacrificial incense? Then, as the pies were taken out and landed on the brick hearth, and a number of pairs of eyes were watching the proceedings with the keenest interest, it would not be strange if pies and eyes sometimes got mixed up. I remember once quite a sensation was produced in the little crowd because brother T. lost his balance, and, for want of a chair to break his fall, sat down on one of the smoking hot pies!

After cooling and sorting, the precious delicacies were put away into the large closets in the front entry or hall, which the foot of the small boy was not permitted to profane.

Wednesday was devoted to chicken pies and raised cake. The making of the latter was a critical operation. If I mistake not, it was begun on Monday. I believe the conditions must be quite exact to have the yeast perform its work perfectly in the rich conglomerated mass. In due time the cake is finished. The chicken pies are kept in the oven, so as to have them still hot for supper. The two turkeys have been made ready for the spit, the kitchen cleared of every vestige of the great carnival that has reigned for the last two days, and there is a profound pause of an hour or two before the scene opens.

The happy meetings, the loaded tables, the hilarity and good cheer that prevailed, checked but not subdued in after years as one and another of the seats are made vacant by their departure to the better land,—these are things to be imagined, but cannot be described. Warner, in his 'Being a Boy,' says that the hilarity of the day is interfered with by going to meeting and wearing Sunday clothes; but our parents managed that wisely by dividing the day, the first half of it being kept religiously, but the afternoon being given up to festivity,—by no means, however, common week-day work. This was wise, I say, because it would be almost cruel to allow a lot of young people to indulge themselves to the very extent of prudence, to say the least, in eating, and then sit down to reading good books. This distinction between relaxation and toil for pelf is, I think, too often forgotten nowadays, founded as it is on both religion and philosophy. I remember well the sad look mother gave my brother and myself after our having spent the afternoon in making a hen-house, a very 'cute operation, we thought, but which found no favor in her eyes, as contrary to the traditions of the forefathers.

But the day after Thanksgiving, it must be admitted, had its peculiar pleasures. I doubt if there was any other of the holidays of the year when we boys felt so strongly the sense of freedom, and it was all the sweeter because it was the last we should have before we were set to our winter tasks. Skating was pretty sure to be one of the sports, if the weather had been cold enough to make the ice strong; and indoors there remained for our keen appetite the broken bits of pie and cake, to say nothing of the remnants of the turkey and fowl of the day before, and which were enjoyed with a keener relish, if possible, than at first.

I forgot in its more appropriate place to speak of the roasting of the turkey. This was done in a tin oven with an iron rod running through it, and also through the meat that was to be cooked. This was the spit. The meat was fastened to the spit with skewers, so that, by means of a small crank at the end, it could be made to revolve in order to cook evenly. The oven was in shape something like a half cylinder, with the open side to face the fire. But there was a still more primitive way of roasting a turkey, and one which was resorted to sometimes when our family was the largest. Room was made at one end of the fireplace, and the turkey was suspended by the legs from the ceiling, where was a contrivance to keep the string turning, and of course with it the turkey. On the hearth was a dish to catch the drippings, and with them the meat was occasionally basted. The thing is accomplished much more easily now, but at an expense, I imagine, in the quality of the work.

It is interesting to observe the universality of some of the customs that were in vogue fifty and one hundred years ago. In looking over the Centennial of the Churches of Connecticut, I came across the remark that the festive board, so crowded with good things on Thursday, gradually took on a plainer and less profuse array of dishes, until it ended off on Saturday evening with a simple bowl of hasty pudding and milk. This was in Revolutionary times; but fifty years later, when I was a boy, the same practices prevailed; in fact, hasty pudding and milk was the standing dish for Saturday evening, as boiled Indian pudding was for Sunday's dinner. I have been reminded since reading this item of a couplet my brother once repeated to me when we were boys:—

> 'For we know Northampton's rule to be
> Fried hasty pudding 'long wi' tea.'

Expressive, if not elegant, and it shows that Northampton, bating the slight innovation of the tea, was true to New England tradition.

The Christmas holidays, as they are now observed, were not known in the country towns then. New Year's presents were often made, and the 'Happy New Year' greeting was passed when neighbors met each other; but with most people we were too near the Puritan age to hear the 'Merry Christmas' so common to-day, without a shock as though it were a profanation.

New England Chronicle, November 1892

THE TURKEY'S LAMENT *by Susan Hubbard Martin*

I'm a melancholy turkey,—sad am I,
For a reign of awful terror draweth nigh.
    How I dread the smell of pie,
    And the cakes and tarts piled high,
    For I know that I must die
        Thanksgiving Day.

What avail my sparkling eyes, just like jet,
Or my slim and stately neck, proudly set?
    Though my glossy feathers shine,
    On my flesh will people dine,
    And pronounce me—luscious—fine,
        Thanksgiving Day.

How I wish I had been hatched some other bird,
Chicken, goose, duck or dove'd be preferred,—
    Any fowl, but what I am,
    In this land of "Uncle Sam,"
    For I'm slaughtered like a lamb
        Thanksgiving Day.

How I sympathize with Marie Antoinette,
How that dark and bloody ax haunts me yet,
    Soon on my neck, 'twill descend,
    Make of me a sudden end.
    Was a sadder verse e'er penned,
        Thanksgiving Day?

American Kitchen Magazine, November 1896

THE AMERICAN ECONOMICAL HOUSEKEEPER AND FAMILY RECEIPT BOOK *by Mrs. E. A. Howland*

This book was published in 1845 in Worcester, Mass., and sold for the magnificent sum of twenty-five cents. Although Thanksgiving was still celebrated only in those states where the governors issued proclamation, this book contained a Thanksgiving dinner menu. It was as follows, along with the recipes for various foods on the menu:

Roast Turkey, stuffed
A Pair of Chickens stuffed, and boiled with cabbage and a piece of lean pork.

A Chicken Pie

Potatoes; turnip sauce; squash; onions; gravy and gravy sauce; apple and cranberry sauce; oyster sauce; brown and white bread.

Plum and Plain Pudding, with sweet sauce.

Mince, Pumpkin, and Apple Pies

Cheese.

P.S. The chickens are to be prepared in the same manner as you would to roast them; fill the bodies and crops full of stuffing, and sew them up close; boil them an hour and a half, or two hours.

FOR TURNIP SAUCE.—Boil your turnips and mash them fine; add the same amount of mealy mashed potatoes; season with salt and pepper, moisten it with cream or butter.

SQUASH.—Boil it, peel it, and squeeze it dry in a colander; mash it fine, season it with salt, pepper, and butter.

ONIONS.—Boil them in milk and water, season them with salt, pepper, and butter.

GRAVY SAUCE.—Boil the neck, wings, gizzard, liver and heart of the fowls, till they are tender; put in a boiled onion, chop it all fine, then add two or three pounded crackers, a piece of butter, and a little flour thickening; season it with pepper and salt.

CRANBERRY SAUCE.—Wash and stew your cranberries in water; add almost their weight in clean sugar, just before you take them from the fire.

OYSTER SAUCE.—Put your oysters into a stewpan, add a little milk and water, and let them boil; season with a little pepper and butter, and salt, if necessary.

BROWN BREAD.—Put the Indian meal in your bread-pan, sprinkle a little salt among it, and wet it thoroughly with scalding water. When it is cool, put in your rye; add two gills of lively yeast, and mix it with water as stiff as you can knead it. Let it stand an hour and a half, in a cool place in summer, on the hearth in winter. It should be put into a very hot oven, and baked three or four hours.

PLUM PUDDING BOILED.—Three quarts of flour, a little salt, twelve eggs, two pounds of raisins, one pound of beef suet chopped fine, one quart of milk; put into a strong cloth floured; boil three hours. Eat with sauce.

PLAIN PUDDING.—Boil half a pint of milk with a bit of cinnamon, four eggs with the whites well beaten, the rind of a lemon grated, half a pound of suet chopped fine, as much bread as will do. Pour your milk on the bread and suet, keep mixing it till cold, then put in the lemon-peel, eggs, a little sugar, and some nutmeg grated fine. It may be either baked or boiled.

COMMON MINCE PIE.—Boil a piece of lean fresh beef very tender; when cold, chop it very fine; then take three times the quantity of apples, pared and cored, and chopped fine; mix the meat with it, and add raisins, allspice, salt, sugar, cinnamon, and molasses, to suit the taste; incorporate the articles well together, and it will improve by standing overnight, and if the weather is cool; a very little ginger improves the flavor. Small pieces of butter sliced over the mince before laying on the top crust will make them keep longer. A tea-cup of grape sirup will give them a good flavor.

PUMPKIN PIE.—Take out the seeds and pare the pumpkin; stew, and strain it through a coarse sieve. Take two quarts of scalded milk and eight eggs, and stir your pumpkin into it; sweeten it with sugar or molasses. Salt it, and season with ginger, cinnamon, or grated lemon-peel to your taste. Bake with a bottom crust. Crackers, pounded fine, are a good substitute for eggs. Less eggs will do.

APPLE PIE.—Peel the apples, slice them thin, pour a little molasses and sprinkle some sugar over them; grate on some lemon-peel, or nutmeg. If you wish to make them richer, put a little butter on the top.

CHICKEN PIE.—Cut up your chicken, parboil it, season it in the pot, take up the meat, put in a flour thickening, and scald the gravy; make the crust of sour milk made sweet with saleratus, put in a piece of butter or lard the size of an egg; cream is preferable to sour milk, if you have it. Take a large tin pan, line it with the crust, put in your meat, and pour in the gravy from the pot; make it nearly full, cover it with crust, and leave a vent; bake it in a moderate oven two hours, or two and a half.

STUFFING.—Take dry pieces of bread or crackers, chop them fine, put in a small piece of butter or a little cream, with sage, pepper, and salt, one egg, and a small quantity of flour, moistened with milk.

ROAST TURKEY.—Let the turkey be picked clean, and washed and wiped dry, inside and out. Have your stuffing prepared, fill the crop and then the body full up, sew it up, put on a spit, and roast it, before a moderate fire, three hours. If more convenient, it is equally good when baked.

DR. CHASE'S THANKSGIVING DINNER

Prior to 1900, the people who wrote cookbooks also included home recipes for the cure of various illnesses for man and beast as well as other little hints for home and farm. At the same time, those who wrote home remedy books included recipes for cooking as well as hints for home and farm.

One of the most popular books was written by Dr. Alvin Chase and was called *Dr. Chase's Receipt Book.* As a young man, Dr. Chase traveled, and it was not until the age of thirty-eight that he decided to study medicine. In 1868 he decided to write a book which not only covered the field of medicine but every field of endeavor possible. He wrote about brewing, farming, cooking, etc.

Here is Dr. Chase on the subject of Thanksgiving Dinner:

THANKSGIVING DINNER, WITH SUITABLE RECIPES, BILL OF FARE, HOW TO SET THE TABLE, ETC.—And now I don't think I can do better than to close the department of dishes for the table than in giving a bill of fare, with suitable recipes for a Thanksgiving dinner, which was sent to the Detroit *Post and Tribune* with the writer's plan for setting the table, etc., which will certainly be found of great assistance to new beginners and very handy to refer to by every one upon such occasion or when quite a number of visitors are to be dined upon any occasion. If the writer's name was given I have it not at this writing; but knowing the directions to be reliable, I will let her speak for herself. She says:

Thanksgiving is almost here, and how shall we celebrate the day? I for one believe in the old-fashioned Thanksgiving dinner. The following bill of fare may be of use to some of your readers:

Oyster Soup, Celery, Pepper Sauce, Roast Turkey, with Currant Jelly, Baked Potatoes, Mashed Turnips, Roast Pig, Carrots with Cream, Boston Baked Beans, Chopped Cabbage, Pumpkin Pie, Plum Pudding, Apples, Nuts, Cheese, Tea and Coffee

For the table I prefer a white cloth with fancy border, and napkins to match. A dash of color livens up the table in the bleak November, when flowers cannot be had in profusion. Casters in the center, of course, flanked by tall celery glasses. At each end, glass fruit dishes filled with apples and nuts. A bottle of pepper sauce near the casters, and a mold of jelly by the platter of turkey, and small side dishes of chopped cabbage garnished with rings of cold boiled eggs. The purple cabbage makes the handsomest-looking dishes. Serve the soup from tureens to soup dishes, handing around to the guests. After this comes the *pièce de résistance,* "Thanksgiving turkey." A piece of dark meat with a spoonful of gravy, and one of white turkey with a bit of jelly and a baked potato. I should prefer a spoonful of mashed turnip should be served on each plate, leaving the other vegetables to be passed afterward with the roast pig. After this the salad, and then the plates should be taken away and the dessert served. Then come the apples and nuts, the tea and coffee, well seasoned with grandpa's old-time stories, grandma's quaint ways and kind words and merry repartee from all.

THANKSGIVING MENU
American Kitchen Magazine, November 1896

Cream of Chestnuts, Croutons, Fricassee of Oysters, Olives, Salted Peanuts, Roast Turkey, Giblet Stuffing, Cranberry Sauce, Mashed Potatoes, Diced Turnips, New Cider, Apollinaris, Lemon Milk Sherbet; Roast Duck, Brussels Sprouts, Plum Jelly, Apple and Celery Salad, Cheese, Water Thin Wafers, Plum Pudding, Hard Sauce, Squash Pie, Mince Pie, Fruit, Nuts, Confectionery, Coffee.

Thanksgiving Dinner as given at Grandmother P.'s from 1830 to 1850.
Boiled Turkey, Roast Turkey, Chicken Pie, Potato Balls, Turnips, Squash, Onions, Cranberry Sauce, Celery, Plum Pudding, Mince Pie, Pumpkin Pie.
Thin gingerbread and crackers were passed late in the afternoon and between eight and nine o'clock; after the little folks were put to bed, the older members of the family had a supper of chicken salad and cold roast duck.

THANKSGIVING DINNER I

Oyster stew, celery, oyster crackers, roast stuffed turkey, brown gravy, cranberry moulds, oak hill sweet potatoes, turnips and carrots in white sauce, boiled onions, chicken pie, mince pie, squash patties, fruit pudding, brandy sauce, assorted nuts and raisins, coffee.

What to Have for Dinner, Fannie Farmer, 1905

THANKSGIVING DINNER II

Oyster soup, celery, roast turkey with cranberry sauce, mashed potatoes, baked sweet potatoes, mashed turnips, roast pig, carrots with cream, Boston baked beans, minced cabbage, pumpkin pie, plum pudding, fruit, nuts, cheese, tea and coffee.

Queen of the Household, 1906

CANDLE-DIPPING PARTY:
Diary of An Early American Housewife

December 10, 1772—Dorcas heard of the candle-dipping parties that are held in New York and she asked whether she could have one. Her father agreed to it since he saw no harm in having something different for a winter's evening entertainment. All we had to do was to be certain that there were enough aprons with long sleeves to protect the clothing of each of Dorcas' guests who was to participate in the candle-dipping. She invited eight couples.

CANDLE-DIPPING PARTY

In early New York, candle-dipping was an amusement that combined work and play. Candles were the main source of illumination in the homes and were too expensive to import from England so that they were made at home from tallow or bayberries.

The guests were invited to come early, about six o'clock in the evening, and as each guest arrived, he or she was given a huge apron with long sleeves to cover the clothing from the melted tallow. The candle-dipping was held in the immense kitchen which usually had heavy ceiling beams, darkened and polished by years of smoke, while bunches of dried herbs, ears of corn for popping, and dried apples hung from the rafters. The huge fireplace took up a large portion of one side of the room. In preparation for the candle-dipping, huge brass kettles were over the blaze on long-armed cranes and contained tallow which was kept liquid so that it could be easily poured. As a result, the room was very warm, but then it was usually midwinter and there was snow on the ground and frost in the air. The warmth of the kitchen was appreciated when one entered from outdoors.

Down the center, the longest way of the room, were set two long ladders lying side by side, supported at either end by a block of wood about the height of a chair seat. Under each ladder, at intervals of a foot or so apart, stood a row of big three-footed iron pots and one of footless brass kettles like those over the fire. On the floor between the pots and kettles were placed dripping pans and other vessels, both to protect the floor from grease and to prevent waste of tallow. On either side of each ladder was a row of chairs placed as closely together as possible. On these chairs were seated the candle-dippers, couple by couple.

The servants helped to set up the tallow kettles. Before the couples were seated, the two young people lifted the brass kettles full of melted tallow from the fire and poured their contents to the depth of two or three inches more than a long candle's length upon the water with which similar vessels on the floor were already half-filled.

As soon as the young folks were seated, each guest was handed the candle rods, four or five to each person. From each rod was suspended the wicks of twisted cotton which had been previously prepared, and the candle-dipping began.

Ordinarily, two pairs of industrious hands, with six kettles between them, could easily have completed as many in half the time as it took that night. There would be much laughter, and a festive air prevailed. By eight o'clock the candles were all finished and a supper was served which was finished off with cookies and hot cider.

If dancing was permitted in that particular household, there might be dancing for another hour or so and then all the guests would leave in the sleighs and one could hear the bells sound lower and lower as the guests went farther and farther from the house. It was an evening enjoyed by young and old alike.

CHRISTMAS IN EARLY AMERICA

There was Christmas in the South from the beginning. America's first recorded Yuletide ceremony took place on Virginia's soil. While Puritan New England shunned the ceremonial Christmas, the Southerners nurtured it and kept it ever before them. From the earliest days, Christmas in Virginia has been a period of jollity.

Captain John Smith and his followers had the Dominion's first real Christmas feast, a gift of the Indians. Calling on one of Powhatan's sons, they enjoyed richer fare than they had known for a long time. It was said that they were "never more merrie, nor fedde on more plentie of good oysters, fish, flesh, wild foule and good bread; nor never had better fires in England than in the warm smokie houses."

Christmas soon became a convenient and appropriate season for the gathering of friends, and one ceremony invited another. At an early date the holidays became a favorite time for weddings. Virginia also marked Christmas with a special ceremony of gunpowder.

A Virginia guest often brought his musket with him when he went to pay a call, and he joined his host in shooting, while the women put their hands over their ears and the children jumped up and down in delight. When a neighbor caught the echo, he took out his own firing piece and answered, and his neighbor did the same. In time an official proclamation cautioned against the overuse of gunpowder at entertainments.

Christmas was the season for punch bowls and balls. The people of Virginia also took greenery to their churches, transforming them in appearance. Christmas was also a succession of observances that went on without a letup from December 15 to January 6. Christmas itself was not December 25, but January 5, according to the old church calendar; it was not until about 1750 that the date was changed to the present one.

Christmas in the colonial period was not a day of great gift-giving. For the children there were a few toys, none of them elaborate; for the adults, a good wish, a kiss, or a handshake. It was not until the 1800's that the Virginians took part in the custom of exchanging gifts.

CHRISTMAS SEASON

Now Christmas comes, 'tis fit that we
Should feast and sing, and merry be:
Keep open house, let fidlers play,
A fig for cold, sing care away;
And may they who thereat repine,
On brown bread and on small beer dine.

Virginia Almanack, 1766

CHRISTMAS IN THE SOUTH—ANTE-BELLUM PERIOD

For several weeks after hog killing, the women of the house worked over boxes and bowls with the help of the cook and her helpers and any of the children who could be pressed into service. Nuts had to be cracked and picked over, raisins seeded, orange peel cut, currants washed. Candied citron was converted along with other delicacies into mincemeat, fruit cakes, and puddings.

Everyone worked in the kitchen to combine ingredients, tasting, thinning, thickening, pouring in the brandy and other spirits, then thrusting the baking tins into the ovens and carefully watching so that they could be removed at the proper moment of readiness. Again the fruit cakes were doused with brandy, cooled, and put into well-covered boxes to "set" and "ripen" during the days that remained before Christmas.

Meanwhile, more cakes were being made, such as layer cakes, wafer-like cakes, thick cakes, citron cakes. As they were baked, they were placed into the storeroom to be kept under lock and key along with the pies made of various fruits and custards.

From England the custom of the old Yule log had been introduced into the Southern states and it was an essential part of the holiday. Slaves were sent out to cut down the finest tree in the woods and it was brought back to the house to be placed into the largest fireplace.

As long as the Yule log glowed, the servants were traditionally freed from work. Even if the wood burned for more than a week, the master usually kept his promise. This resulted in the servants developing all sorts of schemes to prolong the burning of the log. Usually they wetted down the log so that it should burn more slowly, but it was the holiday season and although the master knew what had been done, he said nothing about it.

In the last days before Christmas arrived, hunters rode out to bring back any game within range, such as wild duck, partridges, and wild geese. From nearby waters, oysters were brought to the kitchen, while out in the poultry house the turkeys grew plumper and plumper.

With Christmas in sight, the women of the household sent the young men and boys out to the woods to bring back a plentiful supply of evergreens with which to decorate the house. Of course, mistletoe was always found and placed in hidden corners to be taken advantage of when an attractive young lady was under it.

Meanwhile, carriages filled with relatives and friends arrived at the plantation to spend the holiday. Christmas Eve was the time for toasts and the hanging of stockings before the mantel, while Christmas morning was the time for gift-giving to children and servants.

Christmas day heard fireworks crackling at the crack of dawn outside the house. After a hearty breakfast of ham and eggs, various breads, oysters, fish, fruit, and cheese, the boys went out to join in setting off the fireworks, while the men usually went off on a hunt.

The women of the house now turned their attention to the preparation of the dinner, which was served about three in the afternoon. Some of the family might attend church services before the meal. The dinner lasted anywhere from two to three hours, with second and third helpings the usual thing. There then followed a period of relaxation before there were songs and dancing by all.

Supper was light but supper there was. Then the plantation people attended the Christmas dance given for the servants. This lasted until midnight for the guests, although the servants might dance away until dawn.

Some guests, if they lived nearby, might go home, but usually all the guests remained for several days or a week. With the departure of the last guest, the house returned to normal, but there were enough memories to last at least another year for master and servant alike.

CHRISTMAS IN PHILADELPHIA, 1875

John Lewis was an Englishman who became a permanent resident of New York and who wrote letters to his brothers back home on many aspects of American life.

In 1875 he spent the Christmas holidays with his son in Philadelphia, where he enjoyed both the city and the holidays very much. One of the things that most impressed him there was the Christmas tree:

"... There all the people seem to resolve themselves into Children for the occasion. I may say that the usual arrangement in this country is to have two parlours—be it a large or small house—opening to each other by sliding doors, the first being for state occasion. As large & fine a tree as could be accommodated being procured and set up, it is covered with every conceivable shape into which coloured & gilt paper & card can be cut, and little pictures, glass balls, chains, garlands, etc., anything to make a gay and imposing display. This being finished it is placed mostly in the sliding door way, which allows it to be seen 2 ways. All the light possible is thrown upon it, often by reflectors, the lattice blinds being thrown open & it is thus open to

The horsecar—1890's

inspection by passersby—which, as houses in Phila are only a little above the street, is an easy matter. Where the taste & industry of the owner prompts it, other attractions are added as fancy dictates—at one place I visited, an old doctor's, there was a very handsome river steamboat, perfect, 3 feet long with about 50 passengers (these last small pictures cut out) all of white, colour & gilt card; also a beautiful fire hose carriage. When the show commences people go round with or without their children to see them & frequently knock at the door to be admitted to a closer inspection which is readily granted. I heard of one house where 75 were admitted in about 2 hours. Riding through the better class streets on the cars, the effect is novel & very fine as every 2nd or 3rd may be exhibitors. I believe some keep it up 2 or 3 weeks."

CHRISTMAS DINNER I

Cream of onion soup, fried smelts, sauce tartare, potato balls, roast loin of pork, roast apples, carrots, hominy croquettes, celery salad, mince pie, deep apple pie, cheese, nuts, fruit, coffee.

American Kitchen Magazine, December 1896

CHRISTMAS DINNER II

Clam and tomato consommé, browned soup rings, olives, salted pecans, fillets of sole, mushroom sauce, roast goose, giblet gravy, frozen apples, riced potatoes, glazed silver skins, pimento timbales, chiffonade salad, English plum pudding, sherry sauce, coffee ice cream, almond cakes, bonbons, crackers, cheese, coffee.

What to Have for Dinner, Fannie Farmer, 1905

CHRISTMAS DINNER III

Clam or oyster soup, celery, baked fish with Hollandaise sauce, roast turkey, oyster dressing, celery or oyster sauce, roast duck, onion sauce, baked potatoes, sweet potatoes, baked squash, mashed turnips, canned corn, stewed tomatoes, Graham bread, rolls, salmon or other salad, plum pudding, peach pie, fruit, nuts, coffee, tea or chocolate.

Queen of the Household, 1906

MENUS FOR AUTUMN EATING

OCTOBER

MONDAY. *Breakfast*—Graham gems, broiled mutton chop, baked eggs, croquettes of cold vegetables. *Dinner*—Soup, roast beef with potatoes, carrots, plain boiled rice; baked custard, grapes. *Supper*—Cold beef sliced, bread, rice fritters with sugar.

TUESDAY. *Breakfast*—Hash, fried okra, fried fish, biscuit. *Dinner*—Boiled mutton with soup, celery, slaw, sliced pine-apples, cake. *Supper*—Sliced mutton, cottage cheese, bread, cake, grape jam.

WEDNESDAY. *Breakfast*—Brown bread, corn batter cakes, croquettes of mutton and vegetables. *Dinner*—Beef *a la mode,* mashed potatoes and turnips, succotash; apples, grapes, pie. *Supper*—Sliced beef, bread, cake, baked pears.

THURSDAY. *Breakfast*—Toast, croquettes of cold beef and vegetables. *Dinner*—Soup, fried or smothered chickens, mashed potatoes, Lima beans, pickles; bird's nest pudding, cake. *Supper*—Canned corned beef, sliced, rolls, cake, jam.

FRIDAY. *Breakfast*—Mutton chops, fried potato cakes, muffins. *Dinner*—Baked or boiled fish, boiled potatoes, corn, delicate cabbage; peach meringue, cake. *Supper*—Bologna sausage, toasted muffins, honey, cheese, cake.

SATURDAY. *Breakfast*—Plain bread, veal cutlets, cracked wheat. *Dinner*—Boiled beef with vegetables; cocoanut pudding. *Supper*—Soused beef, light biscuit, fried apples, cake.

SUNDAY. *Breakfast*—Vegetable hash, fried oysters, stewed tomatoes. *Dinner*—Broiled pheasant or chicken, sweet potatoes, tomatoes; peach meringue pie, plum jelly, cake. *Supper*—Cold beef sliced, rusk, baked apples.

NOVEMBER

MONDAY. *Breakfast*—Poached eggs on toast, broiled pork, potato cakes. *Dinner*—Roast beef, sweet potatoes, boiled turnips, chicken salad; economical pudding. *Supper*—Rolls, oatmeal mush, cold roast beef, cranberry tarts, cake.

TUESDAY. *Breakfast*—Graham bread, beef croquettes, potatoes. *Dinner*—Spiced beef tongue, baked potatoes, macaroni with cheese; grapes, pie. *Supper*—Toasted graham bread, cold tongue, baked pears, cake.

WEDNESDAY. *Breakfast*—Griddle cakes, broiled mutton chops, potatoes. *Dinner*—Soup, oyster pie, baked sweet potatoes, diced turnips, celery; apple pie with whipped cream. *Supper*—Cold rolls, chipped beef, custard cakes, marmalade.

THURSDAY. *Breakfast*—Waffles, broiled ham, fried sweet potatoes. *Dinner*—Brown stew, baked potatoes, plain rice, slaw; pumpkin pie. *Supper*—Cold sliced beef, short cake, jam.

FRIDAY. *Breakfast*—Corn batter cakes, broiled sausage, chipped potatoes. *Dinner*—Roast pork, apple sauce, mashed potatoes, turnips, cabbage; prune whip, cake. *Supper*—Light biscuit, bologna sausage, baked quinces, Swiss cakes.

SATURDAY. *Breakfast*—Graham gems, veal cutlets, potatoes. *Dinner*—Chicken pot pie, vegetables; warm apple pie, cake. *Supper*—Toasted gems, dried beef, baked apples, cake.

SUNDAY. *Breakfast*—Cream toast, broiled oysters with pork, fried raw potatoes. *Dinner*—Oyster soup, roast goose, baked potatoes, boiled onions, cranberry sauce, celery; peach pie. *Supper*—Cold biscuit, onions, sliced goose, grapes, cakes.

DECEMBER

MONDAY. *Breakfast*—Graham bread, griddle cakes, breakfast stew, fried potatoes. *Dinner*—Soup, boiled corned beef with turnips, potatoes and cabbage; baked apple dumplings with sauce. *Supper*—Biscuit, cold beef, canned cherries, cake.

TUESDAY. *Breakfast*—Buttered toast, fried apples, cold turkey broiled. *Dinner*—Roast turkey, cranberry sauce, potatoes, canned corn; canned fruit and cream. *Supper*—Cold turkey, mush and milk, buns, jam.

WEDNESDAY. *Breakfast*—Corn muffins, breaded veal cutlets, Saratoga potatoes. *Dinner* —Stewed oysters, roast mutton with potatoes, tomatoes, celery; pine-apple ice-cream, jelly, cake. *Supper*—Toasted muffins, cold mutton sliced, apple croutes.

THURSDAY. *Breakfast*—Hot rolls, scrambled eggs, breakfast stew. *Dinner*—Roast quail or fowl, baked potatoes, Lima beans, celery, pumpkin pie. *Supper*—Cold rolls, cold tongue sliced, baked apples, tea cakes.

FRIDAY. *Breakfast*—Buckwheat cakes, smoked sausage broiled, hominy croquettes. *Dinner*—Baked or boiled fish, mashed potatoes, squash, cabbage salad; hot peach pie with cream. *Supper*—Light biscuit, steamed oysters, canned fruit with cake.

SATURDAY. *Breakfast*—Buckwheat cakes, rabbit stew, potato cakes. *Dinner*—Chicken fricassee, baked potatoes, baked turnips; cottage pudding with sauce. *Supper*—French rolls, Welsh rarebit, cake, jam.

SUNDAY. *Breakfast*—Muffins, broiled spare-ribs, fried potatoes. *Dinner*—Soup, roast turkey garnished with fried oysters, mashed potatoes, turnips; cranberry sauce, celery, pudding. *Supper*—Biscuit sandwiches, cold turkey, jelly and cake.